The Joy of C

THE
JOY
OF
C

Third Edition

Lawrence H. Miller
The Aerospace Corporation

Alexander E. Quilici
University of Hawaii at Manoa

WILEY

New York ☐ Chichester ☐ Brisbane ☐ Toronto ☐ Singapore ☐ Weinheim

Another one for our families and friends

Acquisitions Editor: Regina Brooks
Marketing Manager: Jay Kirsch
Production Manager: Lucille Buonocore
Senior Production Editor: Anthony VenGraitis
Cover Designer: Harry Nolan
Book Designer: Maddy Lesure
Manufacturing Manager: Mark Cirillo

Recognizing the importance of preserving what has been written, it is a policy of John Wiley & Sons, Inc. to have books of enduring value published in the United States printed on acid-free paper, and we exert our best efforts to that end.

The programs presented in this book have been included solely for their instructional value. They have been carefully tested but are not guaranteed for any particular purpose. The publisher does not offer any warranties or representations, nor does it accept any liabilities with respect to the programs.

Library of Congress Cataloging-in-Publication Data

Miller, Lawrence H.
    The Joy Of C / Lawrence H. Miller, Alexander E. Quilici.
       p.   cm.
    Includes index.
    ISBN 0-471-12933-X (pbk.)
    1. C (Computer program language) I. Quilici, Alexander E.
    II. Title.
    QA76.73.C15M54   1997
    005.13'3–dc20   92-23091
                                                                 CIP

Printed in the United States of America

10 9 8 7 6 5 4 3

PREFACE

C is a powerful programming language. It provides a variety of features that help us write clear, concise programs that are portable, efficient, and easy to maintain. But C also has a reputation for being hard to learn and even harder to master. Its conciseness and complexity can overwhelm all but the most experienced programmer. Many programmers, in fact, wind up avoiding many of its most important features and missing out on the true pleasures of programming in C.

The Joy of C is intended to be a step-by-step companion in your journey from novice to expert C programmer. It's a life raft that will keep you from slowly sinking into a sea of confusion, and a gentle guru that will guide you along the path to becoming a true C master. You'll find this book useful as a self-study guide to C if:

- *You've programmed in other high-level languages such as BASIC, FORTRAN, or Pascal and now want to program in C.* We don't start from scratch and try to teach you how to program. Instead, we assume some prior programming experience and expend much of our effort describing and investigating C's unique and unfamiliar features.[1] We've also carefully chosen our examples, wherever possible picking programs similar to those you're likely to have seen written in another language, thus easing the transition to programming in C.

- *You've programmed in C, but you don't yet feel as though you've mastered it.* We cover the language completely, delving deeply into many issues that are often casually examined or completely avoided. You can't be a proficient C programmer without knowing how to put together large programs, how to produce portable and efficient code, or how to use pointers to effectively organize and access data—topics we emphasize rather than ignore.

- *You're familiar with C but not ANSI C.* The ANSI C standard adds many useful features to the original C definition and implementation, including function proto-types, generic pointers, implicit string concatenation, an improved preprocessor, and additional library functions and header files. We don't simply relegate these features to an appendix, nor do we just briefly touch on them as interesting extensions. Instead, we thoroughly examine and exploit these features as integral parts of the language.

---

[1] In particular, we assume that you've at least been exposed to the basic concepts underlying computer programming, and ideally have written programs that use variables, arithmetic, decisions, and loops.

- *You're planning on eventually learning C++.* C++ is an object-oriented programming language that's based on C. It's rapidly gaining in popularity and looks to be the language of the future. Unfortunately, it's all but impossible to learn C++ unless you're completely comfortable with C. We've tried to smooth your likely transition to C++ by including several chapters on the basics of C++ programming. These chapters redo some of our earlier C examples in C++ so that you can get a good feel for some of the key differences between the two languages.

- *You're looking for examples of real-world C programs or are interested in obtaining a set of useful programming tools.* We provide over 200 useful programs and functions, including a base converter, a histogram producer, an electronic address book, a C program cross-referencer, various sorting and searching programs, and more. We also provide implementations of useful libraries such as sets, queues, stacks, lists, and trees. All of these programs have been written, compiled, and executed using a variety of ANSI C compilers on everything from small personal computers to powerful workstations to large mainframes.

Special Features

This book has grown out of over a decade of teaching C courses to a wide range of students—from first-year computer science and electrical engineering majors to life-long assembly language programmers, from casual computer users who've never programmed before to competent C hackers fine-tuning their skills. And we've concluded that there are several ways to ease the often difficult process of mastering a programming language, all of which we've incorporated here:

- *We provide complete, useful programs.* Our examples don't merely illustrate language features, they illustrate them in a realistic way as part of a useful function or program. And our examples are complete—we avoid potentially confusing program fragments and ensure that every function comes with a main program that shows how to call it and how to use its return value. As a result, you won't have to puzzle for hours over how a particular piece of code might actually be used.

- *We provide non-trivial example programs.* Almost every chapter ends with a case study: a significant, real-world application that cements the concepts covered in the chapter. We often construct these case studies from functions and programs written and explained earlier in the text, reinforcing these examples and providing realistic demonstrations of how bigger programs are built from smaller pieces. As a result, you won't be left wondering how non-trivial programs are actually written, and you won't be stuck starting your own programming projects from scratch.

- *We provide multiple versions of our example programs.* Our approach to presenting most of C's constructs is to gradually rewrite and extend our earlier examples. We usually begin with a simple, straightforward function or program and then gradually improve it, showing how we can use various language features to make it more concise or efficient, or more powerful and useful. We've resisted the strong temptation to immediately take advantage of extremely useful but potentially confusing language features. As a result, you won't have to struggle with simultaneously trying to understand a new program and new language features, and you'll come to a deep understanding of exactly why and when certain features are useful.

- *We provide pictorial descriptions of data structures and algorithms.* Numerous illustrations help clarify complex concepts such as pointers, arrays, and dynamic allocation. These pictures simplify seemingly complicated data structures and algorithms and ensure that our explanations are easy to follow. As a result, you won't have to rely on closing your eyes and trying to visualize what pointers, arrays, or structures actually look like, or exactly how a particular searching algorithm really works.

- *We highlight potential trouble spots and likely errors.* C comes loaded with language constructs that can lead to complete chaos when they're not used carefully or their fine points are forgotten. And most C programmers seem to make the same set of mistakes when first learning the language. We address both of these problems by liberally sprinkling over 60 warnings and reminders throughout the text, each set in boldface and in a gray-shaded box. As a result, you can use these boxes both as a checklist of mistakes to avoid when writing your programs and as a list of likely bugs when trying to debug programs you've written.

- *We explicitly discuss practical programming issues.* When writing "real" C programs, it's necessary to worry about how to design them, how to compile and run them, how to debug them, how to test them, and how to ensure that they are readable, maintainable, portable, and efficient. Throughout this book, when we explicitly discuss one of these issues, we place that discussion in a large shadowed box. As a result, it's easy to skip over this material on a first reading, and it's easy to skim through the text looking for these discussions.

- *We provide end-of-chapter summaries.* Each chapter concludes with a short section summarizing its key points. Often these summaries list the most important language features covered in the chapter, along with a few crucial details of their use. As a result, you can use these summaries as a checklist of the topics we expect you to have learned from reading the chapter.

- *We provide plenty of programming exercises.* Each chapter ends with a set of programming exercises, each carefully designed to provide practice in using the particular language features discussed in the chapter. There are over 300 exercises in the text as a whole, spanning a wide range of difficulty. Some are simply modifications to our example programs that make them more robust, more efficient, more concise, more usable, or more user-friendly. Others range from small programs to sizable programming projects, many of which are useful programs in their own right. As a result, you'll obtain important practice in using these features by writing functions or programs that you'll find useful later on.

- *We provide a disk containing the source files for all of our example programs.* All you have to do is compile, link, and execute them. If you're having trouble understanding a particular example, you can easily explore its behavior by executing it within a debugger or modifying it to produce useful tracing information. As a result, you won't waste hours and hours typing in the sample programs and can instead spend that time trying to better understand their behavior.

Organization

We divide the text into six parts. Part I is a gentle tutorial introduction to C. Part II is a detailed discussion of fundamental C features: its basic data types, operators, statements, arrays, and storage classes. Part III addresses advanced data types, such as pointers, strings, structures, multidimensional arrays, and arrays of pointers. Part IV looks at advanced program structure, the preprocessor, advanced use of functions, generic functions, and complex declarations. Part V deals with real-world issues, including external files, advanced data structures, and portability. Finally, Part VI deals with moving from programming in C to programming in C++.

Part I: A Gentle Introduction to C

Chapter 1 presents a pair of introductory programs: one is a variant on the traditional "Hello World" example, the other is a program to do several simple financial calculations. Together, these programs introduce the basics of producing output, declaring variables, performing arithmetic, and the process of compiling and linking C programs. • *Chapter 2* provides a series of different versions of a program that computes the interest accumulating in a bank account and uses them to introduce the basic C data types and statements. For variety, it also provides several versions of a program to assign grades to test scores. • *Chapter 3* concludes our introduction to C with a look at the basics of functions, including the concepts of parameter passing, return values, function prototypes, and separate compilation. These concepts are introduced with variants and extensions of the original interest-computing programs.

Part II: The Basics

Chapter 4 describes integer and floating point numbers, the basic arithmetic operators, the idea of data type conversions, and the most important functions in the math library. Its case study is a program to convert values in bases between 2 and 10. • *Chapter 5* covers the character data type, emphasizing character input and output, character testing, and the intimate connection between characters and integers. Its case study extends the earlier base conversion program to handle bases larger than 10. • *Chapter 6* addresses operators, paying special attention to the shorthand assignment and bitwise operators and highlighting often unexpected features such as integer division or lazy evaluation. Its case study is a pair of programs to compress and uncompress files. • *Chapter 7* studies statements, showing the most appropriate uses for each, and concludes with a case study that prints its input in octal, one byte at a time. • *Chapter 8* introduces arrays, using an input reversal program to illustrate how to use them and pass them as parameters. It also provides several functions for searching and sorting arrays. Its case study is a histogram producer. • *Chapter 9* focuses on program structure, discussing the differences between local and global variables and presenting C's storage classes. Its case study is a useful package that implements sets.

Part III: Advanced Data Types

Chapter 10 presents pointers, showing how they can be used to simulate call-by-reference parameter passing, emphasizing the relationships between arrays and pointers, and introducing the notion of dynamic allocation. Its case study implements dynamically allocated sets. • *Chapter 11* presents strings, showing how to construct them from the input and introducing the standard string functions. Its case study is a useful tool to detect duplicate lines in its input. • *Chapter 12* studies structures, unions, and enumerated types, including arrays of structures and structures whose fields are allocated dynamically. Its case study is a simple electronic address book. • *Chapter 13* discusses multidimensional arrays, showing how we can use pointers to access them efficiently. It dramatically illustrates their use in an implementation of the Game of Life. • *Chapter 14* presents arrays of pointers, showing how we can use dynamic allocation to initialize them and how we can use them to access command-line arguments. Its case study is a string-sorting program that takes advantage of both.

Part IV: Advanced Program Structure

Chapter 15 presents the preprocessor, describing how we can use it to make our programs easier to read and debug, as well as more efficient. Its case study reimplements the earlier set package using macros. • *Chapter 16* discusses advanced details of functions, covering functions that can take variable numbers of arguments, pointers to functions, and recursion. Its case study recursively implements binary search. • *Chapter 17* grapples with generic functions, showing how to use the standard library's generic sorting and searching functions and then implementing several simpler generic functions. Its case study is an implementation of the standard library's binary search function. • *Chapter 18* covers complex declarations, showing several examples using complex types and then focusing on how to construct and understand these declarations. Its case study is a program to translate English type descriptions into C declarations.

Part V: Real-World Programming Issues

Chapter 19 explains external files, providing complete coverage of the standard I/O library, bringing together the ideas of the chapter in an externally stored address book for names, addresses, and phone numbers. • *Chapter 20* discusses dynamic data structures, such as linked lists, trees, stacks, and queues. Its case study combines most of them in a C program cross-referencer. • *Chapter 21* presents common portability problems and suggests some solutions. It concludes with a case study that implements a set of functions for portably managing console displays and performing immediate character input.

Part VI: Moving from C to C++

Chapter 22 discusses C++ features that are particularly useful to C programmers, such as references and function overloading. • *Chapter 23* discusses the basics of objects and operations, including how to correctly implement objects that make use of dynamically allocated fields or have fields that are objects themselves. • *Chapter 24* describes inheritance and the closely related topics of polymorphism and dynamic binding.

Appendices

Appendix A provides the missing details of C libraries discussed earlier in the text. •
Appendix B provides the ASCII and EBCDIC character sets.

Using This Book as a Textbook

We've taught a wide variety of courses using prepublication drafts and earlier editions of this text. These courses have included both semester courses at the university and state college level, as well as numerous short courses for programmers in industry. Here's how we've used the text for various one-semester C courses:

Introduction to C Programming for students who've taken at least one course in another programming language. In this type of course we usually cover Parts I, II, and III in order, then cover Chapter 19 (External Files) from Part V. We then use any remaining time to squeeze in as much of Part IV as possible, concentrating on the key ideas in Chapters 15 (The Preprocessor), 16 (Advanced Functions), 18 (Complex Declarations). How much of these later chapters we can actually cover depends significantly on what programming languages the students have previously used. We tend to cover them in great detail when the students know Pascal and to skim them when the students come from a FORTRAN or BASIC background. We find that using the text for this type of course requires no supplementary material.

Advanced C Programming for students who've done some programming in C. In these courses we usually cover Part I in a day or two, spending most of our time on Chapter 3's discussion of functions, and then fly through Part II, using it mostly as a quick refresher, covering it in at most 2-3 weeks. We then spend the vast majority of our time covering Parts III, IV, and V, at a rate of about one chapter a week. We also usually try to spend a week or so on the standard library functions discussed in Appendix A. If we're short on time, we're most likely to cut out parts of Chapter 20 (Data Structures). Again, we find no supplementary material is necessary, although we occasionally spend several weeks toward the end of the semester discussing how to do operating system calls in C.

Introduction to Programming Using C for students with no previous programming experience. In these courses, we spend the first 4-5 weeks thoroughly covering Part I, usually at the rate of around one example program per day. We then spend the next 5-6 weeks covering Part II and the balance of the semester covering

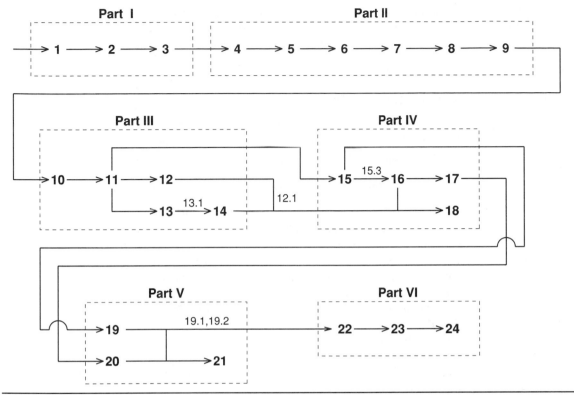

Figure 0.1 The major dependencies between chapters in the text.

as much as possible of Part III, skipping the more difficult material in Chapters 13 (Two-Dimensional Arrays) and 14 (Ragged Arrays). We find that this sort of course requires supplementary material while covering Part I, particularly material on computer hardware and how computers work, as well as detailed line-by-line traces of the execution of our example programs.

No doubt other orderings are possible and reasonable, but any presentation of the material in this text should keep in mind the dependencies between chapters shown in Figure 0.1.

Other Uses of the Text

Our primary goal has been to write a single, stand-alone guide to programming in C. We've tried to produce a text that introductory students would want to keep after finishing the course. We're aware that most introductory courses are likely to cover no more than two-thirds of this text, but we've included the additional material anyway, since it's very useful for those students who plan on really programming in C once the semester is over. To this end, we've been careful to ensure that the entire text is suitable for self-study, especially the chapters on the more advanced topics. A nice side effect is that the text can easily be used as a supplement for other software-related courses, such as Operating Systems, Programming Languages, or Data Structures.

The Joy of C Web Page

Another goal was to make life easier both for instructors teaching from our the text and for students learning C from it. As a result, we have provided a World Wide Web page for the text at:

`http://spectra.eng.hawaii.edu/~alex/TextBooks/JoyOfC/`

Instructors can use the web page to access on-line solutions to the exercises, additional exercises and programming projects, and some sample exams. There is also a complete set of transparency masters for all of the programs, tables, and illustrations in the text, as well as the supplementary material we use when we teach C programming to students who've never before programmed. Instructors can also use this page to obtain the programs in the text for machines other than the PC.

Students can use the web page to access some solutions to the exercises, to see frequently asked questions about the material covered in the text, and to see supplementary material on each chapter, such as program traces, details of how different examples in the text fit together, and so on. Students can also use this page to find out more information about the program disk included with the text, including the details of how to compile and run each of the programs.

Finally, the web page has links to various courses being taught using the text, allowing both instructors and students to explore different approaches to teaching and learning C.

Contacting the Authors

We welcome comments on the text, from both instructors and students. We can currently be reached over the Internet at

`joyofc@wiliki.eng.hawaii.edu`

or through John Wiley and Sons. We will explicitly acknowledge in future text printings and editions everyone who tells us about previously unknown mistakes or makes a suggestion we later adopt.

Changes from the Previous Edition

We have heard many, many suggestions for improvements, from both instructors and students. Many of these suggestions have come from instructors who have been using *The Joy of C* as an introductory programming textbook, not just as a C text for more experienced programmers. As a result, we have made a variety of changes to this edition.

The major additions and deletions are:

- We have significantly slowed the pace of our introductory chapters on C by introducing fewer features in each example and gradually developing many of our example programs, rather than simply presenting them in final form. In addition, we now provide more complete descriptions and additional examples of the C constructs we do introduce.

- We have added a new chapter on functions (Chapter 3). This chapter significantly expands the earlier edition's introduction to functions to cover parameter passing, return values, function prototypes, and separate compilation in much more detail.

- We have added material on program design, development, testing, and debugging. This material is presented as shadowed boxes, allowing it to be skipped by those students for whom it is either too low-level or too high-level. Along with this material, we have moved the material on other topics such as readability, efficiency, and portability that was buried within the chapters into these boxes as well.

- We have expanded our previous C++ coverage to three chapters (Chapters 22, 23, and 24) from one and now cover not only C++ as a better C, but also key issues in using C++ to construct objects, to use inheritance, and to take advantage of polymorphism and dynamic binding.

- We have eliminated our separate chapter on efficiency (our old Chapter 21) and moved the key examples from that chapter to the places where we introduce or discuss the relevant language features.

We have also made a variety of more minor but still important reorganizations. These are:

- Moving the material on less frequently worrisome character-oriented issues (such as trigraphs, wide character types, and signed versus unsigned characters) into a shadowed box at the end of the chapter on characters (Chapter 5). That way this material can be skipped over until it's truly necessary.

- Moving the material on **typedef** in the case study in the chapter on program structure (Chapter 9) into its own expanded section. **typedef** is used often enough in real programs that it is worthy of its own section.

- Moving the discussion of simulating call-by-reference from the chapter on advanced use of functions (the old Chapter 14) to the pointer chapter (Chapter 10). That way this material can be used as an initial example of the use of pointers.

- Exchanging the preprocessor (Chapter 15) and advanced function (Chapter 16) chapters. The advanced function chapter introduces variable argument functions, which are easier to explain after macros have been presented.

- Moving the material on old-style C function definitions and declarations from the beginning of the advanced chapter on functions (Chapter 16) to a shadowed box at the end. That way this material can be skipped unless the students are expected to be able to understand legacy C code.

- Moving the presentation of how to port from ANSI to non-ANSI C compilers from the beginning of the portability chapter (Chapter 21) to the end. This material is becoming less useful now that ANSI compilers are widely available.

We have also changed some presentation details. These include:

- Redrawing all our figures so that they are both more consistent and more easily readable.

- Breaking up programs that had a main program solely to show how a function was called into two separate figures, one with the function and one with the main program.

- Renaming the source files containing different implementations or extensions of the same functions. For example, rather than having all of the files containing our different variants of our **yesOrNo** function simply be named yesorno.c, we now name them yesorno.c, yesorno1.c, and so on.

Acknowledgments

Contributions by several of our friends and colleagues have greatly improved the quality of this text. We're deeply indebted to Robert Quilici for painstakingly plowing through our prepublication drafts, unearthing plenty of problems with our programs and explanations. And we're grateful to David Smallberg for his always perceptive comments and criticisms, and to Dorab Patel for his invaluable wizardry with formatting.

The reviewers of earlier versions of our manuscript made many wonderful suggestions that we have incorporated into this text. We want to extend a special thanks to Thomas Crowe (Arizona State University), Edmund Deaton (San Diego State University), Joyce Harris (DeAnza College), Gary Huckabay (Cameron University), Henry Ruston (Polytechnic University), Wayne Staats (North Carolina State University), and Jieming Zhu (Wichita State University). We also owe our thanks to the many students at UCLA, the University of Hawaii, and a variety of corporations who have used our earlier C textbooks or suffered through the initial drafts of this manuscript. Their many questions and suggestions have improved this text immensely.

We would like to thank the University of Hawaii's Electrical Engineering Department and The Aerospace Corporation for the generous use of their resources and their allowing us the time to produce this work. We would also like to thank the people at John Wiley and Sons, especially Steven Elliot and Regina Brooks, our extremely patient and helpful editors.

This text has benefited from the sharp eyes of the instructors and students who used its early printings. George Durham, Manny Feliciano, and Jim Heavener were especially helpful in finding and fixing our mistakes. Khaled Abdel-Ghaffer, Joy Higa,

Bill Kozick, Y. C. Lee, Richard O'Keefe, Derek Oyama, Sam Rhoads, Bob Roos, Lee Tokuda, Brian Weaver, Kevin Wentzel, and John Witherspoon also helped us root out a variety of embarassing errors.

Finally, we're grateful for the encouragement and support given to us by our families and friends—especially Rita Grant-Miller, Daphne Borromeo, Tammy Franklin, Irene Borromeo, and Doris Perl.

Alex Quilici
Honolulu, Hawaii

Larry Miller
Los Angeles, California

November 1996

Contents

Part I

A GENTLE INTRODUCTION TO C

The first three chapters are a tutorial introduction to basic features of the C language.

- Chapter 1 shows how to produce output, declare variables, and perform calculations, as well as how to compile and link C programs.

- Chapter 2 shows how to write loops, make simple decisions, and read input.

- Chapter 3 presents user-defined functions, showing how they are defined and called.

1 GETTING STARTED WITH C

This chapter is a gentle introduction to C. We begin with a pair of simple programs: one prints a welcoming message, the other calculates the actual cost of purchasing a set of items. We describe these programs in great detail and provide several variants of each. Along the way we introduce the basics of C program organization, the process of compilation and linking, and several fundamental language features: the `printf` function for performing formatted output, variable declaration and assignment, and the arithmetic operators.

1.1 AN INTRODUCTION TO C

C is a general-purpose, high-level programming language.

It is general purpose because there are an incredible variety of C-based application programs running on a wide variety of platforms. These applications include PC-oriented programs—word processors, drawing programs, spreadsheets, databases, personal organizers, and financial accounting packages. They include applications that require much faster, more expensive hardware and perform tasks such as complex simulations and transaction processing. And they include applications that run on specially designed, special-purpose computers and perform tasks such as real-time digital signal processing.

C is high level because a single C language instruction may correspond to many lower-level machine instructions and because a C program can run on a variety of different types of computers, regardless of the specific instructions they provide.

But there are lots of general-purpose, high-level programming languages. Why is C so popular?

Part of the reason is efficiency. Like any high-level language, C requires the use of a *compiler* to translate C instructions into the machine instructions that a computer can actually execute. C, however, was specifically designed to help compilers generate an *efficient* machine language program. It also provides language features that help programmers make their programs more efficient. The result is that the machine language programs that result from compiling C programs tend to execute as quickly as equivalent machine language programs written by hand. This may not seem too exciting, but before C came along, the only way to produce programs that executed quickly enough was often to hand-code them in machine language. These programs, however, took forever to write and after all that work would still run on only a single type of computer. Now that's rarely done, as C programs run quickly, can be written in much less time, and are portable to many different types of computers.

Efficiency, however, isn't the whole story. In fact, as computers have gotten faster, efficiency has become less of a priority. What's stayed very important is the amount of time and effort it takes to write computer programs—the faster we can write a program, the better. C helps here in that it is an *expressive* language—it is possible to say a lot with very little. In particular, C provides a variety of language constructs that allow us to succinctly describe the actions we want our program to perform. Although you may at first struggle to understand the language's syntax, once you master it, you will appreciate the convenience this terseness gives us.

There's one final reason C is popular. It's a stepping stone to a language called C++, which extends C to support object-oriented programming. C++ provides a number of features that go far beyond C in terms of helping us write programs. However, we pay a price: all of those features make C++ incredibly complex, and as a result, it can be a very difficult language to learn. By first learning C and writing lots of C programs, we can much more easily master C++.

1.2   A FIRST C PROGRAM

Figure 1.1 contains a very simple C program. When compiled and run, it prints the message:

```
Welcome to the Joy of C!
```

Let's dive right into this program to see exactly how it works.

The main Program

A C program is a collection of one or more *functions*.[1] A function is a named collection of statements, where each statement is a programming language-specific instruction. When we provide the statements that make up the function, we are said to be *defining* the function.

Our example program defines a single function named **main** that consists of a single **printf**.

```
main()
{
  printf("Welcome to the Joy of C!\n");
}
```

---

[1]C's functions are analogous to functions in Pascal or FORTRAN. However, they can also play the role of Pascal's procedures and FORTRAN and BASIC's subroutines. That is, unlike many other languages, C provides only a single mechanism for grouping statements.

```
main()
{
  printf("Welcome to the Joy of C!\n");
}
```

Figure 1.1 (welcome.c) A program to print a welcome message.

Function definitions have two parts: a header and a body. At a minimum, the header provides the function's name, followed by a pair of parentheses, as in **main**'s header.

```
main()
```

The function's body is a collection of statements. We enclose these statements in braces (**{** and **}**) to group them with the function header. In this case, **main**'s body consists of only a single statement, the **printf**.

When we define a function, we specify what should happen when a function is *executed*. To actually execute the statements within a function, we have to *call* the function. That is, to cause the **printf** statement to execute, we need to call the **main** function that contains it. Fortunately, we don't have to do anything special to call **main**. When a C program starts up, the first thing it does is call **main**, so every program must have a **main**.

The **printf** Statement

Now we've arrived at the heart of our program: the **printf** that does all the work.

```
printf("Welcome to the Joy of C!\n");
```

It turns out that **printf** is itself a function and that this statement is calling **printf**.

In particular, **printf** is a predefined output function. *Predefined* means that it has been written and compiled for you and is linked together with your program after it compiles. C does all input and output through a set of predefined functions that together compose the standard input/output (I/O) library.

We call a function by following its name with a list of *parameters*, which we enclose in parentheses. Parameters provide a function with information it needs to do its job. In this case, **printf** needs to know which characters to write to the output. We tell **printf** what to write by providing it with a single *string* parameter (a list of characters between double quotation marks), and it writes those characters to the standard output. The standard output is usually the terminal (or computer monitor or window) from which you invoked the program.[2]

There are a few details we've ignored. One is the semicolon following our **printf**. In C, whenever a statement consists solely of a call to function, as does our **printf**, we

---

[2]Many operating systems actually let us change where the standard output goes, a process called *output redirection*. To do so, however, we are required to do something special before we run the program. We'll look at this topic in more detail in later chapters.

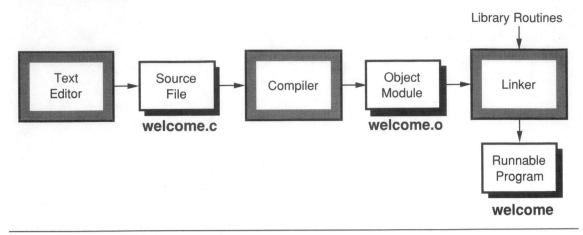

Figure 1.2   The process of constructing, compiling, and executing a C program.

need to end it with a single semicolon. The other is the **\n** at the end of the formatting string. The backslash indicates a special character. **\n** is the newline character; writing a **\n** causes further output to start on the next line. Without it, output continues on the same line. In our example, we write the newline so that when our program finishes, the cursor is sitting at the start of the line following our welcome message.

1.3   COMPILING AND RUNNING C PROGRAMS

The previous section presented the source code for a single C program. But how do we actually arrive at an executable program, one that, when run, produces our earlier output? We have to go through several steps, shown in Figure 1.2:

1. Enter the program into a source file, usually with an *interactive text editor*.

2. Provide this program to the *compiler*, which takes it and produces an *object module*.

3. Give this object module to the *linker*, which produces an executable (or runnable) program.

The *object module* contains compiled code, along with references to any functions, such as **printf**, that the code uses but doesn't define. These references are called *externals*. Before a program can be executed, the compiled versions of these external functions must be linked together with the object module. That's the job of the *linker*. It looks for definitions of these externals in a standard location that contains a library of precompiled standard functions, and links them together with the object module to produce a runnable program.

Aside 1.1: The Details of Compiling C Programs

Although the process of turning C source into executable code sounds simple enough, the details vary widely from system to system. Despite these differences, all C programming environments fall into two general categories: *command-line* and *integrated*.

Traditional C development environments are command-line oriented: they force us to use separate commands to edit, compile, link, and run our programs. Often, however, there's a single command that combines compiling and linking. The workstations we use, for example, provide the popular (and free!) GNU C compiler (gcc), which lets us use

```
gcc -ansi welcome.c -o welcome
```

to form an executable program from the source in Figure 1.1.

This command looks complex. In reality, however, it's quite straightforward. The -ansi tells the GNU compiler to compile welcome.c with ANSI-standard C (as opposed to pre-ANSI C, and without any GNU-specific extensions). The -o welcome tells it to put the resulting executable program in a file named welcome (as opposed to following the UNIX tradition and creating an executable named a.out).

These command-line compilers are easy to learn how to use, provide fast compilation, and let us use our favorite editor to enter our programs. But they have several major drawbacks: incremental program development is time-consuming, and correcting errors is a potentially painful process. Before we can compile our program, we usually have to save our file and leave the editor. If our program contains errors, the compiler provides us with a list of error messages, which we need to record somewhere. To make changes, we have to reenter the editor, reload our file, and work our way through it, trying to find and correct all of our mistakes.

More modern C development environments, such as Turbo C++ under MS-Windows or CodeCenter on UNIX, integrate the editor, compiler, and linker under a single easy-to-use interface. They let us compile and execute programs with a single keystroke—without leaving the editor. But, more important, we can also more easily correct our errors. If the compiler detects any errors, it places us in the editor at the location where the first error occurred, with a message on the screen that describes our mistake. After we fix this error, a single keystroke takes us to the location of the next error, and another keystroke to the error after that, and so on.

These integrated environments make learning C a much less painful process, and we highly recommend them. And because these environments are usually menu-driven, learning how to use them is extremely simple. In Borland's Turbo C++ for Windows, for example, we simply start the development environment with a click on the Turbo C++ icon, enter the program, and choose the Run entry on the Debug Menu to compile, link, and execute our programs. However, it's important not to let this convenience lead you into a "trial-and-error" method of programming, where you write or change code without really understanding what's going on in the hope that eventually point-and-click will lead you to a working solution.

1.4   IMPROVING OUR INITIAL PROGRAM: COMMENTS

Figure 1.3 is an improved version of our initial program. The big difference is that now, like most C programs, it starts with a *comment* that describes what it does.

```
/*
 * A program that prints a welcoming message.
 */
```

A comment begins with a `/*` and ends with a `*/` and can go anywhere blank spaces can occur—at the end of a line, at the beginning, or even in the middle. For readability, however, we usually place comments only at the end of lines or on lines by themselves, as we've done here. When we have comments that extend over multiple lines (like the one above), we usually place a `*` at the beginning of each intermediate line. This isn't necessary, but we like doing so because it visually ties together all of the individual lines making up the comment.

What does the compiler do with our comments? It simply ignores them. That's because comments are directed at the program's reader, not the compiler. In general, we use comments to answer questions that are likely to arise about the program, such as what it does or how it works. Although at first comments may seem to be a luxury rather than a necessity, they're not. It can be difficult to understand another person's program unless they've been kind enough to comment it liberally. In fact, it can even be difficult to understand your own programs after you've put them aside for awhile, unless you were careful to sprinkle helpful comments throughout your code. Don't be afraid to shower a program with comments!

> *Start each program with a comment that describes what it does.*

1.5   FURTHER IMPROVING OUR INITIAL PROGRAM

Despite our adding a comment, our initial C program actually has several sloppy coding practices. Although the program executes and appears to work correctly, many compilers will warn us about possible flaws, and many experienced C programmers will shake their heads sadly when they examine our code. Figure 1.4, for example, shows the warnings we get when we compile it with the gcc compiler we described earlier.[3]

Figure 1.5 contains an improved version of our initial example that makes these compiler warnings go away. What did we have to fix and how did we fix it?

Function Prototypes and Include Files

One problem is that we originally failed to provide a *function prototype* for **printf**. Among other things, a function prototype describes the types of parameters the function

---

[3]Specifically, we compiled the program with the -Wall option on, which forces the compiler to warn us about most potential programming problems it encounters. Many other compilers would check for these flaws without the need for special options.

```
/*
 * A program to print a welcoming message.
 */
main()
{
  printf("Welcome to the Joy of C!\n");
}
```

Figure 1.3   (welcome2.c) A version of our welcoming program with a comment describing what it does.

```
welcome2.c:5: warning: return-type defaults to 'int'
welcome2.c: In function 'main':
welcome2.c:6: warning: implicit declaration of function 'printf'
welcome2.c:7: warning: control reaches end of non-void function
```

Figure 1.4   Some compiler warnings that result from compiling welcome2.c.

```
/*
 * An improved version of our program to print a welcoming message.
 *
 * Revisions:
 *    1) Added includes for function prototypes and EXIT_SUCCESS.
 *    2) Added return value to main's header.
 *    3) Added return statement to main's body.
 */
#include <stdio.h>
#include <stdlib.h>

int main()
{
  printf("Welcome to the Joy of C!\n");
  return EXIT_SUCCESS;
}
```

Figure 1.5   (welcome3.c) A further improved version of our welcoming program.

expects. **printf**'s prototype, for example, indicates that its first parameter must be a string of characters.

Why do we need to provide this information? One reason is so that the compiler can make sure we call the function with the correct parameters. If we accidentally provide **printf** with a number as its first parameter, rather than a string, or if we simply forget to provide that parameter, we want the compiler to point out the error.

Every C programming environment provides a collection of *header files* that contain prototypes for their predefined functions. The file stdio.h, for example, contains prototypes for all of the input and output functions, including **printf**. To use these prototypes, we need to *include* this file, which we do with the line:

```
#include <stdio.h>
```

Lines beginning with a **#** are special. These lines are handled by the *preprocessor*, a special part of the compiler that processes C programs before the "real" compiler sees them. When we invoke the compiler on a source file, it automatically passes that source file through the preprocessor and then works with the result. The line above instructs the preprocessor to include the contents of the file named stdio.h in the program it passes to the compiler (the angle brackets around the name tell the preprocessor this is a special system header file). The compiler sees only the contents of the included file and not the **#include** itself. Including stdio.h provides the necessary prototype for **printf**.

> *When you use a predefined function, be sure to include the appropriate header file.*

Return Values

The second problem is that we ignored **main**'s return value. When a function finishes executing, it can *return* (or give back) a value to its caller. **main** is expected to return a value indicating whether or not the program failed. But who is **main**'s caller? And what value should **main** return?

main's caller is whatever program invoked it, which is normally the operating system command interpreter. Fortunately, most command interpreters ignore **main**'s return value, but not all of them. Some print an error message based on this return value; this means our sloppiness could lead to an error message being written when it shouldn't. It's also possible that our C programs will be run from *command scripts*: programs that are written in a special language and that use other programs as their basic building blocks. These programs often test **main**'s return value to determine what action to take next.

By convention, C programs are supposed to return **EXIT_SUCCESS** when they succeed and **EXIT_FAILURE** when they fail. **EXIT_SUCCESS** and **EXIT_FAILURE** are special symbols defined in another header file, stdlib.h, so we need to include this file as well. It turns out that **EXIT_SUCCESS** is usually defined to be zero, while **EXIT_FAILURE** is defined as some other small, positive integer value, often one.

We don't expect our welcoming program to fail, so we would like **main** to always return **EXIT_SUCCESS** to its caller. We do so with the new statement

```
return EXIT_SUCCESS;
```

at the end of **main**, following the **printf**. The **return** statement terminates the function containing it and returns the specified value to that function's caller. Here, it does what we want: terminates **main** and returns **EXIT_SUCCESS** to its caller.

> *Always return a value from* **main** *indicating whether the program succeeded or failed.*

There's one other detail we have to worry about here. Whenever a function returns a value (like **main** above), we need to tell the compiler what type of value the function returns. In this case, **main** is returning an integral value (as opposed to a real number or a character), which we indicate by preceding **main** with **int**.

```
int main()
```

Don't worry if at this point you find yourself a little bit overwhelmed with all these details. The rest of the book spends plenty of time discussing types and return values. For now, simply remember to include the appropriate header files, use the modified first line of **main**, and add the statement returning **EXIT_SUCCESS**. If you do all that, you'll be writing C programs that look just like the pro's.

1.6   A SECOND C PROGRAM

Let's take a look at a more realistic C program. Figure 1.6 computes the actual cost of a set of items, given a list price per item, a percentage discount, and a sales tax rate. Here is its output when we used it to compute the actual cost of buying 23 compact disks, given that each CD is $13.95, we get an 18% discount for buying more than 20, and the state sales tax is 7.5%:

```
List price per item: 13.950000
List price of 23 items: 320.850000
Price after 18.000000% discount: 263.097000
Sales tax at 7.500000%: 19.732275
Total cost: 282.829275
```

This program begins the same way our earlier programs did: with a comment describing what it does and **#include**s for stdio.h and stdlib.h. But our **main** program is not nearly as simple as before: it now includes variable declarations, assignment statements, and a more complex form of **printf**.

Variable Declarations

Variables are named locations for storing values. Each variable can store a single value of a particular type. C forces us to declare the type of every variable before we can use it. These variable declarations appear at the beginning of a function and specify the variable's name, storage requirements, and internal representation. Here, the first declaration specifies that **items** is an **int**, an abbreviation for the word *integer*, and the next specifies that **list_price** is a **double**, which is short for the phrase "double precision *floating point*".

```
int     items;          /* # of items bought */
double list_price;      /* list price of item */
```

```c
/*
 * Compute the actual cost of buying 23 items at $13.95.  We assume an
 * 18% discount rate and a 7.5% sales tax.
 */
#include <stdio.h>
#include <stdlib.h>

int main()
{
    int     items;                      /* # of items bought */
    double list_price;                  /* list price of item */
    double discount_rate;               /* discount percentage */
    double sales_tax_rate;              /* sales tax percentage */
    double total_price;                 /* total price of all items */
    double discount_price;              /* discount price of all items */
    double sales_tax;                   /* amount of sales tax */
    double final_cost;                  /* cost including sales tax */

    items = 23;
    list_price = 13.95;
    discount_rate = .18;
    sales_tax_rate = .075;

    total_price = items * list_price;
    discount_price = total_price - total_price * discount_rate;
    sales_tax = discount_price * sales_tax_rate;
    final_cost = discount_price + sales_tax;

    printf("List price per item: %f\n", list_price);
    printf("List price of %i items: %f\n", items, total_price);
    printf("Price after %f%% discount: %f\n",
            discount_rate * 100, discount_price);
    printf("Sales tax at %f%%: %f\n",
            sales_tax_rate * 100, sales_tax);
    printf("Total cost: %f\n", final_cost);

    return EXIT_SUCCESS;
}
```

Figure 1.6   (price.c)   Compute the actual cost to purchase a set of items.

The others declare several more variables, all of which are **double**s. In these declarations, the underscore is part of the variable name just as if it were a letter. Using it helps make our variable names easy to understand. We also help our program's readers by following our variable declarations with a comment that explains the variable's purpose.

Why are there these different types? We use integers when we need exact "whole" numbers, since their representation is exact within the range of integers that a given word (memory location) can represent. We also use them when speed of arithmetic operations is important, since most operations are faster with integers than with floating point numbers. In C, an **int** is at least 16 bits, with 1 bit used for the sign; this means that we can *safely* use an **int** to store values between $-32{,}767$ and $+32{,}767$ (that is, between $-2^{15} + 1$ and $+2^{15} - 1$). That seems like a small range of values, and it is. But C provides other types we can use when we need to store larger integral values.[4]

In our example, we use **items** to store the number of items we're going to buy. That number is always whole (we can't buy half a CD) and always small (we can't afford to buy 30,000 compact disks), so we can safely use an **int** to store it.

Floating point numbers, or reals, are numbers with a decimal point. We use them when we need to store fractional values or very large numbers. They differ from integers in that their representations are only approximate and not exact. Their accuracy and range varies from machine to machine, but a **double** has at least 10 significant decimal digits of precision and can hold positive or negative values between 10^{-38} and 10^{+38}. In many machines, however, the number of significant digits and the maximum exponent are much larger.

In our example, all of our **double** variables are used to hold either monetary amounts or percentages. Since all of these quantities potentially involve a fraction, we have to use floating point values rather than integers to store them.[5]

It's a pain to declare all our variables. Many other languages rely on naming conventions to declare variables implicitly. Why doesn't C? Primarily because explicit declarations at the beginning of a function make the program more readable. We need not remember strange, often unintuitive naming conventions. And we can get an idea of the types of data a function manipulates without having to read the entire function.

Assignment Statements

Most of the work in this program is done with a series of *assignment statements*. An assignment statement puts a value into a variable. **main**'s first few assignments store the number of items we want to purchase, the price of each item, the discount rate, and the sales tax rate.

```
items = 23;
list_price = 13.95;
discount_rate = .18;
sales_tax_rate = .075;
```

They work as one might expect. The first assigns the value 23 to the variable **items**, the second assigns the value 13.95 to the variable **list_price**, the third sets **discount_rate** to .18, and the last sets **sales_tax_rate** to .075. As with function calls like **printf**, we must follow assignment statements with a semicolon.

---

[4]Chapter 4 discusses all of C's numeric data types and the ranges of values they can store.

[5]Actually, using real numbers to store monetary amounts is cheating! That's because we usually want exact arithmetic for dollars and cents, but once dollar amounts get into the tens of thousands, we run up against the floating point precision limits of some machines. Solving this problem is tricky. It usually involves storing the dollars and cents in separate integer variables, doing arithmetic separately on the dollars and cents, and then combining the results.

After we've stored our initial values, we need to perform a set of calculations, and store their results.

total list price = list price of an item × number of items
total discount amount = total price of all items × discount rate
total discounted price = total price of all items − total discount amount
total sales tax = total discounted price × sales tax rate
actual cost of all items = total discounted price + total sales tax

We do so with a series of assignment statements. These statements make use of several *arithmetic operators*. C provides the usual **+** (addition), **-** (subtraction), ***** (multiplication), and **/** (division), along with several others, which we will introduce later. ***** and **/** have higher precedence than **+** and **-**. That means C performs multiplication and division before addition and subtraction. As with most other programming languages, however, we can use parentheses to change the order of evaluation.

The first assignment statement computes the total list price. It multiplies the number of items by the price of an item and stores the result in **total_price**.

```
total_price = items * list_price;
```

The second computes the total discounted price. This computation takes two steps. We compute the total discount amount by multiplying the total list price by the discount rate. And we then subtract this discount amount from the total price. Since we're not really interested in the dollar savings, we don't bother storing the discount amount.

```
discount_price = total_price - total_price * discount_rate;
```

This assignment works correctly because C performs multiplications and divisions before additions and subtractions. It does not subtract **total_price** from itself (giving zero) and then multiply the result by the **discount_rate** (again giving zero).

The last two assignments are straightforward, computing and storing the sales tax amount, and then adding it to the discounted price to give us the actual cost.

```
sales_tax = discount_price * sales_tax_rate;
final_cost = discount_price + sales_tax;
```

Formatted Output with `printf`

The last few statements in the program display the results of all these calculations. As you might expect, we use **printf**, but now we take advantage of its ability to perform *formatted output*. Formatted output means that we provide the format in which **printf** writes a set of values. We specify the format as **printf**'s first parameter, called *the formatting control string*. **printf** then writes its other parameters to the standard output according to this specification.

By default, **printf** writes anything in the formatting control string (between the quotation marks) as is. We took advantage of that feature to display our first program's welcoming message. But there's also an exception. When **printf** encounters a **%**, it takes **%** to be the start of a description of how to write a value. **printf** expects the **%**

to be followed by a letter specifying the value's type. **%i** or **%d** indicates a base 10 (or decimal) integer, and **%f** a floating point value.

Consider what happens with the first two **printf** statements in our example:

```
printf("List price per item: %f\n", list_price);
printf("List price of %i items: %f\n", items, total_price);
```

The first **printf** writes the string

```
List price per item:
```

followed by a space. It then encounters the **%f**, which causes it to write the value of **list_price**, and ends by writing the newline. The second **printf** is similar except that when it encounters the **%i**, it writes the value of **items**, and when it encounters the **%f**, it writes the value of **total_price**.

There's no limit to the number of values we can display with a single **printf**; we simply provide a formatting control for each and follow the control string with a comma-separated parameter list. It's not a terrible error to provide more values to write than formatting codes; any extra values will simply be ignored. It's much worse to provide too few values or values of the wrong type. That's likely to cause your program to terminate early or produce output consisting of bizarre values.

> *Make sure there is formatting instruction of the correct type for each value you want to print.*

The next few **printf**s are a bit trickier.

```
printf("Price after %f%% discount: %f\n",
        discount_rate * 100, discount_price);
printf("Sales tax at %f%%: %f\n",
        sales_tax_rate * 100, sales_tax);
```

When we write the discount and sales tax rates, we want to follow them with a percent sign. But we can't simply put a **%** in our formatting string, since a **%** indicates that a formatting code follows. The trick is that to write a percent sign, we use two of them, **%%**.

As these **printf**s illustrate, we're not restricted to passing variables as parameters. We are also free to provide an expression, as we do here. When we do, C simply computes its value and passes it on to the function.

1.7 IMPROVING OUR SECOND PROGRAM

As with our first example, our cost-computing program has several problems. The first is stylistic: the various values that we need to compute prices are buried in the program, making them somewhat difficult to modify.[6] The other is aesthetic: quite frankly, this

---

[6]Of course, it would be even better to have the program read these values from its input. We'll see how to do that in the next chapter.

program's output is ugly. The dollar amounts, for example, have six places after the decimal, rather than the two we would prefer.

Figure 1.7 contains a revised version of this program that fixes these difficulties. Here is its much prettier output:[7]

```
List price per item:              13.95
List price of 23 items:          320.85
Price after 18.0% discount:      263.10
Sales tax at 7.5%:                19.73
Total cost:                      282.83
```

Let's see what changes we had to make.

Defining Constants

Our first change is that we now use a new preprocessor statement, **#define**, to define four *constants*: **ITEMS** is the number of items we want to buy (23), **LIST_PRICE** is the list price of an individual item (13.95), **DISCOUNT_RATE** is our discount (.18), and **SALES_TAX_RATE** is the sales tax (.075).

```
#define ITEMS              23
#define LIST_PRICE         13.95
#define DISCOUNT_RATE       .18
#define SALES_TAX_RATE      .075
```

#define gives a name to a value. Its syntax—that is, the way the statement is constructed—is simple. The keyword **#define** starts in column one and is followed by a *NAME* and a *VALUE*. (We use italics as in *NAME* or *VALUE* to indicate generic symbols; the programmer provides the actual name and its value.)

```
#define NAME    VALUE
```

Unlike assignment statements, we do not follow the **#define** with a semicolon.

NAME doesn't have to be all uppercase letters, but we usually restrict ourselves to uppercase names for our constants so that they stand out when reading the program. There is also no syntactic limitation on where we can place our **#define**s, other than that they must begin in the first column and that they must appear before we use the **#define**d name. Despite this freedom, we usually place them near the beginning of a program, usually immediately following any **#include**s.

#define's semantics—that is, what the statement actually does—are more complex. When the preprocessor encounters a **#define**, it associates the value with the name. Then, whenever the name occurs later in the program, the preprocessor replaces it with its corresponding value.[8]

After the preprocessor has finished its replacements, it passes the program to the compiler proper; this means the compiler never sees the names in the **#define**s. In

---

[7]This program makes use of tab stops. These tab stops are usually set by using an operating system command. This output was produced with tab stops every eight columns (the usual default). Your output may vary if your tab stops are set differently.

[8]In fact, **#define** isn't restricted to replacing names with values. It's actually a general mechanism for replacing a name with a string of characters. Later chapters discuss **#define** in more detail.

```c
/*
 * An improved version of our cost-computing program.
 *
 * Revisions:
 *    1) Placed problem-specific values in defined constants rather
 *       than initialized variables.
 *    2) Modified printf's to produce output in a nicer format by
 *       using field widths and tab stops.
 */
#include <stdio.h>
#include <stdlib.h>

#define ITEMS           23
#define LIST_PRICE      13.95
#define DISCOUNT_RATE    .18
#define SALES_TAX_RATE   .075

int main()
{
  double discount_price;            /* discounted price of item */
  double total_price;               /* total price of all items */
  double sales_tax;                 /* amount of sales tax */
  double final_cost;                /* cost including sales tax */

  total_price = ITEMS * LIST_PRICE;
  discount_price = total_price - total_price * DISCOUNT_RATE;
  sales_tax = discount_price * SALES_TAX_RATE;
  final_cost = discount_price + sales_tax;

  printf("List price per item:\t\t%7.2f\n", LIST_PRICE);
  printf("List price of %i items:\t\t%7.2f\n", ITEMS, total_price);
  printf("Price after %.1f%% discount:\t%7.2f\n",
         DISCOUNT_RATE * 100, discount_price);
  printf("Sales tax at %.1f%%:\t\t%7.2f\n",
         SALES_TAX_RATE * 100, sales_tax);
  printf("Total cost:\t\t\t%7.2f\n", final_cost);

  return EXIT_SUCCESS;
}
```

Figure 1.7   (price2.c)   An improved version of our program to compute the cost of a set of items.

our program, the preprocessor replaces each use of **LIST_PRICE** with its defined value, 13.95, and performs a similar action for the other three defined constants.[9] By using **#define** for our constants, we no longer have to declare variables to hold them, and we

_____

[9]stdlib.h usually **#define**s **EXIT_SUCCESS** as zero (and **EXIT_FAILURE** as one), so the preprocessor makes this substitution for us as well.

highlight which values in our program can be easily changed. This results in a program that's easier to read and easier to change.

Using Field Widths with `printf`

The other change we've made to our program is in how we display values. Now we display dollar amounts with two places after the decimal point and percentages with one, and we line up all of the amounts.

Normally, `%i` and `%d` use just enough space to print the entire value, and `%f` prints floating point values with exactly six digits after the decimal point and however many digits are necessary preceding it. We change these defaults by providing an optional field width and precision, as in our first `printf`.

```
printf("List price per item:\t\t%7.2f\n", LIST_PRICE);
```

Here, to write the value of **LIST_PRICE**, we use `%7.2f`, which tells the compiler that we want floating point output, with seven characters in all and two digits to the right of the decimal point. That is, as xxxx.xx, with the x's replaced by the digits in **LIST_PRICE**.

It's possible that our field width will be too large or too small for the value we're printing. If the field width is too large, **printf** simply *right*-justifies the number within the field. That's the case above, where **LIST_PRICE** is 13.95 and therefore requires a total of five spaces. The result is a pair of leading blanks. (As an alternative, we can add a leading minus sign, as in `%-7.2f`, to have C *left*-justify the number within the field.) If the field width is too small, such as if we were to use `%3.2f` to write our list price of 13.95, **printf** stretches the field so that it's just large enough to write the entire value.

It turns out we get the same behavior if we leave off the field width entirely, as in `%.2f`. In fact, using `%.Nf`, where N stands for a small integer, is the standard way of writing a number with N digits after the decimal point when we don't care how large the number actually is. So `%.1f` means one digit after the decimal point, `%.2f` means two digits after the decimal point, and so on. We take advantage of this ability in later **printf**s to guarantee that the discount and sales tax amounts do not have leading blanks:

```
printf("Price after %.1f%% discount:\t%7.2f\n",
       DISCOUNT_RATE * 100, discount_price);
printf("Sales tax at %.1f%%:\t\t%7.2f\n",
       SALES_TAX_RATE * 100, sales_tax);
```

Perhaps you've noticed that `\t` pops up in most of these **printf**s. The `\t` is a tab character. It behaves like `\n`, except that instead of placing the cursor on the beginning of the next line, it places the cursor at the next tab stop. Usually there are tab stops every eight characters, so by writing tab characters, we can line up all the dollar amounts on one of these tab stops.

printf is actually more powerful than we've let on, and we'll present more of its capabilities later. But because **printf** is so powerful, there are times when it is inefficient and there are better ways to produce output. We'll discuss these methods

Aside 1.2a: The Importance of Program Layout

C is a free-format language—there are few restrictions on the format of C programs. This means we can lay out our programs any way we choose. In fact, there is nothing to prevent us from placing most of our example program on a single, lengthy line. But we didn't, for an obvious reason: the program would have been completely unreadable.

Aside 1.2b shows what happens when we don't lay out our programs carefully. It's a new version of Figure 1.7 without any indentation or white space. On top of that, we didn't bother to use defined constants or descriptive variable names. The result is a program that's an eyesore to examine and a headache to understand.

White space and consistent indentation make our programs easier to understand, so we take care to indent our statements consistently and to place spaces around operators. You don't have to mimic our formatting style, but try to ensure that whatever style you choose is consistent and readable. This may seem like more work than just haphazardly laying out the program—and it is. It takes more time to ensure that statements are indented properly than just starting everything in the first column of the line. It takes more time to define readable names for constants than to just use their underlying values throughout the program. And it takes more time to use a long name that describes a variable's use rather than simply using a short one that leaves the program's reader guessing. But this extra effort pays off in the long run, not only by making life easier for others who have to read your programs, but for you when the time comes for you to find and fix problems or make improvements to your program.

Believe it or not, though, there are actually people who enjoy reading and writing obscure C code—and for whom messy.c isn't anywhere near confusing enough to be interesting. There's an annual *Obfuscated C Code Contest* dedicated to coming up with bizarre, hard-to-understand C programs. And there's even a book, *Obfuscated C and Other Mysteries*, written by Don Libes and published by John Wiley and Sons, that is dedicated to dicussing and explaining weird C code. However, there's a big difference between purposely writing obscure and confusing code as part of a contest and accidentally writing it as part of a hurried effort to complete a program. In the latter case, you'll regret it when the day comes when you are stuck having to figure out what the program did in order to make changes to it.

later, along with other functions in the standard I/O library. Appendix A supplies a more complete description of **printf**'s formatting codes.

A Word to the Wise

Trying to learn how to write C programs simply by reading a book about it is like trying to learn how to play guitar simply by watching music videos—it's completely silly. We can't emphasize enough that the only way to really learn a programming language is to write programs in it—lots and lots of programs!

Aside 1.2b (messy.c) A much less readable version of our program to compute costs.

```
/*
 * A very messy version of our cost-computing program.
 */
#include <stdio.h>
#include <stdlib.h>
int main() {double dp;double tp;double st;double fc;
tp=23*13.95;dp=tp-tp*.18;st=dp*.075;fc=dp+st;
printf("List price per item:\t\t%7.2f\n",13.95);
printf("List price of %i items:\t\t%7.2f\n",23,tp);
printf("Price after %.1f%% discount:\t%7.2f\n",.18*100,dp);
printf("Sales tax at %.1f%%:\t\t%7.2f\n",.075*100,st);
printf("Total cost:\t\t\t%7.2f\n",fc);return EXIT_SUCCESS;}
```

As a result, each chapter in this text ends with a large set of exercises, designed to help you really master the art of programming in C. These exercises are grouped into several different categories. *Explore* involves running the chapter's example programs or making a set of specified changes to them to see what happens. *Modify* involves making changes to the chapter's example programs that are carefully tuned toward exploring how a given language feature works. *Extend* involves adding additional features to the chapter's programs that make them more powerful or robust. *Tune* involves changing the chapter's example programs to increase their portability or efficiency. *Code* involves writing from scratch brand new programs that usually require a subset of the features presented in the chapter and that are similar to the chapter's example programs. And *Build* involves implementing programming projects that are more complex than the text's example programs.

To ensure that you have mastery of the chapter's material, before moving on to the next chapter, you should successfully complete at least one or two of the exercises in each category and implement at least one of the chapter's programming projects.

SUMMARY

- A C program consists of several parts:

      preprocessor statements
      int main()
      {
         declarations
         statements
      }

- Anything between a **/*** and ***/** is treated as a comment and ignored by the compiler.

- All C programs are run through a preprocessor before they are passed to the compiler proper. Preprocessor statements are lines starting with a **#**. There are preprocessor statements to include system header files (**#include**) and to give symbolic names to constants (**#define**).

- We declare variables by providing a type (**int** for integers or **double** for floating point numbers) and a name. We assign values to variables using the = operator.

- C provides the usual arithmetic operators: **+** for addition, **-** for subtraction, ***** for multiplication, and **/** for division. The precedence of ***** and **/** is higher than that of **+** and **-**.

- We perform output by calling the **printf** library function.

  printf("*format string***", *expression-1***, ***expression-2***, ...);**

  It uses special formatting codes in its first parameter to determine how to display subsequent parameters. To use **printf**, we must remember to include stdio.h.

- **main** uses the **return** statement to provide an indication of success or failure to the calling environment. By convention, **EXIT_SUCCESS** indicates success and **EXIT_FAILURE** indicates failure. To use these constants, we must remember to include stdlib.h.

EXERCISES

1–1 Compile and run our initial welcoming program (Figure 1.1) on your computer. Does your compiler warn you about the program's sloppy coding practices? To make the compiler sufficiently picky, you may have to turn on warnings, either through command-line options or menu entries.

1–2 Experiment with making various errors in entering the programs in this chapter. What happens if you add an extra semicolon after the **main()**? Leave out the parentheses? Place an extra semicolon after the **printf**? Leave off the semicolon? Start keeping a list of different error messages and their underlying causes.

Modify

1–3 Modify our final welcoming program (Figure 1.5) to print a different message:

    This is my first C program.

1–4 Modify our initial price-computing program (Figure 1.6) to compute the price of 25 gallons of gas at $1.29 per gallon with a 3% discount and a 5% sales tax.

1–5 Repeat the previous exercise for the improved price-computing program (Figure 1.7).

1–6 Suppose we never received a discount on purchases. How could we simplify the improved price-computing program (Figure 1.7)?

Extend

1–7   Modify our final welcoming program (Figure 1.5) to print the welcome message three times, rather than just once.

1–8   Change the improved price-computing program (Figure 1.7) to print the discount per item and the total discount amount.

Tune

1–9   If your system doesn't have eight characters per tab stop, make appropriate changes to the improved price-computing program (Figure 1.7) so that its output lines up correctly anyway.

Code

1–10   Write a simple program to print the following message five times.

                `I will heed the programming advice in the text.`

1–11   Write a program to compute and print the actual cost of a new Mercedes two-seater convertible. Assume that the sticker price is $89,950, that the dealer will discount the car 12%, that there's a 10% luxury tax on the amount over $30,000, and that the state sales tax is 8.75%.

1–12   Write a program to determine the list price of a car when you know the actual cost is $12,200, the sales tax is 5.5%, and the discount is 11%.

Build

1–13   Write a program to print your net income after taxes, assuming your gross salary is $78,000, you have to pay 7.5% in social security on the first $58,000 of income, your federal tax is $3000 plus 28% of all income over $30,000, and your state tax is 10% of your gross.

Extend this program to also print the total amount paid in taxes, as well as the percentage of the gross salary that amount represents.

2 GETTING COMFORTABLE WITH C

This chapter continues our tutorial introduction to C. We focus on two new example C programs: one that computes interest accumulating in a bank account over time, the other that assigns pass/fail grades based on student scores. We describe how each of these programs works and provide several different extensions. These programs introduce C's **while** and **for** loops, **if** statement, and predefined **scanf** input function. By the chapter's end you'll have been exposed to a wide variety of C's features, and you should feel comfortable writing small but useful C programs.

2.1 A PROGRAM TO COMPUTE SIMPLE INTEREST

Let's write a new C program. This program should calculate and print the interest accumulating in a bank account over a 7-year period, assuming an initial deposit of $5000 and a simple interest rate of 6%. Here's the output we want to see when we compile and run it.

```
Interest Rate:           6.00%
Starting Balance:    $ 5000.00
Period:                  7 years

Year       Balance
   1    $ 5300.00
   2    $ 5618.00
   3    $ 5955.08
   4    $ 6312.38
   5    $ 6691.13
   6    $ 7092.60
   7    $ 7518.15
```

This output includes the account balance at the end of each year in the period. The program should use a simple interest rate compounding formula to do its calculations.

balance at year's end =
   balance at year's start + (balance at year's start × interest rate)

Using Some Familiar Features

We'll construct this program in stages, starting with some familiar C features. In particular, Figure 2.1 is a program that writes the initial headings. Its output is:

```
Interest Rate:              6.00%
Starting Balance:  $ 5000.00
Period:                      7 years

Year        Balance
```

Like most C programs, it begins with a comment describing what the program does and includes stdio.h to obtain **printf**'s prototype and stdlib.h to obtain the definitions of **EXIT_SUCCESS** and **EXIT_FAILURE**. Our program then defines three constants: **PRINCIPAL** is the initial bank balance (5000), **INTRATE** is the interest rate (.06), and **PERIOD** is the number of years our money will remain in the bank (7). We have defined **INTRATE** to be .06 rather than 6.0 to simplify our later interest calculations.

As in our earlier programs, the function **main** follows the constant definitions. **main** simply consists of several **printf**s that use these constants to display the headings.

```
printf("Interest Rate:        %7.2f%%\n", INTRATE * 100);
printf("Starting Balance:  $ %7.2f\n", PRINCIPAL);
printf("Period:                %7i years\n\n", PERIOD);
printf("Year        Balance\n");
```

The first prints the annual interest rate we're assuming, multiplied by a hundred to make it a percentage rather than a fraction. The second displays the starting balance. The third displays the period over which we are accumulating interest. The last writes the labels for the columns of years and balances.

While we could have simply placed the values of these constants directly into the **printf**s, taking the time to define these constants makes our program easy to change to apply to different balances, interest rates, and periods.

The while Loop

So far, we've only taken care of writing the headings. But we also want to print a table of years and balances. Figure 2.2 extends Figure 2.1 to also write each of the years (but not the balances). Its output is:

```
Interest Rate:              6.00%
Starting Balance:  $ 5000.00
Period:                      7 years

Year        Balance
   1
   2
   3
   4
   5
   6
   7
```

```
/*
 * Print headings for table showing interest accumulation.
 */
#include <stdio.h>
#include <stdlib.h>

#define PRINCIPAL   5000.00              /* start with $5000 */
#define INTRATE        0.06              /* interest rate of 6% */
#define PERIOD         7                 /* over 7-year period */

int main()
{
  printf("Interest Rate:      %7.2f%%\n", INTRATE * 100);
  printf("Starting Balance:  $ %7.2f\n", PRINCIPAL);
  printf("Period:             %7i years\n\n", PERIOD);
  printf("Year     Balance\n");

  return EXIT_SUCCESS;                   /* assume program worked! */
}
```

Figure 2.1   (intratp1.c) A program that writes the headings for a table showing interest accumulation.

We now make use of a new C construct: the **while** loop. In particular, to print each of these years, we use this **while** loop:

```
year = 1;
while (year <= PERIOD)
{
  printf("%4i\n", year);
  year = year + 1;
}
```

while is a mechanism for repeating one or more statements. Its syntax is:[1]

```
while (Expression)
{
  Statements
}
```

When we have only a single statement, we can eliminate the surrounding braces, allowing us to write simple loops more concisely.

A **while** evaluates the *Expression* in parentheses and, if the condition is true, executes the *Statements*. The **while** repeats the process until the condition is false, when it skips to the statement that follows it.

---

[1] In a description of the syntax of a C statement, the text in **computer** font is meant to be entered as is, and the text in *italics* should be replaced by a language construct that corresponds to what the text describes. So the **while**, the parentheses, and the braces must be provided, but the *Expression* in the **while**'s condition can be replaced with any legal C language expression and the *Statements* in its body can be replaced with any legal C language statements.

```
/*
 * Print headings and years for table showing interest accumulation.
 */
#include <stdio.h>
#include <stdlib.h>

#define PRINCIPAL  5000.00              /* start with $5000 */
#define INTRATE       0.06              /* interest rate of 6% */
#define PERIOD        7                 /* over 7-year period */

int main()
{
  int    year;                          /* year of period */

  printf("Interest Rate:      %7.2f%%\n", INTRATE * 100);
  printf("Starting Balance:  $ %7.2f\n", PRINCIPAL);
  printf("Period:             %7i years\n\n", PERIOD);
  printf("Year     Balance\n");

  year = 1;                             /* just print years */
  while (year <= PERIOD)
  {
    printf("%4i\n", year);
    year = year + 1;
  }

  return EXIT_SUCCESS;                  /* assume program worked! */
}
```

Figure 2.2   (intratp2.c) A program to write the headings and the years for our interest accumulation table.

Here, as long as **year** is less than or equal to **PERIOD**, we execute the two statements:

```
printf("%4i\n", year);
year = year + 1;
```

The first statement prints **year** and the second updates it.

Before we enter the loop, we set **year** to one, and each time through the loop, we increase **year** by one. The loop exits when **year** is finally greater than **PERIOD**. The result is that this loop runs **year** from one to **PERIOD**, writing **year**'s value each time through the loop.

The test in this **while** loop uses one of C's *relational operators*, **<=**, which tests whether a value is less than or equal to another value (**<=**). There are also operators to test for inequality (**!=**), equality (**==**), less than (**<**), greater than (**>**), and greater than or equal to (**>=**).[2]

---

[2]Chapter 6 provides a complete discussion of C's operators.

This type of use of **while** loop is called a *counting loop*, and it can be used in C whenever we want to do a particular set of statements a fixed number of times. It has the general pattern:

```
int  counting-variable;
  ...
counting-variable = starting-value;
while (counting-variable <= ending-value)
{
   actions-to-repeat
   update counting-variable
}
```

Figure 2.3 is the complete interest rate program that extends Figure 2.2 to print the balances. To do so, it adds a new variable, **balance**, that represents the balance at the end of the year. It initializes it to **PRINCIPAL** before the loop, and then modifies the loop to contain a statement using the interest rate to compute the ending balance for each year. It also changes the **printf** to write the computed balance, not just the year.

2.2   DEALING WITH COMPILE ERRORS

Learning a new programming language can be difficult, so it's likely that your first few C programs will not compile successfully the first time. Figure 2.4 contains a version of our interest rate program that illustrates several common mistakes. Figure 2.5 shows the error messages one popular compiler produces when we compile this file.[3]

Compiler error messages usually include the type of error, the file and line number where the error occurred, and a description of the mistake made. In general, there are two types of error messages: fatal errors and warnings.

Fatal errors indicate a serious problem. So serious, in fact, that no object module is created if one occurs. In our example, there are three fatal errors. The first one, the parse error at line 16, arises because we failed to put a semicolon after the first **printf**. This error message is tricky because the problem is actually with line 15, but the compiler doesn't realize that something is amiss until it sees the **printf** on the next line. But it teaches us a valuable lesson. We should treat any compiler error message as a starting point for locating errors, but we need to be prepared to look at the lines preceding the line that the compiler claims has a problem. It also shows us that some compilers aren't particularly detailed in their descriptions of problems they encounter with our program.

The second error message, the parse error at line 24, arises because we used **:=** instead of **=** in the assignment statement to update **year**. The compiler's message here is more helpful, directing us right to the source of the problem.

The final error message, the undeclared identifier in line 26, arises because we failed to include stdlib.h, the header file that defines **EXIT_SUCCESS**. The compiler simply tells us that this symbol is undefined, but it's up to us to do the detective work required to determine why. Here, we know it's a system symbol and that system symbols are

---

[3]This output comes from gcc, version 2.6.0, run with the -O and -Wall options turned on.

```
/*
 * Generate a table showing interest accumulation.
 */
#include <stdio.h>
#include <stdlib.h>

#define PRINCIPAL  5000.00                /* start with $5000 */
#define INTRATE       0.06                /* interest rate of 6% */
#define PERIOD        7                   /* over 7-year period */

int main()
{
  double balance;                         /* balance at year's end */
  int    year;                            /* year of period */

  printf("Interest Rate:      %7.2f%%\n", INTRATE * 100);
  printf("Starting Balance: $ %7.2f\n", PRINCIPAL);
  printf("Period:             %7i years\n\n", PERIOD);
  printf("Year     Balance\n");

  balance = PRINCIPAL;
  year = 1;
  while (year <= PERIOD)
  {
    balance = balance + balance * INTRATE;
    printf("%4i   $ %7.2f\n", year, balance);
    year = year + 1;
  }

  return EXIT_SUCCESS;                     /* assume program worked! */
}
```

Figure 2.3   (intrate.c) The complete program to calculate accumulated interest.

defined in header files, which gives us a clue to check whether we included all the appropriate header files.

Warnings indicate a potential problem—but not one serious enough to avoid creating an object module. As long as there are no fatal errors, the program will compile, even with warnings. The first warning, the one about **year**, occurs because our incorrect attempt at assigning a value to **year** caused the compiler to assume we were defining **year** as a label.[4] This warning illustrates that one problem can lead to the compiler making assumptions and then generating seemingly unrelated error messages. Simply fixing the problematic assignment to correct the earlier parse error will make this warning go away.

The second warning, the one about **balance**, was generated because we didn't initialize **balance** before using it (so its initial value would be whatever value is

---

[4]Chapter 7 explains what labels are and how they are used.

```
/*
 * Generate a table showing interest accumulation (contains errors).
 */
#include <stdio.h>

#define PRINCIPAL  5000.00            /* start with $5000 */
#define INTRATE    0.06              /* interest rate of 6% */
#define PERIOD     7                 /* over 7-year period */

int main()
{
  double balance;                    /* balance at year's end */
  int    year;                       /* year of period */

  printf("Interest Rate:      %7.2f%%\n", INTRATE * 100)
  printf("Starting Balance: $ %7.2f\n\n", PRINCIPAL);
  printf("Year     Balance\n");
  printf("Period:             %7i years\n\n", PERIOD);

  year = 1;
  while (year <= PERIOD)
  {
    balance = balance + balance * INTRATE;
    printf("%4i    $ %7.2f\n", year, balance);
    year := year + 1;
  }

  return EXIT_SUCCESS;                /* assume program worked! */
}
```

Figure 2.4 (oops.c) A less-than-perfect version of our interest rate program.

```
oops.c: In function 'main':
oops.c:16: parse error before 'printf'
oops.c:25: parse error before '='
oops.c:28: 'EXIT_SUCCESS' undeclared (first use this function)
oops.c:28: (Each undeclared identifier is reported only once
oops.c:28: for each function it appears in.)
oops.c:25: warning: label 'year' defined but not used
oops.c:12: warning: 'balance' might be used uninitialized in this function
oops.c:29: warning: control reaches end of non-void function
```

Figure 2.5 Sample output from compiling our erroneous interest rate program.

in the memory location assigned to it). This occurred because we forgot the statement assigning **PRINCIPAL** to **balance**. Restoring that assignment gets rid of this warning.

The final warning, the one about control, occurs because the **return**'s use of the undeclared **EXIT_SUCCESS** makes the compiler ignore that **return** (and conclude that **main**, which has promised to return an **int**, has violated that promise). Including stdlib.h to obtain **EXIT_SUCCESS**'s definition will also eliminate this warning.

> *Do not take compiler warning messages lightly.*

Compiler warnings inevitably indicate some programming mistake or faulty as-sumption, and failing to take heed of them often leads to disastrous results. Here's the output we got when we fixed our syntax errors and ran our program without fixing the source of the warnings.

```
Interest Rate:            6.00%
Starting Balance:  $ 5000.00
Period:                       7 years

Year       Balance
    1   $     0.00
    2   $     0.00
    3   $     0.00
    4   $     0.00
    5   $     0.00
    6   $     0.00
    7   $     0.00
```

The balance is incorrectly 0.00 at the end of each year. The problem arises because we didn't initialize **balance** before we tried to print its value, and on our machine it happened to be initialized to zero.

2.3   A MORE COMPACT INTEREST COMPUTING PROGRAM

Figure 2.6 contains a slight variant on our initial interest rate computing program. Our previous version used a **while** loop to update the balance.

```
year = 1;
while (year <= PERIOD)
{
  balance = balance + balance * INTRATE;
  printf("%4i    $ %7.2f\n", year, balance);
  year = year + 1;
}
```

```
/*
 * Interest rate program revised to use "for" rather than "while".
 */
#include <stdio.h>
#include <stdlib.h>

#define PRINCIPAL  5000.00              /* start with $5000 */
#define INTRATE       0.06              /* interest rate of 6% */
#define PERIOD        7                 /* over 7-year period */

int main()
{
  double balance;                       /* balance at year's end */
  int    year;                          /* year of period */

  printf("Interest Rate:     %7.2f%%\n", INTRATE * 100);
  printf("Starting Balance: $%7.2f\n\n", PRINCIPAL);
  printf("Period:            %7i years\n\n", PERIOD);
  printf("Year     Balance\n");

  balance = PRINCIPAL;
  for (year = 1; year <= PERIOD; year = year + 1)
  {
    balance = balance + balance * INTRATE;
    printf("%4i   $ %7.2f\n", year, balance);
  }

  return EXIT_SUCCESS;                  /* assume program worked! */
}
```

Figure 2.6   (intrate2.c) A version of our interest rate program that uses a **for** rather than a **while**.

Now we use another looping construct, the **for** loop.

```
for (year = 1; year <= PERIOD; year = year + 1)
{
  balance = balance + balance * INTRATE;
  printf("%4i   $ %7.2f\n", year, balance);
}
```

Most programming languages have a construct that allows us to initialize a loop index to some starting value, increment or decrement it each time through the loop, and terminate the loop when some stopping condition is met. C's **for** loop is similar but much more general. Its basic form is:

```
for ( Start ; Test ; Action )
{
   Statements
}
```

Start, *Test*, and *Action* can be any C expressions. As with the **while**, if we have a loop body containing only one statement, we don't have to provide the braces.

The **for** begins by evaluating *Start*, which usually initializes a counter. Then it evaluates *Test*, which usually tests a counter's value. It exits the loop if the condition checked is false. Otherwise, it executes the *Statements*, evaluates *Action*, and repeats the cycle. *Action* usually increments the counter controlling the loop.

Our **for** initializes **year** to one and then tests to see whether it's less than or equal to **PERIOD**. If it is, it executes the loop body (printing the current balance and computing the next balance), increments **year**, and does the test again. The loop exits when **year** is greater than **PERIOD**.

We prefer **for** to **while** for implementing counting loops. With a **while** loop, it's not always immediately obvious that the point of the loop is to do a particular action *N* times, as the update of the loop counter may be buried in the middle of a sizable loop body. On top of that, the initialization of the variable used as the loop counter may happen long before the **while**. In contrast, with a **for** we can tell at a glance what's happening. The result is that the **for** leads to a more concise, more readable program, even though both loops are appropriate.

> *Use **for** rather than **while** to implement counting loops.*

2.4   EXTENDING OUR INTEREST PROGRAM TO READ VALUES

Let's make our interest accumulation program more flexible. Rather than hard-wiring the initial balance (**PRINCIPAL**), the interest rate (**INTRATE**), and the number of years (**PERIOD**), we'll obtain these values from an interactive user. Figure 2.7 contains the new version of the program. Here's a sample run:

```
Enter interest rate, principal, and period: .04 1000 7
Interest Rate:        4.00%
Starting Balance: $ 1000.00

Year     Balance
   1    $ 1040.00
   2    $ 1081.60
   3    $ 1124.86
   4    $ 1169.86
   5    $ 1216.65
   6    $ 1265.32
   7    $ 1315.93
```

Using **scanf**

To read input, we use a new standard I/O library function, **scanf**, the input analog to **printf** (so, as with **printf**, we need to include stdio.h to use it). **scanf** reads formatted input from the *standard input*, which is usually the keyboard.

```
/*
 * Interest rate program revised to allow user input.
 */
#include <stdio.h>
#include <stdlib.h>

int main()
{
  double intrate;                        /* interest rate */
  double balance;                        /* balance at year's end */
  int    year;                           /* year of period */
  int    period;                         /* length of period */

  printf("Enter interest rate, principal, and period: ");
  scanf("%lf%lf%i", &intrate, &balance, &period);

  printf("Interest Rate:     %7.2f%%\n", intrate * 100);
  printf("Starting Balance: $ %7.2f\n\n", balance);
  printf("Period:            %7i years\n\n", period);
  printf("Year      Balance\n");

  for (year = 1; year <= period; year = year + 1)
  {
    balance = balance + balance * intrate;
    printf("%4i   $ %7.2f\n", year, balance);
  }

  return EXIT_SUCCESS;                    /* assume program worked! */
}
```

Figure 2.7 (intrate3.c) An interest rate program that gets user input.

scanf's arguments are a formatting control string, enclosed in quotation marks, and a list of locations where values are to be stored. The control string uses conventions just similar enough to those of **printf** to cause confusion. As expected, we can use **%i** and **%d** to read a base 10 **int**. But rather than using **%f** to read a **double**, we must use **%lf**, which stands for "long float", a double-precision floating point value.

scanf works by reading input from the user and *scanning* it for values of the types specified in the control string. That is, **scanf** works its way through the control string, and whenever it encounters a field specification, such as **%i** or **%lf**, it skips space characters, such as blanks, tabs, and line boundaries, and tries to read a value of the specified type.

Figure 2.7 begins by using **printf** to write a prompt requesting the starting balance, interest rate, and period. It then uses **scanf** to obtain their values from the user.

```
printf("Enter interest rate, principal, and period: ");
scanf("%lf%lf%i", &intrate, &balance, &period);
```

scanf reads two floating point values and an integer from the program's input. Because **scanf** automatically ignores intervening white space, the input values can be widely separated and do not even have to be on the same line.

In general, the first call a program makes to **scanf** causes it to read a line of input from the user. If **scanf** makes it to the end of a line without reading all the values it is looking for (such as seeing two values when it expects three), it will wait for the user to enter another line of input and then continue by processing it. However, if it finds what it's looking for early (such as receiving a line with five values when it is only trying to read three) and we then call it again, it first examines the rest of the line it last read before moving on to the next line.

scanf ignores space characters in the control string, but expects any other characters that appear in the control string to appear in its input as well.

There's one small—but crucial—detail we've so far ignored. We don't simply provide **scanf** a list of variable names. **scanf** expects to be passed a variable's *address* rather than its name. To obtain a variable's address, we simply precede its name with the address-of operator **&**. Forgetting the address operator **&** causes strange and unforgiving behavior (we'll see why when we examine what addresses actually are and consider how function parameters work).

> *Remember to precede any variables passed to* **scanf** *with an* **&**.

Repeatedly Reading Input

To explore the effects of more than one interest rate, principal, or period, we're now stuck with repeatedly running our interest computing program. We would much rather run it just once. Figure 2.8 is a new version of this program that lets us enter more than one interest rate, principal, and period.

It turns out that **scanf** not only reads values but also tells us how many values it correctly read. It does so by *returning* this value after it finishes executing. One common way to process a return value is to save it in a variable, like this,

```
n = scanf("%lf%lf%i", &intrate, &balance, &period);
```

and then use that variable later on in the program. In this case, we are saving **scanf**'s return value into **n**. The idea is that after **scanf** executes, it returns the number of values it actually read and this number is then placed in the variable **n**. If **n** is two, for example, it means that **scanf** only read the first two values (the interest rate and balance) successfully and ran into trouble trying to read the period (perhaps because the user entered a word rather than a number). Once we've saved this return value, we could, for example, use it to print the number of values the call to **scanf** actually read.

In general, **scanf** succeeded in reading the desired input values only if it returns the number of values we asked it to read. Here, we ask it to read three values, so the **scanf** succeeded only if it returns three, and it failed if it returns zero, one, or two.

Besides returning a value between zero and the number of values we requested, **scanf** might also return the special value **EOF**, a constant (defined in stdio.h) that

```c
/*
 * The interest rate program revised to repeatedly read input values.
 */
#include <stdio.h>
#include <stdlib.h>

int main()
{
  double intrate;                          /* interest rate */
  double balance;                          /* balance at year's end */
  int    year;                             /* year of period */
  int    period;                           /* length of period */
  int    n;                                /* number of values read */

  printf("Enter interest rate, principal, and period: ");
  n = scanf("%lf%lf%i", &intrate, &balance, &period);

  while (n == 3)
  {
    printf("Interest Rate:      %7.2f%%\n", intrate * 100);
    printf("Starting Balance: $ %7.2f\n", balance);
    printf("Period:             %7i years\n\n", period);
    printf("Year     Balance\n");
    for (year = 1; year <= period; year = year + 1)
    {
      balance = balance + balance * intrate;
      printf("%4i    $ %7.2f\n", year, balance);
    }

    printf("\nEnter interest rate, principal, and period: ");
    n = scanf("%lf%lf%i", &intrate, &balance, &period);
  }

  return EXIT_SUCCESS;                      /* assume always succeeds */
}
```

Figure 2.8 (intrate4.c) A version of our interest computing program that allows us to enter more than one set of input values.

indicates that the end of the input has been reached. When the input is coming from the keyboard, the user signals the end of input by typing a special, system-dependent character.[5]

To read all input values, we need to combine **scanf** with **while**. This particular use of **while** is called an *input-reading* loop and has the general form shown on the top of the next page.

---

[5]Usually **EOF** is defined as −1, although its value is system-dependent. By default, on UNIX systems the EOF character is a control-*D*. On MS-DOS, it's a control-*Z* at the start of the line and immediately followed by a carriage return.

```
print prompt
n = scanf( ... );
while ( n == expected-number-of-values )
{
   process just-read input values
   print prompt
   n = scanf( ... );
}
```

Figure 2.8 uses an input-reading loop like this one. It wraps the process of writing the headings and computing the year-ending balances in a **while** loop. Before entering the loop, it prints a prompt, uses **scanf** to read the first set of input values, and records the number of values we read. The loop then tests whether we read the number of values we expected and, if we did, processes those values (printing the headings and the table of years and balances), prints a prompt, and then reads the next set of values.

```
printf("Enter interest rate, principal, and period: ");
n = scanf("%lf%lf%i", &intrate, &balance, &period);
while (n == 3)
{
   compute and print balances
   printf("Enter interest rate, principal, and period: ");
   n = scanf("%lf%lf%i", &intrate, &balance, &period);
}
```

This loop processes input as long as we can successfully read three new values (the interest rate, starting balance, and period). There are two reasons why we might fail: we hit the end of the input or there's an error in the input. In either case, this will cause **scanf**'s return value, which we store in **n**, to be something other than three.

2.5   A PROGRAM TO PROCESS SCORES

We're going tackle a new task: writing a program to read student test scores (values between 0 and 100), to assign pass/fail grades, and to display how many scores we read, how many passed and failed, and the average score. We'll assume that 70 or better is passing and anything less than 70 is failing. Here's some example input and output:

```
Score? 91
91 - Passes
Score? 70
70 - Passes
Score? 60
60 - Fails
Score? 69
69 - Fails
Score? control-D
4 scores entered, 2 pass, 2 fail.
Average: 72
```

Another Input-Reading Loop

There's a lot to writing this program. As a result, we'll start slowly and simply write the part of the program that reads each test score and prints it. This is called *echoing* the input. Figure 2.9 contains this initial grading program. It prompts the user for each test score, and after reading all the input values it prints a count of the number of scores we read. Here is some sample I/O for this program:

```
Score? 91
91
Score? 70
70
Score? 60
60
Score? control-D
3 scores entered.
```

This program consists primarily of an input-reading loop, whose processing of each new input value is simply to print it and then update the count of values read. This program differs from our interest rate program in that each time through we expect to read one score, not three, so we compare **scanf**'s return value to one to check whether we were successful in reading that score.

The **if** Statement

Figure 2.10 extends Figure 2.9 to print "Passes" or "Fails" after each score, depending on whether the score is 70 or greater. It also prints the total number of passes and fails. Here is some sample I/O for this program:

```
Score? 91
91 - Passes
Score? 70
70 - Passes
Score? 60
60 - Fails
Score? control-D
3 scores entered, 2 pass, 1 fail.
```

This program uses a new C construct: the **if** statement.

```
if (Expression)
{
   True-statements
}
else
{
   False-statements
}
```

if evaluates the expression in parentheses and, if the condition is true, executes the *True-statements*. If the condition is false, it executes the *False-statements*. The **else**

```
/*
 * A program to read, print, and count scores.
 */
#include <stdio.h>
#include <stdlib.h>

int main()
{
  int next_score;         /* current input value */
  int n;                  /* input values read with last scanf */
  int score_count;        /* count of scores read */

  score_count = 0;
  printf("Score? ");
  n = scanf("%i", &next_score);
  while (n == 1)
  {
    score_count = score_count + 1;
    printf("%i\n", next_score);
    printf("Score? ");
    n = scanf("%i", &next_score);
  }
  printf("\n%i scores entered.\n", score_count);

  return EXIT_SUCCESS;
}
```

Figure 2.9   (gradep1.c)   A program to read scores and print them.

and the *False-statements* are optional. If we omit them and the condition is false, *True-statements* are simply skipped.[6] As with **while** and **for**, we don't need the braces surrounding the *True-statements* or the *False-statements* when they consist of a single statement.

In particular, our grading program uses this **if** statement:

```
if (next_score >= PASSING_SCORE)
{
  printf("%i - Passes\n", next_score);
  pass_count = pass_count + 1;
}
else
{
  printf("%i - Fails\n", next_score);
  fail_count = fail_count + 1;
}
```

---

[6]Unlike many other programming languages, there is no **then** keyword, and *Expression* must be surrounded with parentheses.

```c
/*
 * Extending our previous program to assign pass/fail grades.
 */
#include <stdio.h>
#include <stdlib.h>

#define PASSING_SCORE 70

int main()
{
  int next_score;          /* current input value */
  int n;                   /* input values read with last scanf */
  int score_count;         /* count of scores read */
  int pass_count;          /* count of passing scores */
  int fail_count;          /* count of failing scores */

  score_count = 0;
  pass_count = 0;
  fail_count = 0;

  printf("Score? ");
  n = scanf("%i", &next_score);

  while (n == 1)
  {
    score_count = score_count + 1;
    if (next_score >= PASSING_SCORE)
    {
      printf("%i - Passes\n", next_score);
      pass_count = pass_count + 1;
    }
    else
    {
      printf("%i - Fails\n", next_score);
      fail_count = fail_count + 1;
    }

    printf("Score? ");
    n = scanf("%i", &next_score);
  }

  printf("\n%i scores entered, %i pass, %i fail.\n",
         score_count, pass_count, fail_count);

  return EXIT_SUCCESS;
}
```

Figure 2.10   (gradep2.c) A program to read scores and identify each as passing or failing.

Aside 2.1: Developing Programs Incrementally

We can view implementing a C program as a three-step process: *code* (writing the necessary C instructions), *compile* (modifying the source as necessary to get rid of compiler errors), *debug* (repeatedly running the program, comparing its behavior to what's expected, locating the source of any errors, and modifying their source).

This view, however, is too simplistic, and it tends to lead us into the trap of trying to code an entire program in one shot (such as simply sitting down and writing the final grading program). But, tempting as it is, one-shot development has proven not to be a workable approach to creating software. Experience has shown that it is much better to build programs as we have been doing in this chapter, using a technique called *incremental program development*. The idea is to start by coding, compiling, and debugging only a small piece of the desired program. Then, once we're sure that works, we go through the same process with a small, incremental extension to the program, and we keep repeating the process until we have implemented the desired solution.

There are several reasons why incremental program development is a good idea. One is that small problems are easier to solve than large ones. By tackling a large, difficult problem one small piece at a time, we are essentially dividing it into a series of smaller, simpler problems. Yet we wind up eventually solving the bigger problem.

Another is that it's easy to make mistakes when we write code. If we write the whole program at once, the problem might lie *anywhere* in the entire program, which makes it very difficult to track down. On the other hand, if we add just a few lines of code each time, any problem that creeps in must be due to the lines we most recently added, and we can focus our attention there.

Finally, coding, compiling, and debugging is a learning process. If we code the whole program and we realize while trying to debug it that we misunderstood a language concept, we may have to rewrite much of our code. If we just code a small piece, we can take advantage of what we learned when we code later portions of the program.

In reality, there is much more to program development than we've let on here. We've left off the key issues of design (taking a problem specification and sketching out the overall pieces of the program) and testing (trying numerous inputs to try to verify that the program always produces the correct results)—areas we will discuss later.

This works by comparing **next_score** to **PASSING_SCORE** (70) using the greater-than-or-equal operator (**>=**). If the test is true, it means the score is greater than or equal to 70, and we execute the group of statements immediately following the test. In this case, those statements print the score and "Passes", and then update a count of passing scores. If the test fails, we execute the group of statements following the **else**, which print the score and "Fails", and update a count of failing scores.

Figure 2.11 shows the final grading program that now also prints the average score.[7] We do so by adding each score to a running total and then dividing this running total

---

[7]To fit this program on a single page, we have taken advantage of C's unrestricted program layout and placed on a single line all of the assignments that set the various counters to zero.

```c
/*
 * The complete grading program.
 */
#include <stdio.h>
#include <stdlib.h>

#define PASSING_SCORE 70

int main()
{
  int next_score;          /* current input value */
  int n;                   /* input values read with last scanf */
  int score_count;         /* count of scores read */
  int pass_count;          /* count of passing scores */
  int fail_count;          /* count of failing scores */
  int avg_score;           /* average score */
  int total_score;         /* total score */

  score_count = 0;  pass_count = 0;  fail_count = 0;  total_score = 0;

  printf("Score? ");
  n = scanf("%i", &next_score);
  while (n == 1)
  {
    score_count = score_count + 1;
    total_score = total_score + next_score;
    if (next_score >= PASSING_SCORE)
    {
      printf("%i - Passes\n", next_score);
      pass_count = pass_count + 1;
    }
    else
    {
      printf("%i - Fails\n", next_score);
      fail_count = fail_count + 1;
    }
    printf("Score? ");
    n = scanf("%i", &next_score);
  }
  if (score_count == 0)
    avg_score = 0;
  else
    avg_score = total_score / score_count;
  printf("\n%i scores entered, %i pass, %i fail.\n",
         score_count, pass_count, fail_count);
  printf("Average: %i\n", avg_score);

  return EXIT_SUCCESS;
}
```

Figure 2.11   (grade.c)   The complete program to assign pass/fail grades.

by the number of scores we've read. But we have to be careful. It's possible that the user won't enter any scores at all, in which case we will be dividing by zero when we compute the average. The problem is that dividing by zero is undefined, which means the behavior of our program is unpredictable—on some computers, we'll simply get the wrong results, but on others our program will terminate with a run-time error.

The bottom line is that we need to avoid dividing by zero. We do so by testing whether the count of scores read is zero. If it is, we assign zero to the average; otherwise, we do the necessary division.

```
if (score_count == 0)
  avg_score = 0;
else
  avg_score = total_score / score_count;
```

Here, we take advantage of the ability to elide the braces surrounding the **if**'s statement lists when they contain a single statement.

2.6   HANDLING INPUT ERRORS

Both of our programs to process their input have a major flaw: they don't say anything if they aren't given the input they expect. The interest accumulator, for example, quietly terminates if it isn't given the two **double**s and the **int** that it expects. Similarly, the grading program simply stops reading any more input and prints the average and the various counts. That's undesirable, since it's easy for the user to accidentally provide three floating point values instead of two, provide letters rather than numbers, or possibly provide no input at all. And if the user does so, the user will be left scratching his or her head trying to figure out why the program didn't produce the expected results. To minimize user confusion, invalid input should at the very least result in an error message.

Figure 2.12 shows how we can address this problem in our interest rate program. For valid input, it produces the same output as Figure 2.8. But for invalid input, such as providing a name rather than the expected numbers, it lets us know there's a problem:

```
Enter interest rate, principal, and period: alex
Warning: Input reading terminated by error.
```

The trick is to take advantage of **scanf**'s return value. Our input-reading loop stops when **scanf** has returned something other than three (the number of values we expect). If there's no input error, that should be because the user entered the end-of-file character and **scanf** returns **EOF**. Otherwise, the user did enter some input and **scanf** was able to read zero, one, or two values successfully before it encountered a problem.

This behavior allows us to easily determine whether an input error has occurred. After the loop terminates, we test whether or not **n** (which we are using to hold **scanf**'s return value) is **EOF**. If it isn't, that means we stopped because of an error, and we write an appropriate error message.

```
if (n != EOF)
  printf("Warning: Input reading terminated by error.\n");
```

```
/*
 * The interest rate program revised to notify about input errors.
 */
#include <stdio.h>
#include <stdlib.h>

int main()
{
  double intrate;                            /* interest rate */
  double balance;                            /* balance at year's end */
  int    year;                               /* year of period */
  int    period;                             /* length of period */
  int    n;                                  /* number of values read */

  printf("Enter interest rate, principal, and period: ");
  n = scanf("%lf%lf%i", &intrate, &balance, &period);

  while (n == 3)
  {
    printf("Interest Rate:     %7.2f%%\n", intrate * 100);
    printf("Starting Balance: $ %7.2f\n", balance);
    printf("Period:            %7i years\n\n", period);
    printf("Year     Balance\n");
    for (year = 1; year <= period; year = year + 1)
    {
      balance = balance + balance * intrate;
      printf("%4i   $ %7.2f\n", year, balance);
    }

    printf("\nEnter interest rate, principal, and period: ");
    n = scanf("%lf%lf%i", &intrate, &balance, &period);
  }

  if (n != EOF)
    printf("Warning: Input reading terminated by error.\n");

  return EXIT_SUCCESS;                        /* assume always succeeds */
}
```

Figure 2.12 (intrate5.c) A version of our interest accumulating program that detects erroneous input.

We don't have an **else** for this **if** because we don't want to print any message if we are terminating because of end of file.

> *Test **scanf**'s return value to verify that the input was read successfully.*

scanf is a useful function, but less useful than it may at first appear. One problem is that we usually can use it only when we can assume that the input is correct, as when our

Aside 2.2a: Debugging Programs

What do you do when your program compiles but produces incorrect output? Aside 2.2b is such a program, a variant of Figure 2.10 that produces this output:

```
Score? 90
90 - Passes
Score? 60
60 - Fails
Score? 40
40 - Fails
Score? 80
80 - Passes
Score? control-D
4 scores entered, 5 pass, 4 fail.
```

Most of this output is fine, except for the pass/fail totals.

Finding and fixing mistakes like these is the process of debugging. The key to debugging is to be able to *explain* why the program produced the incorrect output. Here, the incorrect output is the values of **pass_count** and **fail_count**, so we are apparently not updating those counts correctly. Our program should be updating exactly one of these counts each time through the loop, but clearly isn't doing so. A reasonable way to see exactly what's actually happening is to place a **printf** to print the values of these counts at the bottom of the loop. Aside 2.2c does so, and here's some input and output when we run it.

```
Score? 90
90 - Passes
DEBUG: pass_count=2, fail_count=1
Score? 60
60 - Fails
DEBUG: pass_count=2, fail_count=2
Score? 75
75 - Passes
DEBUG: pass_count=4, fail_count=3
Score? control-D
3 scores entered, 4 pass, 3 fail.
```

Now we have a big clue as to what's happening. After the very first score we process, **pass_count** and **fail_count** are incorrect. **pass_count** should be set to 1, but it's 2! Examining the statement updating **pass_count**, we can see why: We are accidentally setting it to **score_count** + 1, not **pass_count** + 1. The other problem is that **fail_count** is getting updated after every score. Upon closer inspection, we can see why: we forgot the braces around the **else** part of the **if**. As a result, only the **printf** to write "Fails" is part of the **else**, and the update of **fail_count** happens every time through the loop. Fixing these two mistakes leads us to the working program we had before.

In general, when our output is incorrect, we need to place **printf**s in the program to display the values of those variables in the places where they are updated.

Aside 2.2b (badgrade.c) A version of our grading program that contains several mistakes.

```c
/*
 * A new version of our previous program to assign pass/fail grades.
 *
 * This version has several errors that lead it to produce incorrect
 * output.
 */
#include <stdio.h>
#include <stdlib.h>

#define PASSING_SCORE 70

int main()
{
  int next_score;        /* current input value */
  int n;                 /* input values read with last scanf */
  int score_count;       /* count of scores read */
  int pass_count;        /* count of passing scores */
  int fail_count;        /* count of failing scores */

  score_count = 0;
  pass_count = 0;
  fail_count = 0;

  printf("Score? ");
  n = scanf("%i", &next_score);

  while (n == 1)
  {
    score_count = score_count + 1;
    if (next_score >= PASSING_SCORE)
    {
      printf("%i - Passes\n", next_score);
      pass_count = score_count + 1;
    }
    else
      printf("%i - Fails\n", next_score);
      fail_count = fail_count + 1;

    printf("Score? ");
    n = scanf("%i", &next_score);
  }
  printf("\n%i scores entered, %i pass, %i fail.\n",
         score_count, pass_count, fail_count);

  return EXIT_SUCCESS;
}
```

Aside 2.2c (fixgrade.c) Our mistaken grading program instrumented to provide some debugging output.

```
/*
 * Adding debugging printfs to our erroneous grading program.
 */
#include <stdio.h>
#include <stdlib.h>

#define PASSING_SCORE 70

int main()
{
  int next_score;         /* current input value */
  int n;                  /* input values read with last scanf */
  int score_count;        /* count of scores read */
  int pass_count;         /* count of passing scores */
  int fail_count;         /* count of failing scores */

  score_count = 0;
  pass_count = 0;
  fail_count = 0;

  printf("Score? ");
  n = scanf("%i", &next_score);

  while (n == 1)
  {
    score_count = score_count + 1;
    if (next_score >= PASSING_SCORE)
    {
      printf("%i - Passes\n", next_score);
      pass_count = score_count + 1;
    }
    else
      printf("%i - Fails\n", next_score);
      fail_count = fail_count + 1;

    printf("DEBUG: pass_count=%i, fail_count=%i\n",
           pass_count, fail_count);

    printf("Score? ");
    n = scanf("%i", &next_score);
  }

  printf("\n%i scores entered, %i pass, %i fail.\n",
         score_count, pass_count, fail_count);

  return EXIT_SUCCESS;
}
```

input has been generated by another program. Why? Because, as we've seen, **scanf** simply quits reading input at the first unexpected character. The problem is that there's no simple way to use it to skip over illegal input. As a result, many programs that use **scanf** simply terminate as soon they encounter problematic input, and this behavior makes them much less user-friendly than we would like.[8]

Another problem has to do with efficiency. Since **scanf** can read an arbitrary number of values of differing types, its underlying implementation is often large and cumbersome.

In subsequent chapters we'll look at low-level input in detail and develop solutions to these problems.

2.7   THE ASSIGNMENT OPERATOR

One drawback of the input-reading loop we have been using is that we have to repeat the input-reading statement twice, once before we enter the loop and again at the end of each pass through the loop. Unfortunately, repeating code is asking for trouble. Not only do we increase the chances of making an error by failing to repeat the code exactly, but we also make it more difficult to modify the program (such as to read an extra item on each input line), as we have to remember to make the change in more than one place.

Figure 2.13 is a revised version of Figure 2.12 that avoids this problem. Rather than having two separate calls to **scanf**, we use a single call within the loop test.

```
while ((n = scanf("%lf %lf %i", ...)) == 3)
{
    ...
}
```

This loop test is tricky. What's going on here is that assignment, **=**, is an operator; it assigns a value to a variable and then returns the value assigned. This behavior allows us to then use this value in another expression.

In this case, after **scanf** reads the input values, we assign its return value to **n**, just like before. But now we also compare the value we assigned with 3 to determine if the loop should exit.

In general, we can translate any input-reading loop that we saw before into the simpler:

```
print prompt
while ((n = scanf( ...)) == expected-number-of-values)
{
    process just-read input values
    print prompt
}
```

---

[8] It's reasonable to wonder why our program always returns **EXIT_SUCCESS**, even if it has terminated due to an input error. One reason is just to keep our program simple. A more important reason, however, is that the failure could happen after any number of successful input values, so it's not clear that returning **EXIT_FAILURE** would be appropriate.

```
/*
 * The interest rate program made more concise using the "=" operator.
 */
#include <stdio.h>
#include <stdlib.h>

int main()
{
  double intrate;                       /* interest rate */
  double balance;                       /* balance at year's end */
  int    year;                          /* year of period */
  int    period;                        /* length of period */
  int    n;                             /* number of values read */

  printf("Enter interest rate, principal, and period: ");
  while ((n = scanf("%lf%lf%i", &intrate, &balance, &period)) == 3)
  {
    printf("Interest Rate:       %7.2f%%\n", intrate * 100);
    printf("Starting Balance: $ %7.2f\n", balance);
    printf("Period:             %7i years\n\n", period);
    printf("Year      Balance\n");

    for (year = 1; year <= period; year = year + 1)
    {
      balance = balance + balance * intrate;
      printf("%4i    $ %7.2f\n", year, balance);
    }
    printf("Enter interest rate, principal, and period: ");
  }

  if (n != EOF)
    printf("Warning: Input reading terminated by error.\n");

  return EXIT_SUCCESS;                   /* assume always succeeds */
}
```

Figure 2.13 (intrate6.c) A more concise version of our interest computing program that allows us to enter more than one set of input values.

Assignment as an operator is a powerful feature, but it has several potential pitfalls. It can make our programs harder to understand, since an embedded assignment can make a single expression do several different things. Above, we manage to read input, save a function's return value, and determine whether to exit the loop, all in a single expression. It also has very low precedence, which usually gets us into trouble if we don't surround its use with parentheses.

> *Parenthesize any assignment you embed in a larger expression.*

Aside 2.3: Avoiding Common Errors

Debugging programs can be frustrating, difficult, and time-consuming. That's especially true when the program appears to go into an infinite loop, or the program dies with an incomprehensible system error message (such as "Bus Error" or "Segmentation Violation", which are common error messages in the UNIX world, or "Process Stopped Responding", which is a common message in the world of Microsoft Windows).

One way to minimize the frequency of these errors is to examine your program source using a "checklist" of common mistakes. Alternatively, you can wait until your program dies and then use the checklist to help you locate problem code.

Here are the errors that seem to show up the most and their likely symptoms when you run the program.

- Forgetting the **&** in front of a numeric variable being passed to **scanf** (program crashes).

- Not providing enough values for the formatting strings you have provided to **scanf** or **printf** (program crashes or produces strange output values).

- Providing the wrong formatting control for the type of value you are trying to read or write (program crashes or produces strange output values).

- Forgetting to provide the statement to update the counter in a counting loop (program goes into an infinite loop).

- Forgetting to provide a **scanf** inside an input-reading loop (program goes into an infinite loop).

- Forgetting to initialize a numeric variable (program produces strange output values or goes into an infinite loop).

- Accidentally using = instead of == in a test (program never goes through a loop or goes into an infinite loop).

- Failing to put parentheses around the = when it is embedded within a test (program never goes through a loop or goes into an infinite loop).

Many compilers will warn you about the last three, so taking care to understand every warning will help you eliminate these types of mistakes.

SUMMARY

- C provides the **while** and **for** looping constructs. The **while** repeatedly tests an expression and, if it's true, executes the body of the loop. The **for** allows us to initialize a variable before going through the loop and to update it each time we finish executing the loop body.

- We use the **while** primarily for input-reading loops (and other loops that repeat as long as some arbitrary condition is true). We use the **for** primarily for counting loops (and other loops that need to be executed a fixed number of times).

- C provides a variety of operators for doing comparisons (**==, !=, <, <=, >, >=**) and for taking an address (**&**).

- We perform formatted input with the predefined **scanf** function.

  > **scanf** (**"***format string***"**, *address-1*, *address-2*, ...**)**

  To use **scanf**, we need to include stdio.h.

- We make decisions using the **if** statement. The **if** statement evaluates an expression and uses its value to determine which one of two sets of statements to execute. If it's true, the **if** executes the statements immediately following the test, and if it's false, the **if** executes the statements after the **else**.

- In C, assignment is an operator that returns the value assigned. This often lets us write concise code.

EXERCISES

Explore	**2–1** Compile and run each of this chapter's programs on your computer.

2–2 Fix the errors but not the warnings in our erroneous interest rate program (Figure 2.4). What output does the program produce on your machine with your compiler?

2–3 Delete the **&** before **balance** in the **scanf** in the first interest rate program that reads input (Figure 2.7). What happens when you execute the program?

Modify

2–4 Modify the error-checking version of the interest rate program (Figure 2.13) to expect input values separated by a comma. What happens when the user separates the numbers by spaces instead?

2–5 Rewrite Chapter 1's final cost-computing program (Figure 1.7) to read any values it needs, rather than defining them as constants.

Extend

2–6 Make Chapter 1's final welcoming program (Figure 1.3) print the welcoming message over and over, one per line, until it fills the entire screen (that's usually 24 lines on most terminals or PCs in text mode).

2–7 Extend the final version of the interest rate program (Figure 2.13) to verify that the balance and interest rate are both positive numbers. Write appropriate error messages if either is not.

2–8 Extend the final version of the interest rate program (Figure 2.13) to print a count of the number of initial balances that are successfully processed.

Code

2–9 Write a program to print the integers between M and N, inclusive, where M and N are program constants. With an M of 1 and an N of 5, it should write the numbers 1, 2, 3, 4, and 5. Assume $M \leq N$.

2–10 Write a program that prints the integers between M and N, inclusive, in reverse order. That is, with an M of 1 and an N of 5, its output is 5, 4, 3, 2, and 1. Assume $M \leq N$.

2–11 Write a small program to print the sum of the integers between M and N, inclusive, where M and N are program constants. With an M of 1 and an N of 100, your program should print 5050.

Modify the program to use **scanf** to read the two limiting values and to behave sensibly even if $M \geq N$.

2–12 Write a program to print the sum of its input values, assuming that they're **double**s.

2–13 Write a program to print the largest and smallest values in its input. The program should behave reasonably even when there are no input values.

2–14 Write a program that reads two values, **min** and **max**, and then reads the remainder of its input, counting the values less than **min** and those greater than **max**. When the program is done reading its input, it prints these two counts.

Build

2–15 Write a program to print a multiplication table for the integers 1 through 12. The table should have 12 rows of 12 columns. The first row of the table contains the values of $1 \times 1, 1 \times 2, \ldots, 1 \times 12$, the second row of the table contains the values of $2 \times 1, 2 \times 2, \ldots, 2 \times 12$, and so on.

Make sure your program provides labels for the table's rows and columns, as in the table shown below.

```
        1    2    3    4    5    6    7    8    9   10   11   12
    +-----------------------------------------------------------
  1|    1    2    3    4    5    6    7    8    9   10   11   12
  2|    2    4    6    8   10   12   14   16   18   20   22   24
  3|    3    6    9   12   15   18   21   24   27   30   33   36
  4|    4    8   12   16   20   24   28   32   36   40   44   48
  5|    5   10   15   20   25   30   35   40   45   50   55   60
  6|    6   12   18   24   30   36   42   48   54   60   66   72
  7|    7   14   21   28   35   42   49   56   63   70   77   84
  8|    8   16   24   32   40   48   56   64   72   80   88   96
  9|    9   18   27   36   45   54   63   72   81   90   99  108
 10|   10   20   30   40   50   60   70   80   90  100  110  120
 11|   11   22   33   44   55   66   77   88   99  110  121  132
 12|   12   24   36   48   60   72   84   96  108  120  132  144
```

Modify your program to read two input values to use as the bounds for the table. Your program should work regardless of which order the bounds are entered.

2–16 Write a program to print a table of powers. The program should read three values: a **base** and two exponents, **min** and **max**. Assume the input values are positive integers. The program should print $base^n$ for $min \leq n \leq max$.

With a **base** of 2, a **min** of 0, and a **max** of 3, the program's output should be:

```
Base   Exp   Result
   2     0        1
   2     1        2
   2     2        4
   2     3        8
```

Extend your solution to allow negative powers. The result should now be a **double**.

3

AN

INTRODUCTION

TO

FUNCTIONS

This chapter finishes our tutorial introduction to C. We focus on user-defined functions, showing how we can define simple functions and use them to improve upon our earlier interest rate programs. Along the way, we cover function definitions, function calls, function prototypes, and function return values. We also introduce the process of compiling programs that contain functions defined in multiple source files. Finally, we demonstrate how using functions leads to more readable and maintainable programs, and we discuss how to test the functions we've written. By this chapter's end, you should feel comfortable constructing programs from functions you write yourself.

3.1   WRITING OUR OWN FUNCTIONS

A C program is simply a collection of one or more functions (including **main**). Some, such as **scanf** and **printf**, come predefined with the standard C libraries. But the vast majority of functions are user-defined. So far, **main** is the only function we've written. But when we write larger programs, we need to break them into smaller, more manageable pieces. Functions are the mechanism that lets us do so. We can create common, single-purpose routines and use them from the main program, without the main program's having to know how they actually accomplish their task. In fact, we have already used functions that were prewritten and compiled for us, such as **printf** and **scanf**, without knowing what they look like internally.

Figure 3.1 is a new variant of our interest rate program that shows how to create and use our own functions. This program produces output similar to the output generated by our previous interest rate programs. However, we thought you might be getting bored with seeing version after version of the interest rate program, so this version has a slight twist: it now compounds interest monthly rather than annually. And because we wanted this entire program to fit on a single page, we've eliminated the previous version's error

```c
/*
 * A new version of our interest rate program that compounds interest
 * monthly, rather than yearly.
 */
#include <stdio.h>
#include <stdlib.h>

int main()
{
  double yearEndBalance(double monthly_bal,
                        double interest_rate);

  int     period;                          /* length of period */
  int     year;                            /* year of period */
  double  balance;                         /* balance at end of year */
  double  intrate;                         /* interest rate */

  printf("Enter interest rate, principal, and period: ");
  scanf("%lf %lf %i", &intrate, &balance, &period);

  printf("Interest Rate:     %7.2f%%\n", intrate * 100);
  printf("Starting Balance: $ %7.2f\n", balance);
  printf("Period:            %7i years\n\n", period);
  printf("Year     Balance\n");

  for (year = 1; year <= period; year = year + 1)
  {
    balance = yearEndBalance(balance, intrate);
    printf("%4i   $ %7.2f\n", year, balance);
  }

  return EXIT_SUCCESS;                      /* assume program succeeded */
}

/* Compute a year's ending balance, compounding interest monthly */

double yearEndBalance(double monthly_bal,
                      double interest_rate)
{
  double  monthly_intrate;                 /* % interest per month */
  int     month;                           /* current month */

  monthly_intrate = interest_rate / 12;
  for (month = 1; month <= 12; month = month + 1)
    monthly_bal = monthly_bal * monthly_intrate + monthly_bal;

  return monthly_bal;
}
```

Figure 3.1 (intrate7.c) A new variant of our interest rate computing program. This time we compound interest monthly, rather than annually.

checking and reading of multiple input values. Here is some sample input and output for the program.

```
Enter interest rate, principal, and period: .04 1000 7
Interest Rate:          4.00%
Starting Balance: $ 1000.00
Period:                    7 years

Year      Balance
   1    $ 1040.74
   2    $ 1083.14
   3    $ 1127.27
   4    $ 1173.20
   5    $ 1221.00
   6    $ 1270.74
   7    $ 1322.51
```

Creating Functions

This program uses a new function, **yearEndBalance**, to compute a year's ending balance, given the year's starting balance and the annual interest rate. That is, **yearEndBalance** expects us to provide a year's starting balance, such as 1000.00, and a yearly interest rate (as a fraction, such as 0.04, not a percentage, such as 4.0), and it gives us back the year's ending balance of 1040.74. Such a function is nice because instead of doing all of these calculations ourselves, we merely call the function, in the same way we call **printf** to produce output. Unfortunately, however, unlike **scanf** and **printf**, this function had not already been written for us and placed in a library, so we are forced to create it ourselves.

We create a function by *defining* it. Defining a function involves providing a *function header*, which specifies its parameters and the type of value it returns, and a *function body*, which declares its local variables and provides the code executed when the function is called.

```
return-type function-name (parameter-1, parameter-2, . . . , parameter-N)
{
     Local declarations

     Statements
}
```

A function header consists of the function's return type, its name, and a parenthesized parameter list. The function's *return type* is the type of value the function actually returns, such as **int** or **double**.[1] The function's *parameter list* consists of variable declarations that specify each parameter's name and type. These parameters will be given values when we execute the function.

---

[1] We're actually allowed to omit the return type, in which case the compiler assumes that the function returns an **int**. In fact, that's what we originally did with **main**, but our programs are more readable if we always provide a return type.

Keeping this in mind, here's the header for **yearEndBalance**:

```
double yearEndBalance(double monthly_bal,
                      double interest_rate)
{
    ...
}
```

This part of the function definition specifies that **yearEndBalance** is a function that returns a **double**. This makes sense, as we want it to give us back the year's final balance, which is a **double**. It also specifies that **yearEndBalance** takes two parameters: **monthly_bal** is the balance for the first month of the year, **interest_rate** is the yearly interest rate. Both of these parameters are **double**s.

We follow the function's header with the function's body. This is where we declare any variables local to the function (such as loop counters). These *local variables* can be accessed only within that function. The statements executed when the function is called follow these declarations. We must supply the braces surrounding the function's body even if it contains no variable declarations or statements.

yearEndBalance declares a pair of local variables: **monthly_intrate** and **month**.

```
double  monthly_intrate;        /* % interest per month */
int     month;                  /* current month */
```

These variables are local to **yearEndBalance** in that only that function can access them by name. We will get a compiler error, for example, if we try to access either of these variables in **main**. Similarly, the variables defined in **main**, such as **period**, **year**, and so on, are local to **main**, which means we get an error if we try to access them in **yearEndBalance**.

yearEndBalance's body consists of an assignment statement, a loop, and a **return** statement. The assignment statement simply calculates the monthly interest rate by dividing the yearly interest rate (which was provided as a parameter) by 12.

```
monthly_intrate = interest_rate / 12;
```

The loop updates the monthly balance in the same way we updated the yearly balance in the earlier interest rate programs.

```
for (month = 1; month <= 12; month = month + 1)
   monthly_bal = monthly_bal * monthly_intrate + monthly_bal;
```

We end **yearEndBalance**'s body with a **return** statement.

```
return monthly_bal;
```

return is how a function gives back a single value to its caller. In general, **return**'s syntax is:

```
return Expression;
```

A **return** evaluates *Expression*, exits the function, and returns its value to the function's caller. In Figure 3.1, **yearEndBalance** returns **monthly_bal**, which at that point contains the monthly balance for the last month of the year.

Calling Functions

We actually execute the functions we create by *calling* them. A function calls another function by specifying its name and providing a list of values, the function's *actual* parameters or *arguments*. Each time **main** goes through the **for** loop, it calls **yearEndBalance** with two arguments: **balance** and **intrate**, the current balance and annual interest rate just read from the user,

```
balance = yearEndBalance(balance, intrate);
```

When we call a function, C assigns its argument values to its formal parameters and executes the function's statements until it encounters a return (or ending brace). This parameter-passing mechanism is known as *call by value* because each argument's *value* is *copied* and given to the function. In fact, we tend to think of a function's formal parameters as local variables that happen to be conveniently initialized when the function is called.

Figure 3.2 illustrates just what happens when **yearEndBalance** is called. C assigns **balance**'s value to **monthly_bal** and **intrate**'s value to **interest_rate**. Because **monthly_bal** and **interest_rate** are copies of the variables in **main** that were passed as parameters, changing their values doesn't affect those variables.

> *Changes to a function's parameters do not affect its arguments.*

Even though **yearEndBalance** repeatedly modifies **monthly_bal**, this doesn't affect **balance**, since only a copy of **balance** was passed to it. This behavior has its good points and bad points. Score one point because it makes it hard for functions to *accidentally* change values in their callers. This helps keep our programs modular and eases debugging. Score another point because it lets us pass constants and expressions to functions without having to store them in temporary variables first. But take away a point because it's now hard for functions to *intentionally* change values in their callers. They can do so only indirectly through addresses (as does **scanf**, for example).

Return Values

After C executes a function, it substitutes its return value, if any, for the function call. You should think of a function's return value as replacing the function's call. In Figure 3.1, **yearEndBalance** returns **monthly_bal**, so this value conceptually replaces the call to the function in **main**. That is, C executes the call

```
balance = yearEndBalance(balance, intrate);
```

by executing **yearEndBalance** and substituting the value it returns for its call, which results in **balance** being assigned the value of **monthly_bal**, as shown in Figure 3.3.

main

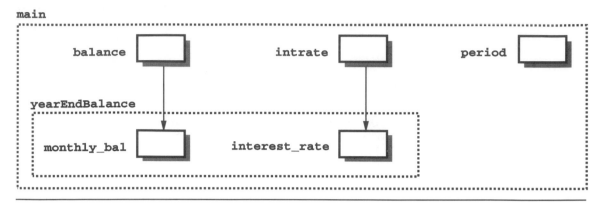

Figure 3.2 What happens when **yearEndBalance** is called. The values of **balance** and **intrate** in **main** are copied into **monthly_bal** and **interest_rate** in **yearEndBalance**.

main

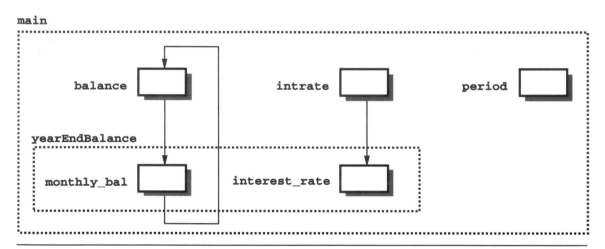

Figure 3.3 What happens when **yearEndBalance** returns.   The value in its local variable **monthly_bal** is returned and assigned to **balance** in **main**.

It may seem strange to pass **balance** as a parameter and then assign it the function's return value. But there's no easier way to update it. We've already seen that call by value means that changing **monthly_bal**'s value doesn't affect **balance**. And changing **monthly_bal**'s name to **balance** isn't a simpler alternative: the function's formal parameters are distinct, local variables, so all we would be doing is creating two different variables named **balance**, one in **main** and the other in **yearEndBalance**, just as we've done with **intrate**.

Providing Function Prototypes

As usual, **main** starts with a set of declarations, but this time one of them is new:

```
double yearEndBalance(double monthly_bal,
                      double interest_rate);
```

This declaration, called a *function prototype*, looks just like the function's header except for the trailing semicolon. You should be wondering why we need it. After all, don't we provide the same information when we define the function?

The problem is that we often define functions after we define their callers, as we did here, defining **yearEndBalance** after we define **main**. But to process function calls, the compiler needs to know the expected type of the function's arguments and return value. This declaration tells the compiler how **yearEndBalance** is supposed to be called; it describes the types of its return value and parameters. Without it, how could the compiler check whether we were passing the right arguments to the function or using its return value correctly? The compiler needs the above declaration to detect common mistakes such as passing an incorrect number of arguments to **yearEndBalance**.

> *Make sure to provide a prototype for every function you call.*

So what happens if we don't provide a prototype? If we've defined the function before its caller, we're fine, as the compiler can get the necessary type information from the function's definition. But if we haven't, the compiler assumes that the function has some unknown set of arguments and that it returns an **int**. That assumption can lead to trouble. It means that the compiler won't be able to do type checking on our function calls. And it often leads to "type mismatch" error messages at the point where we define the function we were calling. Life is simpler if we always provide a prototype.

It's important for every function to provide a prototype for each of the functions it calls. So if we call **yearEndBalance** from two different functions, each of those functions should include a prototype for **yearEndBalance**.[2] You'll likely get a strange compiler error message if only some of a function's callers provide its prototype.

To verify that a function call is reasonable, the compiler actually need not know the parameter names, only their types. In the prototypes we can omit the names entirely or include different names—the names we supply are *dummies*, so they need not correspond in any way to the names used as the function's parameters or function arguments when it is called. Many programs take advantage of this to provide long descriptive names in the protoypes and use short names in the function itself. For example, we could have instead provided this more descriptive prototype for **yearEndBalance**:

```
double yearEndBalance(double balance_at_start_of_year,
                      double annual_interest_rate);
```

---

[2] In subsequent chapters, we'll see how we can use header files to avoid providing prototypes in all of the calling functions. This is the trick that lets us avoid explictly providing prototypes for all of the standard I/O library functions like **printf** and **scanf** in the functions that use them.

By providing descriptive names in the prototype, we make it clear just how the caller is using the function. But in the function itself, where the purpose of the parameters is more obvious, we use the shorter names for convenience.

There's no reason why we couldn't have also written the above prototype this way:

```
double yearEndBalance(double, double);
```

The problem with this form is that it provides no information to program's reader about the purpose of this function's parameters. As a result, we usually take the trouble to provide names, since they help document what the function does.

It turns out there's a nice trick to allow us to easily provide prototypes. A function prototype can be thought of as the function definition without a body and with a terminating semicolon. So all we have to do is copy the function's header to its caller's declaration section and then follow it with a semicolon. In fact, that's just what we did to construct Figure 3.1. We copied **yearEndBalance**'s header from its definition, placed it in **main**, and added a semicolon.

Functions without Return Values

Sometimes we write functions that do not have a useful return value. Figure 3.4 is a revision of Figure 3.1 that encapsulates the printing of the headings in a new function **printHeadings**. This function expects to be given the interest rate, the starting balance, and a number of years, and prints each of their values, along with the heading line for the table of balances. As a result, it takes three parameters. However, this function doesn't return anything. That's because it's entire job is printing the headings; there's no information it needs to provide the caller after it's done with its task. There is a special type, **void**, we use as the return type for functions such as **printHeadings** that never return a useful value. So **printHeadings**'s function prototype looks like:

```
void printHeadings(parameter declarations);
```

We usually use **void** when the primary job of a function is to perform output or when it performs its job by calling a series of other functions to do the real work.[3]

printHeadings didn't have any **return** statement. That's because when control reaches a function's final curly brace, it automatically returns to the calling function. Alternatively, functions that are declared to return **void** can use a **return** statement with no expression:

```
return;
```

Ignoring Function Return Values

Just because a function returns a value, we're not obligated to do anything with it. Sometimes functions return a value, but we don't particularly care what it is. In these cases, we're allowed to simply ignore it. We have been doing so all along in many of

---

[3]These **void** functions behave like Pascal procedures or FORTRAN subroutines.

```
/*
 * A new version of our interest rate program using multiple functions.
 */
#include <stdio.h>
#include <stdlib.h>

int main()
{
  void printHeadings(double intrate, double balance, int period);
  double yearEndBalance(double balance_at_start_of_year,
                        double annual_interest_rate);

  int     period;                        /* length of period */
  int     year;                          /* year of period */
  double  balance;                       /* balance at end of year */
  double  intrate;                       /* interest rate */

  printf("Enter interest rate, principal, and period: ");
  scanf("%lf %lf %i", &intrate, &balance, &period);
  printHeadings(intrate, balance, period);
  for (year = 1; year <= period; year = year + 1)
  {
    balance = yearEndBalance(balance, intrate);
    printf("%4i   $ %7.2f\n", year, balance);
  }
  return EXIT_SUCCESS;                   /* assume program succeeded */
}

/* Print the headings for a table of interest accumulation */

void printHeadings(double intrate, double balance, int period)
{
  printf("Interest Rate:     %7.2f%%\n", intrate * 100);
  printf("Starting Balance: $ %7.2f\n", balance);
  printf("Period:            %7i years\n\n", period);
  printf("Year      Balance\n");
}

/* Compute a year's ending balance, compounding interest monthly */

double yearEndBalance(double monthly_bal, double interest_rate)
{
  double  monthly_intrate;               /* % interest per month */
  int     month;                         /* current month */

  monthly_intrate = interest_rate / 12;
  for (month = 1; month <= 12; month = month + 1)
    monthly_bal = monthly_bal * monthly_intrate + monthly_bal;
  return monthly_bal;
}
```

Figure 3.4 (intrate8.c) A variant of our interest rate computing program that uses several functions.

our calls to **scanf**, where we assume that the input was read successfully and simply ignore its return value.

```
scanf("%lf %lf %i", &intrate, &balance, &period);
```

A common mistake when using functions is to ignore their return values by mistake. An example would be a call such as:

```
yearEndBalance(balance, intrate);
```

This implicitly ignores **yearEndBalance**'s return value, but doing so here is silly, since the only reason we're calling the function is to compute the new balance. Ignoring a function's return value is really only sensible when the function has a useful side effect. Fortunately, many compilers will warn us when they detect us ignoring a non-**void** function's return value.

> *Make sure you don't accidentally ignore a function's return value.*

Functions without Parameters

There is one last special type of function: a function that takes no parameters. An example is **writePrompt**, a function that takes care of writing the prompt asking the user to enter the interest rate, principal, and period.

```
void writePrompt(void)
  { printf("Enter interest rate, principal, and period: "); }
```

When we have a function, such as **writePrompt**, that takes no parameters, we specify a parameter list of **void** or simply leave the list empty, as we've done with **main**.[4]

Why write such a simple function? When we have a loop reading multiple interest rates, principals, and periods, we need to write the prompt twice, once before the loop and once at the loop body's end. Putting the **printf** that writes the prompt in a function guarantees that we'll have exactly the same prompt in both places. (We'll use **writePrompt** in a new version of the interest rate program.)

3.2   SEPARATE COMPILATION

Our programs have so far resided in single files. But C also allows us to spread a program's source over a set of files. We can compile each file separately and link at a later time, or compile and link all at one time.

Figure 3.5 shows what happens when we compile a program composed of several source files. Each source file compiles into an *object module* containing its machine language code, along with a list of its references to external functions and variables. The

---

[4]In Chapter 16, we'll see that there is actually a subtle and important distinction between these two approaches. Until then, however, stick to using a **void** parameter list to indicate a function that takes no parameters, with **main** as the one exception.

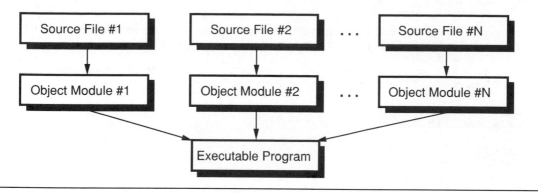

Figure 3.5 The process of separate compilation and linking.

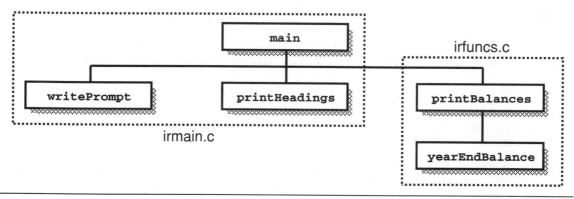

Figure 3.6 How we have organized our latest interest-accumulating program.

linker then creates an executable file from these object modules by filling in external references and adding any referenced library functions.

To illustrate separate compilation, we provide a new version of the final interest rate program from the previous chapter. This one reads multiple sets of interest rates, balances, and periods from the user, and uses monthly compounding of interest. It consists of a collection of functions, and it is split into several source files.

Figure 3.6 shows how we have organized this program. In this diagram, the shadowed boxes represent functions, and the lines indicate function calls. **main** calls **writePrompt**, **printHeadings**, and **printBalances**, which in turn calls **yearEndBalance**. The larger dashed boxes group functions into source files. Our program consists of two source files, irmain.c and irfuncs.c. Figure 3.7 shows irmain.c, which contains **main**, **writePrompt**, and **printHeadings**. Figure 3.8 shows irfuncs.c, which contains **printBalances** and **yearEndBalance**.

```c
/*
 * The main program of our interest rate program and the two functions
 * it uses for writing the prompt and the headings.
 *
 * It also uses another function to print the balances, but that
 * function is defined in another source file.
 */
#include <stdio.h>
#include <stdlib.h>

int main()
{
  void writePrompt(void);
  void printHeadings(double intrate, double balance, int period);
  void printBalances(double intrate, double balance, int period);

  int     period;                       /* length of period */
  double  balance;                      /* balance at end of year */
  double  intrate;                      /* interest rate */
  int     n;                            /* number of values read */

  writePrompt();
  while ((n = scanf("%lf %lf %i", &intrate, &balance, &period)) == 3)
  {
    printHeadings(intrate, balance, period);
    printBalances(intrate, balance, period);

    writePrompt();
  }

  if (n != EOF)
    printf("Warning: Encountered error in reading input.\n");

  return EXIT_SUCCESS;
}

/* Prompt the user for all necessary input values */

void writePrompt(void)
  { printf("Enter interest rate, principal, and period: "); }

/* Print the headings that will precede the interest table */

void printHeadings(double intrate, double balance, int period)
{
  printf("Interest Rate:    %7.2f%%\n", intrate * 100);
  printf("Starting Balance: $ %7.2f\n", balance);
  printf("Period:           %7i years\n\n", period);
  printf("Year      Balance\n");
}
```

Figure 3.7   (irmain.c)   The function **main** of our latest interest-computing program.

```
/*
 * Functions useful for dealing with interest accumulation.
 */
#include <stdio.h>

/* Print a table showing interest accumulation */

void printBalances(double intrate, double balance, int period)
{
  double yearEndBalance(double monthly_bal, double interest_rate);

  int year;

  for (year = 1; year <= period; year = year + 1)
  {
    balance = yearEndBalance(balance, intrate);
    printf("%4i   $ %7.2f\n", year, balance);
  }
}

/* Compute a year's ending balance, compounding interest monthly */

double yearEndBalance(double monthly_bal, double interest_rate)
{
  double  monthly_intrate;              /* % interest per month */
  int     month;                        /* current month */

  monthly_intrate = interest_rate / 12;
  for (month = 1; month <= 12; month = month + 1)
    monthly_bal = monthly_bal * monthly_intrate + monthly_bal;
  return monthly_bal;
}
```

Figure 3.8 (irfuncs.c) The file containing the functions **printBalances** and **yearEndBalance**.

Figure 3.9 shows how all these files and functions are combined to form a final executable program named ir. irmain.c is compiled into an object module that contains the code implementing **main**, **writePrompt**, and **printHeadings**. Between them, these functions call three functions that have no code supplied in this object module: **printBalances**, **printf**, and **scanf**. Similarly, irfuncs.c is compiled into an object module that contains the code for **printBalances** and **yearEndBalance**. **printBalances** calls only one function that has no code in this object module, **printf**.

The linker's job is to make an executable program by connecting the calls to functions defined in other object modules to the functions themselves. That is, the linker must connect the call to **printBalances** in the object module for irmain.c to the actual code for **printBalances** in the object module for irfuncs.c. Similarly, it must

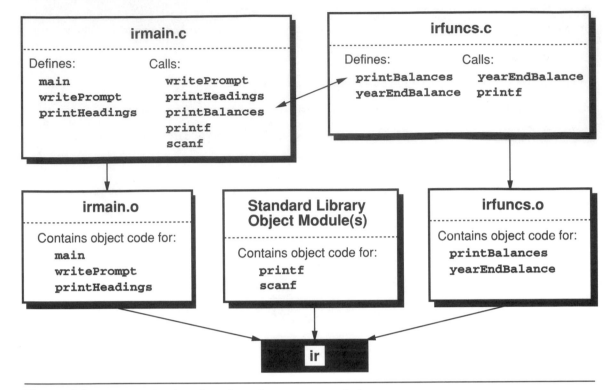

Figure 3.9   The organization of our latest interest-accumulating program.

connect the calls to **printf** and **scanf** to the code for them contained in the object modules created for the standard library.

Recompiling When Fixing Mistakes

Splitting up a program into multiple source files has many benefits. One is that it speeds program development and debugging. When we update a function—perhaps to fix a newly discovered mistake—we do not have to recompile the entire program. Instead, we simply recompile the source file containing the change and relink it with the object modules for the program's other source files.[5]

Suppose, for example, that we decide to update one of the functions in irfuncs.c (either **printBalances** or **yearEndBalance**). We need not recompile irmain.c, but instead simply recompile irfuncs.c and link the object module that results with the

---

[5]Of course, splitting a program into multiple files also leads to a new problem: How do we decide which source files must be recompiled when we make a change? Fortunately, most integrated environments take care of determining this for us, and many command-line environments provide additional tools (such as make in UNIX) that come to our rescue.

Aside 3.1: The Details of Separately Compiling C Programs

Which commands and options we use to compile and link files separately vary from system to system. The overall process, however, is the same. We first invoke the compiler individually on each of the source files that make up our program. This process usually involves using a special command option or menu selection to tell the compiler not to invoke the linker after creating the object module. Once we've created all the necessary object modules, we then invoke the linker to tie them together. So to put the interest rate program together, we would compile irfuncs.c and irmain.c into object modules and then link those object modules together.

On our gcc compiler, we used the following commands to construct our executable program.

```
gcc -ansi -c irfuncs.c
gcc -ansi -c irmain.c
gcc -ansi -o ir irfuncs.o irmain.o
```

The -c option tells the compiler to compile only and not try to resolve any external references. So the first two commands compile our two source files into object modules named irfuncs.o and irmain.o. The last command invokes the linker to combine those two object modules into a single executable program named ir.

Most compilers provide a shortcut. If we simply provide a list of source file names, they will compile each into an object module (the equivalent of the -c option) and then link them together. As a result, we could also create our ir executable using this command:

```
gcc -ansi -o ir irfuncs.c irmain.c
```

Normally, however, we compile each file separately and link them together. That's because we fix all the compile problems in each individual source file before moving on to the next file.

Most compilers also allow us to mix source files and object modules on the same command line. For example, we can use

```
gcc -ansi -o ir irfuncs.c irmain.o
```

compile irfuncs.c and link the resulting object module with the object module created by compiling irmain.c. This is useful when we make changes to only some of our source files, or when we want to link with object modules provided by someone else.

Separately compiling files in integrated environments is also straightforward. For example, in Turbo C++ there is a menu option for compile-only, rather than compile and link. We can use that entry to compile each of the source files. Linking files together is a bit trickier. We have to create a *project* file (a file with the suffix .prj). In its simplest form, a project file contains a list of source file names. When we select the make-executable menu entry, it will compile all of these files (if they're not already compiled) and then link the resulting object modules together. The result is an executable program named *project*.exe, where *project* is the name of the project file (without the .prj).

```
Enter interest rates, principal, and period: .06 .08 .01 1000 5
Year      Balance    (Starting balance: $ 1000.00, Interest rate: 6.00%)
   1    $ 1061.68
   2    $ 1127.16
   3    $ 1196.68
   4    $ 1270.49
   5    $ 1348.85
Year      Balance    (Starting balance: $ 1000.00, Interest rate: 7.00%)
   1    $ 1072.29
   2    $ 1149.81
   3    $ 1232.93
   4    $ 1322.05
   5    $ 1417.63
Year      Balance    (Starting balance: $ 1000.00, Interest rate: 8.00%)
   1    $ 1083.00
   2    $ 1172.89
   3    $ 1270.24
   4    $ 1375.67
   5    $ 1489.85
Enter interest rates, principal, and period: control-D
```

Figure 3.10   Some sample input and output from our latest interest-accumulating program.

object module originally compiled from irmain.c. With a small program like this one, we don't really save a lot of compilation time. But as our programs grow larger and larger and contain more and more functions, the time savings become quite noticeable.

Reusing Object Modules

Separate compilation allows us to easily use the same set of functions in more than one program. In particular, we need compile the source file containing these functions only once, and then link the resulting object module with whatever programs find them useful.

To illustrate, we'll write a new interest-accumulating program. This one reads a balance, a starting interest rate, an ending interest rate, an increment, and a period. It then prints a set of tables, one for each interest rate in the given range. Figure 3.10 shows some sample I/O for the program.

To write this program, we must supply a new **main**, but we can continue to use our existing **printBalances** and **yearEndBalance** functions (since the input and headings differ, but the table of interest accumulation still looks the same). Figure 3.11 shows the file, irtables.c, that contains the new main program. We can generate a new executable program simply by compiling this file and linking the resulting object module with the object module that results from compiling the source file, irfuncs.c, that contains the definitions of **printBalances** and **yearEndBalance**.

```
/*
 * A program to print tables of interest accumulation under
 * different interest rates.
 */
#include <stdio.h>
#include <stdlib.h>

int main()
{
  void writePrompt(void);
  void printTables(double start, double finish, double incr,
                   double balance, double period);

  int     period;                       /* length of period */
  double  balance;                      /* balance at end of year */
  double  start_ir;                     /* starting interest rate */
  double  end_ir;                       /* ending interest rate */
  double  incr;                         /* interest rate increment */
  int     n;                            /* number of values read */

  writePrompt();
  while ((n = scanf("%lf %lf %lf %lf %i",
                    &start_ir, &end_ir, &incr, &balance, &period)) == 5)
  {
    printTables(start_ir, end_ir, incr, balance, period);
    writePrompt();
  }
  if (n != EOF)
    printf("Warning: Encountered error in reading input.\n");

  return EXIT_SUCCESS;
}

void writePrompt(void)
  { printf("Enter interest rates, principal, and period: "); }

void printTables(double start, double finish, double incr,
                 double balance, double period)
{
  void printBalances(double intrate, double balance, int period);

  double ir;

  for (ir = start; ir <= finish; ir = ir + incr)
  {
    printf("Year     Balance   (Starting balance: $ %7.2f,", balance);
    printf(" Interest rate: %.2f%%)\n", ir * 100);
    printBalances(ir, balance, period);
  }
}
```

Figure 3.11 (irtables.c) Print tables of interest accumulation for various interest rates.

Aside 3.2: Top-Down Design

When we write a program, we usually start with a specification: a detailed description of what the program should do. At a minimum, specifications describe the program's expected input and output, as well as the general form of its calculations. A key part of the process of turning specifications into source code is *design*. Design involves determining the program's organization—what functions it requires and how they should fit together.

We used a technique called *top-down design* to break our latest interest-accumulating program into functions. The idea is simple. We start with a high-level, sketchy description of a solution to the problem we are trying to solve. We then break it into pieces, and break those pieces into smaller pieces, and so on, until the pieces that remain are small, simple tasks that we can see at once how to implement.

Our first cut at the interest-accumulating program was to break **main** into these pieces:

> *write the prompt*
> *while we can successfully read the input values*
>   *print the headings for that input*
>   *print the balance table for that input*
>   *write the prompt*

This sketchy outline is called *pseudo-code* (because it freely mixes C constructs and English). Once you have pseudo-code like this, it is reasonable to use a function call to implement each of the actions it describes. For example, we can "write the prompt" by calling a **writePrompt** function, "print the headings" by calling a **printHeadings** function, and so on.

Once we decide which functions we need, we must decide what information they require. For example, **printHeadings** requires a balance, interest rate, and period, so that it can display them. In contrast, **writePrompt** needs no parameters, as for this program the prompt is always the same. We also need to decide upon any return values (although here our initial functions can all return **void**).

The next step is to determine what additional functions we need by repeating the top-down design process. Sometimes we get lucky and the function is so simple that we need little, if any, design to implement it. It's obvious, for instance, that **writePrompt** and **printHeadings** are just one or more calls to **printf**. It's less clear, however, how to implement **printBalances**. Its sketchy outline is:

> *for each year*
>   *compute the year's ending balance*
>   *print the year and the updated balance*

This immediately suggests that we provide a function, **yearEndBalance**, to compute and return the year's ending balance. At this point, we've essentially implemented the program.

Support for Testing Functions

Separate compilation allows us to construct our programs one function at a time, thoroughly testing each function before moving on to the next. Figure 3.12 illustrates this idea with a new source file containing a main program to test **yearEndBalance**.

Its **main** consists of a set of calls to a function **testIt**, with each call supplying a balance and an interest rate. **testIt** simply calls **yearEndBalance** and prints the result. We are careful to check cases that are likely to cause trouble, such as a zero balance and a zero or negative interest rate. To perform the tests, we compile this new **main**, link it with the object module containing **yearEndBalance**, and execute it to verify that each of the calls produces the output or return value we expect. Here is the output this program produces:

```
Balance: 1000.00, Rate:  0.04, End balance: 1040.74
Balance: 1000.00, Rate:  0.12, End balance: 1126.83
Balance:    0.00, Rate:  0.06, End balance:    0.00
Balance: 1000.00, Rate:  0.00, End balance: 1000.00
Balance: 1000.00, Rate: -0.05, End balance:  951.13
```

Writing a separate main to test **yearEndBalance** allows us to be reasonably sure that it is working correctly before we try to use it in an interest-accumulating program. In addition, if we make changes to **yearEndBalance**, we can then use this testing main program to ensure that **yearEndBalance** still produces the same results, before we link its object module in with other programs.

> *Write a testing main for each function before using it.*

Testing functions one at a time is much better than trying to construct a complete program and then seeing if the whole thing works. The odds are that it won't, and finding and fixing any problems can be very time-consuming. In contrast, by testing each function individually, any problem we detect is almost certainly with that function, making it much easier to figure out what went wrong.

3.3   SOME ADDITIONAL FEATURES OF FUNCTIONS

Figure 3.13 illustrates a few additional useful features of functions in a new version of irmain.c. The first is that there is no need to supply a prototype if we define a function before it is called. In particular, we have now defined the three functions **main** calls (**writePrompt**, **printHeadings**, and **notifyIfError**) before **main**. As a result, the compiler knows what parameters and return value these functions expect when we call them in **main**, and we no longer are required to supply their prototypes.

Just because we can sometimes omit prototypes, however, does not make doing so a good idea, and we usually supply prototypes regardless of where we define the function. The reason is that we may want to rearrange the functions within the source file, or maybe even move some of them to another file. In doing so, we may wind up trying to call one of them before its definition appears and without a prototype. Explicitly

```c
/*
 * A program to test yearEndBalance.
 */
#include <stdio.h>
#include <stdlib.h>

int main()
{
  void testIt(double starting_balance, double interest_rate);

  /* Expected inputs */

  testIt(1000.00, 0.04);
  testIt(1000.00, 0.12);

  /* Potential problematic cases */

  testIt(0.00,    0.06);          /* zero balance */
  testIt(1000.00, 0.00);          /* zero interest rate */
  testIt(1000.00, -0.05);         /* negative interest rate */

  return EXIT_SUCCESS;
}

/* Try one test of our yearEndBalance function. */

void testIt(double starting_balance, double interest_rate)
{
  double yearEndBalance(double starting_balance, double interest_rate);

  double resulting_balance;

  resulting_balance = yearEndBalance(starting_balance, interest_rate);
  printf("Balance: %7.2f, Rate: %5.2f, End balance: %7.2f\n",
          starting_balance, interest_rate, resulting_balance);
}
```

Figure 3.12   (testyear.c) A program to test **yearEndBalance**.

supplying the prototypes rather than relying on the order in which functions are defined eliminates these sorts of problems. In addition, supplying prototypes explicitly lets the program's reader see at a glance what functions a given function is calling.

The next new feature is that we are not required to save a function's return value in a variable before using it. We take advantage of this in the **return** that terminates **main**.

```c
        return notifyIfError(n);
```

Here, **main** is calling a function named **notifyIfError** and then taking whatever

```c
/*
 * A version of our interest rate program without function prototypes.
 * The function definitions appear before their calls.
 */
#include <stdio.h>
#include <stdlib.h>

void writePrompt(void)
  { printf("Enter interest rate, principal, and period: "); }

void printHeadings(double intrate, double balance, int period)
{
  printf("Interest Rate:       %7.2f%%\n", intrate * 100);
  printf("Starting Balance: $ %7.2f\n", balance);
  printf("Period:              %7i years\n\n", period);
  printf("Year      Balance\n");
}

int notifyIfError(int values_read)
{
  if (values_read != EOF)
  {
    printf("Warning: Encountered error in reading input.\n");
    return EXIT_FAILURE;
  }
  return EXIT_SUCCESS;
}

int main()
{
  void printBalances(double intrate, double balance, int period);

  int     period;                    /* length of period */
  double  balance;                   /* balance at end of year */
  double  intrate;                   /* interest rate */
  int     n;                         /* number of values read */

  writePrompt();
  while ((n = scanf("%lf %lf %i", &intrate, &balance, &period)) == 3)
  {
    printHeadings(intrate, balance, period);
    printBalances(intrate, balance, period);
    writePrompt();
  }

  return notifyIfError(n);
}
```

Figure 3.13 (irmain2.c) A final version of our interest-accumulating main program that illustrates several new features of functions.

Aside 3.3a: Improving Program Quality with Functions

Breaking programs into collections of small functions makes our programs easier to understand and maintain.

Consider Aside 3.3b, a new version of Figure 3.4 that is written entirely without any user-defined functions. It's smaller, but despite its decreased size, it's considerably more complex and harder to understand. A quick glance at Figure 3.4's **main** told us what the program is doing: writing a prompt, reading values, printing balances, and notifying us if there is an error. With Aside 3.3b, however, we must somehow figure out this behavior from examining the underlying statements. We have to understand that the innermost **for** is updating monthly balances, and the outermost **for** is printing a table of balances. In addition, we could immediately see the purpose of each variable before. For example, we could quickly see that **year** was only used in **printBalances**. Now, however, we must examine the entire **main** to determine exactly where **year** is used. In general, it is much easier to understand a **main** that consists of a set of function calls than a **main** that contains the internals of those functions instead.

To see how one way of using functions results in programs that are easier to change, suppose we decide to compute the balances daily, rather than monthly. All we have to do is make a few changes within **yearEndBalance** (specifically, changing **monthly_bal** to **daily_bal**, computing a daily interest rate by dividing by 365, and running through the loop 365 times instead of 12). If we then decide to use an interest-compounding formula, we can again simply modify the internals of **yearEndBalance**—without having to change the main program using it.

Another way that using functions makes our programs easier to change is by minimizing redundancy. Suppose we decide to change our prompt. With a **writePrompt** function, we need change only the single **printf**. Otherwise, we have to locate and modify both **printf**s that write a prompt. Unfortunately, it's possible that we'll fail to find one of them, or we won't change both prompts exactly the same way. When code appears in only one place, it tends to eliminate these types of incorrect program updates.

It's well worth the extra effort it takes to break a program into functions.

value it returns and returning that value to the calling environment. In general, if a function's return value is only going to be used once, we just use it directly without saving it in an intermediate variable.

Our motivation for this **return** statement is that our previous **main**s assume the program succeeds and always return **EXIT_SUCCESS**. However, if the program terminates early because of bad user input, it seems reasonable to have the program not only print an error message, but also indicate the failure through its return value. **notifyIfError** is a new function that takes **scanf**'s return value and writes an error message if it's not equal to **EOF**. In addition, it returns **EXIT_SUCCESS** or **EXIT_FAILURE**, depending on whether an error occurred. As a result, the call to **notifyIfError** takes care both of writing the error message if it's necessary and determining what **main**'s return value should be.

Aside 3.3b (intrate9.c) A single-file, no-function version of our interest rate program.

```
/*
 * An interest rate program without user-defined functions.
 */
#include <stdio.h>
#include <stdlib.h>

int main()
{
  int     period;                    /* length of period */
  double  balance;                   /* balance at end of year */
  double  intrate;                   /* interest rate */
  int     year;                      /* next year or period */
  int     n;                         /* number of values read */
  double  monthly_intrate;           /* % interest per month */
  int     month;                     /* current month */

  printf("Enter interest rate, principal, and period: ");
  while ((n = scanf("%lf %lf %i", &intrate, &balance, &period)) == 3)
  {
    printf("Interest Rate:     %7.2f%%\n", intrate * 100);
    printf("Starting Balance: $ %7.2f\n\n", balance);
    printf("Year     Balance\n");
    for (year = 1; year <= period; year = year + 1)
    {
      monthly_intrate = intrate / 12;
      for (month = 1; month <= 12; month = month + 1)
        balance = balance * monthly_intrate + balance;
      printf("%4i    $ %7.2f\n", year, balance);
    }
    printf("Enter interest rate, principal, and period: ");
  }
  if (n != EOF)
    printf("Warning: Encountered error in reading input.\n");
  return EXIT_SUCCESS;
}
```

The final feature is that C allows us to have as many **return** statements as we want in a function. We take advantage of this in **notifyIfError**. It has a pair of **return** statements that differ solely in the value they return. If there's an error, we write an error message and return **EXIT_FAILURE**. Otherwise, if we get past the **if**, we know there wasn't an error, so we return **EXIT_SUCCESS**. However, in any call of this function, only one **return** will be executed, since the **return** terminates its execution.

Having two **return** statements simplifies **notifyIfError**'s definition. If we had only a single **return**, we would have to have a variable, such as **status**, and a more complex **if** that decides which value to assign to **status** (as we have been doing in most of our programs so far). However, there's a tradeoff here. Many programmers

Aside 3.4a: Helping Detect Bugs In Functions

Common sources of bugs in using functions are passing them incorrect parameters or using their return values incorrectly. These bugs can be difficult to track down, since it's often not clear whether the problem is in the function itself or in how it was used.

There are several tricks to help us detect these sorts of bugs. One is to have our functions *trace* their calls. To do that, we have our functions print their parameters when they are called and display their return value immediately before they return. This allows us to run the program, examine the trace, and verify that we called the functions with the correct parameters and that they computed the correct result.

Another trick is to make explicit any assumptions the function makes. We can do this by providing **if** statements that check each assumption, print an error message if it doesn't hold, and then return a special value. This guarantees that if we somehow violate a basic assumption of the function, we will get a nice error message, rather than strange results or an infinite loop.

Aside 3.4b illustrates both techniques in a new function, **determinePeriod**. It takes a starting balance, an interest rate, and a desired amount and determines the number of years required to achieve the desired amount. It prints all three parameters when it is called and prints the number of years it computed right before it returns. It also verifies that the balance and the interest rate are positive and prints an error message and returns −1 (an impossible number of years) if they aren't. If it didn't make this check, we would be in trouble, since a negative interest rate or balance could cause an infinite loop.

Aside 3.4c is a main program showing various correct and incorrect calls from **determinePeriod**. Here is the output that results:

```
DEBUG: determinePeriod called with parameters:
DEBUG: intrate=0.05, balance=1000.00, desired=2000.00
DEBUG: determinePeriod normal return: 15
Achieved in 15 years
DEBUG: determinePeriod called with parameters:
DEBUG: intrate=0.05, balance=2000.00, desired=1000.00
DEBUG: determinePeriod normal return: 1
Achieved in 1 years
DEBUG: determinePeriod called with parameters:
DEBUG: intrate=1000.00, balance=2000.00, desired=0.05
DEBUG: determinePeriod normal return: 1
Achieved in 1 years
DEBUG: determinePeriod called with parameters:
DEBUG: intrate=-0.05, balance=1000.00, desired=2000.00
DEBUG: determinePeriod failure (interest_rate <= 0)
Achieved in -1 years
DEBUG: determinePeriod called with parameters:
DEBUG: intrate=0.05, balance=-1000.00, desired=2000.00
DEBUG: determinePeriod failure (balance <= 0)
Achieved in -1 years
```

Of course, we don't always want debugging output. Once we know that our function and the program using it work, we simply remove (or comment out) the **printf**s.

Aside 3.4b (period.c) A function that provides debugging information and validates its parameters.

```c
/*
 * Calculate length of time to achieve desired amount.
 */
#include <stdio.h>

int determinePeriod(double intrate, double balance, double desired)
{
  double yearEndBalance(double monthly_bal, double interest_rate);

  int year;

  printf("DEBUG: determinePeriod called with parameters:\n");
  printf("DEBUG: intrate=%.2f, balance=%.2f, desired=%.2f\n",
         intrate, balance, desired);
  if (intrate <= 0)
  {
    printf("DEBUG: determinePeriod failure (interest_rate <= 0)\n");
    return -1;      /* period of -1 indicates problem */
  }
  if (balance <= 0)
  {
    printf("DEBUG: determinePeriod failure (balance <= 0)\n");
    return -1;      /* period of -1 indicates problem */
  }
  year = 1;
  while (balance < desired)
  {
    balance = yearEndBalance(balance, intrate);
    year = year + 1;
  }
  printf("DEBUG: determinePeriod normal return: %i\n", year);
  return year;
}
```

would have a harder time understanding this version of **notifyIfError**. That's because they are forced to figure out which circumstances caused which exit. In general, you should try to have a single **return** in any function unless multiple **return**s simplify it significantly.

SUMMARY

- We can define our own functions by providing the function's return value, parameters, and statements to be executed when the function is called.

- C uses call-by-value parameter passing, copying the values of the actual arguments into

Aside 3.4c (useperiod.c) A main program that sometimes incorrectly uses **determinePeriod**.

```c
/*
 * Determine how many periods it takes to accumulate X dollars.
 * This program is erroneous.
 */
#include <stdio.h>
#include <stdlib.h>

int main()
{
  int determinePeriod(double intrate, double balance, double desired);

  int period;

  /* Use correctly: How many years to go from $1000 to $2000 at 5%  */
  period = determinePeriod(.05, 1000, 2000);
  printf("Achieved in %i years\n", period);

  /* Use incorrectly: parameters in wrong order */
  period = determinePeriod(.05, 2000, 1000);
  printf("Achieved in %i years\n", period);

  /* Use incorrectly: parameters in wrong order */
  period = determinePeriod(1000, 2000, .05);
  printf("Achieved in %i years\n", period);

  /* Use incorrectly: bad interest rate parameter */
  period = determinePeriod(-.05, 1000, 2000);
  printf("Achieved in %i years\n", period);

  /* Use incorrectly: bad balance parameter */
  period = determinePeriod(.05, -1000, 2000);
  printf("Achieved in %i years\n", period);

  return EXIT_SUCCESS;
}
```

the function's formal parameters. Changing the parameters within the function has no effect on the values passed to it.

- The variables within a function are local to that function and can't be directly accessed by any other function.

- Every call to a function should be preceded by a function prototype. The compiler uses the information in the prototype to verify that we are passing the function the right number and types of arguments and that we are using its return value correctly.

- We can divide our programs into multiple source files, compile them separately, and then link the resulting object modules together.

EXERCISES

Explore

3–1 Compile and run this chapter's interest rate programs on your computer. Try separately compiling, linking, and executing Figures 3.7 and 3.8 and Figures 3.13 and 3.8.

3–2 What happens if you eliminate the function prototype for **yearEndBalance** from Figure 3.1?

3–3 What happens if you move **notifyIfError**'s definition after **main** in Figure 3.13 without supplying a prototype for it?

Modify

3–4 Modify the final version of the interest rate program (Figures 3.7 and 3.8) to compute the interest daily rather than monthly.

3–5 Modify Figure 3.12 so that it doesn't save **yearEndBalance**'s return value in a variable.

3–6 Modify irfuncs.c (Figure 3.8) so that **yearEndBalance** displays its parameters and return values and **printBalances** displays its parameters.

Extend

3–7 Extend the version of the interest rate program in Figures 3.7 and 3.8 to verify that the balance and interest rate are both non-negative numbers. Write an appropriate error message if either is not. You should write a function to do the verification.

3–8 There are a variety of ways user input can make Figure 3.11 go into an infinite loop. Extend the program to check for those inputs and print an error message if any of those conditions occur. You should do so by writing a function **verifyInput** that performs the various necessary checks and returns an indication of whether the input was acceptable or not. You should also modify **printTables** to verify that its parameters are sensible before it attempts to produce any output.

Code

3–9 Write a function, **sumRange**, to calculate the sum of the integers between m and n, inclusive, where m and n are passed to it as parameters. With an m of 1 and an n of 100, the function should print 5050. Supply a simple main program that tests it. Your function should behave sensibly even if it is given an n larger than m, or n and m are negative.

3–10 Write a function, **cylVolume**, that computes the volume of a cylinder given its height and radius. The formula for volume of a cylinder is $\pi \times radius^2 \times height$.

Use this function to write a program to read the radius and height of a cylinder and print its volume.

Build

3–11 Write a function, **printPowers**, that takes two parameters, **value** and **n**, and prints the first **n** powers of **value**. For example, with **value** equal to 1 and **n** equal to 12, it would print the value of $1 \times 1, 1 \times 2, \ldots, 1 \times 12$, and with **value** equal to 2 and **n** equal to 12, it would print the values of $2 \times 1, 2 \times 2, \ldots, 2 \times 12$.

Once you have **printPowers** written, use it in a program that prints a multiplication table for the integers 1 through 12. The table should have 12 rows of 12 columns.

3–12 Take the **printPowers** function you wrote in the previous exercise and extend it to print negative powers as well as positive ones.

3–13 Write a function, **printStars**, to print **n** stars where **n** is passed as a parameter. For example, the call **printStars(10)** should produce ********** as output.

Use this function in a new function, **printBar**, which should be passed the width and height of the bar to print. So the call **printBar(5, 3)** should produce this output:

```
*****
*****
*****
```

Finally, write a main program to test this function.

3–14 Write a function, **printBlanks**, to print **n** spaces. Combine this with **printStars** from the previous exercise to write a new function, **printBox**, that is passed the width and height of a box to display. Boxes differ from bars in that they have blanks in the center rather than stars. So the call **printBox(5, 3)** should produce this output:

```
*****
*   *
*****
```

3–15 Write a function, **printDigit**, that takes a number from 0 to 9 and a size n, and displays it an $n \times n$ box. For example, the call **printDigit(3, 7)** would display the number 3 in a 7×7 box, like this:

```
*******
      *
      *
*******
      *
      *
*******
```

To help you out, you may want to write auxiliary functions to do things like draw horizontal and vertical lines.

Part II

THE BASICS

The next six chapters go into great detail on the core features of the C language.

- Chapter 4 looks at C's different numeric types.

- Chapter 5 shows how to manipulate characters in C.

- Chapter 6 focuses on C's large collection of operators.

- Chapter 7 presents C's small collection of statements.

- Chapter 8 examines the basics of one-dimensional arrays of C's basic data types.

- Chapter 9 discusses storage classes and program organization.

4 NUMBERS

This chapter delves into the details of C's numerical data types and arithmetic operators. We begin with the rules for composing identifiers and then move on to the various integer and real data types. We show how to create numerical constants and declare numerical variables and how to read and print these values. Along the way we study the range of values each type can hold, and when each type is most appropriate. After looking at the numerical data types, we introduce C's arithmetic operators and examine conversions between different data types. The chapter concludes with a case study that converts decimal numbers to other bases.

4.1   IDENTIFIERS AND NAMING CONVENTIONS

Variable and function names are known as *identifiers*. But not every combination of characters is a legal identifier. First, identifiers consist only of lowercase and uppercase letters, digits, and underscores (_)—no other characters are allowed. Second, the first character must be a letter or an underscore—it can't be a digit. Though legal, we avoid names beginning with an underscore, as they are "reserved for the implementation." That is, they exist (as the name of a system-provided library function, for example), but the lowly programmer is not supposed to create new ones. Finally, there's a set of keywords that are reserved, so we can't use them as identifiers. Table 4.1 lists the standard keywords.[1]

In addition, all names in the standard libraries are reserved. That means, for example, that we can't legally write our own function named **printf**.

Case is significant in identifiers: **var** refers to a different identifier than **Var**, which refers to a different identifier than **VAR**. C's keywords must be in lowercase, so an identifier like **INT** or **Double** is perfectly legal, though perhaps somewhat confusing.

There is no limit on the length of an identifier. There is, however, a limit to the number of significant characters. Originally, only the first 8 characters were significant, implying that **var_name1** and **var_name2** referred to the same identifier. Now things have improved significantly, and we're guaranteed that at least the first 31 characters are significant in an internal name, such as a local variable. But for an external name, such as a function call, only the first 6 characters are guaranteed to be significant, and

---

[1] Each implementation may have a few additional reserved words; some of the more common ones we've run into include **asm**, **far**, **fortran**, **huge**, **near**, and **pascal**. In addition, if you intend to eventually compile your C programs under a C++ compiler, you should also avoid using the C++ keywords. These are **catch**, **class**, **delete**, **inline**, **friend**, **namespace**, **new**, **operator**, **private**, **protected**, **public**, **template**, **this**, **throw**, **try**, **using**, and **virtual**.

auto	break	case	char	const	continue	default	do
double	else	enum	extern	float	for	goto	if
int	long	register	return	short	signed	sizeof	static
struct	switch	typedef	union	unsigned	void	volatile	while

Table 4.1 C's reserved words.

case differences may be ignored. That's problematic, since it means that in some implementations any function name starting with **display** (such as **displayValues** or **displayBalances**) refers to the same function. Fortunately, most implementations don't have this painful restriction. For readability, most of the programs in this book assume that external names are no different from internal names. In a later chapter on portability, however, we show an easy way to relax this assumption.

4.2 INTEGERS

Integers are whole numbers. There are three classes of integers: **short int**, **int**, and **long int**, in both **signed** and **unsigned** forms. We can write **short int** and **long int** more concisely as **short** and **long**, respectively.

These classes vary in size and efficiency of use. Table 4.2 lists the minimum sizes and ranges of these values. On most systems, a **short** is 16 bits, an **int** is either 16 or 32 bits, and a **long** is 32 bits. The language, however, guarantees only that **int**s and **short**s will be at least 16 bits, that **long**s will be at least 32, and that a **short** is not going to be larger than an **int**, which is not going to be larger than a **long**.

Why do we have all of these different classes? Because they all have different uses. **int**s occupy one word of storage and are generally the most efficient data type to use. **long**s provide a portable way to store values that require more than 16 bits, but often are much slower than **int**s when used to perform arithmetic. And **short**s provide a portable way to save space when a variable's value always falls within a small range. To keep things simple, however, we usually try to avoid **short**s unless our program is running out of space and to avoid **int**s unless it's running out of time.

> *Unless efficiency is crucial, make all integer variables* **long***s.*

Integers can be either signed or unsigned. Signed integers use one bit for the sign of the number (where the bit is usually zero if it's positive and one if it's negative). A **signed int** (or just **int**, the default) uses one bit for the sign and 15 bits for the magnitude on 16-bit machines or 31 bits for the magnitude on 32-bit machines.

Bits: 0   1-15 (or 1-31)

Sign	Magnitude

INTEGER TYPE	BITS	MINIMUM RANGE
short	16	−32,767 to +32,767
int	16	−32,767 to +32,767
long	32	−2,147,483,647 to +2,147,483,647
unsigned short	16	0 to 65,535
unsigned int	16	0 to 65,535
unsigned long	32	0 to 4,294,967,295

Table 4.2 The *minimum* sizes and values of the integer data types. Their specific values can vary on different machines, but they're required to be greater than or equal to these values in magnitude.

This explains why 16-bit **int**s can range in value from −32,767 to 32,767: 15 bits can represent any value from 0 to $2^{15} - 1$ (or 32,767).

Unsigned integers have no sign bit and use all the bits for the magnitude, doubling the range of positive values they can represent.

Bits: 0-15 (or 0-31)

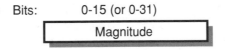

This explains why unsigned 16-bit **int**s can range in value from 0 to 65,535: 16 bits can represent any value from 0 up to $2^{16} - 1$ (or 65,535). When a variable will only hold non-negative values, as in a loop counter, making it unsigned increases the range of values it can hold. We declare unsigned integers with **unsigned int** (or simply, **unsigned**), **unsigned short**, and **unsigned long**.

Most C programs rarely use **unsigned**. In this text, we use it primarily to help the program's reader see that a loop index (or other counter) is never negative.

Integer Constants

Integer constants are expressed as a string of digits. We can have decimal (base 10), octal (base 8), and hexadecimal (base 16) integers. A leading '0' indicates an octal number; a leading '0x' or '0X' indicates a hexadecimal (hex for short). Regardless of how the value is specified, it is stored in its binary equivalent. For example, the decimal value **63**, the octal value **077**, and the hex value **0x3f** are all stored as 0...0111111.

All constants in C have a type. By default, if the constant fits in an **int**, it's of type **int**, just as we might expect. So **63** is always an **int**, as are **077** and **0x3f**.

Where it gets tricky is in deciding the type of a value that doesn't fit in an **int**, such as 99,999, on a machine with 16-bit **int**s. We have to worry about two cases: decimal, and octal or hex. If it's decimal, it's automatically treated as a **long** or as an **unsigned long** if it's too large for a **long**. And if it's octal or hex, it has the first type it fits in from among **unsigned int**, **long**, or **unsigned long**. Table 4.3 shows some values and their types.

CONSTANT VALUE	BITS IN AN **int**	CONSTANT TYPE
1000	16 or 32	**int**
100000	16	**long**
100000	32	**int**
2500000000	16 or 32	**unsigned long**
0x7FFF	16	**int**
0xFFFF	16 or 32	**unsigned int**
0x7FFFFFFF	16	**long**
0x7FFFFFFF	32	**int**
0xFFFFFFFF	16	**unsigned long**
0xFFFFFFFF	32	**unsigned int**

Table 4.3   Some example integer constants and their types. A constant's type depends on the number of bits in the underlying type on the particular machine being used.

These rules are complex and we would rather not worry about them. C provides several suffixes that let us specify the particular type we want. A suffix of **l** or **L** forces the constant to be a **long** (that is, to take at least 32 bits), so **255L** and **0xFFL** both are **long** constants. We force a constant to be treated as **unsigned** with a suffix of **u** or **U**, so **255U** is an **unsigned int**. Finally, we can force a constant to be an **unsigned long** by combining the suffixes for **unsigned** and **long**. **100000ul** is an **unsigned long** constant. There are no **short** constants.

Most of the time, we can safely ignore a constant's type. However, later on in the text, we'll show where being able to explicitly specify their types proves handy.[2] For now, we'll be careful to specify types whenever we have a constant that falls into the range where it's a **long** on some machines and an **int** on others, or whenever it's to be placed in an **unsigned int** or **unsigned long**.

C provides us with a unary minus operator, **-**, which we can use to change the sign of our constants.[3] As expected, **-15** gives us negative **15**.

Reading and Writing Integers

We read and write integers with **scanf** and **printf**; Table 4.4 shows the appropriate formatting codes.

We have to be careful to use the correct formatting codes for the values we are trying to write, as using an incorrect formatting code may cause strange results. The little program in Figure 4.1 provides an example of what can go wrong. It writes an **unsigned long** as both an **unsigned long** (which is how we should write it)

---

[2]For those who can't wait, we can use explicit types to avoid some type conversions, to specify which operator behavior we want for operators that behave differently depending on a value's type, and to ensure that a function's arguments match its parameters when constants are passed without the function's prototype in scope.

[3]As an extension to ANSI C, many compilers also provide a unary plus operator, **+**.

TYPE	READING WITH **scanf**	PRINTING WITH **printf**
short	**%hd** or **%hi**	**%d** or **%i**
int	**%d** or **%i**	**%d** or **%i**
long	**%ld** or **%li**	**%ld** or **%li**
unsigned short	**%hu**	**%u**
unsigned int	**%u**	**%u**
unsigned long	**%lu**	**%lu**
octal **short**	**%ho**	**%o**
octal **int**	**%o**	**%o**
octal **long**	**%lo**	**%lo**
hex **short**	**%hx**	**%x**
hex **int**	**%x**	**%x**
hex **long**	**%lx**	**%lx**

Table 4.4 Common formatting codes for reading and printing integers.

```
/*
 * A program using the wrong formatting code to write several values.
 */
#include <stdio.h>
#include <stdlib.h>

int main()
{
  unsigned long value;

  /* Write a large value as both an unsigned long (which it is supposed
     to be) and as a long (which is a mistake) */

  value = 2500000000ul;
  printf("%lu %li\n", value, value);

  /* Write a small value as both an unsigned long (which it is supposed
     to be) and as a long (which is a mistake) */

  value = 25000ul;
  printf("%lu %li\n", value, value);

  return EXIT_SUCCESS;
}
```

Figure 4.1 (outerr.c) A program to write a large unsigned value as both unsigned and signed. The value comes out negative when written as signed.

Aside 4.1: Numbering Systems

Real-world C programs sometimes have to deal with binary (base 2), octal (base 8), and hexadecimal (base 16) numbers. That makes it important to understand how to write numbers in these bases and how to convert from one base to another.

A value in any base system is represented by a string of symbols. In base 10, the base you're most familiar with, we build numbers out of the digits 0 through 9. In binary, however, we can only use 0 and 1. Similarly, in octal, we can only use 0 through 7. In hexadecimal, not only can we use all ten digits, but also the letters A through F. Those letters represent the values 10 through 15, respectively. Each base system is centered on an integer, called the *base* or *radix*. For binary it's base 2, for octal it's base 8, and for hexadecimal it's base 16.

Each place occupied by a symbol corresponds to a power of the base. The rightmost place corresponds to $base^0$ (which is 1 for any base). Each move to the left multiplies the current place by the base's value. In decimal, that means the rightmost place corresponds to 1s, the next place to the left to 10s, the place to left of that to 100s, and so on. In octal, the rightmost place corresponds to 1s; the next place to the left to 8s, the one after that to 64s, and so on. In hexadecimal, the rightmost place also corresponds to 1s, but the next place on the left to 16s, the one after that to 256s, and so on. Here's the correspondance between position and value in binary, octal, decimal, and hexadecimal:

BASE		POSITION				
	n	4	3	2	1	0
Binary	2^n	16	8	4	2	1
Octal	8^n	4096	512	64	8	1
Decimal	10^n	10000	1000	100	10	1
Hexadecimal	16^n	65536	4096	256	16	1

We compute the base 10 value of a number $a_n a_{n-1} \cdots a_1 a_0$ in base B by computing $\sum_{i=0}^{n} a_i \times B^i$. For example, to convert 724_8, we need to compute $(7 \times 8^2) + (2 \times 8^1) + (4 \times 8^0)$, which gives us 482_{10}. To convert $A2C_{16}$ to base 10, we evaluate $(10 \times 16^2) + (2 \times 16^1) + (12 \times 16^0)$, which evaluates to 2604_{10}.

There's a simple relationship between binary, octal, and hexadecimal numbers. To convert from binary to octal, group the number from the right in three-bit units and convert each group to an octal number. To convert to hexadecimal, group the number from the right in four-bit units and convert each group to a hexadecimal number (for hexadecimal, remember that 10 converts to A, 11 to B, 12 to C, 13 to D, 14 to E, and 15 to F). Here's an example:

Binary	0	100	001	110	111	010
Octal	0	4	1	6	7	2

Binary		0100	0011	1011	1010
Hex		4	3	B	A

To convert a number X from base 10 to base B, divide X by B. The remainder becomes the rightmost digit of the converted number. The quotient becomes the next X, and is divided by B. The process ends when the new quotient is finally zero.

and as a **long** (which is a mistake).

```
printf("%lu %li\n", value, value);
```

When we run it on a machine with 32-bit **long**s, we get this output.

```
2500000000 -1794967296
25000 25000
```

The first value is the expected result when we write 2,500,000,000, and the other is a strange, signed value. The problem is that when we write a value with **%li**, it's taken as a **signed long**, and since this value's leftmost bit is on, it's taken as a negative value. But when we write it with **%lu**, the leftmost bit isn't treated as a sign and we get the value we expect. There's no problem when we write 25,000, since its leftmost bit is off.

> *Make sure your formatting codes correspond to the types of the values that you're trying to read or write.*

4.3   REALS

Reals, or floating point numbers, are stored differently than integers. Internally, they are broken into a fraction and an exponent. The number of bits for each is machine-dependent, but a typical representation for a 32-bit real uses 23 bits plus a sign bit for the fraction (or mantissa) and 8 bits for the exponent, as shown below.

Bits:	0	1-8	9-31
	Sign	Exponent	Mantissa

Bit 0 is the sign of the fraction, bits 1 through 8 are the exponent, and bits 9 through 31 contain the fraction.[4]

We normally write real numbers with a decimal point, as in 13.45 or −211.0, but we can also write them in 'e' notation, giving both a fraction and a base 10 exponent. 'e' notation is similar to scientific notation, except that the letter 'e' replaces the times sign and the base. Here are several examples.

FLOATING POINT	'E' NOTATION	SCIENTIFIC NOTATION
12.45	1.245e1	1.245×10^1
-211.0	-2.110e2	-2.110×10^2
0.0056	5.600e-3	5.600×10^{-3}
-0.000123	-1.230e-4	-1.230×10^{-4}
1000000.0	1e6	1.000×10^6

---

[4]The value of the exponent is usually encoded using an "excess" notation. The trick is that an "excess" amount is added to the exponent's value before storing it, guaranteeing that the stored value is positive. That excess is then subtracted when the value is retrieved. Fortunately, we almost never have to worry about these low-level details.

Aside 4.2a: Integral Values and Portability

The sizes and ranges of values of the integer types vary from machine to machine. The range of values on a particular implementation can be determined using the standard header file limits.h, which contains constants defined for the smallest and largest values of each of the integer types (among other things). Here are the more important constants in that file, their meaning, and their largest and smallest acceptable values.

CONSTANT	VALUE	DESCRIPTION
INT_MAX	+32767	largest value of an **int**
INT_MIN	-32767	smallest value of an **int**
LONG_MAX	+2147483647L	largest value of a **long**
LONG_MIN	-2147483647L	smallest of a **long**
SHRT_MAX	+32767	largest value of a **short**
SHRT_MIN	-32767	smallest value of a **short**
UINT_MAX	65535U	largest value of an **unsigned int**
ULONG_MAX	4294967295UL	largest value of an **unsigned long**
USHRT_MAX	65535U	largest value of an **unsigned short**

The specific values on your machine are required to be greater than or equal to these values in magnitude.

Aside 4.2b is a little program that prints the minimum and maximum values we can store in each of the signed integer types, as well as the maximum values for the unsigned types (the minimum values for these types is 0, so there's little reason to print them out). It works by simply including limits.h and displaying the constants it contains, carefully using the appropriate formatting code for each. Here is its output when we run it on a 32-bit machine (an HP 700-series workstation):

```
Range of ints:   -2147483648 to 2147483647
Range of longs:  -2147483648 to 2147483647
Range of shorts: -32768 to 32767
Largest unsigned int:   4294967295
Largest unsigned long:  4294967295
Largest unsigned short: 65535
```

In contrast, here's the output when we run it on a 16-bit personal computer.

```
Range of ints:   -32768 to 32767
Range of longs:  -2147483648 to 2147483647
Range of shorts: -32768 to 32767
Largest unsigned int:   65535
Largest unsigned long:  4294967295
Largest unsigned short: 65535
```

The two outputs are similar, except that the range of **int**s (and **unsigned int**s) on a 16-bit machine is much smaller than it is on a 32-bit machine. If we write the program on the 32-bit machine and plan to compile and run it on the 16-bit machine, we had better make sure we aren't storing any values larger than 32767 in an **int**, or our program isn't going to work when we port it.

Aside 4.2b (limits.c) A program to print the ranges of integer values on our machine.

```
/*
 * Display the ranges of values of different types.
 */
#include <stdio.h>
#include <stdlib.h>
#include <limits.h>

int main()
{
  printf("Range of ints:    %i to %i\n",    INT_MIN, INT_MAX);
  printf("Range of longs:   %li to %li\n", LONG_MIN, LONG_MAX);
  printf("Range of shorts: %i to %i\n\n", SHRT_MIN, SHRT_MAX);
  printf("Largest unsigned int:    %u\n",  UINT_MAX);
  printf("Largest unsigned long:   %lu\n", ULONG_MAX);
  printf("Largest unsigned short: %u\n",   USHRT_MAX);

  return EXIT_SUCCESS;
}
```

Unlike integers, which are represented exactly, a floating point value is represented approximately. Consider the fraction $\frac{100}{3}$, which we write as $33.333\overline{3}$ and which contains an infinite number of 3s after the decimal point. Unfortunately, the internal representation for floating points can only support a fixed number of *significant* digits. A representation that guarantees only 6 significant digits could store this fraction as any value beginning with 33.3333. The result is that with real numbers we care not only about the smallest and largest value we can store in them, but also how many digits of that value are significant.

C provides three types of real values: **double**, which we've already seen, **float**, and **long double**. A **double** provides at least 10 significant digits and usually requires 64 bits of storage. A **float** provides at least 6 significant digits and usually requires 32 bits of storage. And a **long double** potentially provides even more significant digits and a larger range of values. Many implementations, however, treat **double**s and **long double**s as synonyms.

Why are there all of these types? We use **float**s when we want to save storage or avoid the overhead of double-precision operations. We use **double**s when we want more significant digits and storage isn't a problem. And we use **long double**s when our implementation provides even more significant digits or a wider range of values for them. As with integers, we try to keep things simple and use only one type.

> *Unless efficiency is a major concern, make all of your floating point variables* **double***s.*

```
/*
 * Compute the area of a circle.
 */
#include <stdio.h>
#include <stdlib.h>

#define  PI   3.1415926            /* our favorite constant! */

int main()
{
  double radius;                   /* user-entered radius of a circle */
  double area;                     /* computed area of that circle */

  printf("Enter radius: ");
  if (scanf("%lf", &radius) == 1)
  {
    area = PI * radius * radius;
    printf("Area in floating point notation: %f\n", area);
    printf("Area in exponential notation:    %e\n", area);
    printf("Area in smallest notation:       %g\n", area);
  }
  else
    printf("Error: expected numeric radius.\n");

  return EXIT_SUCCESS;             /* always return success */
}
```

Figure 4.2 (area.c) A program to compute the area of a circle.

By default, any real constant is a **double**. To have **float** constants, we follow the number with an 'f' or 'F', as in **3.1415926F**. To have **long double** constants, we follow it with an 'l' or 'L', as in **3.1415926L**.

As with integers, we use **scanf** to read reals and **printf** to print them. With **scanf**, **%f** indicates a **float**, **%lf** a **double**, and **%Lf** a **long double**. With **printf**, **%f** indicates a **float** or **double**, and **%Lf** indicates a **long double**. If we need output in 'e' notation (1.3e4 instead of 13000), we use **%e** instead of **%f**. If we want whichever form can be displayed in the fewest characters, we use **%g**.

Figure 4.2 is a short program that uses the simple formula

$$area = \pi \times radius^2$$

to compute the area of a circle, given its radius. It uses **double**s for all of its calculations and prints its answer in several different formats. Here's an example run:

```
Enter radius: 34.5
Area in floating point notation: 3739.280592
Area in exponential notation:    3.739281e+03
Area in smallest notation:       3739.28
```

Aside 4.3a: Real Values and Portability

For reals, as with integers, there's a header file that contains constants for their implementation-defined limits. This header file is float.h. Here are its important constants, their minimum values (if any), and their purpose.

CONSTANT	VALUE	DESCRIPTION
FLT_DIG	6	decimal digits of precision for float
FLT_EPSILON	1E-5	smallest x such that $1.0 + x \neq 1.0$
FLT_MAX	1E+37	largest float
FLT_MIN	1E-37	smallest float
FLT_MAX_10_EXP	+37	largest integer power of 10 in a float
FLT_MIN_10_EXP	-37	smallest integer power of 10 in a float
DBL_DIG	10	decimal digits of precision for double
DBL_EPSILON	1E-9	smallest x such that $1.0 + x \neq 1.0$
DBL_MAX	1E37	largest double
DBL_MIN	1E-37	smallest double
DBL_MAX_10_EXP	+37	largest integer power of 10 in a double
DBL_MIN_10_EXP	-37	smallest integer power of 10 in a double
LDBL_DIG	10	decimal digits of precision for long double
LDBL_EPSILON	1E-9	smallest x such that $1.0 + x \neq 1.0$
LDBL_MAX	1E37	largest long double
LDBL_MIN	1E-37	smallest long double
LDBL_MAX_10_EXP	+37	largest integer power of 10 in a long double
LDBL_MIN_10_EXP	-37	smallest integer power of 10 in a long double

Aside 4.3b is a little program that uses these constants to print the ranges and significant digits of the various real values. Here is its output when run on our workstation.

```
Range of floats:          1.17549e-38 to 3.40282e+38
Range of doubles:         2.22507e-308 to 1.79769e+308
Range of long doubles:    3.3621E-4932 to 1.18973E+4932
Precision of floats:      6 digits
Precision of doubles:     15 digits
Precision of long doubles: 15 digits
```

These constants exist primarily so that sophisticated programs can detect and prevent potential problems with their floating point arithmetic. One common example is computing a running total from a large number of small floating point values. After the total gets large enough, it's possible for the addition of the small number to not increase the total correctly. For example, adding $0.50 to $222,500, may not change $222,500 to $222,500.50 if there are only six significant digits. Fortunately, we can detect this problem before it occurs by ensuring that $v \geq t \times$ **DBL_EPSILON** $\times 10^d$, where v is the value we're adding, t is the running total, and d is the number of significant digits.

This sort of code is difficult to write but, fortunately, it tends to be necessary only in certain well-understood situations, and we can look up appropriate techniques in books on issues in performing floating point arithmetic.

Aside 4.3b (floats.c) A program to print the ranges of real values on our machine.

```
/*
 * Display the ranges and properties of real values of different types.
 */
#include <stdio.h>
#include <stdlib.h>
#include <float.h>

int main()
{
  printf("Range of floats:          %g to %g\n",    FLT_MIN, FLT_MAX);
  printf("Range of doubles:         %g to %g\n",    DBL_MIN, DBL_MAX);
  printf("Range of long doubles:    %LG to %LG\n",
         LDBL_MIN, LDBL_MAX);
  printf("\n");
  printf("Precision of floats:       %i digits\n",  FLT_DIG);
  printf("Precision of doubles:      %i digits\n",  DBL_DIG);
  printf("Precision of long doubles: %i digits\n",  LDBL_DIG);

  return EXIT_SUCCESS;
}
```

4.4 ARITHMETIC OPERATORS

C has only a small set of integer and real data types and only a few arithmetic operators we can use on them. These operators are: + (addition), – (subtraction), * (multiplication), / (division), and % (modulus or remaindering—for integers only). All these operators take two operands, and except for %, operate on both integer and real operands. They associate (are evaluated) left to right, with *, /, and % having higher precedence than either + or –. This means that

```
balance = balance + balance * INTRATE;
```

is evaluated as though it were written as

```
balance = balance + (balance * INTRATE);
```

Signed Integer Arithmetic

Integer arithmetic is always exact within the limits of the number of values that can be represented within the integral data type used—so you don't have to worry about precision problems. Unfortunately, you do have to worry about overflow, since C provides no run-time indication that a signed integer overflow has occurred.

Officially, the result of an overflow is undefined. In reality, the arithmetic usually takes place and gives an incorrect result. Overflow can also be caused by multiplying two large numbers together, regardless of their signs. While it is possible to detect overflow after the fact—perhaps by noting that adding two positive numbers produced a negative result—it is better to try and avoid any overflow in the first place.[5] Use data types appropriate to the range of values the result *might* cover. If you are adding two **int**s and their result might not fit in an **int**, use **long**s instead. As an alternative, use a **double** and then test to see if the result is greater than **INT_MAX**.

> *Avoid arithmetic overflows by carefully choosing your data types.*

Integer addition, subtraction, and multiplication (both operands are integers) behave just like in other programming languages or your home calculator. Integer division (both operands are integers) produces a *truncated* result. That is, it simply throws away the real part of the result: **10/3** is 3, as is **17/5**. This truncation means that "fractional" division of integers always returns zero: **1/3**, for example, evaluates to zero, as does **25/26**. One subtlety, however, is that the direction of truncation is machine-dependent for negative numbers. That is, **-4/3** might return either -1 or -2.

> *Avoid division involving negative integers and division by zero.*

The remaindering operator, **%**, takes two integer operands and returns the remainder when the first is divided by the second: **5%3**, for example, is 2, and **1%3** is 1. For positive integers, this is the familiar modulus operation. The sign of the result is machine dependent for negative numbers. For this reason, **%** is best used only with positive values. Regardless of the sign of **a** and **b**, however, **(a/b) * b + a%b** will always equal **a** (assuming, of course, that **a/b** is possible).

Unsigned Integer Arithmetic

Unsigned integer arithmetic is similar to signed integer arithmetic, except that there are no negative results and no overflow. Instead, all unsigned integer arithmetic takes place modulo 2^n, where n is the number of bits in the unsigned operands. This means that adding 1 to the largest unsigned value gives zero, and conversely, subtracting 1 from zero gives the largest unsigned value. Figure 4.3 contains a program that illustrates unsigned arithmetic. It simply adds 1 and 2 to the largest possible **unsigned int**. To obtain the largest **unsigned int**, we include the standard header file limits.h, which contains its value in the constant **UINT_MAX**. Its output, on a 16-bit machine, is:

```
Largest unsigned int: 65535
Largest plus one:     0
Largest plus two:     1
```

[5]On most machines, adding 1 to the largest positive number yields the smallest negative value, and conversely, subtracting 1 from the smallest negative value yields the largest positive value (both operations cause the sign bit to change).

```
/*
 * Display largest unsigned int and the numbers following it.
 */
#include <stdio.h>
#include <stdlib.h>
#include <limits.h>                    /* for UINT_MAX */

int main()
{
  unsigned int i;

  i = UINT_MAX;
  printf("Largest unsigned int: %u\n", i);
  printf("Largest plus one:     %u\n", i+1);
  printf("Largest plus two:     %u\n", i+2);

  return EXIT_SUCCESS;
}
```

Figure 4.3   (unsign.c)   A program that adds several values to the largest unsigned integer.

Floating Point Arithmetic

Floating point arithmetic is an approximation of the correct result, since floating point values are rounded or truncated to the number of significant digits allowable in the representation. Typically, this is 6 digits for **float**s and 15 digits for **double**s. Both overflow and underflow can occur with real arithmetic; the action taken is machine dependent. For example, adding to the largest possible **float** will produce overflow, and dividing the smallest possible **float** by a large value will cause underflow. The hardware of most machines traps floating point overflow, causing a run-time error and termination of the program. Technically, the result of floating point underflow is undefined, although it usually gives us a zero result.

Floating point division differs from integer division in that the real part of the result is not thrown away. As long as either operand of **/** is real, floating point division is used. That means **1.0/3.0**, **1/3.0**, and **1.0/3** all give the result **0.333333**.

Arithmetic Functions

C has a sparse set of arithmetic operators when compared with many other languages. Where, for example, is FORTRAN's exponentiation operator? How do we obtain a floating point remainder? And how do we obtain an absolute value?

C's philosophy is to keep the language small and to have library functions that perform any missing operations. It's easy to write a **power** function to compute x^y, assuming that **x** is a **double** and that **y** is an **int**. Figure 4.4 contains **power**, and Figure 4.5 contains a main program that uses it to read **x**, **y** pairs (without checking for input errors), compute x^y, and print the result. Here's some example input and output:

```
/*
 * A function to compute x to the y.
 */
double power(double x, int exp)
{
  double p;                              /* power computed so far */

  p = 1;
  if (exp > 0)
    while (exp > 0)                      /* positive exponent */
    {
      p = p * x;
      exp = exp - 1;
    }
  else
    while (exp < 0)                      /* negative exponent */
    {
      p = p / x;
      exp = exp + 1;
    }
  return p;
}
```

Figure 4.4   (power.c)   A simple function to compute integer exponents.

```
/*
 * Using our own function to compute exponents (no error checking).
 */
#include <stdio.h>
#include <stdlib.h>

int main()
{
  double power(double base, int exp);

  double x;                              /* user-supplied base */
  int    y;                              /* user-supplied exponent */

  while (scanf("%lf %i", &x, &y) == 2)
    printf("%g^%i = %g\n", x, y, power(x, y));

  return EXIT_SUCCESS;
}
```

Figure 4.5   (usepwr.c)   A main program using our **power** function. It's restricted to **int** exponents.

Aside 4.4: Compiling Programs That Use the Math Library

It turns out that many compilers force us do something special at compile time in order to use the functions in the math library. In particular, we often have to tell them explicitly that we are actually going to be using the math library. This is so they can ensure that its functions will be linked together with our program. For our old friend, the GNU C compiler, we have to use the -lm option on the command line. The "l" stands for library, and the "m" for math. (This is also true of many other compilers that run under the UNIX operating system.) For example, we compiled Figure 4.6 this way:

```
gcc -ansi usepow.c -o usepow -lm
```

Why do we have to explicitly specify that we are using the math library, but not the standard I/O library? Because almost all programs perform I/O and will therefore need to be linked with the I/O library functions, but not all programs need the math library functions, and it would therefore be wasteful to always try to link them in.

```
3.567 4
3.567^4 = 161.887
3.4 20
3.4^20 = 4.26166e+10
```

Many other functions, such as **sin** and **cos**, aren't as easy to write, and most of us have little desire to write them ourselves. Fortunately, C comes complete with a large library of math functions. Table 4.5 provides a brief description of the more commonly used ones (and Appendix A describes the others and discusses how these functions indicate errors in their arguments or results).

Here, however, we'll be content to use just one of them: **pow**. This function is a generalization of **power** that takes two **double** arguments and returns the first raised to the power of the second. To use it, all we have to do is include the math library header file, math.h, and call **pow** with appropriate arguments. Figure 4.6 is a rewrite of Figure 4.5, which uses the math library **pow** to compute the same results. The **main** programs are almost identical except that when we call **pow**, we can pass it a **double** exponent, whereas **power** is restricted to processing an **int** exponent.

4.5   TYPE CONVERSIONS

Our discussion of arithmetic operators has ignored an important question: What happens when an operator's operands are not both the same type? This occurred, for example, in our **power** function when we assigned an **int** (**1**) to a **double** (**p**). It also happened in Chapter 3's **yearEndBalance** function (Figure 3.8) when we sneakily divided a **double** (**intrate**) by an **int** (**12**). In these cases, automatic type conversions occurred. There are two types of automatic conversions: *assignment* and *arithmetic*.

FUNCTION	COMPUTES	RESTRICTIONS
`exp(x)`	e^x	
`ldexp(x,n)`	$x \times 2^n$	
`log(x)`	$\log_e x$	$x > 0$
`log10(x)`	$\log_{10} x$	$x > 0$
`pow(x,y)`	x^y	$x \neq 0$ if $y \leq 0$, and $x > 0$ if y not integer
`sqrt(x)`	$\sqrt{x}$	$x \geq 0$
`ceil(x)`	nearest whole number $\geq x$	
`floor(x)`	nearest whole number $\leq x$	
`fabs(x)`	$\lvert x \rvert$ (absolute value)	
`fmod(x,y)`	real remainder of x/y	$y \neq 0$
`sin(x)`	sine of x in radians	
`cos(x)`	cosine of x in radians	
`tan(x)`	tangent of x in radians	
`asin(x)`	$\sin^{-1} x$, in range $[-\pi/2, \pi/2]$	$-1 \leq x \leq 1$
`acos(x)`	$\cos^{-1} x$, in range $[0, \pi]$	$-1 \leq x \leq 1$
`atan(x)`	$\tan^{-1} x$, in range $[-\pi/2, \pi/2]$	
`atan2(x,y)`	$\tan^{-1} x/y$, in range $[-\pi, \pi]$	$x \neq 0$ and $y \neq 0$
`sinh(x)`	hyperbolic sine of x	
`cosh(x)`	hyperbolic cosine of x	
`tanh(x)`	hyperbolic tangent of x	

Table 4.5 The most frequently used math library functions. **x** and **y** are **double**s; **n** is an **int**. All angles are expressed in radians. All functions return a **double**.

```
/*
 * Using the math library to compute exponents (no error checking).
 */
#include <stdio.h>
#include <stdlib.h>
#include <math.h>

int main()
{
  double x;                              /* user-supplied base */
  double y;                              /* user-supplied exponent */

  while (scanf("%lf %lf", &x, &y) == 2)
    printf("%g^%g = %g\n", x, y, pow(x, y));

  return EXIT_SUCCESS;
}
```

Figure 4.6 (usepow.c) A program using **pow** to compute exponents. It's not restricted to **int** exponents.

Assignment Conversions

Whenever we assign one value to another, C automatically converts the assigned value to the type on the left-hand side of the assignment, if possible. Sometimes these conversions involve truncating a value or changing its internal representation, as when we assign an **int** to a **double**.

These automatic *assignment conversions* are convenient. In **power**, we assigned a **1** (an **int**) to **p** (a **double**) and it was automatically converted to **1.0** before the assignment took place.[6] But these conversions can cause problems when we assign a value of one type to a value with a shorter type. Consider the program shown in Figure 4.7. It first multiplies two **long**s together, assigns them to an **int**, and prints the result. Then it assigns a large negative **long** to the same **int** and prints that result. Here's its output when run on a machine with 32-bit **int**s and 32-bit **long**s.

```
First answer: 100000000
Second answer: -1691154500
```

And here's its strange output when run on a machine with 16-bit **int**s and 32-bit **long**s.

```
First answer: -7936
Second answer: 1980
```

How did multiplying two positive values give a negative result? And how did assigning a negative value give a positive result? When we multiply the two **long**s, we obtain the correct result, 100,000,000 in this case. But when we assign this value to an **int**, only its least significant bits were actually assigned (because we ran this on a machine with 16-bit **int**s and 32-bit **long**s). The same thing happens when we assign the negative **long** to the **int**, as shown below.

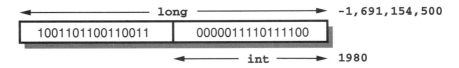

The sign bit (the leftmost bit) is on in the **long** and off in the **int**.

In general, converting from a longer type to a shorter type usually leads to loss of significance or, worse, meaningless results. Fortunately, most compilers will produce a warning when we try to assign a value from a larger type to a shorter type.

> *Avoid converting from a longer type to a shorter type.*

Assignment conversions actually happen in two places other than explicit assignment. The first occurs whenever we call a function with arguments that differ in type from those of its prototype. The other occurs when the expression in a function's **return** statement differs in type from that of the function's return type.

---

[6]Of course, we could have avoided this conversion entirely by assigning 1.0 to **p**.

```
/*
 * Example of automatic conversions: multiplying two longs together
 * and storing them in an int.
 *
 * This program isn't portable.
 */
#include <stdio.h>
#include <stdlib.h>

int main()
{
  int answer;
  long i;
  long j;

  i = 10000;
  j = 10000;
  answer = i * j;
  printf("First answer: %i\n", answer);
  answer = -1691154500L;
  printf("Second answer: %i\n", answer);

  return EXIT_SUCCESS;
}
```

Figure 4.7   (conex.c) A program illustrating potential problems with automatic conversions.

Figure 4.8 illustrates both of these conversions with a pair of functions, **round** and **trunc**, and a simple **main** program to call them. **round** and **trunc** do the obvious things: **round(10.6)** returns **11**, **round(10.2)** returns **10**, and both **trunc(10.6)** and **trunc(10.2)** return **10**.

How do these functions work? **round** simply adds **0.5** to its **double** argument and returns the result. But because **round** is defined to return an **int**, that result is automatically converted to an **int** (by truncation) before it returns. **trunc** does even less work. We define it to take an **int**, rather than a **double**. Since we provide a prototype before calling it, the **double** we pass it is automatically converted to an **int** before **trunc** is called. **trunc** then simply returns that converted value.

There are actually even simpler ways to round and truncate variables. We'll see those in the next section.

Arithmetic Conversions

In addition to assignment conversions, C performs the conversions listed in Figure 4.9 whenever it evaluates expressions, such as when it performs arithmetic or compares values. These rules may seem complicated, but essentially all C does is convert the value of the operand with the smaller type to the type of the operand with the larger

```
/*
 * The round and trunc functions (for positive values only) and a
 * minimal test program using them.
 */
#include <stdio.h>
#include <stdlib.h>

int main()
{
  int round(double);
  int trunc(int);

  double x;

  printf("Enter a series of positive real numbers, followed by EOF\n");
  while (scanf("%lf", &x) == 1)
    printf("value=%f,rounded=%i,truncated=%i\n", x, round(x), trunc(x));

  return EXIT_SUCCESS;
}

int round(double v)
  { return v + 0.5; }              /* round value up or down */

int trunc(int v)
  { return v; }                    /* get rid of fractional part */
```

Figure 4.8   (round.c) Taking advantage of assignment conversions to implement **round** and **trunc**.

type. So, for example, if we multiply an **int** by a **double**, C will convert the **int**'s value to a **double** and the multiplication will then take place in double precision.

Table 4.6 gives an idea of what happens during some of these conversions, assuming a machine with 16-bit **int**s, 32-bit **long**s, 32-bit **float**s, and 64-bit **double**s.

Casts

As we've just discovered, C performs some type conversions automatically. At times, however, we want to force a type conversion in a way that is different from the automatic conversion. We call such a process *casting* a value. We specify a cast by giving a type in parentheses followed by the expression to be cast:

    (*type*) *expression*

The cast causes the result of the expression to be converted to the specified type.

Casts eliminate the need for truncation and rounding functions. We can replace **trunc** with a cast to an **int**.

    (int) x

1. If either operand is a **long double**, convert the other to a **long double**.

2. Otherwise, if either operand is a **double**, convert the other to a **double**.

3. Otherwise, if either operand is a **float**, convert the other to a **float**.

4. Otherwise, convert any **short** (or **char**, discussed in the next chapter) operand to an **int** if it fits in an **int** or an **unsigned int** if it doesn't. Then, if either operand is an **unsigned long**, convert the other to an **unsigned long**.

5. Otherwise, if one operand is a **long** and the other is an **unsigned int**, convert the **unsigned int** to a **long** if it fits in a **long**, or convert them both to **unsigned long**s if it doesn't.

6. Otherwise, if either operand is a **long**, convert the other to a **long**.

7. Otherwise, if one operand is an **unsigned int**, convert the other to an **unsigned int**.

8. Otherwise, both operands must be of type **int**, so no additional conversion takes place.

Figure 4.9   C's rules for automatic conversions.

FROM	TO	REPRESENTATION CHANGE
short	**int**	none
float	**double**	pad mantissa with 0s
signed int	**signed long**	sign-extended high word
unsigned int	**unsigned long**	zero-fill high word
long	**int**	truncate high word
signed long	**unsigned long**	none
signed int	**unsigned int**	none
unsigned int	**signed int**	none

Table 4.6   What may happen when we convert one type to another. Most conversions from a longer to a shorter type produce undefined results.

This expression turns **x**'s value into an **int** by truncation. If **x** is **12.7**, the expression's value is **12**. We can replace **round** by adding 0.5 to the value and then casting the entire expression to an **int**.

```
(int) (x + 0.5);
```

If **x** is **12.7**, adding 0.5 to it yields **13.2**; casting this to an **int** truncates the result to **13**. Of course, the variable or expression being cast is not changed; a cast simply returns a value of the cast type. The cast operator has high precedence, so we had to parenthesize the expression to be cast. Had we failed to do so, as in

```
(int) x + 0.5;
```

the result would have been **12.5** instead.

Another typical use of a cast is in forcing division to return a real number when both operands are **int**s. Figure 4.10 is a program to average a series of integers (assuming that there are less than **INT_MAX** of them). Here is some sample input and output for the program (we hit the EOF character after entering five values):

```
97 76 85 91 98
Average of 5 values is 89.400000.
```

This program accumulates a total in an integer variable **sum**, and a count of the number of values read in the integer **n** (which we declare as **unsigned**, as it is a counter and therefore will never be negative). We compute the average with:

```
avg = (double) sum / n;
```

Casting **sum** to a **double** causes the division to be carried out as floating point division. Without the cast, integer division is performed, since both **sum** and **n** are integers.

The statement above is the same as:

```
avg = ((double) sum) / n;
```

It is not the same as:

```
avg = (double) (sum / n);
```

This statement would divide **sum** by **n** using integer division and then convert the result to a **double** (exactly the same behavior it would have without the cast, since the assignment would cause a conversion anyway). To get real division, we must cast one of the operands to a real.

Our final uses of the cast are for a different purpose. We mentioned before that it's a bad idea to convert a longer type to a shorter type. But sometimes we know it's a safe conversion. Assuming that **i** and **j** are **int**s and **l** is a **long**,

```
i = l % j;
```

is safe. That's because we know **%** will return a value between 0 and **j** − 1, a value which fits safely in an **int**. The problem here is that many compilers would give a warning; after all, we are assigning a **long** result to an **int**. But we know it's safe, and we can tell the compiler and the program's reader we know that by casting the resulting **long** to an **int**.

```
i = (int) (l % j);
```

Doing this cast explicitly requests a conversion from **long** to **int**, which turns off any compiler warnings about unsafe conversions.

Another similar situation occurs when we want to ignore a function's return value. In many of our earlier programs, for example, we didn't do anything with **scanf**'s

```c
/*
 * Compute average of its input values.
 */
#include <stdio.h>
#include <stdlib.h>

int main()
{
  int          next;              /* next input value */
  long         sum;               /* running total */
  unsigned int n;                 /* number of input values */
  int          result;            /* did we read another value? */
  double       avg;               /* average of input values */

  sum = 0;
  n = 0;
  while ((result = scanf("%i", &next)) == 1)
  {
    sum = sum + next;
    n = n + 1;
  }

  if (result != EOF)
    printf("Warning: bad input after reading %u values\n", n);

  if (n == 0)
    avg = 0.0;
  else
    avg = (double) sum / n;
  printf("Average of %u values is %f.\n", n, avg);

  return EXIT_SUCCESS;
}
```

Figure 4.10   (avg.c) A program to compute the average of its input values.

return value; we just quietly ignored it by not assigning it to a variable or using it in a test.

```c
        scanf("%lf", &radius);
```

In these situations, it's better style to cast **scanf**'s return value to **void**. Some compilers will give a warning here, fearing that we're accidentally throwing away a useful value. To turn off those warnings, we can cast the function's return value to **void**.

```c
        (void) scanf("%lf", &radius);
```

A cast to **void** simply states that we know we're ignoring the value returned by the function and not simply overlooking it by mistake.

Aside 4.5: Improving Efficiency by Avoiding Conversions

Conversions are convenient, but they are also potentially costly, and we want to avoid them as much as possible. Unfortunately, they creep in without our realizing it, unnecessarily slowing down our program. They most often creep in through assignments, parameter passing, and arithmetic expressions.

Consider this assignment, taken from Figure 4.10.

```
sum = sum + next;
```

Since **sum** is a **long** and **next** is an **int**, **next**'s value gets converted to a **long** in order to do the addition. That's not too painful and, in fact, can likely be done without requiring an extra machine instruction. But imagine that we had instead made **sum** a **double** (which would be reasonable if we're trying to eliminate the cast following the loop). Then **next**'s value would be converted to a **double** each time we do the addition, an operation that requires a representation change, which will likely involve at least one extra machine instruction. Fortunately, we can eliminate the conversion above simply by making **next** a **long** (and remembering to change the **scanf** formatting code where we read it in). In this particular loop, this change makes little difference, since the I/O and call to **scanf** take most of the time. But in a frequently executed loop that's only doing calculations, the extra time could be noticeable.

In general, automatic conversions take place whenever we have two different data types within the same expression. So the obvious solution is to try to limit expressions to a single data type. When that's not possible, the best we can hope for is to minimize the number of conversions that take place, either by rearranging the expression or by making use of explicit temporary variables.

Parameter passing is another likely source of unnecessary conversions. When we supply function prototypes, C automatically converts the actual parameter to whatever type the function expects. So passing an **int** to a function expecting a **double** results in a conversion. These automatic conversions during parameter passing are both good and bad. They're good because we can write a function that handles any numeric data type simply by declaring it to take **double**s and then passing it whatever type we want. But they're bad because expensive conversions take place whenever we fail to pass **double**s.

We can avoid some conversions by writing one version of our function for each numeric data type. The standard libraries, for example, provide several different functions to compute absolute values: **abs** returns the absolute value of an **int**, **labs** returns the absolute value of a **long**, and **fabs** returns the absolute value of a **double**.

Eliminating conversions requires careful coding and in many cases makes little visible difference in our program's total execution time. However, it's reasonable to strive to avoid them anyway, because in many programs the cost of conversions quickly adds up and it can be painful to hunt them down and remove them if it later turns out to be necessary.

Aside 4.6: Making Our Arithmetic More Efficient

Programs frequently spend much of their execution time doing arithmetic. To make them more efficient, we want to avoid arithmetic whenever we can, and when that's impossible, we want to use integer arithmetic rather than floating point arithmetic. Floating point arithmetic is especially slow, since it must often be emulated in software, rather than directly executed in hardware.

As with unnecessary conversions, unnecessary floating point arithmetic often occurs in expressions involving constants. Consider the following expression, assuming **diameter** is a **double** and **radius** is an **int**.

```
diameter = 2.0 * radius;
```

Here **radius**'s value is converted to a **double** and then multiplied by 2.0 using **double** arithmetic, and the result is stored in **diameter**. That's a lot of unneeded work. We could have written this more simply as

```
diameter = 2 * radius;
```

There's still an automatic conversion (in the assignment), but overall this expression is faster because we're now using only integer arithmetic.

4.6   CASE STUDY—A BASE CONVERSION PROGRAM

This section is optional!

We conclude this chapter with a program that converts an input value from base 10 to a user-selectable base between 2 and 10. The program repeatedly reads value/base pairs, converts the value into that base, and prints the result. Like many of our earlier programs, it stops when it encounters an error in the input or the end of file. Figure 4.11 contains some sample input and output, in which we gave the program the value 175 and determined its value in each of the bases 2 through 9. Figure 4.12 contains the main program, and Figure 4.13 contains the function it uses to convert and display the value.

How do we convert a base 10 value v to a value in another base b? We work from left to right, producing the most-significant digit in b first and the least-significant digit last. The algorithm is:

1. Set k to the number of digits the result will have.

2. While $k > 0$,

   (a) Display v/b^{k-1} (the most significant remaining digit).

   (b) Set v to $v \% b^{k-1}$ (the remaining part of the base 10 value to display).

   (c) Subtract 1 from k (the number of digits in the result we still have to display).

To see how this algorithm works, consider converting 175 to its value in octal (base 8). The most significant digit in the result is $175/(8^2)$, which is 175/64, or 2. The remaining value to display is 175 % 64, or 47. Now we repeat the cycle and compute

```
175 2
175 in base 10 is 10101111 in base 2
175 3
175 in base 10 is 20111 in base 3
175 4
175 in base 10 is 2233 in base 4
175 5
175 in base 10 is 1200 in base 5
175 6
175 in base 10 is 451 in base 6
175 7
175 in base 10 is 340 in base 7
175 8
175 in base 10 is 257 in base 8
175 9
175 in base 10 is 214 in base 9
```

Figure 4.11   Some sample input and output for our base conversion program.

```c
/*
 * Convert base 10 values into values in a specified base between
 * 2 and 10.
 */
#include <stdio.h>
#include <stdlib.h>

int main()
{
  void displayValueInBase(unsigned long value, unsigned int base);

  unsigned long value;              /* next input value */
  unsigned int  newbase;            /* base to convert it to */
  int  n;                           /* number of values read in */

  while ((n = scanf("%lu %u", &value, &newbase)) == 2)
  {
    printf("%lu in base 10 is ", value);
    displayValueInBase(value, newbase);
    printf(" in base %u\n", newbase);
  }
  if (n != EOF)
    printf("Error: Expected pair of integer values.\n");

  return EXIT_SUCCESS;
}
```

Figure 4.12   (convert.c)   A program to convert from base 10 to other bases.

```
/*
 * Display a value in a specified base between 2 and 10.
 */
#include <stdio.h>
#include <math.h>

void displayValueInBase(unsigned long v, unsigned int b)
{
  unsigned int  k;                    /* digits needed in result */
  unsigned long divisor;              /* initially b^(# of digits - 1) */

  if (v == 0)                         /* zero is the same in any base */
    printf("0");
  else
  {
    k = floor(log10(v)/log10(b)) + 1;
    divisor = pow(b, k - 1);          /* first divisor is b^(k - 1) */

    /* Run through value, calculating and displaying the value of each
       of the digits in the new base (left to right) */

    while (divisor >= 1)
    {
      printf("%lu", v / divisor);
      v = v % divisor;
      divisor = divisor / b;
    }
  }
}
```

Figure 4.13   (convfnc.c)   A function to print a base 10 value in another base.

the next most significant digit as $47/(8^1)$, which is $47/8$, or 5. The remaining value to display is 47 % 8, or 7. So the least significant digit in the result is $7/(8^0)$, or 7, and we're finished. Our final result is 257_8. We can test this result by calculating $2 \times 8^2 + 5 \times 8^1 + 7 \times 8^0$, which is 175, as it should be.

There are actually several problems with directly implementing this algorithm. One is that it assumes we magically know how many digits are in the result. It turns out there's a simple formula we can use: the number of digits needed to display a positive value v in base b is $\lfloor \log_b v \rfloor + 1$. The math library provides the **floor** function, but doesn't provide any function to compute $\log_b v$. Fortunately, however, the math library does provide the function **log10**, and $\log_b v$ is equivalent to $\log_{10} v / \log_{10} b$.

Another problem is that it's inefficient: we have to compute an exponent (a power of b) each time through the loop. Fortunately, we can solve this problem by calculating b^{k-1} before we enter the loop and storing it in a variable **divisor**. Then instead of using k to index the loop, we can just use **divisor**, dividing it by the base each time and stopping once it reaches zero.

SUMMARY

- C provides several different types of whole numbers: **int**s, **short**s, and **long**s, in both **signed** and **unsigned** variations. We use **short**s to save space, **int**s to save time, and **long**s to prevent portability problems.

- C allows several different types of integer constants: decimal (begins with a digit other than zero), octal (begins with a 0), and hex (begins with 0x or 0X), **long** (trailed by **l** or **L**) and **unsigned** (trailed by **u** or **U**).

- C provides several different types of real numbers: **float**s, **double**s, and **long double**s. We use **float**s to save space, **double**s to maximize precision, and **long double**s to take advantage of the extra range and precision provided by some machines.

- C provides only the arithmetic operators **+**, **-**, *****, **/**, and **%**. Operators common to other languages are often found as functions in the math library.

- C performs automatic conversions whenever we mix types in arithmetic expressions, assignments, or function calls (when we've provided a prototype).

- We can use the cast operator (a type surrounded by parentheses) to request specific conversions.

EXERCISES

Explore

4–1 Find out what the smallest and largest values for each integer type are on your machine. Also find out what the range of each floating point type is on your machine.

4–2 What happens if you pass **displayValueInBase** a negative value to display? A base other than 2 through 10?

4–3 What is the output of the exponent-computing program (Figure 4.6) when we use **%f** to display its output? What about when we use **%e**?

Modify

4–4 Rewrite Chapter 3's **yearEndBalance** function to use the interest-computing formula:

$$balance\ at\ end\ of\ period =$$
$$balance\ at\ start\ of\ period \times (1.0 + monthly\ interest\ rate)^{months}$$

This formula assumes that the interest is compounded monthly, rather than annually as we did in our earlier programs.

Extend

4–5 Make **round** and **trunc** (Figure 4.8) work correctly for both positive and negative numbers.

4–6 The average-calculating program (Figure 4.10) produces incorrect results if the number of values is greater than **INT_MAX**, if any input value is greater than **INT_MAX**, or if the sum is greater than **LONG_MAX**. Rewrite the program to avoid these problems.

4–7 Extend the base conversion program (Figure 4.12) so that it detects bases that aren't between 2 and 10 and prints an appropriate error message.

4–8 Extend the program using the **power** function (Figure 4.5) to display powers in bases other than base 10. That is, the program should prompt for a base and then print the powers it computes in that base.

Tune

4–9 Eliminate all unnecessary conversions from the average-computing program (Figure 4.10).

Code

4–10 Use the routines in our base converter (Figures 4.12 and 4.13) to write a program that reads a pair of values and prints all the values between them in bases 2 through 10.

4–11 Write a program to read Fahrenheit temperatures and print them in Celsius. The formula is $°C = (5/9)(°F - 32)$.

4–12 Write a program to read Celsius temperatures and print them in Fahrenheit.

4–13 Write a function, **isLeapYear**, that determines whether a particular year is a leap year. Assume that a year is a leap year if it's divisible evenly by 4, except when it's divisible by 100 but not 400. Make sure you write a test program to check whether **isLeapYear** works correctly.

4–14 Write a function, **safeDivide**, that takes two integer parameters and returns the result (as a **double**) of using real division to divide them. It should return 0.0 if the divisor is zero.

4–15 Write a program to read the coefficients a, b, and c of a quadratic equation and print its roots: the values of x such that $ax^2 + bx + c = 0$. The roots are given by

$$\frac{-b \pm \sqrt{b^2 - 4ac}}{2a}$$

4–16 Write a program to read two endpoints of a line and print their midpoint. Given two points, $P_1(x_1, y_1)$ and $P_2(x_2, y_2)$, their midpoint is $P_m(x_m, y_m)$, where x_m is $(x_1 + x_2)/2$ and y_m is $(y_1 + y_2)/2$.

4–17 Write a program that reads in an integral value and prints all powers from 1 until n, where n is the last power that can be computed without causing overflow. Use only integral variable types.

4–18 Write a program to produce a table of square roots. The program reads the range of values (m and n) and an increment (i), all of which are integers. The program prints the square roots for m, $m + i$, $m + 2 \times i$, through n.

4–19 Write a program to print a table of logs. Its input is a range of values and an increment. Its output is $\log_e x$ and $\log_{10} x$ for each x in the specified range.

4–20 The math library **sin**, **cos**, and **tan** functions expect their argument to be an angle in radians. Write a program to read an angle in degrees and print its **sin**, **cos**, and **tan**. Convert from degrees to radians by multiplying by $\pi/180$.

Build

4–21 Write a program to read the vertices of a triangle and determine whether or not it is a right triangle. Assume each vertex is a pair of integer coordinates. A triangle with vertices A, B, and C is a right triangle if $d(A, B)^2 \equiv d(B, C)^2 + d(A, C)^2$, where

$d(P_1, P_2)$ represents the distance between two points, P_1 and P_2. A, B, and C may be given in any order.

You will find it useful to write a function that takes two points (x_1, y_1) and (x_2, y_2) and returns the distance between them. Use the formula:

$$\sqrt{(x_1 - x_2)^2 + (y_1 - y_2)^2}$$

4–22 Write a program to read two points on a line, then two points on another line, and determine whether the lines are parallel or whether they intersect, and if they intersect, whether they are perpendicular. Two lines are parallel if their slopes are equal. Two lines are perpendicular if the product of their slopes is -1.

You will find it useful to write a function, **slope**, that takes two points on the line and calculates their slope. Given two points, $P_1(x_1, y_1)$ and $P_2(x_2, y_2)$, the line's slope is:

$$\frac{y_2 - y_1}{x_2 - x_1}$$

Watch out for the case where the line is parallel to the y axis.

5   CHARACTERS

This chapter discusses characters, the one basic data type we've so far ignored. As with integers and reals, we study how to create character constants and define character variables, and we examine the range of values they can hold and present several different ways to read and print them. As part of this discussion, we introduce C's library functions for efficient character-at-a-time input and output and for testing whether a character falls into a particular class, such as uppercase or lowercase. Along the way, we'll also study what happens when we convert back and forth between characters and integers and discover that characters are little more than a special type of integer. The chapter concludes by extending the previous chapter's base conversion program to handle conversions from any base to any other base.

5.1   REPRESENTING AND STORING CHARACTERS

We usually think of characters as letters of the alphabet, but they encompass more than that. There are characters for digits and punctuation, as well as special *control characters*, for actions such as ringing a *bell* or causing a *form feed*.

Internally, every character is represented by a small integer. What characters are available and how they are represented internally depends on the machine on which the program runs. The most common character sets are ASCII (American Standard Code for Information Interchange) and EBCDIC (Extended Binary Coded Decimal Interchange Code). ASCII is the character set used on most personal, micro, and minicomputers, as well as several large mainframes, while EBCDIC is used on large IBM mainframes. There are 128 ASCII and 256 EBCDIC characters. That means ASCII characters are 7 bits (values between 0 to 127) but are usually put into an 8-bit byte, whereas EBCDIC requires the full 8 bits (values between 0 and 255). Appendix B describes both of these character sets.

We obtain character variables by declaring them to be of type **char**:

```
char c;
```

The **char** type corresponds to a single byte and can hold the representation for a single character, stored internally as an 8-bit integer (on most machines). In fact, as we'll see shortly, **char**s are just a special case of C's integral data types.

Character Constants

Just as we can have numeric constants, we can have character constants. We create one by placing a character between quotation marks, as in `'A'`, `'z'`, `'7'`, or `'?'`. Character constants are stored as their value in the machine's character set.

Some characters aren't printable, or perform special actions when they're displayed. We represent these characters with *escape sequences*, a backslash (`\`) followed by a special character, an octal number, or a hex number. Table 5.1 provides a complete list of these escape sequences.

Without knowing it, we've already been using one of them: `\n` to obtain a newline. As another example, we can produce a bell by writing a `\a`.

```
printf("Wake up!\a\n");
```

The `\'` and `\"` escape sequences are particularly useful. We use `\'` when we want a single quote as a character constant, as in `'\''`. We use `\"` when we want a double quote inside a quoted string of characters, as in `printf`'s formatting control string.[1]

```
printf("How do you like \"The Joy of C\" so far\?\n");
```

The last two codes in Table 5.1—the `\`*ddd* and `\x`*ddd*—don't look like characters at all, but exist because we need a flexible mechanism to specify all available characters, including ones that don't print. Following a backslash by one to three octal digits (0 through 7) specifies a single character based on its octal representation. So, on ASCII machines, we can also ring a bell by writing a `\007`.

A backslash followed by an `x` or `X`, followed by one to three hexadecimal digits (`0` through `9`, `A` through `F`, `a` through `f`), specifies a single character based on its hexadecimal representation. We can make our code more obscure by writing `\x3F` instead of `\?`, though we probably wouldn't want to do so.

```
printf("Huh\x3F\n");
```

Actually, the hexadecimal form is just a convenient alternative to octal for specifying unprintable characters. Some programmers prefer octal, others hexadecimal.

Formatted Reading and Writing of Characters

We can read a value into a character with `scanf` using the `%c` formatting code:

```
scanf("%c", &c);
```

Unlike other formatting codes, `%c` doesn't cause `scanf` to ignore leading white space. If the next character in the input is a blank, tab, or newline, that's what we read. We can write a character with `printf` in a similar way:

```
printf("%c", c);
```

---

[1] Why there is a need to have an escape sequence for "?" is more difficult to explain, and we tackle it later on in this chapter.

CODE	CHARACTER	ASCII HEX VALUE
`\0`	null character	0
`\a`	audible alert	0x07
`\b`	backspace	0x08
`\f`	form feed	0x0C
`\n`	newline	0x0A
`\r`	carriage return	0x0D
`\t`	horizontal tab	0x09
`\v`	vertical tab	0x0B
`\'`	single quote	0x27
`\"`	double quote	0x22
`\\`	backslash	0x5C
`\?`	question mark	0x3F
`\`*ddd*	up to 3-digit octal value	
`\x`*ddd*	up to 3-digit hexadecimal value	

Table 5.1 Characters available using backslash escape sequences.

Figure 5.1 puts everything together in a little program that prints several bells to obtain the user's attention, asks a question, and then prints the response.

5.2   CHARACTERS VERSUS INTEGERS

Because characters are stored in an integer representation, we're allowed to treat them as small integers. In fact, **char**s *are* simply 1-byte integers, and C automatically converts back and forth between **char**s and **int**s whenever it's necessary, as in assignments, arithmetic expressions, or comparisons. Unlike languages such as Pascal, we don't need built-in functions to explicitly convert between characters and integers.

> *Automatic conversions between characters and integers are safe only with legal integer representations in the machine's character set.*

To illustrate a safe conversion, let's consider a common problem: converting an uppercase character into lowercase. Suppose we have a **char** variable **lower** that contains a character between **'a'** and **'z'**, and we want to assign its corresponding uppercase character to another **char** variable **upper**. That is, if **lower** is **'q'**, we want to assign **'Q'** to **upper**. Here's how we do it, assuming that we're using the ASCII character set.

```
upper = (lower - 'a') + 'A'
```

```
/*
 * Example program using the various character codes.
 */
#include <stdio.h>
#include <stdlib.h>

#define MAXBEEP 10u

int main()
{
  unsigned int  i;                          /* index to write beeps */
  char c;                                   /* character we read */

  for (i = 0; i < MAXBEEP; i = i + 1)       /* lots of beeps */
    printf("Wake up!\a\n");

  printf("Are you awake yet\?\?\? ");       /* query user */
  if (scanf("%c", &c) == 1)                 /* obtain response */
  {
    printf("You responded with a '%c'\n", c);
    if (c == 'y')
      printf("We're glad you're awake!\n");
    else
      printf("Well, we tried!\n");
  }
  else                                      /* couldn't read character */
    printf("Huh\x3F\n");

  return EXIT_SUCCESS;
}
```

Figure 5.1 (wakeup.c) An example program using the various character codes.

This assignment seems strange—are we doing arithmetic with characters? Actually, we're not. C converts all **char**s to **int**s and then operates on these **int**s. After the calculations it converts the resulting **int** to a **char** and assigns it to **upper**.

The expression converts from lowercase to uppercase by computing the difference between the ASCII code for the lowercase character in **lower** and the ASCII code for **'a'**. This difference will be 0 for **'a'**, 1 for **'b'**, 2 for **'c'**, and so on. We then add this difference to the code for **'A'**, which gives us the code for the corresponding uppercase character. Of course, this technique assumes that the lowercase and uppercase letters are contiguous, which is true of ASCII, but not of EBCDIC. We'll see a more portable way to do this conversion in a little while.

These automatic conversions also allow us to print **char**s as integers, and vice versa. When we write a **char** as an **int**, we see its character set representation. And when we write an **int** as a **char**, we see the character with that integer representation. So assuming that **c** is a **char**, we can use a single **printf** to display **c**'s internal representation in both decimal and octal and to display the character **c** contains. We do so simply by writing the character using the integer, octal, and character formatting codes.

```
printf("%4i\t%4o\t%c\n", c, c, c);
```

5.3 CHARACTER INPUT AND OUTPUT

Just as there are prewritten routines for formatted input and output of numerical and string data, there are predefined functions for character input and output. The two character-equivalent functions of **scanf** and **printf** are **getchar** and **putchar**, respectively.

getchar reads the next character in the standard input. It takes no arguments and returns the character's integer representation. Like **scanf**, **getchar** returns **EOF** if it encounters the end-of-file character. As we saw earlier, **EOF** is usually -1, a value that does not represent a legal character. That's why **getchar** returns an **int** rather than a **char**: it must be able to return any normal character, plus **EOF**, which must be a value outside the machine's character set. Because **getchar** returns an **int**, we usually store its return value into an **int** variable, rather than a **char**.

putchar is a similar function for writing a character. It takes the integer representation for a character in the machine's character set and writes it as a character to the standard output. We get machine-dependent results if the number does not represent a legal character, although most machines simply use its least significant bits (equivalent to the local character representation). **putchar** returns the character it wrote, or **EOF** if for some reason it fails.

Figure 5.2 uses **getchar** and **putchar** in a program to copy its input to its output. Figure 5.3 shows sample input and output for the program. At first glance, this program seems utterly useless. However, we'll see shortly that with input and output redirection we can use it to display and copy files.

The program simply reads characters with **getchar** and writes them with **putchar**, stopping when **getchar** returns **EOF**. We include stdio.h because it contains the prototypes for **getchar** and **putchar** and the definition of **EOF**.[2] Because **getchar** can return either a legitimate character or **EOF**, we declare the variable **c**, which holds the character we're reading or writing, as an **int**. The loop test is especially compact because we take advantage of the assignment operator's ability to return the value it assigned:

```
while ((c = getchar()) != EOF)
```

This reads a character, stores it into **c**, and then compares it with **EOF** to determine whether to go through the loop.

This technique for reading input should seem familiar, as it is very similar to the input-reading loop we have been using to read numbers with **scanf**. The primary

---

[2]In many standard library implementations, **getchar** and **putchar** are actually macros, rather than functions, a topic covered in Chapter 15. In that case, stdio.h contains their definitions rather than their prototypes.

```
/*
 * Copy the input to the output.
 */
#include <stdio.h>
#include <stdlib.h>

int main()
{
  int c;                                        /* next character */

  while ((c = getchar()) != EOF)
    putchar(c);

  return EXIT_SUCCESS;
}
```

Figure 5.2   (display.c)   A program to copy its standard input to its standard output.

```
Don't you
Don't you
just love
just love
programming
programming
in C?
in C?
We thought so!
We thought so!
```

Figure 5.3   Sample input and output for character-copying program. The output is written only when an entire input line has been read.

difference is that **getchar** returns what it read, while **scanf** uses its parameters to tell it where to save what it read.

Look carefully at the output in Figure 5.3. Do you notice something strange? You should: the input characters aren't printed until after an entire line has been read. How can this be when we're reading a character at a time? Shouldn't each character be printed right after it is input?

The reason for this behavior is that standard I/O library functions such as **getchar** and **scanf** *buffer* their input. In other words, when we read from the keyboard, the operating system collects characters in a special location until we type a carriage return or hit the enter key. It does something similar when we read from a file, except that it reads a larger chunk of characters each time. All **getchar** does is return the next character in the buffer. This buffering is also done when we do output to a file. When

Aside 5.1a: Input/Output Redirection

Most programming environments provide a mechanism, called *I/O redirection*, by which we can change where a program's input comes from and where its output goes to. This ability makes many programs much more useful than they might at first appear.

display is an example. It's just not that useful to have a program that reads and displays the characters we type. It is much more useful to have a program that can read those characters from a file or write them to a file. And that's where I/O redirection comes in. It allows us to specify where a program's input comes from and where its output goes to.

Of course, the actual details vary from system to system, but the principles are the same. Here we show how to do redirection in two of the most popular systems: UNIX and MS-DOS.

Suppose we've successfully compiled and linked display.c and obtained an executable program named display. When we execute it, normally by typing display at the command interpreter's prompt, the system sets things up so that the program's standard input comes from our keyboard and so that its standard output goes to the terminal or display. But if we follow the command with a < and a file name, the program's standard input is the named file rather than the keyboard. That means we can use

    display < *somefile*

to display the contents of *somefile*. This command executes display so that every time it reads a character with **getchar**, it is reading from somefile rather than the keyboard.

Similarly, following a command with a > and a file name causes the program's standard output to be the named file rather than the console monitor. So the command

    display > *somefile*

will cause whatever we type at the keyboard to be entered into *somefile*, rather than being displayed on the screen. That's because now, whenever we use **putchar** to write to the standard output, we're really writing to *somefile*. When we're all done entering our input, we need to hit the end-of-file character.

We're allowed to combine both input and output redirection when invoking a command. So we can use display to copy oldfile into newfile with

    display < *oldfile* >*newfile*

In this case, **getchar** is set up to read from oldfile, and **putchar** to write to newfile.

It's important to keep in mind that although we have used **getchar** and **putchar** to describe I/O redirection, it actually works with all I/O functions, including **scanf** and **printf**. This means that we can run any of our example programs that read values from the user with their input redirected so that they read values from a file, and we can run them with their output redirected to save their output in a file.

Aside 5.1b further illustrates what happens when we redirect display's input and output.

Aside 5.1b: How input/output redirection works.

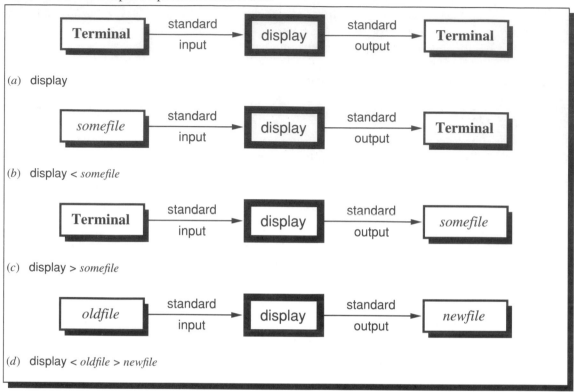

(a) display

(b) display < *somefile*

(c) display > *somefile*

(d) display < *oldfile* > *newfile*

we write to a file, the operating system collects characters and writes them to the file in large groups. And when we write to the standard output, our output is usually only written when the buffer is full (normal buffering), when we write a newline, or when we request input. Buffering allows us to use backspace to edit our input and makes input and output more efficient.[3]

We can extend our character-copying program to perform more complex input transformations. The program in Figure 5.4 prints each input line preceded with a line number. Like Figure 5.2, this program reads one character at a time until it reaches the end of the input, writing each character to its output. But this program also remembers the last character read. Whenever it is about to print a character, it first checks whether the preceding character it wrote was a newline (**\n**). If it is, it means that it's at the beginning of a new line, and so it prints the line number before writing the next character. Figure 5.5 shows the output of running the line-numbering program on itself.

---

[3]There are no unbuffered I/O operations in the standard I/O library. That doesn't mean you can't do real character-at-a-time I/O, you just have to do it using operating-system-specific routines, not standard portable ones.

```
/*
 * Copy input to output, giving each line a number.
 */
#include <stdio.h>
#include <stdlib.h>

int main()
{
    int  c;                             /* current and */
    int  lastch;                        /*    previous characters */
    unsigned long lineno;               /* lines printed so far */

    lineno = 0;
    lastch = '\n';
    while ((c = getchar()) != EOF)
    {
        if (lastch == '\n')
        {                               /* hit end of line */
            lineno = lineno + 1;
            printf("%8lu ", lineno);
        }
        putchar(c);
        lastch = c;
    }

    return EXIT_SUCCESS;
}
```

Figure 5.4   (lineno.c)   A program to line-number its input.

Because **getchar** buffers its input, it isn't well suited for interactive programs such as editors or menu-driven interfaces. These programs need to read a character as soon as the user types it—without waiting for a carriage return. An interactive screen editor shouldn't make the user type a carriage return after entering an editor command. Similarly, an interactive database interface shouldn't force the user to enter a carriage return after making a menu selection. In fact, we usually don't want buffering whenever we read input from the keyboard or write output to the display.

Unfortunately, obtaining unbuffered input is often a chore, as there's no standard library function that does this for us. That's because turning the buffering on and off generally involves complicated interactions between C and the operating system.[4]

Fortunately, many implementations of C provide special functions for reading characters immediately that hide all the nasty interactions with the operating system. Unfortunately, these functions aren't portable, and they're not part of standard C.

---

[4]On UNIX systems, for example, it takes at least two complex system calls to set things up so that we can access characters as soon as they're typed. In fact, in Chapter 21's discussion on portability we show how to obtain unbuffered input and output on both UNIX and MS-DOS systems. That discussion also shows how to manage unbuffered input and output in a portable way.

```
1 /*
2 * Copy input to output, giving each line a number.
3 */
4 #include <stdio.h>
5 #include <stdlib.h>
6
7 int main()
8 {
9   int  c;                              /* current and */
10   int  lastch;                         /*    previous characters */
11   unsigned long lineno;                /* lines printed so far */
12
13   lineno = 0;
14   lastch = '\n';
15   while ((c = getchar()) != EOF)
16   {
17     if (lastch == '\n')
18     {                                  /* hit end of line */
19       lineno = lineno + 1;
20       printf("%8lu ", lineno);
21     }
22     putchar(c);
23     lastch = c;
24   }
25
26   return EXIT_SUCCESS;
27 }
```

Figure 5.5   The output of running the line-numbering program on itself.

5.4   CHARACTER-TESTING FUNCTIONS

When we read a character, we often need to know what type of character it is. Is it an uppercase or lowercase character? A digit? Is it printable or a control character? And so on.

One way to find out this information is to check whether the character falls within a particular range of characters. We could determine whether **c** is a lowercase letter by checking whether the expression

```
c >= 'a' && c <= 'z'
```

is true. But this method works only when the lowercase letters are contiguous within the local character set. Unfortunately, while this is true of ASCII, it is not true of EBCDIC. If we want our program to work regardless of the underlying character set, we need another method. Fortunately, C provides a set of functions, listed in Table 5.2, that we can use to perform these comparisons. To use them, we include another system-supplied header file, ctype.h.

FUNCTION	CHARACTER TYPE
`isalnum`	a letter or digit (a–z, A–Z, 0–9)
`isalpha`	a letter (a–z, A–Z)
`iscntrl`	a control or delete character (in ASCII, 0x00–0x1F and 0x7F)
`isdigit`	a digit (0–9)
`isgraph`	printable, not including space (in ASCII, 0x21–0x7E)
`islower`	a lowercase letter (a–z)
`isprint`	printable, including space (in ASCII, 0x20–0x7E)
`ispunct`	punctuation (**isprint** and **!isalnum** and not space)
`isspace`	a white space, \t, \v, \f, \r, or \n
`isupper`	an uppercase letter (A–Z)
`isxdigit`	a hexadecimal digit (0–9, a–f, A–F)

Table 5.2 The character-testing functions defined in ctype.h.

Each of these functions takes an **int**, which must be a valid character in the character set or **EOF**, and returns true (a nonzero value) if it falls into the given class and false (zero) if it doesn't. For example, we can use **islower** to portably determine whether a character is lowercase:

```
if (islower(c) != 0)
```

We can verify that a character is not an uppercase letter in a similar way.

```
if (isupper(c) == 0)
```

In Figure 5.6, we use one of these functions in a program that writes its input to its output, one word per line. A word is defined as a group of letters. The input

```
here is 1 short line!
```

produces the output

```
here
is
short
line
```

This program is yet another extension to our earlier character copier. It reads its input one character at a time, writes any character that is part of a word, and writes a newline when it reaches the end of a word. To test whether a character is part of a word, we use **isalpha**.

There are two other useful routines available in the character-type library, **tolower** and **toupper**. Both take a character and return a character. **tolower** converts an uppercase character to its lowercase equivalent. If the character isn't uppercase, **tolower** simply returns it. **toupper** is similar, except it converts a lowercase character to uppercase.

```
/*
 * Break input into words (groups of letters).
 */
#include <stdio.h>
#include <stdlib.h>
#include <ctype.h>

#define TRUE    1
#define FALSE   0

int main()
{
  int c;                        /* next input character */
  int in_word;                  /* flag: are we dealing with a word? */

  in_word = FALSE;
  while ((c = getchar()) != EOF)
    if (isalpha(c) != 0)
    {                           /* it's a letter */
      putchar(c);               /* write it and note we're in word */
      in_word = TRUE;
    }
    else                        /* it's not a letter */
      if (in_word == TRUE)      /* write a newline if we were in word */
      {
        putchar('\n');
        in_word = FALSE;
      }

  return EXIT_SUCCESS;
}
```

Figure 5.6   (brkwd.c) A program to print its input to its output, one word per line.

Figure 5.7 uses **tolower** in a function called **yesOrNo** that gets a "yes" or "no" response, and Figure 5.8 is a short main program that shows how it is used.

A "yes" is any response beginning with an uppercase or lowercase 'y'; anything else is a "no" (including the end-of-file character). We take the user's input character and map it into lowercase to make the test a little simpler. We then skip the remaining characters on the input line. We do this because the input is buffered, so the user has to enter a newline character before we see any of the input. That means there's a newline waiting to be read, so we read it, along with any extra characters that might precede it.[5]

---

[5]This program subtly assumes that all input lines end with a newline, and not with an end-of-file character. That's a safe bet when the input comes from the terminal, but dangerous if it's been redirected to come from a file. This program will go into an infinite loop in that situation, as it is looking only for a newline character when it is trying to skip to the end of the input line. We'll see how to fix that problem in later chapters, but the remaining programs in this chapter share this minor flaw.

```
/*
 * Obtain a "yes" or "no" answer from the user.
 */
#include <stdio.h>
#include <ctype.h>

int yesOrNo(void)
{
  int c;                               /* holds input character */
  int answer;                          /* holds YES or NO answer */

  c = getchar();
  if (tolower(c) == 'y')
    answer = 1;                        /* 1 (YES) for 'Y' or 'y' */
  else
    answer = 0;                        /* 0 (NO) for anything else */
  if (c != EOF)
    while (c != '\n')                  /* skip other characters on line */
      c = getchar();
  return answer;
}
```

Figure 5.7   (yesorno.c)   A function to get a yes or no answer from the user.

```
/*
 * Print a prompt and then use "yesOrNo" to get a yes or no answer.
 */
#include <stdio.h>
#include <stdlib.h>

int main()
{
  int yesOrNo(void);

  printf("Enter a YES or NO answer: ");
  if (yesOrNo() != 0)
    printf("That was a YES!\n");       /* non-zero return */
  else
    printf("That was a NO!\n");        /* zero return */

  return EXIT_SUCCESS;
}
```

Figure 5.8   (useyn.c)   A program that uses our **yesOrNo** function.

yesOrNo returns a one if it detects a "yes" and a zero if it detects a "no". That means we can take care of reading the response and checking if it's a "yes" with this simple **if**:

```
if (yesOrNo() != 0)
  printf("That was a YES!\n");
else
  printf("That was a NO!\n");
```

5.5   CONVERTING CHARACTERS INTO NUMBERS

We often want to read characters and convert them into integers. Our first thought is to use **scanf**—but unfortunately it handles input errors poorly. An alternative is to read characters one at a time and to convert them into a single integer ourselves. This type of input scanning is important in many different programming problems; the efficiency we gain by writing our own scanners, plus the better error control, is well worth the effort.

Figure 5.9 contains a program to read a single digit from the user and then print its value. Here's some sample input and output:

```
Select an entry: 8
Enter a value between 0 and 5: what?
Enter a value between 0 and 5: 4
You chose 4!
```

This program uses the function **getDecimalDigit**, a variant of **yesOrNo** that obtains a single digit from the user and returns its numeric value. **getDecimalDigit** takes a single parameter, the largest acceptable input value. So the call

```
getDecimalDigit(5)
```

indicates that the user must enter a digit between 0 and 5. If we've displayed a menu, **getDecimalDigit** is a convenient way to obtain the user's choice.

Figure 5.10 contains **getDecimalDigit**. It uses a new function, **getFirst**, to read an input line and return its first character, and **isdigit** to verify that it is indeed a digit. As you might expect, **getFirst** works by using **getchar** to read the individual characters, skipping over extra input characters until it hits the line-ending newline (as did **yesOrNo**).

getDecimalDigit then converts the character to its integer equivalent and verifies that the resulting value is acceptable. If it isn't, **getDecimalDigit** writes an error message and repeats the process until it gets one of the desired digits. If for some reason the user enters the end-of-file character, **getDecialDigit** returns **EOF**.[6]

To perform the conversion, we need not know the character's internal representation. We use a similar technique to the one we used earlier to convert from a lowercase

---

[6]The logic here is a little tricky because the function contains two **return**s: one exits the loop—and the function—if it successfully converted a digit's value, the other appears after the loop and exits the function if the user enters the end-of-file. While multiple **return**s can make a function hard to read, here we've made an exception, since there are really two completely different circumstances when we want to leave the function: we've found a value, or we know we'll never find a value.

```
/*
 * Program illustrating converting a character to a number.
 */
#include <stdio.h>
#include <stdlib.h>

#define MAX_DIGIT    5u         /* largest possible input value */

int main()
{
  int getDecimalDigit(unsigned int max);

  int digvalue;                 /* value of user-entered digit */

  printf("Select an entry: ");
  if ((digvalue = getDecimalDigit(MAX_DIGIT)) != EOF)
    printf("You chose %i!\n", digvalue);

  return EXIT_SUCCESS;
}
```

Figure 5.9 (getdigmn.c) A program to read a digit from the user and print its value.

character to an uppercase one. To convert a digit character to an integer, we simply subtract the character `'0'` from it.[7]

```
value = c - '0'
```

For example, in ASCII, the code for `'7'` is 55 and the code for `'0'` is 48; the subtraction yields the integer value 7.

getDecimalDigit is useful, but it's not general—it handles only single-digit numbers. Figure 5.11 contains **getDecimalNumber**, which extends it to read and convert a *sequence* of characters. The function uses **getchar** to read characters and **isdigit** to determine whether the character is a digit. As each character is read, it's checked to determine whether it's a digit. If it is, **getDecimalNumber** updates a sum representing the value of the sequence by multiplying the current sum by 10 and then adding the digit the new character represents:

```
sum = 10 * sum + (c - '0');
```

It may not be immediately clear why this conversion works. The basic idea is that the value of an n-digit number is the value of the first $n - 1$ digits times 10, plus the value of the nth digit. So 34 is 3 (the value of its first digit) times 10, plus 4 (the value of its second digit). And 345 is 34 (the value of its first two digits) times 10, plus 5 (the value of its third digit). Since we're reading numbers one digit at a time, each time we encounter a new digit we must multiply the current value by 10 and add the new digit.

---

[7]This assumes that all digits are represented by contiguous codes, which is the case with both ASCII and EBCDIC.

```
/*
 * Functions to read a character and convert it to a number.
 *    getDecimalDigit - get a digit between 0 and "max" from user.
 *    getFirst - read an input line, returning its first character.
 */
#include <stdio.h>
#include <ctype.h>

int getDecimalDigit(unsigned int max)
{
  int getFirst(void);

  int c;                     /* character that might be a digit */
  int value;                 /* value of character as number */

  while ((c = getFirst()) != EOF)
  {
    if (isdigit(c) != 0)
      if ((value = c - '0') <= max)
        return value;        /* return value of character */
    printf("Enter a value between 0 and %u: ", max);
  }
  return c;
}

int getFirst(void)
{
  int first;                 /* first character on line */
  int junk;                  /* holds other characters */

  if ((first = getchar()) != EOF)
  {
    junk = first;            /* skip remaining characters */
    while (junk != '\n')
      junk = getchar();
  }
  return first;
}
```

Figure 5.10   (getdig.c) Read a digit from the user and compute its integer value.

How does **getDecimalNumber** know when to stop converting? The trick is that it stops as soon as it hits a character that's not a digit. It then checks whether that character is a newline and, if it is, returns the value of the sequence. Otherwise, it skips over the rest of the line and returns −1 to indicate an error.

Reading numerical data one character at a time and doing our own conversions may seem wasteful when we already have **scanf**, but it isn't. **scanf** has several problems: it compiles into a large amount of runnable code, and it is often slower than using our own conversions. More importantly, **scanf** makes error handling difficult by telling us

```c
/*
 * Read a line's worth of characters and convert them into a number,
 * one character at a time.  It only works for positive numbers.  It's
 * an error if the line contains anything other than digits.
 */
#include <stdio.h>
#include <stdlib.h>
#include <ctype.h>

int main()
{
  long getDecimalNumber(void);

  long val;                                /* input value read */

  printf("Enter a number: ");
  if ((val = getDecimalNumber()) == -1)
    printf("You didn't enter a number.\n");
  else
    printf("You entered %li\n", val);

  return EXIT_SUCCESS;
}

long getDecimalNumber(void)
{
  int  c;                                /* next input character */
  long sum;                              /* running total */

  sum = -1;                              /* simplify error handling */
  if ((c = getchar()) != EOF)            /* EOF is an error! */
  {
    if (isdigit(c) != 0)                 /* digit, so keep processing */
    {                                    /* if number, convert it */
      sum = 0;
      while (isdigit(c) != 0)
      {
        sum = 10L * sum + (c - '0');     /* convert value */
        c = getchar();
      }
    }
    if (c != '\n')                       /* not ending with a newline? */
    {
      sum = -1;                          /* it's an error */
      while (c != '\n')                  /* skip rest of line */
        c = getchar();
    }
  }
  return sum;
}
```

Figure 5.11 (getnum.c) Read a group of characters and turn them into a single integer.

Aside 5.2a: Characters and Portability

The integral types—**short**, **int**, and **long**—are **signed** by default. But what about **char**s—are they **signed** or **unsigned**? That is, what values do **char**s store? −128 to 127? Or 0 to 255?

Whether **char** is **signed** or **unsigned** is implementation defined. The only thing we're guaranteed is that a legitimate character in the machine's character set is always treated as nonnegative. EBCDIC uses all 8 bits to represent characters, so with it we're guaranteed to have **unsigned char**s. ASCII requires only 7 bits, however, so some implementations may have **char** default to **signed char**, and others to **unsigned char**. As with integers, we can explicitly request a particular type by preceding **char** with **signed** or **unsigned**.

Here are the constants in limits.h that represent the minimum ranges of the various **char** types. That is, the specific values on your machine are required to be greater than or equal to these in magnitude.

CONSTANT	VALUE	DESCRIPTION
CHAR_BIT	8	maximum bits in a byte
CHAR_MAX	127	maximum value of a **char**
CHAR_MIN	0	minimum value of a **char**
SCHAR_MAX	+127	maximum value of a **signed char**
SCHAR_MIN	−127	minimum value of a **signed char**
UCHAR_MAX	255	maximum value of an **unsigned char**

Why do we care whether **char**s are **signed** or **unsigned**? Most of the time we don't. It really matters only when we're on ASCII machines and put a value into a **char** that's outside the legal character set (less than 0 or greater than 127). The program in Aside 5.2b illustrates this distinction. It runs through all the ASCII characters and prints their decimal and octal values and displays the characters themselves when they're printable (so we can avoid printing those characters that do strange things such as erasing the screen or causing a form feed).

Aside 5.2b uses a variable **c** to run through the character set. We initially set it to 0 and keep incrementing it until we've printed all the characters. We know the loop is complete when **c** is one greater than the last ASCII character (128). What type should **c** have? One possibility is **char**, but then we're in trouble if **char** defaults to **signed**. That's because the largest **signed char** is 127, and we would have an overflow, which would cause **c** to become negative. But we're safe with **c** as an **unsigned char**.

Of course, we could have eliminated worrying about this whole problem simply by declaring **c** as an **int**. In fact, we need to make that change to process EBCDIC with our program, since there are 256 EBCDIC characters, and 257 doesn't fit into an **unsigned char**. We've really just used **unsigned char** here to make a point, not because it's the best way to do things. In fact, C's automatic conversions and I/O functions that return integers make **char** variables less useful than one might think, and we ordinarily use them only with arrays of characters, a topic covered in later chapters.

Aside 5.2b (charset.c) A program to print the local character set.

```
/*
 * Print character set in decimal, octal, and character (ASCII only).
 */
#include <stdio.h>
#include <stdlib.h>
#include <ctype.h>
#include <limits.h>

int main()
{
  unsigned char c;

  for (c = 0; c <= SCHAR_MAX; c = c + 1)
  {
    printf("%4i\t%4o", c, c);
    if (isprint(c) != 0)
      printf("\t%c", c);
    putchar('\n');
  }

  return EXIT_SUCCESS;
}
```

only how many values it correctly converted and providing no information about why a failure might have occurred. To provide suitable error messages or error recovery when a failure occurs, we still have to deal with the input one character at a time.

5.6   CASE STUDY—A MORE GENERAL BASE CONVERTER

This section is optional!

We conclude this chapter with a more general version of the base converting program we wrote in the last chapter. This version differs in that it's not restricted to converting decimal numbers into other bases. Instead, it lets us convert from any base to any base, from binary through base 36. Bases larger than 10 use letters as placeholders for their digits—a is 10, b is 11, c is 12, all the way up through z, which is 35. Figure 5.12 contains one example run of the program, where we use it to convert values from base 16 into base 2.

Figure 5.13 contains the main program. It reads the desired input and output bases and then reads a sequence of values in the input base, displaying those values in the desired output base. It terminates reading the input when an invalid value is entered or it encounters the end-of-file character.

The program makes use of several other source files and borrows heavily from what we've written before.

```
Enter initial base: 16
Enter target base: 2
Enter number to convert: FFFF
FFFF in base 16 is 1111111111111111 in base 2.
Enter number to convert: AAAA
AAAA in base 16 is 1010101010101010 in base 2.
Enter number to convert: 1111
1111 in base 16 is 1000100010001 in base 2.
Enter another base 16 number to convert: FAFA
FAFA in base 16 is 1111101011111010 in base 2.
Enter another base 16 number to convert: A8B4
A8B4 in base 16 is 1010100010110100 in base 2.
Enter another base 16 number to convert: 8EF5
8EF5 in base 16 is 1000111011110101 in base 2.
Enter another base 16 number to convert: 15
15 in base 16 is 10101 in base 2.
Enter another base 16 number to convert: A
A in base 16 is 1010 in base 2.
Enter another base 16 number to convert: 1
1 in base 16 is 1 in base 2.
Enter another base 16 number to convert: 2
2 in base 16 is 10 in base 2.
Enter another base 16 number to convert:
```

Figure 5.12   Some sample input and output from our extended program to convert from one base to another.

It reads its input values using a pair of functions. The first, **getNumberInBaseN**, is a variant on **getDecimalNumber** that reads a value in any base, up to base 36, rather than just up to base 10. Like the original, however, it still returns a base 10 value. The other, **getBase**, reads in the input and output bases using **getNumberInBaseN** and then does some error checking to ensure the specified bases are reasonable. Figure 5.14 contains **getBase** and Figure 5.15 contains **getNumberInBaseN**.

How does **getNumberInBaseN** differ from **getDecimalNumber**? One change is that it now takes the base of the input number as a parameter, rather than having base 10 hardwired into its code. Another change is that it makes use of a new function, **toDecimal**, to turn a character into its appropriate base 10 value. That is, if the input character is an 'f', **toDecimal** returns 15. Before we knew we had a digit, so we converted it simply by subtracting '0'. Now the conversion is more complex, since letters are legitimate digits in bases greater than 10. When we have a letter, we have to subtract 'a' from it and then add 10. This conversion is, of course, ASCII dependent.

toDecimal actually takes a pair of parameters: the character to convert and a base. That way it can ensure that the character is a legitimate digit in the specified base before attempting the conversion. It returns −1 if there's an error.

We still use **displayValueInBase** to convert the number from base 10 to the output base—with one change. Now we have to convert values other than 0 through 9 to an appropriate character. If we're displaying a base 16 number and one of its

```
/*
 * Convert from any base to any other base.
 */
#include <stdio.h>
#include <stdlib.h>

#define   MINBASE   2u                 /* smallest base */
#define   MAXBASE   36u                /* largest base */

int main()
{
  void displayValueAndBases(unsigned long num, int base, int newbase);
  long getNumberInBaseN(unsigned int b);
  int  getBase(unsigned int minbase, unsigned int maxbase);

  int  base;                           /* initial base */
  int  newbase;                        /* final base*/
  unsigned long num;                   /* initial value, in base 10 */

  printf("Enter initial base: ");   /* grab initial base (in base 10) */
  if ((base = getBase(MINBASE, MAXBASE)) != -1)
  {
    printf("Enter target base: ");                /* grab target base */
    if ((newbase = getBase(MINBASE, MAXBASE)) != -1)
    {
      printf("Enter number to convert: ");     /* grab number */
      while ((num = getNumberInBaseN(base)) != -1)
      {
        displayValueAndBases(num, base, newbase);
        printf("Enter another base %i number to convert: ", base);
      }
      putchar('\n');
    }
  }

  return EXIT_SUCCESS;
}


void displayValueAndBases(unsigned long num, int base, int newbase)
{
  void displayValueInBase(unsigned long v, unsigned int b);

  displayValueInBase(num, base);
  printf(" in base %i is ", base);
  displayValueInBase(num, newbase);
  printf(" in base %i.\n", newbase);
}
```

Figure 5.13   (convert2.c)   The main program for our more general base converter program.

```
/*
 * Read in the base using getNumberInBaseN
 */
#include <stdio.h>

int getBase(unsigned int minbase, unsigned int maxbase)
{
  long getNumberInBaseN(unsigned int b);

  long base;

  if ((base = getNumberInBaseN(10)) == -1)
    printf("Error: nonnumeric base detected\n");
  else
  {
    if (base < minbase)                /* set to -1 if too small */
    {
      printf("Error: Smallest base is %u.\n", minbase);
      base = -1;
    }
    if (base > maxbase)                /* set to -1 if too large */
    {
      printf("Error: Largest base is %u.\n", maxbase);
      base = -1;
    }
  }
  return (int) base;                   /* base is in range of int */
}
```

Figure 5.14   (getbase.c)   A function to read in a base and perform some basic error checking on it.

digits is a 15, we write an 'F' rather than 15. To do this conversion, we use another new function, **toChar**, which takes an **int** and returns the appropriate character to display. It uses a technique that's similar to the one we showed for converting lowercase characters to uppercase. And, as in **toDecimal**, **toChar** is now ASCII dependent. We'll provide more portable versions of these functions in later chapters. Figure 5.16 contains **toDecimal** and **toChar**; Figure 5.17 contains the new version of **displayValueInBase**.

SUMMARY

- C provides a special integral type, **char**, for holding the integer representations of characters.

- C provides character constants, a character enclosed in single quotes, as well as escape sequences to identify special characters.

```
/*
 * Read a base N number, one character at a time.
 */
#include <stdio.h>

long getNumberInBaseN(unsigned int base)
{
  int   toDecimal(int c, int b);

  int   c;                              /* next input character */
  int   value;                          /* decimal value of next char */
  long  sum;                            /* running total */

  sum = -1;
  if ((c = getchar()) != EOF)           /* EOF is error */
  {
    if ((value = toDecimal(c, base)) != -1)
    {                                   /* within number, compute sum */
      sum = 0;
      while (value != -1)
      {                                 /* valid next digit in base */
        sum = base * sum + value;   /* update number */
        c = getchar();
        value = toDecimal(c, base);
      }
    }
    if (c != '\n')
    {
      sum = -1;                         /* indicate error! */
      while (c != '\n')                 /* skip rest of line */
        c = getchar();
    }
  }
  return sum;
}
```

Figure 5.15   (getbasen.c)   A function that reads a value in a specified base.

- C automatically converts back and forth between **char**s and **int**s.

- The standard library contains a pair of functions for doing I/O a character at a time: **getchar** reads the next character in the standard input, and **putchar** writes a character to the standard output.

- The library also provides a set of character-testing functions used to determine whether a particular character has certain properties, such as being a lower- or uppercase letter.

- Reading numerical data a character at a time and doing our own conversions allows us to improve on **scanf**'s error-handling abilities.

```
/*
 * Functions to convert digits to and from characters (ASCII ONLY).
 *    toDecimal - convert char to equivalent decimal number.
 *    toChar - convert decimal number to equivalent character.
 */
#include <ctype.h>

int toDecimal(int c, int base)
{
  int value;

  if (isdigit(c))                   /* set value if the input is anything */
    value = c - '0';                /* we know how to handle */
  else
    if (islower(c))
      value = c - 'a' + 10;
    else
      if (isupper(c))
        value = c - 'A' + 10;
      else                          /* if not, it's an error */
        value = -1;

  if (value >= base)                /* make sure it's legal for base */
    value = -1;

  return value;
}

int toChar(int value)
{
  int c;

  if (value < 10)
    c = '0' + value;
  else
    c = 'A' + value - 10;
  return c;
}
```

Figure 5.16 (convchar.c) Functions for converting characters to and from decimal values.

EXERCISES

 5–1 Compile and run the programs in this chapter.

5–2 What happens if you remove the check for printable characters from Aside 5.2b?

Modify 5–3 Change the line-numbering program (Figure 5.4) to avoid numbering blank lines (it counts them, but doesn't display a number in front of them).

```
/*
 * Display a value in a specified base between 2 and 36.
 */
#include <stdio.h>
#include <math.h>

void displayValueInBase(unsigned long v, unsigned int b)
{
  int toChar(int value);               /* Addition to Chapter 4 */

  unsigned int k;                      /* digits needed in result */
  unsigned long divisor;               /* initially b^(# of digits - 1) */

  if (v == 0)                          /* zero is the same in any base */
    printf("0");
  else
  {
    k = floor(log10(v)/log10(b)) + 1;
    divisor = pow(b, k - 1);           /* first divisor: b^(k - 1) */

    /* Run through value, calculating and displaying the value of each
       of the digits in the new base (left to right) */

    while (divisor >= 1)
    {
      putchar(toChar((int)(v / divisor)));  /* Change from Chapter 4 */
      v = v % divisor;
      divisor = divisor / b;
    }
  }
}
```

Figure 5.17   (convfnc2.c) Function for displaying a value in a specified base.

5–4 The one-word-per-line program (Figure 5.6) uses a definition of a word that will break a line such as

```
#include <ctype.h>
```

into:

```
include
ctype
h
```

Modify this program to recognize special characters such as **#**, **<**, **>**, and **.** as part of a word. Handling **.** is tricky—it should be part of a word only if it's surrounded by letters.

Aside 5.3: Character Set Differences and Portability

The character sets used in many places, such as large parts of Europe, don't include some special punctuation characters, such as the curly braces ({ and }), square brackets ([and]), and a few others. C programs can be written with these deficient character sets using the *trigraphs* shown below.

TRIGRAPH	CHARACTER
??=	#
??/	\
??'	^
??(	[
??)	]
??!	|
??<	{
??>	}
??-	~

A *trigraph* is a three-character sequence beginning with a pair of question marks that stands for a particular character. Whenever the preprocessor encounters a trigraph, it substitutes that character. (This explains the need for the **\?** escape sequence. It exists to prevent pairs of question marks being accidentally interpreted as the beginning of a trigraph.)

In other places, such as Asia, that have an enormous number of different characters, implementations have extended character sets that don't fit into a single byte. C provides an additional character type, **wchar_t** (*wide character type*), for characters in these extended character sets. **wchar_t** is a synonym for an implementation-dependent integral type. To use it, we need to include a new standard header file, stddef.h, that provides definitions for several useful data types. We can use **wchar_t** just as we use **char**, with one exception: we write constants with a preceding **L**. So **L'q'** is a constant of type **wchar_t**.

Most of us will be able to get by quite comfortably without ever using **wchar_t**. Nonetheless, it's important to keep in mind that the traditional American character sets are not the only ones out there.

5–5 Modify **getDecimalNumber** (Figure 5.11) so that it reads and converts real numbers (that is, numbers containing a decimal point) instead of integers. Extend the function to handle numbers in scientific notation as well.

5–6 Modify any version of our previous interest rate program to use the extension to **getDecimalNumber** you wrote in the previous exercise instead of **scanf**.

Extend

5–7 Extend the program that prints its input to its output one line at a time (Figure 5.2) to do new things. It should now print its output in lower case, and it should strip out any digits and punctuation characters.

5–8 Extend the line numbering program (Figure 5.4) to number pages. That is, place a line with "PAGE *N*" at the beginning of each page, with a blank line between the page-numbering line and the next line of the output. Assume that a page has a maximum of 66 lines (use a constant **PAGE_LEN**).

5–9 Change **getDecimalDigit** (Figure 5.10) to verify that there is nothing but trailing spaces after the digit. Any other characters should result in an error message.

5–10 Extend **getDecimalNumber** (Figure 5.11) to allow a **+** or **-** before the number. Then extend it to allow leading and trailing blanks or tabs.

| Tune |

5–11 The conversion in **toDecimal** (Figure 5.16) depends on the ordering of lowercase letters—it works for ASCII but not for EBCDIC. Modify it so that it works with any character-set encoding scheme.

| Code |

5–12 Write a program that copies its input to its output but eliminates all blank lines. A blank line is any line that contains only white space. This task is not the same as simply eliminating all newline characters.

5–13 Write a program that reads a single character and prints its integer equivalent. Then write a program that reads an integer and prints its character equivalent. Be sure to do appropriate error and range checking.

5–14 Write a program to read an **int** and print its octal, decimal, hexadecimal, and unsigned decimal equivalents.

5–15 Write a program to print the decimal, octal, and hex values of the characters that have special escape sequences.

5–16 Write a program that prints the number of control characters in its input.

5–17 Write a program to print each number found in its input on a line by itself, preceded by the line number on which it was located. A number is simply a sequence of digits.

5–18 Write a function, **getLetter**, that reads an upper- or lowercase letter and tests to see whether it is within the minimum and maximum letters provided as arguments.

| Build |

5–19 Write a program to count the number of words, lines, and characters in its input. A word is any sequence of non-white-space characters.

5–20 A range is a sequence of characters of the form [*character-character*], such as **[a-d]** or **[r-u]**. Write a program to find ranges and replace them with the characters contained in the range. That is, the program should replace **[a-d]** with **abcd**.

Make sure the program prints an appropriate error message if it can't decipher a range or if the range doesn't make sense.

5–21 Write a package of simple drawing functions. This package should include functions for drawing filled and hollow rectangles, squares, and triangles. These functions should take a description of the object to draw (such as the height and width for a rectangle) and a character to use to draw the object. For example, a 3-by-5 filled rectangle with a '+' as the drawing character would look like:

```
+++++
+++++
+++++
```

Similarly, a hollow 5-by-5 filled square drawn with '@' as the drawing character would look like:

```
@@@@@
@   @
@   @
@   @
@@@@@
```

This package is easy to construct if you start by writing low-level utility functions. One example is **writeN**, which takes a character and a number of times to write it.

6 OPERATORS

This chapter takes a long look at C's rich set of operators. We examine more closely the operators we've already introduced, and we introduce the operators we previously ignored. We pay special attention to the operators that have no analog in most other programming languages, such as the shorthand assignment and bit-manipulation operators. Many of C's operators are just similar enough to those of other programming languages to cause problems, so we spend much of our time on their caveats and quirks. The chapter concludes with a case study: a pair of programs that compress and uncompress their input.

6.1 OPERATORS, OPERANDS, AND PRECEDENCE

Much of a programming language's power derives from the operators it provides. And C provides a wide selection of operators. Table 6.1 summarizes them, their relative precedence, associativity, and the operations they perform.

The table is organized in order of decreasing precedence. We saw earlier that in C, as in most programming languages, we can use parentheses to override the default order of evaluation. What we didn't discuss earlier is associativity. Associativity of an operator describes how expressions are grouped when they contain operators of similar precedence. For example, consider the expression below (which we used in Figure 4.2 to compute the area of a circle).

```
area = PI * radius * radius;
```

We have two **'s, which are both the same operator and therefore have the same precedence. As a result, it's their associativity that determines the order of evaluation. In this case, * associates left to right, which means this expression is evaluated as if it were written:

```
area = (PI * radius) * radius;
```

Another, more complex example results if we take this expression (which is used in Figure 5.11 to convert character digits into integers),

```
sum = 10L * sum + (c - '0');
```

and rewrite it without the parentheses.

```
sum = 10L * sum + c - '0';
```

OPERATOR	DESCRIPTION	ASSOCIATES
x[i], **f(x)**	array subscripting and function call	left to right
., **->**	direct and indirect structure field selection	left to right
++, **--**	postfix increment/decrement	right to left
++, **--**	prefix increment/decrement	right to left
sizeof, (*type*)	size of a variable or type (in bytes), cast to *type*	right to left
+, -, !, ~	unary plus, unary minus, logical and bitwise NOT	right to left
&, *	address of and dereferencing	right to left
*, /, %	multiply, divide, modulus	left to right
+, -	addition, subtraction	left to right
>>, <<	right, left shift	left to right
<, >, <=, >=	test for inequality	left to right
==, !=	test for equality, inequality	left to right
&	bitwise AND	left to right
^	bitwise XOR (exclusive OR)	left to right
|	bitwise OR	left to right
&&	logical AND	left to right
||	logical OR	left to right
? :	conditional operator	right to left
=	assignment	right to left
+=, -=, *=, /=, %=	add to, subtract from, multiply to, divide by, assign remainder	right to left
<<=, >>=, ^=, &=, |=	shift right and left, assign bitwise XOR, AND, OR	right to left
,	sequential expression evaluation	left to right

Table 6.1   C's operators and their precedence. All operators within a set of lines have equal precedence.

Because the ***** has higher precedence than either the **+** or the **-**, the multiplication will be evaluated first. But since the **+** and **-** have the same precedence, it's their associativity that determines the order of their evaluation. They associate left to right, so this expression is evaluated as if it were written:

```
sum = ((10L * sum) + c) - '0';
```

By default, the addition would happen before the subtraction. Using the parentheses, we change things so that the subtraction comes before the addition, which makes it clear that we intend to convert the character to an integer, then add that integer to the sum.

Most operators share two properties. First, they expect their operands to have the same type and will perform the arithmetic conversions we described earlier if they don't. There are a few operators that require specific types of operands, but unless we point out otherwise, assume an operator works with any integral or real data type. Second, most operators don't impose an order of evaluation on their operands. When we multiply two expressions together, there's no guarantee that the operand on the left will be evaluated before the operand on the right. That rarely matters—we need to worry about the order of evaluation only when it involves a side effect, such as a function call. There are several operators that do impose an order of evaluation, but again, unless we point out otherwise, assume an operator's operands aren't evaluated in any particular order.

The remainder of this chapter describes the operators in Table 6.1, although we do skip several of them. We ignore the arithmetic and type-casting operators, since we've already discussed them in some detail. And we skip over the structure, array, and pointer accessing operators, since we devote the better part of several later chapters to them.

6.2   THE RELATIONAL OPERATORS

We use relational operators to test whether a particular relationship holds between two values. There are relational operators to compare values for equality (**==**), inequality (**!=**), greater than (**>**), less than (**<**), greater than or equal (**>=**), and less than or equal (**<=**). A relational operator returns an **int**: 1 (true) if the relation holds, 0 (false) if it doesn't. They return **int**s because the statements that perform tests, such as **if** or **while**, don't actually test whether the test is true or false. Instead, they test whether it evaluates to 0 (false) or something other than 0 (true).

As a result, we never need to explicitly check whether values are zero. Figure 6.1 avoids doing so in a new version of our earlier program to display its input one word per line. We've rewritten the **if** that tests whether the next character is a letter,

```
if (isalpha(c) != 0)
```

more compactly as:

```
if (isalpha(c))
```

Similarly, we've rewritten our test that compares **in_word** with the constant **TRUE** (1),

```
if (in_word == TRUE)
```

more simply as:

```
if (in_word)
```

That's because **in_word** has to be either **TRUE** (1) or **FALSE** (0). If it's not 0, which is what we're testing for here, we know it's 1.

Figure 6.2 is another example. It's a new version of our main program showing how to use **yesOrNo** to get a yes or no answer from the user. Since **yesOrNo** returns one if it's a yes and zero if it's a no, we can test for a yes answer with:

```
if (yesOrNo())
    printf("That was a YES!\n");      /* non-zero return */
else
    printf("That was a NO!\n");       /* zero return */
```

It is well worth the effort to understand this particular shortcut. It is convenient, it results in more readable code (once you are familiar with it), and it frequently appears in real-world programs.

```
/*
 * Break input into words (groups of letters).
 */
#include <stdio.h>
#include <stdlib.h>
#include <ctype.h>

#define TRUE   1
#define FALSE  0

int main()
{
  int c;                        /* next input character */
  int in_word;                  /* flag: are we dealing with a word? */

  in_word = FALSE;
  while ((c = getchar()) != EOF)
    if (isalpha(c))
      {                         /* it's a letter */
        putchar(c);             /* write it and note we're in word */
        in_word = TRUE;
      }
    else                        /* it's not a letter */
      if (in_word)              /* write a newline if we were in word */
      {
        putchar('\n');
        in_word = FALSE;
      }

  return EXIT_SUCCESS;
}
```

Figure 6.1 (brkwd2.c) A more compact program to break its input into one word per line. We've eliminated all explicit comparisons with zero.

We can write compact code by using the relational operators to test the result of an assignment—but we have to be careful. That's because the relational operators have higher precedence than assignment. In our loop to read input characters, we had to parenthesize the assignment:

        (c = getchar()) != EOF

What happens if we leave off the parentheses?

        c = getchar() != EOF   /* OOPS! */

Table 6.1 tells us that != has higher precedence than =. That means we assign to c the result of comparing the newly read character with EOF. So c will be zero or one, depending on whether or not we read EOF, and putchar would write whatever character

```
/*
 * Print a prompt and then use "yesOrNo" to get a yes or no answer.
 */
#include <stdio.h>
#include <stdlib.h>

int main()
{
  int yesOrNo(void);

  printf("Enter a YES or NO answer: ");
  if (yesOrNo())
    printf("That was a YES!\n");       /* non-zero return */
  else
    printf("That was a NO!\n");        /* zero return */

  return EXIT_SUCCESS;
}
```

Figure 6.2   (useyn2.c)   A new version of our main program using the **yesOrNo** function.

has an internal representation of **\001**, which is probably something unprintable.

> ***Don't forget to parenthesize assignments when using the relational operators to compare their results.***

In fact, it's generally a good idea to parenthesize the operands of relational operators, since they fall in the middle of the precedence hierarchy.

Figure 6.3 contains another common mistake made by novice C programmers. Can you spot it? The program is a new version of our earlier program to print the average of its input values. The problem is in the **if** statement that protects against dividing by zero.

```
if (n = 0)
  avg = 0.0
else
  avg = (double) sum / n;
```

Our mistake is that we used the assignment operator, **=**, rather than the test-for-equality operator, **==**. This expression now mistakenly assigns 0 to **n**, which the **if** then treats as false. The result is that we *always* do the division by zero we were trying to prevent!

> ***Watch out for accidentally using = to test for equality.***

One final mistake often made is attempting to compare real numbers with **==** and **!=**. Figure 6.4 is a program that makes this mistake. It has a loop index that repeatedly

```
/*
 * Compute average of its input values.  Contains error!
 */
#include <stdio.h>
#include <stdlib.h>

int main()
{
  int           next;                    /* next input value */
  long          sum;                     /* running total */
  unsigned int n;                        /* number of input values */
  int           result;                  /* did we read another value? */
  double        avg;                     /* average of input values */

  sum = 0;    n = 0;
  while ((result = scanf("%i", &next)) == 1)
  {
    sum = sum + next;
    n = n + 1;
  }
  if (result != EOF)
    printf("Warning: bad input after reading %u values\n", n);
  if (n = 0)                             /* MISTAKE! */
    avg = 0.0;
  else
    avg = (double) sum / n;
  printf("Average of %u values is %f.\n", n, avg);

  return EXIT_SUCCESS;
}
```

Figure 6.3   (avgerr.c) A buggy version of Chapter 4's program to compute the average of its input values.

updates a floating point counter (**f**) by a small value (**0.1**). To stop the loop, it uses the test **f != EXIT_VALUE**, where **EXIT_VALUE** is a floating point constant. Here's the program's output, when we run it on a machine with 7 significant digits.

```
        0.0000000000
        0.1000000015
        0.2000000030
        0.3000000119
        0.4000000060
        0.5000000000
        0.6000000238
        0.7000000477
        0.8000000715
        0.9000000954
        1.0000001192
        Loop exit test failed.
```

```
/*
 * Illustrate problems with floating point equality testing.
 */
#include <stdio.h>
#include <stdlib.h>

#define EXIT_VALUE  1.0f

int main()
{
  float f;

  for (f = 0.0; f != EXIT_VALUE; f = f + 0.1)
  {
    printf("%.10f\n", f);          /* print out value */
    if (f > EXIT_VALUE)
    {
      printf("Loop exit test failed.\n");
      return EXIT_FAILURE;
    }
  }

  return EXIT_SUCCESS;
}
```

Figure 6.4 (floaterr.c) A program to illustrate problems with testing for floating point equality.

The problem is that adding 0.1 isn't adding exactly 0.1, but a value that is approximately 0.1. As a result, the counter is never exactly 1.0, but a value that is approximately 1.0 (although interestingly enough 0.5 is represented exactly). Fortunately, our program has a test inside the loop that exits if the counter somehow becomes larger than 1.0, preventing an infinite loop.

> *Don't compare floating point numbers with == or !=.*

6.3　　THE LOGICAL OPERATORS

We often need to combine relational tests in a single expression. To do so, we use the logical operators: logical AND (&&), logical OR (| |), and logical negation (!). Like the relational operators, these return an **int**, 1 (true) or 0 (false). Table 6.2 shows how they determine what's true and false. Logical AND and OR interpret non-zero operands as true and zero operands as false. An expression such as **x && y** will evaluate to true only if both **x** and **y** aren't zero. Similarly, an expression such as **x | | y** will evaluate to true if either **x** or **y** isn't zero. Logical negation returns 1 if its operand is zero, and zero otherwise.

	OPERANDS		RESULT	
OP1	OP2	&&	||	
nonzero	nonzero	1	1
nonzero	zero	0	1
zero	nonzero	0	1
zero	zero	0	0

Table 6.2　Results of using the logical operators.

Figure 6.5 uses them both in a new version of our **yesOrNo** function. Now we use ‖ to check whether the next input character is an upper- or lowercase 'y', rather than first using **tolower** to convert the input character to lowercase:

```
if ((c = getchar()) == 'y' || c == 'Y')
```

And in our loop to skip the remaining characters on a line, we now enter the loop only if the character we read is not **EOF** *and* is not a newline.

```
while (c != EOF && c != '\n')
```

Doing so guarantees that our program doesn't go into an infinite loop if for some reason the input has an end of file without a preceding newline.

The logical operators **&&** and ‖ associate left to right, and their precedence is low, so we rarely need to parenthesize when we combine them with the relational operators. As we might expect, the expression

```
c != '\n' && c != EOF
```

is evaluated as though we wrote

```
(c != '\n') && (c != EOF)
```

Figure 6.6 shows how this **yesOrNo** program can be written even more compactly. We now compute the function's return value with a single assignment:

```
answer = (c = getchar()) == 'y' || c == 'Y';
```

Like the relational operators, the logical operators return 1 for true and 0 for false. What this assignment does is read a character, store it into **c**, and then place a 1 into **answer** if it's a 'y' or a 'Y' and a 0 otherwise. By taking advantage of this feature, we've eliminated entirely the need for the special constants **TRUE** and **FALSE**.

This assignment is a good example of C's power and its drawbacks, all wrapped up in a single line. This same code can be written more clearly but less concisely as:

```
c = getchar();
answer = (c == 'y' || c == 'n');
```

```
/*
 * Function to obtain a yes/no answer from the user and return 1 if
 * it's a yes, and 0 if it's a no.
 */
#include <stdio.h>
#include <ctype.h>

int yesOrNo(void)
{
  int c;                           /* holds input character */
  int answer;                      /* holds 1 (YES) or 0 (NO) */

  if ((c = getchar()) == 'y' || c == 'Y')
    answer = 1;                    /* 1 (YES) for 'Y' or 'y' */
  else
    answer = 0;                    /* 0 (NO) for anything else */
  while (c != EOF && c != '\n')    /* skip other characters on line */
    c = getchar();
  return answer;
}
```

Figure 6.5 (yesorno2.c) A new and improved version of Chapter 5's **yesOrNo** function.

```
/*
 * Function to obtain a yes/no answer from the user and return 1 if
 * it's a yes, and 0 if it's a no (more concise version).
 */
#include <stdio.h>
#include <ctype.h>

int yesOrNo(void)
{
  int c;                           /* holds input character */
  int answer;                      /* holds 1 (yes) or 0 (no) */

  answer = (c = getchar()) == 'y' || c == 'Y';
  while (c != EOF && c != '\n')    /* skip other characters on line */
    c = getchar();
  return answer;                   /* 1 for 'Y' or 'y', otherwise 0 */
}
```

Figure 6.6 (yesorno3.c) An even more concise version of our **yesOrNo** function. It takes advantage of the assignment operator and the integer return values of the logical operators.

(We added the parentheses to make clear that the result of the logical entire expression is being assigned to **answer**). There's often a tradeoff like this one between clarity and conciseness. It's up to individual programmers to decide whether they—and their program's readers—are comfortable with writing and reading the more concise version.

We have to be careful when we combine logical operators. The program in Figure 6.7 revises Figure 6.1 to allow words to contain digits as well as letters, so long as the first character is still a letter. For example, the input

```
w8 4 me 2go with you.
```

produces

```
w8
me
go
with
you
```

as its output. This program now contains a more complex test to determine whether the character we read is part of a word:

```
if (isalpha(c) || in_word && isdigit(c))
```

Because the precedence of **&&** is higher than that of **||**, this test actually evaluates as though it were written as:

```
if (isalpha(c) || (in_word && isdigit(c)))
```

That is, this expression is true if **c** is a letter, or if **c** is a digit and we're already in a word. That's very different than if it were evaluated as:

```
if ((isalpha(c) || in_word) && isdigit(c))
```

In fact, since **isalpha(c)** and **isdigit(c)** can't both be true at the same time, this **if** will be false if either is true!

Because combining logical operators can be confusing, it's a good idea to surround their use with parentheses.[1]

It's possible that **&&** and **||** may never evaluate one of their operands, a process called *lazy* or *short-circuit* evaluation. The reason is that we often know their value after evaluating only the first operand—eliminating the need to evaluate the other operand. In C, if we have a series of clauses connected by logical AND, the first false one terminates the evaluation. Consider the logical AND in our earlier test:

```
while (c != '\n' && c != EOF)
    c = getchar();
```

The clause **c != \n** is evaluated first. If it's false, the entire logical expression is false, regardless of the value of the second clause—so the second clause is not evaluated. More

---

[1] In fact, many compilers will warn us about expressions like these and suggest we use parentheses to clarify what's happening.

```
/*
 * Break input into words (letter followed by letters or digits).
 */
#include <stdio.h>
#include <stdlib.h>
#include <ctype.h>

#define TRUE  1
#define FALSE 0

int main()
{
  int c;                        /* next input character */
  int in_word;                  /* flag: are we dealing with a word? */

  in_word = FALSE;
  while ((c = getchar()) != EOF)
    if (isalpha(c) || in_word && isdigit(c))
    {                           /* it's a letter */
      putchar(c);               /* write it and note we're in word */
      in_word = TRUE;
    }
    else                        /* it's not a letter */
      if (in_word)              /* write a newline if we were in word */
      {
        putchar('\n');
        in_word = FALSE;
      }

  return EXIT_SUCCESS;
}
```

Figure 6.7   (brkwd3.c) An extension to our program to write words one per line. Now a word can include digits, as long as it begins with a letter.

to the point, **c** isn't compared with **EOF**. That's not all that important here, but we'll take advantage of this feature frequently in later programs.

Logical OR, ||, is similar: the first true clause terminates the evaluation of all succeeding clauses. Here,

```
    answer = (c = getchar()) == 'y' || c == 'Y';
```

c is not compared with 'Y' when **c** is 'y'.

> *Unlike the relational operators, && and || impose an order of evaluation on their operands.*

Logical NOT, !, takes one operand, which it always evaluates. Figure 6.8 uses it in a program to shrink its input by deleting all leading and trailing white space and by turning other groups of white space into a single blank. The ! appears in this test:

```
while (!isspace(c))
```

isspace(c) returns a 1 if **c** is a white space character and a 0 otherwise. The ! in front of it turns the 1 into a 0 and the 0 into a 1. The result is that we enter the loop only if **c** is not a white space character.

Logical negation has high precedence, so we have to be careful to parenthesize its operand when it contains other operators. Those cases are rare, however, since we can often eliminate the need for logical negation entirely by carefully rewriting our tests. For example, suppose we are writing a loop to skip trailing spaces. We might think of the loop as stopping if we either encounter a character that is not a space or we hit a newline. Since we want a loop that executes when the stopping condition is not true, we can negate the stopping expression like this:

```
while (! (!isspace(c) || c == '\n') )
    c = getchar();
```

Fortunately, we can simplify this complex test to the test in Figure 6.8:

```
while (isspace(c) && c != '\n')
    c = getchar();
```

6.4   BITWISE OPERATORS

The operators we've seen so far are found in most high-level programming languages. There are also less-common operators for accessing bits. We can shift bits left (<<) or right (>>), invert bits (~), and do bitwise AND (&), OR (|), and XOR (^). All of these operators require integral operands. In fact, we usually restrict our use of them to **unsigned** operands.

These operators let us deal with the details of the machine, and they help us write more efficient programs. We must often set specific bits to request various hardware operations, such as direct writing to and from a disk. When these operations complete, they often set status bits to tell us whether they succeeded or failed. We use the bitwise operators to set and examine these bits. In addition, we can often use these operators to store our data compactly and to provide fast versions of some numerical operations.

Bit Shifts

The left (<<) and right (>>) shift operators take an operand and return its value shifted left or right by a specified number of bits. The operand itself is not affected. The form of the operators is *op* >> *n* and *op* << *n*. *n* should be a positive integer less than the number of bits in the value being shifted.

```
/*
 * Removes leading and trailing white space from its input and
 * turns runs of white space into a single blank.
 *
 * It assumes lines end with a newline character.
 */
#include <stdio.h>
#include <stdlib.h>
#include <ctype.h>

int main()
{
  int c;                                /* next input character */

  while ((c = getchar()) != EOF)
    {            /* each pass through loop takes care of one input line */
    while (isspace(c) && c != '\n')
      c = getchar();                    /* skip leading spaces */
    while (c != '\n')
      {                                 /* process any words */
      while (!isspace(c))
        {                               /* dump out word */
        putchar(c);
        c = getchar();
        }
      while (isspace(c) && c != '\n')   /* skip trailing spaces */
        c = getchar();
      if (c != '\n')                    /* not trailing, write space */
        putchar(' ');
      }
    putchar('\n');                      /* trailing, write newline */
    }

  return EXIT_SUCCESS;
}
```

Figure 6.8 (shrink.c) A program to shrink its input by removing white space.

As an example,

   x = v << 1;

takes **v**'s value, shifts it 1 bit to the *left*, and assigns it to **x**. The result is that **x** is assigned $v \times 2$. In general, shifting to the left n places is the same as multiplying by 2^n. Similarly,

   x = v >> 1;

takes **v**'s value, shifts it 1 bit to the *right*, and assigns it to **x**. The result is that **x** is assigned $v / 2$. In general, shifting to the right n places is the same as dividing by 2^n.

Assuming **v** is 6, here is what **v**'s value looks like, shifted left by 1 bit and right by 1 bit:

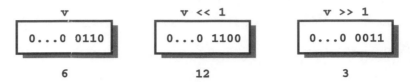

This diagram gives the impression that C always fills the vacated bits with zero. That's usually—but not always—true. Whenever we do a *left* shift, zero bits are shifted in from the right. But when we do a *right* shift, the replacement for the vacated bits on the left depends on the variable's type. If the variable is unsigned, the replacement bits are zero. If it's signed, the replacement bits usually share the sign bit's value (sign extension). But it's possible that on some machines zeros are shifted in for signed values, which would have the (most likely undesired) effect of changing the value's sign.

> *Whenever possible, avoid right shifts on signed values.*

Bitwise Logical Operators

There are three bitwise logical operators that take a pair of operands: bitwise AND (**&**), bitwise OR (**|**), and bitwise XOR (**^**). They work on their operands bit by bit, setting each bit in the result. Table 6.3 shows the results of these operators: bitwise AND is 1 only when both bits are 1, bitwise OR is 1 if either bit is 1, and bitwise XOR (exclusive OR) is 1 if exactly one of the bits is 1.

There's one other bitwise logical operator: bitwise NOT (**~**). It takes only one operand and returns its value with each of its bits inverted—any 1 bit becomes zero, and any zero bit becomes 1. That means, for example, that **~0** is an integer with all 1 bits. Table 6.4 shows an example of these bitwise operators. It highlights one key difference between the logical and the bitwise logical operators. Although **&&** and **||** always return 0 or 1, there's no such restriction on their bitwise logical counterparts.

We use these bitwise operators primarily to test and set individual bits or groups of bits in a word. This ability is often needed to manipulate devices that use individual bits as controlling signals or status indications. When manipulating bits, we create a *mask* that selects particular bits. A mask is simply an integer with only those bits we are interested in turned on, as in:

```
#define OURBIT  0x80          /* bit 7: (...00 1000 0000) */
```

Given this mask, we can turn on the desired bit in an integer **x** with:

```
x = x | OURBIT              /* turn on bit 7 */
```

On the other hand, we can turn off that bit with:

```
x = x & ~OURBIT            /* turn off bit 7 */
```

OPERANDS			RESULTS	
Op1	Op2	&	|	^
1	1	1	1	0
1	0	0	1	1
0	1	0	1	1
0	0	0	0	0

Table 6.3 Results of using the bitwise logical operators.

EXPRESSION	BINARY VALUE			
A:	1001	0110	0001	0001
B:	0001	1010	1101	1001
A & B:	0001	0010	0001	0001
A | B:	1001	1110	1101	1001
A ^ B:	1000	1100	1100	1000
~A:	0110	1001	1110	1110
~B:	1110	0101	0010	0110

Table 6.4 An example of the bitwise logical operators

This works because `~OURBIT` is a word with all bits on except for the one in which we're interested. When we do the AND, we're turning off that bit and keeping all the other bits the same. Finally, we can test whether our bit is on or off with:

```
x & OURBIT          /* nonzero if bit on */
```

The expression returns a non-zero value if the bit is on and zero if it's off. Table 6.5 shows what's happening with these expressions.

The bitwise operators have very low precedence. Bitwise `&` and `|`, for example, have lower precedence than the relational operators. That means to be safe, we generally parenthesize all uses of bitwise operators that are part of more complicated expressions.

> *Parenthesize all uses of the bitwise operators in larger expressions.*

Figure 6.9 uses these operators in a function `printBinary` to print an integer's value in binary. It takes two parameters: `x` is the value we want to print in binary (`unsigned int`), and `nbits` is the number of bits in an `int`. It works by running through the bits in `x`, going from left (bit $n - 1$) to right (bit 0). To print bit `i`, it first shifts `x`'s value `i` bits to the right, making the value's rightmost bit the one we're

EXPRESSION	BINARY VALUE			
x:	0000	0000	1100	1011
OURBIT:	0000	0000	1000	0000
~OURBIT:	1111	1111	0111	1111
x & ~OURBIT:	0000	0000	0100	1011

Table 6.5   An example using the bitwise logical operators to turn bits off

```
/*
 * A pair of useful bit-manipulating functions.
 *    intBits - returns number of bits in an unsigned int.
 *    printBinary - prints an unsigned int in binary.
 */
#include <stdio.h>

unsigned int intBits(void)
{
  unsigned int x;                         /* word being shifted */
  unsigned int i;                         /* count of shifts */

  i = 0;
  for (x = 1; x != 0; x = x << 1)
    i = i + 1;
  return i;
}

void printBinary(unsigned int x, unsigned int nbits)
{
  int i;                                  /* index of desired bits */

  for (i = nbits - 1; i >= 0; i = i - 1)
    printf("%i", (x >> i) & 01);
  putchar('\n');
}
```

Figure 6.9   (prbin.c)   Print the underlying binary representation of an **unsigned int**.

interested in. It then turns off the other bits by ANDing the result of the shift with a word with just the rightmost bit on.

```
        printf("%i", (x >> i) & 01);
```

printBinary assumes we know how many bits are in **int**. To figure that out, we use a function **intBits**. The trick we use is to start with an **int** with just its rightmost bit on. We then keep shifting it to the left, a bit at a time, and count how many shifts we can do before the bit disappears off the left end. That count's final value is the number of bits in an **int**. This technique is clever, but it's actually not the easiest way to determine how many bits a particular type has. We'll see a better way later in the chapter.

Why did we write a new function rather than simply using our earlier base-converting functions? For the special case of printing values in binary, the bit-shifting operators result in a simpler, more efficient function.

Figure 6.10 is a program that uses **printBinary** and **intBits** to show what happens to an input value when we shift it to the right and to the left and when we turn various bits on and off. Here's some sample input and output for the program when run on a machine with 16-bit **int**s.

```
Enter value: 15487
In binary: 0011110001111111
15487 >> 1 = 7743: 0001111000111111
15487 << 1 = 30974: 0111100011111110
Bit 7 was off, now on = 15615: 0011110011111111
```

Getting and Setting Bits

Sometimes it seems as though there's an operator for everything. But that impression is misleading. There are many useful operations for which no built-in operator exists. One important example is accessing a bit or group of bits within a word. We can create our own mask and then do a bitwise AND or OR to access them, but that's painful. What we really want is an easy way to specify the bits of interest and have the appropriate masks created for us automatically.

Figure 6.11 contains implementations of a set of functions for accessing bits that let us do just that. **getBit** and **setBit** get or set the value of the **n**th bit within a word. **getBits** and **setBits** are similar, but work with a group of **k** bits, starting at position **n** within a word. All of these functions assume the *rightmost* bit in the word is bit number zero.

Here are the results of a series of example calls to these functions, given a variable **word** whose value is 181 (0...10110101).

CALL	RETURN VALUE	BIT PATTERN		
getBit(word, 1)	0	0...0	0000	0000
getBit(word, 2)	1	0...0	0000	0001
setBit(word, 3, 1)	189	0...0	1011	1101
setBit(word, 4, 0)	165	0...0	1010	0101
getBits(word, 3, 2)	2	0...0	0000	0010
getBits(word, 0, 4)	5	0...0	0000	0101
setBits(word, 2, 5, 16)	193	0...0	1100	0001
setBits(word, 0, 4, 7)	183	0...0	1011	0111

Figures 6.12 and 6.13 show exactly what happens with the calls **getBits(word,3,2)** and **setBits(word,2,5,16)**, respectively.

```
/*
 * Program illustrating some basic bit-manipulating operations.
 */
#include <stdio.h>
#include <stdlib.h>

#define OURBIT   0x80                    /* bit 7: (...00 1000 0000) */

int main()
{
  unsigned int intBits(void);
  void         printBinary(unsigned value, unsigned int intbits);

  unsigned int nbits;                    /* bits in an int */
  unsigned int v;                        /* input value */
  unsigned int x;                        /* modified input value */

  nbits = intBits();                     /* get # of bits in an int */
  printf("Enter value: ");               /* get value to display */
  scanf("%u", &v);                       /* assume no errors */
  printf("In binary: ");
  printBinary(v, nbits);                 /* display in binary */
  x = v >> 1;
  printf("%u >> 1 = %u: ", v, x);        /* show right-shifted */
  printBinary(x, nbits);
  x = v << 1;                            /* show left-shifted */
  printf("%u << 1 = %u: ", v, x);
  printBinary(x, nbits);
  x = v;
  if ((x & OURBIT) != 0)                 /* show with bit 7 off and on */
    printf("Bit 7 was on, now off = %u: ", x = x & ~ OURBIT);
  else
    printf("Bit 7 was off, now on = %u: ", x = x | OURBIT);
  printBinary(x, nbits);

  return EXIT_SUCCESS;
}
```

Figure 6.10   (useprbin.c)   A program that uses **printBinary** to illustrate the bit-shifting operators.

How do these functions work? **getBit** shifts **word** *right* **n** places, so that the rightmost bit, bit 0, holds the desired bit value. As with **printBinary**, it then ANDs the entire word with a mask containing a single 1 in its rightmost bit, effectively turning off all of **word**'s other bits. **setBit** behaves differently depending on whether it is turning on or turning off the desired bit. To turn on the **n**th bit, **setBit** ORs the word with a mask containing a single 1 in the **n**th position. It is easy to create this mask: **setBit** simply shifts a 1 *left* **n** places. To turn off the **n**th bit, **setBit** ANDs the word with a mask containing a single 0 in the **n**th position, the negation of the mask above.

```
/*
 * Functions to get and set bit values.  All assume suitable parameters.
 *   getBit:  get value of bit n in word.
 *   setBit:  return value with bit n set to v (0 or 1).
 *   getBits: get value of k bits at position n in word.
 *   setBits: return value with k bits starting at bit n assigned v.
 */

unsigned int getBit(unsigned int word, int n)
  { return (word >> n) & 01; }

unsigned int setBit(unsigned int word, int n, unsigned int v)
{
  if (v != 0)
    return word | (01 << n);     /* turn on the bit */
  else
    return word & ~(01 << n);    /* turn off the bit */
}

unsigned int getBits(unsigned int word, int n, int k)
  { return (word & (~(~0 << k) << n)) >> n; }

unsigned int setBits(unsigned int word, int n, int k, unsigned int v)
  { return (word & ~(~(~0 << k) << n)) | (v << n); }
```

Figure 6.11   (bits.c) Functions to determine and set the value of bits in a word.

We could write **getBits** and **setBits** on top of repeated calls to **getBit** or **setBit**—which is acceptable if we don't care how quickly our program runs. Instead, however, both functions work by creating a mask that isolates the desired group of bits. They do so by taking a word of all 1s (**~0**), shifting it left **k** places, and inverting it bitwise. This results in a group of 1 bits in the **k** rightmost bits of the mask. Then they shift this group left **n** places, which puts them in the correct place.

getBits simply ANDs this mask with the word, shifts the result right **n** places, and returns the desired bits. **setBits** ANDs the *negation* of the mask to turn off the relevant bits, and then ORs the word with the new value shifted left **n** places.

Figure 6.14 provides a main program that uses these functions to store several integers—representing an employee's sex, age, marital status, and years employed—into an **unsigned short**, as shown below.

15-14	13-7	6	5-0
STATUS	AGE	SEX	YEARS

By compressing this information into a single word, we make the most efficient use of our available memory. The tradeoff is that we are making assumptions about the ranges of values that could come to haunt us later.

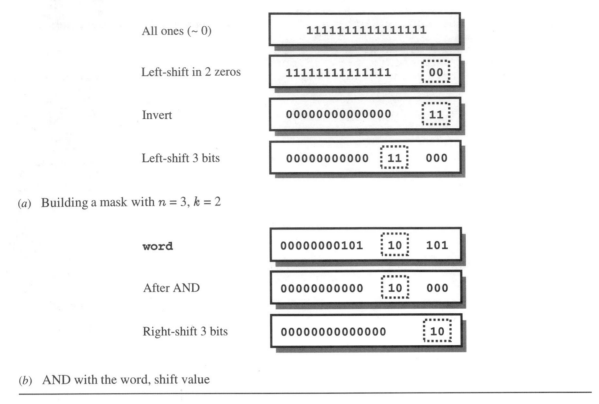

All ones (~ 0)

1111111111111111

Left-shift in 2 zeros

11111111111111   00

Invert

00000000000000   11

Left-shift 3 bits

00000000000   11   000

(a) Building a mask with $n = 3$, $k = 2$

word

00000000101   10   101

After AND

00000000000   10   000

Right-shift 3 bits

00000000000000   10

(b) AND with the word, shift value

Figure 6.12   How **getBits(word,3,2)** builds and uses a mask to get a group of bits within a word.

Using Exclusive OR

We have used all of the bitwise operators except exclusive OR. One use for it is in data encryption. Encrypting a file makes its contents unreadable while preserving the information it contains. And one of the simplest ways to encrypt text is to exclusive OR the text with a lengthy key. If the text is larger than the key (which is usually the case), just cycle through the key repeatedly until the entire file has been encrypted. The nice aspect of this scheme is that we use the same method and the same key to decrypt the encrypted version of the file: we just take the exclusive OR with the key one more time.

As an example, suppose we have an 8-bit piece of data to be encrypted and an 8-bit key. Taking the exclusive OR with the key produces the encrypted data.

```
DATA (ASCII 'P')    0101  0000
KEY                 0001  0010
DATA xor KEY        0100  0010   (encrypted data)
```

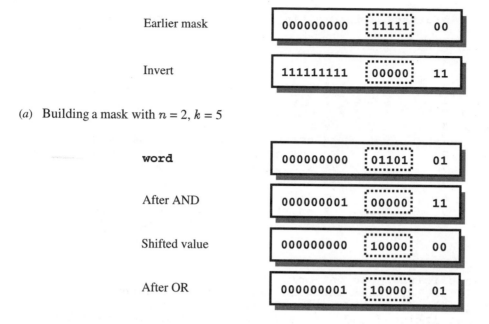

Earlier mask   `000000000` `11111` `00`

Invert   `111111111` `00000` `11`

(a) Building a mask with $n = 2$, $k = 5$

word   `000000000` `01101` `01`

After AND   `000000001` `00000` `11`

Shifted value   `000000000` `10000` `00`

After OR   `000000001` `10000` `01`

(b) AND with the word and OR with shifted value v

Figure 6.13 How `setBits(word,2,5,16)` builds and uses a mask to set a group of bits within a word.

Taking the exclusive OR with the key again produces the original data.

DATA xor KEY	0100 0010	(encrypted data)
KEY	0001 0010	
DATA	0101 0000	

Figure 6.15 contains a program that encrypts (or decrypts) its input. It's virtually identical to our earlier character-copying program, except that instead of copying each character directly to the output (via **putchar**), we take the exclusive OR of the current character with the next character of the key. This is actually a bit tricky, since we store the key in a single 4-byte **unsigned long**. To grab the next character, we need to shift the key over 1 byte. The bit-shifting operators, however, require the number of bits to shift, not the number of bytes. Fortunately, the system header file limits.h contains a constant **CHAR_BIT** that represents the number of bits in a byte, so we shift **CHAR_BIT** bits × the number of the byte we want.

There's actually one more tricky detail. Before we do the exclusive OR, we turn on the high bit in the key character. That's because it turns out that many systems use

```c
/*
 * Pack employee information into a single word (no error checking).
 */
#include <stdio.h>
#include <stdlib.h>

#define SINGLE     0                /* codes for marital status */
#define MARRIED    1
#define SEPARATED  2
#define DIVORCED   3
#define MSBIT      14               /* starting bit for marital status */
#define MSBITS     2                /* number of marital status bits */
#define AGEBIT     7                /* starting bit for age */
#define AGEBITS    7                /* number of bits for age */
#define SEXBIT     6                /* bit number for sex */
#define YRSBIT     0                /* starting bit for employed years */
#define YRSBITS    6                /* number of bits for years */

int main()
{
  unsigned int getBit(unsigned int word, int n);
  unsigned int setBit(unsigned int word, int n, unsigned int v);
  unsigned int getBits(unsigned int word, int n, int k);
  unsigned int setBits(unsigned int word, int n, int k, unsigned int v);

  unsigned int   mstat;
  unsigned int   sex;
  unsigned int   age;
  unsigned int   years;
  unsigned short info;            /* holds info on one person */

  printf("male=1, female=0? ");
  scanf("%u", &sex);
  info = setBit(0, SEXBIT, sex);
  printf("age? ");
  scanf("%u", &age);
  info = setBits(info, AGEBIT, AGEBITS, age);
  printf("single=%u, married=%u, separated=%u, divorced=%u? ",
         SINGLE, MARRIED, SEPARATED, DIVORCED);
  scanf("%u", &mstat);
  info = setBits(info, MSBIT, MSBITS, mstat);
  printf("years employed? ");
  scanf("%u", &years);
  info = setBits(info, YRSBIT, YRSBITS, years);
  printf("Sex: %u\n", getBit(info, SEXBIT));
  printf("Age: %u\n", getBits(info, AGEBIT, AGEBITS));
  printf("Marital status: %u\n", getBits(info, MSBIT, MSBITS));
  printf("Years employed: %u\n", getBits(info, YRSBIT, YRSBITS));

  return EXIT_SUCCESS;
}
```

Figure 6.14 (usebits.c) A program using bit shifting to store employee information efficiently.

```
/*
 * Encrypt standard input using built-in encryption key (0xABCD).
 */
#include <stdio.h>
#include <stdlib.h>
#include <limits.h>

#define MAXKEY    2L      /* length of the key (2 bytes) */
#define HIGHBIT   0x80    /* mask to access high bit only */

int main()
{
  unsigned long key;        /* the encryption key */
  unsigned char keybyte;    /* the next byte in the key */
  int           c;          /* next character */
  unsigned long j;          /* character count */

  key = 0xABCD;        /* 1st 4 bits = 10, 2nd 4 bits = 11, and so on */
  j = 0;
  while ((c = getchar()) != EOF)
  {
    keybyte = (unsigned char) (key >> ((int) (j % MAXKEY) * CHAR_BIT));
    putchar(c ^ (keybyte | HIGHBIT));
    j = j + 1;
  }

  return EXIT_SUCCESS;
}
```

Figure 6.15 (encrypt.c) A program to encrypt a file, using exclusive OR with a built-in key.

a special control character, such as a *control*-Z, to indicate the end of the file, and this pattern can result from doing an exclusive OR with a key character—but only if its high bit is off. Turning it on prevents a potentially nasty problem.

To simplify the program's structure, we've built the key into it. In a more secure encryption program, of course, the program's user would provide the key.

Other Uses of Bitwise Operators

Sometimes bitwise operators can make integer arithmetic unnecessary. Since left-shifting n bits is equivalent to multiplying by 2^n, we can replace such multiplications with a bit-shifting operation. Similarly, right-shifting n bits is equivalent to dividing by 2^n, so we can replace those divisions as well.

There is another place where the bitwise operators can potentially lead to a more efficient program. Consider Figure 6.16's **isOdd** and **isEven** functions for determining whether a particular unsigned integer is odd or even. These functions are doing an integer division, hidden in the usual implementation of the **%** operator they use.

Figure 6.17 shows a better implementation of these functions that avoids arithmetic entirely by directly checking whether the rightmost bit is on or off. **isOdd** checks whether that bit is on, and **isEven** checks whether that bit is off. The bit-shifting and logical operations are usually somewhat faster than the equivalent arithmetic operation. But we pay a price for this speed: these functions are now harder to read than before.

Figure 6.18 is a simple main program that shows how to use these functions.

6.5   ASSIGNMENT OPERATORS

We have seen that in C, unlike most other programming languages, assignment not only assigns the result of an expression to a variable but also returns this value. One benefit is that we can assign values during tests, as in our now familiar loop to read the input one character at a time.

```
while ((c = getchar()) != EOF)
  putchar(c);
```

Another benefit is that we can use assignment operators more than once in a single statement. We can initialize more than one variable to some initial value (say, 0) with

```
sum = i = 0;
```

The assignment operator associates right to left, so this multiple assignment is equivalent to

```
sum = (i = 0);
```

Shorthand Assignment Operators

C doesn't just provide a single assignment operator—it provides an entire collection. These operators have the form

   lhs op= rhs

where *lhs* is the left-hand side of the assignment, *rhs* is an expression, and *op* is any one of C's arithmetic or bit-shift operators (so the shorthand operators are **+=**, **-=**, ***=**, **/=**, **%=**, **>>=**, **<<=**, **&=**, **|=**, and **^=**). The shorthand form is equivalent to

   lhs = lhs op (rhs)

with *lhs* evaluated once. Like **=**, the shorthand assignment operators return the value assigned, and we can use them in other expressions.

These shorthand operators are mostly for convenience—they save a large amount of typing. In fact, the shorthand operators are so convenient that after using them for just a little while, you'll find it hard to program in any language that doesn't have them. With the shorthand operators, for example, we can multiply **p** by **x** with

```
p *= x;
```

```
/*
 * An initial implementation of functions to tell whether a
 * given value is odd or even.
 */

int isOdd(unsigned int x)     { return (x % 2) == 1; }
int isEven(unsigned int x)    { return (x % 2) == 0; }
```

Figure 6.16   (oddeven1.c) A naive implementation of functions to determine whether a number is odd or even.

```
/*
 * A better implementation of functions to determine whether a
 * given value is odd or even.
 */
int isOdd(unsigned int x)  { return (x & 01); }
int isEven(unsigned int x) { return !(x & 01); }
```

Figure 6.17   (oddeven2.c) A more clever implementation of functions to determine whether a number is odd or even.

```
/*
 * A program to test our isOdd and isEven functions.
 */
#include <stdio.h>
#include <stdlib.h>

int main()
{
  int isOdd(unsigned int x);
  int isEven(unsigned int x);

  unsigned int value;

  while (scanf("%u", &value) == 1)
    printf("isOdd(%u) is %i, isEven(%u) is %i\n",
           value, isOdd(value), value, isEven(value));

  return EXIT_SUCCESS;
}
```

Figure 6.18   (useodd.c) A simple program that uses **isOdd** and **isEven**.

a terse equivalent of

```
p = p * x;
```

Similarly, we can divide **p** by **x** with

```
p /= x;
```

the shorthand for

```
p = p / x;
```

Figure 6.19 uses almost all of the shorthand arithmetic operators in a new version of our earlier **power** function.

These operators not only save typing, they lead to more concise and, perhaps surprisingly, more readable code. To see why, consider the assignment:

```
balance = balance + balance * intrate;
```

We can write this assignment more concisely using an assignment operator:

```
balance += balance * intrate;
```

The latter is more likely to be correct because we have to type **balance** once less, lowering the chance of typing a different name by mistake. And it's more readable because it makes it clear that the point of this multiplication is to add it to **balance**.

Postfix and Prefix Assignment

C also provides two special sets of shorthand operators for the common operations of incrementing and decrementing by 1: **++** adds 1 to its operand and **--** subtracts 1 from its operand. There are two forms of these operators, *prefix* (preceding its operand) and *postfix* (following its operand).

The form doesn't matter, *so long as the operator and its operand are not part of a larger expression.* By itself, **exp++** or **++exp** is equivalent to **exp += 1**, and **exp--** or **--exp** is equivalent to **exp -= 1**. Figure 6.20 uses these operators to write our most concise version of **power**. The function is now significantly more compact than the original version, without suffering any significant loss in readability. Here, we wrote it using the postfix form, but we could have written it using the prefix form as well.

We can use postfix and prefix operators as a piece of a more complicated expression. The problem is that it then makes a big difference which form we use. When we use **++** as a postfix operator, it first evaluates the operand, provides its value to the rest of the statement or expression, and then adds 1 to it. As a prefix operator, it does the additions first and makes the new value of the variable available to the expression. Prefix and postfix **--** behave similarly to **++**, except that they decrement their operand.

In Figures 6.21 and 6.22, we have two new versions of the previous chapter's line numbering program. The first initializes **lineno** to zero and uses

```
printf("%8lu ", ++lineno);
```

```
/*
 * A more concise version of our power-computing function.
 */
double power(double x, int exp)
{
  double p;

  p = 1.0;
  if (exp > 0)                                /* positive exponent */
    while (exp > 0)
    {
      p *= x;   exp -= 1;
    }
  else                                        /* negative exponent */
    while (exp < 0)
    {
      p /= x;   exp += 1;
    }
  return p;
}
```

Figure 6.19   (power2.c)   Chapter 4's **power** made concise using shorthand assignment operators.

```
/*
 * Most concise version of our power-computing function.
 */
double power(double x, int exp)
{
  double p;

  p = 1.0;
  if (exp > 0)                                /* positive exponent */
    while (exp > 0)
    {
      p *= x;   exp--;
    }
  else                                        /* negative exponent */
    while (exp < 0)
    {
      p /= x;   exp++;
    }
  return p;
}
```

Figure 6.20   (power3.c)   Our most concise version of **power**.

```
/*
 * Copy input to output, giving each line a number.
 */
#include <stdio.h>
#include <stdlib.h>

int main()
{
  int           c;                  /* current and */
  int           lastch;             /*    previous characters */
  unsigned long lineno;             /* lines printed so far */

  lineno = 0;  lastch = '\n';
  while ((c = getchar()) != EOF)
  {
    if (lastch == '\n')             /* hit end of line */
      printf("%8lu ", ++lineno);
    putchar(lastch = c);
  }

  return EXIT_SUCCESS;
}
```

Figure 6.21   (lineno2.c) Our line numbering program made more concise with prefix increment.

to print it. This increments **lineno** *before* passing its value to **printf**. It's equivalent to the two statements:

```
++lineno;
printf("%8lu ", lineno);
```

The second version initializes **lineno** to 1 and uses

```
printf("%8lu ", lineno++);
```

to print it. This increments **lineno** *after* passing its value to **printf**. It's equivalent to

```
printf("%8lu", lineno);
lineno++;
```

We will use these forms of the prefix and postfix operators frequently in later chapters.

6.6   OTHER OPERATORS

There are three other operators of interest: the comma operator (**,**), the **sizeof** operator, and the conditional operator (**?:**).[2]

---

[2]None of of these operators have analogs in other high-level languages like Pascal or BASIC.

```
/*
 * Copy input to output, giving each line a number.
 */
#include <stdio.h>
#include <stdlib.h>

int main()
{
  int             c;                 /* current and */
  int             lastch;            /*    previous characters */
  unsigned long lineno;              /* lines printed so far */

  lineno = 1;  lastch = '\n';
  while ((c = getchar()) != EOF)
  {
    if (lastch == '\n')              /* hit end of line */
      printf("%8lu ", lineno++);
    putchar(lastch = c);
  }

  return EXIT_SUCCESS;
}
```

Figure 6.22   (lineno3.c) Our line numbering program made more concise with postfix increment.

The Comma Operator

C treats a comma-separated list of expressions as a single expression and evaluates it left to right, returning the value of the rightmost expression as the expression's value.

One use for the comma operator is to eliminate embedded assignments from tests. Figure 6.23 uses it in a new version of the previous chapter's program to copy its input on its output. We can rewrite

```
while ((c=getchar()) != EOF)
  putchar(c);
```

as

```
while (c = getchar(), c != EOF)
  putchar(c);
```

The latter separates reading the character from testing for end of file. Because the comma operator evaluates left to right, the rightmost expression's value (here, the test for end of file) controls the **while**'s execution. That is, C first evalutes the expression `c = getchar()`, and then the expression `c != EOF`, and finally uses the value of this expression to determine whether or not to execute the loop body. Either method is acceptable, and we find ourselves using them interchangeably; use the one you find easiest to read.

```
/*
 * Copy the input to the output.
 */
#include <stdio.h>
#include <stdlib.h>

int main()
{
  int c;                                    /* next input character */

  while (c = getchar(), c != EOF)
    putchar(c);

  return EXIT_SUCCESS;
}
```

Figure 6.23   (display2.c)   A new version of our earlier character-copying program.

Another use is to allow us to prompt for input in the same expression in which we read it. Figure 6.24 is a version of our Chapter 4's program to read x, y pairs and display x^y. This time we prompt for each x, y pair.

```
Enter x,y:  10  4
10^4 = 10000
Enter x,y:  2.5  8
2.5^8 = 1525.88
Enter x,y:
```

To do so, we use the comma operator in the test expression of the **while**.

```
while (printf("Enter x,y: "), scanf("%lf %i", &x, &y) == 2)
```

What happens is that C evaluates the first expression, the **printf**, which writes the prompt. C then evaluates the second expression, the **scanf**, which reads the input values. Finally, it compares **scanf**'s return value with two and returns the result as the value of the entire expression.

Yet another use is to provide multiple expressions where the language allows only one, such as in the *Start* and *Action* expressions for the **for** loop. We'll see examples of this in the next chapter.

The comma operator has the lowest precedence of any of C's operators, so we can safely use it to turn any list of expressions into a single statement. Don't do so, however, unless the expressions are closely related, or the program will become harder to understand and maintain.[3]

---

[3]The comma in function calls is simply a syntactic separator, not an operator. The order of evaluation of the arguments of function calls is implementation-dependent (unspecified); sometimes it's right to left, other times it's left to right, or it may even be completely random.

```
/*
 * Using our own function to compute exponents.
 */
#include <stdio.h>
#include <stdlib.h>

int main()
{
  double power(double base, int exp);

  double x;                              /* user-supplied base */
  int    y;                              /* user-supplied exponent */

  while (printf("Enter x,y: "), scanf("%lf %i", &x, &y) == 2)
    printf("%g^%i = %g\n", x, y, power(x, y));

  return EXIT_SUCCESS;
}
```

Figure 6.24 (usepwr2.c) A new version of our earlier exponent-computing program.

The sizeof Operator

sizeof returns the number of bytes necessary to store an object with the type of its operand. The operand can either be a type enclosed in parentheses or an expression (which is usually a variable or constant). By definition, **sizeof(char)** is 1.

sizeof is unique because it's evaluated at compile time, not run time. In fact, it actually doesn't evaluate its operand; it simply figures out what type it is, how much room it requires, and then replaces itself with a constant.

What's the type of **sizeof**'s return value? Obviously, it's an unsigned integer—no data type in C requires less than 1 byte—but which unsigned integer? That depends on the implementation; what **sizeof** returns is a value of type **size_t**, which is defined in the system header file stddef.h. Whenever we store the result of a **sizeof** in our programs, we need to include this header file.

Figure 6.25 is a program that uses **sizeof** to compute and print the size of several different data types, including the standard types **short**, **int**, and **long**. Here is the program's output when we ran it on a 16-bit machine.

```
short:   2
int:     2
long:    4
float:   4
double:  8
```

Before printing an object's size, we cast **sizeof**'s return value to an **unsigned long**. That way we're safe regardless of what type **sizeof** returns. We didn't bother to print the size of a **char**, since by definition that is 1 byte.

```
/*
 * Print the sizes of various types.
 */
#include <stdio.h>
#include <stdlib.h>

int main()
{
  printf("short:    \t%lu\n", (unsigned long) sizeof(short));
  printf("int:      \t%lu\n", (unsigned long) sizeof(int));
  printf("long:     \t%lu\n", (unsigned long) sizeof(long));
  printf("float:    \t%lu\n", (unsigned long) sizeof(float));
  printf("double:   \t%lu\n", (unsigned long) sizeof(double));

  return EXIT_SUCCESS;
}
```

Figure 6.25   (sizeof.c) A program that prints the sizes of the basic data types.

You might be wondering what **sizeof** is good for. One use is the one illustrated by Figure 6.25: we can use it to determine how many bytes each of our data types requires. But we'll see some more compelling uses of **sizeof** in later chapters when we discuss the topics of dynamic allocation and more complex data types.

The Conditional Operator

The final operator is the *conditional operator*, which is an **if** statement in disguise.

> *expression* **?** *true-expression* **:** *false-expression*

It first evaluates *expression*, and if it is true (non-zero), it then evaluates and returns *true-expression*. Otherwise, it evaluates and returns *false-expression*. No matter what, it evaluates only one of either *true-expression* or *false-expression*.

The conditional operator provides a convenient shorthand for **if** statements that decide which of two values a particular variable should be assigned. Figure 6.26 uses it in a more concise version of Figure 4.10, our program to compute the average of its input values. Originally, we had an **if** statement to protect against dividing by zero when there were no input values.

```
if (n == 0)
  avg = 0.0;
else
  avg = (double) sum / n;
```

But with the conditional operator we can turn this **if** into a single assignment statement.

```
avg = (n == 0) ? 0.0 : (double) sum / n;
```

```c
/*
 * Compute average of its input values.
 */
#include <stdio.h>
#include <stdlib.h>

int main()
{
  int           next;           /* next input value */
  long          sum;            /* running total */
  unsigned int  n;              /* number of input values */
  int           result;         /* did we read another value? */
  double        avg;            /* average of input values */

  sum = n = 0;
  while ((result = scanf("%i", &next)) == 1)
  {
    sum += next;
    n++;
  }
  if (result != EOF)
    printf("Warning: bad input after reading %u values\n", n);
  avg = (n == 0) ? 0.0 : (double) sum / n;
  printf("Average of %u values is %f.\n", n, avg);

  return EXIT_SUCCESS;
}
```

Figure 6.26 (avg2.c) A more concise version of our earlier program to compute the average of its input values.

It's not necessary to parenthesize the test, but doing so is a good idea, since the parentheses help distinguish the test from the values returned.

Using conditional operators leads to programs that are more concise and possibly more efficient. Unfortunately, it's easy to go overboard with them, which leads to programs that are definitely less readable. Anything with more than a single nested conditional operator is better written using **if**s. Should you decide, despite our warnings, to use nested conditional operators, you can make them more readable by not only parenthesizing the expressions tested by the conditional operators, but also wrapping parentheses around the nested conditional operators themselves. Again, you don't have to do that, but it's a good habit to get into since it protects against possible precedence problems.

> *Avoid writing nested conditional operators.*

Aside 6.1a: Deciding When to Take Shortcuts

You can get through life quite nicely without ever using a shortcut operator. And there's an unfortunate tendency of many C programmers to do exactly that; they treat shortcut operators as unnecessary and confusing and simply avoid them. On the other hand, some C programmers seem to fall in love with the shortcut operators and try to use them everywhere they can, doing such nasties as using many of them in the same expression, leading to code that's painful to read. The correct attitude, however, lies somewhere in the middle.

Ideally, you should use a shortcut operator when it simplifies the code without sacrificing readability. For example, using **++** is a clear win over its more traditional "add one and assign" counterpart: it's simpler, clearer, and less prone to error. Avoiding it in a case like this is silly. Similarly, there's no reason not to use **+=** (or any of the other arithmetic shortcut operators) instead of doing arithmetic and then assigning. It's perfectly reasonable to use multiple assignment when you are initializing a series of variables being used for a similar purpose (such as a set of counters). Its use actually improves the program since it highlights the relationship between those variables. And it's even quite reasonable to use the conditional operator as a replacement for an **if** statement that's deciding between two different assignments for a variable when that variable is only used once after that. Using the conditional operator in the place where the variable would have been used eliminates the need for the variable, simplifying the program.

Aside 6.1b illustrates the proper use of shortcut operators. It's a new version of Chapter 2's grading program that uses shortcut operators. This program is as readable as the original, slightly simpler, and slightly shorter.

However, it's clearly possible to go overboard and write programs that become painful to read. Before using **++** or **--** as part of a larger expression, you should ensure that its use simplifies the program rather than complicates it. When in doubt about whether to use a shortcut operator, write the expression with and without it, and examine both carefully to decide whether the shortcut operator leads to clearer, simpler code, or instead to code that's just going to confuse its reader.

6.7   CASE STUDY—DATA COMPRESSION

This section is optional!

We conclude this chapter with a pair of programs to compress and uncompress their input. Data compression reduces the amount of storage needed to hold a particular piece of information, such as a file, saving disk space and shortening the time required to copy or move the file. This is especially important for many graphics and video-related applications, which require enormous amounts of storage.

There are all sorts of techniques for file compression that vary greatly in complexity and efficiency. We've chosen one of the simplest, called run-length encoding: simply replace any sequence of identical bytes (or characters) with 2 bytes, one containing the repeated byte and the other containing the length of the sequence. With this method, for

Aside 6.1b (grade2.c) Our earlier grading program rewritten to use shortcut operators.

```
/*
 * The grading program rewritten to use shortcut operators.
 */
#include <stdio.h>
#include <stdlib.h>

#define PASSING_SCORE 70

int main()
{
  int next_score;        /* current input value */
  int score_count;       /* count of scores read */
  int pass_count;        /* count of passing scores */
  int fail_count;        /* count of failing scores */
  int total_score;       /* total score */

  total_score = pass_count = fail_count = 0;
  while (printf("Score? "), scanf("%i", &next_score) == 1)
  {
    total_score += next_score;
    if (next_score >= PASSING_SCORE)
    {
      printf("%i - Passes\n", next_score);
      pass_count++;
    }
    else
    {
      printf("%i - Fails\n", next_score);
      fail_count++;
    }
  }
  score_count = pass_count + fail_count;
  printf("\n%i scores entered, %i pass, %i fail.\nAverage: %i\n",
         score_count, pass_count, fail_count,
         (score_count == 0) ? 0 : (total_score / score_count));

  return EXIT_SUCCESS;
}
```

example, a group of eight blanks becomes a single blank followed by an 8. Since many files, programs, image data, and so on have frequent runs of duplicated characters, this encoding scheme can provide substantial savings.

Unfortunately, this scheme also has a problem: What do we do with a single byte surrounded by different characters? We certainly don't want to replace it with 2 bytes (the character and a count of one), as the file would grow rather than shrink. Ideally, in fact, we would like to simply leave it alone. But then how do we tell whether a particular byte is a character or a count? One possibility is to precede the count by a special character that means "here comes a character/count pair," an approach that takes 1 *byte* per sequence. We can do better, however, if we assume that our input is ASCII characters. Then there is an alternative that takes 1 *bit* per sequence. ASCII characters take 7 bits and C characters are stored in 8-bit bytes, so we can use the extra (high-order) bit to identify groups. Of course, this means our compression program only works with text files and cannot be used to compress binary files, such as object modules.

Figure 6.27 contains compress, a program that implements this compression scheme. The assumption is that the program will be run with its standard input redirected to the file to be compressed, and its standard output redirected into some other file. It reads groups of identical characters, a character at a time, counting the characters in the group. As long as the group is larger than some minimum that makes it worthwhile to compress (in our case, three or more characters), the program writes the repeated character once, first turning its high-order bit on, and follows it with the count. The program simply writes shorter groups directly.

We have to uncompress a compressed file to access its original contents. Figure 6.28 contains uncmprss, a program to accomplish this task. It reads a character at a time and examines the character's high-order bit. If the bit is off, it simply writes the character. Otherwise, the bit is on, and the next byte must be the count. It reads the count, and then writes that many characters (with their high bit turned off).

We ran compress on a collection of source programs and achieved space savings ranging from 10 to 20 percent. While this is commendable—we now have more available disk space and our files transmit faster over phone lines—other, more complex methods do much better. Most of these work by creating a frequency distribution of characters in the file, and using varying length bit strings to encode the different characters.

SUMMARY

- C provides relational operators for testing whether one value is equal (**==**), not equal (**!=**), less than (**<**), greater than (**>**), less than or equal (**<=**), or greater than or equal (**>=**) another value.

- C provides logical operators for combining relational expressions: **&&** ANDs the results of the expressions and **||** ORs them. Both make use of short-circuit evaluation. There is one other logical operator, **!**, that inverts the logical value of an expression.

- C provides operators for shifting bits (**<<** and **>>**), inverting bits (**~**), and doing logical operations on bits (**&**, **|**, and **^**).

- C provides a set of shorthand assignment operators. There are both arithmetic shorthand operators (**+=**, **-=**, ***=**, **/=**, and **%=**) and bitwise shorthand operators (**&=**, **|=**, **<<=**, **>>=**, and **^=**). Careful use of these operators often leads to more readable and efficient code. Poor use of these operators often leads to confusing code.

```c
/*
 * Simple data-compression program.
 *
 * This program assumes ASCII characters.
 */
#include <stdio.h>
#include <stdlib.h>
#include <limits.h>

#define MINSIZE    3              /* smallest group to compress */
#define HIGHBIT   0x80            /* high bit indicates compressed char */

int main()
{
  int c;                         /* last character read */
  int newc;                      /* new character read */
  int cntc;                      /* count of last character */

  c = getchar();
  while (c != EOF)
  {
    cntc = 1;                    /* count occurrences of c */
    while (cntc < UCHAR_MAX && (newc = getchar()) == c)
      cntc++;
    if (cntc >= MINSIZE)
    {                            /* write count (high bit on) */
      putchar(c | HIGHBIT);
      putchar(cntc);
    }
    else                         /* write chars (high bit off) */
      while (cntc-- > 0)
        putchar(c & ~HIGHBIT);
    c = newc;
  }

  return EXIT_SUCCESS;
}
```

Figure 6.27   (compress.c)   A program to compress its input.

- C provides increment (++) and decrement (--) operators, in both prefix and postfix forms. As prefix operators, the operation happens before the value is used. As postfix operators, the operation happens after the value is used.

- C provides a conditional operator (?:) for selecting between a pair of expressions, a comma operator (,) for sequentially evaluating a list of expressions, and a **sizeof** operator for determining the number of bytes in a variable or type.

```
/*
 * Simple uncompress program.
 */
#include <stdio.h>
#include <stdlib.h>

#define HIGHBIT   0x80       /* high bit on indicates compressed char */

int main()
{
  int getCount(int c);

  int c;                     /* new character read */
  int cntc;                  /* count of times char should appear */

  while ((c = getchar()) != EOF && (cntc = getCount(c)) != 0)
    while (cntc-- > 0)
      putchar(c & ~HIGHBIT);

  return EXIT_SUCCESS;
}

int getCount(int c)          /* determine # of times to write char */
{
  if (! (c & HIGHBIT))
    return 1;                             /* once - not compressed */
  return ((c = getchar()) == EOF) ? 0   /* zero - EOF followed char */
                                  : c;  /* next char is count */
}
```

Figure 6.28   (uncmprss.c) A program to uncompress its input.

EXERCISES

6–1 Compile and run the programs in this chapter.

6–2 What happens if you attempt to right-shift a signed value on your computer?

6–3 Modify the file-shrinking program (Figure 6.8) to eliminate completely any lines containing nothing but white space (this includes lines consisting only of a newline).

6–4 Modify our earlier interest-computing programs to take advantage of C's shortcut operators. Does this change make those programs more or less readable?

6–5 Rewrite Chapter 5's base converter to take advantage of shortcut operators. Does this change make this program more or less readable?

6–6 Our compression program (Figure 6.27) is restricted to ASCII characters because we use the high bit to indicate compressed strings. Write a new version that instead indicates sequences by preceding them with an extra byte, one that contains a null character. Your program should work on any input, even one with null characters. Of course, you have to modify the uncompression program (Figure 6.28) to decode this new scheme.

Extend

6–7 Extend the data-packing program (Figure 6.11) to check for input errors such as entering a value other than 0 or 1 for the person's sex.

6–8 Extend the data-packing program (Figure 6.11) to read a series of values and compute the average age and average length of employment. Then modify it to print all female employees before any male employee. Finally, modify it to print only the unmarried employees.

Tune

6–9 In the encryption program (Figure 6.15), **j** will eventually overflow on very large files. Is this a problem? If so, how can it be fixed?

Code

6–10 Write a pair of functions, **bitsOn** and **bitsOff**, that return the number of bits that are on and off in a word. Use the shorthand bit-manipulating operators.

6–11 Write a program that verifies that every character in its input is an ASCII character. A non-ASCII character (a character with its high-order bit set) causes an error message containing its octal code and position in the file (line number and character). We can use this program to verify that a file contains only ASCII characters before trying to compress it with our compression program (Figure 6.27).

6–12 Write a function, **invBits**, that inverts a group of bits within a word. **invBits** should be passed a word, the position (from the right) of a group of bits within the word, and the number of bits to invert.

6–13 Use **?:** to write expressions that return the smaller and larger of two values. Then use it to write expressions that return the smallest and largest of three values.

Build

6–14 Write a program to produce a sales report. The input is in the form of a product code (an **int**), a sales price (a **double**), and a number of units sold (an **int**). Print the total sales and units sold for each product, along with the average price per unit. Also print the total sales of all products. Assume the products are grouped together by sales code.

Extend your solution to print the highest and lowest sales item by volume and by units.

6–15 Write a concise program to compute student grade point averages (GPAs). Its input is a list of grades ('A', 'B', 'C', 'D', or 'F'). Grades are separated by spaces. Each input line contains the grades for a single student. When computing a student's GPA, an A is worth 4 points, a B is worth 3 points, and so on. Here's some sample input and output:

```
A A A A
4.0
A C B
3.0
B B B A
3.2
```

Extend this program to print the average GPA. The average GPA should be computed by summing the individual GPAs and then dividing by the number of students. For the example input above, that would be 3.4.

6–16 Write a concise program to extract all the integers from its input. It should print each integer it detects on a line by itself. The input

```
w8  4  mc  2  finish  2!
```

should result in the output

```
8
4
2
2
```

6–17 Write a program to compress its input data. Each input line contains a child's age (between 3 and 18), grade in school (between 0 and 12), sex (either 'M' or 'F'), and grade point average (a number between 0.0 [all F's] and 4.0 [all A's]). Assume the GPA has exactly one digit after the decimal point. Your program should convert each input line into a single 16-bit integer. Its output is the integers that result.

7 STATEMENTS

This chapter covers C's rather small set of statements. We present the fine points of the statements we have already used and describe in detail those we have so far overlooked. While doing so, we improve and extend many of the programs we wrote in earlier chapters, and we write new programs to simulate a simple calculator and to print various breakdowns of input characters. The chapter concludes by tying several topics together in a program that prints an octal dump of its input.

7.1 EXPRESSION STATEMENTS

C's simplest statement is the *expression statement*, an expression followed by a semi-colon:

expression;

We can use it anywhere C's syntax requires a statement. Both assignment statements and function calls, such as

```
lineno = 0;
```

and

```
printf("%8lu ", ++lineno);
```

are expression statements.[1]

An expression statement executes by evaluating the expression and throwing away the result. To be useful, it must have a side effect, such as invoking a function or changing a variable's value. The legal but useless expression statement

```
p * x;
```

multiplies **p**'s value by **x**'s value but does nothing with the result. Why would we ever write such a silly statement? Simply because of a typo—we probably meant to write ***=** instead of *****. Fortunately, many compilers will warn us about this sort of statement.[2]

---

[1] They are not special statement types, as in other programming languages such as FORTRAN, BASIC, and Pascal.

[2] The warning is usually something along the lines of "Statement has no effect at line ...".

> *Watch out for accidentally writing syntactically legal expression statements that accomplish nothing.*

"Do-nothing" expression statements are most likely to cause problems when they appear in loops. If instead of updating a loop counter, with **i++**, we accidentally write

```
i+1;
```

the symptom is likely to be an infinite loop. Make you sure you understand the source of any compiler warnings about your expression statements.

7.2   COMPOUND STATEMENTS

A *compound statement* or *block* is a group of statements surrounded by braces.

```
{
    statement
    . . .
    statement
}
```

Compound statements, like expression statements, can go anywhere C's syntax requires a statement. We *don't*, however, follow compound statements with a semicolon.

We can take any compound statement containing only expression statements and use the comma operator to rewrite it as a single, more compact expression statement. For example, we can replace the compound statement

```
{
    putchar(c);
    in_word = TRUE;
}
```

with the more compact expression statement

```
putchar(c), in_word = TRUE;
```

Figure 7.1 takes advantage of this feature in a new version of our earlier program to write its input to the output, one word per line. All of its compound statements have been replaced with expression statements.

Are changes like this one worth it? They certainly lead to more compact programs, but at a cost: the resulting program is less readable and harder to modify and debug. In general, leave compound statements alone unless they consist of closely related expression statements or unless the lines saved make the function fit on a single page, aiding readability. While Figure 7.1 is a nice example of how it is possible to replace some compound statements with expression statements, it's actually not a good idea to make that change to this program, since the **putchar** and the assignment to **in_word** are really not that closely related.

```
/*
 * Break input into words (letter followed by letters or digits).
 */
#include <stdio.h>
#include <stdlib.h>
#include <ctype.h>

#define TRUE  1
#define FALSE 0

int main()
{
  int c;                         /* next input character */
  int in_word;                   /* flag: are we dealing with a word? */

  in_word = FALSE;
  while ((c = getchar()) != EOF)
    if (isalpha(c) || (in_word && isdigit(c)))       /* write letter */
      putchar(c), in_word = TRUE;
    else
      if (in_word)                 /* write newline if we were in word */
        putchar('\n'), in_word = FALSE;

  return EXIT_SUCCESS;
}
```

Figure 7.1   (brkwd4.c)   A terse version of our program to print its input to its output, one word per line.

7.3   SIMPLE DECISIONS—THE IF

We've already seen two forms of the **if** statement, one with an **else**,

```
if (Expression)
{
   True-statements
}
else
{
   False-statements
}
```

and one without.

```
if (Expression)
{
   True-statements
}
```

There is, however, one common combination of **if**s that we haven't seen: the *nested if*, one **if** inside another, as in this **if** that converts military time (**mhour**), a 24-hour clock, to standard time (**stdhour**).

```
if (mhour <= 12)
  if (mhour == 0)
    stdhour = 12;              /* midnight */
  else
    stdhour = mhour;           /* AM */
else
  stdhour = mhour - 12;        /* PM */
```

The idea is that if the hour is less than or equal to 12, it's left alone, unless it's 0, in which case it's converted to 12. If the hour is greater than 12, it's converted by subtracting 12 from it.

We've seen that we can elide the braces around the statements when we have only a single statement. But doing so has the potential to lead us into trouble when we are using nested **if**s and the inner **if** doesn't have an **else**. Consider this mistaken alternative to the previous **if**:

```
stdhour = mhour;              /* assume AM */
if (mhour <= 12)
  if (mhour == 0)
    stdhour = 12;             /* midnight */
else
  stdhour = mhour - 12;       /* PM */
```

To which **if** does the **else** belong? From the indentation, we might assume the outer. But the compiler ignores the indentation and simply assumes that any **else** attaches to the closest nonterminated **if**. So, despite this program's misleading indentation, the **else** associates with the *inner* **if** and the program does the time conversion incorrectly. We avoid the problem by placing the inner **if** in braces:

```
stdhour = mhour;              /* assume AM */
if (mhour <= 12)
{
  if (mhour == 0)
    stdhour = 12;             /* midnight */
}
else
  stdhour = mhour - 12;       /* PM */
```

In fact, we can avoid this problem entirely by always wrapping nested **if**s within braces.

Figure 7.2 is a short program using this fragment. It reads in military time and prints standard time. Figure 7.3 shows some sample input and output.

To print the minutes, we make use of a new feature of **printf**: if a field width begins with a leading zero, then the field is filled with zeros rather than blanks. So we write the hours and minutes with

```
printf("Standard time: %u:%02u\n", stdhour, min);
```

This writes **min** in a field two digits wide, padded with leading zeros instead of blanks.

```
/*
 * Convert military time to standard time.  No error checking.
 */
#include <stdio.h>
#include <stdlib.h>

int main()
{
  unsigned int mhour;               /* input: military hour */
  unsigned int min;                 /* input: military minutes */
  unsigned int stdhour;             /* standard hour */

  while (printf("Enter military time (as xx:xx): "),
         scanf("%u:%u", &mhour, &min) == 2)
  {
    stdhour = mhour;                        /* assume AM or noon */
    if (mhour <= 12)
    {
      if (mhour == 0)
        stdhour = 12;                       /* midnight */
    }
    else
      stdhour = mhour - 12;          /* PM */
    printf("Standard time: %u:%02u\n", stdhour, min);
  }

  return EXIT_SUCCESS;
}
```

Figure 7.2   (mtime.c) Convert military time to standard time.

```
Enter military time (as xx:xx): 21:15
Standard time: 9:15
Enter military time (as xx:xx): 12:05
Standard time: 12:05
Enter military time (as xx:xx): 0:05
Standard time: 12:05
Enter military time (as xx:xx): 3:30
Standard time: 3:30
Enter military time (as xx:xx): 15:30
Standard time: 3:30
Enter military time (as xx:xx): 23:59
Standard time: 11:59
```

Figure 7.3   Some sample output for our program to convert military time to standard time.

7.4   MULTIWAY DECISIONS—THE ELSE-IF

There's one other interesting form of **if**—the **else**-**if**:

```
if (first-expression)
    first-statement
else if (second-expression)
    second-statement
    . . .
else if (final-expression)
    final-statement
else
    default-statement
```

The final **else** and *default-statement* are optional.

So far we've used **if**s to select one of two alternatives. The **else**-**if** comes in handy when we want to decide among many alternatives. It evaluates each expression in turn until one evaluates to something other than zero and then executes the statement associated with that expression. If all the expressions evaluate to zero, it executes the *default-statement* if any. In either case, control then passes to the statement following the **else**-**if**. Of course, **else**-**if** really isn't a special statement; it's simply a common way of writing **if**s in which the statement associated with each **else** happens to be another **if**:

```
if (first-expression)
    first-statement
else
  if (second-expression)
      second-statement
  else
      . . .
    if (final-expression)
        final-statement
    else
        default-statement
```

Figure 7.4 provides an example. It's a program that counts the number of characters in its input that fall into different classes, such as white space, letters, digits, punctuation, and so on. Here's its output when run with its source file as its input (using redirection):[3]

```
Total        1791

spaces        571   31.9%
letters       930   51.9%
digits         20    1.1%
puncts        270   15.1%
others          0    0.0%
```

---

[3] It makes sense that "others" is zero for this example, as we wouldn't expect to find unprintable characters in a source file.

```c
/*
 * Print counts of various types of characters appearing in the input.
 */
#include <stdio.h>
#include <stdlib.h>
#include <ctype.h>

#define  CNT_WIDTH  11     /* field width for displaying counts */

int main()
{
  double pct(unsigned long count, unsigned long total);

  int           c;                         /* next input character */
  unsigned long spaces;                    /* white-space characters */
  unsigned long letters;                   /* a-z, A-Z */
  unsigned long digits;                    /* 0-9 */
  unsigned long puncts;                    /* punctuation characters */
  unsigned long others;                    /* anything else */
  unsigned long t;                         /* total characters */

  spaces = letters = digits = puncts = others = 0;
  while ((c = getchar()) != EOF)
    if (isspace(c))
      spaces++;                            /* white space */
    else if (isalpha(c))
      letters++;                           /* upper- or lowercase letter */
    else if (isdigit(c))
      digits++;                            /* digit */
    else if (ispunct(c))
      puncts++;                            /* punctuation */
    else
      others++;
  t = spaces + letters + digits + puncts + others;
  printf("Total    %*lu\n\n", CNT_WIDTH, t);
  if (t != 0)
  {
    printf("spaces  %*lu %5.1f%%\n", CNT_WIDTH, spaces, pct(spaces, t));
    printf("letters %*lu %5.1f%%\n", CNT_WIDTH, letters, pct(letters, t));
    printf("digits  %*lu %5.1f%%\n", CNT_WIDTH, digits, pct(digits, t));
    printf("puncts  %*lu %5.1f%%\n", CNT_WIDTH, puncts, pct(puncts, t));
    printf("others  %*lu %5.1f%%\n", CNT_WIDTH, others, pct(others, t));
  }

  return EXIT_SUCCESS;
}

double pct(unsigned long count, unsigned long total)
  { return count * 100.0 / total; }        /* compute/return percentage */
```

Figure 7.4 (countem.c) A program to print a breakdown of the different types of characters in its input.

The program reads its input one character at a time. It uses a single **else-if** to determine the type of character we have and to update the appropriate counter.[4]

```
if (isspace(c))
    spaces++;                    /* whitespace */
else if (isalpha(c))
    letters++;                   /* upper- or lowercase letter */
else if (isdigit(c))
    digits++;                    /* digit */
else if (ispunct(c))
    puncts++;                    /* punctuation */
else
    others++;
```

The **else-if** checks if the character is white-space, a letter, a digit, or a punctuation character, stopping as soon as it falls into one of those classes. Then it updates the appropriate counter and exits. If the character doesn't fall into one of these classes, it updates the default counter, **others**. We're careful to make all of these counters **unsigned long**, since files can easily have more characters than we can count with an **int**.

To display the counters, we take advantage of another new feature of **printf**.

```
printf("Total    %*lu\n\n", CNT_WIDTH, t);
```

If the field width is a *****, as in **%*lu**, we must supply two parameters, not just one. The first parameter is the desired field width, and the second is the value to write. Here, since **CNT_WIDTH** is 11, it means we're writing **t** in a field that's 11 digits wide.

7.5   MULTIWAY DECISIONS—THE SWITCH

Occasionally we have an **else-if** that tests for different values of the same expression. We might, for example, have an **else-if** that compares a single-letter, user-entered command with the program's legal commands to determine which action to take. But there's a better way: the **switch** statement.

```
switch(expression)
{
    case case-label-1 :        statement-list
    case case-label-2 :        statement-list
        . . .
    case case-label-n :        statement-list
    default:                   statement-list
}
```

---

[4]From running this program on our files, we've discovered that C programs are typically about 50% letters, 25% to 35% spaces, and around 15% punctuation; executable programs are 75% control characters; and input files to text-formatting programs are 70% letters, 10% punctuation. It's relatively straightforward to use this information to make educated guesses about the contents of files.

switch works by evaluating *expression*, passing control to the case labeled with its value (or to **default** if there is no such case), and executing the case's *statement-list*. There are several restrictions on the labels. They have to be expressions that the compiler can evaluate to an integer constant, and all of the labels within a single **switch** must be unique, although they can appear in any order. Each case's *statement-list* can contain zero or more statements; there is no need to put braces around them.

After executing these statements, control automatically passes through to the next label. This falling through is almost always undesirable, so we usually place a **break** statement at the end of each **case**'s statement list. A **break** exits the enclosing **switch**.[5]

Figure 7.5 illustrates **switch** with a simple calculator program. Its input is a series of triplets containing a floating point operand, a single-character operator (such as **+**, **-**, *****, or **/**), and another floating point operand. The calculator prints the result of applying the operator to its operands. Here's some sample input and output for the calculator program:

```
35.6+23.9
59.500000
67/69
0.971014
87.12-56.11
31.010000
10*15
150.000000
1/0
Warning: division by zero.
0.000000
```

We use **scanf** to read the operand-operator-operand triplets. Because **scanf** doesn't automatically skip white space before single characters, there can be no spaces between the operator and its operands (eliminating this restriction is left as an exercise). The program simply quits if the user enters bad input.

Most of the program is a giant **switch** that selects the appropriate action for the user-entered operator. There is one case for each legal operator, along with a default case that prints an error message for any invalid operator. The case for division is careful to verify that the denominator isn't 0 before doing the division.[6]

We end the actions for each case with a **break** statement; without it, control would automatically pass to the following case. We don't need a **break** after the **default**, since that's the last case and we don't have to worry about control falling through.[7]

---

[5] Unless the **break** is within a loop within a **switch**, but we'll worry about that possibility later in the chapter.

[6] It does this by testing whether the second operator is not equal to 0.0, which appears to violate our earlier recommendation not to test floating point numbers for equality. Here, however, the test is reasonable. The reason is that as long as the operand isn't exactly equal to 0.0, our division will be acceptable. It's only 0.0 that gives us the problem.

[7] **default** does not have to be the last case, but for stylistic reasons it should be. If for some reason it's not, it will need a **break** too.

```c
/*
 * Simple calculator program.
 */
#include <stdio.h>
#include <stdlib.h>

int main()
{
  int    vals;                          /* scanf return value */
  double op1;                           /* the operand on the right */
  double op2;                           /* the operand on the left */
  char   operator;                      /* operator */
  double result;                        /* result */

  while ((vals = scanf("%lf%c%lf", &op1, &operator, &op2)) == 3)
  {
    switch(operator)
    {
      case '+':
        result = op1 + op2;
        break;
      case '-':
        result = op1 - op2;
        break;
      case '*':
        result = op1 * op2;
        break;
      case '/':
        if (op2 != 0.0)                  /* watch out for divide by 0 */
          result = op1 / op2;
        else
        {
          printf("Warning: division by zero.\n");
          result = 0.0;
        }
        break;
      default:
        printf("Unknown operator: %c\n", operator);
        result = 0.0;                    /* default result */
    }
    printf("%f\n", result);
  }

  if (vals != EOF)
    printf("Error detected in the input: program terminated.\n");

  return vals == EOF ? EXIT_SUCCESS : EXIT_FAILURE;
}
```

Figure 7.5   (calc.c)   A simple calculator program that illustrates **switch**.

Aside 7.1: Making Decisions

C provides several different mechanisms for making decisions: **if**, **else-if**, and **switch**. When is each appropriate?

You should use **switch** whenever you need to select an action based on specific values of a variable. Each value corresponds to a case in the **switch**. This happens frequently when you have one-letter commands and want to map them to actions. If you find yourself writing an **else-if**, where each test is comparing the same variable to a different value, you should really be using **switch** instead. Even though that might make your program longer, **switch** more clearly illustrates what you are doing.

else-if is appropriate when you need to select an action based on more complex tests than simply comparing a variable to a set of values. This happens frequently when you are doing a different action for different ranges of values of a variable (such as assigning letter grades based on test scores), or when the tests involve calling functions (such as doing different things depending on whether a character is digit, or a letter, and so on). In these cases, using **else-if** makes clear that you are selecting one action from a set of possible actions.

A regular **if** is appropriate when you are selecting between two actions (such as determining whether a grade is a pass or a fail).

> *Don't forget to place a* **break** *at the end of each case to prevent accidentally falling through.*

This automatic falling through cases leads to serious problems when we forget the **break**. But it's useful when we want numerous cases to select the same action. Figure 7.6 takes advantage of it in a program to provide a breakdown by group (quotes, brackets, and the usual delimiters) of the punctuation characters in its input. Here's the output when we run the program on itself.

```
Quotes          41
Brackets        28
Delimiters      51
Others        1171
```

The program has one counter for each group, and a **switch** to select the counter to be updated. Each character within a group has a case label, with all labels for a group placed above the single statement that increments its counter. When control passes to the label for any character in the group, it falls through to the statement updating the group's counter.

Falling through cases is appropriate only when the same action occurs for many different constants. Don't use it to execute statements in one case followed by statements in another.

```c
/*
 * Count various types of punctuation characters.
 */
#include <stdio.h>
#include <stdlib.h>

#define  CNT_WIDTH  11   /* field width for displaying counts */

int main()
{
  int            c;                  /* next input character */
  unsigned long quotes;              /* counts quotation marks */
  unsigned long brackets;            /* counts parens/brackets */
  unsigned long delims;              /* counts punctuation */
  unsigned long others;              /* counts everything else */

  quotes = brackets = delims = others = 0L;
  while ((c = getchar()) != EOF)
    switch(c)
    {
      case '\'':
      case '"':
      case '`':
        quotes++;                    /* single and double quotes */
        break;
      case '(':
      case ')':
      case '{':
      case '}':
      case '[':
      case ']':
        brackets++;                  /* punctuation brackets */
        break;
      case ',':
      case '.':
      case ';':
      case ':':
      case '!':
      case '?':
        delims++;                    /* nonpunctuation chars */
        break;
      default:
        others++;
    }
  printf("Quotes     %*lu\n", CNT_WIDTH, quotes);
  printf("Brackets   %*lu\n", CNT_WIDTH, brackets);
  printf("Delimiters %*lu\n", CNT_WIDTH, delims);
  printf("Others     %*lu\n", CNT_WIDTH, others);

  return EXIT_SUCCESS;
}
```

Figure 7.6   (countpct.c)   A program to count special input characters.

7.6 LOOPS

C provides three looping mechanisms: **while**, **do-while**, and **for**. We're already well acquainted with **while**, and we've been introduced to **for**. **do-while** is similar to **while**, except that it's guaranteed to execute its body at least once.

The **do-while** Statement

Unlike the **while**, which tests before it executes its body, the **do-while** tests afterward.

```
do
    statement
while (expression);
```

A **do-while** repeatedly executes *statement* and evaluates *expression*. As with the **while**, the cycle comes to an end when *expression* evaluates to zero. But unlike the **while**, *statement* is always executed at least once.

Figure 7.7 uses **do-while** in a new version of our earlier **yesOrNo** function. Originally, **yesOrNo** took anything other than a 'y' or a 'Y' as a "no". This new version instead forces the user to enter an appropriate answer (unless the user enters the end-of-file character, which we then treat as a "no"). The heart of **yesOrNo** is a single **do-while**. It keeps reading input lines until it finds one whose first character is appropriate. We use a **do-while** because we know we have to read at least one line of input.

We have made one other change to this version of **yesOrNo**. It now handles the skipping of characters until the end of the input line by calling a new function, **skipToEOL**, shown in Figure 7.8. Using a separate function significantly simplifies **yesOrNo** by eliminating the need for nested loops (the **while** to skip characters would have been inside the **do-while** to repeatedly ask for a yes or no answer).

The **for** Statement

The last looping construct is the **for** statement:

```
for (Start ; Test ; Action )
    statement
```

We've seen that a **for** evaluates *Start* and then enters a cycle of evaluating *Test*, executing *statement*, and evaluating *Action*. The cycle terminates when *Test* evaluates to zero.

Usually, *Start* and *Action* are assignments or function calls and *Test* is a relational test—but all expressions are arbitrary and optional. *Arbitrary* means that we can fill them with any legal expression—we're not restricted to simply updating and testing a variable. *Optional* means that we can omit an expression whenever we want.

We omit both *Test* and *Action* when we want to write an infinite loop. That's because a missing *Test* is taken to be nonzero, which means that such a loop is infinite and we

```
/*
 * Obtain a yes or no answer from the user.
 */
#include <stdio.h>
#include <ctype.h>

#define TRUE  1
#define FALSE 0

int yesOrNo(void)
{
  void skipToEOL(int c);

  int c;                                 /* holds input character */
  int answer;                            /* holds YES or NO answer */
  int keep_going;                        /* do we have to ask again? */

  do
  {
    keep_going = FALSE;
    switch (c = tolower(getchar()))
    {
      case EOF:  answer = FALSE;  break;     /* treat EOF as a NO */
      case 'y':  answer = TRUE;   break;
      case 'n':  answer = FALSE;  break;
      default:   printf("Please answer with a YES or NO: ");
                 keep_going = TRUE;
    }
    skipToEOL(c);                        /* skip rest of line */
  }
  while (keep_going);
  return answer;
}
```

Figure 7.7 (yesorno4.c) A new way to get a yes or no answer from the user.

```
/*
 * Skip over remaining characters on the input line.
 */
#include <stdio.h>

void skipToEOL(int c)
{
  while (c != '\n' && c != EOF)
    c = getchar();
}
```

Figure 7.8 (skip.c) A function to ignore the remaining characters on the input line.

expect to exit it with a **return** or some other *jump* statement (which we discuss in subsequent sections). So,

```
for(;;)
     statement
```

will execute *statement* forever.

> *Remember that we need the semicolons in the* **for** *even when we leave out the expressions.*

Figure 7.9 uses an infinite **for** in another version of **yesOrNo**. It repeatedly reads a character, skips the remaining characters on the input line, and writes an error message. We leave the loop (by returning from the function) only when the first character is an appropriate answer or an end of file.

You should think carefully before writing an infinite **for**. Loops like the one in Figure 7.9 can be difficult to read, as they can exit from anywhere inside the loop. In fact, that loop has three different exit conditions (end of file, a "yes", or a "no") instead of the usual one! The entire loop body must be read to understand these conditions, rather than just the loop's control expression, as in our other loops. It's a good idea to save the infinite **for** where you really want a loop to go on and on, unless some special, erroneous condition occurs.

We often omit *Start* when we've already done any needed initializations before entering the loop, such as when the loop counter is passed as a parameter. Figure 7.10 does so in an even more concise version of our earlier **power** function. Because the exponent **exp** is passed as a parameter, there's no need to initialize it:

```
for (; exp > 0; exp--)
  p *= x;
```

Start, *Test*, and *Action* are truly arbitrary expressions and are in no way limited to the simple testing or updating of counter variables. Figure 7.11 is a new version of our line-numbering program, rewritten to take full advantage of this feature. Almost all of the program fits in a single **for**:

```
for (lineno = 0, lastch = '\n';
     c = getchar(), c != EOF;
     lastch = c, putchar(c))
  if (lastch == '\n')                 /* hit end of line */
    printf("%8lu ", ++lineno);
```

Here, *Start* initializes **lineno**, the variable that holds the last line number written, and **lastch**, the variable that holds the last character written. *Test* reads a new character and verifies that it's not end of file. And *Action* remembers this character and writes it out. All that's left in the body of the loop is to write out line numbers at the beginning of each new line.

```
/*
 * Obtain a yes or no answer from the user (using infinite loop).
 */
#include <stdio.h>
#include <ctype.h>

#define TRUE    1
#define FALSE   0

int yesOrNo(void)
{
  void skipToEOL(int c);

  int answer;                           /* holds input character */

  for (;;)
  {
    if ((answer = tolower(getchar())) == EOF)
      return FALSE;                     /* EOF is NO */

    skipToEOL(answer);
    if (answer == 'y')
      return TRUE;
    else if (answer == 'n')
      return FALSE;

    printf("Please answer with a YES or NO: ");
  }
}
```

Figure 7.9   (yesorno5.c)   A version of **yesOrNo** that uses an infinite **for**.

7.7   THE NULL STATEMENT

C has a statement that does nothing: a lone semicolon with no preceding expression is a *null statement*. It's merely a placeholder that we use when the syntax requires a statement but we don't need to do any action. This situation occurs most frequently when side effects in a loop's control expression obviate the need for the loop body.

Figure 7.12 takes advantage of this feature in a new version of our **skipToEOL** function. Rather than a **while**, we use a **for**:

```
for (; c != '\n' && c != EOF; c = getchar())
   ;
```

Because all the body of the original **while** did was read a character, moving that read into the **for** loop's action part leaves its loop body empty, allowing us to provide a null statement as its body.

```
/*
 * Compute powers, more concise version.
 */
double power(double x, int exp)
{
  double p;

  p = 1.0;
  if (exp > 0)                              /* positive exponent */
    for (; exp > 0; exp--)
      p *= x;
  else                                      /* negative exponent */
    for (; exp < 0; exp++)
      p /= x;
  return p;
}
```

Figure 7.10   (power4.c)   A very concise version of **power**.

```
/*
 * Copy input to output, giving each line a number.
 */
#include <stdio.h>
#include <stdlib.h>

int main()
{
  int           c;                  /* current and */
  int           lastch;             /*    previous characters */
  unsigned long lineno;             /* lines printed so far */

  for (lineno = 0, lastch = '\n';
       c = getchar(), c != EOF;
       lastch = c, putchar(c))
    if (lastch == '\n')             /* hit end of line */
      printf("%8lu ", ++lineno);

  return EXIT_SUCCESS;
}
```

Figure 7.11   (lineno4.c)   Yet another version of our line-numbering program.

```
/*
 * Skip over remaining characters on the input line (using for instead
 * of while).
 */
#include <stdio.h>

void skipToEOL(int c)
{
  for (; c != '\n' && c != EOF; c = getchar())
    ;
}
```

Figure 7.12 (skip2.c) A more concise version of a function to skip any remaining characters on a line.

As a more complex example, Figure 7.13, a new version of our program to average its input, takes advantage of this feature in the **for** loop to sum the input:

```
for (sum=n=0; scanf("%i", &next) == 1; sum += next, n++)
    ;                      /* compute total of input values */
```

By using the comma operator, we turn the two statements that were in the loop body into a single expression, which then becomes the *Action* of the loop. Once again, that leaves nothing to do in the loop body, so we simply use a null statement there.

> *Avoid placing a null statement on the same line as a* **for** *or a* **while**.

Placing the null statement on the same line as the **for** or **while** is legal, and it makes the program more compact, but it also makes the program more difficult to decipher. It's far too easy for the program's reader to ignore the semicolon at the end of the line and mistake the following lines for the loop's body. Always place the null statement on a line by itself, indented slightly and followed by a comment. Failing to do so makes it hard to find mistakes like the one in this loop:

```
while (scanf("%i", next) == 1);
    printf("%i\n", next);
```

It was supposed to echo each value it read. But it doesn't. The semicolon on the line containing the **while** is a null statement that forms the loop's body. The **printf** that was meant to be the loop body executes only after the loop exits, printing the value of the last number read.

7.8   JUMP STATEMENTS

Statements ordinarily execute sequentially. Several statements alter this normal flow of control: **break**, **continue**, and **goto**. These *jump* statements violate some of the

```
/*
 * Compute average of its input values with no error checking.
 */
#include <stdio.h>
#include <stdlib.h>

int main()
{
  int          next;                   /* next input value */
  long         sum;                    /* running total */
  unsigned int n;                      /* number of input values */
  double       avg;                    /* average of input values */

  for (sum=n=0; scanf("%i", &next) == 1; sum += next, n++)
    ;                      /* compute total of input values */
  avg = (n == 0) ? 0.0 : (double) sum / n;
  printf("Average of %u values is %f.\n", n, avg);

  return EXIT_SUCCESS;
}
```

Figure 7.13 (avg3.c) An input averaging program that uses a **for** with an empty loop body.

basic principles of structured programming and should be used with care.[8] In fact, many programmers avoid these statements like the plague, since they are always avoidable and their abuse leads to impenetrable programs. Carefully used, however, they can simplify otherwise complex code and contribute to making our programs more readable.

The break Statement

We've already used **break** to exit a **switch**. But **break** actually exits the nearest enclosing **for**, **while**, and **do-while**, as well.

Figure 7.14 provides an example of **break**. It contains a new version of Chapter 4's program to prompt for and read x, y pairs and then compute x^y. The program uses a loop that reads values until the end of file is reached:

```
while (printf("Enter x,y: "), (r = scanf(...)) != EOF)
  if (r != 2)
  {
    printf("Error: Didn't read two input values.\n");
    break;
  }
```

---

[8] When it appears in the middle of a function, the **return** statement also alters the normal flow of control. At the end of a function, however, **return** is necessary, since it's the only way for a function to provide a value to its caller.

```
/*
 * Using our own function to compute exponents.
 */
#include <stdio.h>
#include <stdlib.h>

int main()
{
  double power(double base, int exp);

  double x;                            /* user-supplied base */
  int    y;                            /* user-supplied exponent */
  int    r;                            /* scanf return value */

  while (printf("Enter x,y: "), (r = scanf("%lf %i", &x, &y)) != EOF)
  {
    if (r != 2)
    {
      printf("Error: Didn't read two input values.\n");
      break;
    }

    printf("%g^%i = %g\n", x, y, power(x, y));
  }

  return r == EOF ? EXIT_SUCCESS : EXIT_FAILURE;
}
```

Figure 7.14 (usepwr3.c) Our main program for **power** rewritten to handle errors using **break**.

Ostensibly, the **while** takes us through the entire set of input values. But the first thing in the body of the loop is a check to determine whether **scanf** actually read two values successfully. If there was a problem, we print an error message and use **break** to exit the loop and pass control to the statement following it. In this case, that statement is the return from **main**.

Why write it this way? Simply because using **break** highlights failing to read a pair of input values as a special case. In general, we can use **break** to simplify a loop's test by separating out special cases or error conditions.

The continue Statement

A **continue** skips the rest of the loop body and causes the loop test to be immediately evaluated (except in the **for**, which evaluates *Action* first).

When do we use **continue**? Usually, to help prevent excessive nesting within a loop. Figure 7.15 uses the **continue** shown on the top of the next page in a slight revision of our earlier program to convert from military time to standard time.

```
/*
 * Convert military time to standard time, now with error checking.
 */
#include <stdio.h>
#include <stdlib.h>

int main()
{
  unsigned int mhour;              /* input: military hour */
  unsigned int min;               /* input: military minutes */
  unsigned int stdhour;           /* standard hour */

  while (printf("Enter military time (as xx:xx): "),
         scanf("%u:%u", &mhour, &min) == 2)
  {
    if (mhour >= 24 || min >= 60)
    {
      printf("Error: military time is from 0:00 to 23:59\n");
      continue;
    }

    stdhour = mhour;                      /* assume AM */
    if (mhour <= 12)
    {
      if (mhour == 0)
        stdhour = 12;                     /* midnight */
    }
    else
      stdhour = mhour - 12;               /* PM */
    printf("Standard time: %u:%02u\n", stdhour, min);
  }

  return EXIT_SUCCESS;
}
```

Figure 7.15 (mtime2.c) A version of our program to convert from military time to standard time that uses a **continue**.

```
if (mhour >= 24 || min >= 60)
{
  printf("Error: military time is from 0:00 to 23:59\n");
  continue;
}
```

Now the program prints an error message if it encounters an invalid input (such as an hour field that's greater than 23 or a minutes field that's larger than 59). It then uses this **continue** to skip further processing of that input.

This **continue** is actually somewhat silly, since we can eliminate it simply by adding an **else** to our **if**. In fact, we can always avoid using a **continue** by adding

Aside 7.2: Selecting an Appropriate Loop

C provides us with several different choices for loops: **while**, **do-while**, and **for**. It can be difficult to determine which is the most appropriate loop to use, especially since the **for** is more general than the **while**.

Use **for** whenever there is a single variable that's initialized, tested, and updated. By doing so, all the control information winds up on a single line and need not be searched for in the body of the loop. Counting loops fall into this category (since they assign a value to the counting variable, test if it has reached the desired value, and increment or decrement it each time through the loop). Perhaps surprisingly, many other loops fall into this category as well. Any loop that accumulates a value until it reaches a given range can also reasonably be written as a **for**, such as a loop to read and sum input values until they hit some predetermined maximum or our earlier loop to skip over the remaining characters on the input line.

Some programmers also use the **for** more generally, whenever the loop control expressions are simple and related. A common example is to write a loop that reads and counts input values as a **for** (which involves initializing a counter, reading a value and testing if it's end of file, and incrementing the counter). Whether or not to write this sort of loop as a **for** or a **while** is really a matter of personal preference.

Don't use a **for** when it would contain unrelated computations (such as initializing one counter, testing another, and incrementing or decrement a third). And don't use a **for** if it would be missing both its *Start* and *Action*.

Use **do-while** when the loop action must repeat at least once. These loops are surprisingly rare, however, since most of the time there are circumstances we want to check for that would prevent us from ever going through the loop.

That leaves the **while** loop for practically all the remaining cases. When in doubt, write the code for both the **while** and **for** loops and use the more readable one.

an **else** and making the code to be skipped a separate function. We use it only when we check for errors at the beginning of a loop and find it convenient to leap over the rest of the loop body if an error occurs.

> *Avoid* **continue** *except when checking for error conditions at the top of a loop.*

The goto Statement

The **goto** is the final jump statement. It simply transfers control to a labeled statement:

```
goto label
   . . .
label: statement
```

A *label* has the same syntax as an identifier and must be in the same function as the **goto**. If we want a label at the end of the function, we need to follow it with a null statement (but in that case we should probably be using a **return** rather than a **goto**).

One reasonable use of a **goto** is to rapidly bail out of nested loops when an error occurs.

```
for (...)
  for (...)
  {
    ...
    if (error condition) goto error;
    ...
  }
  ...
error:
  printf("Serious error detected -- bailing out\n");
```

When the error condition occurs, control simply transfers to the label **error** and the error message is printed. To see why **goto** is useful in this situation, consider trying to avoid it. We can't use **break** because it only exits a single loop. We could let a boolean variable note the error condition and then test its value each time through the loop, or we could make the code fragment containing the loops a function that returns a special value when an error condition occurs—but these alternatives seem to be more work than they're worth.

The above **goto** is reasonable, but in general the fewer **goto**s in your programs, the better. Most compilers generate less efficient code for loops implemented with **goto** instead of the structured loop constructs. In addition, rampant **goto**s render a program unreadable. **goto**s are rarely used in well-written programs, and we haven't needed any in the programs in this book.

> *Avoid gotos whenever possible.*

7.9   CASE STUDY—OCTAL DUMP

This section is optional!

We end this chapter with a program to print an octal dump of its input. The input

```
this is    a test
```

(which has two invisible tab characters between the "is" and the "a") produces

```
000000  164 t   150 h   151 i   163 s
000004  040     151 i   163 s   011 \t
000008  011 \t  141 a   040     164 t
000012  145 e   163 s   164 t   012 \n
```

The program reads the input one character at a time, writing it in octal and as a character if it is printable. It displays special characters, such as tabs and form feeds, as escape sequences. An octal dump is useful for displaying text files containing strange characters, directories that contain files whose names have unprintable characters, and binary files.

Figure 7.16 contains the entire octal dump program, which happens to use several of the special features of C's statements discussed in this chapter. The **main** program handles reading the characters and keeping track of when it's time to go to the next line of output. It uses a function **printChar** to actually display the character's octal and text representations. To print the count of characters and to print each character's octal representation, we again use the ability of **printf** to provide leading zeros instead of blanks.

SUMMARY

- C provides expression statements (any expression followed by a semicolon) and compound statements (any set of statements surrounded by braces).

- C provides an **if** statement for doing different actions if an expression is true or false.

- C provides a **switch** statement for selecting an action based on different values of a single expression.

- C provides three looping constructs: **while**, which tests before the loop body; **for**, which in addition lets us specify actions to perform before we enter the loop and each time we complete the loop body; and **do-while**, which tests after the loop body.

- C provides several control-flow-altering statements: **break**, **continue**, and **goto**. **break** exits the nearest enclosing loop or **switch**, **continue** skips the rest of a loop, and **goto** transfers control to an arbitrary label. These statements should be avoided if at all possible.

- Finally, C provides a **return** statement, which generally should appear only at the end of a function.

EXERCISES

7–1 Compile and run the programs in this chapter.

7–2 What happens if you eliminate all **break** statements from our punctuation-counting program (Figure 7.6)?

7–3 Locate the bugs in our buggy loop example (Aside 7.3b).

Modify

7–4 Rewrite our military time to standard time conversion program (Figure 7.2) to use the conditional operator.

7–5 Rewrite our **break** and **continue** examples (Figures 7.14 and 7.15) without using a **continue** or **break**.

```
/*
 * Dump input in octal (and character if printable).
 */
#include <stdio.h>
#include <stdlib.h>
#include <ctype.h>

#define MAXCHARS  4                         /* max # of chars on a line */

int main()
{
  void printChar(int c);

  int           c;                          /* next character */
  int           linecnt;                    /* # of chars on line */
  unsigned long inpcnt;                     /* # of chars in input */

  for (linecnt = 0, inpcnt = 0; (c = getchar()) != EOF; inpcnt++)
  {
    if (linecnt++ == 0)
      printf("%06li  ", inpcnt);
    else
      printf("   ");
    printChar(c);
    if (linecnt == MAXCHARS)
    {
      putchar('\n');
      linecnt = 0;
    }
  }
  if (linecnt > 0)                          /* finish up last line */
    putchar('\n');

  return EXIT_SUCCESS;
}

void printChar(int c)
{
  printf("%03o ", c);               /* write octal code for character */
  switch (c)                        /* write escape sequence or char */
  {
    case '\a':  printf("\\a");  break;
    case '\b':  printf("\\b");  break;
    case '\f':  printf("\\f");  break;
    case '\n':  printf("\\n");  break;
    case '\r':  printf("\\r");  break;
    case '\t':  printf("\\t");  break;
    case '\v':  printf("\\v");  break;
    default:    printf("%c ", isprint(c) ? c : ' ');
  }
}
```

Figure 7.16 (octdump.c) A program to produce an octal dump of its input.

Aside 7.3a: Debugging Loops

Many programmers struggle to write their loops correctly. There are three common problems with loops: never executing the loop body, never leaving the loop, and leaving the loop too early. These errors occur for obvious reasons. Never going through a loop means that the loop condition wasn't true when the loop was first executed. Never leaving a loop occurs because the loop condition never becomes false. And leaving the loop too early occurs because the loop condition unexpectedly became true.

Surprisingly, a few carefully placed **printf**s are usually all it takes to have our program provide all the information we need to quickly detect and correct these errors. The trick is to print the values of any variables involved in the loop test before the loop is ever executed, at the beginning of the loop body, at end of the loop body, and right after the loop exits.

By printing the values before the loop is entered, we see what the conditions were before the loop test was evaluated (and why we never entered the loop, if that's what happened). By printing the values at the start and end of the loop body, we can see how the variables controlling our loop change as the loops executes (and why our loop never exits, or exits earlier, if that's what's happening). And by printing the values after the loop exits, we can verify exactly why the loop exited.

Aside 7.3b illustrates the technique in a little program whose job is to read and count input values until they sum to 1000 (placed in the constant **MaxValues**). Unfortunately, it has several errors, and when we run it, it never goes through the loop! Fortunately, however, we have placed our **printf**s in the program, so we get this helpful output:

```
DEBUG: Before loop entered: sum=0, MAX_SUM=1000
20
DEBUG: After loop exits: n=1, sum=0, MAX_SUM=1000
DEBUG: n == 2? 0, sum > MAX_SUM? 0
First 0 values
```

This output tells us that both loop tests were false: **n** wasn't equal to 2, and sum wasn't greater than **MAX_SUM**! Careful examination tells us that was because we wrote those tests wrong (we are reading one value with **scanf** and want to keep executing the loop as long as **sum** is *less than* **MAX_SUM**.

That's not the only mistake however. Fixing the **while** leads to a problem within the loop. Run the program and examine its output to see how helpful it is in detecting that mistake!

7–6 Rewrite a **while**, a **do-while**, and a **for** using only **if**s and **goto**s. Are the **goto** versions more or less readable than the standard loop constructs?

7–7 Many programmers work in hex rather than octal. Modify the octal dump program (Figure 7.16) to produce a hex dump instead.

Extend

7–8 Extend our military time to standard time conversion program (Figure 7.2) to also print "AM", "PM", "Noon", or "Midnight".

Aside 7.3b (loopbug.c) A buggy loop and some well-placed **printf**s to help us locate the bug.

```c
/*
 * Print count of inputs that sum to below desired amount (buggy).
 */
#include <stdio.h>
#include <stdlib.h>

#define MAX_SUM 1000

int main()
{
  int count;
  int sum;
  int n;
  int x;

  count = 0;   sum = 0;
  printf("DEBUG: Before loop entered: sum=%i, MAX_SUM=%i\n",
          sum, MAX_SUM);
  while ((n = scanf("%i", &x)) == 2 && sum > MAX_SUM)
  {
    printf("DEBUG: Start of loop body: n=%i, sum=%i, MAX_SUM=%i\n",
            n, sum, MAX_SUM);
    sum += count;
    count++;
    printf("DEBUG: End of loop body: sum=%i, MAX_SUM=%i\n",
            sum, MAX_SUM);
  }
  printf("DEBUG: After loop exits: n=%i, sum=%i, MAX_SUM=%i\n",
          n, sum, MAX_SUM);
  printf("DEBUG: n == 2? %i, sum > MAX_SUM? %i\n",
          n == 2, sum > MAX_SUM);
  printf("First %i values\n", count);

  return EXIT_SUCCESS;
}
```

7–9 Change our character counting program (Figure 7.4) to print the number of upper- and lowercase characters in its input and to print the number of vowels and the number of consonants.

7–10 Modify the calculator (Figure 7.5) to allow the operands to be preceded and followed by an arbitrary amount of white space and to try to recover from input errors.

7–11 Rewrite the calculator (Figure 7.5) to use an **else-if** instead of a **switch**. Which version is more readable? Which version makes it easier to add synonyms for operators?

7–12 Modify the calculator (Figure 7.5) to allow synonyms for its operators (**a** for **+**, **s** for **-**, **m** for *****, and **d** for **/**), along with two new operators, **%** (remainder) and **^** (exponentiation).

7–13   Modify the octal dump program (Figure 7.16) to print control characters in the form `^X`. For example, a *control-G* prints as `^G`.

Code **7–14**   Using nested **if**s, write a function **min3** that returns the smallest of three **int** values passed to it as parameters. Also, write a function **max3** that returns the largest of its three **int** parameters.

7–15   Write a program that prints the line numbers of those lines in its input that are over 80 characters long (those lines that are too big to fit on the typical terminal screen). Modify the program so that it also prints the length of those lines.

7–16   Write a program that prints the line numbers of those lines that contain only white-space characters. Modify this program so that it also prints the line number of any line containing control characters, along with any control characters that line contains.

7–17   Write a program that prints all the prime numbers between 1 and 1000. A prime number is exactly divisible only by 1 and itself.

Build **7–18**   Write a simple program to aid in balancing a checkbook. The program's input is single-letter commands followed by an amount. The legal commands are **d** (deposit), **c** (check), **s** (service charge), **w** (withdrawal), and **b** (set starting balance). The program should print the balance after each transaction. Make sure your program is well behaved even when the input is in error.

7–19   Write a simple program to assign a grade. The program's input is a single test score and its output is a letter grade. Assume the traditional grading scale: 90-100 is an 'A', 80-89 is a 'B', 70-79 is a 'C', 60-69 is a 'D', and 0-59 is an 'F'. Make sure your program checks for input errors.

Extend this program to read a series of scores for each student rather than a single score. Each input line now contains the scores for a single student. Print the average score and the final grade.

Further extend the grading program from the previous exercise to expect each score to be followed by a weight. Make sure all the weights for a particular student add up to 100. Now the program prints both the weighted average and the final grade.

7–20   Write a program to determine whether a series of purchases come in over or under a budget. The program starts by reading a budget and a sales tax rate. It then reads a series of input lines containing the price of an item, the number purchased, and a discount rate. The program computes and prints the cost of each item. After reading all the input, it then prints the total cost and how it compared to the budget.

8 ARRAYS

This chapter introduces arrays. Our focus is on declaring arrays, accessing their elements, and passing them as parameters. We introduce arrays with a program that reverses its input and show how to pass arrays as parameters by rewriting this program, building it on top of a pair of user-defined functions. We further illustrate arrays by writing several useful functions: one reads values into an array until it encounters a sentinel, another searches an array for a particular value, and the last reads values into an array using a technique known as insertion sort. The chapter concludes with a case study that makes use of almost all the C features we've seen so far: a program that produces a histogram of its input.

8.1 USING ARRAYS—A PROGRAM TO REVERSE ITS INPUT

Figure 8.1 is a program to reverse its input. It reads all of its input values and then writes them in reverse order; the last value read is the first one written. If the program's input is these five values:

```
10 20 18 68 1
```

its output is:

```
1
68
18
20
10
```

Reversing the input may seem senseless, but we can use this program to take values sorted in ascending order and print them in descending order. This program introduces the *array*, a convenient method for storing a large collection of values.

An array is a named collection of values, called *elements*, all of which have the same underlying type. C supports arrays of any of its data types. We can do only two things with arrays: declare an array, which involves specifying how many elements it contains and what their type is, and access a particular element.

We declare an array by giving the type of its elements, its name, and the number of elements it will contain:

element-type name [*n*]

This allocates space for *n* array elements of the specified *element-type*.

```
/*
 * An initial program to read values and print them in reverse order.
 */
#include <stdio.h>
#include <stdlib.h>

#define MAXVALS 100        /* max number of values we can reverse */

int main()
{
  int table[MAXVALS];      /* array to hold input values */
  int n;                   /* number of values in "table" */
  int i;                   /* index used in writing values */
  int next;                /* next input value */

  n = 0;
  while (scanf("%i", &next) == 1)
  {
    table[n] = next;
    n++;
  }
  for (i = n - 1; i >= 0; i--)
    printf("%i\n", table[i]);

  return EXIT_SUCCESS;
}
```

Figure 8.1   (revintp1.c) A program that prints its input in reverse order, one value per line.

Once we have allocated this space, we can access the individual array elements by following the array's name with an *index* enclosed in square brackets, as in *name* [*index*]. An index is any expression that evaluates to an integer. Arrays are indexed starting at 0 and going up to one less than the number of elements in the array, so we can access elements of an array with *name* [**0**], *name* [**1**], *name* [**2**], and so on, up through *name* [*number-of-elements* -1], as shown below.

So far, our description of arrays has been somewhat abstract. Let's examine a specific example of their use. In Figure 8.1, the declaration

```
    int table[MAXVALS];
```

declares **table** to be an array, consisting of **MAXVALS int**s (where **MAXVALS** has been **#define**d as 100). Arrays are indexed from 0, so in this example we can access **table[0]** through **table[99]**.

> *Arrays are indexed starting with 0, not with 1 as in many other programming languages.*

Figure 8.1 reverses its input by reading values into an array and then printing the array in reverse order. The program stores the first input value in **table[0]**, the second input value in **table[1]**, and so on.

A single **while** loop controls the reading of the program's input values.

```
n = 0;
while (scanf("%i", &next) == 1)
{
  table[n] = next;
  n++;
}
```

This looks like our usual input-reading loops, reading each input value into a variable **next** and stopping when there is an error or end of file. The loop body takes **next** and places it in the next available place within the array. It does so by having a counter **n** keep track of the index where the next value should go, using that counter to specify the array element into which we should place **next**,

```
table[n] = next;
```

and then incrementing **n**. When the loop terminates, **n** will be the number of elements actually in the array.[1]

The program concludes with a **for** loop that prints **table**'s elements in reverse order.

```
for (i = n - 1; i >= 0; i--)
  printf("%i\n", table[i]);
```

We use **i** to index through **table**'s elements backward from its last element to its first. The loop is straightforward, with one subtlety. Even though **n** is the number of array elements, when we initialize **i** as the index of **table**'s last element, we initialize it to **n-1**, not **n**. We do this because arrays are indexed from 0, not 1. We want to ensure we access only **table[0]** through **table[n-1]**. In fact, **table[n]** is not a value we've read into the array.

Preventing Illegal Array Accesses

Our input reversal program has a flaw: it doesn't worry about running out of room in the array. Figure 8.2 is an improved version that takes care of this problem by verifying that there is room in the array before storing the input value it read into the array.

---

[1] There are more concise ways to read the input into the array, but they have problems when there are errors in the input or the array fills up.

```
/*
 * An initial program to read values and print them in reverse order.
 */
#include <stdio.h>
#include <stdlib.h>

#define MAXVALS 100          /* max number of values we can reverse */

int main()
{
  int table[MAXVALS];        /* array to hold input values */
  int n;                     /* number of values in "table" */
  int i;                     /* index used in writing values */
  int next;                  /* next input value */

  n = 0;
  while (scanf("%i", &next) == 1)
  {
    if (n >= MAXVALS)                /* Make sure there's room */
    {
      printf("No more room after reading %i values.\n", n);
      break;
    }
    table[n++] = next;
  }
  for (i = n - 1; i >= 0; i--)
    printf("%i\n", table[i]);

  return EXIT_SUCCESS;
}
```

Figure 8.2   (revintp2.c)   An improved version of our input-reversal program.

We do this by revising the loop body to test whether there's room before storing the next value read.

```
if (n >= MAXVALS)                /* Make sure there's room */
{
  printf("No more room after reading %i values.\n", n);
  break;
}
table[n++] = next;
```

If we didn't have this test and we ran out of room, we would be storing a value in the nonexistent memory location, **table[100]**.

There is no run-time array bounds checking, so we are responsible for doing our own bounds checking in our programs.[2] If we don't, and we attempt to access an invalid

---

[2]This differs from languages such as Pascal, where an illegal array access is guaranteed to terminate the program with a reasonable error message from the run-time environment.

Aside 8.1: Portability and Undefined Behavior

C officially describes the results of an access outside an array's bounds as *undefined*. But what exactly does that mean?

In February 1989 the ANSI standards committee, and subsequently ISO, adopted a standard for C. One important result was clarifying a lot of fine points, especially when doing something invalid. The standards committee defined the term "undefined behavior" to mean:

> ... behavior, upon use of a nonportable or erroneous program construct, of erroneous data, or of indeterminately valued objects, for which the standard imposes no requirements. Permissible undefined behavior ranges from ignoring the situation completely with unpredictable results, to behaving during translation [compilation] or program execution in a documented manner characteristic of the environment (with or without the issuance of a diagnostic message), to terminating a [compilation] or execution (with the issuance of a diagnostic message).

What this really means is that *anything* can happen with an undefined array access, from writing a reasonable error message to crashing the system. A really nice compiler, for example, might insert code in your object module to test for the problem at run time and then let you know about the problem; a nasty one might send a message about your competence as a programmer to your professor or your boss. On many typical compilers, accessing a subscript like `table[100]` when `table` has been declared to have 100 elements is likely to access or modify the value at the memory location immediately following our table, which is likely to be the location reserved for another variable. This type of error can be incredibly hard to track down, even in small programs like the one in Figure 8.1.

There are a number of other places where the result is officially "undefined", such as having `%` formats that don't match in number or type with the values to be read or printed or right-shifting signed values. We have to keep them in mind when we program and carefully avoid them.

location, such as `table[100]`, it's likely that neither the compiler nor the run-time environment will complain.

> *Make sure any value used as array subscript is a legal array subscript.*

This program takes advantage of postfix incrementing to make the program more concise, combining the update of the index with storing a value in the array.

```
table[n++] = next;
```

Because we are using postfix increment, it first stores the value in **table[n]** and then increments **n**.

Using `for` Loops to Process Arrays

Because processing arrays so often involves initializing, using, and then updating an index variable, we often use **for** loops when processing arrays, even when reading values into them. Figure 8.3 revises our previous input-reversal program to use a **for** as its input-reading loop. This loop now ostensibly reads input values until it hits **EOF**. Internally, however, it tests for an input error or full array within the loop and uses **break** to leave early if one of those situations is encountered.

We initialize and update **n** as part of the initialization and action parts of the **for**. This makes it clear to a program's reader that **n** represents the number of values read and stored in the array.

8.2   PASSING ARRAYS AS PARAMETERS

We can pass arrays as parameters, but the details are more complex than with the data types we've passed before. To illustrate this process, we rewrite our input reversal program to use two new functions, **tableFill** and **tablePrintRev**. **tableFill** reads data into an array and counts the number of elements read. We pass it the array to fill and the number of values it can hold. It returns the number of elements read. **tablePrintRev** prints an array in reverse order. We pass it the array to print and the number of values it contains. Figure 8.4 contains the main program for our new input-reversing program, showing how the functions are called, and Figure 8.5 contains the function definitions.

It's straightforward to pass an array to a function: all we do is provide its name. The heart of the **main** program is two function calls. The first passes the array **table** and the number of elements it can hold to **tableFill**, and the second passes the array and the number of values actually read into it to **tablePrintRev**.

```
n = tableFill(table, MAXVALS);
tablePrintRev(table, n);
```

Now let's look at how these functions work.

A Function to Read Values into an Array

tableFill takes two parameters: the array where the input values are to go (**a**) and the maximum number of values to read (**max**). As usual, we declare these parameters in the function header; **a** is an array of integers and **max** is an integer.

```
int tableFill(int a[], int max)
{
   ...
}
```

```
/*
 * An initial program to read values and print them in reverse order.
 */
#include <stdio.h>
#include <stdlib.h>

#define MAXVALS 100        /* max number of values we can reverse */

int main()
{
  int table[MAXVALS];      /* array to hold input values */
  int n;                   /* number of values in "table" */
  int i;                   /* index used in writing values */
  int next;                /* next input value */
  int r;                   /* return code from trying to read values */

  for (n = 0; (r = scanf("%i", &next)) != EOF ; n++)
  {
    if (r != 1)
    {
      printf("Input error after reading %i values.\n", n);
      break;
    }
    if (n >= MAXVALS)              /* Make sure there's room */
    {
      printf("No more room after reading %i values.\n", n);
      break;
    }
    table[n] = next;
  }
  for (i = n - 1; i >= 0; i--)
    printf("%i\n", table[i]);

  return EXIT_SUCCESS;
}
```

Figure 8.3 (revint.c) A version of our input-reversal program that uses a **for** loop to read input values.

With array parameters we leave out the size of the array, as we did with **a**. We'll see why shortly.

Two things happen when we execute **tableFill**: it reads values into the array **a**, and it keeps track of the number of values read in a local variable **cnt**. When it finishes, **a** contains values at **a[0]** through **a[cnt-1]**. There's a problem though: because **cnt** is local, no other function, such as **main** or **tablePrintRev** can access it. **tableFill** therefore returns **cnt**'s value (the number of values read into **a**), so that the main program can use it.

At this point alarm bells should be ringing. **tableFill** reads values into the array **a** that is declared as one of its parameters. But aren't we expecting **tableFill** to read

```
/*
 * Read values and print them in reverse order using functions.
 */
#include <stdio.h>
#include <stdlib.h>

#define MAXVALS 100          /* max number of values we can reverse */

int main()
{
  int  tableFill(int a[], int max);
  void tablePrintRev(int a[], int max);

  int  table[MAXVALS];       /* array to hold input values */
  int  n;                    /* number of values in "table" */

  n = tableFill(table, MAXVALS);
  tablePrintRev(table, n);

  return EXIT_SUCCESS;
}
```

Figure 8.4   (revint2.c)   A new version of our input reversal program.

values into an array that's located in **main**? How is this possible if C always passes parameters using call by value?

It's possible because we've kept something hidden: an occurrence of an array name doesn't really refer to the entire array. In fact, an array name is merely an address, the address of the array's first element. When we pass **table** to **tableFill** what we're really passing is the address of **table[0]**, **&table[0]**. And it's that address that's copied into **a** and used in subsequent subscript calculations. Within **tableFill**, accessing **a[cnt]** is really accessing **table[cnt]**. So when we change **a[cnt]** within **tableFill** with the assignment

```
    a[cnt] = next;
```

we change **table[count]** in **main**.

> *Changing an array parameter changes the corresponding array argument.*

Now we can better understand the parameter list in **tableFill**'s header:

```
    int tableFill(int a[], int max)
```

The first parameter, **a**, is described as an array (of some unknown number) of **int**s. We don't give a size because **a** really isn't an array at all—it's just a copy of the address of the array's first element.

```
/*
 * Functions to fill a table and print it in reverse order.
 *    tableFill - read values into a table
 *    tablePrintRev - print a table in reverse order
 */
#include <stdio.h>

int tableFill(int a[], int max)
{
  int next;                  /* next input value */
  int r;                     /* return from trying to read values */
  int cnt;                   /* count of values read */

  for (cnt = 0; (r = scanf("%i", &next)) != EOF; cnt++)
  {
    if (r != 1)              /* bad return from scanf */
    {
      printf("Error in the input after reading %i values.\n", cnt);
      break;
    }
    if (cnt == max)          /* no room to store this value */
    {
      printf("No more room in array after reading %i values.\n", cnt);
      break;
    }
    a[cnt] = next;           /* save element in array */
  }
  return cnt;
}

void tablePrintRev(int a[], int n)
{
  int i;                     /* index used in writing values */

  for (i = n - 1; i >= 0; i--)
    printf("%i\n", a[i]);
}
```

Figure 8.5 (tabfill.c) Functions for reading a table and printing it in reverse order.

Passing an address rather than the entire array can be a bit bewildering, but it has one nice benefit: functions aren't tuned to a particular size array. We can, for example, use **tableFill** to read in any size array of integers. It doesn't matter if the array has 10 or 100 or even 1000 elements. When we declare an array parameter, we need only declare that it's an array of a particular type, but can omit how many elements it contains. Of course, these functions do need to know how many elements are actually in the particular arrays they are passed. But we can easily supply that information in an additional parameter, as we did with **tableFill**.

You might think that an alternative to passing an array as a parameter would be to somehow have **tableFill** return an array. However, C does not allow functions to return arrays.

The function **tablePrintRev** is similar to **tableFill**. It takes two arguments, the array to print and the number of values in the array, and its header follows the same format as **tableFill**:

```
tablePrintRev(int a[], int max)
```

And like **tableFill**, it's a general function. We can use it to print any size array of integers in reverse order.

Arrays and Function Prototypes

Before we called **tableFill** and **tablePrintRev** from **main**, we supplied prototypes for them.

```
int tableFill(int a[], int size);
void tablePrintRev(int a[], int items);
```

We mentioned earlier that with function prototypes only the type information is important, not the names, which allows us to leave the names out. With arrays, however, doing so makes the prototypes especially ugly and hard to understand.

```
int tableFill(int [], int);
void tablePrintRev(int [], int);
```

In C, the type information is everything in the type declaration without the variable name. So these declarations say that **tableFill** and **tablePrintRev** take two parameters: an **int** array of any size and an **int**. When our prototypes involve arrays, we generally provide a dummy name to keep them readable.

Arrays and the `sizeof` Operator

In Chapter 6, we introduced the **sizeof** operator as a mechanism for determining how many bytes a particular variable requires. We can also use it with arrays. On a 16-bit machine, modifying Figure 8.4 by inserting this statement before the call to **tableFill**

```
printf("Table requires %lu bytes.\n",
        (unsigned long) sizeof(table));
```

causes the program to print

```
Table requires 200 bytes.
```

The 200 is the number of elements in **table** (100) × the number of bytes per element (2).

> **sizeof** *returns the number of bytes in the array, not the number of elements.*

You might think that **sizeof** gives us a way to calculate the number of elements in an array parameter, allowing us to avoid passing that information explicitly as an additional argument. But it doesn't. The reason is that taking **sizeof** of an array parameter gives the number of bytes in the address that's actually passed, not in the entire array. Although inconvenient, this behavior makes sense because **sizeof** is a compile-time operator, so it has no way of knowing how many items are actually passed at run time.

8.3 SOME EXAMPLE PROGRAMS USING ARRAYS

Arrays play a role in most programs. The most frequent operations we perform on arrays are reading values into them, searching them for a value, putting them into sorted order, and printing them. This section contains a pair of example programs that illustrate these common operations. The first reads values into an array and then uses sequential search to determine whether or not it contains certain values. The second reads values into an array, using a special technique called insertion sort. Both of these examples work only with arrays of **int**, but you can use them as a model for similar functions that work with other types of arrays.

Searching an Array with Sequential Search

Figure 8.6 contains our first example. It reads values into an array until encountering a zero, then determines whether subsequent input values are in the array. Here's some sample input and output:

```
10 45 67 16 0
67
Found 67 as element 2.
10
Found 10 as element 0.
76
Didn't find 76.
```

We've already seen how to read values into an array until we encounter end of file or run out of room. But we can't use **tableFill** here, since we need to read additional values after filling the array. Instead, we have to write a new function that reads values into the array only until the user enters a special value indicating the end of the input. That value is called a *sentinel*.

Figure 8.7 contains **tableFillSentinel**, our new input-reading function. It's similar to **tableFill**, but with several key differences. One is that it takes an extra parameter: the sentinel indicating the end of the input. The other is that it now prints an error message if it encounters **EOF**. We're still careful to check whether there's an error

```
/*
 * Search table for the target value, returning its position.
 */
#include <stdio.h>
#include <stdlib.h>

#define MAXVALS   10                    /* max # of entries in table */
#define SENTINEL   0                    /* terminating input value */

int main()
{
  int tableSearch(int a[], int n, int target);
  int tableFillSentinel(int a[], int n, int termval);

  int table[MAXVALS];                   /* table of values */
  int target;                           /* value to find */
  int found;                            /* target position */
  int n;                                /* number of items */
  int r;                                /* scanf return value */

  n = tableFillSentinel(table, MAXVALS, SENTINEL);

  while ((r = scanf("%i", &target)) == 1)
    if ((found = tableSearch(table, n, target)) != -1)
      printf("Found %i as element %i.\n", target, found);
    else
      printf("Didn't find %i.\n", target);

  if (r != EOF)
    printf("Illegal value to search for.\n");

  return EXIT_SUCCESS;
}
```

Figure 8.6   (usetable.c)   A program to read values into an array and then search it for particular values.

in the input or the array is full and to place the value we read into the array only after we're sure it's safe to do so.

Once we fill the array, we need to search the array for subsequent input values. To do so, we use a new function, **tableSearch**, shown in Figure 8.8. It takes three parameters: the array to search, the number of elements actually in the array, and the target value we're trying to find. It works by simply running through the array, comparing each array element with the target. It returns the index of the matching element, or -1 if a matching element isn't found. For small arrays, searching the entire array for the target value is sufficiently fast. For large arrays, however, this sequential search method is likely to be too slow, since on average it's going to examine half of the elements in the array. Fortunately, we'll eventually see a much more efficient approach we can use for large sorted arrays.

```
/*
 * Read values into an array until a sentinel value is read.
 */
#include <stdio.h>

int tableFillSentinel(int a[], int max, int sentinel)
{
  int next;                         /* next input value */
  int r;                            /* return from trying to read values */
  int cnt;                          /* count of values read */

  cnt = 0;
  while ((r = scanf("%i", &next)) == 1 && next != sentinel)
  {
    if (cnt == max)                 /* no room to store this value */
    {
      printf("Array full after reading %i values.\n", cnt);
      break;
    }
    a[cnt++] = next;                /* save element in array */
  }
  if (r == EOF)                     /* never saw sentinel */
    printf("End of file before encountering %i\n", sentinel);
  else if (r != 1)                  /* bad return from scanf */
    printf("Error in the input after reading %i values.\n", cnt);
  return cnt;
}
```

Figure 8.7 (tabsent.c) A function to fill an array until a sentinel is reached.

```
/*
 * A function to search for a target in an array of integers.
 */
int tableSearch(int a[], int n, int target)
{
  int i;

  for (i = 0; i < n && a[i] != target; i++)
    ;                                       /* search for matching value */
  return (i != n) ? i : -1;
}
```

Figure 8.8 (tabsrch.c) A function to perform sequential search on an array.

Aside 8.2: Writing Readable Functions

Our examples so far, especially in this chapter, have shown you a large collection of different functions. We have, however, spent little time discussing what makes a good function. Here are some of the characteristics well-written functions should have:

- *Cohesiveness*: A function should perform only one task, and all statements in the function should be related to that task. If the actions of a function cannot be described in a single sentence, the function is trying to do too much and it should be split up into separate functions.

- *Generality*: A function should perform its one task well. A sorting routine, for example, should work well for all sizes of input, handling error cases (such as being given no elements to sort) reasonably. A function shouldn't count on being passed sensible parameters and should verify that any assumptions it makes about its parameters hold.

- *Simplicity*: A function should perform its task in the simplest manner possible; do not try to fine-tune the code to save an instruction or two. Usually, changing the algorithm (for example, using a quicksort instead of an insertion sort) will contribute much more to efficiency than any amount of code manipulation.

- *Small Size*: A function that performs a single task in a simple manner is generally not lengthy. Limiting functions to a screen or page (about 25 to 50 lines) works well. Of course, too many small functions can also fragment a program and obscure program readability and efficiency. Most programmers, however, write functions that are too long rather than too short.

Sorting an Array with Insertion Sort

The other example of using arrays is a sorting program. This program reads integers, keeps them sorted in an array (in ascending order), and prints the array when it is done reading. The program reads from its standard input and writes to its standard output, but we can use redirection to use it to sort a file.

The program in Figures 8.9 and 8.10 uses a sorting technique known as *insertion sort*; it is easy to understand and to code and usually works with little debugging effort. Its drawback is that it is not the fastest sorting routine; the computing time increases as the *square* of the number of values to be sorted. Double the number of values and the computing time goes up by a factor of 4; triple the number and the computing time goes up by a factor of 9. Even so, insertion sort is suitable when we have to sort fewer than 50 to 100 values.

Insertion sort works by assuming that the array is already sorted and its job is to take each new value and insert it into the appropriate place in the array. We compare the new value with the last, "largest" element in the array. If the new value is smaller than the largest, we shift the largest over one place in the array and compare the new value

```
/*
 * Read values and sort them using "insertion sort."
 */
#include <stdio.h>
#include <stdlib.h>

#define   MAXVALS  100                  /* max # of values to sort */

int main()
{
  void tableInsert(int [], int, int);
  void tablePrint(int [], int);

  int   table[MAXVALS];                 /* table of values */
  int   n;                              /* number of values in table */
  int   r;                              /* value returned by scanf */
  int   v;                              /* current value */

  for (n = 0; (r = scanf("%i", &v)) != EOF; n++)
  {
    if (r != 1)
    {
      printf("Input error after reading %i values\n", n);
      break;
    }
    if (n == MAXVALS)
    {
      printf("Table full after reading %i values\n", n);
      break;
    }
    tableInsert(table, n, v);
  }

  tablePrint(table, n);

  return EXIT_SUCCESS;
}
```

Figure 8.9 (isort.c) A program to sort integers using insertion sort.

with the next largest value. When the new number is finally larger than some value in the array, we have found the appropriate place to insert it. If the new value is smaller than every value in the array, it goes into the first position. The entire operation can be characterized as "compare, shift; compare, shift; ..." until we find the appropriate place. Figure 8.11 illustrates the technique.

We use two functions to implement insertion sort: **tableInsert** places a value in its correct place in the array, and **tablePrint** prints the array.

tableInsert needs to determine where the new element should go and put it there. To insert a value in the array, we compare it with each array element, starting

```
/*
 * Functions for manipulating a table.
 *    tableInsert - insert an integer into correct place in table
 *    tablePrint  - print table in sorted order
 */
#include <stdio.h>

void tableInsert(int a[], int num, int val)
{
  int pos;

  for (pos = num; pos > 0 && val < a[pos-1]; pos--)
    a[pos] = a[pos-1];
  a[pos] = val;
}

void tablePrint(int a[], int num)
{
  int i;

  for (i = 0; i < num; i++)
    printf("%i\n", a[i]);
}
```

Figure 8.10 (tabins.c) Functions to insert in and print a sorted table.

with the largest, or last, element and shifting values one place whenever it is smaller than the element we are comparing. Eventually, it will be greater than or equal to some array element, or we will have reached the start of the array. In either case we insert it into the newly created hole. Finding the place for the new element is accomplished with a single **for** loop, whose body consists of a single statement:

```
for (pos = num; pos > 0 && val < a[pos - 1]; pos--)
  a[pos] = a[pos - 1];
```

A great deal is taking place within this **for** loop; we suggest trying to work through it by hand to see its effect.

tablePrint is almost identical to **tablePrintRev**; the only difference is in the order in which the table is printed. Like **tablePrintRev**, **tablePrint** is passed the number of elements in the array it is printing, so it also works for any size array.

8.4 CASE STUDY—A HISTOGRAM PRODUCER

This section is optional!

All of the examples of arrays in this chapter have manipulated them sequentially. This chapter concludes with a program that instead accesses individual elements directly. This program produces a histogram of its input. A histogram is a way to visualize a

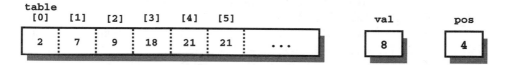

(a) The value is smaller than **table[pos - 1]**, so copy **table[pos - 1]** to **table[pos]** and decrement **pos**.

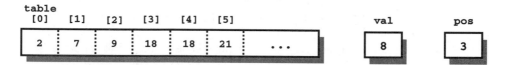

(b) The value is smaller than **table[pos - 1]**, so copy **table[pos - 1]** to **table[pos]** and decrement **pos**.

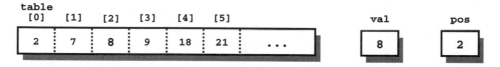

(c) The value is not smaller than **table[pos - 1]**, so copy **table[pos - 1]** to **table[pos]** and decrement **pos**.

(d) Copy the value into **table[pos]**.

(e) The final array after inserting the value.

Figure 8.11   Stages in insertion sort. The new value is eventually put between the 7 and the 9.

frequency distribution using a set of bars, with each bar's length representing the relative frequency of a group of values. Figure 8.12 shows a sample histogram generated from the data in Figure 8.13.

The usual approach to generating histograms is to maintain an array whose elements count the values falling within each range. After reading and counting the input values, the bars can be generated by writing one asterisk (or other desired character) for each value that falls within that range. There are two tricky parts: mapping the input value to the appropriate counter within the array and producing reasonable output when one group has a large number of values.

To keep things simple, we assume that each group of values (or *bucket*) has one counter and that every bucket is the same size. Given an input value, we can map it to the appropriate counter by subtracting the smallest value from it and dividing the result by the size of a bucket. If we have a data value of 45, a minimum value of 0, and 10 values per bucket, we should update bucket number 4.

Our other worry is how to produce reasonable output, even if there are more values in a bucket than there are columns available on the output device. The trick is to scale the output so that the row with the most asterisks covers the available width, and the other rows are proportionally shorter. It's possible, however, that this scaling will cause a row with proportionally few values to appear as though it has none. To fix that, we write at least one asterisk for each row that has one or more values. We also write an exact count at every row's end.

The histogram program is broken into several different files. Figure 8.14 contains the main program. Figure 8.15 contains the function **fillBuckets**, which reads the input values and updates the appropriate counter. Figure 8.16 contains **printHistogram**, which writes the histogram, after first scaling the counters to determine how many asterisks to print. Finally, the histogram program uses a set of generally useful utility functions such as **inRange**, **min**, **max**, and **putNChars**. Since we want to use these functions in other programs, we've placed them in a separate file, shown in Figure 8.17.

SUMMARY

- C provides arrays whose sizes must be specified at compile time.

- Arrays are indexed from 0 through the number of elements in the array minus one.

- We are responsible for making sure that we use only legitimate subscripts on a given array. Access outside those subscripts produces *undefined* behavior.

- When we pass an array to a function, only the address of its first element is copied, not the entire array. There's no need to specify the number of elements.

- Unlike the other variables we've seen, changes to array parameters affect the passed array.

- Some common operations on arrays are to read values into them, search for a value, sort the array, and print the values they contain.

```
  0-   9 |
 10-  19 |**                              (3)
 20-  29 |*                               (1)
 30-  39 |
 40-  49 |*                               (1)
 50-  59 |***                             (5)
 60-  69 |*******                         (11)
 70-  79 |************************         (37)
 80-  89 |********                        (13)
 90-  99 |**                              (3)
100-100  |***                             (5)
```

Figure 8.12   Sample histogram output.

```
89   87   56   89   67   78   79   80
85   97  100  100   23   45   12   14
87   88   84   84   84   84   77   77
72   73   68   69   69  100  100   11
75   71   71   72   79   84   71   72
70   74   75   73   71   79   72   55
55   68   65   67   72   71   75   73
71   74   71   71   78   79   80  100
91   92   66   61   61   57   57   65
71   74   78   78   78   78   78
```

Figure 8.13   Sample histogram input.

EXERCISES

Explore   8–1   Compile and run each of the programs in this chapter on your machine.

8–2   What happens if you modify **table[10]** in an array that has only 10 elements?

Modify   8–3   Modify the programs in this chapter to work with **double**s.

8–4   Modify the insertion sort program (Figure 8.9) to sort its input in descending rather than ascending order.

8–5   Modify the insertion sort program (Figure 8.9) to first find the appropriate place to insert the new value and then shift everything after it one place before inserting the value. That is, break the loop we're currently using into two separate loops.

8–6   Rewrite the histogram program (Figures 8.14 and 8.16) to read its input using **getDecimalNumber** (Figure 5.11) rather than **scanf**.

```
/*
 * Produce a histogram of its input values.
 */
#include <stdlib.h>

#define NUMBCKTS   11          /* reasonable number of buckets  */
#define MINVAL      0          /* range of values is 0-100      */
#define MAXVAL    100          /*   (assumption is test scores) */

int main()
{
  void fillBuckets(unsigned long buckets[],
                  int bucket_size, int numbuckets,
                  int minval, int maxval);
  void printHistogram(unsigned long buckets[],
                    int bucket_size, int numbuckets,
                    int minval, int maxval);

  unsigned long buckets[NUMBCKTS];
  int           bucket_size;

  bucket_size = (MAXVAL - MINVAL) / (NUMBCKTS - 1);
  fillBuckets(buckets, bucket_size, NUMBCKTS, MINVAL, MAXVAL);
  printHistogram(buckets, bucket_size, NUMBCKTS, MINVAL, MAXVAL);

  return EXIT_SUCCESS;
}
```

Figure 8.14   (histo.c)   The main program for our histogram producer.

Extend

8–7 Extend the insertion sort program (Figure 8.9) to count and print the number of elements moved. For a random set of n input values, there should be somewhere between 0 and $n(n + 1)/2$ exchanges. That is, the best case is when the input is already in order, in which case each new element will be added at the end and no exchanges will take place. The worst case will be when the values are in reverse order, in which we will be forced to exchange all the elements that are currently in the array each time we add a new element.

8–8 Modify the histogram program (Figures 8.14 and 8.16) to read the minimum and maximum values, bucket size, and number of rows per bar from the user. Obviously there needs to be some internal maximum bucket count; the program should verify that the desired bucket count is not too large.

Code

8–9 Write a function, **tableInit**, that sets every element of an array of integers to a given value. The function takes three parameters: the array, its size, and the initial value.

8–10 Write a function **tableSum**, that returns the sum of the first **n** values in an array.

Use **tableSum** to write a function, **tableAverage**, that computes and returns the average of the first **n** elements in an array of **int**s.

```
/*
 * Place each input value in an appropriate bucket.
 */
#include <stdio.h>

void fillBuckets(unsigned long buckets[],
                 int bucket_size, int numbuckets,
                 int minval, int maxval)
{
  int inRange(int min, int max, int value);

  int next;                              /* next input value */
  int r;                                 /* scanf return value */
  int i;                                 /* index */

  for (i = 0; i < numbuckets; i++)       /* zero out buckets */
    buckets[i] = 0;

  while ((r = scanf("%i", &next)) != EOF)
    if (r != 1)
    {
      printf("Error while reading input values\n");
      break;
    }
    else if (!inRange(minval, maxval, next))
      printf("Out of range input value: %i\n", next);
    else
      buckets[(next - minval) / bucket_size]++;
}
```

Figure 8.15   (histoin.c) The function to read the input and update the buckets.

Test **tableSum** with a small program that uses **tableFill** (Figure 8.5) to fill the array with values.

8–11 Write a function to determine whether an array of **int**s is symmetrical. That is, its first element is the same as its last element, its second element is the same as its next-to-last element, and so on.

8–12 Write a function, **getDecimalNumbers**. It should read values from a single input line, stopping when it reads a **\n** or when the maximum number of values have been read. It returns the number of values read, and it takes two arguments. The first tells it how many values to read, and the second is an array in which to place those values. Use blanks and tabs to delimit numbers.

8–13 Write a function, **tableDelete**, that removes all occurrences of a given value from the first n elements of an array.

8–14 Write a function, **tableReplace**, that replaces all occurrences of a given value in an array with a different, provided value.

```
/*
 * Print the histogram.
 */
#include <stdio.h>

#define MAXMARKS   25                   /* maximum marks per bucket */
#define MARKER     '*'                  /* marker for values */

void printHistogram(unsigned long buckets[],
                    int bucketsize, int numbuckets,
                    int minval, int maxval)
{
  int            min(int x, int y);
  int            max(int x, int y);
  void           putNChars(char c, int n);
  unsigned long tableMax(unsigned long a[], int n);

  int            b;                     /* bucket index */
  int            bmin;                  /* smallest value in a bucket */
  int            bmax;                  /* largest value in a bucket */
  double         scale;                 /* scaling factor */
  int            marks;                 /* # of marks to write on line */
  unsigned long most;                   /* # of marks in largest bucket */

  most = tableMax(buckets, numbuckets);
  scale = (most > MAXMARKS) ? (double) MAXMARKS / most : 1.0;
  for (b = 0, bmin = minval; b < numbuckets; b++, bmin = bmax + 1)
  {                                           /* print each row to scale */
    bmax = min(bmin + bucketsize - 1, maxval);
    marks = (buckets[b] > 0) ? max(buckets[b] * scale, 1) : 0;
    printf("%3i-%3i |", bmin, bmax);        /* write label */
    putNChars(MARKER, marks);               /* write markers */
    putNChars(' ', MAXMARKS - marks);       /* write spaces */
    if (buckets[b])                           /* write count */
      printf(" (%lu)", buckets[b]);
    putchar('\n');
  }
}

unsigned long tableMax(unsigned long a[], int n)
{
  int            i;
  unsigned long largest;                        /* largest count */

  for (largest = 0, i = 0; i < n; i++)
    if (a[i] > largest)
      largest = a[i];
  return largest;
}
```

Figure 8.16   (histoout.c)   The function to print the histogram.

```
/*
 * Some useful utility functions.
 *    min - returns smaller of two values.
 *    max - returns larger of two values.
 *    inRange - check whether one value is between two others.
 *    putNChars - write a character "n" times.
 */
#include <stdio.h>

int min(int x, int y)
  { return (x < y) ? x : y; }

int max(int x, int y)
  { return (x > y) ? x : y; }

int inRange(int min, int max, int v)
  { return v >= min && v <= max; }

void putNChars(char c, int n)
{
  while (n-- > 0)
    putchar(c);
}
```

Figure 8.17 (utils.c) Some generally useful utility functions.

Build 8–15 One way to avoid overflow is to use an array to represent the numbers, with one integer in the array corresponding to one digit in the number. Write a function, **addBigNum**, that adds two numbers represented by digit arrays, and fills in a third digit array with the result. Also write its counterpart, **subBigNum**, that subtracts two numbers represented by digit arrays.

Add two additional functions, **multBigNum** and **divBigNum**, which multiply and divide two numbers represented by digit arrays.

8–16 Write a program that reads its input into an array and then uses selection sort to sort the array. In selection sort, we first find the smallest element in the array and exchange it with the first array element's value; then we find the next smallest element in the array and exchange it with the second array element's value; and so on, until the array is sorted.

8–17 Write a program that uses insertion sort to sort an array in place.

8–18 Write a program that reads values from its input and counts the occurrences of each unique value in the input. Assume the values are between 1 and 100. Once the input has been read, write each value and the number of its occurrences. Ignore values that didn't appear in the input.

Modify this program so that there's no limit on the number or range of the input values. You'll need to keep two arrays, one containing the input values and the other containing their corresponding counts.

8–19 Write a program that prints the 10 smallest values in its input. Extend the program to print the 10 largest values.

8–20 Write a program that reads test scores into an array. Once it's read the scores, have it print the mean (the average score), median (the score that half the students are less than and the other half are better than), and mode (the score the most students had).

Make your program print the scores in sorted order.

8–21 Write a program that reads pairs of values and prints them, both sorted by the first value and sorted by the second. One use of this program would be to read student ID numbers and test scores and then print them sorted by student numbers and student scores.

9 PROGRAM
STRUCTURE

Our previous programs have had a simple structure. This chapter deals with more complex program organizations. We finish up our description of variables local to particular functions and introduce variables accessible by any function. While discussing variables, we present the storage classes that control their lifetime, location, and visibility. We then show how header files simplify accessing variables and functions defined in other files, and how we can have variables and functions accessible only within a single file. This chapter concludes with a case study: an initial implementation of a set data type.

9.1   LOCAL VARIABLES

Local variables are those declared within a function body. We've so far ignored two of their most useful features. First, there's a shortcut for declaring more than one variable with the same type. Second, we're able to provide an initial value whenever we declare a variable. And third, we're not restricted to declaring local variables only at the start of functions (although this feature is used much less frequently than the other two).

Concise Variable Declarations

So far, we have declared each variable by preceding it with a type and following it with a semicolon, even if the variables had the same type:

```
int c;                  /* current and */
int lastch;             /*    previous characters */
```

However, there's a short cut, and Figure 9.1 takes advantage of it in a slightly more concise version of our earlier program to line-number its input. C lets us factor out common type information and then connect the declarations up with commas, instead of separating them with semicolons.

```
int c, lastch;          /* current and previous characters */
```

The obvious advantage to this more concise form is less typing, since we don't have to repeat the type in every variable declaration. But there are disadvantages as well.

```
/*
 * Copy input to output, giving each line a number.
 */
#include <stdio.h>
#include <stdlib.h>

int main()
{
  int           c, lastch;        /* current and previous characters */
  unsigned long lineno = 0;       /* lines printed so far */

  for (lastch = '\n'; (c = getchar()) != EOF; lastch = c, putchar(c))
    if (lastch == '\n')           /* hit end of line */
      printf("%8lu ", ++lineno);

  return EXIT_SUCCESS;
}
```

Figure 9.1   (lineno5.c)   A more concise version of our program to line-number its input.

One is that we now have no obvious place to comment on what the variable does, unless we place names on separate lines and lose some of the conciseness.

```
int c,                  /* current and */
    lastch;             /* previous characters */
```

The other is that it's not as easy to change a variable's type. For this reason, we generally prefer the more verbose form, unless we happen to be declaring a few temporary variables.

Initializing Local Variables

What's the default initial value of local variables we don't initialize explicitly? You might guess zero, since that's the value they would have in many other languages, but you would be wrong. Instead, they simply start with whatever was previously in the memory location allocated for them—usually garbage.

> *Don't count on local variables automatically being initialized to zero.*

To prevent hard-to-find problems, we must explicitly initialize all our local variables before we use them.[1] Conveniently, we can initialize a local variable when we declare it. All we have to do is follow its name with an equal sign and an arbitrary expression.

---

[1] Some compilers generate code that sets local variables to zero but the language has no such requirement; if a program depends on this behavior, it may fail when we compile it on another machine or compiler or even when we use different compiler options.

We took advantage of this in Figure 9.1 when we declared **lineno**:

```
unsigned long lineno = 0;           /* lines printed so far */
```

This declares **lineno** as an **unsigned long** and then initializes it to zero. It's essentially the equivalent of a declaration immediately followed by an assignment.

```
unsigned long lineno;

lineno = 0;
```

These initializations take place each time the function containing them executes. Here, that's just once, when **main** is first called.

It's a good idea to initialize most variables when they are declared, as it prevents the common mistake of forgetting to initialize them before using them. Of course, there are several exceptions. It doesn't make sense to initialize a variable that will be filled in when it is passed as a function argument (such as the input variables we pass to **scanf**) or will be filled in and updated as part of a **for** loop (such as counters or array indices).

We aren't restricted to initializing variables to zero. We can, in fact, initialize them with any legal C expression, which means that we can include function calls, parameters, and already-declared local variables. We'll use this feature frequently in subsequent programs.

We initialize arrays by supplying a brace-enclosed, comma-separated list of expressions. The values in this list become the initial values of the corresponding array elements. There's one restriction, however: the initial values for the array elements must be computable at compile time, so they can't involve other variables or functions. As an example,

```
int days[12] = {31, 28, 31, 30, 31, 30,
                31, 31, 30, 31, 30, 31};
```

declares **days** as an array of 12 **int**s and initializes **days[0]** to 31, **days[1]** to 28, and so on. When we provide initial values, we don't have to specify explicitly how many items an array has—the compiler will allocate just enough space for the initialized elements. So

```
int days[] = {31, 28, 31, 30, 31, 30,
              31, 31, 30, 31, 30, 31};
```

is equivalent to the previous declaration.

> *Make sure any array size you provide is large enough to hold the initial elements.*

This declaration of **days**,

```
int days[10] = {31, 28, 31, 30, 31, 30,
                31, 31, 30, 31, 30, 31};
```

will result in a compiler error message, since we're specifying more than 10 values. If our specified array size is larger than the number of elements (and we provide at least one explicit value), the extra elements are assigned zero.

```
int days[13] = {31, 28, 31, 30, 31, 30,
                31, 31, 30, 31, 30, 31};
```

Here, the extra element **days[12]** is assigned a zero. Unfortunately, there's no convenient way to initialize only selected elements.

We use the initialization of arrays with a little program to read dates (month, day, and year) and to print the day of the year. Here is some sample input and output for the program.

```
Enter date (month day year): 6 24 1992
176
Enter date (month day year): 6 24 1995
175
Enter date (month day year): 2 19 1996
50
Enter date (month day year): 4 7 1995
98
Enter date (month day year): 12 31 1995
365
Enter date (month day year): 12 31 1996
366
```

Figure 9.2 is the program itself. Most of the work is done by the function **dayCalc**, which takes a date and returns the corresponding day of the year. It uses **days** to hold the number of days in each month. Given a date, it runs through the table summing the entries, until it reaches the entry for the given month. It then adds the provided days and adds one more day if the specified year is a leap year.

Declaring Variables within Blocks

We've seen that we can declare and initialize local variables at the beginning of any function. But we can also declare and initialize local variables at the beginning of any compound statement or *block*. These variables are initialized each time we enter the block. This feature is useful whenever we need a variable in only a small part of a function, such as a loop index, or a temporary variable to hold the result of a calculation.

Figure 9.3 provides an example in a new version of Chapter 7's program to compute the average of its input values. Like the previous version, it uses a variable **avg** to hold the average of the input values. Now, however, we declare **avg** in a block following the loop to read the input values:

```
{ /* compute and print input avg */
  double avg = (n == 0) ? 0.0 : (double) sum / n;

  printf("Average of %i values is %f.\n", n, avg);
}
```

```c
/*
 * Given month, day, year, return day of year (no error checking).
 *    dayCalc - calculate day or year, given month, day, and year.
 *    isLeapYear - returns 1 if current year a leap year, 0 otherwise.
 */
#include <stdio.h>
#include <stdlib.h>

int main()
{
  int dayCalc(int month, int day, int year);

  int month, day, year;                          /* current input date */

  while (printf("Enter date (month day year): "),
         scanf("%i %i %i", &month, &day, &year) == 3)
    printf("%i\n", dayCalc(month,day,year));

  return EXIT_SUCCESS;
}

int dayCalc(int month, int day, int year)
{
  int isLeapYear(int year);

  int days[] = {31, 28, 31, 30, 31, 30,
                31, 31, 30, 31, 30, 31};
  int i;
  int total = day + (month > 2 && isLeapYear(year));

  for (i = 0; i < month - 1; total += days[i++])
    ;                                  /* sum days in preceding months */
  return total;
}

int isLeapYear(int year)
  { return (year % 4 == 0 && year % 100 != 0) || year % 400 == 0; }
```

Figure 9.2 (daycalc.c) A program to determine on which day of the year a particular date falls. The program takes into account whether or not it's a leap year.

We initialize **avg** at the same time we declare it, using the same expression to protect against dividing by zero we used in earlier versions of the program.

Why not simply declare **avg** at the beginning of the function? By declaring variables only within the small portion of the program where they are needed, we lessen the chances of accidentally using or changing them in other places. Of course, this program is relatively small, so it's probably not worth the extra effort to declare variables right where they are used. But in a larger function, declaring variables local to particular blocks can greatly improve the program's readability and maintainability.

```
/*
 * Compute average of its input values with no error checking.
 */
#include <stdio.h>
#include <stdlib.h>

int main()
{
  int     next, n;                    /* next input, number of inputs */
  long    sum = 0;                    /* running total */

  for (n = 0; scanf("%i", &next) == 1; n++)
    sum += next;
  { /* compute and print input average */
    double avg = (n == 0) ? 0.0 : (double) sum / n;

    printf("Average of %u values is %f.\n", n, avg);
  }

  return EXIT_SUCCESS;
}
```

Figure 9.3   (avg4.c)   Yet another version of our program to compute the average of its input values.

Local variables do not have a long lifetime: they live only from block entry to block exit. When we enter a block, space is reserved for its local variables. When we exit the block, this space is freed. As a result, the next time we enter a block its local variables may not even use the same physical memory locations—so we can't count on them still having the values they had before.

Local variables have limited visibility, only from the point of their declaration until the end of the block in which they are declared. We can't directly access a local variable outside of the block in which it's declared. Trying to access **avg** before or after the block computing and printing the average results in an error message from the compiler.

9.2   GLOBAL VARIABLES

So far we have declared variables only at the beginning of blocks. But we can also declare variables outside any function, anywhere in the source file. These *global* variables are visible from where they are declared until the end of the file.[2] We can access them simply by referring to them by name, without our needing to pass them as parameters. Global variables differ from local variables in several other ways as well: they exist throughout the life of the program, rather than just the life of a block, and they start off at zero by default, rather than at some unknown value.

---

[2]C's global variables resemble Pascal's global variables and FORTRAN's common variables.

Figure 9.4 uses global variables in a program that counts occurrences of each unique character in its input. Given the input,

```
this is a test
```

which contains two invisible tab characters between the words "is" and "a", the program produces this output.

```
\011    : 2
\012    : 1
\040 ( ): 2
\141 (a): 1
\145 (e): 1
\150 (h): 1
\151 (i): 2
\163 (s): 3
\164 (t): 3
```

How does this program work? It reads each new character and uses it as an index into a table of counters, **charcnts**.

```
while (c = getchar(), c != EOF)
  charcnts[c]++;
```

There is one entry in this table for each character code, from zero to the number of possible character codes on the machine (**UCHAR_MAX**, from limits.h). The counters themselves are **unsigned long**s.

```
unsigned long charcnts[UCHAR_MAX + 1];
```

Once the program has read its entire input, it uses **printCounters** to run through **charcnts** and print each of the counts.

```
for (i = 0; i < UCHAR_MAX; i++)
  if (charcnts[i])
  {
    printf("\\%03o ", i);
    isprint(i) ? printf("(%c)"", i) : printf("   ");
    printf(": %lu\n", charcnts[i]);
  }
```

This loop takes advantage of several subtle C features. The first is an implicit test against zero in the **if** statement. If the count is zero, we don't print any information about that character. The second is the use of the **%03o** formatting code, which writes the character's value in a field three digits wide, padded with zeros rather than blanks. The last is the use of the conditional operator to select which **printf** we use. If the character is printable, we write the character, but if it isn't, we write blanks instead.

Since that table is declared outside of any function, it's a global variable, and both **main** and **printCounters** can use it simply by referring to it by name.

Since global variables start at zero, we don't bother to initialize the elements in **charcnts**. This implicit initialization is convenient and countless programs take advantage of it. Of course, we can also explicitly initialize global variables in the same

```c
/*
 * Counts the different characters in its input.
 */
#include <stdio.h>
#include <stdlib.h>
#include <ctype.h>
#include <limits.h>

unsigned long charcnts[UCHAR_MAX + 1];          /* 0...UCHAR_MAX */

int main()
{
  void printCounters(void);

  int  c;

  while(c = getchar(), c != EOF)
    charcnts[c]++;
  printCounters();

  return EXIT_SUCCESS;
}

void printCounters(void)
{
  int i;

  for (i = 0; i < UCHAR_MAX; i++)
    if (charcnts[i])                  /* write count only when nonzero */
    {
      printf("\\%03o ", i);
      isprint(i) ? printf("(%c)", i) : printf("    ");
      printf(": %lu\n", charcnts[i]);
    }
}
```

Figure 9.4 (charcnt.c) A program to count different characters in its input.

way we initialize their local counterparts, with one exception: the initializing expression must evaluate to a constant at compile time. That means it cannot make use of function calls or references to other variables.

Even though global arrays are automatically initialized to zero, we can use this idiom

```c
unsigned long charcnts[UCHAR_MAX + 1] = {0};
```

to make explicit our reliance on the array's elements starting with zero. This explicitly initializes the first element to zero; the others are zero by default.[3]

---

[3]We can also use this form with local arrays to sneakily guarantee that the entire array is initialized to 0.

We used a global variable here because it saved us from having to explicitly initialize any of the table elements. It also simplifies the call to **printCounters**, since we don't have to provide any parameters. There's a cost though: our program is now less general, since **printCounters** now only works with a particular global array named **charcnts**.

> *Avoid global variables wherever possible.*

Global variables have several drawbacks. They obscure the connections between functions, decreasing readability and modular independence. Because any of a program's functions can easily change a global variable, an accidental change can lead to subtle, hard-to-find errors. In addition, the storage for global variables must be allocated before the program begins executing and is tied up for the entire program. That's wasteful when compared to local variables, whose space is tied up only during the execution of the function containing their declaration.

When using global variables, consider carefully the trade-off between readability and convenience. A little extra effort to avoid globals and to have all functions communicate through parameters increases modularity and aids readability. We try to use globals only for tables or for variables shared between routines when it is inconvenient to pass them as parameters.

9.3 STORAGE CLASSES

We've seen that every variable has a type, such as **int**, **double**, and so on. But what we haven't seen yet is that every variable also has a *storage class*. A variable's storage class provides information about its visibility, lifetime, and location. So far, we've been relying on the compiler's default storage classes. There are, however, several explicit storage class specifiers: **auto**, **register**, **static**, and **extern**. We can explicitly provide a storage class simply by preceding a variable's declaration with one of these keywords.

The Storage Class auto

Our local variables have the default storage class **auto**. The name **auto** derives from their *automatic* creation and removal on block entry and exit. We can use the keyword **auto** to make the storage class of a local variable explicit, but no one does, since a declaration such as

```
{
  auto int x, y;
    . . .
}
```

is exactly equivalent to

```
{
   int x, y;
     . . .
}
```

The Storage Class register

Automatic variables are stored in memory. We can suggest to the compiler that specific variables be stored in the machine's high-speed registers by declaring them with the storage class **register**. The declaration

```
register int i;
```

declares **i** as a **register** variable. Making frequently accessed variables **register** usually leads to faster and slightly smaller programs. But **register** is really only a hint, and the compiler is free to ignore our advice.

There are several restrictions on **register** variables. First, we can declare only local variables and function parameters to be **register**, not global variables. Second, since a machine register is usually a single word, many compilers allow only those variables that fit into a single word to be placed in registers. This means that we can normally place only integers or addresses into registers, although the actual types vary from machine to machine. Third, a **register** variable is not kept in memory, so we can't take its address with **&**. That means, for example, that we can't use **scanf** to read a value directly into a **register** variable. And finally, most machines have only a few registers available to user programs, as few as two or three. If we declare a **register** variable that isn't of the right type, or if there aren't enough registers, the compiler simply ignores our advice.

Figure 9.5 uses **register** in a new version of **tableSearch** (from Figure 8.8). This time we place into registers any variable that is accessed each time we go through a loop, such as an index variable. The exception is the table we're searching, since we can't declare an array as **register**.

When we call a function with **register** parameters, we aren't required to supply the **register** as part of its prototype. Even though the function **tableSearch** declares **n** and **t** as **register** parameters,

```
int tableSearch(int a[], register int n, register int t);
```

we can still use its earlier prototype:

```
int tableSearch(int a[], int n, int t)
```

C also allows us one other shortcut. The declaration

```
register i;
```

is a terse equivalent to

```
register int i;
```

```
/*
 * Faster version of array-searching function.
 */
int tableSearch(int a[], register int n, register int t)
{
  register int i;

  for (i = 0; i < n && a[i] != t; i++)
    ;                                         /* search for matching value */
  return (i != n) ? i : -1;
}
```

Figure 9.5 (tabsrch2.c) A new version of the previous chapter's table-searching function. It takes advantage of **register** declarations.

Since there are usually few available registers, carefully select the variables you place in them—if you don't, the compiler will select them for you. If efficiency is an issue, you need to determine which variables are most often used in the functions that take the most time and declare them as **register**.

The Storage Class static

Local variables live only as long as the block in which they reside. But sometimes we need a local variable to retain its value between function calls. Suppose, for example, that we want to modify a function to print a message that includes the number of times it is called. This might be useful when debugging: any output the function produces is then labeled by the call that produced it. To do so, however, the function must somehow maintain a count that it updates each time we call it. One approach is to use a global variable to hold the count, but then the count can be modified by any function.

Figure 9.6 shows our first attempt at writing this function. We simply use a local variable **cnt**, initialized to zero when we declare it,

```
int cnt = 0;
```

and we increment it each time the function is called. Unfortunately, it doesn't work, since **cnt** is initialized to zero *every* time we call **testFunc**. No matter how many times we call it, it still writes a 1.

The trick to fixing this problem is to give **cnt** the storage class **static**,

```
static int cnt = 0;
```

as we've done in Figure 9.7. A **static** local variable lives as long as the program containing it does. Space for it is allocated and initialized once, conceptually at compile time. The rules for **static** initialization are the same as for globals: they start at zero by default, but we can provide an initializing action that will take effect once, when the program begins execution.

```
/*
 * Keep a count of times function is called (buggy version).
 */
#include <stdio.h>
#include <stdlib.h>

int main()
{
  void testFunc(void);

  testFunc(); testFunc(); testFunc();

  return EXIT_SUCCESS;
}

void testFunc(void)
{
  int cnt = 0;

  printf("testFunc call #%i\n", ++cnt);
}
```

Figure 9.6   (tstfnc1.c) An incorrect try at counting function calls. No matter how many times we call it, it always writes a 1.

```
/*
 * Keep a count of times function is called (working version).
 */
#include <stdio.h>
#include <stdlib.h>

int main()
{
  void testFunc(void);

  testFunc(); testFunc(); testFunc();

  return EXIT_SUCCESS;
}

void testFunc(void)
{
  static int cnt = 0;

  printf("testFunc call #%i\n", ++cnt);
}
```

Figure 9.7   (tstfnc2.c) Correct version of a function that counts and prints the number of times it's called.

Aside 9.1a: Registers and Efficiency

So just how important is using **register**? With many compilers, it is much less important that you might think.

To help us gauge the effect of using **register** with the C compilers on our machines, we wrote a simple program, shown in Aside 9.1b, that performs 10,000 searches of a 10,000-element table using our **tableSearch** function. We then formed a variety of different executables for each of the compilers available on our machine. In particular, we compiled versions of **tableSearch** with and without using **register** and with and without compiler optimization turned on, and we linked each of these different versions with our main program. This allowed us to assess the impact of **register** on the efficiency of the **tableSearch** function. Here are the results of this effort.

WHICH COMPILER	USING **register**?	TURNED ON OPTIMIZATION?	TIME IN **tableSearch**
gcc	off	no	23.32
gcc	on	no	14.90
gcc	off	yes	5.09
gcc	on	yes	5.08
cc	off	no	16.19
cc	on	no	8.09
cc	off	yes	5.07
cc	on	yes	5.06

It turns out that with unoptimized compiles, using **register** makes a big difference, cutting the execution time by 40–50%, depending on the compiler. However, for optimized compiles, using **register** results in only a tiny improvement, not even 1%. The real improvement comes from requesting an optimized compilation (which makes sense, as many compilers spend significant time in register allocation as part of the optimization process). The bottom line is that we should compile our programs using optimization before worrying about **register**, and only if our program is still executing too slowly do we need to start worrying about placing variables in registers.

In the new version of **testFunc**, **cnt** is assigned a zero when the program starts. Each time we call **testFunc**, it increments and prints **cnt**. Since **cnt** is **static**, its value is preserved across calls. So the first time we call **testFunc**, it writes a 1, the next time a 2, and so on.

Figure 9.8 provides a more realistic use of **static** variables. It's a little program that line-numbers its input and writes a page number on the top of every page. This program is broken into two pieces: a **main** program that reads a character at a time and a function **dumpChar** to print each character, keeping track of the number of lines and pages written and writing a page number at the top of every new page. The idea behind

Aside 9.1b (usesrch.c) A program that repeatedly calls our table-searching function.

```
/*
 * A main program to use our table searching function.
 */
#include <stdio.h>
#include <stdlib.h>

#define MAX_ENTRIES 10000

int main()
{
  int tableSearch(int a[], int n, int t);

  int table[MAX_ENTRIES];
  int i;

  for (i = 0; i < MAX_ENTRIES; i++)     /* initialize the table */
    table[i] = i;

  /* loop to do MAX_ENTRIES searches, each time going further
     in the table */

  for (i = 0; i < MAX_ENTRIES; i++)
    if (i != tableSearch(table, MAX_ENTRIES, i))
      printf("Problem: table[i] != i\n");

  return EXIT_SUCCESS;
}
```

dumpChar is to encapsulate all line numbering and page handling in a single function, so that the main program worries only about reading and writing characters. **dumpChar** keeps the page number and line numbers in **static** variables, **pageno** and **lineno**, so that their values remain between successive calls to it. They are initialized to zero once, before we ever call **dumpChar**. Because **static** and global variables are initialized to zero by default, explicitly setting them to zero is not necessary, but for readability we do so anyway.

The Storage Class **extern**

In our character-counting program, we conveniently defined the global table **charcnts** before either of the functions **main** and **printCounters** that used it.

```
unsigned long charcnts[UCHAR_MAX + 1];
```

This definition does two things. It allocates storage for the table, and it provides the type information necessary to access the table simply by referring to it by name.

```
/*
 * Print lines with automatic page and line numbering.
 */
#include <stdio.h>
#include <stdlib.h>

#define PAGELEN  60                              /* page length */

int main()
{
  void dumpChar(int c);

  int  c;                                        /* next input character */

  for (; (c = getchar()) != EOF; dumpChar(c))
    ;

  return EXIT_SUCCESS;
}

void dumpChar(int c)
{
  static int pageno = 0;                         /* current page number */
  static int lastch = '\n';                      /* last char read */
  static unsigned long lineno = 0;               /* current line number */

  if (lastch == '\n')                            /* beginning of line */
  {
    if (lineno % PAGELEN == 0)
      printf("\fPage: %i\n\n", ++pageno);        /* new page */
    printf("%8lu ", ++lineno);
  }
  putchar(lastch = c);
}
```

Figure 9.8 (pagenum.c) A program to page-number its input.

If **charcnts** is defined later in the file or in another file, we need some other mechanism to provide the necessary type information to the functions accessing it. To do so, we declare each global variable within the functions using it, preceded by the storage class specifier **extern** (but without size information for arrays):

```
extern unsigned long charcnts[];
```

This *external declaration* tells the compiler the type of the variable and that the compiler should assume space for it is allocated elsewhere. Because external declarations don't allocate space, we need not provide bounds for the array.

Figures 9.9 and 9.10 contain a new version of our character-counting program that's split into a pair of files. In charcnt1.c, we define the array of counters, **charcnts**,

```
/*
 * Counts the different characters in its input (separate compilation).
 */
#include <stdio.h>
#include <stdlib.h>
#include <limits.h>

unsigned long charcnts[UCHAR_MAX + 1];          /* 0...UCHAR_MAX */
int            chars = UCHAR_MAX + 1;

int main()
{
  void printCounters(void);

  int   c;

  while(c = getchar(), c != EOF)
    charcnts[c]++;
  printCounters();

  return EXIT_SUCCESS;
}
```

Figure 9.9   (charcnt1.c) A character-counting program that uses global variables.

```
/*
 * Function to print the character counts.
 */
#include <stdio.h>
#include <ctype.h>

void printCounters(void)
{
  extern unsigned long charcnts[];              /* table of counts */
  extern int           chars;                   /* entries in table */
  int                  i;

  for (i = 0; i < chars; i++)
    if (charcnts[i])                   /* write count only when nonzero */
    {
      printf("\\%03o ", i);
      isprint(i) ? printf("(%c)", i) : printf("   ");
      printf(": %lu\n", charcnts[i]);
    }
}
```

Figure 9.10   (prcnt1.c) The function to print the table of character counts. It uses external declarations to access the global variables for the table and the count of items in it.

and the **main** program. We also define a new global, **chars**, which holds the number of items in the array. In prcnt1.c, we define **printCounters**, the function used to display the table. To access the globals defined in the other file, it contains a pair of external declarations:

```
extern unsigned long charcnts[];
extern int            chars;
```

These declarations leave the linker to resolve the references.

Similarly, **main** provides an external declaration for the function **printCounters**, leaving the linker to fill in that reference as well. For function decalarations, however, we need not provide the **extern**, as these declarations are **extern** by default.

An **extern** within a function provides type information to just that one function. We can provide the type information to all functions within a file by placing external declarations before any of them. We've done so in the new version of our character-counting program shown in Figures 9.11 and 9.12.

> *Define a global variable exactly once and use external declarations everywhere else.*

A global definition (where we don't preface the variable's type with **extern**) allocates storage. But we can declare a global with **extern** as often as needed, since a global declaration merely provides type information and doesn't allocate any storage. We don't need these declarations, however, if the global variable is defined before the functions that use it. That's because a global variable definition also declares the variable's type.

The distinction between *definition* and *declaration* also applies to functions. We *define* a function when we specify its parameters and function body, which causes the compiler to allocate space for the function's code and provides type information for its parameters. We *declare* a function when we provide a prototype, but we don't need the **extern**, since functions are external by default. The declaration

```
void printCounters(void);
```

is equivalent to

```
extern void printCounters(void);
```

Function declarations outside of any function work the same way as variable declarations outside of any function—they provide the necessary type information to all functions in the source file. So if we supply prototypes once, at the top of the source file, we don't have to supply them within each of the functions. Of course, a function definition also supplies that type information, which means we can avoid providing prototypes by defining a function before any of the functions that use them.

What happens when we fail to provide the necessary external declarations? If we don't declare a global variable, the compiler complains about its being undefined the first time it encounters it. Here, that means failing to declare **charcnts** results in

```
/*
 * A new version of our character counting program.
 */
#include <stdio.h>
#include <stdlib.h>
#include <limits.h>

unsigned long charcnts[UCHAR_MAX + 1];   /* 0...UCHAR_MAX */
int            chars = UCHAR_MAX + 1;

void printCounters(void);

int main()
{
  int c;

  while(c = getchar(), c != EOF)
    charcnts[c]++;
  printCounters();

  return EXIT_SUCCESS;
}
```

Figure 9.11   (charcnt2.c) A simpler version of our character-counting program.

```
/*
 * A new version of the function to print the character counts.
 */
#include <stdio.h>
#include <ctype.h>

extern unsigned long charcnts[];   /* table of counts */
extern int            chars;       /* entries in table */

void printCounters(void)
{
  int i;

  for (i = 0; i < chars; i++)
    if (charcnts[i])        /* write count only when nonzero */
    {
      printf("\\%03o ", i);
      isprint(i) ? printf("(%c)", i) : printf("   ");
      printf(": %lu\n", charcnts[i]);
    }
}
```

Figure 9.12   (prcnt2.c) A simpler version of the function to print the table of character counts.

an "undefined variable" error the first time we use it. With a function, however, the compiler assumes it returns an **int** and knows nothing about its arguments, which means that it can't do any type checking or assignment conversions of its parameters. Here, that's not a problem, although we generally want those features. We provide prototypes for *all* our functions, even those that take no arguments and return **int**.

9.4   TYPE QUALIFIERS

Storage classes provide information about a variable's lifetime and visibility. *Type qualifiers* provide additional information about how the variable is going to be used. There are two type qualifiers: **const** and **volatile**. We use them by placing one of these keywords in front of the variable's type.

const specifies that a particular object is not supposed to change. For example,

```
const int PAGELEN = 60;
```

declares **PAGELEN** as an **int** and tells the compiler that its value should remain constant throughout its lifetime. This causes the compiler to forbid any assignments to **PAGELEN** (including trying to increment or decrement it), except for the initializing declaration. This means we have to provide initial values for objects declared as **const**.

We can also use **const** to declare constant arrays; that is, arrays whose elements won't be modified. Our earlier function **dayCalc** could be improved with a new declaration for **days**.

```
const int days[] = {31, 28, 31, 30, 31, 30,
                    31, 31, 30, 31, 30, 31};
```

It's now an error to attempt to change an element of **days**, as in

```
days[1] = 29;
```

We aren't limited to declaring array variables as **const**; we can also use **const** to indicate that a function doesn't change its array parameters. We do so in Figure 9.13, a new version of our earlier character-counting program. This time we have the array of counters as a local variable, rather than as a global, and pass it to the function **printCounters** to print. The function doesn't modify the array it's passed, so we've now defined it to take a constant array of integers:

```
void printCounters(const unsigned long charcnts[])
```

When we create a function with a **const** parameter, the function's prototype must also declare that parameter as **const**.

We're allowed to pass a non-**const** array to a function expecting a **const** array; C simply treats the array as a **const** inside the function. The array, **charcnts**, we pass **printCounters** is not a **const** array. But the compiler will warn us if we pass a **const** array when the corresponding array parameter hasn't been declared as **const**, as in

```
n = tableFill(days, 12);
```

```
/*
 * A version of the character-counting program carefully using const.
 */
#include <stdio.h>
#include <stdlib.h>
#include <ctype.h>
#include <limits.h>

int main()
{
  void printCounters(const unsigned long charcnts[]);

  static unsigned long charcnts[UCHAR_MAX + 1];        /* 0...UCHAR_MAX */
  int    c;

  while(c = getchar(), c != EOF)
    charcnts[c]++;
  printCounters(charcnts);

  return EXIT_SUCCESS;
}

void printCounters(const unsigned long charcnts[])
{
  int i;

  for (i = 0; i < UCHAR_MAX; i++)
    if (charcnts[i])                        /* write count only when nonzero */
    {
      printf("\\%03o ", i);
      isprint(i) ? printf("(%c)", i) : printf("   ");
      printf(": %lu\n", charcnts[i]);
    }
}
```

Figure 9.13 (charcnt3.c) Yet another version of our character-counting program. This time we're careful to make sure the array is passed to **printCounters** as a constant.

We prefer **const** to **#define** for defining named constants, since it allows us to easily limit the constant's scope. **const** also allows the compiler to flag as an error any attempt to assign a value to that variable.[4]

const, however, doesn't completely eliminate the need for **#define**. We can't use a **const** in any expression that must be evaluated at compile time, such as a subscript in an array declaration or an initializing expression for a global variable. In Chapter 8's array-manipulating programs, for example, we used

        #define MAXVALS 100

---
[4]In fact, it lets the compiler put the constant in read-only memory.

to define the number of elements in **table**. We can't replace that definition with

```
const int MAXVALS = 100;
```

The other type qualifier, **volatile**, is the opposite of **const**. It means that the value could change at any time and that the compiler should be aware of this when doing optimizations. We use **volatile** only when we have a variable that's being updated by external sources, such as operating system functions or interrupt routines.

9.5   USER-DEFINED TYPES

Type qualifiers are useful, but they can also make our type declarations rather lengthy. One way to simplify these declarations is with a new C facility, **typedef**, which allows us to define synonyms for existing types. A **typedef** looks like a variable declaration except that we replace the variable name with the name of the new type. For example, we can define **Counter** as a synonym for **unsigned long** with

```
typedef unsigned long Counter;
```

Similarly,

```
typedef int Index;
```

defines **Index** as as synonym for **int**.

We can then use these types as if they are built-in types such as **int** or **double**. The declaration

```
Index i;
```

declares **i** to be an **int**.

Figure 9.14 takes advantage of these **typedef**s to improve Figure 9.13.   For example, we define the **Counter** type and use it in declaring **main**'s table of counters,

```
static Counter charcnts[UCHAR_MAX + 1];
```

and **printCounters**'s parameter.

```
void printCounters(const Counter charcnts[])
```

In this case, **Counter** is not only less typing than **unsigned long**, but it also makes clear what the underlying type is being used for, increasing the readability of our program.

typedefs usually appear outside of any function, at the top of the source file, and are in effect from the **typedef** until the end of the file. It is also possible to define types known about only within a particular function, but this technique is infrequently used.

```
/*
 * One final version of the character-counting program.
 */
#include <stdio.h>
#include <stdlib.h>
#include <ctype.h>
#include <limits.h>

typedef unsigned long Counter;
typedef int Index;

int main()
{
  void printCounters(const Counter charcnts[]);

  static Counter charcnts[UCHAR_MAX + 1];      /* 0...UCHAR_MAX */
  int     c;

  while (c = getchar(), c != EOF)
    charcnts[c]++;
  printCounters(charcnts);

  return EXIT_SUCCESS;
}

void printCounters(const Counter charcnts[])
{
  Index i;

  for (i = 0; i < UCHAR_MAX; i++)
    if (charcnts[i])                      /* write count only when nonzero */
    {
      printf("\\%03o ", i);
      isprint(i) ? printf("(%c)", i) : printf("   ");
      printf(": %lu\n", charcnts[i]);
    }
}
```

Figure 9.14 (charcnt4.c) A final version of our character-counting program. This time we use **typedef**s to try to improve the program's readability.

9.6   HEADER FILES

We've seen how to use explicit external declarations to access variables and functions defined in other files. Another approach is to put those declarations into header files.

We'll illustrate the difference between these approaches with a pair of multi-file versions of our earlier **yesOrNo** program: the first using explicit declarations, the second using a header file. Figure 9.15 is useyn3.c, the **main** function that uses

```
/*
 * Main program using yes or no.
 */
#include <stdio.h>
#include <stdlib.h>

int main()
{
  int yesOrNo(void);

  extern const int YES, NO, BAD;

  int answer;

  printf("Enter a YES or NO answer: ");
  if ((answer = yesOrNo()) == YES)
    printf("YES!\n");
  else if (answer == NO)
    printf("NO!\n");
  else if (answer == BAD)
    printf("END OF FILE!\n");
  else
    printf("UNKNOWN!\n");

  return EXIT_SUCCESS;
}
```

Figure 9.15 (useyn3.c) A main program accessing **yesOrNo** using explicit external declarations.

yesOrNo to obtain a yes or no answer from its user. Figure 9.16 is a source file that contains the **yesOrNo** function and a pair of global constants, **YES** and **NO**, that it returns. Since **main** calls **yesOrNo**, it must provide its prototype,

```
int yesOrNo(void);
```

along with external declarations for the constants **YES** and **NO**.

```
extern const int YES, NO;
```

One problem with this approach is that every function (or source file) using **yesOrNo** must provide these declarations. Another problem is that if we want to use **typedef** to define a type for **yesOrNo**'s return value (such as **Response**), we have to repeat the **typedef** in every source file.

A better approach is to put these declarations into a header file, which we then include in any source file calling **yesOrNo**. Figure 9.17 is this header file, yesorno.h. This header file also defines a new type **Response**, a synonym for **int**, which we use to declare **yesOrNo**'s return value.

Figure 9.18 is useyn4.c, a file containing a new version of the main program using **yesOrNo** that simply includes this header file.

```
/*
 * Get a yes or no answer from the user.
 */
#include <stdio.h>
#include <ctype.h>

const int YES = 1, NO = 0, BAD = -1;

int yesOrNo(void)
{
  void skipToEOL(int current_char);

  int answer;                                /* holds input character */

  while ((answer = tolower(getchar())) != EOF)
  {
    skipToEOL(answer);
    if (answer == 'y' || answer == 'n')
      return (answer == 'y') ? YES : NO;
    printf("Please answer with a YES or NO!\n");
  }
  return BAD;
}
```

Figure 9.16   (yesorno6.c) Our **yesOrNo** function.

```
/*
 * Prototypes and constants for "yesorno".
 */
typedef int Response;

extern const Response YES;
extern const Response NO;
extern const Response BAD;

Response yesOrNo(void);
```

Figure 9.17   (yesorno.h) A header file defining a prototype for **yesOrNo** and providing external declarations for the constants it uses.

```
/*
 * Main program using yesOrNo, this time using a header file
 * to provide external declarations.
 */
#include <stdio.h>
#include <stdlib.h>
#include "yesorno.h"

int main()
{
  Response answer;

  printf("Enter a YES or NO answer: ");
  if ((answer = yesOrNo()) == YES)
    printf("YES!\n");
  else if (answer == NO)
    printf("NO!\n");
  else if (answer == BAD)
    printf("END OF FILE!\n");
  else
    printf("UNKNOWN!\n");

  return EXIT_SUCCESS;
}
```

Figure 9.18 (useyn4.c) A main program accessing **yesOrNo** using a header file. This is substantially less effort than providing the necessary declarations explicitly.

We now use a slightly different form of **#include**.

```
#include "yesorno.h"
```

We surround yesorno.h by quotation marks instead of angle brackets to indicate that it is our own include file, and not one that is system supplied. That way the preprocessor will search our files first, before searching the standard system locations for it.

Figure 9.19 is yesorno7.c, a new version of the **yesOrNo** function that uses the **Response** type. As a result, it also includes yesorno.h. However, we would want to include this header file even if **yesOrNo** didn't require the **Response** definition. Why? Because by including yesorno.h in yesorno7.c, we guarantee that its prototype matches its definition and that the compiler will catch any inconsistencies. If we don't, it's possible that the prototype we include in **main** won't match the function's actual definition, leading to hard-to-find errors.

> *Include a header file containing a function's prototype in both the files that call the function and the file that defines it.*

```
/*
 * Get a yes or no answer from the user.
 */
#include <stdio.h>
#include <ctype.h>
#include "yesorno.h"

const Response YES = 1, NO = 0, BAD = -1;

Response yesOrNo(void)
{
  void skipToEOL(int current_char);

  int answer;                              /* holds input character */

  while ((answer = tolower(getchar())) != EOF)
  {
    skipToEOL(answer);
    if (answer == 'y' || answer == 'n')
      return (answer == 'y') ? YES : NO;
    printf("Please answer with a YES or NO!\n");
  }
  return BAD;
}
```

Figure 9.19 (yesorno7.c) A new version of our **yesOrNo** function that makes use of a header file to define shared constants and to provide its prototype.

9.7   PRIVATE VARIABLES AND FUNCTIONS

So far, we've had two types of variables: local variables accessible only within a function and global variables accessible to any function, even one in a different file. For modularity, however, we sometimes want to have variables and functions that are accessible only to the functions within a single file, not to functions in other files.

We'll illustrate these *private* globals with a program that computes the average time riders must wait for a bus. Its input describes the time that either a person or bus arrived at the bus stop, and consists of triplets of integers. The first integer is a code (0 indicates a person, 1 a bus), the second is the arrival time, and the third indicates how many people arrived or how many seats were available on the bus. The program's output identifies the arrivals and prints the total number of riders and the average waiting time. Figure 9.20 contains some sample input and output for the program.

Implementing Queues

The program simulates a line of people waiting for a bus. When a person arrives, it saves their arrival time. When a bus arrives, it lets those who have waited the longest onto

```
0 2 2
2 people arrived at time 2
0 6 1
1 people arrived at time 6
0 7 4
4 people arrived at time 7
1 7 5
Bus arrived at time 7 (5 seats)
0 8 2
2 people arrived at time 8
0 8 9
9 people arrived at time 8
1 15 13
Bus arrived at time 15 (13 seats)
18 riders waited 104, average wait 5.78
```

Figure 9.20   Some sample I/O for our program to simulate arrivals and departures at a bus stop.

the bus first and updates a count of the total waiting time. We use a queue to store these arrival times. A queue is a "first-in, first-out" data structure that behaves like a line for a movie: the people who arrive first are at the front, and those who arrive last are at the back. We implement three queue operations: **enqueue** adds an item to the rear of the queue, **dequeue** takes an item off the front of the queue, and **emptyqueue** returns nonzero if the queue is empty. Queues are generally useful, so we place these functions in a separate file, queues.c, and provide a header file, queues.h, that contains their prototypes. Figure 9.21 contains queues.h and Figure 9.22 contains queues.c.

How can we implement a queue? The simplest way is as an array and a count. Adding an item is easy: we increment the count and add the item to the array's end. But deleting an item is difficult: not only do we have to decrement the count, but we also have to shift all array elements over one place. Alternatively, we can maintain two indices into the array: **f** indexes its first item, and **r** indexes its last. Adding an element is still easy: we increment **r** and place a value at the location it indexes. But now deleting an item is also easy: we simply increment **f** and return the item it indexed.

Actually, we've ignored something: the queue is actually a moving subsection of the array. After enqueueing three items and dequeueing two of them, the first item in the queue is actually the third item in the array. This queue movement means that whenever **f** or **r** indexes the array's last element, updating either should cause the index being updated to index the array's first element. To handle this case, **enqueue** and **dequeue** both use a function **next** to return the appropriate index value.

How and where should we declare the queue and its indices? All of the functions in queues.c use them, so we must declare them outside of any of these functions. The problem is that functions in other files can also access these globals. All they have to do is provide an appropriate external declaration.

```
extern int queue[], f, r;
```

```
/*
 * Prototypes for our queue functions.
 */
void enqueue(int item);              /* add item to queue */
int  dequeue(void);                  /* take item away from queue */
int  emptyqueue(void);               /* is queue empty? */
```

Figure 9.21   (queues.h)   The header file for the queues package.

```
/*
 * Simple queue manager, no error checking.
 */
#include "queues.h"               /* queue prototypes */

#define MAXQUEUE 100              /* number of queue items */

static int queue[MAXQUEUE];       /* the queue itself */
static int f, r;                  /* indices to queue front and end */

static int next(int i);

void enqueue(int item)            /* add item to end of queue */
{
  queue[r] = item;
  r = next(r);
}

int dequeue(void)                 /* delete first item in queue */
{
  int temp = queue[f];

  f = next(f);
  return temp;
}

int emptyqueue(void)              /* is queue empty? */
  { return f == r; }

/* PRIVATE: returns index to next item, handling wraparound */

static int next(int i)
  { return (i + 1 < MAXQUEUE) ? i + 1 : 0; }
```

Figure 9.22   (queues.c)   The source file for managing queues.

We would prefer to have these variables visible only to the functions implementing the queue operators, not to the entire outside world. That's because we want to be able to change how we implement queues without having to worry about whether some function, somewhere, takes advantage of our particular implementation. But how can we limit access to the queue variables to the single source file in which they're defined?

The trick is to declare those variables as **static**.

```
static int queue[MAXQUEUE];
static int f, r;
```

static variables and functions are not made available to the linker. Since the linker doesn't know about them, it can't resolve any external references to them made in other files. That means only the queue-handling functions can access **queue**, **f**, and **r**. For the same reason, we also declare the function **next** to be **static**. That way it can't be called directly from functions in other files, preventing accidental name conflicts and keeping outside functions from sneakily accessing the queue.

We've placed **next**'s prototype before any of its callers. Unfortunately, we're not allowed to place prototypes for **static** functions inside other functions, so the only other alternative would be to define **next** before defining its callers.

Implementing Our Bus Stop Simulator

Besides queues.c and queues.h, our program consists of files containing definitions for global variables and other functions (wait.c and handle.c), external declarations for the global variables (wait.h), and prototypes for the other functions (handle.h).

wait.c contains the **main** program and definitions for two global counters: one for the total number of riders, another for the total number of minutes they've waited.

```
unsigned long riders;
unsigned long waiting;
```

main handles reading the input, invokes the functions **person** or **bus** to process each new arrival, and prints the final statistics.

handle.c contains **person** and **bus**. These functions handle the arrival of new riders or buses by using **enqueue** and **dequeue** to add or delete arrival times from the queue. They also update the counts of riders and the total waiting time. That means these counters have to be accessed in two source files: wait.c, where we define and print them, and handle.c, where we update them.

One way to share these variables among files is to include external declarations for the counters in **person** and **bus**, the functions that access them. That's similar to what we did in our character-counting program. But, in general, a better to way to share globals in a set of source files is to define them in one file and to create a header file that provides their external declarations. We then include this header file whenever we reference the globals.

wait.h is the header file that contains the needed external declarations:

```
extern unsigned long riders;
extern unsigned long waiting;
```

We include this header file in both places that refer to these globals: wait.c and handle.c. In a small program with only a few globals, it's not clear how we're better off with the added complications of a header file. But in larger programs it's much easier to include a header file than it is to explicitly provide the external declarations. In addition, by including the header file in the source file defining the globals, we guarantee our external declarations are correct.

handle.h is the final file in our program. It contains the prototypes for **person** and **bus**. We include this file in both source files. In wait.c, it supplies the prototypes we need to successfully call the functions. In handle.c, it causes the compiler to make sure our prototypes match our function definitions.

Figure 9.23 contains wait.h, Figure 9.24 contains wait.c, Figure 9.25 contains handle.h, and Figure 9.26 contains handle.c. To make the executable program, we need to link together the object modules for queues.c, wait.c, and handle.c.

9.8   CASE STUDY—ABSTRACT DATA TYPES

This section is optional!

One possible criticism of C compared with other high-level languages is its lack of a "set" data type. A set is simply an unordered collection of values, without duplications, with certain operations defined on it. Some of the more common operations are adding and deleting values and testing to determine if a value is in a set. We conclude this chapter by implementing these set operations and a program that uses them.

We implement sets as an *abstract data type* by creating a **Set** data type and functions for the various set operations. Programs using sets know only the names of these operations, restrictions on their use, and the order and expected type of their parameters. To hide the details of their implementation from their users, we package the set operations in a single module we compile separately. This allows us to change the implementation or add operations without having to rewrite the programs using them.

The concept of an abstract data type shouldn't seem strange. We have been using **float**s and **double**s without knowing either their internal representation or the implementation details of operators such as **+** or **/**.

Implementing Sets

We implement sets as a bit array, one bit per set element. C doesn't provide bit arrays, but we can simulate them using an array of **unsigned short**s. To access the bit corresponding to a given set element, we have to determine its location: the array element that contains the bit, and where that bit is located within that array element. We do so by dividing the set element by the number of bits in an **unsigned short**; the remainder is the bit's position within the array element. Figure 9.27 shows a sample computation. With this representation, the set operations are simple. We add an element to a set by turning on the bit it indexes and delete it by turning that bit off. And we check membership by examining the bit's value.

```
/*
 * Declarations for shared counters.
 */
extern unsigned long riders;            /* people on bus */
extern unsigned long waiters;           /* people waiting for bus */
```

Figure 9.23   (wait.h) Definitions of shared counters of bus riders and people waiting for a bus.

```
/*
 * Compute average waiting time of riders of a bus.
 */
#include <stdio.h>
#include <stdlib.h>
#include "wait.h"
#include "handle.h"

unsigned long riders;                   /* total riders */
unsigned long waiters;                  /* total waiting time */

int main()
{
  int  code,                            /* transaction code */
       time,                            /* event time */
       count;                           /* room on bus, people at stop */

  while (scanf("%i %i %i", &code, &time, &count) == 3)
    switch(code)
      {
      case 0:  person(time, count);
               break;
      case 1:  bus(time, count);
               break;
      default: printf("Invalid code of %i\n", code);
               break;
      }
  if (riders == 0)
    printf("No riders ever showed up.\n");
  else
    printf("%lu riders waited %lu, average wait %.2f\n",
           riders, waiters, (double) waiters / riders);

  return EXIT_SUCCESS;
}
```

Figure 9.24   (wait.c) The main program for bus simulator.

```
/*
 * Prototypes for functions to update appropriate counters.
 */
void person(int time, int persons);
void bus(int time, int capacity);
```

Figure 9.25 (handle.h) The prototypes for the functions to handle updating counters.

```
/*
 * Functions to update riders and waiting time.
 *    person - add a new set of riders to a bus stop.
 *    bus - take away a set of riders from a bus stop.
 */
#include <stdio.h>
#include "queues.h"
#include "wait.h"
#include "handle.h"

void person(int time, int newpeople)
{
  riders += newpeople;
  printf("%i people arrived at time %i\n", newpeople, time);
  while (newpeople--)
    enqueue(time);
}

void bus(int time, int capacity)
{
  printf("Bus arrived at time %i (%i seats)\n", time, capacity);
  while (!emptyqueue() && capacity--)
    waiters += time - dequeue();
}
```

Figure 9.26 (handle.c) The functions to handle updating counters.

The Set Type and Its Operations

Programs using sets don't have to know that they are implemented as a bit array. In fact, we want programs to be able to declare a **Set** type as if the language provided one. To do so, we define our **Set** data type using **typedef**:

```
typedef unsigned short Set[MAXELEMS/US_BITS];
```

This **typedef** makes **Set** a synonym for an array of **unsigned short**s. The number of elements in the array is the number of items in the set divided by the number of bits in an **unsigned short**.

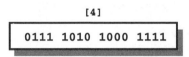

[0]	[1]	[2]	[3]	[4]
0-15	16-31	32-47	48-63	64-79	· · ·

(*a*)   Element 69 is in word 4 (69 / 16)

[4]

```
0111 1010 1000 1111
```

(*b*)   Element 69 is bit 5 in word 4 (69 % 16)

Figure 9.27   Locating the bit representing a set element, here, 69. First we select the array element and then the bit within it.

Figure 9.28 shows the header file sets.h, in which we've defined the **Set** type, as well as the prototypes for the set operations. As expected, we have to include sets.h in all files containing functions that manipulate sets.

Figure 9.29 is the file sets.c, containing the set operations: initializing a set (setting all entries in the representation to zero), adding an element to a set (turning its bit on), deleting an element from a set (turning its bit off), and determining whether an element is a member of a set (checking whether its bit is on).

We build the basic set operations on top of a pair of functions: **word** returns the index of the array element containing the desired set element, and **bit** returns its bit position within that **unsigned short**. Because these functions are internal to the **Set** type's implementation, we keep them hidden by declaring them as **static**.[5]

Most of the set operations modify the **Set** passed to them (since a **Set** is an array, they can modify its elements). The sole exception is **setMember**, so we've made its **Set** parameter a **const** to protect against accidental change.

Using Sets

Figure 9.30 uses sets in a program that partitions its input into values that appear once and those that appear many times. We could use this program to verify that no identification number appears more than once. Figure 9.31 shows the program's output for the input:

```
8 99 99 245 0 99 501 99 309 17 410 17
```

The program uses two **Set**s: **unique** contains the values appearing once, and **dup** contains the duplicates. The program reads each value and checks whether it is a

---

[5]We've placed the **static** functions in the file before the definition of their callers. This eliminates the need to provide prototypes for them. We've done that simply to shrink the program's size.

```
/*
 * Definitions to use "sets" of integers.
 */
#define US_BITS     16             /* bits in unsigned short */
#define MAXELEMS   512             /* set items, must be multiple of 16 */

typedef unsigned short Set[MAXELEMS/US_BITS];

extern void setInit(Set s);
extern void setAdd(Set s, int e);
extern void setDelete(Set s, int e);
extern int  setMember(const Set s, int e);
```

Figure 9.28   (sets.h) The header file for sets.

```
/*
 * The functions to handle sets.
 */
#include "sets.h"

static int word(int elem)                  /* word # containing element */
  { return elem / US_BITS; }

static int bit(int elem)
  { return elem % US_BITS; }                /* bit # containing element */

void setInit(Set s)                        /* initialize set to empty */
{
  int i;

  for (i = 0; i < MAXELEMS / US_BITS; s[i++] = 0)
    ;
}

void setAdd(Set s, int elem)               /* add element to set */
  { s[word(elem)] |= 1 << bit(elem); }

void setDelete(Set s, int elem)            /* delete element from set */
  { s[word(elem)] &= ~(1 << bit(elem)); }

int setMember(const Set s, int elem)    /* is element in set? */
  { return ((unsigned) s[word(elem)] >> bit(elem)) & 01; }
```

Figure 9.29   (sets.c) An implementation of a simple sets package.

```
/*
 * Identify duplicates in the input.
 */
#include <stdio.h>
#include <stdlib.h>
#include "sets.h"
#include "setutils.h"              /* for setPrint, setSwitch */

int main()
{
  Set   unique, dup;              /* unique and duplicate elements */
  int   r, inp;                   /* scanf return, input value */

  setInit(unique);  setInit(dup);
  while ((r = scanf("%i", &inp)) != EOF)
  {
    if (r != 1)                   /* verify read value at all */
    {
      printf("Value in error.\n");
      break;
    }
    if (inp < 0 || inp >= MAXELEMS)
    {
      printf("Value out of range.\n");
      continue;
    }
    if (setMember(unique, inp))        /* a value in unique already */
      setSwitch(dup, unique, inp);     /*   gets moved to dup */
    else if (!setMember(dup, inp))     /* a value not in either */
      setAdd(unique, inp);             /*   gets added to unique */
  }
  printf("Unique values\n");
  setPrint(unique);
  printf("Duplicate values\n");
  setPrint(dup);

  return EXIT_SUCCESS;
}
```

Figure 9.30 (usesets.c) A program to check for duplicate input values.

member of **unique**. If it is, we remove it from **unique** and add it to **dup**. Otherwise, we simply add it to **unique**. When finished, we print the members of these two sets. To print a set, we run through all possible set values, printing those values that are set members.

The program uses two new functions built on top of the existing **Set** operations. **setSwitch** moves an element from one set to another, modifying both of the **Set**s passed to it. **setPrint** runs through a set, printing all of its elements. It doesn't modify

```
Unique values
0
8
245
309
410
501
Duplicate values
17
99
```

Figure 9.31   Sample output for our program to use sets.

the **Set** passed to it, so we've made that **Set** a **const**. We place these functions in a separate source file and provide a header file with their prototypes. Figure 9.32 is the header file; Figure 9.33 is the source file.

SUMMARY

- C lets us declare variables in any block. These variables have visibility only within that block and exist only throughout the life of the block.

- C also lets us declare variables outside of any function. These variables are visible throughout the remainder of the source file. They can also be accessed from other files through the use of external declarations.

- C lets us initialize variables when we declare them. With local variables, we can provide any expression. With global variables, we're restricted to those expressions that are evaluable at compile time.

- C allows us to specify that variables are constants. When we do so, we must initialize them when we declare them.

- We can place external declarations and constant definitions in header files that are included by the modules requiring them.

- We can have variables and functions local to a single source file by declaring them outside of any function and prefacing them with the storage class **static**.

- We implement abstract data types by defining the operations in a single source file and putting their external declarations in a header file. This way the functions using the data type aren't privy to the details of their implementation.

```
/*
 * Prototypes for set utility functions
 */
void setSwitch(Set new, Set old, int value);
void setPrint(const Set set);
```

Figure 9.32 (setutils.h) The prototypes for a pair of useful utility functions for manipulating sets.

```
/*
 * Utility functions for manipulating sets.
 */
#include <stdio.h>
#include "sets.h"
#include "setutils.h"

void setSwitch(Set new, Set old, int value)
{
  setDelete(old, value);
  setAdd(new, value);
}

void setPrint(const Set set)
{
  int i;                              /* next potential element */

  for (i = 0; i < MAXELEMS; i++)
    if (setMember(set, i))
      printf("%i\n", i);
}
```

Figure 9.33 (setutils.c) Two useful utility functions for manipulating sets.

EXERCISES

9–1 Compile and run the programs in this chapter.

9–2 Can you determine what values local variables start out with on your machine? Is it a good idea to rely on that behavior?

Modify

9–3 Modify the programs in this chapter to limit the scope of any index variables used. Does this make those loops more readable? Does this make these programs more or less compact?

9–4 Rewrite several programs from earlier chapters to initialize variables where they're declared and use **const** where appropriate. Does this make these programs more or less readable?

Aside 9.2: The Benefits of Abstract Data Types

The key idea underlying abstract data types is that we should separate the details of a data type's implementation from the details of its use, a concept called *information hiding*. We do this in C by breaking our definition of a data type into two pieces: a header file describing it, and the source file that actually implements it. The header file contains the prototypes for the functions that work on the data type, along with a **typedef** that defines a name for the data type. Programs that use the data type need only include this header file and link in the object module that implements the functions that manipulate the type. If we don't provide the source file, programmers using the type will not know exactly how the type is implemented!

This separation leads to simpler, more readable, more maintainable programs. The program in Figure 9.30, for example, would be considerably more complex and consequently harder to understand if it also contained the definition of each of the set operations. We can understand how it works without knowing that sets happen to be implemented as bit arrays. That program would also be much harder to change. By implementing sets as a separate module, we've made it easy to change the implementation of sets without having to make changes in the programs using it.

Abstract data types are also nice because they can often be used, unchanged, in many different programs. Building a program on top of code we have already written is called *software reuse*, and is a powerful technique for developing software quickly. One way to do this is to create modules, like our sets, that can easily be used by new programs. Doing so effectively adds features to the language, allowing us to build programs much more quickly than we could if we had to start from scratch each time.

9–5 Rewrite our earlier histogram program (Figure 8.14) to use global variables for the bucket array, the bucket size, and the number of buckets. Use header files rather than explicit declarations.

Extend

9–6 Modify our program to calculate the day of the year (Figure 9.2) to do error checking on its input. It should make sure that the month is between 1 and 12 and that the day of the month is legal for that month.

9–7 Our bus stop simulator (Figures 9.23 and 9.24) doesn't print a count of how many people are left waiting at the bus station when the program ends. This can be fixed by adding and using a new queue-handling function, **queuelen**, which returns the number of items in the queue.

9–8 Another problem with our bus stop simulator (Figures 9.23 and 9.24) is that it doesn't behave sensibly if the arrival times aren't increasing in sequential order. Fix the program so that it does something reasonable instead.

9–9 Modify the final character-counting program (Figure 9.13) to break its output into groups corresponding to the different *ctype* categories. For example, it should have one group for lowercase letters, another for uppercase letters, another for digits, and so on. That is, rather than simply printing a count for each character in lexicographic order by characters, group the characters so that it prints the counts for the lowercase characters, then for the uppercase characters, and so on.

9–10 With our queue-handling functions (Figures 9.21 and 9.22), what happens when we add items to an already full queue? What about deleting an item from an empty queue? Modify these functions to return an appropriate value if we attempt one of these operations.

`Tune` **9–11** Modify our earlier histogram program (Figure 8.14) to use registers where appropriate. Does it make a noticeable difference in program speed?

`Code` **9–12** Our implementation of sets (Figures 9.28 and 9.29) is incomplete. Other common set operations include union and intersection. **setUnion** is a function that takes two sets and returns a set containing all the items in either of those two sets. **setInter** is similar, but returns a set containing the items that are in both of those sets. Implement these operations.

9–13 The difference of two sets is defined as the elements in the first set that are not also present in the second set. Write a function, **setDiff**, that places the difference of two sets into a third set.

9–14 Write a function, **setPrintElems**, that prints the elements of a set in traditional set notation. A set containing the elements 3, 7, and 14 should print as {**3, 7, 14**}. Can this be implemented without adding set operations?

`Build` **9–15** Write a program to fill its input. Assuming we want a line width of 40 characters, given the input:

```
this is a test
of our program to do filling
of its input
so that its output
never exceeds the
40 character margin but is as close as possible to
it.
```

the program's output should be:

```
this is a test of our program to do
filling of its input so that its output
never exceeds the 40 character margin
but is as close as possible to it.
```

9–16 Our implementation of sets (Figures 9.28 and 9.29) isn't particularly space efficient for sets containing only a few elements. An alternative is to use sorted arrays of **int**s rather than bit arrays. Now when we add an element to the set, we place it in its correct place in the array. We check for membership by searching the array. And we delete an element by shifting array items. Implement sets using sorted arrays.

9–17 Write a program to print the calendar for a particular month. Its input should be a pair of integers: the number of the month and the number of the day of the week of the first day of the month (0 for Sunday, 1 for Monday, and so on).

9–18 A stack is the reverse of a queue: The first thing placed on it is the last thing taken off, just like a stack of cafeteria trays. Stacks generally have a small set of operations: **stackPush** adds an item to a stack, **stackPop** takes the top item off and returns it, **stackTop** returns the top item, and **stackEmpty** returns nonzero if the stack is empty. Write these operations using an array to implement the stack.

Use these stack operations to write a program to reverse its input. The program should never access the stack elements except through the stack operations.

Use these stack operations to write a program that prints out the location in the input of any unbalanced parentheses. That is, if it detects that a left parenthesis has no matching right parenthesis, it should print its position in the input (character number is sufficient).

Part III

ADVANCED DATA TYPES

The next five chapters of this text focus on C's advanced mechanisms for organizing data.

- Chapter 10 presents pointers and their common use in parameter passing, array traversal, and dynamic memory allocation.

- Chapter 11 focuses on strings.

- Chapter 12 examines constructed types (structures, unions, and enumerated types).

- Chapter 13 describes arrays of arrays (two and higher dimensioned arrays).

- Chapter 14 discusses arrays of pointers (ragged arrays).

10 POINTERS

This chapter introduces pointers, a data type that can hold addresses. We study how to use them to provide call-by-reference parameter passing and to traverse arrays efficiently. We also see how to use them to access dynamically allocated arrays, arrays for which space is allocated at run time rather than compile time. The chapter concludes with a new implementation of sets, this time with dynamically allocated sets of varying sizes.

10.1   POINTERS

A *pointer* is simply the address of a memory location. Whenever we declare a variable, as in

```
int i;
```

the compiler reserves a memory location for it. The compiler might, for example, set aside memory location 10000 for **i**. When we subsequently refer to **i**, we are really referring to this location. Assigning zero to **i** with

```
i = 0;
```

places a zero in memory location 10000. We say that 10000 is **i**'s address or, in other words, a *pointer* to **i**. In C, we can access a value directly by providing its name or indirectly through a pointer. We will soon see how this indirect pointer access allows us to simulate call-by-reference parameter passing, to traverse arrays more efficiently, and to manipulate dynamically allocated arrays.

Declaring and Obtaining Pointers

Pointers are a basic data type. We can declare pointer variables, variables that contain addresses of (or pointers to) other values. We have to declare a pointer as pointing to a value of a particular type, such as an **int**, a **double**, a **char**, and so on. We must do so because when we access a value through a pointer, the compiler needs to know the value's type.

We declare a variable as a pointer to a particular type with

```
type *name;
```

This declares *name* as a pointer to *type*. The following declares **iptr** as a "pointer to **int**," **fptr** as a "pointer to **float**," **cptr** as a "pointer to **char**," and **dptr** as a "pointer to **double**."

```
int    *iptr;        /* pointer to int */
float  *fptr;        /* pointer to float */
char   *cptr;        /* pointer to char */
double *dptr;        /* pointer to double */
```

Each of these declarations allocates space for the named pointer variable, but doesn't make it point to anything (just as declaring **i** as an **int** allocates room for an integer but doesn't initialize that space). To do so, we use the operator, **&**, that returns the address of its operand. We can initialize **iptr** to point to **i** with

```
iptr = &i;
```

Assuming **i** is stored in memory location 10000, after this assignment **iptr** contains the address 10000, a pointer to **i**.

Dereferencing Pointer Variables

Once we have made a pointer point to something, we access the pointed-to value using the indirection operator *****, a process called *dereferencing*. In the example above, ***iptr** is **i**. Since **i** is zero, so is ***iptr**.

Because **iptr** is of type "pointer to **int**," ***iptr** is of type **int**, and we can use it anywhere an **int** variable can occur, such as in assignments. So,

```
n = *iptr;
```

assigns to **n** whatever **iptr** points to (zero in this example),

```
*iptr = j;
```

assigns **j**'s value to whatever **iptr** points to (**i** in this case), and

```
*iptr = *iptr + 10;
```

adds 10 to whatever ***iptr** points to. Figure 10.1 illustrates what's going on with these assignments.

The Generic Pointer Type

Figure 10.2 is a short program that plays around with pointers. Here's its output when we run it on our machine:

```
Addresses: &i=FFB6 &n=FFB8 &j=FFBA
Initial values: iptr=0000 i=0 n=17 j=23
Later values: iptr=FFB6 i=0 n=0 j=23
Final values: iptr=FFB6 i=33 n=0 j=23
```

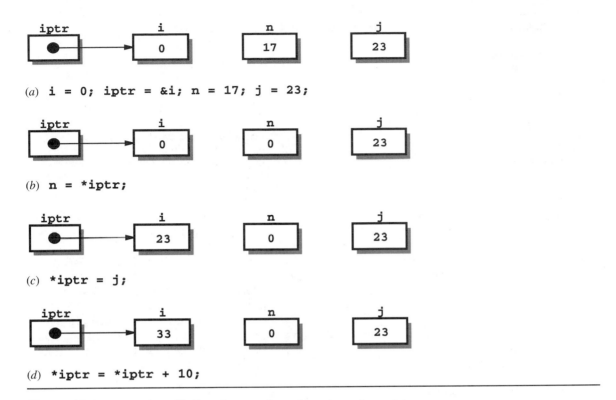

(a) `i = 0; iptr = &i; n = 17; j = 23;`

(b) `n = *iptr;`

(c) `*iptr = j;`

(d) `*iptr = *iptr + 10;`

Figure 10.1 Examples of indirectly accessing values through a pointer.

Among other things, it prints the values of several pointers, as well as what they point to. To do so, we use a new **printf** formatting code, **%p**, that writes a pointer's value in hexadecimal. But how does **%p** know what type of pointer we're passing to it? That's an issue because there are many types of pointers, and these pointers can vary in size.[1] **printf** needs to know the type of pointer to know how many bytes to write.

The trick is that **%p** always expects the same type of pointer—a pointer to **void**. A pointer to **void** is a *generic* pointer: it is simply an address, but not the address of any particular type of object. So to print a pointer, we first cast it to a pointer to **void**, which we then pass to **printf**:

```
printf("&i=%p\n", (void *) &i);
```

This works because we're guaranteed that a generic pointer is large enough to safely hold a pointer to *any* type of object. We're also guaranteed that we can cast any pointer

---

[1]On some machines, for example, a pointer to a **char** takes up two words, whereas a pointer to an **int** takes only one.

```
/*
 * Examples of assigning, following, and printing pointers.
 */
#include <stdio.h>
#include <stdlib.h>

int main()
{
  int *iptr = NULL;
  int i = 0;                              /* some useful value */
  int n = 17;                             /* another value */
  int j = 23;                             /* still another value */

  printf("Addresses: ");                  /* display addresses: */
  printf("&i=%p", (void *) &i);           /*    i's address */
  printf(" &n=%p", (void *) &n);          /*    n's address */
  printf(" &j=%p\n", (void *) &j);        /*    j's address */

  printf("Initial values: ");             /* display initial values */
  printf("iptr=%p i=%i n=%i j=%i\n", (void *) iptr, i, n, j);
  iptr = &i;                              /* place i's address in iptr */
  n = *iptr;                              /* place i's value into n */
  printf("Later values: ");               /* display changed values */
  printf("iptr=%p i=%i n=%i j=%i\n", (void *) iptr, i, n, j);
  *iptr = j;                              /* place j's value in i */
  *iptr = *iptr + 10;                     /* update i */
  printf("Final values: ");
  printf("iptr=%p i=%i n=%i j=%i\n", (void *) iptr, i, n, j);

  return EXIT_SUCCESS;
}
```

Figure 10.2   (ptrex.c)   A program that declares, assigns to, dereferences, and prints pointers.

type to and from a pointer to **void** without loss of information.[2] The drawback, of course, is that we can't do operations that need to know the size of the pointed-to thing.

Generic pointers are a very powerful tool that we'll explore in much greater detail later in this chapter.

The Null Pointer

There's one pointer we can't dereference. It's illegal to dereference a pointer with the value zero, and doing so usually causes a run-time error that terminates the program.[3] We use such a pointer as a placeholder to indicate explicitly that a pointer variable doesn't

---

[2]On many machines, all pointers are the same size, so a cast from one type of pointer to another doesn't really do anything—but not on *all* machines. We need the cast to ensure that our program is portable.

[3]Officially, dereferencing such a pointer causes *undefined* behavior, but it's always a programming mistake.

point anywhere. In fact, we use it so frequently that there's a special constant **NULL**, defined in the system header file stddef.h, that's exactly equivalent to the constant **0**.

Local pointer variables, like other local variables, are not automatically initialized. In fact, they start off with a random value—whatever happens to be in the memory location reserved for the pointer—and could therefore point anywhere. Following these pointers will likely lead us into areas of memory into which we don't want to go. On the other hand, global and **static** pointers are initialized, but to zero, which we've just seen is illegal to dereference. So ***iptr** is meaningless until **iptr** has been made to point to something, regardless of whether **iptr** is global or local.

> *Don't dereference a pointer variable until you've assigned it an address.*

One way to prevent problems with using uninitialized pointer variables is to initialize all of them to **NULL**. In fact, we did so with **iptr** in Figure 10.2. Of course, we still need to initialize them to some other value before we follow them, but this way we're less likely to damage some random memory location. We'll see other uses for **NULL** later in the chapter.

10.2   USING POINTERS TO SIMULATE CALL BY REFERENCE

We have seen the mechanics of declaring, initializing, and dereferencing pointers. We will now look at one of the most common use of pointers in real programs: simulating call-by-reference parameter passing.

We have seen that C passes parameters by value. When we call a function, C allocates space for its parameters and copies the values passed as the function's arguments. When the function returns, this space is deallocated. This means that *a function cannot change the values of its arguments*. In fact, we can treat parameters as though they are local variables, conveniently initialized by the calling function. This allows us to pass arbitrary expressions and prevents us from accidentally modifying a function's arguments.

But what do we do when we have a function like **scanf** that needs to modify a variable in its caller? Simply changing the value of a parameter doesn't work, since such changes are local. Instead, we must use **&** to pass a pointer to the variable. The function then dereferences the pointer with ***** to access or modify the variable's value.

The swap Function

Figure 10.3 contains a function **swap** that's designed to exchange the values of two integer variables. Because of *call by value*, however, this version of **swap** doesn't do what we want. Here's the program's unpleasant output:

```
Before swap, s=5, t=10
After swap, s=5, t=10
```

```
/*
 * A program that doesn't exchange two values.
 */
#include <stdio.h>
#include <stdlib.h>

int main()
{
  void swap(int x, int y);

  int s = 5, t = 10;

  printf("Before swap, s=%i, t=%i\n", s, t);
  swap(s, t);
  printf("After swap, s=%i, t=%i\n", s, t);

  return EXIT_SUCCESS;
}

/* Incorrectly exchanges only values of its parameters */

void swap(int x, int y)
{
  int temp;

  temp = x;
  x = y;
  y = temp;
}
```

Figure 10.3   (badswap.c)   An incorrect version of swapping function along with a program that uses it.

The problem is that it swaps the values of its parameters **x** and **y**, but does not affect the values **s** and **t** passed to it by the main program.

To get **swap** to exchange the values of variables in its calling function, we have to pass it their addresses and modify it to exchange the values indirectly through these pointers. Figure 10.4 contains a corrected version of **swap** and an example call. Now the program's more pleasing output is:

```
Before swap, s=5, t=10
After swap, s=10, t=5
```

Figure 10.5 illustrates how this new version of **swap** works, assuming that the addresses of **s** and **t** are 1000 and 2000, respectively, **s** is 5, and **t** is 10. When **swap** is called, **xptr** becomes 1000 and **yptr** becomes 2000, the addresses of **s** and **t**. The first assignment,

```
temp = *xptr;
```

```
/*
 * A program that does exchange two values.
 */
#include <stdio.h>
#include <stdlib.h>

int main()
{
  void swap(int *xptr, int *yptr);

  int s = 5, t = 10;

  printf("Before swap, s=%i, t=%i\n", s, t);
  swap(&s, &t);
  printf("After swap, s=%i, t=%i\n", s, t);

  return EXIT_SUCCESS;
}

/* Correctly exchanges a pair of values in caller */

void swap(int *xptr, int *yptr)
{
  int temp;

  temp = *xptr;
  *xptr = *yptr;
  *yptr = temp;
}
```

Figure 10.4   (swap.c)   Correct version of the swapping function and a program that uses it.

places the value in location 1000 (5) into **temp**. Similarly, the next assignment,

```
*xptr = *yptr;
```

assigns to location 1000 the value in location 2000 (10), and the final assignment,

```
*yptr = temp;
```

completes the exchange by placing **temp**'s contents (5) in location 2000.

Some Common Mistakes

There are several common mistakes when dealing with pointer parameters. Most of these mistakes, however, are simply type mismatches that the compiler will detect for us so long as we supply appropriate prototypes.[4]

---

[4]This means that, whenever we are using pointers, it's especially important for us to make the effort to provide prototypes.

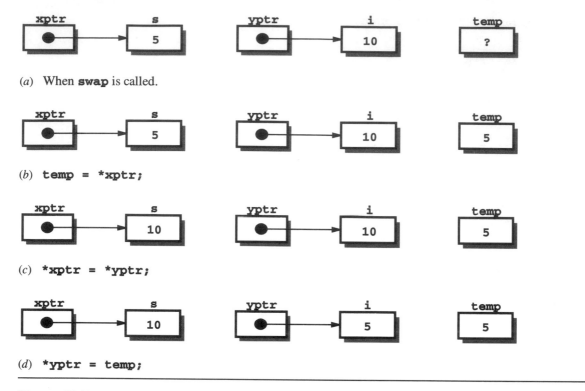

(a) When **swap** is called.

(b) `temp = *xptr;`

(c) `*xptr = *yptr;`

(d) `*yptr = temp;`

Figure 10.5 Exchanging two variables using pointers.

The first is failing to pass a pointer to a function that expects one. Doing so here, as in

```
swap(s, t);
```

would cause **swap** to try to exchange the values in addresses 5 and 10, which is not at all what we want. For **swap** to work correctly, we must pass it the *addresses* of the variables whose values are to be exchanged, not the values themselves. Passing the variables themselves is likely to cause an addressing exception.

> *Don't fail to pass a pointer to a function that expects one.*

The second common mistake is to use a pointer as an integer in one place and as a pointer in another. One way we can avoid this problem is by first writing the function without any pointer parameters. We can then transform the appropriate parameters into pointers by renaming them to reflect their new use and then replacing all their uses with the appropriate pointer name, preceded by a *****. In fact, this is how we got the correct version of **swap** from the incorrect one. We replaced the **int** variables **x** and **y** with the pointer variables **xptr** and **yptr** and preceded all uses of these pointers with *****. Although it is not necessary for **swap**, we may have to parenthesize references through pointer variables to guarantee the desired order of evaluation.

> *Don't forget to dereference pointer parameters when you need to access their values.*

There are actually several other ways to avoid problems with using pointers. Figure 10.6 illustrates one of these. It contains **minmax**, a function that takes a table of **int**s and determines its minimum and maximum values. That means it needs some way to return both these values. One way is to directly return the minimum as its value and return the maximum indirectly through a pointer parameter. But we prefer using the same mechanism for returning both values, so we return both through pointer parameters. The problem is that having several pointer parameters increases our chances of making a mistake such as forgetting to dereference the pointer. So we want to minimize our accesses through the pointers. Our trick is to use local variables, **min** and **max**, throughout the function and only at the end of the function to return their values through the pointers.

Figure 10.7 shows another approach that seemingly eliminates the pointers entirely. We pass a two-element array to **minmax** and let it store the minimum and maximum values in the array. Of course, we're still using a pointer, but it's completely hidden. The drawback is that **main** has to refer to these values through the array, which requires subscripting and is somewhat less convenient than accessing **int** variables directly. Another drawback is that this approach makes sense only when trying to return more than one value of the same type, so there are times when you're going to be stuck using pointers anyway.

10.3   TRAVERSING ARRAYS USING POINTERS

We can use arrays in C in the same way we use arrays in other languages. But doing so ignores some of their most important features and leads to slower, less powerful programs. It turns out that to take full advantage of arrays, we're stuck using pointers.

In C, arrays and pointers are intimately intertwined. When we declare an array, the compiler not only allocates a block of storage large enough to hold the array, but also defines the array's name as a (constant) pointer to its first element (element 0).

Figure 10.8 shows what happens when we declare **t** to be an array of 100 **int**s with

```
int t[100];
```

The compiler first allocates 100 contiguous storage locations, each holding one **int**. It then defines **t** as the address of its zeroth element. Since array indexing begins with 0, **t** is equivalent to **&t[0]**. Here, **t** is the constant 1000, the location where **t[0]** is stored.

```
/*
 * Return largest and smallest array values through
 * pointer parameters.
 */
#include <stdio.h>
#include <stdlib.h>
#include <limits.h>

int main()
{
  void minmax(const int table[], int n, int *minptr, int *maxptr);

  const int table[] = {10, 56, 79, -21, 51, 5, 64, 70, 0, -10};
  const int entries = sizeof(table)/sizeof(table[0]);
  int       min, max;

  minmax(table, entries, &min, &max);
  printf("min=%i, max=%i\n", min, max);

  return EXIT_SUCCESS;
}

void minmax(const int table[], int n, int *minptr, int *maxptr)
{
  int i;
  int min = INT_MAX, max = INT_MIN;

  for (i = 0; i < n; i++)
    if (table[i] < min)
      min = table[i];
    else if (table[i] > max)
      max = table[i];
  *minptr = min;
  *maxptr = max;
}
```

Figure 10.6   (minmax.c) A function to find the smallest and largest values in an array, along with a main program that uses it.

There are two ways to access array elements. One is through the direct array indexing we've been using in earlier array-manipulating programs. To access an array element, we provide the array name and a bracket-enclosed index. To traverse the array, we can use an index variable that runs through the possible index values.

We use this traditional array indexing in a program to read its input into a table, compute the average, and then print the number of items in the table less than and greater than the average. If the program's input is:

```
10 40 20 30 30 100 20 10 20 20
```

```
/*
 * Return largest and smallest array values thru
 * an array parameter.
 */
#include <stdio.h>
#include <stdlib.h>
#include <limits.h>

#define MIN_INDEX 0
#define MAX_INDEX 1

int main()
{
  void minmax(const int table[], int n, int results[]);

  const int table[] = {10, 56, 79, -21, 51, 5, 64, 70, 0, -10};
  const int entries = sizeof(table)/sizeof(table[0]);
  int       results[2];

  minmax(table, entries, results);
  printf("min=%i, max=%i\n", results[MIN_INDEX], results[MAX_INDEX]);

  return EXIT_SUCCESS;
}

void minmax(const int table[], int n, int results[])
{
  int i;
  int min = INT_MAX, max = INT_MIN;

  for (i = 0; i < n; i++)
    if (table[i] < min)
      min = table[i];
    else if (table[i] > max)
      max = table[i];
  results[MIN_INDEX] = min;
  results[MAX_INDEX] = max;
}
```

Figure 10.7 (minmax2.c) A new version of our function to find the smallest and largest values in an array, along with a main program that uses it. This time it returns these values in another array instead of returning them through pointers.

its output is:

```
There are 10 values.
The average is 30.
There are 2 values above average.
There are 6 values below average.
```

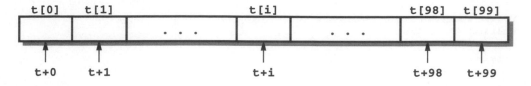

Figure 10.8 What happens when we declare **t** as an array containing 100 **int**s.

We divide the program into several source files. Figure 10.9 contains the main program, along with a pair of functions to read the table and print the values less than or greater than the average. Figure 10.10 contains the function **tableAverage**, which uses traditional indexing to sum an array of integers:

```
for (i = 0; i < n; i++)
    sum += a[i]
```

Traditional array indexing is simple to use, easy to understand, and similar to the way we process arrays in other languages. But there's another, often more efficient, way to traverse arrays: accessing array elements indirectly through pointers. We can do so because C provides pointer arithmetic—the ability to add integers to or subtract integers from a pointer. We're now going to rewrite this program to use pointers rather than array subscripting.

Pointer Arithmetic

In C, pointer arithmetic is automatically done in units of the pointer's underlying base type. That is, adding 1 to a pointer to an array element gives a pointer to the next element—regardless of whether we have an array of **int**s, an array of **double**s, or an array of any other type. In the declaration for **t**, an array of **int**s, **t** is a pointer to its first element (**&t[0]**). That means **t + 1** is a pointer to its second element (**&t[1]**), **t + 2** is a pointer to its third element (**&t[2]**), and so on. In general, **t + i** is the address of element **t[i]**.

Since **t + i** is the address of **t[i]**, ***(t + i)** is equivalent to **t[i]**. So we can initialize **t[3]** to 0 with array indexing,

```
t[3] = 0;
```

or with pointer indexing,

```
*(t + 3) = 0;
```

In fact, the compiler converts array subscripts into pointer dereferences—**t[i]** *becomes* ***(t + i)**. Why are these equivalent? Because in the pointer dereference, ***(t + i)**, the addition **t + i** is carried out in **sizeof(int)** increments. Selecting the *i*th element of an array involves calculating its address, given the array's base address (the location of **t[0]**). When we write **t[3]**, C multiplies the index (3) by

```c
/*
 * Compute average and print interesting counts.  Uses:
 *    tableFill - reads in table entries (same tableFill as before).
 *    tableAvgCnts - compute average statistics.
 */
#include <stdio.h>
#include <stdlib.h>

#define MAXVALS 100

int main()
{
  int    tableFill(int a[], int max);
  void   tableAvgCnts(int a[], int n, double avg);
  double tableAverage(int a[], int n);

  int    t[MAXVALS];
  int    n   = tableFill(t, MAXVALS);
  double avg = tableAverage(t, n);

  printf("There are %i values.\n", n);
  printf("The average is %g.\n", avg);
  tableAvgCnts(t, n, avg);

  return EXIT_SUCCESS;
}

int tableFill(int a[], int max)
{
  int count = 0;

  for (; count < max; count++)
    if (scanf("%i", &a[count]) != 1)
      break;                                  /* kick out on error */
  return count;
}

void tableAvgCnts(int a[], int n, double avg)
{
  int i;                                      /* index */
  int above = 0;                              /* above average */
  int below = 0;                              /* below average */

  for (i = 0; i < n; i++)
    if (a[i] > avg)
      above++;
    else if (a[i] < avg)
      below++;
  printf("There are %i values above average.\n", above);
  printf("There are %i values below average.\n", below);
}
```

Figure 10.9 (usetavg.c) Our average-computing and -printing program.

```
/*
 * Compute average of an array, array subscripting version.
 */
double tableAverage(int a[], int n)
{
  double sum = 0.0;                              /* running total */
  int    i;                                      /* count of items */

  for (i = 0; i < n; i++)
    sum += a[i];
  return (n != 0) ? sum / n : 0.0;
}
```

Figure 10.10 (tavg.c) Compute average of an array.

the size of an **int** and adds the result to the base address of the array. In our example, assuming **t** is 1000 and **int**s are 2 bytes long, the computation results in an address of 1006, which is where we find **t[3]**.

What have we gained with this pointer manipulation? So far it may seem that we've simply discovered a more complicated way to access array elements. But consider the new version of **tableAverage** shown in Figure 10.11. It uses a pointer, **ptr**, to traverse the array rather than an array index.

```
ptr = a;
for (i = 0; i < n; i++)
{
    sum += *ptr;
    ptr++;
}
```

We access the individual elements with ***ptr**, rather than through an array subscript. And we traverse the array by simply adding 1 to **ptr** each time we go through the loop. This works because incrementing a pointer makes it point to the next array element.

Why is this pointer-accessing method potentially faster? The main reason is that we eliminate an address computation. When we write **t[i]**, the compiler turns it into ***(t + i)**, which requires an addition (and possibly a multiplication) to locate the desired element. In the pointer version, the pointer is incremented each time we go through the loop—which can often be done as part of the machine instruction that dereferences the pointer—and no other calculation is necessary.[5]

There is one final form of pointer arithmetic: subtracting two pointers. We use this most frequently to calculate the subscript of a pointed-to array element. That's because the result of subtracting a pointer **q** from a pointer **p** is j such that **p** + j gives **q** (that is, j is the number of elements between them). So if **p** is **&t[0]** and **q** is **&t[3]**, **q** - **p** is 3. Of course, this operation gives a portable result only if both operands point to the same array.

---

[5] In the next section, we'll show how to improve this loop even more.

```
/*
 * Compute average of an array, pointer version.
 */
double tableAverage(int a[], int n)
{
  double sum = 0.0;                              /* running total */
  int    i;                                      /* count of items */
  int    *ptr;                                   /* traversing pointer */

  ptr = a;
  for (i = 0; i < n; i++)
  {
    sum += *ptr;
    ptr++;
  }
  return (n != 0) ? sum / n : 0.0;
}
```

Figure 10.11   (tavg2.c)   A pointer version of **tableAverage**.

> *The only legal arithmetic operators on pointers are adding or subtracting an integer, or subtracting one pointer from another.*

We can't add, multiply, or divide two pointers, and we can't multiply or divide a pointer by an **int**. This restriction is occasionally irritating. Suppose we need the value of the middle element in an array of **n** elements (the element halfway between the array's first and last element). We can easily find it using array indexing: it's **t[n/2]**. And we might think that we could also easily find it using pointer arithmetic (assuming **minptr** points to the array's first element and **maxptr** points to its last element):

```
* ((minptr + maxptr) / 2)
```

But this fails because we can't legally *add* pointers. Fortunately, we can legally *subtract* pointers, so we can instead use

```
* (minptr + (maxptr - minptr) / 2)
```

Although this may look like pointer addition, it's not. Subtracting two pointers yields an integer, as does dividing an integer by 2. And adding an integer to a pointer gives a pointer. We'll make use of this computation in a later chapter when we present an implementation of binary search.

Pointer Comparison

Pointers can be compared. We can test whether a pointer is equal (**==**), not equal (**!=**), less than (**<**), less than or equal (**<=**), greater than (**>**), or greater than or equal (**>=**) to another.

Two pointers are equal only if they point to the same location. One pointer is less than another if it points to a lower location in memory, so **&t[3]** is less than **&t[5]**. Conversely, one pointer is greater than another if it points to a higher location in memory, so **&t[5]** is greater than **&t[3]**.

Where different arrays reside in memory is machine dependent and is likely to vary from implementation to implementation.[6] That means it's not portable to compare pointers into different arrays.

> *Don't compare pointers that don't access the same array.*

Figure 10.12 shows how we can use pointer comparisons to write **tableAverage** more efficiently. This loop is more efficient because it no longer tests a counter to determine when the array has been traversed. Instead, we compare the indexing pointer with a pointer to the location just past the array's last element. When they're equal, we leave the loop. We declare and initialize the ending pointer with

```
int *endptr = a + n;
```

which is identical to the separate declaration and assignment

```
int *endptr;

endptr = a + n;
```

That is, it assigns the address **a + n** to **endptr** and not to what **endptr** points to.

Having a pointer to just past the last element seems strange. But we're guaranteed that a pointer to *one* element past the end of an array is legal. It's not legal to follow that pointer; the guarantee is merely that the *address* is legal. Even so, why didn't we just have a pointer to the last element, not one past it? The main reason is that we want our pointer traversal of an array to resemble our array-subscripting traversal. With array subscripting, we stopped the loop when the index was 1 more than the index of the array's last element.

Concise Pointer Loops

We haven't been writing our loops as concisely as we could. Figure 10.13 rewrites **tableAverage**'s loop to sum up **a**'s values as

```
while (ptr < endptr)
    sum += *ptr++;
```

Because of the precedence and evaluation order of ***** and **++**, ***ptr++** means "obtain the value that **ptr** points to (***ptr**), return the value, and then increment the pointer".

---

[6]On the PC, for example, different arrays may be stored in different memory segments. Two pointers could compare as equal when they point to completely different locations.

```
/*
 * Compute average of an array, concise pointer version.
 */
double tableAverage(int a[], int n)
{
  double sum = 0.0;                      /* running total */
  int    *ptr;                           /* traversing pointer */
  int    *endptr = a + n;                /* pointer to just past end */

  for (ptr = a; ptr < endptr; ptr++)
    sum += *ptr;
  return (n != 0) ? sum / n : 0.0;
}
```

Figure 10.12 (tavg3.c) A more concise pointer version of **tableAverage**.

```
/*
 * Function to compute average of array, most concise version.
 */
double tableAverage(int *ptr, int n)
{
  double sum = 0.0;
  int  *endptr = ptr + n;    /* pointer to just past last element */

  while (ptr < endptr)
    sum += *ptr++;
  return (n != 0) ? sum / n : 0.0;
}
```

Figure 10.13 (tavg4.c) The most concise version of our function to find the average of an array.

This differs from **(*ptr)++**, which increments *the value* pointed to by **ptr**, after returning its original value, as shown in Figure 10.14. The result is that

```
sum += *ptr++;
```

is equivalent to

```
sum += *ptr;
ptr++;
```

Similarly, ***ptr--** decrements the pointer after returning the pointed-to value. The prefix forms increment (***++ptr**) or decrement (***--ptr**) the pointer and return whatever value it then points to.

Combining a dereference with a prefix or postfix operator leads to more concise but more confusing code. In general, it's a good idea to avoid this combination.

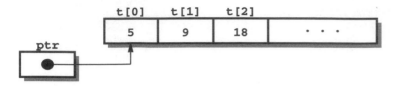

(*a*) Initial assignment: **ptr = &t[0]** (or equivalently, **ptr = t**).

(*b*) Subsequent increment: ***ptr++** increments **ptr** and returns what **ptr** previously pointed to (5), so **v = *ptr++** sets **v** to 5.

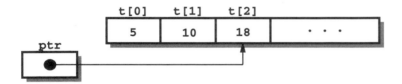

(*c*) Another subsequent increment: **(*ptr)++** increments **t[1]** (setting it to 10) and returns its value before the increment (9), so **v = (*ptr)++** sets **v** to 9.

Figure 10.14   The difference between ***ptr++** and **(*ptr)++**.

Pointers and Other Types of Arrays

Pointers can be used to traverse an array of any type. Figures 10.15 and 10.16 take advantage of pointer arithmetic in a version of our input reversal program that assumes our input values are **double**s rather than **int**s. The program works because pointer arithmetic for references to an element in an array of **double**s is done in terms of **double**s, units of 8 bytes (assuming 8-byte **double**s). We did little more than change all of the pointer and function declarations.

10.4 ARRAY PARAMETERS AND POINTERS

We saw earlier that when we pass an array parameter, we really only pass the address of its first element—in other words, a pointer. This means that a function header or

```
/*
 * Input-reversal program using pointers.  For doubles, not ints.
 */
#include <stdlib.h>

#define MAXVALS 100

int main()
{
   int    dblTableFill(double d[], int max);
   void   dblTablePrintRev(double d[], int num);

   double table[MAXVALS];

   dblTablePrintRev(table, dblTableFill(table, MAXVALS));

   return EXIT_SUCCESS;
}
```

Figure 10.15   (drevtab.c)   A program to reverse its input **double**s.

```
/*
 * Table-handling functions using pointers.  For doubles, not ints.
 *    dblTableFill - read values into table.
 *    dblTablePrintRev - print table in reverse order.
 */
#include <stdio.h>

int dblTableFill(double a[], int max)
{
   double *ptr = a;                  /* pointer to first element */
   double *endptr = ptr + max;       /* pointer to just after last element */

   for (ptr = a; ptr < endptr; ptr++)
     if (scanf("%lf", ptr) != 1)
       break;
   return ptr - a;                   /* # of values read successfully */
}

void dblTablePrintRev(double a[], int num)
{
   double *ptr = a + num;

   while (ptr-- > a)
     printf("%f\n", *ptr);
}
```

Figure 10.16   (dtabfill.c)   Functions to fill and print in reverse order an array of **double**s.

Aside 10.1a: Portability, Pointers, and Traversing Arrays Backwards

We have seen that the standard technique for forward array traversals is to set up pointers to the first element and to *just past* the last element. But what about when we want to traverse the array backwards?

One example is printing an array in reverse order. The obvious solution is to have a pointer to the last element and to keep decrementing as long as it's greater than or equal to the first element's address:

```
for (ptr = &a[num-1]; ptr >= a; ptr--)
  printf("%i\n", *ptr);
```

But this solution has a problem: it's not legal to have a pointer to the element just before the start of an array. And since this loop terminates only when **ptr** becomes less than **a**, we're in trouble. That's not guaranteed to be a legal address, which means the comparison may fail.

As a result, we must take a different approach: test whether **ptr** is greater than **a**, and decrement it before we dereference it.

```
ptr = a + num;
while (ptr-- > a)
  printf("%i\n", *ptr);
```

Aside 10.1b does so in a pointer version of the function **tablePrintRev** from Chapter 8's input reversal program. For completeness, Aside 10.1b also contains a pointer version of **tableFill**. But since that function traverses the array in forward order, we don't have to worry about this issue there.

prototype, such as

```
double tableAverage(int a[], int n)
```

is equivalent to

```
double tableAverage(int *a, int n)
```

We can use these forms interchangeably. In fact, the compiler automatically translates any array parameter into a pointer parameter.

We don't explicitly declare an array parameter's size, so functions that process arrays need to know how many array elements to process. That means that when we pass an array, we usually also pass the number of elements in the array, as when we pass **n** in **tableAverage**.[7]

One benefit of an array's being passed as a pointer is that we can pass the address of any array element. This effectively allows us to pass only part of an array. We can use our **tableAverage** function to compute the average of **k** elements of **t**, starting with

---

[7]We cannot use **sizeof** in **tableAverage** because **sizeof**(*a pointer*) returns the size of the pointer, not of the entire array.

Aside 10.1b (tabfill2.c) Pointer versions of the table-handling routines.

```
/*
 * Pointer versions of table-handling functions.
 *   tableFill - read values into table.
 *   tablePrintRev - print values in reverse order.
 */
#include <stdio.h>

int tableFill(int a[], int max)
{
  int *ptr = a;                    /* pointer to first element */
  int *endptr = ptr + max;         /* pointer to just past last element */

  for (ptr = a; ptr < endptr; ptr++)
    if (scanf("%i", ptr) != 1)
      break;
  return ptr - a;                  /* # of values read successfully */
}

void tablePrintRev(int a[], int num)
{
  int *ptr = a + num;              /* pointer to just past last element */

  while (ptr-- > a)
    printf("%i\n", *ptr);
}
```

`t[i]`, with either

```
        avg = tableAverage(&t[i], k);
```

or the equivalent

```
        avg = tableAverage(t + i, k);
```

In both cases we pass `t[i]`'s address. Figure 10.17 shows how **tableAverage** can still access any element of **t** through appropriate negative or positive offsets of **ptr**.

> *Don't pass an array element to a function expecting an array parameter.*

A function expecting an array must be passed an array name or an element's address. The call

```
        avg = tableAverage(t[i], k);      /* wrong! */
```

is a serious mistake, since **tableAverage** expects a pointer and instead receives an **int**. So long as you provided a prototype, the compiler should catch this error for you.

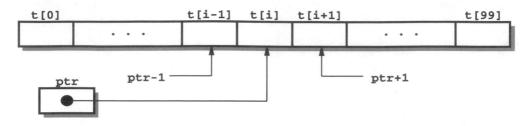

Figure 10.17 What happens when we have a pointer into the middle of an array containing 100 **int**s.

10.5   POINTERS AS FUNCTION RETURN VALUES

Not only do we often pass pointers as parameters, but we also often return pointers from functions. There are two common uses of this feature.

One use is to return a pointer to a particular element within an array. An example is the new version of Chapter 8's **tableSearch**, shown in Figure 10.18. This version searches an array of **int**s for a matching value and returns a pointer to its location or **NULL** if the value can't be found. Its prototype is:

```
int *tableSearch(int table[], int n, int value);
```

It is especially convenient to return a pointer, as this version of **tableSearch** is using a pointer to traverse the array. This way it can simply return that pointer.

Figure 10.19 has an example main program that calls **tableSearch**, checks whether the returned pointer is non-**NULL**, and then uses that pointer to access the desired element and to calculate its position.

The other use is to return a pointer to an array. We use this in one final version of **minmax**, shown in Figure 10.20. This time, after **minmax** determines the smallest and largest values in the array, it stores them in a **static**, internal, two-element array and returns a pointer to the first element in this array. Its caller can then dereference this pointer to access those elements. That works because whenever we subscript a pointer, as in **resptr[MIN_INDEX]** or **resptr[MAX_INDEX]**, the pointer in essence behaves just like an array name: C uses pointer arithmetic to add the subscript to the pointer and then dereferences the result. Of course, we have to be careful that the pointer actually points to an element in an allocated array.

This is yet another way to return more than one piece of information from a function. One advantage over other approaches is that we now have fewer parameters to worry about than in previous versions and the function appears as though it returns an array. However, we're still dealing with a pointer as the return value, and we have to refer to the minimum and maximum values through the pointer. In addition, returning a pointer to a **static** makes our program more fragile. That's because it forces us to save the values if we will need them after we call the function again.

```
/*
 * A function to search for a target in an array of integers.
 */
#include <stddef.h>                 /* for NULL pointer */

int *tableSearch(int a[], int n, int target)
{
  int *ptr;
  int *endptr = a + n;

  for (ptr = a; ptr < endptr && *ptr != target; ptr++)
     ;                                 /* search for matching value */
  return ptr != endptr ? ptr : NULL;
}
```

Figure 10.18   (tabsrch3.c) A version of **tableSearch** that returns a pointer to the element rather than its subscript.

10.6   CONSTANTS AND POINTERS

Just as we have integer and real variables that are constants, we can also have pointers to constants and constant pointers. The declaration

```
const int *ptr;
```

declares **ptr** to be a pointer to a constant **int**. That means that although we can modify **ptr**, we can't modify what it points to. An operation such as

```
*ptr = 0;
```

is illegal. One use for **ptr** would be to traverse a constant array, perhaps to print each of its elements.

We can assign a pointer to a non-**const** to a pointer to a **const** of the same basic type. So if we have an **int ***, we can assign it to a **const int ***. This allows us to write functions whose parameters are pointers to constants (forbidding the function from modifying the values pointed to by the pointers), while allowing us to pass those functions pointers to non-constants (allowing us to use those functions with any type of array).

Assigning the other way, however, requires a cast. That is, we can't simply assign a **const int *** to an **int ***. Even with the cast, however, we're courting danger, as we can now modify a value originally declared to be constant.[8]

---

[8]One common use of this conversion, however, is to write search functions that treat the array they're searching as a constant but return a non-**const** pointer to the matching array element. That way their caller can use this pointer to modify the array without doing a cast.

```
/*
 * Search table for the target value, returning its position.
 */
#include <stdio.h>
#include <stdlib.h>

#define MAXVALS   10                    /* max # of entries in table */
#define SENTINEL   0                    /* terminating input value */

int main()
{
  int *tableSearch(int a[], int n, int target);
  int tableFillSentinel(int a[], int n, int termval);

  int table[MAXVALS];                   /* table of values */
  int target;                           /* value to find */
  int *foundptr;                        /* target position */
  int n;                                /* number of items */
  int r;                                /* scanf return value */

  n = tableFillSentinel(table, MAXVALS, SENTINEL);
  while ((r = scanf("%i", &target)) == 1)
    if ((foundptr = tableSearch(table, n, target)) != NULL)
      printf("Found %i as element %i.\n", target, foundptr - table);
    else
      printf("Didn't find %i.\n", target);
  if (r != EOF)
    printf("Illegal value to search for.\n");

  return EXIT_SUCCESS;
}
```

Figure 10.19   (usetable2.c) A main program using our new version of **tableSearch**.

The syntax for declaring pointers that are constants is strange:

```
int *const endptr = ptr + max;
```

This makes **endptr** a constant pointer to an **int** and initializes it with the address **ptr + max**. We can't modify a constant pointer, so we must initialize constant pointers when we declare them. We can, however, modify what they point to.

Finally, we can declare a constant pointer to a constant item. This happens most frequently when we pass an array to a function that uses a pointer to traverse it and doesn't change its items. This declaration,

```
const int *const firstptr = a;
```

declares **firstptr** as a constant pointer to a constant integer. That means we can neither modify **firstptr** nor modify the value it points to. Since the pointer itself is

```
/*
 * Return largest and smallest array values through a pointer
 * to an internal static array.
 */
#include <stdio.h>
#include <stdlib.h>
#include <limits.h>

#define MIN_INDEX 0
#define MAX_INDEX 1

int main()
{
  int *minmax(const int table[], int n);

  const int table[] = {10, 56, 79, -21, 51, 5, 64, 70, 0, -10};
  const int entries = sizeof(table)/sizeof(table[0]);
  int        *resptr = minmax(table, entries);

  printf("min=%i, max=%i\n", resptr[MIN_INDEX], resptr[MAX_INDEX]);
  return EXIT_SUCCESS;
}

int *minmax(const int table[], int n)
{
  static int results[2];
  int i;
  int min = INT_MAX, max = INT_MIN;

  for (i = 0; i < n; i++)
    if (table[i] < min)
      min = table[i];
    else if (table[i] > max)
      max = table[i];
  results[MIN_INDEX] = min;
  results[MAX_INDEX] = max;
  return results;
}
```

Figure 10.20   (minmax3.c) One final version of the **minmax** function..

constant, we must initialize it when we declare it.

The syntax for declaring constants seems tricky. Just remember that if the pointer is constant, place the **const** immediately preceding the identifier. And if the pointed-to object is constant, place the **const** before that object's type.

Figures 10.21 and 10.22 contain a new version of our program to reverse its input, modified to use **const** for its pointer parameters and local variables.

```
/*
 * Pointer version of input-reversal program, using constants.
 */
#include <stdlib.h>

#define MAXVALS   100                    /* max values in "table" */

int main()
{
  int  tableFill(int *ptr, int max);
  void tablePrintRev(const int a[], int num);

  int  t[MAXVALS];                       /* table for input values*/

  tablePrintRev(t, tableFill(t, MAXVALS));

  return EXIT_SUCCESS;
}
```

Figure 10.21   (revint3.c) A version of our reverse program modified to use **const** pointers.

```
/*
 * Pointers versions of table-handling functions (with const).
 *    tableFill - read values into table.
 *    tablePrintRev - print values in reverse order.
 */
#include <stdio.h>

int tableFill(int *ptr, int max)
{
  int *const firstptr = ptr;        /* pointer to first element */
  int *const endptr = ptr + max;    /* pointer to just past end */

  for ( ; ptr < endptr && scanf("%i", ptr) == 1; ptr++)
    ;
  return ptr - firstptr;            /* # of values read successfully */
}

void tablePrintRev(const int a[], int num)
{
  const int *const firstptr = a;
  const int *ptr = firstptr + num;

  while (ptr-- > firstptr)
    printf("%i\n", *ptr);
}
```

Figure 10.22   (tabfill3.c) Versions of **tableFill** and **tablePrintRev** that use **const** pointers.

Aside 10.2a: Pointers and Efficiency

Most programmers would agree that it is more difficult to run through arrays using pointer indexing instead of array subscripting. The payoff for this extra effort, however, is in efficiency: carefully rewriting array-processing code using pointers tends to make our programs run faster.

To see just how much improvement pointers give us, we wrote a test program, shown in Aside 10.2b, that calls our **tableAverage** function 10,000 times to compute the average of a 10,000-element table. Here are the results.

FILE NAME	TRAVERSAL METHOD	TIME IN SECONDS	SPEED UP
tavg1.c	Array subscripting	20.59	
tavg2.c	Pointer indexing (separate counter)	13.25	35.6%
tavg3.c	Pointer indexing (pointer comparison)	12.20	7.9%
tavg4.c	Pointer indexing (most concise)	12.19	0.1%

Going from an initial array version to a pointer version shows an improvement of around 35%. Modifying the pointer version to use pointer comparisons rather than an extra index improved performance by another 8% or so. Finally, combining the pointer increment and the dereference in a single expression leads to only a very minute improvement of about a tenth of one percent.

The bottom line from this little experiment is that going to pointers can lead to large savings, at least for programs like this one that repeatedly traverse an array.

10.7 GENERIC POINTERS AND POINTER CONVERSIONS

We often find ourselves wanting to copy one array into another. The obvious way to do it would be to simply assign one array name to another.

```
double f[MAXVALS], g[MAXVALS];

f = g;                          /* illegal! */
```

The only problem is that this assignment doesn't work. In fact, it doesn't even compile. It's an illegal assignment because we're trying to modify a constant. The name of an array is a *constant* pointer to its first element, so **f** is a constant address. Even if it weren't a constant, however, we would still only be modifying a pointer, and not the pointed-to elements. To copy one array into another, we're stuck with running through the arrays and copying one element at a time.

While we could write a loop to do this copy ourselves, there's a library function, **memcpy**, that we can use instead. It simply copies a block of bytes from one location to another, so we can use it to copy arrays containing elements of any type. In fact, the standard libraries provide a set of easy-to-use functions that perform tasks such as

Aside 10.2b (manyavgs.c) A program that repeatedly calls `tableAverage`.

```
/*
 * A main program to use our table-averaging function.
 */
#include <stdio.h>
#include <stdlib.h>

#define MAX_ENTRIES 10000       /* # of entries in table */
#define MAX_AVERAGES 10000      /* # of average calculations */

int main()
{
  double tableAverage(int *ptr, int n);

  int table[MAX_ENTRIES];
  int i;
  double avg;

  for (i = 0; i < MAX_ENTRIES; i++)    /* initialize the table */
    table[i] = i;

  /* loop to do MAX_AVERAGES searches, each time going further
     in the table */

  for (i = 0; i < MAX_AVERAGES; i++)
    avg = tableAverage(table, MAX_ENTRIES);

  return EXIT_SUCCESS;
}
```

copying, searching, or initializing blocks of bytes. Table 10.1 lists these functions. To use these functions, we need to include the standard header file string.h.

To copy one array into another, we pass **memcpy** pointers to the first element of the arrays, along with the number of *bytes* we want to copy. **memcpy** copies its second argument into its first, 1 byte at a time. So we can copy **g** into **f** with

```
memcpy(f, g, sizeof(g));
```

f and **g** are pointers to the first elements of those arrays, and since **g** is declared as an array, `sizeof(g)` is the number of bytes in that array.[9]

How can we implement a function like **memcpy** that doesn't care what type of pointers we pass to it? The trick is that we declare **memcpy**'s two pointer parameters as pointers to **void** (declared as **void ***). Pointers to **void** differ from other pointers in several ways. Ordinarily, there are no automatic conversions between pointers. To assign a pointer of one type to a pointer of another type, we're forced to insert an explicit

---

[9]The call **memcpy(f, g, MAXVALS)** is incorrect. Why? Because the third argument must be in *bytes*, not *elements*.

FUNCTION	WHAT IT DOES
`void *memcpy(d,s,n)`	Copy **n** bytes from the location pointed to by **s** into the location pointed to by **d**. Returns **d**. Don't use it when the memory locations overlap.
`void *memmove(d,s,n)`	Exactly like **memcpy** except that the memory locations may overlap.
`int memcmp(s1,s2,n)`	Compare the first **n** bytes in **s1** with the first **n** bytes in **s2**. Returns a negative value if **s1** < **s2**, zero if they're equal, and a positive value if **s1** > **s2**.
`void *memchr(s,c,n)`	Find the first occurrence of **c** in the first **n** bytes of **s**. Returns a pointer to the character if found, or the null pointer otherwise.
`void *memset(d,c,n)`	Copy the byte **c** into the first **n** locations pointed to by **d**. Returns **d**.

Table 10.1 Functions that access blocks of bytes. **d** is a pointer to a **void**; **s**, **s1**, and **s2** are pointers to **const void**; **n** is a **size_t**; and **c** is an **int** cast to an **unsigned char** for comparison purposes.

cast. But we can assign any pointer to and from a pointer to **void** without a cast. That's what happens when we call **memcpy**: the pointers we pass are automatically converted to pointers to **void**.

The other difference is that we can't dereference a pointer to **void** or do pointer arithmetic with it. We first have to convert it to some other pointer type. **memcpy** treats the pointer it's passed as a pointer to a byte and goes through the blocks of bytes it's passed, copying 1 byte at a time.

Figure 10.23 shows one possible implementation of **memcpy**, called **ourmemcpy** to prevent name conflicts with the standard library function. We also provide a main program that uses it to copy an array of **double**s.

We've declared the two pointer parameters **xptr** and **yptr** as pointers to **void**, so it's illegal to dereference them with ***xptr** or ***yptr**. Before we can access the bytes to which they point, we must turn them into pointers to bytes (**unsigned char**s). That's easy to do: we simply assign them to variables declared as pointers to **Byte** (a **typedef** to **unsigned char**).

```
Byte        *destptr = xptr;
const Byte *srcptr = yptr;
```

There are a couple of subtleties about **memcpy**. First, it returns the generic pointer passed as a first argument. So far, however, we've simply ignored this return value. Second, the parameter holding the number of bytes to copy has type **size_t**. That's because we usually pass it the result of doing **sizeof** on the array we're copying. And third, we can't use **memcpy** if the copied arrays overlap. That situation arises when we copy one part of an array to earlier or later in the array. In these situations, we need to use a separate function, **memmove**, that's identical to **memcpy**, except that it *always* works correctly. Why are there two functions? Because sometimes we want **memcpy**'s efficiency and other times we want **memmove**'s generality.

```
/*
 * One possible implementation of memcpy, along with a program that
 * uses it to copy one array into another.
 */
#include <stdio.h>
#include <stdlib.h>

#define MAXVALS 10              /* number of items in array */

typedef unsigned char Byte;    /* BYTE's a synonym for unsigned char */

int main()
{
  void ourmemcpy(void *xptr, const void *yptr, size_t n);

  double f[MAXVALS];
  double g[MAXVALS] = {7.5, 4.5, 5.4, 9.8, 9.5,
                       8.2, 9.1, 9.9, 4.5, 6.3};
  int    i;

  ourmemcpy(f, g, sizeof(g));            /* copy g into f */
  for (i = 0; i < MAXVALS; i++)          /* print f to see result */
    printf("f[%i]=%f\n", i, f[i]);

  return EXIT_SUCCESS;
}

void ourmemcpy(void *xptr, const void *yptr, size_t n)
{
  Byte        *destptr = xptr;
  const Byte *srcptr  = yptr;
  const Byte *endptr  = srcptr + n;

  while (srcptr < endptr)
    *destptr++ = *srcptr++;
}
```

Figure 10.23   (memcpy.c) One possible implementation of **memcpy**, called **ourmemcpy** to prevent name conflicts.

10.8   DYNAMICALLY ALLOCATING ARRAYS

Many programming languages let us specify an array's size at run time. That feature is convenient, since we don't always know at compile time exactly how many elements an array should have. Unfortunately, C requires the number of items in an array to be known at compile time. The problem is that the arrays we allocate at compile time often turn out to be much too big, which wastes space, or much too small, which makes our programs fail.

Luckily, there are several library functions we can use to get around this restriction. Table 10.2 lists these functions and provides brief descriptions. The two we use most frequently are **malloc** (for "memory allocation"), which allocates storage space from a system-maintained pool of memory, and **free**, which returns the space allocated by **malloc** to this pool for reuse later. The idea is that we can use **malloc** to allocate space for an array and **free** to return it. Prototypes for these functions are defined in the system header file stdlib.h, which must be included to use them.

Allocating Storage with **malloc**

malloc is passed a single argument of type **size_t** specifying the number of bytes to allocate. It allocates a block of bytes of at least the desired size and returns a pointer to it or **NULL** if a large enough chunk could not be found. For example, we can allocate an array large enough for **n double**s with

```
double *tptr = malloc(n * sizeof(double));

if (tptr = NULL)
  printf("Couldn't allocate %i doubles\n", n);
```

malloc allocates bytes, not integers or floating points. If we want to allocate an array of 100 **double**s, we can't simply pass it 100. Instead, we must pass it the number of bytes an array of 100 **double**s requires, the size of a **double** times 100.

We can use **malloc** to allocate space for an array of any type. **malloc** simply returns a pointer to the first byte in a block of bytes and guarantees that the returned block satisfies the alignment considerations for all of C's data types. This returned pointer is a pointer to **void**, so we must place it into a pointer to a **double** before we can actually dereference it to access the allocated array elements. There's no need for a cast, though, since C does the appropriate automatic conversion when we do the assignment.

Deallocating Storage with **free**

free takes a pointer to an array of bytes allocated by **malloc** or **calloc** and makes that storage available to be reallocated. We can return the memory used by the array **tptr** that we allocated above with

```
free(tptr);
```

Because **free** can be used to free any block of bytes allocated by **malloc**, its argument is declared as a pointer to **void**. But we don't have to cast **tptr**, as it's automatically converted to a pointer to **void**.

An Example of Dynamic Allocation

We use **malloc** and **free** in one final variant of our input-reversing program. In particular, we package **malloc** in a function **dblTableCreate**, which allocates a table of **n double**s and prints an error if **malloc** fails, and **free** in a function

FUNCTION	WHAT IT DOES
`void *calloc(n,size)`	Allocates space for **n** items, each of **size** bytes. Sets the allocated space to zero. Returns a pointer to the beginning of the allocated space or **NULL** if the space can't be allocated.
`void free(p)`	Allows allocated space pointed to by **p** to be allocated again.
`void *malloc(size)`	Allocate space for **size** bytes. Doesn't initialize the allocated space. Returns a pointer to the beginning of the allocated space or **NULL** if the space can't be allocated.
`void *realloc(p,size)`	Changes the space allocated by **p** to be **size** bytes. Returns a pointer to the beginning of the allocated space or **NULL** if the space can't be allocated. The contents of the space pointed to by **p** are unchanged.

Table 10.2 Functions for managing dynamically allocated storage. **n** and **size** are both **size_t**, and **p** is a pointer to **void**.

dblTableDestroy, which deallocates the table after verifying that it wasn't accidentally passed a null pointer. Figure 10.24 contains these functions.

The input-reversing program itself, shown in Figure 10.25, expects its input to be broken into groups, with each group preceded by a count of the items in it. The program reads and reverses each of these groups. Unlike most of our earlier versions, however, it expects **double**s as its input values, not **int**s. Here's some sample input and output:

```
8 19.8 35.5 25.3 45.5 31.8 40.5 50.2 12.9
12.900000
50.200000
40.500000
31.800000
45.500000
25.300000
35.500000
19.800000
5 15.4 20.2 12.6 19.9 16.5
16.500000
19.900000
12.600000
20.200000
15.400000
```

How can the program read and reverse a group? It needs to read the group into an array large enough to hold it and then print this array in reverse order. After the program reads the group's size, it uses **dblTableCreate** to allocate a large enough array. It then uses **dblTableFill** to fill it and **dblTablePrintRev** to print it in reverse order. Once the program is done with a group, it uses **dblTableDestroy** to release the group's storage, so it can be reused for the next group.

```
/*
 * Allocate and free a table of arrays of doubles, with error checking.
 */
#include <stdio.h>
#include <stddef.h>                 /* definition of NULL */
#include <stdlib.h>                 /* declaration for malloc/free */

double *dblTableCreate(int n)
{
  double *tptr = malloc(n * sizeof(double));

  if (tptr == NULL)
    printf("Couldn't allocate %i doubles\n", n);
  return tptr;
}

void dblTableDestroy(double *tptr)
{
  if (tptr != NULL)
    free(tptr);
}
```

Figure 10.24 (dmaketab.c) Functions to allocate and free a table of **double**s.

Some Common Mistakes

malloc is a powerful function, but we have to be careful when we use it. One problem arises when we run out of memory. If there isn't enough memory to honor our request, **malloc** will fail and will return **NULL** instead of a legitimate pointer. That means it's crucial to check whether the pointer **malloc** returned is **NULL** before using it.

> *Don't assume **malloc** will always succeed.*

Another problem arises if we fail to initialize the storage **malloc** allocates. This space starts off with whatever happens to be in memory at the time it's allocated. That means we have to be careful to initialize it ourselves. There is, however, a variant of **malloc** that allocates the storage and fills it with zeros. This function, **calloc**, takes two arguments rather than one. The first is the number of items (an **unsigned int**); the second is the size of each item (a **size_t**). Like **malloc**, it returns a pointer to the first byte in the storage it allocated.

> *Don't assume the storage **malloc** provides is initialized to zero.*

One final problem arises if we modify the pointer **malloc** returns. If we increment that pointer, for example, it no longer points to the beginning of the storage we allocated,

```
/*
 * Read and reverse groups within the input.
 */
#include <stdio.h>
#include <stdlib.h>                    /* definition of malloc */

int main()
{
  double *dblTableCreate(int n);
  void dblTableDestroy(double *tptr);
  int  dblTableFill(double a[], int max);
  void dblTablePrintRev(double a[], int n);

  int n;                        /* elements in group, table */
  int res;                      /* scanf result */

  while ((res = scanf("%i", &n)) == 1)
  {
    double *tptr = dblTableCreate(n);

    if (tptr)
      dblTablePrintRev(tptr, dblTableFill(tptr, n));
    dblTableDestroy(tptr);
  }
  if (res != EOF)
    printf("Couldn't read all elements\n");

  return (res == EOF) ? EXIT_SUCCESS : EXIT_FAILURE;
}
```

Figure 10.25   (grprev.c)   A program to reverse groups within its input.

and we can no longer pass that pointer to **free** to return that storage. We're best off treating that pointer like a constant, just as if it were the name of an array.

> *Don't modify the pointer returned by* **malloc**.

Similarly, there are several common mistakes made when using **free**. One is to use it to deallocate storage that wasn't originally obtained from **malloc**, such as local or global variables. This causes general chaos, since **free** assumes that it's releasing storage obtained from **malloc**. Another is to try to access storage after it's been released with **free**. Some implementations will let us get away with this, but it's a bad idea, since it's possible that storage has already been reallocated elsewhere.

> **free** *only pointers obtained from* **malloc**, *and don't access the storage after it's been* **free***d.*

10.9   CASE STUDY—DYNAMICALLY ALLOCATED SETS

*This section
is optional!*

This chapter concludes with a case study in which we extend our sets package from the previous chapter to allow varying set sizes. Surprisingly, we need only make a few changes to our earlier version. Figure 10.26 shows our new version of sets.h, renamed sets2.h, and Figure 10.27 shows our new version of sets.c, renamed sets2.c.

First, we need to add two new functions: **setCreate** creates a new set capable of handling a specified number of elements; **setDestroy** gets rid of a set once we no longer need it. **setCreate** dynamically allocates the storage needed for a **Set**; **setDestroy** releases it. Their prototypes are:

```
Set setCreate(unsigned int n);
void setDestroy(Set s);
```

Since we want sets to start out empty, we use **calloc** to allocate storage rather than **malloc**. This guarantees that all bytes used for the set are initially zero.

Second, we need to redeclare **Set** as a pointer, rather than as a fixed-size array. Specifically, we define **Set** as a pointer to **void**. That way we keep the details of what a **Set** actually is hidden from its callers. They don't need to know that a **Set** is a dynamically allocated array of **unsigned short**s. Unfortunately, this complicates the functions implementing sets, since they now have to cast the **Set** pointer to a pointer to an **unsigned short** before dereferencing it.

Third, we have to modify the other set functions, the ones that access the individual set elements. They're still passed a **Set**, but now they have to cast it into a pointer to an **unsigned short**, so that they can dereference it to get to the bits representing the set values.

To redo our earlier program that printed the unique and duplicate values in its input, we have only to make two minor changes. There is no longer a constant **MAXELEMS** defined in sets2.h, so we now define it appropriately in the programs that use sets. And it's no longer sufficient to simply declare **Set** variables. Now we need to call **setCreate** to actually allocate space for the **Set** elements. Figure 10.28 shows a revised version of that earlier program.

Since all our sets are no longer exactly the same size, we were forced to modify the **setPrint** function to take an additional parameter: the size of the set it's printing. Figure 10.29 contains an updated version of our earlier setutils.h and Figure 10.30 contains an extension to setutils.c.

) SUMMARY

- C provides pointers, a data type that can hold addresses. We obtain pointers with **&** and obtain the value they point to with *****.

- There is a generic pointer type, **void ***, that can contain any type of pointer. But before we can make use of that pointer, we must cast it to another type.

```
/*
 * Improved definitions to use "sets" of integers.
 */
typedef void *Set;

extern Set    setCreate(unsigned int n);
extern void   setDestroy(Set s);
extern void   setAdd(Set s, int e);
extern void   setDelete(Set s, int e);
extern int    setMember(const Set s, int e);
```

Figure 10.26   (sets2.h) The revised header file for sets.

- We can add or subtract an integer and a pointer, and we can subtract one pointer from another. The arithmetic takes place in units of the pointed-to type. We can also compare two pointers, so long as they point to the same array.

- To print a pointer, we cast it to **void *** and use **printf**'s **%p** formatting code.

- We can combine pointer arithmetic and comparisons to traverse arrays more efficiently than with array subscripting. Pointer arithmetic takes place in units of the pointed-to type.

- C has several library functions to manage dynamic memory allocation: **malloc**, which allocates a chunk of memory; **calloc**, which allocates and sets to zero a chunk of memory; and **free**, which returns a chunk of memory to the system.

EXERCISES

Explore **10–1** Compile and run the programs in this chapter.

10–2 We provided a main program to compile and run the different versions of our function to compute the average of an array (Aside 10.2b). Compare the performance of the pointer and array indexing versions on your machine.

Modify **10–3** Rewrite all of Chapter 8's programs and functions to use pointers to traverse their arrays. This is a sizable exercise, but well worth doing!

10–4 Rewrite **tableSearch** (Figure 10.18) to use pointers to search backward from the end of the array rather than forward from the front.

Extend **10–5** Rewrite Chapter 9's queue-manipulating functions (Figure 9.22) to use pointers rather than array indexing. Then extend it to allocate the queues dynamically by providing a **createQueue** function that should be called before the queue is accessed with **enqueue** or **dequeue**.

```
/*
 * Functions to handle dynamically allocated sets.
 */
#include <stdlib.h>
#include "sets2.h"

#define US_BITS 16

static int word(int elem);
static int bit(int elem);

Set setCreate(unsigned int n)            /* create an empty set */
{
  return calloc((n / US_BITS) + ((n % US_BITS) != 0),
                sizeof(unsigned short));
}

void setDestroy(Set s)                   /* get rid of a set */
  { free(s); }

void setAdd(Set s, int elem)             /* add element to set */
  { * ((unsigned short *) s + word(elem)) |= 1 << bit(elem); }

void setDelete(Set s, int elem)          /* delete element from set */
  { * ((unsigned short *) s + word(elem)) &= ~(1 << bit(elem)); }

int setMember(const Set s, int elem)     /* is item in set? */
{
  const unsigned int temp = * ((const unsigned short *) s + word(elem));

  return (temp >> bit(elem)) & 01;
}

static int word(int elem)
  { return elem / US_BITS; }             /* word # containing element */

static int bit(int elem)
  { return elem % US_BITS; }             /* bit # representing element */
```

Figure 10.27 (sets2.c) The revised source for the set operations.

10–6 Extend the group reversal program to allocate more space only if the existing array is too small.

Code **10–7** Write `tableReverse`, a function to reverse an array in place. First write it using array subscripting and then using pointers.

10–8 Write `tableDelete`, a function that deletes all occurrences of a particular item from an array of `int`s. It does the delete by shifting array elements. First write it using array subscripting and then using pointers.

```
/*
 * Identify duplicates in the input.
 */
#include <stdio.h>
#include <stdlib.h>
#include "sets2.h"
#include "setutls2.h"

int main()
{
  const int MAXELEMS = 512;                  /* # of set elements */
  Set    unique = setCreate(MAXELEMS),       /* unique and */
         dup    = setCreate(MAXELEMS);        /*   duplicate sets */
  int    r, inp;                             /* scanf return, input value */

  while ((r = scanf("%i", &inp)) != EOF)
  {
    if (r != 1)
    {
      printf("Value in error.\n");
      break;
    }
    if (inp < 0 || inp >= MAXELEMS)
    {
      printf("Value out of range.\n");
      continue;
    }
    if (setMember(unique, inp))
      setSwitch(dup, unique, inp);
    else if (!setMember(dup, inp))
      setAdd(unique, inp);
  }
  printf("Unique values\n");
  setPrint(unique, MAXELEMS);
  printf("Duplicate values\n");
  setPrint(dup, MAXELEMS);

  return EXIT_SUCCESS;
}
```

Figure 10.28   (usesets2.c)   The revised program to use the set operations.

10–9   Write **calloc**, assuming **malloc** exists.

10–10   Write **mymemmove**, an implementation of **memmove**, the variant of **memcpy** that can handle an overlap between the copy's source and destination.

10–11   Write **tableDiff**, a function that compares two arrays of integers and returns the subscript of the first place they differ. If the arrays are the same, the function returns −1. First write it using array subscripting and then using pointers.

```
/*
 * Revised prototypes for set utility functions.
 */
void setSwitch(Set new, Set old, int value);
void setPrint(const Set set, int max);
```

Figure 10.29   (setutls2.h)   The revised header file for the set utilities.

```
/*
 * Set utility functions.
 *
 *    Revisions:
 *      1) Now includes sets2.h
 *      2) Now has additional argument for number of items to print
 *      3) The passed in Set is a constant.
 */
#include <stdio.h>
#include "sets2.h"

void setSwitch(Set new, Set old, int value)
{
  setDelete(old, value);
  setAdd(new, value);
}

void setPrint(const Set set, int max)
{
  int i;                                    /* next potential element */

  for (i = 0; i < max; i++)
    if (setMember(set, i))
      printf("%i\n", i);
}
```

Figure 10.30   (setutls2.c)   The revised definitions of the set utilities.

10–12 Write **tableSym**, a function that tests whether an array of **int**s is symmetrical. That is, it returns a 1 if the array would print the same forward and backward, and a zero otherwise. Use pointers. How concise a function can you create?

10–13 Write **tableMax**, a function to find the largest value in an array. Use pointers to traverse the array.

10–14 Write **tableDup**, a function to create a dynamically allocated copy of an existing array of **int**s. It takes the name of the array it's copying and the number of elements in the array and returns the new array.

10–15 Write **tableDump**, a function that prints all of the elements in an array and their addresses, one per line.

11 STRINGS

This chapter presents strings, a special type of array of characters. We introduce string constants and variables and examine the close relationship strings have with pointers. We present the standard library functions for manipulating strings and provide array-subscripting and pointer-indexing implementations of several of the more commonly used ones. We also present an implementation of a useful function for reading an input line into a string and rework several of our earlier programs to use it. We conclude with a case study: a program that strips consecutive duplicate lines from its input.

11.1   STRING CONSTANTS

A *string* is simply an array of characters, terminated with an extra character, the null character, `'\0'` (backslash zero). We can create a *constant* string by enclosing a group of characters in double quotation marks.

```
"Enter YES or NO: "
```

C folds consecutive constant strings into a single string, so

```
"Enter " "YES " "or" " NO: "
```

is equivalent to the string above. We take advantage of this automatic folding when we have to store strings too long to fit on a single line.

When the compiler sees a constant string, it tacks on a terminating null character, allocates spacc for the string, and returns a pointer to its first character. Typically, we assign this pointer to a pointer variable.

```
char *q = "Enter YES or NO: ";
```

This declares **q** as a pointer to a character and initializes **q** to point to the first character in our constant string.

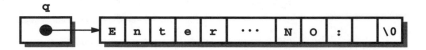

The result is that **q** points to a string containing 18 characters: the 17 between the double quotation marks and the final null character inserted by the compiler.

Why does the compiler insert the terminating null? Primarily to make it easier for us to pass strings to functions—we don't have to pass their length. C has a library of useful string functions, all of which expect a string to be null-terminated. We can, for example, print a string using **printf**'s **%s** format without explicitly supplying its length.

A string constant has type "pointer to **char**", and a value equal to a pointer to its first character. That means we can use a constant string anywhere we can use a pointer to a **char**. We can, for example, separate the variable declaration from the assignment.

```
char *q;

q = "Enter YES or NO: ";
```

And we can pass strings as function arguments, as we've been doing all along with **printf**.

```
printf("That wasn't a valid response\n");
```

One thing we can't do is change the characters within a string constant. For the pointer **q** above, it's illegal to do

```
q[5] = 'x';
```

This restriction arises because compilers are free to place string constants in read-only memory and to merge duplicate string constants.

Figure 11.1 takes advantage of string constants in a new version of **yesOrNo** that is passed a prompt to write. Figure 11.2 is a header file that supplies its prototype and defines the constants it uses. And Figure 11.3 is a main program that uses it. The main program takes advantage of being able to treat constant strings as pointers to characters. In particular, it uses the conditional operator to select which string to pass to **printf**.

```
printf("%s!\n", (yesOrNo(q) == YES) ? "YES" : "NO");
```

This works because both **"YES"** and **"NO"** are pointers to the first character in the string, and the conditional operator is really selecting which pointer to pass to **printf**.

11.2   STRING VARIABLES

So far our strings have been constants, for which the compiler allocates space. But we can also create strings by allocating an array and then providing the individual characters ourselves.

```
char q[18] = {'E', 'n', 't', 'e', 'r', ' ', 'Y', 'E', 'S',
              ' ', 'o', 'r', ' ', 'N', 'O', ':', ' ', '\0'};
```

This declares **q** as an array of 18 characters and then initializes those characters from the list we provide. When we take this approach, we have to be careful to explicitly provide the trailing null. The advantage to allocating the array ourselves is that we can then change the characters within it.

```
/*
 * Obtain a yes or no answer from the user, prompting for response.
 */
#include <stdio.h>
#include <ctype.h>
#include "yesorno2.h"

const int YES = 1, NO = 0, BAD = -1;

int yesOrNo(const char *prompt)
{
  void skipToEOL(int c);

  int answer;

  while (printf(prompt), (answer = tolower(getchar())) != EOF)
  {
    skipToEOL(answer);
    if (answer == 'y')
      return YES;
    if (answer == 'n')
      return NO;
    printf("That's not a reasonable answer.\n");
  }
  return BAD;
}
```

Figure 11.1   (yesorno8.c)   A new version of **yesOrNo** that's passed a prompt to write.

```
/*
 * Prototypes and constants for prompting version of yesOrNo
 */
int yesOrNo(const char *prompt);

extern const int YES, NO, BAD;
```

Figure 11.2   (yesorno2.h)   The prototype for **yesOrNo**, along with some constant definitions.

> *Don't forget to supply the trailing null character when creating a string.*

Listing all the characters is somewhat tedious, especially for large arrays. Fortunately, there's a special shortcut for initializing character arrays: we simply surround the initial characters by double quotes, just as if they were a string constant.

```
char q[18] = "Enter YES or NO: ";
```

```
/*
 * Main program using our new yesOrNo function.
 */
#include <stdio.h>
#include <stdlib.h>
#include "yesorno2.h"

int main()
{
  char *q;                                    /* question for user */

  q = "Enter YES or NO: ";

  printf("%s!\n", (yesOrNo(q) == YES) ? "YES" : "NO");

  return EXIT_SUCCESS;
}
```

Figure 11.3   (useyn5.c) A new main program that uses **yesOrNo**.

But this isn't a real string constant, even though it looks like one. That is, its value is not an address. When we declare an array and provide a string constant as its initial value, the constant is simply a shorthand to save us from having to provide the entire list of characters and the trailing null. As with other arrays, we can omit the subscript and the compiler will allocate just enough space for the elements we provide. This declaration

```
char q[] = "Enter YES or NO: ";
```

is exactly equivalent to the one above.

> *We can't simply assign one character string to another, just as we couldn't assign arrays.*

Although it seems as if the following set of declarations and assignments should work, they don't.

```
char  *q = "Enter YES or NO: ";
char  qcopy[100];
    . . .
qcopy = q;
```

The reason is that even though **qcopy** is indeed a pointer to the first character in the array, it is a *constant*. Its value, the address of **qcopy[0]**, may not change. If we really want to copy the characters in **q** into **qcopy**, we have to do so one at a time. Luckily, as we'll see shortly, there's a standard library function to do this operation for us.

11.3 BUILDING STRINGS FROM THE INPUT

We often want to build strings from a program's input instead of creating them at compile time. Figure 11.4 contains a new version of our line-numbering program that needs this ability. It works a line at a time, rather than a character at a time. It reads each line into a string and then prints the line number and the string. To do this, it makes use of a new function: **getline**.

Figure 11.5 contains **getline**. It reads a line of input, with a maximum length of **max** characters, into a character array **line**. The string passed to **getline** must be large enough to hold **max** + 1 characters (the characters on the line, plus the trailing null).

How does **getline** work? It repeatedly reads characters and places them into the array **line**. It stops when it encounters the end of the input line (a **\n**) or finds that the array is full. It does *not* place the newline character into the array. But it does terminate the string with a null. Since there must be room for this extra null character, **getline** stops filling the array after it has read **max** characters—but it continues reading until it hits the end-of-line character, effectively ignoring any other characters on the line. This guarantees that the next time the function is called, it begins reading characters from the start of a new line. **getline** returns the number of characters it placed in the string, not counting the added null character, or **-1** when it reaches end of file.

11.4 STRING FUNCTIONS FROM THE STANDARD LIBRARY

C provides no operators that work on strings directly, such as string assignment, string comparison, or string concatenation. Instead, we have to rely on a set of standard string library functions. Table 11.1 lists the string-handling functions we use most frequently. The standard library actually contains several other functions, but we leave the more obscure and more complicated functions for Appendix A.

All of these functions expect the strings they're passed to be terminated with a null character. Our programs will fail miserably when we pass these functions character arrays without the terminating null. Similarly, if we use the **%s** format to **printf** and mistakenly provide it with a character array that's not null-terminated, it will display whatever characters it finds in the memory following the array, stopping only when it finally encounters a null or gets a memory error.

> *Make sure to null-terminate any character arrays you pass the standard string functions.*

The copying and concatenating functions also expect the destination string to be large enough to contain the result and to not overlap with the source string.

```
/*
 * Line number its input, one line at a time.
 */
#include <stdio.h>
#include <stdlib.h>

#define MAXLEN  80                          /* longest line */

int main()
{
  int getline(char line[], int max);

  char          line[MAXLEN + 1];           /* input line (plus \0) */
  unsigned long lines = 0L;                 /* line count */

  while (getline(line, MAXLEN) != -1)
    printf("%8lu %s\n", ++lines, line);

  return EXIT_SUCCESS;
}
```

Figure 11.4   (lineno6.c)   A version of our line-numbering program that reads its input a line at a time.

```
/*
 * Read a single input line into an array.
 */
#include <stdio.h>

int getline(char line[], int max)
{
  int c;                                /* current character */
  int i = 0;                            /* character count */

  while ((c = getchar()) != '\n' && c != EOF)
    if (i < max)
      line[i++] = c;
  line[i] = '\0';                       /* terminate with null */
  return (c == EOF) ? -1 : i;
}
```

Figure 11.5   (getline.c)   The function **getline**, which reads an input line into a string.

NAME	WHAT IT DOES
`char *strcat(s1,s2)`	Concatenates **s2** to the end of **s1**, returning **s1**.
`char *strncat(s1,s2,n)`	Concatenates at most **n** characters from **s2** to the end of **s1**, returning **s1**.
`char *strcpy(s1,s2)`	Copies **s2** to **s1**, including the null character, returning **s1**.
`char *strncpy(s1,s2,n)`	Copies at most **n** characters from **s2** to **s1**, returning **s1**. If it stops copying before the null, the null isn't added to **s1**.
`int strcmp(s1,s2)`	Compares **s1** and **s2**, returning less than 0, 0, or greater than 0, depending on whether **s1** is less than, equal to, or greater than **s2**, respectively.
`int strncmp(s1,s2,n)`	Compares at most **n** characters; same return as **strcmp**.
`size_t strlen(s)`	Returns number of characters in **s**, *not* counting trailing null.
`char *strchr(s,c)`	Returns a pointer to the first occurrence of **c** in **s**, or **NULL**.
`char *strrchr(s,c)`	Returns a pointer to the last occurrence of **c** in **s**, or **NULL**.
`char *strstr(s1, s2)`	Returns a pointer to the first occurrence of the string **s2** in **s1**, or **NULL**.
`size_t strspn(s1,s2)`	Returns length of prefix of **s1** consisting of characters in **s2**.
`size_t strcspn(s1,s2)`	Returns length of prefix of **s1** consisting of characters not in **s2**.
`char *strpbrk(s1,s2)`	Returns pointer to first occurrence in **s1** of any character in **s2**, or **NULL** if there are no such occurrences.

Table 11.1 Commonly used standard string functions (**s**, **s1**, and **s2** are pointers to **char**, **c** is an **int** treated as a **char** during comparisons, and **n** is a **size_t**). string.h contains their prototypes.

Using the Standard String Functions

Figure 11.6 is a small program that uses several of these standard library string functions. It reads input lines containing people's names and converts them to a last name, first name format. For the input:

```
Alex Quilici
Larry Miller
```

it produces the output:

```
Quilici, Alex
Miller, Larry
```

The program also does a little error checking, making sure that each input line fits the format it expects.

```
/*
 * Name conversion program
 */
#include <stdio.h>
#include <stdlib.h>
#include <string.h>
#include <stddef.h>

#define MAXLEN    80

int main()
{
  int    getline(char line[], int maxlen);

  char   inpline[MAXLEN + 1];     /* input line */
  int    len;                     /* length of input line */
  char   newname[MAXLEN + 2];     /* converted name (extra char for ,) */
  char   *blankptr;               /* pointer to blank separator */

  while ((len = getline(inpline, MAXLEN)) != -1)
    if (len == 0 ||
        (blankptr = strchr(inpline, ' ')) == NULL ||
        strlen(blankptr + 1) == 0)
      printf("ERROR: bad format input line\n");
    else
    {                                      /* split into two strings */
      strcpy(newname, blankptr + 1);       /* make last name first */
      strcat(newname, ", ");               /* append comma */
      *blankptr = '\0';
      strcat(newname, inpline);            /* put first name last */
      printf("%s\n", newname);             /* write new name */
    }

  return EXIT_SUCCESS;
}
```

Figure 11.6   (convnam.c)   Convert names from first name/last name to last name/first name.

How does this program work? It begins by reading the input line into a character array, **inpline**. It then locates the blank separating the first and last names, copies the characters after the blank (the last name) into another character array **newname**, appends a comma and a blank to **newname**, and finally copies the characters preceding the blank (the first name) onto the end of this array. After all this work it prints **newname**.

We make heavy use of the string library functions. First, we use **strchr** to locate the separating blank.

```
                blankptr = strchr(inpline, ' ')
```

strchr takes a string and a character and returns a pointer to the first occurrence of that character in the string. It returns **NULL** if it can't find the character. We use **strlen** to make sure that we have a last name following the separating blank.

```
strlen(blankptr + 1) == 0
```

strlen takes a string and returns the number of characters in it, *not counting the trailing* **'\0'**. Here, we make sure at least one character follows the blank and precedes the trailing null.

Once we've gotten a pointer to the blank, we start constructing the new name. We first use **strcpy** to copy the characters after the blank into **newname**.

```
strcpy(newname, blankptr + 1);  /* make last name first */
```

strcpy takes two arguments, both strings, and copies the second into the first, returning a pointer to its first argument. Here, we pass **blankptr + 1** because we want to start copying with the character after the blank. Figure 11.7 shows the result of performing these calls.

strcpy assumes that the second string is null terminated and that the first string is large enough. Here, that's a safe assumption, since the string we're copying into (**newname**) is at least as large as the string we're copying from (**inpline**). The order of **strcpy**'s arguments may seem strange, but it is intended to mimic assignment.

After we've copied the last name, we need to append a comma and a blank to it. To do that, we use one other standard string function: **strcat**.

```
strcat(newname, ", ");         /* append comma */
```

strcat copies its second argument onto the end of its first argument, overwriting the terminating null. It terminates the entire string with a null character. Like **strcpy**, **strcat** assumes there's enough room for all the characters it appends.

Finally, we again use **strcat** to copy the first name onto the end of **newname**.

```
*blankptr = '\0';
strcat(newname, inpline);
```

Both **strcat** and **strcpy** copy characters until they hit a null. Since we want to copy only the characters before the separating blank, we replace it with a null before calling **strcat**.

Figure 11.8 is an improved version of our name conversion program. This time we allow more varied input—we let one or more blanks and tabs precede, separate, and follow the names. This makes our program considerably more complex. We now have to search for where the first and last name begin. The first name can be preceded by blanks and tabs. To locate it, we use a new function: **strspn**.

```
fnameptr = inpline + strspn(inpline, Spaces);
```

strspn takes two arguments, both strings. It returns the length of the longest prefix of the first argument that contains only characters found in its second argument. Here, we want the length of the prefix containing only blanks and tabs (the contents of a global constant **Spaces**). We obtain a pointer to the beginning of the name by adding the number of these leading blanks to **inpline**, the address of the beginning of the string.

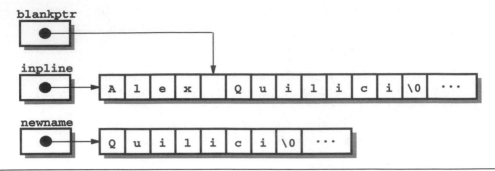

Figure 11.7 The pointers after finding the blank separating the names and copying the last name.

Our next task is to find the blank following the first name. We do that using **strcspn**:

```
blankptr = fnameptr + strcspn(fnameptr, Spaces);
```

strcspn is similar to **strspn**. The difference is that it returns the length of the longest prefix not containing any of the characters in its second argument. Here, we're trying to determine the number of non-blanks and non-tabs, since those characters constitute the characters in the first name.

We use these functions again to obtain pointers to the beginning and end of the last name. Once we have pointers to the first and last names and where they begin and end, we can start building the converted name, again using **strcpy** and **strcat**. Figure 11.9 shows the pointers that result.

Figure 11.10 implements a new version of the **yesOrNo** function. This version improves the most recent version by requiring the user to enter entire words such as "yes" or "no" instead of single letter responses. To compare the user's response with the various "yes" or "no" responses, we use one final library function: **strcmp**.

```
if (strcmp(line, "yes") == 0 || strcmp(line, "YES") == 0)
  return YES;
if (strcmp(line, "no") == 0 || strcmp(line, "NO") == 0)
  return NO;
printf("That's not a reasonable answer\n");
```

strcmp takes two strings and returns a negative value if the first is lexicographically less than the second, zero if they are equal, and a positive value if the first is lexicographically greater than the second.[1] Here, we use it to compare the user's input line with various reasonable positive and negative responses.

---

[1] What this means is that **strcmp** orders strings by comparing their characters using the character codes in the underlying character set.

```c
/*
 * Name conversion program, more free-format version.
 */
#include <stdio.h>
#include <stdlib.h>
#include <string.h>
#include <stddef.h>

#define MAXLEN  80                      /* longest input line */

const char *const Spaces = " \t";

int main()
{
  int    getline(char line[], int maxlen);

  char   inpline[MAXLEN + 1];     /* input line */
  int    len;                     /* input line length */
  char   newname[MAXLEN + 2];     /* converted name (extra char for ,) */
  char   *fnameptr, *lnameptr;    /* ptr to first and last name */
  char   *blankptr;               /* ptr to separating blank */
  char   *followptr;              /* ptr to char after last name */
  char   *finalptr;               /* ptr to end of trailing blanks */

  while ((len = getline(inpline, MAXLEN)) != -1)
    if (len == 0)
      printf("ERROR: empty input line\n");
    else
    {                                   /* compute needed pointers */
      fnameptr = inpline + strspn(inpline, Spaces);
      blankptr = fnameptr + strcspn(fnameptr, Spaces);
      lnameptr = blankptr + strspn(blankptr, Spaces);
      followptr = lnameptr + strcspn(lnameptr, Spaces);
      finalptr = followptr + strspn(followptr, Spaces);
      if (fnameptr == blankptr || blankptr == lnameptr ||
        lnameptr == followptr || finalptr != inpline + len)
        printf("ERROR: not exactly two names on input line\n");
      else
      {                                 /* do the actual conversion */
        *followptr = '\0';              /* delete trailing blanks */
        *blankptr = '\0';               /* separate into two strings */
        strcpy(newname, lnameptr);
        strcat(newname, ", ");
        strcat(newname, fnameptr);
        printf("%s\n", newname);     /* display new name */
      }
    }

  return EXIT_SUCCESS;
}
```

Figure 11.8 (convnam2.c) An improved version of our name conversion program.

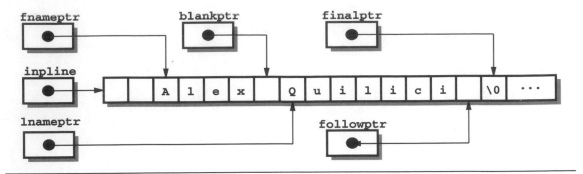

Figure 11.9 The pointers to the beginning and end of the first and last names.

```
/*
 * Obtain a yes or no answer, requiring multicharacter responses.
 */
#include <stdio.h>
#include <string.h>
#include "yesorno2.h"

#define MAXLEN  80

const int YES = 1, NO = 0, BAD = -1;

int yesOrNo(const char *prompt)
{
  int getline(char line[], int max);

  char line[MAXLEN + 1];                      /* input line */

  while (printf(prompt), getline(line, MAXLEN) != -1)
  {
    if (strcmp(line, "yes") == 0 || strcmp(line, "YES") == 0)
      return YES;
    if (strcmp(line, "no") == 0 || strcmp(line, "NO") == 0)
      return NO;
    printf("That's not a reasonable answer.\n");
  }
  return BAD;
}
```

Figure 11.10 (yesorno9.c) An even better version of our old **yesOrNo** function.

Implementing the Standard String Functions

Why does C provide all of these different string functions? It's not because they're difficult to write. In fact, most of these functions are short and simple. The real power of the standard string library is that it implements frequently used routines, simplifying our job of program construction.

Figure 11.11 shows one way to write functions like **strcpy**, **strcmp**, and **strlen**.[2] The actual code used by the standard string functions, however, differs from one environment to another. Our version of **strcpy** works by walking through the two strings, copying the next character in the second into the next character in the first. It stops when it hits the terminating null.

strcmp is similar, but as it walks through the two strings it compares the corresponding characters. It stops if the characters differ, because that means one of the strings is alphabetically less than the other. And it stops if it reaches null in both strings, because that means the strings are the same. **strcmp** returns the difference between the characters. Subtracting two characters yields zero if they are the same, a negative value when the first is alphabetically less than the second, and a positive value when it is greater.

strlen simply walks through the provided string, counting characters and stopping when it hits the null. It returns the count of characters it visited.

Additional String Functions

The standard I/O library provides two functions, extensions to **printf** and **scanf**, that allow output to and input from a string. These functions are **sprintf** and **sscanf**, respectively. Both take a string for input or output, a control string, and a list of variables. As with **scanf**, **sscanf** returns the number of values correctly converted.

We can use **sscanf** together with **getline** to avoid some of the problems associated with illegal input using **scanf**. We can read an entire input line using **getline** and then use **sscanf** to extract the values of the variables: Figure 11.12 is a new version of our earlier calculator program that reads the operands and operators using this technique. This method automatically ignores input lines containing invalid or missing data items, so we no longer have to quit the first time we encounter bad data.

We can use **sprintf** to build strings without having to resort to **strcpy** and **strcat**. We can rewrite this sequence from our name converting program

```
strcpy(newname, blankptr + 1);
strcat(newname, ", ");
*blankptr = '\0';
strcat(newname, inpline);
```

more compactly with **sprintf**.

```
*blankptr = '\0';
sprintf(newname, "%s, %s", blankptr + 1, inpline);
```

---

[2] We're not supposed to redefine library functions. In fact, most compilers warn us if we do. But we've redefined these functions so that you can easily link our implementations in with other programs in this chapter.

```
/*
 * Implementations of several standard string functions.
 */
#include <stddef.h>

char *strcpy(char d[], const char s[])              /* copy "s" -> "d" */
{
  int i;

  for (i = 0; (d[i] = s[i]) != '\0'; i++)
    ;
  return d;
}

int strcmp(const char s[], const char t[])      /* compare "s" and "t" */
{
  int i;

  for (i = 0; s[i] == t[i] && s[i] != '\0'; i++)
    ;
  return s[i] - t[i];
}

size_t strlen(const char s[])                       /* length of "s"? */
{
  size_t i;

  for (i = 0; s[i] != '\0'; i++)
    ;
  return i;
}
```

Figure 11.11   (string.c) Implementations of several of the standard string library functions.

While **sscanf** is similar to **scanf**, there is one important difference. With **scanf**, we can use a series of identical calls to process all of the input values. That's not true of **sscanf**, since each call to **sscanf** starts at the beginning of the string we give it.

Figure 11.13 provides one final example of these string functions in action. It's a new version of our earlier program to count the occurrences of various punctuation characters. The old version was a giant **switch** statement. Now, however, we have one string for each category of punctuation, and we do table lookup to determine which counter to update. In addition, we now display the counters using a function, **displayCounter**, that's passed a string identifying the counter and a counter to write. It uses a new feature of **printf** to write the identifying string:

```
printf("%-*s", LabelWidth, label);
```

The minus sign in a **printf** formatting code requests left justification (rather than the default right justification).

```
/*
 * Simple calculator program (uses getline) to read its input.
 */
#include <stdio.h>
#include <stdlib.h>

#define MAXLEN 80

int main()
{
  int    getline(char line[], int max);

  double op1, op2, result;            /* operands and result */
  char   operator;                    /* operator */
  char   inpline[MAXLEN + 1];         /* to hold input line */

  while (getline(inpline, MAXLEN) != -1)
    if (sscanf(inpline, "%lf%c%lf", &op1, &operator, &op2) != 3)
      printf("Input line in error.\n");
    else
    {
      switch(operator)
      {
        case '+':
          result = op1 + op2;
          break;
        case '-':
          result = op1 - op2;
          break;
        case '*':
          result = op1 * op2;
          break;
        case '/':
          if (op2 != 0.0)             /* watch out for divide by 0 */
            result = op1 / op2;
          else
          {
            printf("Warning: division by zero.\n");
            result = 0.0;
          }
          break;
        default:
          printf("Unknown operator: %c\n", operator);
          continue;
      }
      printf("%f\n", result);
    }
  return EXIT_SUCCESS;
}
```

Figure 11.12 (calc2.c) A new version of the calculator program that reads one line of input at a time.

```c
/*
 * Counts various types of punctuation characters.
 */
#include <stdio.h>
#include <stdlib.h>
#include <string.h>
#include <stddef.h>

const char *const Puncts    = ",.;:!?";
const char *const Brackets  = "(){}[]";
const char *const Quotes    = "'\"";

const int PrintWidth = 11;                      /* width of counter */
const int LabelWidth = 12;                      /* width of id string */

int main()
{
  void displayCount(char *label, unsigned long counter);

  int          c;
  unsigned long quotes = 0, brackets = 0, delims = 0, others = 0;

  while ((c = getchar()) != EOF)
    if (strchr(Quotes, c) != NULL)
      quotes++;                                 /* single & double quotes */
    else if (strchr(Brackets, c) != NULL)
      brackets++;                               /* punctuation brackets */
    else if (strchr(Puncts, c) != NULL)
      delims++;                                 /* usual punctuation */
    else
      others++;                                 /* other characters */

  displayCount("Quotes", quotes);
  displayCount("Brackets", brackets);
  displayCount("Delimiters", delims);
  displayCount("Other", others);

  return EXIT_SUCCESS;
}

void displayCount(char *label, unsigned long counter)
{
  printf("%-*s", LabelWidth, label);
  printf("%*lu\n", PrintWidth, counter);
}
```

Figure 11.13 (countpct2.c) A new version of our earlier program to count quotation, bracket, and punctuation characters in its input.

This version is considerably more compact and more easily extensible, but at a cost. All of its string searching makes it run more slowly than our original version.

11.5   USING POINTERS TO TRAVERSE STRINGS

Strings are simply arrays, so we can process them using pointers, and doing so tends to lead to the expected gains in efficiency.

Figure 11.14 provides a new version of **getline** that uses a pointer, **ptr**, to traverse the string. As it reads each character, it places the character into the location pointed to by **ptr** and then increments **ptr**. This version of **getline** also uses two other pointers: **startptr**, which points to the first character in the array, and **endptr**, which points to the last. We compare **ptr** with **endptr** to determine whether there is still room in the array. When we've read a line, we subtract **startptr** from **ptr** to determine how many characters we read. Figure 11.15 shows the relationship between all of these pointers.

Figure 11.16 shows how to rewrite our earlier versions of **strcpy**, **strcmp**, and **strlen** to use pointers. Our original version of **strcpy** used an array index **i** to walk through the strings **source** and **dest**. But we can also write the function to treat these strings as pointers (initialized to the first element of the respective arrays) rather than as arrays. When we do so, we access the elements indirectly through pointers rather than directly through array indices. We use **dest** and **source** to traverse the destination and source strings, respectively. Each pass through the loop begins by placing the character to which **source** points in the location to which **dest** points. We then compare this character with **\0** to see if we've reached the end of the string. If we haven't, we increment both pointers and continue the loop. **strcmp** and **strlen** use similar techniques.

11.6   CASE STUDY—ELIMINATING DUPLICATE LINES

This section is optional!

To further illustrate strings, we will write a program (called uniq) that takes text as input and copies it to its output, minus any lines that are the same as the line they follow. If the input consists of the lines

```
c
c
is
wonderful
wonderful
wonderful
```

we want the output to be

```
c
is
wonderful
```

```
/*
 * Read input line into an array, pointer version.
 */
#include <stdio.h>

int getline(char *ptr, int max)
{
  int         c;                     /* current character */
  char *const startptr = ptr;        /* pointer to line start */
  char *const endptr   = ptr + max;  /* pointer to line end */

  while ((c = getchar ()) != '\n' && c != EOF)
    if (ptr < endptr)
      *ptr++ = c;
  *ptr = '\0';                       /* terminate with null */
  return (c == EOF) ? -1 : ptr - startptr;
}
```

Figure 11.14   (getline2.c) Pointer version of **getline**.

When is this program useful? We used a variation, suggested in the exercises, to create a list of the number of different words that appear in this book. We first broke the input into individual words, one per line (using a program we wrote earlier), then sorted these lines (using a program we'll see in a later chapter), and finally ran uniq.

uniq is a useful program created from small, already existing pieces. It uses **getline**, **strcmp**, and **strcpy**, each of which we have already written. It processes its input a line at a time, using **strcmp** to compare the current and previous input lines. If they differ, it prints the current line and copies the current line into the previous one using **strcpy**. The process ends when we've read all the input (**getline** returns −1). Figure 11.17 contains uniq.

SUMMARY

- A string is an array of characters, terminated with the null character, '\0'. When we create a string, we must provide the terminating null ourselves.

- We initialize strings by declaring an array and providing a list of characters, or by declaring a pointer and assigning it to a string constant.

- We can easily write a function to read an input line into a string, then use **sscanf** to read individual values from this string. This allows us to easily recover from input errors.

- Since strings are arrays, we can run through them using either array subscripting or pointer indexing.

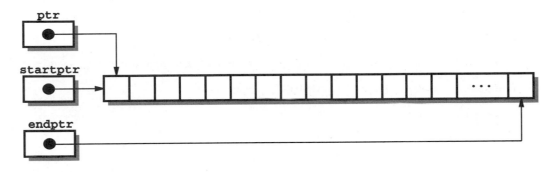

(a) The pointers when **getline** starts up.

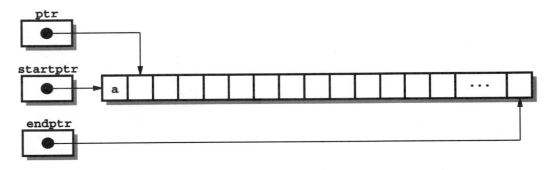

(b) The pointers after reading one character.

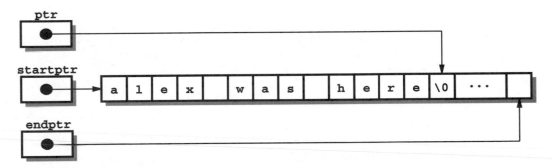

(c) The pointers after reading the input line "alex was here".

Figure 11.15 Pointers used in **getline**.

```
/*
 * Pointer versions of our string functions
 */
#include <stddef.h>

char *strcpy(char *dptr, const char *sptr)
{
  char *const startptr = dptr;         /* save starting pointer */

  for (; (*dptr = *sptr) != '\0'; dptr++, sptr++)
    ;
  return startptr;
}

int strcmp(const char *sptr, const char *tptr)
{
  for (; *sptr == *tptr && *sptr != '\0'; sptr++, tptr++)
    ;
  return *sptr - *tptr;                 /* difference of two chars */
}

size_t strlen(const char *ptr)
{
  const char *const startptr = ptr;

  for (; *ptr != '\0'; ptr++)
    ;
  return ptr - startptr;
}
```

Figure 11.16   (string2.c) Pointer versions of some of the string library functions.

- C provides a large library of functions for manipulating strings. To use them, we need to include string.h. They all expect the string to be null-terminated.

EXERCISES

Modify   **11–1** Modify Chapter 8's insertion sort program (Figure 8.9) to read its input with **getline** and **sscanf**. It should expect one value per line and report errors for any input lines not containing exactly one value.

Extend   **11–2** Extend the final version of **yesOrNo** (Aside 11.1d) to recognize answers such as "Ok", "Yeah", "Sure", and "Affirmative" as "yes" answers. Also recognize "Nope", "Nah", and "Negative" as "no" answers.

11–3 Write a variation of uniq (Figure 11.17) that prints only duplicated lines and another that prints only the first occurrence of each repetition.

```
/*
 * Strip consecutive duplicate lines from the input.
 */
#include <stdio.h>
#include <stdlib.h>
#include <string.h>

#define MAXLEN    80                            /* longest input line */
#define FALSE     0
#define TRUE      1

int main()
{
  int  getline(char *buf, int bufsize);

  char curr[MAXLEN + 1],                        /* current line */
       prev[MAXLEN + 1];                        /* previous line */
  int  first = TRUE;

  for (; getline(curr, MAXLEN) != -1; strcpy(prev, curr))
    if (first || strcmp(prev, curr) != 0)
    {
      printf("%s\n", curr);
      first = FALSE;
    }
  return EXIT_SUCCESS;
}
```

Figure 11.17   (uniq.c)   A program to remove duplicate lines from its input.

11–4   Write a variation of uniq (Figure 11.17) that prints one instance of each line, preceded by a count of the number of times the line is repeated.

Tune   **11–5**   Write compact pointer versions of the other string library functions we used in this chapter. Are these more efficient than straightforward array versions?

Code   **11–6**   Write **putline**, a function that takes a string and writes it and a trailing newline. Use **putchar** rather than **printf**.

11–7   Write the function **stringUpper** that takes a string as an argument and converts all of its characters into uppercase characters.

11–8   Write **stoi** (for string to integer), a function that takes a null-terminated string (array of **char**) containing all digit characters and converts the characters to an integer.

11–9   Write **itos**, a function that takes an integer and a character array and converts the integer into characters and places them into the array.

11–10   Implement **strchr**, **strrchr**, **strspn**, and **strcpsn**.

11–11   Using pointers and avoiding unnecessary local variables, write a function, **rmchr**, that takes a string and a character as arguments, removing all occurrences of the character

Aside 11.1a: Effectively Using Existing Libraries

While the standard library provides a set of extremely useful string functions, they tend to be difficult to use. It can be hard to remember, for example, to check for string equality by testing whether **strcmp**'s return value is zero. Similarly, we may have to stare for a while at a particular call to **strspn** before we figure out that it's looking for the first non-blank in a string.

We can improve our ability to write and understand code that manipulates strings by creating a package of useful functions on top of those in the standard library. Asides 11.1b and 11.1c provide an example. They contain a small set of high-level string functions and their prototypes. These include **firstNonBlank** (which returns a pointer to the first non-blank character in the string) and **stringEmpty** (which returns a 1 or 0 depending on whether or not the string is null), among others. They are simple functions written on top of the library functions, but code using them is significantly clearer than code that directly uses the string functions.

Not all of the functions in Aside 11.1c merely hide the ugly details of using the string library functions. Some also provide high-level functions that capture sequences of library calls, such as **stripBlanks** (which removes all leading and trailing blanks from a string). Others take care of common tasks for which we would otherwise have to traverse the string ourselves, such as **stringLower** (which lowercases all of the characters within a string) and **lastNonBlank** (which locates the last non-blank character in the string, but which, unlike **firstNonBlank**, cannot be directly built on top of standard library functions).

Aside 11.1d uses these functions in an extended version of our old friend **yesOrNo**. We now extend it to obtain "yes" or "no" answers even when the lines contain leading or trailing blanks or tabs and to treat an entirely blank line as a "yes". This function is considerably easier to understand than it would be if we had used all of the string library calls directly, without packaging them into our own functions.

The string functions are not a special case. Many libraries can be improved by layering a set of task-specific functions on top of them. That includes operating-system-dependent libraries, such as those that support displaying our output in graphical windows, as well as some commerical packages, such as those that access databases or allow us to easily manipulate dates and times.

That's true simply because language (and operating system) libraries are designed to supply *generally useful* but *primitive* functions. So the functions one builds on top of these libraries are naturally going to be tuned to the task at hand, and therefore less general but simpler to use. For example, the string library provides functions to search for sets of characters in general, while our function **firstNonBlank** locates the first non-blank character. Not as many applications will have a need to do this task, but for those that do, it's much clearer than using **strspn**.

The bottom line is that you shouldn't simply sprinkle library calls throughout your program. Instead, figure out what higher-level tasks you are using them for, and package the calls into functions that reflect this use. Then use those higher-level functions in your program. This will allow you to reuse those higher-level functions in other programs you write, as well as make your programs much more readable.

Aside 11.1b (sutils.h) The prototypes for our useful string functions.

```
/*
 * Some string utilities written on top of the standard library.
 */
#include <string.h>

char *firstNonBlank(char *s);
char *lastNonBlank(char *s);
void stringLower(char *s);
void stripBlanks(char *s);
int emptyString(char *s);
int stringEqual(char *sx, char *sy);
```

Aside 11.1c (sutils.c) A set of useful string functions.

```
/*
 * Some string utilities written on top of the standard library.
 */
#include "sutils.h"

static const char *Spaces = " \t";

int stringEqual(char *sx, char *sy) { return strcmp(sx, sy) == 0; }
int emptyString(char *s) { return *s == '\0'; }
char *firstNonBlank(char *s) { return s + strspn(s, Spaces); }

char *lastNonBlank(char *s)
{                                /* return ptr to just past last non-blank */
  const int len = strlen(s);
  int i = len;

  while (i-- > 0)
    if (s[i] != ' ' && s[i] != '\t')
      return s[i + 1];
  return s + len;
}

void stripBlanks(char *s)
{                                /* remove leading/trailing blanks */
  *(lastNonBlank(s)) = '\0';
  strcpy(s, firstNonBlank(s));
}

void stringLower(char *s)
{                                /* lowercase string */
  for (; *s != '\0'; s++)
   *s = tolower(*s);
}
```

Aside 11.1d (yesorno10.c) Yet another version of our **yesOrNo** function.

```
/*
 * Obtain a yes or no answer, requiring multicharacter responses,
 * ignoring leading/trailing blanks, and treating an empty line
 * as a YES.
 */
#include <stdio.h>
#include "sutils.h"
#include "yesorno2.h"

#define MAXLEN 80

int yesOrNo(const char *prompt)
{
  char line[MAXLEN + 1];

  while (printf(prompt), getline(line, MAXLEN) != -1)
  {
    stripBlanks(line);    /* remove leading/trailing blanks */
    if (emptyString(line))
      return YES;
    stringLower(line);
    if (stringEqual(line, "YES"))
      return YES;
    if (stringEqual(line, "NO"))
      return NO;
    printf("That's not a reasonable answer.\n");
  }
  return BAD;
}
```

from the string (watch out for sequential occurrences of the character). **rmchr** should not leave holes in the string. What should **rmchr** return?

11–12 Write a function, **rmstr**, that takes two strings as arguments, removing all occurrences of any characters in the second string from the first string. Like **rmchr**, **rmstr** should not leave holes in the string. What should **rmstr** return?

11–13 Write a function **question** that takes a string and writes the string, followed by a question mark and a space. Use **putchar** rather than **printf**.

11–14 Write a function **palstr** that determines whether or not a string is a palindrome (reads the same forward and backward).

11–15 Write a function **strrev** to reverse a string in place.

11–16 Write a function **stradd** that takes two strings and returns a new, dynamically allocated string. This new string should contain the concatenation of these two strings.

12   CONSTRUCTED

TYPES

Arrays are the only type of structure we have used so far. But arrays are limited—all their elements must share the same underlying type. This chapter examines three new ways to represent collections of values: structures, unions, and enumerated types. We introduce structures and show how they group different values in a single variable. We introduce unions and show how they allow us to have a single variable whose value varies in type. And finally, we introduce enumerated types and show how they provide a convenient way to define a set of constants. The chapter concludes with a small database program for storing employee names and phone numbers that comes complete with a menu-driven front end.

12.1   STRUCTURES

Sometimes we want to combine data of different types into a single variable. We might, for example, want a variable to hold all the information on a particular employee: the employee's name, employee number, phone number, and age. Unfortunately, we can't use an array because array elements all share the same underlying type. Instead, we must use a structure.[1]

Defining Structure Types

The first step in using a structure is to define a structure type. We do so by following the keyword **struct** with the name of the structure type (called the *structure tag*) and declarations for each of the items it contains (called *fields* or *members*). We define a structure type to hold our employee information with

```
struct employee
{
  long number;                /* employee number */
  char name[MAXNAME];         /* first and last name */
  char phone[MAXDIGITS];      /* at least xxx-xxx-xxxx\0 */
  int age;                    /* age */
};
```

---

[1] A structure is very similar to a Pascal record.

This declares a new type, **struct employee**, consisting of four fields: **number** (a **long**), **name** (an array of **MAXNAME** characters), **phone** (another array of characters), and **age** (a single **int**). Field names are in a special "name class" kept separate from variable names, so we can have field names that are the same as existing variable names, and we can use the same field name in different structure definitions without fear of conflict.

The fields within a structure can have any legal type, which means they themselves can be structures. The following

```
struct date                      /* to hold a single date */
{
  int month, day, year;
};

struct period                    /* to hold two dates */
{
  struct date start, end;        /* starting, ending dates */
};
```

defines a **date** structure type containing three integers, one each for the month, day, and year, and a **period** structure type that contains a starting and ending date.

Where do these structure type definitions go? Typically, we place them in our source file, outside any function, and preceding any of the functions that make use of them. A structure definition is like a **typedef**; it's known from the point of definition until the end of the source file. As with external declarations, if we need a structure type in more than one source file, we can place its definition in a header file.

Declaring Structure Variables

Once we've defined the structure type, we can declare variables with that type as if it were one of C's built-in data types. For example,

```
struct employee emp;
```

declares a single variable, **emp**, with type **struct employee**. This forces the compiler to allocate at least enough storage for **emp** to hold the four fields within a **struct employee**. Similarly,

```
struct period x;
```

declares a variable **x** with two fields, **start** and **end**, each of which is a structure containing three integers. We can use structure variables like any others: we can assign to them, pass them to functions, and so on.

As a shortcut, we can combine declaring a variable with defining a type. That's because a structure type definition can go anywhere a type can appear.

```
struct date { int month, day, year; } d;
```

This declaration combines defining a new type, **struct date**, and declaring a variable **d** with that type. If we only need the structure type in this one place, we can omit the structure tag.

```
struct { int month, day, year; } d;
```

We usually use this form only when we have a nested structure or when we combine it with **typedef**.

```
typedef struct { int month, day, year; } Date;
```

This defines a type **Date** that's synonymous with a structure containing the three **int** fields **month**, **day**, and **year**. We can then declare variables with the type **Date**:

```
Date birthday;        /* month, day, and year of birth */
```

Accessing Structure Fields

Although it is convenient to treat a structure variable as a single unit, we also need a way to access its individual fields. To access a field, we follow the structure name with the field selection operator, '**.**', and the name of the desired field. Assuming that we've declared **emp** as a **struct employee**, we can assign values to **emp**'s fields with:

```
emp.number = 1001;
emp.age = 29;
strcpy(emp.name, "franklin, tammy");
strcpy(emp.phone, "714-555-5741");
```

The result is shown below.

	number	name	phone	age
emp	1001	franklin, tammy\0	714-555-5731\0	29

The dot operator associates left to right. With **x** declared as a **struct period**, **x.start.month** refers to the month field within the start field of **x**. We can initialize **x**'s fields with

```
x.start.month = 7;
x.start.day   = 20;
x.start.year  = 1981;
x.end.month   = 7;
x.end.day     = 30;
x.end.year    = 1984;
```

Initializing Structures at Compile Time

Like other data types, we can initialize structures when we declare them. As far as initialization goes, structures obey the same set of rules as arrays. We initialize the fields of a structure by following the structure's declaration with a list containing values for each of its fields. As with arrays, these values must be evaluable at compile time. We could initialize **emp** at compile time with:

```
struct employee emp =
{
  1001,                          /* number */
  "franklin, tammy",             /* name */
  "714-555-5741",                /* phone */
  29                             /* age */
};
```

This initializes the **number** field to **1001**, the **name** field to "**franklin, tammy**," the **phone** field to "**714-555-5741**", and the **age** field to **29**. Since the values for the **name** and **phone** fields are string constants, they are automatically terminated with a null character.

When we have fields that are themselves structures, we enclose the values of their fields in brackets.

```
struct period x = { {7,20,1981}, {7,30,1984} };
```

We can omit the brackets surrounding a field when we provide all of its elements, but leaving them in clarifies which values are going to what fields.

Structures and Functions

We can pass structures as arguments to functions. Unlike array names, however, which are always pointers to the start of the array, structure names are not pointers. When we pass a structure, C copies the entire structure and assigns it to its corresponding parameter. As a result, when we change a structure parameter inside a function, we don't affect its corresponding argument.

Actually, we usually pass pointers to structures, rather than structures themselves, as it's faster to pass a pointer: only the pointer has to be copied, not the entire structure.

Figure 12.1 illustrates both methods in a small program that declares, initializes, and prints the fields of several **struct employee**s. We initialize the fields in the first employee, **emp**, by assigning them values at run time, and we print it by passing the entire structure to a function **writeEmp**.

```
writeEmp(emp);
```

We initialize the other employee, **other_emp**, at compile time rather than run time. We print **other_emp** by passing its address to a function **printEmp**.

```
printEmp(&other_emp);
```

The **printf** statements within **printEmp** must dereference the pointer to the structure and then select the appropriate field. Assuming **ep** is a pointer to the structure, one way to do this is

```
printf("Employee: %li\n", (*ep).number);
```

```c
/*
 * Display employee information.
 */
#include <stdio.h>
#include <stdlib.h>
#include <string.h>

#define MAXNAME   40                          /* longest name */
#define MAXDIGITS 27                          /* longest phone */

struct employee
{
  long number;                               /* employee number */
  char name[MAXNAME];                        /* first and last name */
  char phone[MAXDIGITS];                     /* at least xxx-xxx-xxxx\0 */
  int  age;                                  /* age */
};

int main()
{
  void writeEmp(struct employee e);
  void printEmp(struct employee *ep);

  struct employee emp;
  struct employee other_emp = {1023, "perl, doris", "213-555-6917", 29};

  emp.number = 1001;
  emp.age = 29;
  strcpy(emp.name, "franklin, tammy");
  strcpy(emp.phone, "714-555-5741");
  writeEmp(emp);                             /* write the first employee */
  printEmp(&other_emp);                      /* write the second employee */

  return EXIT_SUCCESS;
}

void writeEmp(struct employee e)
{         /* write employee given structure */
  printf("Employee: %li\n", e.number);
  printf("Name:     %s\n",  e.name);
  printf("Age:      %i\n",  e.age);
  printf("Phone:    %s\n",  e.phone);
}

void printEmp(struct employee *ep)
{         /* write employee given pointer to structure */
  printf("Employee: %li\n", ep->number);
  printf("Name:     %s\n",  ep->name);
  printf("Age:      %i\n",  ep->age);
  printf("Phone:    %s\n",  ep->phone);
}
```

Figure 12.1   (prstruct.c) Initialize and print a structure one field at a time.

Why the parentheses? The selection operator binds tighter (has higher precedence) than dereferencing. Without the parentheses, as in `*ep.number`, we're trying to dereference the value of a field in the structure (which makes no sense in this case, as the field isn't a pointer).

Dereferencing a pointer to a structure and selecting one of its fields is such a common operation that C provides a special shorthand operator for it, a right arrow, made up of a minus sign and a "greater than" symbol: `->`. We can use this operator to write the `printf` statements in `printEmp` more concisely:

```
printf("Employee: %li\n", ep->number);
```

Not only can we pass structures to functions, but we can return them as well. We rarely do, however, for the same reason we rarely pass structures to functions: it's too slow. We return pointers to structures instead.

Structures and Operators

Only a few operators apply to structure variables. We've already used `&` to take a structure's address. Another operator, `sizeof`, determines the number of bytes used by the structure. We could compute the size of a **struct employee** by taking the size of a variable with that type

```
sizeof(emp)
```

or by taking the size of the structure type itself

```
sizeof(struct employee)
```

You might think that we could also compute the size by summing up the sizes of each of the structure's fields:

```
sizeof(emp.number) + sizeof(emp.name) +
    sizeof(emp.phone) + sizeof(emp.age)
```

But we don't get the same result. Why? Because each data type has alignment restrictions, which may force the compiler to leave "holes" in a structure so that it can satisfy all the alignment constraints of the various fields within the structure. Although a **char** can start on a byte or word boundary, **int**s, **long**s, and other data types can usually begin only on a word boundary. In our structure, the 27-byte array containing the phone number ends on a byte boundary, so the single byte that follows it and precedes the age field (which must start on a word boundary) is likely to be left unused.

> *Don't assume the size of a structure is the sum of the size of its fields.*

There's only one other operator we can apply to structures: = (assignment), which copies the contents of one structure into another.

```
struct date old_date, date;

old_date = date;
```

This assignment is equivalent to

```
old_date.day = date.day;
old_date.month = date.month;
old_date.year = date.year;
```

There are no operators for comparing structures, so we're stuck with writing functions to perform these types of comparisons. Figures 12.2 and 12.3 provide a set of functions for comparing **struct date**s, along with their prototypes, and Figure 12.4 is an example program using them.

> *We're not allowed to compare structures directly.*

Arrays of Structures

Earlier we mentioned that we can have arrays of any type. That includes structures. One use for an array of structures would be to store a table of personnel records.

```
struct employee emptab[SIZE];
```

This declares an array of **SIZE** elements, with each element in the array a **struct employee** containing **number**, **name**, **phone**, and **age** fields.

emptab is an array of structures, so we use the usual array-accessing methods to reach individual records and then the dot field selection operator to reach their fields. We can, for example, assign a value to **emptab[1]** with

```
emptab[1].number = 1023;
emptab[1].age = 29;
strcpy(emptab[1].name, "perl, doris");
strcpy(emptab[1].phone, "213-555-6917");
```

We can also initialize an array of structures when we declare it.

```
struct employee emptab[] =
{
  {1001, "franklin, tammy",    "714-555-5741", 29},
  {1023, "perl, doris",        "213-555-6917", 29},
  {1033, "pham, gisele",       "714-555-2559", 29},
  {1036, "borromeo, daphne",   "818-555-2042", 26},
  {1039, "borromeo, irene",    "213-555-2718", 29},
  {1047, "stevens, diane",     "213-555-4854", 29},
  {1048, "ockert, veronica",   "213-555-4741", 29}
};
```

```
/*
 * Provides DATE type and prototypes for functions that compare DATEs.
 */
typedef struct { int month, day, year; } Date;

int areDatesEqual(const Date *xptr, const Date *yptr);
int isDateBefore(const Date *xptr, const Date *yptr);
int isDateAfter(const Date *xptr, const Date *yptr);
```

Figure 12.2   (date.h)   Prototypes for functions to compare dates.

```
/*
 * Functions for comparing dates.
 *    areDatesEqual - are two dates the same?
 *    isDateBefore - is the first date before the second?
 *    isDateAfter - is the first date after the second?
 */
#include "date.h"                          /* date type and prototypes */

int areDatesEqual(const Date *xptr, const Date *yptr)
{
  return xptr->year  == yptr->year  &&
         xptr->month == yptr->month &&
         xptr->day   == yptr->day;
}

int isDateBefore(const Date *xptr, const Date *yptr)
{
  if (xptr->year < yptr->year)
    return 1;
  if (xptr->year > yptr->year)
    return 0;

  return (xptr->month < yptr->month ||
         (xptr->month == yptr->month && xptr->day < yptr->day));
}

int isDateAfter(const Date *xptr, const Date *yptr)
  { return !isDateBefore(xptr, yptr) && !areDatesEqual(xptr, yptr); }
```

Figure 12.3   (date.c)   Functions for comparing dates.

```
/*
 * A program to test our date comparison routines.  Uses:
 *    cmpDates - compare two dates and print message describing results.
 *    dateStr - convert date to string format for output.
 */
#include <stdio.h>
#include <stdlib.h>
#include "date.h"

#define MONTH_CHARS   2        /* number of chars in a month */
#define DAY_CHARS     2        /* number of chars in a day */
#define YEAR_CHARS    4        /* number of chars in a year */

int main()
{
  void cmpDates(const Date *ptr1, const Date *ptr2);

  Date day1 = {10, 4, 1965}, day2 = {10, 18, 1963};
  Date day3 = {6, 24, 1963}, day4 = day1;

  cmpDates(&day1, &day2);    cmpDates(&day1, &day3);
  cmpDates(&day2, &day1);    cmpDates(&day2, &day3);
  cmpDates(&day3, &day2);    cmpDates(&day2, &day3);
  cmpDates(&day4, &day1);

  return EXIT_SUCCESS;
}

void cmpDates(const Date *d1ptr, const Date *d2ptr)
{
  char *dateStr(const Date *ptr);

  printf("Comparing %s ", dateStr(d1ptr));
  printf("with %s: ", dateStr(d2ptr));
  if (isDateBefore(d1ptr,d2ptr))
    printf("it's earlier.\n");
  if (isDateAfter(d1ptr,d2ptr))
    printf("it's later.\n");
  if (areDatesEqual(d1ptr,d2ptr))
    printf("they're the same.\n");
}

char *dateStr(const Date *dptr)
{
  static char d[MONTH_CHARS + DAY_CHARS + YEAR_CHARS + 3];

  sprintf(d, "%0*i/%0*i/%*i", MONTH_CHARS, dptr->month,
                              DAY_CHARS, dptr->day,
                              YEAR_CHARS, dptr->year);
  return d;    /* ptr to first character of date */
}
```

Figure 12.4   (datetest.c)   A main program to test our date comparison routines.

1001	franklin, tammy\0	714-555-5731\0	29
1023	perl, doris\0	213-555-6917\0	29
1033	pham, gisele\0	714-555-2559\0	29
1036	borromeo, daphne\0	818-555-2042\0	26
1039	borromeo, irene\0	213-555-2718\0	29
1047	stevens, diane\0	213-555-4854\0	29
1048	ockert, veronica\0	213-555-4741\0	29

Figure 12.5   Array of **struct employee**s showing the contents of each individual element.

This declares and initializes **emptab**, which is an array of employee structures. We don't provide a size for the array, so the compiler determines it from the number of items we provide, seven in this case. Figure 12.5 shows what this array looks like.

We can index an array of structures in the same way we index any other array—either by array subscripting or by using pointers.

We illustrate arrays of structures with a program that initializes and prints an array of **struct employee**s. The program has three parts. Figure 12.6 is a header file that defines a **struct employee**. Figure 12.7 is a main program that initializes the array and then calls the function **printEmps** to print each of the names. And Figure 12.8 is an array-subscripting version of **printEmps**.

printEmps takes two arguments—the address of the first element to print and the number of items we want to print. So to use **printEmps** we need to know how many items are in the array. But how can we figure this out automatically? We do so the same way we figure out how many items are in any other array—we divide the total number of bytes in the array by the number of bytes in an individual item. So we can print the entire table with

```
printEmps(emptab, sizeof(emptab)/sizeof(emptab[0]));
```

or

```
printEmps(emptab, sizeof(emptab)/sizeof(struct employee));
```

The former is more concise but the latter is more readable.

Figure 12.9 shows an alternative version of **printEmps** that uses pointer indexing rather than array subscripting. We can use pointer indexing because pointer arithmetic is always done in units of the pointed-to type, so incrementing a pointer to a structure causes it to point to the next structure in the array.

```
/*
 * Define a struct employee.
 */
#define MAXNAME    40
#define MAXDIGITS  27

struct employee                    /* same definition as before */
{
  long number;                     /* employee number */
  char name[MAXNAME];              /* first and last name */
  char phone[MAXDIGITS];           /* at least xxx-xxx-xxxx\0 */
  int  age;                        /* age */
};
```

Figure 12.6 (premps.h) Header file defining the **struct employee** type.

```
/*
 * Print the name field of each element in a structure.
 */
#include <stdio.h>
#include <stdlib.h>
#include "premps.h"

int main()
{
  void printEmps(struct employee table[], int);

  struct employee emptab[] =
  {
    {1001, "franklin, tammy",    "818-555-5741", 29},
    {1023, "perl, doris",        "213-555-6917", 29},
    {1033, "pham, gisele",       "714-555-2559", 29},
    {1036, "borromeo, daphne",   "818-555-2042", 26},
    {1039, "borromeo, irene",    "213-555-2718", 29},
    {1047, "stevens, diane",     "213-555-4854", 29},
    {1048, "ockert, veronica",   "213-555-4741", 29}
  };

  printEmps(emptab,sizeof(emptab)/sizeof(emptab[0]));

  return EXIT_SUCCESS;
}
```

Figure 12.7 (premps.c) A program to print an array of **struct employee**s.

```
/*
 * Array-printing function, using array subscripting.
 */
#include <stdio.h>
#include "premps.h"                        /* for structure definition */

void printEmps(struct employee table[], int n)
{
  int i;                                   /* array index */

  for (i = 0; i < n; i++)
    printf("Name: %s\n", table[i].name);
}
```

Figure 12.8   (premps1.c) A function **printEmps** to print an array of structures using array indexing.

```
/*
 * Better array-printing function, using pointer indexing.
 */
#include <stdio.h>
#include "premps.h"

void printEmps(struct employee *ptr, int n)
{
  struct employee *endptr = ptr + n;

  for (; ptr < endptr; ptr++)
    printf("Name: %s\n", ptr->name);
}
```

Figure 12.9   (premps2.c) A version of **printEmps** that uses pointer indexing.

12.2   BITFIELDS

So far, the integer fields in our structures have been at least one word in size. But this wastes space when we are dealing with integers requiring less than 16 bits. Fortunately, C lets us specify the number of bits required by an integer field, which lets us pack several different fields into a single word, saving space. Fields specified in terms of their size in bits are called *bitfields*.

How do we declare bitfields? In the same way we declare any other structure field, with one exception and one restriction. The exception is that we must follow the field's name with a colon and the number of bits we need. The restriction is that bitfields must be signed or unsigned **int**s, from one to the number of bits in an **int**. Signed bitfields use the leftmost bit as the sign bit.

We can represent our **date** structure more compactly as a set of bitfields. That's because we really only need to store months between 1 and 12, days between 1 and 31, and years between 0 and 99 (assuming years are an offset into this century).[2]

```
struct date
{
    unsigned int year  : 7;    /* year is 7 bits */
    unsigned int day   : 5;    /* day is 5 bits */
    unsigned int month : 4;    /* month is 4 bits */
};
```

This declares a structure with three bitfields: **year**, **day**, and **month**, as shown below.[3]

The entire structure fits in a single 16-bit word. **year** takes up 7 bits, **day** takes up 5 bits, and **month** takes up 4 bits.

The name of a bitfield is optional; an anonymous bitfield simply uses up space. A bitfield with no name and a size of zero causes the following field to be aligned on a word boundary.

How do we access bitfields? In the same way we access any other structure field: by using the **.** and **->** operators.

```
struct date bday;       /* holds a birthday */
    . . .
bday.month = 6;  bday.day = 24;  bday.year = 63;
```

Essentially, bitfields behave as extremely small integers, and we can use them almost anywhere we can use an integral type.

One restriction is that we can't take the address of a bitfield. This restriction arises because the vast majority of machines aren't bit-addressable. Practically, this means that we can't use **scanf** to read values into a bitfield. Instead, we have to read into a temporary variable and then assign its value to the bitfield.

The other restriction is that we can't apply **sizeof** to a bitfield. That would be silly to do, anyway, since we explicitly declare how many bits we want. But the restriction also arises because **sizeof** returns an integer number of bytes an object takes.

Figure 12.10 uses bitfields in a new version of our Chapter 6 program to pack employee information in a single word (Figure 6.14). We prefer the simplicity of using bitfields to the complexity of using our earlier bit-manipulating functions. But this doesn't mean that those functions are useless. They're still convenient when we don't know at compile time which combinations of bits we need to access or when we care exactly how the bits are packed.

---

[2] This is actually a problematic assumption, since it will be violated as soon as the year 2000 rolls around.

[3] It's machine dependent whether fields are allocated right to left or left to right within a word. Our picture above assumes that it's left to right, but that's not always the case. As a result, we can't assume bitfields are allocated in a particular way. This becomes an issue when we use bitfields for data that's to be transferred from machine to machine. In that case, we're stuck using the bit-shifting operators we saw earlier.

```
/*
 * New version of our earlier program to pack employee info
 * into a single word.  This time we use bitfields.
 */
#include <stdio.h>
#include <stdlib.h>

#define SINGLE     0                 /* marital status flags */
#define MARRIED    1
#define SEPARATED  2
#define DIVORCED   3
#define MALE       1                 /* sex */
#define FEMALE     0

struct emp
{
  unsigned int mstat : 2;            /* marital status */
  unsigned int age   : 7;            /* employee age */
  unsigned int sex   : 1;            /* male or female */
  unsigned int years : 6;            /* years employeed */
};

int main()
{
  unsigned int mstat, sex, age, years;
  struct emp info;                   /* holds info on one person */

  printf("male=%i, female=%i\? ", MALE, FEMALE);
  scanf("%u", &sex);
  info.sex = sex;
  printf("age\? ");
  scanf("%u", &age);
  info.age = age;
  printf("single=%i, married=%i, separated=%i, divorced=%i\? ",
         SINGLE, MARRIED, SEPARATED, DIVORCED);
  scanf("%i", &mstat);
  info.mstat = mstat;
  printf("years employed\? ");
  scanf("%i", &years);
  info.years = years;
  printf("Here's the info:\n");
  printf("Sex: %i\n", info.sex);
  printf("Age: %i\n", info.age);
  printf("Marital status: %i\n", info.mstat);
  printf("Years employed: %i\n", info.years);

  return EXIT_SUCCESS;
}
```

Figure 12.10   (usebits2.c) A new version of our program to pack employee information within a word.

12.3 UNIONS

Structures allow us to package different types of values as a single unit. But we also often want to use the same location to store values of different types at different times. The mechanism that allows us to do this is called a *union*. A union may contain one of many different types of values, but can store only one value at a time.

We declare and use **union**s in the same way we declare and use **struct**s. To declare a union type, we follow the keyword **union** with an optional union tag and the alternative names and types it may hold. For example, we can declare a union type that can hold either a **long** or a **double** with

```
union number
{
  long   l;
  double d;
};
```

Once we've declared a union type, we can declare variables with that type.

```
union number x;
```

This declares a variable **x**, with type **union number**, which may contain either a **long** or a **double**. As with structures we can combine the type definition with the variable declaration.

```
union number
{
  long   l;
  double d;
} x;
```

With **union**s we usually only do so when we declare a union as a field within a structure.

We can initialize a union when we declare it by following it with a brace-enclosed initializing expression.

```
union number x = {69};
```

The expression is evaluated and assigned to the first field of the union.

How do we access a union's individual fields? As with structures, we use the dot operator. To assign to the **long** field of **x** we use **x.l**

```
x.l = 1234;
```

and to assign to the **double** field we use **x.d**

```
x.d = -123.345;
```

We can also access the fields of a union indirectly though a pointer, using the **->** operator.

```
union number *xptr;
   ...
xptr = &x;
xptr->d = 98.76;
```

What does a union look like internally? It's allocated enough storage to hold its largest field. The variable **x**, a **union number**, is allocated space sufficient for a **double**, as shown below.

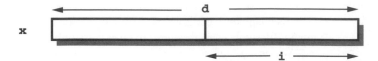

That means we should never assign to one field of a union and then retrieve from another. A series of operations such as

```
x.d = 45.67;                    /* assign a float */
printf("%li\n", x.l);           /* print field as long */
```

is likely to produce results that differ from machine to machine. Whenever we retrieve a field from a union, it should be the last field we assigned.

> *Don't assign to one field of a union and then retrieve from another.*

Figure 12.11 puts all of these operations together in a little program that first assigns an integer into a union and prints it, and then assigns a floating point value into the same union and prints it. The program finishes by erroneously assigning a new floating point value to the union and printing it as an integer, which produces machine-dependent behavior. Here are the results of running this program on our machine:

```
69
1234
-123.345000
98.760000
1078384066
```

As a more realistic use of unions, we will now write a function, **getValue**, that prints a prompt and obtains a value—either a **long**, a **double**, or a string—from the user. The idea is that we pass **getValue** a prompt string and an indication of the type of value we want to read. It returns a pointer to a union that can contain either a **long**, a **double**, or a pointer.

How does **getValue** work? It reads a line of input and fills an internal, **static** union with the desired type. If the type is numeric, **getValue** uses **sscanf** to translate the characters it reads into the desired type. If the type is a string, **getValue** uses a new utility function, **strndup**, to make a dynamically-allocated copy of the string. That **union** must be **static** because the function returns a pointer to it, and otherwise it would be destroyed when the function exits, leaving a dangling pointer. If there's a problem, such as the user's entering a value of an inappropriate type or the end-of-file character, **getValue** returns **NULL**.

Figure 12.12 is getvalue.h, which defines the union type and provides a prototype for **getValue**. Figure 12.13 is getvalue.c, which defines the function itself. And Figure 12.14 is a short main program that uses **getValue** to read a person's name, age, and salary.

```
/*
 * Program to test basic union operations.
 */
#include <stdio.h>
#include <stdlib.h>

union number                           /* define the union type */
{
  long    l;
  double d;
};

int main()
{
  union number x = {69};               /* a union and a pointer to it */
  union number *xptr;

  printf("%li\n", x.l);                /* print the initial value */

  x.l = 1234;
  printf("%li\n", x.l);                /* print the long we put in it */

  x.d = -123.345;
  printf("%f\n", x.d);                 /* print the double we put in it */

  xptr = &x;
  xptr->d = 98.76;
  printf("%f\n", xptr->d);             /* access it through the pointer */

  x.d = 45.67;
  printf("%li\n", x.l);                /* oops: print the double as int */

  return EXIT_SUCCESS;
}
```

Figure 12.11 (union.c) A program illustrating the basic union operations.

12.4 ENUMERATED TYPES

Sometimes we know a variable will have only one of a small set of values. In the function **getValue**, for example, we know that the parameter describing the type of value to read should hold only the constants **INTEGER**, **REAL**, or **STRING**. In these situations, we can use an *enumerated type* to specify the possible values.

We define an enumerated type by giving the keyword **enum** followed by an optional *type designator* and a brace-enclosed list of identifiers. So

```
        enum itype {INTEGER, REAL, STRING};     /* input types */
```

defines an enumerated type, **enum itype**, that has three possible values: **INTEGER**,

```
/*
 * Define types for getValue.
 */
#define MAXLEN 80                  /* longest input line */

#define INTEGER 0
#define REAL    1
#define STRING  2

union value                        /* can hold a long, double, or char */
{
  long    l;
  double  d;
  char    *s;
};

typedef int ItemChoice;

union value *getValue(const char *prompt, ItemChoice value_type);
```

Figure 12.12   (getvalue.h) Header file for **getValue**.

REAL, and **STRING**. Internally, these are defined as constants with an integer value equal to their position in the list: **INTEGER** is zero, **REAL** is 1, and **STRING** is 2. Of course, we could have defined these as constants with **#define**s or **const**, but we find **enum**s more convenient to use.

We are allowed to assign specific integer values to the items in an enumerated type. We do so by following the item with an equal sign and a value. The default value for any item is 1 more than the value of the item preceding it. So

```
enum itype {STRING = 2, INTEGER = 0, REAL};
```

assigns **STRING** a 2, **INTEGER** a zero, and **REAL** a 1, just like before.

All we've done so far is declare an enumerated type. We declare variables with that type in the same way we declared structures and unions.

```
enum itype type;
```

This declares a variable, **type**, that can contain only **INTEGER**, **REAL**, or **STRING**.

The distinction between enumerated types and integers is a fuzzy one. Essentially, we can use any enumerated type as if it were an integer. We don't need to cast it to and from **int**. So why not use simply use integers instead of enumerated types? Because enumerated types highlight variables that only hold one of a limited set of values, making our programs more readable. Because enumerated types provide a convenient way to define integer constants, making our programs more concise. And because some compilers will warn us when we stick inappropriate values in an enumerated type, lessening the chance of error.

```c
/*
 * Read a value from the user.
 */
#include <stdio.h>
#include <string.h>
#include <stddef.h>
#include <stdlib.h>
#include "getvalue.h"

static char *strndup(const char *string, int n);

union value *getValue(const char *prompt, ItemChoice value_type)
{
  int getline(char *buf, int bufsize);

  static union value v;
  char line[MAXLEN + 1];
  int len;

  printf("%s", prompt);
  if ((len=getline(line, MAXLEN)) == -1)
    return NULL;
  switch(value_type)
  {
    case INTEGER:  if (sscanf(line, "%li", &v.l) != 1)
                     return NULL;
                   break;
    case REAL:     if (sscanf(line, "%lf", &v.d) != 1)
                     return NULL;
                   break;
    case STRING:   if ((v.s = strndup(line, len)) == NULL)
                     return NULL;
                   break;
    default:       return NULL;
  }

  return &v;       /* succeeded */
}

static char *strndup(const char *string, int n)
{                  /* new string with first n chars of old string */
  char *ptr = malloc(n + 1);

  if (ptr != NULL)
  {
    strncpy(ptr, string, n);
    ptr[n] = '\0';
  }
  return ptr;
}
```

Figure 12.13 (getvalue.c) A function to read different types of data.

```c
/*
 * A program that uses getValue (quits on first error).
 */
#include <stdio.h>
#include <stdlib.h>
#include <stddef.h>
#include "getvalue.h"

int main()
{
  union value *uptr;            /* return value from getValue */
  char        *name;           /* holds name */
  int          age;            /* holds age */
  double       salary;         /* holds salary */
  int          status;         /* did program succeed? */

  if ((uptr=getValue("Enter name: ", STRING)) == NULL)
  {
    printf("Couldn't get name\n");
    status = EXIT_FAILURE;                        /* name failure! */
  }
  else
  {
    name = uptr->s;              /* save name before getting age */
    if ((uptr=getValue("Enter age: ", INTEGER)) == NULL)
    {
      printf("Couldn't get age\n");
      status = EXIT_FAILURE;                      /* age failure! */
    }
    else
    {
      age = (int) uptr->l;       /* save age before getting salary */
      if ((uptr=getValue("Enter salary: ", REAL)) == NULL)
      {
        printf("Couldn't get salary\n");
        status = EXIT_FAILURE;                    /* salary failure! */
      }
      else
      {
        salary = uptr->d;
        printf("Name: %s\nAge: %i\nSalary: %.2f\n",
                name, age, salary);
        status = EXIT_SUCCESS;
      }
    }
  }

  return status;
}
```

Figure 12.14 (useit.c) A main program that uses our **getValue** function.

Aside 12.1: Using Constructed Types

At first, many C programmers tend to avoid structures, unions, and enumerated types. They seem confusing, and you can usually get by without them. But these constructed types contribute to more readable, more maintainable programs. Here are some suggestions for when and how to use each of these types.

- The point of a structure is to group together related information. Any time you find yourself working with data that is logically related, it should be placed in a structure. One benefit of doing so is that you now only have to pass the structure around, not all the individual fields. Another benefit is that structures allow us to hide information, since they can be processed as a whole without worrying about the contents of their fields.

- Define the structure type and a suitable **typedef** for it in a header file, place all functions that directly access its fields into a single source file (or group of related source files), and compile and link that source file separately. This minimizes the dependencies on the internals of the structure in the remainder of the program and allows you to make changes to the structure without having to make changes throughout your entire program.

- Use a union when you have a single location that will store different types of values at a different times. Remember that the difference between structures and unions is that space is allocated for every member of the structure, but only for the largest member of a union. You cannot store values for more than one field of a union at one time.

- Use enumerated types whenever a variable can have one of a limited set of values. They also provide a convenient way to define constants. While we can get by using integer variables and **#define**, enumerated types greatly aid readability, and allow the compiler to provide potentially additional type checking.

> *Use enumerated types whenever a variable will hold only a small set of integer values.*

It turns out we need not change **getValue** itself to use enumerated types. getvalue.h used a **typedef** to define a new type **ItemChoice** for the parameter controlling what we try to read. As a result, all we need to do is modify this header file to define **enum itype** and to change that **typedef** from an **int** to an **enum itype**.[4] Figure 12.15 shows this revised header file.

---

[4] If we simply revise getvalue.h, we need not make any other changes. However, if we use a new header file with a different name, as we do here, we also have to modify getvalue.c to include this alternative header file, a change we haven't shown.

```
/*
 * Define types for getValue.
 */
#define MAXLEN 80               /* longest input line */

enum itype {LONG, REAL, STRING};

union value                     /* can hold a long, double, or char */
{
  long    l;
  double d;
  char   *s;
};

typedef enum itype ItemChoice;

union value *getValue(const char *prompt, ItemChoice value_type);
```

Figure 12.15 (getvalue2.h) The revised header file for **getValue**.

12.5   CASE STUDY—A DATABASE APPLICATION

*This section
is optional!*

This chapter concludes with a small program to manage a database of employee records. Its users can interactively add, delete, and print records, accessing the desired record by providing the corresponding employee number. When the program finishes, it prints the resulting table. The program has a simple menu-driven interface, one that we'll extend in later chapters.

Storing the Database

How do we store the database? It's kept as an array of **struct employee**s—but now the structure's definition is more general.

```
typedef struct employee          /* one personnel record */
{
  long number;
  char *name;
  char *phone;
  int age;
} Employee;
```

The employee **name** and **phone** numbers are now pointers to **char** rather than arrays of **char**. This means that when we add a record we have to dynamically allocate the space for these fields. When we delete a record, we deallocate this space. We find this extra effort worthwhile, since it allows us to have arbitrarily long names and phone numbers without wasting storage. Figure 12.16 shows a sample session with the program.

```
Main Menu
  (1) Add
  (2) Delete
  (3) Print
  (0) Quit
Enter choice: 1
Add employee number? 10
Employee name: Alex Quilici
Employee phone: 808-555-2115
Employee age: 30
  ...
Enter choice: 1
Add employee number? 5
Employee name: Larry Miller
Employee phone: 213-555-2738
Employee age: 42
  ...
Enter choice: 1
Add employee number? 29
Employee name: Tony Quilici
Employee phone: 408-555-7764
Employee age: 28
  ...
Enter choice: 2
Delete employee number? 29
  ...
Enter choice: 0

10, Alex Quilici, 30, 808-555-2115
5, Larry Miller, 42, 213-555-2738
2 employees
```

Figure 12.16   Some sample input and output for our database program.

To keep things simple, we don't bother to keep the array in sorted order. Instead, we add a new record by placing it after the last record, and we delete an existing record by replacing it with the last record. This organization allows us to quickly insert or delete a record, but slows searching: on the average we'll examine half of the items in the array. Figure 12.17 shows how the sample database is stored.

The Database Program

We break the database program into several different files.

Figure 12.18 contains db.h, which defines the **struct employee** data type and uses a **typedef** to define a type **Employee** that's a shorthand for it. It also supplies the external declarations for the database and prototypes for the functions that manage it. Figure 12.19 contains db.c, the main program that prints the menu, obtains the user's

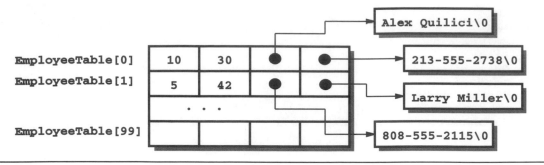

Figure 12.17   Diagram of the array reading in and allocating several records.

```
/*
 * Prototypes for database functions, externals for table.
 */
#define MAXEMPS   100

typedef struct employee                /* one personnel record */
{
  long number;
  char *name;
  char *phone;
  int  age;
} Employee;

extern Employee EmployeeTable[];       /* all personnel records */
extern int      Employees;             /* count of employees */

void addEntry(void);
void deleteEntry(void);
void printEntry(void);
void printEntries(void);
```

Figure 12.18   (db.h) The external declarations for the employee database and the operations on it.

choice, and calls the functions that actually access and update the database. It also contains the definition of the database itself.

Figures 12.20 and 12.21 contain **dbupdate.c** and **dbprint.c**, respectively. These files define the functions that update and display the database. These functions utilize several utility functions to look up items in a table and print an appropriate message depending on whether or not we actually wanted to find the item. Figure 12.22 contains **dbfind.h**, which defines the prototypes for these utilities, and Figure 12.23 contains **dbfind.c**, which defines the utilities themselves.

```
/*
 * Program to manage an employee database.
 */
#include <stdio.h>
#include <stdlib.h>
#include "db.h"
#include "dbinp.h"

Employee EmployeeTable[MAXEMPS];          /* table of employees */
int      Employees;                       /* count of employees */

int main()
{
  for (;;)
  {
    printf("Main Menu\n"
           "  (1) Add\n  (2) Delete\n  (3) Print\n  (0) Quit\n");
    switch ((int) getLong("Enter choice? "))
    {
      case 0:  printEntries();   return EXIT_SUCCESS;
      case 1:  addEntry();       break;
      case 2:  deleteEntry();    break;
      case 3:  printEntry();     break;
      default: printf("Bad choice.\n");
    }
  }

  return EXIT_SUCCESS;
}
```

Figure 12.19   (db.c) The main program and the definitions of the employee database.

The rest of the program is concerned with reading the input. Figures 12.24 and 12.25 contain the files dbinp.h and dbinp.c, which together supply the functions we use for reading input values and their prototypes. These functions, **getLong** and **getStr**, repeatedly prompt for and read input values until they encounter an appropriate value, writing error messages for any inappropriate input values. They are built on top of the version of our earlier **getValue** function, which in turn was built on top of another earlier function, **getline**.

Obviously our database program is far too simplistic to be suitable for any real-world application. The individual records aren't kept in any particular order, so finding a desired record can be time-consuming. And the database is kept in memory, which means it must be reentered every time we run the program. But we'll soon provide mechanisms for fixing these problems. Later chapters look at alternative data structures for storing tables and for dealing with external files.

```c
/*
 * Operations to update the database.
 *    addEntry - add a new entry to the employee table.
 *    deleteEntry - delete an entry from the employee table.
 */
#include <stdio.h>
#include <stdlib.h>
#include "dbfind.h"
#include "dbinp.h"

void addEntry(void)
{
  Employee *empptr;
  long     newnum;

  if (Employees == MAXEMPS)
    printf("Employee table is full.\n");
  else
  {
    newnum = getLong("Add employee number? ");
    if ((empptr = dontFindEmployee(newnum)) == NULL)
    {                                    /* add at end of table */
      empptr = &EmployeeTable[Employees++];
      empptr->number = newnum;
      empptr->name    = getStr("Employee name: ");
      empptr->phone   = getStr("Employee phone: ");
      empptr->age     = (int) getLong("Employee age: ");
    }
  }
}

void deleteEntry(void)
{
  Employee *empptr;
  long     empnum;

  if (Employees == 0)
    printf("Employee table is empty.\n");
  else
  {
    empnum = getLong("Delete employee number? ");
    if ((empptr = findEmployee(empnum)) != NULL)
    {                                  /* replace with last employee */
      free(empptr->name);
      free(empptr->phone);
      *empptr = EmployeeTable[--Employees];
    }
  }
}
```

Figure 12.20 (dbupdate.c) The functions to update the employee database.

```
/*
 * Functions to display entries in the employee database.
 *    printEntry - print a single table entry.
 *    printEntries - print all table entries.
 */
#include <stdio.h>
#include "dbinp.h"
#include "dbfind.h"

void printEntry(void)
{
  const Employee *empptr;
  long           empnum;

  if (Employees == 0)
    printf("Employee table is empty.\n");
  else
  {
    empnum = getLong("Print employee number? ");
    if ((empptr = findEmployee(empnum)) != NULL)
      printf("Employee #%li\n\tName: %s\n\tAge: %i\n\tPhone: %s\n",
             empptr->number, empptr->name,
             empptr->age, empptr->phone);
  }
}

void printEntries(void)
{
  const Employee *ptr           = EmployeeTable;
  const Employee *const endptr = ptr + Employees;

  for (; ptr < endptr; ptr++)
    printf("%li, %s, %i, %s\n",
           ptr->number, ptr->name, ptr->age, ptr->phone);
  printf("%i employee%s\n", Employees, Employees == 1 ? "" : "s");
}
```

Figure 12.21 (dbprint.c) The functions to display the employee database.

SUMMARY

- Structures allow us to combine data of different types into a single variable.

- Unions allow us to store different types in the same variable location.

- Enumerated types allow us to have a variable whose values fall within a specific list of values and provide a nice shortcut for defining a set of constants.

```
/*
 * Prototypes for lookup functions.
 */
#include "db.h"

Employee *findEmployee(long employee_number);
Employee *dontFindEmployee(long employee_number);
```

Figure 12.22   (dbfind.h)   The prototypes for the functions to search the employee database.

```
/*
 * Functions to search employee table.
 *    findEmployee - write error message if employee not found.
 *    dontFindEmployee - write error message if employee found.
 */
#include <stdio.h>
#include "dbfind.h"

static const Employee *lookup(long target)
{
  const Employee *ptr          = EmployeeTable;
  const Employee *const endptr = ptr + Employees;

  for (; ptr < endptr; ptr++)            /* find employee in table */
    if (ptr->number == target)
      return ptr;
  return (Employee *) NULL;
}

Employee *findEmployee(long employee_number)
{
  const Employee *const temp = lookup(employee_number);

  if (temp == NULL)
    printf("There is no such employee.\n");
  return (Employee *) temp;
}

Employee *dontFindEmployee(long employee_number)
{
  const Employee *const temp = lookup(employee_number);

  if (temp != NULL)
    printf("There is an employee with that number.\n");
  return (Employee *) temp;
}
```

Figure 12.23   (dbfind.c)   The functions for searching the employee database.

```
/*
 * Prototypes for functions built on top of getValue.
 */
#include "getvalue2.h"

long getLong(const char *prompt);
char *getStr(const char *prompt);
```

Figure 12.24   (dbinp.h)   Prototypes for interface functions on top of **getValue**.

```
/*
 * Nice interface on top of getValue.
 */
#include <stdio.h>
#include <stddef.h>
#include "dbinp.h"

long getLong(const char *prompt)     /* prompt for and read a long */
{
  union value *up;

  while ((up = getValue(prompt, LONG)) == NULL)
    printf("Bad input.  Expected an integer.\n");
  return up->l;
}

char *getStr(const char *prompt)     /* prompt for and read a string */
{
  union value *up;

  while ((up = getValue(prompt, STRING)) == NULL)
    printf("Bad input.  Expected a string.\n");
  return up->s;
}
```

Figure 12.25   (dbinp.c)   Nice interface on top of **getValue**.

- We can have arrays of any of these types, and we can use pointers to traverse them.

- The only operations we're allowed to perform on a structure are accessing its fields, assigning it to another structure, taking its address, and determining its size.

- We can specify fields in a structure to have a particular size in bits, which allows us to reduce our program's need for space.

EXERCISES

Explore

12–1 Compile and run all of the programs in this chapter.

12–2 Create a **union** with one field for each of C's basic data types. Store various values in the **union** and print each of the fields.

12–3 How can we define a **boolean** enumerated type? Is using an enumerated **boolean** type preferable to using **typedef** or **#define**?

Modify

12–4 Rewrite the functions to compare and print dates (Figures 12.3 and 12.4) to work with a date stored as a collection of bitfields.

12–5 Modify a **struct employee** so that the phone number is stored as a structure, with separate integer fields for the area code, the local prefix, and the final four digits. Change the functions that print the employee table (Figures 12.8 and 12.9) to print phone numbers along with the names.

12–6 Write a new version of the employee database functions that maintains the database in sorted order.

Extend

12–7 Extend **getValue** to read values of other types such as **short** and **float**.

12–8 Extend our package of date-related functions with functions to read a date, to print a date in a nice format, to determine if a date is valid, and to determine the number of days between two **struct dates**.

Code

12–9 Write a program to read and sort an array of **struct employees**. Sort by employee name.

12–10 Write a program to read and sort an array of **struct dates**. Then write a function to search an array of **struct dates** for a particular date.

12–11 Define a structure type, **struct point**, for two-dimensional space coordinates (consisting of real values of x and y). Write a function, **distance**, that computes the distance between two **struct points**.

12–12 Define a structure type, **struct rational**, for rational numbers (consisting of the integer values x and y). Write functions for rational arithmetic.

12–13 Define an enumerated type for the days of the week. Write functions to retrieve the next and previous days. These functions should return an enumerated type.

Build

12–14 Write a program to handle a database of events. An event includes the name of the event and its corresponding date. Provide operations to add, delete, and print events.

12–15 Write a program to manage a database of information about an individual compact disc collection. Each entry includes the name of the group, the name of the CD, the year it was released, the price paid for it, and the total playing time. Allow the user to search for all the CDs released by a given group or for all the information on a particular CD. The user should also be able to print the database sorted by group name, by playing time, by year of release, or by price paid. Finally, allow the user to print aggregate information: the total cost of the collection, the number of CDs, the number of different groups, and so on.

13 ARRAYS

OF

ARRAYS

So far our programs have needed only simple, one-dimensional arrays. This chapter introduces arrays of arrays, concentrating on how we can use pointers to gain performance improvements. We present several programs that manipulate these arrays using traditional subscripting and then rewrite them more efficiently using pointers. We conclude by implementing the Game of Life, once with array subscripting and once using pointers. This chapter is detailed, but studying it carefully will result in faster programs and a deep understanding of arrays and pointers.

13.1　　　**TWO-DIMENSIONAL ARRAYS**

We can have arrays of any type, even arrays whose elements are themselves arrays. These more complex arrays correspond to the multidimensional arrays found in other languages. We can, for example, treat an array whose elements are arrays of integers as a two-dimensional array of integers.

How do we declare an array of arrays? The declaration

```
#define   MAX_STUDENTS    10
#define   MAX_TESTS        3

int   scores[MAX_STUDENTS][MAX_TESTS];
```

makes **scores** an array of 10 elements, with each element an array of 3 **int**s. That means **scores** contains a total of 30 **int**s and corresponds to a traditional two-dimensional array containing 10 rows of 3 columns each. One use of **scores** is to hold test scores for students in a class. Each row corresponds to the test scores for a particular student, each column corresponds to the scores for a particular test. In this case, that means that we have up to 10 students who have taken up to 3 tests.

We access a particular **int** within **scores** by specifying its row and column, which we do by using double sets of brackets. The first index selects the row, and the second selects the column within that row. Each dimension of the array can be indexed from zero to its maximum size minus 1, so the legal indexes for **scores** range from

scores[0][0]	scores[0][1]	scores[0][2]
scores[1][0]	scores[1][1]	scores[1][2]
scores[2][0]	scores[2][1]	scores[2][2]
scores[3][0]	scores[3][1]	scores[3][2]
scores[4][0]	scores[4][1]	scores[4][2]
scores[5][0]	scores[5][1]	scores[5][2]
scores[6][0]	scores[6][1]	scores[6][2]
scores[7][0]	scores[7][1]	scores[7][2]
scores[8][0]	scores[8][1]	scores[8][2]
scores[9][0]	scores[9][1]	scores[9][2]

Figure 13.1   How we index two-dimensional arrays.

scores[0][0] to **scores[9][2]**. Figure 13.1 illustrates this two-dimensional array indexing.

We illustrate this array accessing with a simple program that reads items into a two-dimensional array and then prints the array elements. Two functions do most of the work. **readScores** reads the items into the array, and **printScores** prints them, one row per line. Each input line contains a single score, with all of the scores for a given student preceding those of the next. Each output line contains the test scores for a particular student. Both functions use two variables, **student** and **test**, to index the array; **student** selects the row and **test** selects the element within that row.

Figure 13.2 is the header file, ioscores.h, that contains the prototypes for these functions. Figure 13.3 is the source file, ioscores.c, that contains the functions themselves. And Figure 13.4 is a main program using them.

readScores and **printScores** are straightforward—except for their first parameter declaration.[1]

```
int s[][MAX_TESTS]
```

Why is there a single subscript? As we saw in earlier chapters, when we pass an array, the compiler need know only the size of its elements, not how many elements it has. Here, the compiler needs to know that we're passing an array, each of whose elements is an array of **MAX_TESTS int**s. But it doesn't care how many of those elements we're passing.

---

[1]It's reasonable to expect that **printScores** would declare its array parameter as **const**. But to keep our example programs as simple as possible, we're ignoring that issue until this chapter's case study.

```
/*
 * Prototypes for score-manipulating functions.
 */
#define MAX_TESTS 3

extern int readScores(int s[][MAX_TESTS], int maxrow);
extern void printScores(int s[][MAX_TESTS], int maxrow);
```

Figure 13.2 (ioscores.h) Header file containing the prototypes for our input and output functions.

```
/*
 * Functions to read and print a 2-D array of student test scores.
 *    readScores - read scores into array, one input score per line.
 *    printScores - write scores from array, one line per student.
 */
#include <stdio.h>
#include "ioscores.h"

#define  MAXLEN    80

int readScores(int s[][MAX_TESTS], int maxrow)
{
  int  getline(char *buf, int len);

  int  student, test;                    /* our indices */
  char line[MAXLEN + 1];

  for (student = 0; student < maxrow; student++)
    for (test = 0; test < MAX_TESTS; test++)
      if (getline(line, MAXLEN) == -1 ||
            sscanf(line, "%i", &s[student][test]) != 1)
        return -student;             /* negative indicates problem */
  return maxrow;                     /* successfully read all scores */
}

void printScores(int s[][MAX_TESTS], int maxrow)
{
  int student, test;                     /* our indices */

  for (student = 0; student < maxrow ; student++)
    for (test = 0; test < MAX_TESTS; test++)
      printf("%i%c", s[student][test],
                (test != MAX_TESTS - 1) ? ' ' : '\n');
}
```

Figure 13.3 (ioscores.c) Reading and printing test scores using conventional array subscripting.

```
/*
 * Read and print student scores.
 */
#include <stdio.h>
#include <stdlib.h>
#include "ioscores.h"

#define MAX_STUDENTS 10

int main()
{
  int scores[MAX_STUDENTS][MAX_TESTS];

  if (readScores(scores, MAX_STUDENTS) == MAX_STUDENTS)
    printScores(scores, MAX_STUDENTS);
  else
    printf("Couldn't read all students successfully\n");

  return EXIT_SUCCESS;
}
```

Figure 13.4   (tstscrs.c) A main program that uses **readScores** and **printScores**.

In general, with two-dimensional arrays this means that we must tell the compiler only how many columns the array has, but not how many rows. That means any function we write works with a particular two-dimensional array: one whose rows have a particular number of items of a particular type. We can't write functions that can be passed two-dimensional arrays with varying length rows. That's why we put the definition of **MAX_TESTS** in ioscores.h, since both **readScores** and **printScores** work only with two-dimensional arrays with **MAX_TESTS** columns.

As with all other arrays, when we pass an array of arrays as a parameter, we're really only passing a pointer to its first element. **readScores** takes advantage of that feature in filling the array we pass it. But, as we'll soon see, with two-dimensional arrays we're passing a pointer to its first *row*, not to its first element.

Initializing Two-Dimensional Arrays

Because two-dimensional arrays are really just arrays of arrays, we can initialize them in the same way we initialize their one-dimensional counterparts: by following their declaration with a list of values enclosed in braces. For example,

```
int scores[10][3] = {{90, 75, 85}, {99, 99, 95},
                     {65, 69, 66}, {100, 100, 100},
                     {56, 60, 70}, {78, 85, 90},
                     {87, 82, 97}, {65, 80, 70},
                     {75, 78, 56}, {80, 80, 100}};
```

initializes the items in **scores'** first row to 90, 75, and 85; the items in **scores'** second row to 99, 99, and 95; and so on. Figure 13.5 shows the resulting array.

We're allowed to eliminate the braces surrounding the values in each row if we are specifying every element in the row, so

```
int scores[10][3] =
    {90, 75, 85, 99, 99, 95, 65, 69, 66, 100, 100, 100,
     56, 60, 70, 78, 85, 90, 87, 82, 97, 65,  80,  70,
     75, 78, 56, 80, 80, 100};
```

is a terse equivalent to the initialization above. But there's a problem with this form: it's not immediately apparent which values go with which elements. We prefer the more readable but longer form.

If we don't supply all the elements in the initialization list, the missing elements start off as zero. The declaration

```
int scores[10][3] =
    {{90, 75}, {99, 99}, {65, 69}, {100, 100}, {56, 60},
     {78, 85}, {87, 82}, {65, 80}, {75, 78},   {80, 80}};
```

explicitly initializes the first two elements of each row and implicitly initializes the last element in each row to zero. Unfortunately, there's no way to initialize only selected rows. The simplest way to skip over rows that don't require initialization is to initialize their first element to zero.

Since the compiler can determine the size and structure of an array from the values we provide, we don't have to specify its first dimension (the number of rows). We can rewrite our initial declaration of **scores** as

```
int scores[][3] = {{90, 75, 85}, {99, 99, 95},
                    {65, 69, 66}, {100, 100, 100},
                    {56, 60, 70}, {78, 85, 90},
                    {87, 82, 97}, {65, 80, 70},
                    {75, 78, 56}, {80, 80, 100}};
```

Storing Two-Dimensional Arrays

All arrays in C have their elements stored sequentially in memory. With two-dimensional arrays that means the elements of the first row are stored consecutively in memory, followed by the elements of the second row, and so on. Figure 13.6 shows how **scores** is stored.

When we refer to an array element, as with **scores[7][2]**, the compiler finds its location from the two subscripts and its knowledge of the number of columns in each row and of the location of the first item in the array. Using our earlier declaration of **scores** and assuming that **scores** starts at location 1000, we find **scores[7][2]** at

    &scores[0][0] + words for 3×7 elements in rows 0 through 6
      + words for the 2 elements preceding it in row 7

scores[0][0]

90	75	85
99	99	95
65	69	66
100	100	100
56	60	70
78	85	90
87	82	97
65	80	70
75	78	56
80	80	100

scores[0][2]

scores[9][0]

scores[9][2]

Figure 13.5   The resulting initialized two-dimensional array.

scores[0][0]	90
scores[0][1]	75
scores[0][2]	85
scores[1][0]	99
	⋮
scores[8][2]	56
scores[9][0]	80
scores[9][1]	80
scores[9][2]	100

Figure 13.6   Internal representation of **scores**.

or, in other words, $1000 + 21 \times$ **sizeof(int)** $+ 2 \times$ **sizeof(int)**, which is 1046 (assuming 2-byte **int**s). In general, we find **scores[i][j]** at

$$\texttt{\&scores[0][0]} + i \times \texttt{MAX\_TESTS} \times \texttt{sizeof(int)} + j \times \texttt{sizeof(int)}$$

13.2   POINTERS AND TWO-DIMENSIONAL ARRAYS

The name of an array of arrays, like the name of a one-dimensional array, is the address of the array's first element. For these arrays, however, that first element is not simply an **int** or a **double**, but is itself an array. What that means is that the name of a two-dimensional array of **int**s is not a pointer to its first **int** but to its first row.

Why is this distinction important? Because, as we discovered earlier, any array access is automatically converted to an equivalent pointer expression. Whenever we use two subscripts to reference an element in a two-dimensional array, C converts the array access into an equivalent pointer expression. **scores[i][j]**, for example, is converted into the equivalent pointer expression

```
*(*(scores + i) + j)
```

Figure 13.7 shows how this extremely bizarre-looking expression obtains the value of **scores[i][j]**. The rest of this section clarifies why this expression works and how we can use pointers to efficiently traverse two-dimensional arrays.

Traversing Columns

We illustrate the relationship between pointers and two-dimensional arrays with a simple function, **testAvg**, that computes the average of the values in a given column of an array. The call

```
testAvg(scores, MAX_STUDENTS, i)
```

returns the average of the **i**th column in the first **MAX_STUDENTS** rows, which is the average score on a particular test. **testAvg** works correctly only if **i** is less than **MAX_TESTS**, but to simplify things, we don't bother with error checking.

Figure 13.8 contains a main program that uses **testAvg** to compute the average of each of the columns in an array. Here's the program's output:

```
Average on test 0 is 79.50
Average on test 1 is 80.80
Average on test 2 is 82.90
```

Rather than using a defined constant, we compute the number of students we have with:

```
sizeof(scores) / (sizeof(int) * MAX_TESTS)
```

We've written two versions of **testAvg**. Figure 13.9 contains the first version, which uses array subscripting. Figure 13.10 contains the second version, which uses pointers.

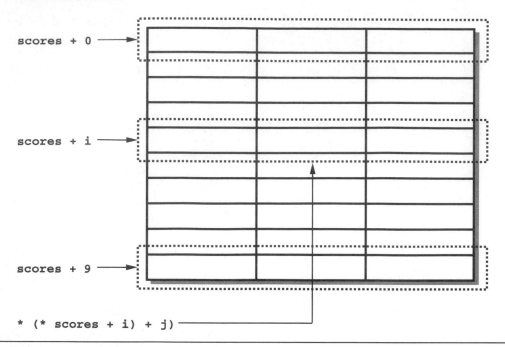

scores + 0 ──►

scores + i ──►

scores + 9 ──►

* (* scores + i) + j) ────────────

Figure 13.7   Using `*(*(scores + i) + j)` to access `scores[i][j]`. Here `i` is 4 and `j` is 1.

> *The name of a two-dimensional array is a pointer to its first row, not its first element.*

When we declare a two-dimensional array, C automatically declares its name as a constant pointer to the array's first row. This declaration,

```
int scores[MAX_STUDENTS][MAX_TESTS];
```

allocates space for a two-dimensional array and defines **scores** as a constant pointer to its first row. So we can declare the parameter in **testAvg** as

```
int (*rowptr)[MAX_TESTS]
```

that is, as a pointer to an array of **MAX_TESTS int**s. We need the parentheses around ***rowptr** because ***** has lower precedence than **[]**. Without them, as in

```
int *rowptr[MAX_TESTS];
```

we would be declaring **rowptr** as an array of **MAX_TESTS** elements, each a pointer to an **int**, a topic we cover in the next chapter.

Because pointer arithmetic is done in units of the pointed-to thing, incrementing a pointer to a row makes it point to the next row. This allows us to traverse a two-

```
/*
 * Print average on each test.  For simplicity, the initial scores
 * are hard-coded into the array rather than read.
 */
#include <stdio.h>
#include <stdlib.h>
#include "ioscores.h"

int main()
{
  double testAvg(int s[][MAX_TESTS], int rows, int n);

  int scores[][MAX_TESTS] = {{90, 75, 85}, {99, 99, 95},
                             {65, 69, 66}, {100, 100, 100},
                             {56, 60, 70}, {78, 85, 90},
                             {87, 82, 97}, {65, 80, 70},
                             {75, 78, 56}, {80, 80, 100}};
  const int n = sizeof(scores) / (sizeof(int) * MAX_TESTS);
  int i;

  for (i = 0; i < MAX_TESTS; i++)
    printf("Average on test %i is %.2f\n", i, testAvg(scores, n, i));

  return EXIT_SUCCESS;
}
```

Figure 13.8 (usetest.c) A program to use **testAvg** to compute the average of each of the columns.

```
/*
 * Compute the average of a column in a 2-D array using subscripting.
 */
#include "ioscores.h"

double testAvg(int s[][MAX_TESTS], int rows, int n)
{
  double sum = 0.0;                        /* column total */
  int    i;                                /* row index */

  for (i = 0; i < rows; i++)
    sum += s[i][n];
  return sum / rows;
}
```

Figure 13.9 (testavg1.c) An array-subscripting version of **testAvg**.

```
/*
 * Compute the average of a column in a 2-D array using pointers.
 */
#include "ioscores.h"

double testAvg(int (*rowptr)[MAX_TESTS], int rows, int n)
{
  double sum = 0.0;                     /* column total */
  int (*endptr)[MAX_TESTS];             /* will point to last row */

  for (endptr = rowptr + rows; rowptr < endptr; rowptr++)
    sum += (*rowptr)[n];
  return sum / rows;
}
```

Figure 13.10   (testavg2.c) A pointer-indexing version of **testAvg**.

dimensional array by initializing a pointer (**rowptr**) to the first row of the array and incrementing the pointer (**rowptr++**) each time we need to get to the next row. Figure 13.11 illustrates this process.

But once we have a pointer to a row, how do we get at its elements? The expression **(*rowptr)[n]** gives us the *n*th element in a row pointed to by **rowptr**. Figure 13.12 shows why this expression works.

> *Dereferencing a pointer to a row gives us the row itself, not its first element.*

More accurately, dereferencing a pointer to a row gives us a pointer to the row's first element. Since **rowptr** points to a particular row, ***rowptr** is a pointer to that row's first element. What's weird is that **rowptr** and ***rowptr** refer to identical addresses. The difference is their type: **rowptr** is a pointer to an array of **int**s, but ***rowptr** is a pointer to the first **int** in that array (the row). That difference in type means that **rowptr + n** is a pointer to the *n*th row past **rowptr**, whereas ***rowptr + n** is a pointer to the *n*th column in the array pointed to by **rowptr**. We can use ***rowptr** as though it were the name of an array (the array containing the **MAX_TESTS** elements in that row), which means that **(*rowptr)[n]** accesses the *n*th element in the row.

We compiled and ran both versions of **testAvg** on several different computers. On the average, the pointer version took less than two-thirds the time of the straightforward array-subscripting version. Why is there so much improvement? Normally when we do a two-dimensional array access, such as **scores[i][j]**, to locate the desired element, the compiler must do the complicated address calculation we saw earlier. This calculation first figures out which row the element is in and then where it is in that row. But when we use the row pointer, the compiler already knows which row the element is in, eliminating a major portion of the address calculation. Later exercises suggest ways to improve this function even further.

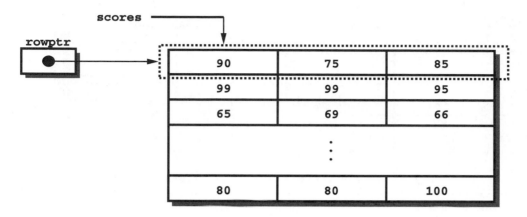

(a) **rowptr** starts off pointing to the first *row* in **scores**.

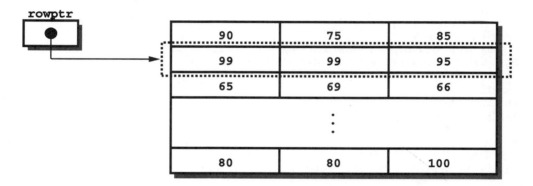

(b) Incrementing **rowptr** causes it to point to the next row of **scores**.

Figure 13.11   What happens when we increment a pointer to a row.

Traversing Rows

We can use pointers to process rows as well as columns. Figure 13.13 is a program that uses a new function, **studentAvg**, to compute the average of a row. Figures 13.14 and 13.15 contain array-subscripting and pointer-indexing versions of **studentAvg**, respectively. Here's the program's output when run on a sample set of student scores:

```
83.33 97.67 66.67 100.00 62.00 84.33 88.67 71.67 69.67 86.67
```

When we use pointers, we traverse a row of a two-dimensional array just as we traverse a one-dimensional array: We initialize a pointer to the row's first element and

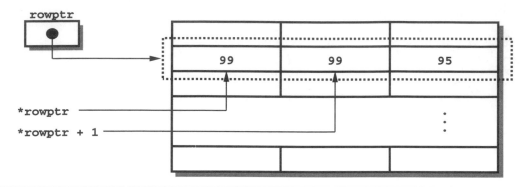

Figure 13.12 How we access an element through a pointer to a row.

```
/*
 * Read scores and print average for each student.  As before,
 * for simplicity the test scores are hard-coded, not read.
 */
#include <stdio.h>
#include <stdlib.h>
#include "ioscores.h"

int main()
{
  double studentAvg(int s[][MAX_TESTS], int n);

  int i;
  int scores[][MAX_TESTS] = {{90, 75, 85}, {99, 99, 95},
                             {65, 69, 66}, {100, 100, 100},
                             {56, 60, 70}, {78, 85, 90},
                             {87, 82, 97}, {65, 80, 70},
                             {75, 78, 56}, {80, 80, 100}};
  int n = sizeof(scores) / (sizeof(int) * MAX_TESTS);

  for (i = 0; i < n; i++)
    printf("%.2f ", studentAvg(scores, i));
  putchar('\n');

  return EXIT_SUCCESS;
}
```

Figure 13.13 (userow.c) A program that prints the average of each of the rows in a two-dimensional array.

```
/*
 * Compute row average using array subscripting.
 */
#include "ioscores.h"

double studentAvg(int s[][MAX_TESTS], int n)
{
  int i = 0;                              /* index to next row */
  long sum = 0L;                          /* total so far */

  for (; i < MAX_TESTS; sum += s[n][i++])
    ;
  return (double) sum / MAX_TESTS;
}
```

Figure 13.14   (rowavg1.c) An array-subscripting version of **studentAvg**.

```
/*
 * Compute row average using pointer indexing.
 */
#include "ioscores.h"

double studentAvg(int s[][MAX_TESTS], int n)
{
  const int *colptr = &s[n][0];                 /* ptr to first item */
  const int *const endptr = colptr + MAX_TESTS; /* ptr to last item */
  long sum = 0L;                                /* total so far */

  for (; colptr < endptr; sum += *colptr++)
    ;
  return (double) sum / MAX_TESTS;
}
```

Figure 13.15   (rowavg2.c) A pointer-indexing version of **studentAvg**. It obtains a pointer to the first element in a row and uses it to traverse the row.

increment it until it points to the row's last element. Again we find a large performance improvement. The pointer version takes less than one-third the time of the array-subscripting version. Why? Because we now access the various elements within a row simply by incrementing a pointer—completely eliminating any address calculations.

Accessing Rows

We just wrote a specialized function to compute the average of a row within a two-dimensional array. But we could also have used **tableAverage** (from Chapter 10).

Aside 13.1a: Efficiently Traversing Two-Dimensional Arrays

It turns out that the internal layout of two-dimensional arrays allows us to traverse them with pointers as if they were giant one-dimensional arrays. This often leads to *dramatic* time savings.

Aside 13.1b contains a program that calls two different functions to initialize all of the elements in a large two-dimensional array. The first function, **twodInitSub**, takes three parameters: a two-dimensional array with **MAXCOLS** columns in each row, the number of rows in the array, and the value with which to initialize each of its elements. It uses two indices, **row** and **col**, and straightforward two-dimensional array subscripting. To obtain some data on its execution time, we had the program initialize the array 500 times. On our workstation that took approximately 3 seconds.

The other function, **twodInitPtr**, much more quickly accomplishes this task. It's designed to initialize every item in a one-dimensional array to a particular value. It expects to be passed pointers to the array's first and last **int**s, along with the initializing value. It then uses pointers to traverse the array. We call **twodInitPtr** with:

```
twodInitPtr(&t[0][0], &t[MAXROWS - 1][MAXCOLS - 1], 5);
```

&t[0][0] and **&t[MAXROWS - 1][MAXCOLS - 1]** are pointers to the first and last **int**s in our two-dimensional array.

Why do we pass **t** to **twodInitSub** and **&t[0][0]** to **twodInitPtr**? Because although both pointers refer to the same address, they have different types. **&t[0][0]** is a pointer to an **int**, and **t** is a pointer to an array of **int**s. **twodInitSub** expects to be passed a pointer to the first *row* of the two-dimensional array, and **twodInitPtr** expects to be passed a pointer to its first *element*.

This version took approximately 1.8 seconds to perform the same task, which is a reduction in time of about 40%. Why is it so much faster? Before, we did two-dimensional array subscripting each time we wanted to access an element. That subscripting potentially involves a great deal of arithmetic: a multiplication to locate the element's row and an addition to find the item's column. Now, however, we're using a pointer to traverse it, which eliminates the need to compute each array element's location.

In general, whenever we sequentially traverse a segment of a two-dimensional array, we should pretend that segment is a one-dimensional array and traverse it using pointers.

We simply pass it the address of the desired row's first element, along with the number of elements in that row. To sum up the values in row 5, for example, we use

```
tableAverage(&scores[5][0], MAX_TESTS)
```

There is, however, an even more concise way to provide the address of the first element in a row. We simply follow the array name with a single subscript: the row number. We can rewrite the call above as

```
tableAverage(scores[5], MAX_TESTS)
```

Aside 13.1b (init2d.c) Initializing a two-dimensional array using array subscripting and pointer indexing.

```c
/*
 * A program that uses two different ways to initialize a 2-D array.
 */
#include <stdlib.h>

#define ITERATIONS   500
#define MAXROWS      150
#define MAXCOLS      200

int main()
{
  void twodInitSub(int table[][MAXCOLS], int rows, int value);
  void twodInitPtr(int *ptr, int *endptr, int value);

  int t[MAXROWS][MAXCOLS];                /* table to initialize */
  int i;                                  /* count */

  for (i = 0; i < ITERATIONS; i++)      /* first try slow way */
    twodInitSub(t, MAXROWS, 5);
  for (i = 0; i < ITERATIONS; i++)      /* then try faster way */
    twodInitPtr(&t[0][0], &t[MAXROWS - 1][MAXCOLS - 1], 5);

  return EXIT_SUCCESS;
}

void twodInitSub(int table[][MAXCOLS], int rows, int value)
{                    /* initialize 2-D array using subscripting */
  int row, col;

  for (row = 0; row < rows; row++)
    for (col = 0; col < MAXCOLS; col++)
      table[row][col] = value;
}

void twodInitPtr(int *ptr, int *endptr, int value)
{                    /* initialize 2-D array using pointer indexing */
  for (; ptr < endptr; *ptr++ = value)
    ;
}
```

There are two ways to understand how this works. One way relies on remembering that a two-dimensional array is really an array of arrays. So when we access **scores[i]**, we're accessing the **i**th element in **scores**, which happens to be an array of **int**s. The other way is to remember that C turns any array access into a pointer expression. **scores[i]** is turned into ***(scores + i)**. Adding **i** to **scores** gives us a pointer to the **i**th row, dereferencing it gives us a pointer to the first element in the **i**th row. So **scores[i]** is exactly equivalent to **&scores[i][0]**.

Figure 13.16 contains a new version of our earlier program to compute the average student score. This version uses **tableAverage**. The primary advantage of this version is that it uses an existing function that works with one-dimensional arrays of any size, rather than requiring a special function that only works with rows in two-dimensional arrays of a particular size.

13.3   MULTIDIMENSIONAL ARRAYS

It turns out that C also allows three- and higher-dimensional arrays. We declare, initialize, and subscript these as we do two-dimensional arrays. For example,

```
#define MAX_CLASSES   2
#define MAX_STUDENTS 10
#define MAX_TESTS     3

int classes[MAX_CLASSES][MAX_STUDENTS][MAX_TESTS];
```

declares an array of 2 elements, each of which is itself an array of 10 elements, each of which is an array of 3 **int**s. This corresponds to a three-dimensional array holding 60 **int**s organized into 2 two-dimensional arrays of 10 rows and 3 columns each. We could use it to store the test scores for students in two different classes, with each of the two-dimensional arrays holding the scores for the students in one class. As you may have guessed, the name of a three-dimensional array is a constant pointer to the first two-dimensional array inside it.

We access the elements of a three-dimensional array using three subscripts, so **classes[0][1][2]** refers to the third column of the second row of the first two-dimensional array, or, in plain English, the third test score of the second student in the first class.

N-Dimensional Arrays and Parameters

When we declare an N-dimensional array parameter, we must supply all dimensions except the first, regardless of what N actually is. This is because when we pass an N-dimensional array as a parameter, we really pass a pointer to its first element (the first $(N - 1)$-dimensional array it contains).

Figure 13.17 provides an example with a program that reads values into **classes** and then prints them. To do so, it makes use of the two functions **readClasses** and **printClasses**. Figure 13.18 contains their prototypes, and Figure 13.19 contains the function themselves.

Both functions are passed two parameters: a three-dimensional array and the number of two-dimensional arrays it contains. The functions expect to be passed **classes**, but since we're really passing only a pointer, we can declare the prototypes using cither array indexing notation

```
void printClasses(int c[][MAX_STUDENTS][MAX_TESTS], int n)
```

or pointer notation

```
/*
 * Print average for each student, using our earlier tableAverage
 * function (again, scores are hard-coded rather than read).
 */
#include <stdio.h>
#include <stdlib.h>
#include "ioscores.h"

int main()
{
  double tableAverage(int *ptr, int n);

  int i;
  int scores[][MAX_TESTS] = {90, 75, 85, 99, 99, 95, 65, 69, 66, 100,
                             100, 100, 56, 60, 70, 78, 85, 90, 87, 82,
                             97, 65, 80, 70, 75, 78, 56, 80, 80, 100};
  const int n = sizeof(scores) / (sizeof(int) * MAX_TESTS);

  printf("Student\t   Average\n");
  for (i = 0; i < n; i++)
    printf("%4i\t%10.2f\n", i, tableAverage(scores[i], MAX_TESTS));

  return EXIT_SUCCESS;
}
```

Figure 13.16 (avgtab.c) A second version of our program to print average student scores.

```
void printClasses(int (*ptr)[MAX_STUDENTS][MAX_TESTS], int n)
```

The latter form declares **ptr** as a pointer to a two-dimensional array. But because **readClasses** and **printClasses** use array indexing to process **classes**, we've used the first form.

N-Dimensional Arrays and Pointers

readClasses uses **readScores** to read the scores into each of the individual two-dimensional arrays in **classes**. It first reads the scores for the first class, then the scores for the second class, and so on. And **printClasses** does something similar, except that it uses **printScores** to print these arrays. But both **readScores** and **printScores** expect a pointer to the first row in a two-dimensional array. How can we provide them with one when we're running through a three-dimensional array?

C treats any N-dimensional array as an array of $(N - 1)$-dimensional arrays: a two-dimensional array as an array of one-dimensional arrays, a three-dimensional array as an array of two-dimensional arrays, and so on. By "treats", we mean several things. First, regardless of the number of dimensions in it, C stores any array as a single one-dimensional array. What differs are the elements inside that one-dimensional array.

```
/*
 * Read and print student scores, one student per line.
 */
#include <stdio.h>
#include <stdlib.h>
#include "ioclass.h"                  /* for readClasses/printClasses */

#define MAX_CLASSES  2

int main()
{
  int classes[MAX_CLASSES][MAX_STUDENTS][MAX_TESTS];

  if (readClasses(classes, MAX_CLASSES) == MAX_CLASSES)
    printClasses(classes, MAX_CLASSES);
  else
    printf("Couldn't read all classes successfully\n");

  return EXIT_SUCCESS;
}
```

Figure 13.17   (classes.c) A program to read and print three-dimensional arrays.

```
/*
 * Prototypes for functions to read and print class scores.
 */
#include "ioscores.h"

#define MAX_STUDENTS 10

int readClasses(int c[][MAX_STUDENTS][MAX_TESTS], int n);
void printClasses(int c[][MAX_STUDENTS][MAX_TESTS], int n);
```

Figure 13.18   (ioclass.h) Header file defining prototypes for our I/O functions.

Figure 13.20 shows how a three-dimensional array is stored: it's an array, each element of which is a two-dimensional array. Similarly, a two-dimensional array is an array of one-dimensional arrays. Second, C defines any array name as a constant pointer to the first $(N - 1)$-dimensional array within it. **classes**, for example, is a constant pointer to its first two-dimensional array. Third, C translates any N-dimensional array into a sequence of pointer additions and dereferences, with one addition and dereference for each dimension of the array. And finally, C calculates pointer arithmetic for any N-dimensional array based on the size of the $(N - 1)$-dimensional arrays it contains.

One result of all these features is that C automatically translates **classes[i]** into ***(classes + i)**, which is a pointer to the first row in the **i**th two-dimensional

```
/*
 * Functions to read/print a 3-d array.
 *    readClasses - use read_scores to read scores for each class.
 *    printClasses - use print_scores to print scores for each class.
 */
#include <stdio.h>
#include "ioclass.h"

int readClasses(int c[][MAX_STUDENTS][MAX_TESTS], int n)
{
  int class;

  for (class = 0; class < n; class++)
    if (readScores(c[class], MAX_STUDENTS) != MAX_STUDENTS)
      return -class;
  return class;
}

void printClasses(int classes[][MAX_STUDENTS][MAX_TESTS], int n)
{
  int class;

  for (class = 0; class < n; class++)
  {
    printScores(classes[class], MAX_STUDENTS);
    putchar('\n');
  }
}
```

Figure 13.19 (ioclass1.c) Functions to read and print a three-dimensional array using array subscripting.

1000	x[0][0][0]	x[0][0][1]	x[0][0][2]	x[0][0][3]	*First*
1008	x[0][1][0]	x[0][1][1]	x[0][1][2]	x[0][1][3]	*2D-Array*
1016	x[1][0][0]	x[1][0][1]	x[1][0][2]	x[1][0][3]	*Second*
1024	x[1][1][0]	x[1][1][1]	x[1][1][2]	x[1][1][3]	*2D-Array*
1032	x[2][0][0]	x[2][0][1]	x[2][0][2]	x[2][0][3]	*Third*
1042	x[2][1][0]	x[2][1][1]	x[2][1][2]	x[2][1][3]	*2D-Array*

Figure 13.20 Storage layout for a $3 \times 2 \times 4$ three-dimensional array of **int**s.

array within **classes**. And that's exactly what we want to pass to **readScores** and **printScores**.

```
printScores(classes[i], MAX_STUDENTS);
```

Another result is that we can use pointers to traverse any *N*-dimensional array—although the code can be confusing and hard to read when we traverse higher-dimensional arrays. If we have a pointer **ptr** that points to some two-dimensional array within **classes**, incrementing it with **ptr++** causes it to point to the next two-dimensional array. And because dereferencing a pointer gives a pointer to the array's first element, ***twodptr** is a pointer to the first row of a two-dimensional array and ****twodptr** is a pointer to its first element. Figure 13.21 provides an example, with pointer versions of **readClasses** and **printClasses**.

Initializing *N*-Dimensional Arrays

We can initialize any array, regardless of its dimension, by providing a brace-enclosed list of elements. If any of these elements are arrays, we can also enclose their values in braces. For example,

```
int x[3][2][4] =
  { { { 0,   1,   2,   3},
      { 4,   5,   6,   7} },
    { { 8,   9,  10,  11},
      {12,  13,  14,  15} },
    { {16,  17,  18,  19},
      {20,  21,  22,  23} } };
```

As with any array, we could just list the array's elements.

```
int x[3][2][4] =
  {  0,   1,   2,   3,
     4,   5,   6,   7,
     8,   9,  10,  11,
    12,  13,  14,  15,
    16,  17,  18,  19,
    20,  21,  22,  23 };
```

For higher-dimensional arrays, we use the longer form, since it's just too easy to make a mistake and forget a desired array element.

13.4   CASE STUDY—THE GAME OF LIFE

This section is optional!

This chapter concludes with an illustration of the power of pointers. We implement the Game of Life, a simulation of population growth dynamics developed by British mathematician John Horton Conway. In Life, a board represents the world, and each cell represents a single location. A cell is either empty or contains a single inhabitant. The game uses three simple rules to model population changes:

```
/*
 * Pointer version of 3-D array-reading and -printing functions.
 *    readClasses - use readScores to read scores for each class.
 *    printClasses - use printScores to print scores for each class.
 */
#include <stdio.h>
#include "ioclass.h"

int readClasses(int (*ptr)[MAX_STUDENTS][MAX_TESTS], int n)
{
  int (*saveptr)[MAX_STUDENTS][MAX_TESTS] = ptr;
  int (*endptr)[MAX_STUDENTS][MAX_TESTS];

  for (endptr = ptr + n - 1; ptr <= endptr; ptr++)
    if (readScores(*ptr, MAX_STUDENTS) != MAX_STUDENTS)
      return saveptr - ptr;    /* negative value on error */
  return ptr - saveptr;
}

void printClasses(int (*ptr)[MAX_STUDENTS][MAX_TESTS], int n)
{
  int (*endptr)[MAX_STUDENTS][MAX_TESTS];

  for (endptr = ptr + n - 1; ptr <= endptr; ptr++)
  {
    printScores(*ptr, MAX_STUDENTS);
    putchar('\n');
  }
}
```

Figure 13.21   (ioclass2.c)   Pointer-indexing versions of our I/O functions.

Survival An inhabited cell remains inhabited if exactly two or three of its neighboring cells are inhabited. (A cell has eight neighbors, four adjacent orthogonally and four adjacent diagonally.)

Death An inhabited cell becomes uninhabited if fewer than two or more than three of its neighbors are inhabited.

Birth An uninhabited cell becomes inhabited if exactly three of its neighbors are inhabited.

All births and deaths occur simultaneously, together causing the creation of a new generation.

Figure 13.22 shows some sample configurations and their first few generations. Sadly, most worlds eventually become uninhabited. But don't worry—some worlds develop a stable, inhabited population, whereas others reach a dynamically stable population that oscillates between states.

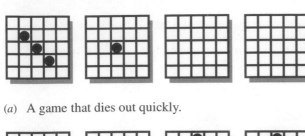

(*a*) A game that dies out quickly.

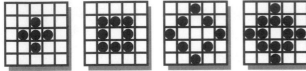

(*b*) A game that starts by growing rapidly.

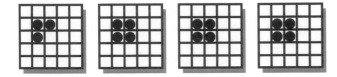

(*c*) A game that rapidly reaches a stable state.

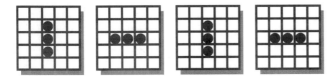

(*d*) A game that reaches an oscillating state.

Figure 13.22   Various worlds for the Game of Life and their population changes.

An Array-Subscripting Version

life divides nicely into three separate tasks: reading an initial description of a world, computing the next generation, and displaying the next generation. Each of these corresponds to a single function, placed into its own source file. **getWorld** reads a description of a world and records its initial inhabitants. **nextWorld** examines the current generation to determine the contents of the next generation. And **putWorld** displays the current generation.

The world itself is a two-dimensional array of **Boolean**s; **TRUE** indicates an inhabited cell, and **FALSE** an uninhabited cell. A **Boolean** is simply a **typedef** to **short**. For convenience and readability, we've also used **typedef** to define a type

```
/*
 * Header file for Life game.
 */
#include <stdio.h>

#define   BORDER     'X'                /* border around world */
#define   MARKER     '#'                /* occupied cell marker */
#define   MAXROW     20                 /* legal rows: 1...20 */
#define   MAXCOL     78                 /* legal columns: 1...78 */
#define   NUMROWS    22                 /* extra cells surrounding */
#define   NUMCOLS    80                 /* (simplify neighbors) */
#define   MAXLEN     80                 /* longest input line */

typedef   short Boolean;
typedef   Boolean World[NUMROWS][NUMCOLS];

typedef   Boolean (*PtrToWorld)[NUMCOLS];
typedef   const Boolean (*PtrToConstWorld)[NUMCOLS];

#define   TRUE       1
#define   FALSE      0

extern Boolean getWorld(PtrToWorld x);
extern int nextWorld(PtrToConstWorld x, PtrToWorld y);
extern void putWorld(PtrToConstWorld x);

extern int Rows, Cols, Gen, EndGen, Inhabs;
```

Figure 13.23 (life.h) Header file for the Game of Life program.

World as a two-dimensional array of **Boolean**s, a type **PtrToWorld** as a pointer to a row within a **World**, and a type **PtrToConstWorld** as a pointer to a row within a **World** that we aren't going to change. A special header file, life.h, contains these **typedef**s, along with definitions of various useful constants for the size of the world and the characters used to display cells. To simplify counting a cell's neighbors, a **World** actually includes room for an extra uninhabited border of cells. The displayable world is 20 by 78, the space available on the average display after writing a border around the world and a line identifying the current generation. Figure 13.23 contains life.h.

Figure 13.24 contains the main program, life.c. It begins by using **getWorld** to read the initial world, and **putWorld** to display the updated world. It then repeatedly uses **nextWorld** to calculate the contents of the next world, and **putWorld** to display it. It stops when it has displayed the requested number of generations or the world has reached a stable state.

Figure 13.25 contains **getWorld**. It expects the first input line to describe the desired number of rows and columns for the world, along with the number of generations to compute and display. And it expects each remaining input line to contain the row

```
/*
 * Main program for the Game of Life.
 */
#include <stdlib.h>
#include "life.h"

int Rows;                              /* # of rows used */
int Cols;                              /* # of columns used */
int Inhabs;                            /* # of inhabitants */
int Gen;                               /* current generation */
int EndGen;                            /* last generation */

int main()
{
  static World world1,                 /* one is current world */
               world2;                 /* other is future world */
  PtrToWorld   currptr = world1,       /* pointers to current and */
               nextptr = world2;       /*   future worlds */
  int          status;

  if (!getWorld(currptr))              /* bad input */
  {
    printf("No input world or input errors -- stopping\n");
    status = EXIT_FAILURE;             /* error exit */
  }
  else
  {
    putWorld(currptr);                 /* write initial world */
    for (Gen = 2; Inhabs && Gen <= EndGen; Gen++)
    {
      PtrToWorld temp;

      if (!nextWorld(currptr, nextptr))
        break;                         /* no changes! */
      putWorld(nextptr);               /* write next world */
      temp = currptr;                  /* exchange worlds */
      currptr = nextptr;
      nextptr = temp;
    }
    if (!Inhabs)
      printf("All inhabitants are dead\n");
    else if (Gen <= EndGen)
      printf("Reached stable state\n");
    else
      printf("Computed requested generations.\n");
    status = EXIT_SUCCESS;
  }

  return status;
}
```

Figure 13.24   (life.c)   The main program for the Game of Life.

```c
/*
 * Life input handler (quits on first error)
 */
#include <stdio.h>
#include "life.h"

static int inRange(int min, int max, int value);

Boolean getWorld(PtrToWorld world)
{
  int getline(char *ptr, int len);

  char buf[MAXLEN + 1];                           /* input line */
  int r, c;                                       /* next position */

  if (getline(buf, MAXLEN) == -1 ||
      sscanf(buf, "%i %i %i", &Rows, &Cols, &EndGen) != 3)
  {
    printf("Didn't provide ROWS, COLS, FINAL GENERATION\n");
    return FALSE;
  }

  printf("Rows=%i Cols=%i, Final Generation=%i\n",
         Rows, Cols, EndGen);

  if (!inRange(1, MAXROW, Rows))
    printf("Invalid Rows, set to %i\n", Rows = MAXROW);
  if (!inRange(1, MAXCOL, Cols))
    printf("Invalid Columns, set to %i\n", Cols = MAXCOL);
  while (getline(buf, MAXLEN) != -1)
    if (sscanf(buf, "%i %i", &r, &c) != 2)
      printf("Non-numeric cell position -- ignored\n");
    else if (!inRange(1, Rows, r) || !inRange(1, Cols, c))
      printf("%i,%i is out of range -- ignored\n", r, c);
    else if (!world[r][c])
    {
      printf("Cell %i,%i is now occupied\n", r, c);
      world[r][c] = TRUE;
      Inhabs++;
    }
  return TRUE;
}

static int inRange(int min, int max, int value)
{
  return min <= value && value <= max;
}
```

Figure 13.25   (getworld.c) A function to read the description of the world.

and column position of an inhabitant. **getWorld** reads input lines with our old friend **getline** and uses **sscanf** to grab the various values. It verifies that each value is in range using a **static** function named **inRange** and writes an appropriate error message when one isn't.[2]

getWorld assumes that its standard input has been redirected to come from a file, since there's likely to be too much input to enter directly. So although **getWorld** does check for input errors, it doesn't bother to prompt for its input.

Figure 13.26 contains **nextWorld**. It computes the next generation by examining each cell of the current generation, counting how many inhabited neighbors it has, and applying the rules to see whether it is inhabited in the next generation. **nextWorld** needs to make all the changes at the same time, so it expects to be passed a pointer to another world where it can record the next generation. When it returns, the main program exchanges the next and current worlds. **nextWorld** updates a counter of inhabitants and returns a count of changes so the main program can easily determine if a generation has been annihilated or has reached a stable state.

Figure 13.27 contains the final piece of the program. **putWorld** displays the current generation. It indicates the world's border with **X**'s, inhabited cells with a **#**, and uninhabited cells with a blank.

Neither **nextWorld** nor **putWorld** should change the world containing the current generation. We want the compiler to enforce this restriction, so these functions declare that parameter as a **PtrToConstWorld**, rather than simply as a **PtrToWorld**. Because the **typedef** for **PtrToConstWorld** indicates that the pointed-to world is a **const**, the compiler will flag as an error any attempt to change the world through that pointer. This prevents these functions from accidentally changing a cell in the world.[3]

A New Version Using Pointers

All of the functions in the current version of Life use traditional two-dimensional array subscripting. That makes it easy to write and easy to understand—and unbearably slow. When simulating large worlds, there is an annoying pause between successive generations. So we need to speed up the program. But how?

The program spends most of its time in **nextWorld**, calculating the next generation. **nextWorld** is devoted almost entirely to traversing a two-dimensional array. Since it accesses rows sequentially within the array, and array elements sequentially within rows, we should find a performance improvement if we use pointers to traverse the array.

Figure 13.28 contains the pointers we need. The basic idea is straightforward. We traverse the current world one row at a time, using a single row pointer, **cwrptr** (which stands for current world row pointer). We use another pointer, **colptr**, to process each row. The tricky part comes when we count the neighbors—we need to access elements in the rows preceding and following the one pointed to by **cwrptr**. To do this efficiently, we need two additional pointers, **pcolptr** and **ncolptr**, that point

---

[2] We've placed the prototype for **inRange** before **getWorld** rather than inside of it because **inRange** is a **static** function.

[3] The disadvantage is that many compilers give us warnings when we pass non-**const** two-dimensional arrays to functions expecting **const** two-dimensional arrays. To get rid of these warnings, it's necessary to explicitly cast the problematic argument to a constant or to go out and buy a better compiler.

```
/*
 * Compute the next generation.
 */
#include "life.h"

int nextWorld(PtrToConstWorld curr, PtrToWorld next)
{
  int changed = 0;                        /* cells that changed */
  int r, c;                               /* row, column index */

  Inhabs = 0;
  for (r = 1; r <= Rows; r++)
    for (c = 1; c <= Cols; c++)
    {
      int neighbors =  curr[r - 1][c - 1] + curr[r - 1][c] +
                       curr[r - 1][c + 1] + curr[r + 1][c - 1] +
                       curr[r + 1][c]     + curr[r + 1][c + 1] +
                       curr[r][c - 1]     + curr[r][c + 1];

      if ((neighbors == 3) || (neighbors == 2 && curr[r][c]))
      {
        next[r][c] = TRUE;
        Inhabs++;
      }
      else
        next[r][c] = FALSE;

      changed += next[r][c] != curr[r][c];
    }
  return changed;
}
```

Figure 13.26 (nxtworld.c) Compute the next generation.

to the same column as **colptr**, but in the rows before and after it. As we traverse the current row, we increment these pointers as well.

Figure 13.29 contains the pointer version of **nextWorld**. This new version takes less than one-fifth the time of the original, an impressive savings. We leave making similar changes to **putWorld** as an exercise for the reader.

SUMMARY

- C lets the elements of an array be arrays themselves.

- When we pass two-dimensional arrays as parameters, we have to specify the number of elements in each row, but not the number of rows.

```
/*
 * Handle printing the generation.
 */
#include "life.h"

static void putBorder(int n);

void putWorld(PtrToConstWorld world)
{
  int c, r;

  printf("Generation %i out of %i\n", Gen, EndGen);
  putBorder(1 + Cols + 1);
  for (r = 1; r <= Rows; r++)
  {
    putchar(BORDER);
    for (c = 1; c <= Cols; c++)
      putchar(world[r][c] ? MARKER : ' ');
    putchar(BORDER);
    putchar('\n');
  }
  putBorder(1 + Cols + 1);
  putchar('\n');
}

static void putBorder(int n)
{
  int i;

  for (i = 1; i <= n; i++)
    putchar(BORDER);
  putchar('\n');
}
```

Figure 13.27 (outworld.c) Display the contents of a generation.

- The name of a two-dimensional array is a pointer to its first element, which happens to be its first row.

- We can have pointers to rows and use them to traverse a two-dimensional array a row at a time. This lets us efficiently access a column.

- When we traverse a sequence of elements within a two-dimensional array, we can use pointers to items as if it were a one-dimensional array. This allows us to efficiently access each item in a row.

- We can often process rows of a two-dimensional array using existing functions designed to work with a one-dimensional array.

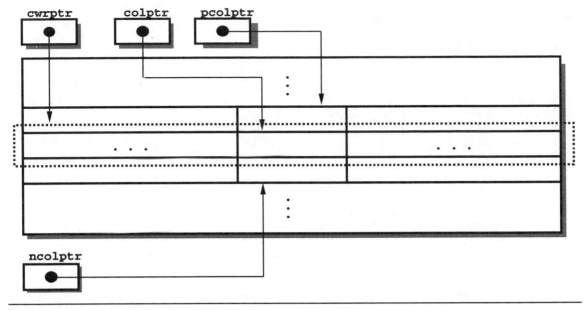

Figure 13.28   The pointers used to traverse a Life world.

- All of the techniques for accessing two-dimensional arrays can be generalized and used for higher-dimensional arrays.

- It's reasonable to use normal subscripting rather than pointers to traverse the elements of multidimensional arrays. Then, if the resulting program needs to be sped up, these traversals should be rewritten to use pointers.

EXERCISES

13–1   Rewrite **readScores** and **printScores** (Figure 13.3) to use pointers.

13–2   We can improve **testAvg** (Figures 13.9 and 13.10) by treating it as a one-dimensional array and traversing it with a pointer. We initialize a pointer to the **n**th column and increment by **MAX_TESTS** to access the **n**th column of subsequent rows. Make this improvement.

13–3   Rewrite **putWorld** (Figure 13.27) to traverse its array using pointers. Is it now more efficient?

13–4   Change life (Figure 13.24) so that it dynamically allocates space for the world. Can you make this version run even faster than ours?

```
/*
 * Compute next generation, this time using pointers.
 */
#include "life.h"

int nextWorld(PtrToConstWorld curr, PtrToWorld next)
{
  PtrToConstWorld  cwrptr = curr + 1;         /* 1st row curr world */
  PtrToWorld       nwrptr = next + 1;         /* 1st row next world */
  PtrToConstWorld  endcwrptr = cwrptr + Rows; /* last row curr world */
  int changed = 0;                            /* changes to world */
  int neighbors;                              /* # of cell neighbors */

  for (Inhabs = 0; cwrptr <= endcwrptr; cwrptr++, nwrptr++)
  {
    const Boolean *colptr    = cwrptr[0]  + 1;  /* current col */
    const Boolean *pcolptr   = cwrptr[-1] + 1;  /* previous row */
    const Boolean *ncolptr   = cwrptr[1]  + 1;  /* next row */
    const Boolean *endcolptr = colptr + Cols;   /* last col */
    Boolean *nxtptr          = nwrptr[0] + 1;   /* col in next */

    for (; colptr <= endcolptr; colptr++, nxtptr++, pcolptr++, ncolptr++)
    {
      neighbors =  pcolptr[-1] + pcolptr[0] + pcolptr[1] + colptr[-1] +
                   ncolptr[-1] + ncolptr[0] + ncolptr[1] + colptr[1];
      if ((neighbors == 3) || (neighbors == 2 && *colptr))
      {
        *nxtptr = TRUE;
        Inhabs++;
      }
      else
        *nxtptr = FALSE;
      changed += *nxtptr != *colptr;
    }
  }
  return changed;                             /* non-zero if not stable */
}
```

Figure 13.29   (nxtwrld2.c) A new version of **nextWorld** that uses pointers to traverse the array.

Extend

13–5 Extend life (Figure 13.24) to check for an oscillating stable state in any of the last 10 generations. Use a three-dimensional array to hold the necessary generations.

Tune

13–6 To keep things simple, we've avoided using **const** in many of the programs in this chapter. Fix them to use **const** where it's appropriate.

Code

13–7 Write a function to print the total values of each of the two-dimensional arrays contained in the three-D array **classes** (Figure 13.17) There should be one value output for each two-dimensional array that **classes** contains.

13–8 Write a function, **readStudent**, that reads in a student ID number, followed by the student's test scores. Use the student number to select the row in the array. Implement an appropriate error-testing and flagging mechanism.

13–9 Write a function, **printTests**, that prints the elements of **scores**, one column per line. Each line of output contains all of the scores for a particular test.

13–10 Write a function to determine whether a particular square two-dimensional array is a magic square (all rows, columns, and diagonals add to the same value). Use a constant to define the size of the square, and make the function work no matter what the constant is set to. For example, if the size is 3, the following is a magic square:

```
4 9 2
3 5 7
8 1 6
```

13–11 Write a function to determine whether a particular square two-dimensional array is an identity matrix (1s on the diagonal and 0s everywhere else). Can you write this function treating the array as though it is one-dimensional?

13–12 Write a fast function to initialize an identity matrix.

13–13 Write a function, **print2dRev**, that prints the values in a two-dimensional array in reverse order, last row first and first row last. First, write it using the usual array subscripting; then rewrite it so that the rows are indexed with a pointer. Finally, rewrite it so that all elements are indexed with pointers. Which of the three versions is the fastest?

13–14 Write a function, **sortScores**, that takes a two-dimensional array of **int**s and a column to sort on and modifies the array so that the specified column is sorted from low to high.

13–15 Write a fast function to compare a pair of two-dimensional arrays. The function should return a pointer to the first place where the arrays differ.

13–16 Write a function that dynamically allocates a two-dimensional array with the appropriate number of rows and columns. This function must be declared to return a pointer, and its return value must be assigned to a pointer to a one-dimensional array containing the appropriate number of columns.

13–17 Write a function that sums the elements in a three-dimensional array using a single pointer to traverse the array. How much faster is this than using three-dimensional subscripting?

Repeat the previous exercise for some higher-dimensional array. Can you generalize your function to work on any N-dimensional array? Explain why the function is substantially faster when pointers are used.

13–18 Write a function to calculate and print the average of each test by class. It should be passed a three-dimensional array of classes as an argument, as in Figure 13.17. The order of output should be all the scores for the first test in the first class, then all the scores for the first test in the second class, and so on.

Build 13–19 Write a set of functions that allows us to write to a two-dimensional array rather than the screen. The idea is that we perform numerous updates on this array (such as adding and deleting characters) and then do a function call to replace the screen with the contents of the array. Modify life so that it uses this set of functions.

13–20 Write a program to supervise a tic-tac-toe game between two human players. It should request moves, display them, and notify them when the game is over. It should also be able to print a trace of all the moves the players made.

13–21 Write a program to play dealer in a blackjack game. Allow up to seven players.

13–22 Write a program to produce large block letters of the strings it's given as input. Represent each letter as a set of 1s and 0s in an 8-by-8 two-dimensional array. For example, an "I" would have all 1s in the top and bottom rows and 1s down the middle two columns of each row.

14 ARRAYS

OF

POINTERS

Our earlier programs have made ample use of arrays, We've seen arrays of integers, characters, and reals, as well as arrays of structures and arrays of arrays. This chapter examines another kind of array, arrays of pointers, concentrating on arrays of strings. We show how to initialize these arrays at compile time, how to construct them dynamically at run time, and how to use pointers to traverse them efficiently. We provide array-subscripting and pointer-indexing versions of functions to print and search arrays of strings. And we examine command-line argument processing, an important application of these arrays. The chapter concludes with an implementation of a string-sorting program.

14.1   ARRAYS OF POINTERS—RAGGED ARRAYS

Two-dimensional arrays contain the same number of elements in each row. But same-size rows can be inefficient. Suppose we define a table that holds character strings for each of the days of the week.

```
char day_table[][10] =
  {
    {'m', 'o', 'n', 'd', 'a', 'y', '\0'},
    {'t', 'u', 'e', 's', 'd', 'a', 'y', '\0'},
    {'w', 'e', 'd', 'n', 'e', 's', 'd', 'a', 'y', '\0'},
    {'t', 'h', 'u', 'r', 's', 'd', 'a', 'y', '\0'},
    {'f', 'r', 'i', 'd', 'a', 'y', '\0'},
    {'s', 'a', 't', 'u', 'r', 'd', 'a', 'y', '\0'},
    {'s', 'u', 'n', 'd', 'a', 'y', '\0'}
  };
```

We have to declare each row to hold enough characters in the longest string. The problem is that we waste space in the rows containing shorter strings.

What we really want is an array whose rows can vary in length, called a *ragged array*. We can build a ragged array out of an array of pointers, making each entry in the array a pointer to a string.

We declare and initialize a ragged array by supplying a list of character strings.

```
char *days[] =
{
  "monday",  "tuesday", "wednesday", "thursday",
  "friday", "saturday", "sunday"
};
```

This declares **days** to be an array of pointers to characters.

Since we omitted the subscript from **days**, the compiler makes the array just large enough to hold the elements we supply. In this case, the compiler allocates space for an array containing seven pointers and assigns each element a pointer to the corresponding string. Figure 14.1 shows a table of days stored as a two-dimensional array and Figure 14.2 shows that same table stored as a ragged array.

We access the elements of this array in exactly the same way we access the elements of an array of any other type.

Figure 14.3 contains a program that prints a table of strings, one per line. To do so, it makes use of a function, **printStrings**, that is passed a table of character strings, along with the number of entries in the table, and prints the pointed-to strings, one per line. We're lazy, so we let the compiler calculate the number of items in **days** for us.

```
printStrings(days, sizeof(days)/sizeof(char *));
```

Figure 14.4 contains **printStrings**. It does the actual printing with **printf**, using the **%s** formatting code. The **%s** format expects a pointer to the first character of a string, which is exactly what each of the entries in **days** is.

Actually, because both the pointers **days** contains and the characters they point to are constant, we should really declare **days** with

```
const char * const days[]
```

Similarly, we should declare the **table** parameter in **printStrings** the same way. But using **const** with arrays of pointers tends to be confusing, so for now we'll just stick with our original declaration. However, these strings are constants and shouldn't be changed.

Accessing Individual Items

We haven't yet worried about accessing the individual items within a ragged array. In **printStrings**, for example, we simply pass a pointer to the beginning of the row (or string) we want to print. But imagine for the moment that we didn't have **printf**, and instead had to use **putchar** to write the characters. Then we would need to access each of the items in the string. Figure 14.5 contains a new implementation of **printStrings** written this way.

We're doing something curious in this version of **printStrings**: using two-dimensional subscripting to access individual characters in an array, even though it's only a one-dimensional array. If **table** is an array of pointers to characters, **table[i][j]** refers to the **j**th character in its **i**th row. Why does this work? **table[i]** is a pointer

day_table

m	o	n	d	a	y	\0			
t	u	e	s	d	a	y	\0		
w	e	d	n	e	s	d	a	y	\0
t	h	u	r	s	d	a	y	\0	
f	r	i	d	a	y	\0			
s	a	t	u	r	d	a	y	\0	
s	u	n	d	a	y	\0			

Figure 14.1 A two-dimensional array of characters with wasted space at the end of each row.

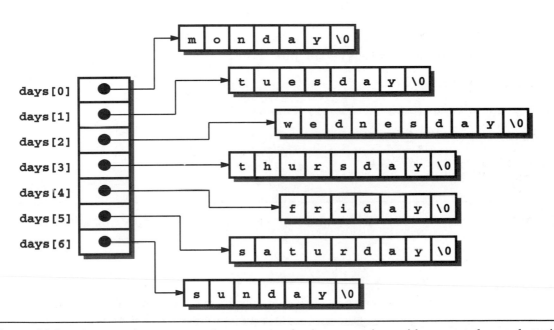

Figure 14.2 The same data now stored as an array of pointers to strings with no wasted space but with extra space used for the pointers.

```
/*
 * Main program that prints a table of days.
 */
#include <stdio.h>
#include <stdlib.h>

char *days[] =
{
   "monday",  "tuesday", "wednesday", "thursday",
   "friday", "saturday", "sunday"
};

int main()
{
   void printStrings(char *table[], int n);

   printStrings(days, sizeof(days)/sizeof(char *));

   return EXIT_SUCCESS;
}
```

Figure 14.3 (prdays.c) A program to print a table of days of the week, one per line.

```
/*
 * Print a table of strings, one per line.
 */
#include <stdio.h>

void printStrings(char *table[], int n)
{
   int i;

   for (i = 0; i < n; i++)
     printf("%s\n", table[i]);
}
```

Figure 14.4 (prstr1.c) Print a table of character strings, one per line, using **printf** to write the strings.

to the first character in a string, so adding **j** to it gives a pointer to the **j**th character in the string. We can access the **j**th character with

```
*(table[i] + j)
```

which is equivalent to **table[i][j]**. Figure 14.6 provides a picture of how this expression works. More concretely, since **table[0]** is a pointer to the string **monday**, we can access the **'n'** with **table[0][2]**.

```
/*
 *  Print a table of strings, one per line, using putchar.
 */
#include <stdio.h>

void printStrings(char *table[], int n)
{
  int i, j;

  for (i = 0; i < n; i++)
  {
    for (j = 0; table[i][j] != '\0'; j++)
      putchar(table[i][j]);
    putchar('\n');
  }
}
```

Figure 14.5   (prstr2.c) Another version of our array-printing function; this one uses **putchar**.

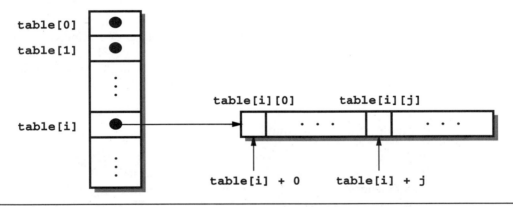

Figure 14.6   Accessing an individual character with an array of pointers to character strings.

Although we can use two-dimensional accessing, we saw in the previous chapter it is faster to avoid it wherever possible and use pointers instead. Figure 14.7 does just that in a new version of **printStrings**. This version uses a single pointer to a character, **ptr**, to traverse the individual strings it prints. We initialize **ptr** to point to the string's first character with

        ptr = table[i]

This initialization works because each entry in **table** is a pointer to the first character in a string. Once we've assigned that pointer to **ptr**, we can traverse the string as we would

```
/*
 * Print table of strings using pointers to traverse the string.
 */
#include <stdio.h>

void printStrings(char *table[], int n)
{
  int i;
  char *ptr;

  for (i = 0; i < n; i++)
  {
    for (ptr = table[i]; *ptr != '\0'; ptr++)
      putchar(*ptr);
    putchar('\n');
  }
}
```

Figure 14.7   (prstr3.c) A version of **printStrings** that uses a pointer to traverse the strings.

traverse any other string. We dereference the pointer to access the individual characters and increment it to go on to the next one. This version takes about one-fourth the time of the previous version, making it worthwhile to try to eliminate two-dimensional array accessing wherever possible.

Dynamic String Allocation

Up to now, we have initialized our arrays of pointers at compile time, leaving the task of allocating space for the pointed-to strings to the compiler. We did this because we knew the contents of the table at compile time. But that's not always the case. Suppose we want to write a program that sorts its input lines. The program must read its input into some kind of table in order to sort it. But what kind? Since some input lines are likely to be much longer than others, we don't want to use a two-dimensional array—it would waste too much space. Instead, we need to read the input into an array of strings and allocate the space for each entry ourselves.

We write this sorting program at the end of the chapter. For now we illustrate runtime string allocation with a simple program, shown in Figure 14.8, to reverse its input. This program uses two functions, shown in Figure 14.9: **readStrings**, which reads its input into a table of strings, one line per string, and **printStringsRev**, which prints the table of strings in reverse order.

readStrings takes a pair of parameters: an empty table of pointers and the maximum number of pointers that can fit in the table. It fills in the table with pointers to dynamically allocated strings containing the input lines and returns the number of lines read. **readStrings** uses **getline** to read each input line into an array **line**, and a new utility function, **makeDupStr**, to make a dynamically allocated copy of **line**.

```
/*
 * Reverse input, one line at a time.
 */
#include <stdio.h>
#include <stdlib.h>
#include <stddef.h>

#define   MAXLINES       100          /* lines to store */

int main()
{
  void printStringsRev(char *table[], int n);
  int  readStrings(char *table[], int max);

  int  lines;                          /* input lines read */
  char *strings[MAXLINES];             /* array of pointers to strings */

  if ((lines = readStrings(strings, MAXLINES)) < 0)
    printf("Out of memory after reading %i lines\n", -lines);
  else
  {
    if (lines >= MAXLINES)
      printf("Only %i out of %i lines stored\n", MAXLINES, lines);
    printStringsRev(strings, lines > MAXLINES ? MAXLINES : lines);
  }

  return (lines < 0 || lines >= MAXLINES) ? EXIT_FAILURE : EXIT_SUCCESS;
}
```

Figure 14.8   (revinp.c)   A program to reverse its input, one line at a time.

If for some reason there's not enough memory to store the number of lines in the table, **readStrings** returns the negative of the lines read, leaving it to its caller to decide how to handle that situation.

makeDupStr takes a pointer to a string, calls **malloc** to allocate enough storage for a copy of the string, uses **strcpy** to copy the string into the newly allocated storage, and returns a pointer to this newly created copy. **readStrings** takes this pointer and places it in the table. The result is that each table entry becomes a pointer to a block of storage allocated by **malloc** and containing a single input line. Figure 14.10 illustrates this process of reading a line and storing it in the table.

printStringsRev is similar to **printStrings**, except that it prints the last element first and the first element last.

This program relies heavily on dynamic allocation, and on a small microcomputer it might easily run out of storage. What should we do when **makeDupStr** (really **malloc**) fails? Unfortunately, there is no general solution, so we have to decide what to do on a case-by-case basis. Here, we take the easy way out: when **makeDupStr** fails, we simply stop reading input and print an error message.

```c
/*
 * Functions to read and print string table.
 *    readStrings - Read strings into table, dynamically allocating
 *       space for each string.  It indicates an out-of-memory error
 *       by returning the negative number of lines it successfully read.
 *    printStringsRev - Print table in reverse order.
 *    makeDupStr - Duplicate a single string.
 */
#include <stdio.h>
#include <string.h>
#include <stddef.h>                    /* for NULL */
#include <stdlib.h>                    /* for malloc */

#define  MAXLEN   80                   /* chars per line */

static char *makeDupStr(const char *str);

int readStrings(char *table[], int max)
{
  int    getline(char *line, int n);

  int    lines;                        /* lines read */
  char   *sptr;                        /* ptr to space from malloc */
  char   line[MAXLEN + 1];             /* current input line */

  for (lines = 0; getline(line, MAXLEN) != -1; lines++)
    if (lines < max)
      if ((sptr = makeDupStr(line)) != NULL)
        table[lines] = sptr;
      else
        return -lines;                 /* indicate out-of-memory error */
  return lines;
}

void printStringsRev(char *table[], int n)
{
  while (--n >= 0)
    printf("%s\n", table[n]);
}

static char *makeDupStr(const char *str)
{
  char *newstr = malloc(strlen(str) + 1);

  if (newstr != NULL)
    strcpy(newstr, str);
  return newstr;
}
```

Figure 14.9   (strtab.c) Our functions to read and print tables of strings.

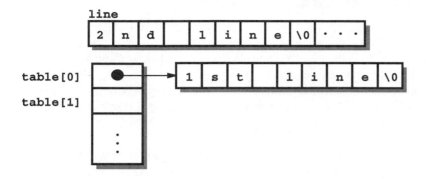

(*a*) The array after placing the first input line in it and reading the second input line.

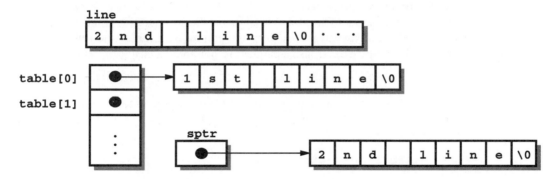

(*b*) The array after allocating space for the second input line and copying the line into that space.

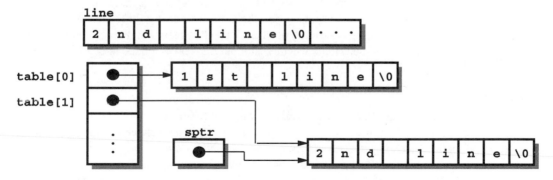

(*c*) The array after copying the line into that space and hooking the line into the table.

Figure 14.10 How we can build a table of strings dynamically at run time.

14.2   POINTERS AND ARRAYS OF POINTERS

In the previous section, we used normal array subscripting to traverse our arrays of pointers. We can, however, use pointers to traverse these arrays, just as we can with any other array. We do so in Figure 14.11, a new version of **printStrings**, our function to print a table of strings, one per line.

As before, we call **printStrings** by passing it an array of pointers to strings and the number of items in the array. But now we declare the array parameter differently.

```
printStrings(char **ptr, int n)
```

We've seen that when we pass an array, we are really passing a pointer to its first element. So when we pass an array of **int**s, we pass a pointer to an **int**. When we pass an array of **char**s, we pass a pointer to a **char**. And when we pass an array of pointers to characters, we pass a pointer to a pointer to a **char**, **ptr**'s type.

printStrings uses our standard method for traversing an array: we set a pointer, **ptr**, to the array's first element and keep incrementing it until it points just past the array's last element. As usual, we keep the pointer to just past the last element in **endptr**, which, like **ptr**, is also a pointer to a pointer to a character.

```
char **endptr = ptr + n;
```

Each time through the loop we want to pass **printf** a pointer to the first character in the next string in the table. Since **ptr** points to the string, we have to dereference it when we pass it to **printf**.

```
printf("%s\n", *ptr);
```

Figure 14.12 shows the relationship between these pointers.

As an additional example, we'll write a function, **searchStrings**, to search an array of strings for a particular string. The function takes three arguments: a string to find, an array of pointers to **char**, and the number of strings in the array. It returns a pointer to the matching table entry or **NULL** if no entry matches. We could, for example, use this function to determine whether an input line corresponded to one of the days of the week with:

```
searchStrings(line, days, 7)
```

Just like **printStrings**, it runs a pointer through a table of strings. The only difference is that now, instead of calling **printf**, it calls **strcmp**, the string library function that compares strings. Figure 14.13 contains a main program that shows how to use **searchStrings**, Figure 14.14 shows an array-subscripting version of it, and Figure 14.15 shows a pointer-indexing version.

Both **printStrings** and **searchStrings** simply pass a pointer to the next string to a function that processes it—they don't access the individual characters in the strings directly. But we can't always avoid doing that. Imagine once again that we don't have **printf**. Figure 14.16 is yet another version of **printStrings** that uses **putchar** to print the individual characters in the strings, this time using a pointer to traverse the array.

```
/*
 * Print a table of strings, one per line.
 */
#include <stdio.h>

void printStrings(char **ptr, int n)
{
  char **endptr = ptr + n;            /* ptr to just past last element */

  for (; ptr < endptr; ptr++)
    printf("%s\n", *ptr);
}
```

Figure 14.11   (prstr4.c) Yet another version of **printStrings**. This one uses a pointer to traverse the table of strings.

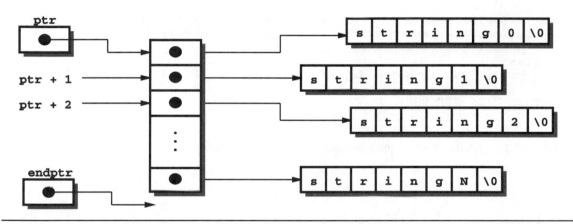

Figure 14.12   Using pointers to traverse an array of strings.

We access the individual characters in the string the same way we accessed individual elements when we had a row pointer. If we use a pointer **ptr** to traverse the array of strings, **(*ptr)[j]** refers to the **j**th character in whatever string **ptr** points to. Why? Because **ptr** points to an item in the table of pointers, ***ptr** is the value of that pointer, which means that ***ptr** is the address of the first character in the string. Adding **j** to ***ptr** gives us the address of the **j**th character, and dereferencing that with

```
*(*ptr + j)
```

gives us the character. This expression is equivalent to **(*ptr)[j]**. Figure 14.17 shows what's going on here in more detail.

```
/*
 * Main program to test our string-searching function.
 */
#include <stdio.h>
#include <stdlib.h>

#define MAXLEN 80

char *days[] = {"monday", "tuesday", "wednesday", "thursday",
                "friday", "saturday", "sunday"};
const int numdays = sizeof(days)/sizeof(days[0]);

int main()
{
  int       getline(char *line, int max);
  char      *searchStrings(const char *target, char *t[], int n);

  const char *match;
  char       line[MAXLEN + 1];

  while (printf("Enter day of week: "), getline(line, MAXLEN) != -1)
    if ((match = searchStrings(line, days, numdays)) != NULL)
      printf("%s is a day of the week\n", match);
    else
      printf("%s is not a day of the week.\n", line);

  return EXIT_SUCCESS;
}
```

Figure 14.13   (testsrch.c)   A main program using our string-searching function.

```
/*
 * Search table for given string, array-subscripting version.
 */
#include <stddef.h>
#include <string.h>

char *searchStrings(const char *string, char *table[], int n)
{
  int i = 0;

  for (; i < n; i++)
    if (strcmp(table[i], string) == 0)
      return table[i];                      /* return pointer to match */
  return NULL;                              /* no match */
}
```

Figure 14.14   (srchstr1.c)   An array subscripting version of **searchStrings**.

```
/*
 * Search table for a given string, pointer-indexing version.
 */
#include <stddef.h>
#include <string.h>

char *searchStrings(const char *string, char **ptr, int n)
{
  char **const endptr = ptr + n;

  for (; ptr < endptr; ptr++)
    if (strcmp(*ptr, string) == 0)
      return *ptr;                        /* return pointer to match */
  return NULL;                            /* no match */
}
```

Figure 14.15   (srchstr2.c) A pointer-indexing version of **searchStrings**.

```
/*
 * Print a table of strings, one per line, using a pointer to
 * traverse the table.
 */
#include <stdio.h>

void printStrings(char **ptr, int n)
{
  char **endptr = ptr + n;     /* pointer to just past last element */
  int j;                       /* index to individual items */

  for(; ptr < endptr; ptr++)
  {
    for (j = 0; (*ptr)[j] != '\0'; j++)
      putchar((*ptr)[j]);
    putchar('\n');
  }
}
```

Figure 14.16   (prstr5.c) Our final version of **printStrings**, which traverses the array using a pointer and accesses the characters in the strings indirectly through that pointer.

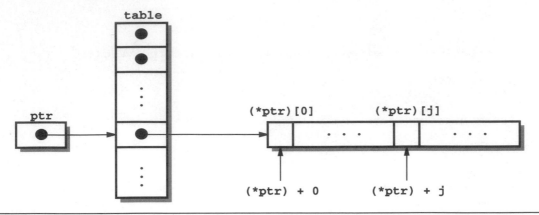

Figure 14.17 Accessing an individual character within an array of pointers to character strings when we're using a pointer to traverse them.

14.3 COMMAND-LINE ARGUMENTS

Arrays of pointers have an important application that we haven't yet examined: they are used to store command-line arguments. When we run a program, such as a compiler or text editor, we often provide not only the program's name but also the names of files the program will work with. The command, along with those file names, is known as a *command-line*, and its individual components are known as *command-line arguments*.

How can a program access these arguments? It turns out that when **main** is called, it is passed two parameters that together describe the command-line that invoked the program. The first is the number of arguments on the command-line. The second is an array of pointers to strings containing the various arguments. Traditionally, these are called **argc** and **argv**, respectively. We declare **main**'s parameters in the same way as those of any other function.

```
int main(int argc, char *argv[])
```

By convention, **argv[0]** points to the first character of the program's name, so **argc** is always at least 1.[1] We use the other arguments to specify various program options, as well as external files the program should process.

A Program to Echo Its Arguments

We illustrate command-line argument processing with a program called echo, which simply prints each of its arguments minus the program name. Figure 14.18 contains a first, straightforward implementation of echo. It uses array indexing to traverse **argv**

---

[1]Even so, some versions of C set the program's name to the null string.

```
/*
 * Echo arguments, using array subscripting.
 */
#include <stdio.h>
#include <stdlib.h>

int main(int argc, char *argv[])
{
  int next;                                 /* index to next argument */

  for (next = 1; next < argc; next++)
    printf("%s%c", argv[next], (next < argc - 1) ? ' ' : '\n');

  return EXIT_SUCCESS;
}
```

Figure 14.18   (echo.c)   Echo the program's arguments using array indexing.

and prints each of the entries except the first (the program name). We write the arguments separated by spaces, with the last argument followed by a newline.

If we supply the command-line

    echo c programming is really fun

echo's output is

    c programming is really fun

For this command line, when **main** is called, **argc** is six and **argv** is an array of six strings, as shown in Figure 14.19.

Figure 14.20 contains a second, trickier version. It uses a pointer to traverse **argv**. We can do this because **argv**, like any other array parameter, is really a pointer to the array's first element. We use our standard technique, setting a pointer, **argptr**, to point to the first array item in which we're interested (in this case, the one pointed to by **argv + 1**, since we want to skip the program name), repeatedly incrementing it to traverse the arguments, and stopping when it points to the end of the array.

As with other arrays, using a pointer to traverse command-line arguments makes our programs run faster—but harder to read and understand. Either method of command-line argument processing is acceptable, but you should master the pointer method, even if it isn't your favorite, as you will encounter it frequently in existing programs.

Command-Line Options

We'll illustrate the full power of command-line arguments with a program called ws, for word search. By default, ws prints all of the lines in its input that contain any of the strings provided as its arguments. So running with its source file as input and **Boolean**,

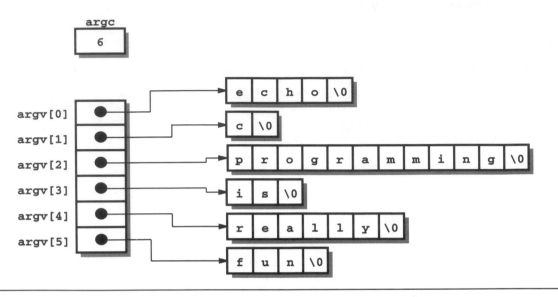

Figure 14.19 The initial values of **argc** and **argv** for our sample use of echo.

```
/*
 * Echo arguments, using pointer indexing.
 */
#include <stdio.h>
#include <stdlib.h>

int main(int argc, char *argv[])
{
  char **argptr       = argv + 1;      /* pointer to first argument */
  char **const endptr = argv + argc;   /* pointer to last argument */

  for (; argptr < endptr; argptr++)
    printf("%s%c", *argptr, (argptr < endptr - 1) ? ' ' : '\n');

  return EXIT_SUCCESS;
}
```

Figure 14.20 (echo2.c) Echo the program's arguments using pointer indexing.

Aside 14.1: Supplying Command-Line Arguments

Users have historically executed C programs by typing commands to a command interpreter, called a *shell*. Programs were run by entering a *command-line*, which contained the program's name, followed by specific information we wanted to supply that command, such as a pattern to search for or a file name to work with. The primary alternative to this approach was to have the program prompt for the information. However, that had a major drawback: programs that prompt for information are much less useful as components of *command files* or *shell scripts* (files containing sequences of commands for the shell to execute). In addition, for some tasks, it's considerably more convenient to type a single command-line than to respond to a series of prompts.

In many environments, such as UNIX, we still execute programs the same way. However, what about those of us who work with graphical environments, such as Windows? In these environments, we invoke programs by clicking on icons or choosing the program to run from a list of programs. There, the concept of a command-line appears to make little sense, except when we are constructing command files.

Command-line arguments, however, haven't disappeared; they've just been hidden from us. When we select an icon associated with a program, it's also often been pre-associated with default command-line arguments; when the system invokes the program, it supplies those arguments to the program. That's also true when we execute a program by dragging a file and then dropping it onto an icon. What really happens is that the program is invoked with that file name as its argument.

Visual C++ development environments, such as Borland's Turbo C++, also usually provide a mechanism for us to explicitly supply command-line arguments, even though we are not running the program from a command-line. The approach is to allow us to select a menu entry, which prompts for default arguments. When we later select the menu entry to execute our newly created program, the environment executes it and provides it with the arguments we supplied earlier.

Exactly what constitutes a command-line argument varies from system to system, but individual arguments are usually delimited by white space. And if you want white space within an argument, place the argument in quotes. It is a good idea to consult your own compiler's documentation before heavily using command-line arguments.

TRUE, and **FALSE** as its arguments results in its printing any line in ws.c that contains the words "Boolean", "TRUE", or "FALSE".

ws also allows some optional arguments. Traditionally, optional arguments begin with a dash ("-") or a slash ("/"), depending on which operating system you're using.[2] ws's options are -n to print only those lines that don't match, -c to print only a count of those lines that do or don't match (depending on whether -n is used with it), and -l to precede its output with a line number.

ws's design is typical of most programs that have options. The main program handles the options and a separate function handles all the real work, in this case doing the search.

---

[2]UNIX, for example, uses the dash, whereas MS-DOS uses the slash.

```
/*
 * Header file defining useful search constants and types.
 */
#include <stdio.h>
#include <stdlib.h>
#include <string.h>

#define MAXLEN 80

typedef short Boolean;

#define TRUE   1
#define FALSE  0

extern Boolean PrintNumber;          /* current line number */
extern Boolean PrintNoMatch;         /* print unmatched lines? */
extern Boolean PrintCountOnly;       /* print match count only? */
```

Figure 14.21   (ws.h)   Definitions of useful constants, types, and externals for the word-searching program.

The two pieces communicate through constants and external variables declared in the header file. Figure 14.21 contains the header file ws.h, Figure 14.22 contains the main program, and Figure 14.23 contains the functions to do the actual searching.

main first processes the optional arguments. We know we're done with the optional arguments when we encounter an argument that doesn't begin with a dash. When an argument does begin with a dash, we examine the next character and set a flag to record the option's value. An unrecognized option causes us to write an error message and quit. (Our program could be improved by allowing more than one option to follow a single dash, but we leave that as an exercise.)

Once the options have been processed, we assume that any subsequent arguments are strings to process. We call a function **searchInput** to do the searching, passing it a pointer to the first argument representing a word to find, along with the number of different words we're trying to find. It reads input lines with **getline** and uses a new function, **findMatch**, to determine whether any of those words are in its input line. **findMatch** simply runs through the various words, using **strstr** to see if any of them is a substring of the input line.

As before, we use pointers to process the arguments. Figure 14.24 shows the relationships among the various pointers used to process the arguments.

Command-line options are a powerful and useful idea. Many programs, however, use them to provide different and often unrelated features. These extra features are used infrequently, if at all, but they make the program significantly harder to read and debug. To avoid falling into this trap, first write a simple version of the program that performs its main task correctly. Add options only after the program has been in use for a while and it's become clear that adding certain features will make the program more useful.

```
/*
 * Search for strings provided in program's arguments.
 */
#include "ws.h"

Boolean PrintNumber;                    /* line number */
Boolean PrintNoMatch;                   /* print lines that don't match */
Boolean PrintCountOnly;                 /* just print match count */

int main(int argc, char *argv[])
{
  void  searchInput(char *strtab[], int n);

  char **argptr            = &argv[1];          /* pointer to next arg */
  char **const endptr      = &argv[argc - 1]; /* pointer to last arg */
  Boolean badopt           = FALSE;             /* bad option flag */
  int      status          = EXIT_SUCCESS;      /* return value */

  for (; argptr <= endptr && (*argptr)[0] == '-'; argptr++)
    if ((*argptr)[1] == '\0')
      badopt = TRUE;
    else
      switch ((*argptr)[1])
      {                                 /* process next option */
        case 'c':
          PrintCountOnly = TRUE;
          break;
        case 'l':
          PrintNumber    = TRUE;
          break;
        case 'n':
          PrintNoMatch   = TRUE;
          break;
        default:
          printf("ws: bad option %c\n", (*argptr)[1]);
          badopt         = TRUE;
      }

  if (badopt || argptr > endptr)                /* oops */
  {
    printf("usage: ws [-c][-l][-n] patterns...\n");
    status = EXIT_FAILURE;
  }
  else
    searchInput(argptr, endptr - argptr + 1);

  return status;
}
```

Figure 14.22 (ws.c) The main part of our program to search its input for the words provided as its arguments.

```
/*
 * Do the actual search.
 *    searchInput - see if any of the strings passed to it are in the
 *      program's input.
 *    findMatch - find out if string is substring of any entry in table.
 *    displayLine - write any matching lines.
 */
#include "ws.h"

static Boolean findMatch(const char *str, char *tab[], int n);
static void    displayLine(const char *line, long lines);

void searchInput(char *strptrs[], int n)
{
  int     getline(char *line, int maxlen);

  char    line[MAXLEN + 1];          /* holds next line */
  long    lines;                     /* count lines */
  long    matched_lines = 0L;        /* matched lines */
  Boolean found;

  for (lines = 1; getline(line, MAXLEN) != -1; lines++)
  {
    found = findMatch(line, strptrs, n);
    if ((found && !PrintNoMatch) || (!found && PrintNoMatch))
    {
      matched_lines++;
      if (!PrintCountOnly)
        displayLine(line, lines);
    }
  }
  if (PrintCountOnly)
    printf("%li\n", matched_lines);
}

static Boolean findMatch(const char *str, char *tab[], int n)
{
  int i;

  for (i = 0; i < n; i++)
    if (strstr(str, tab[i]) != NULL)
      return TRUE;
  return FALSE;
}

static void displayLine(const char *line, long lines)
{
  if (PrintNumber)
    printf("%li ", lines);
  printf("%s\n", line);
}
```

Figure 14.23   (wssrch.c)   The functions that handle the actual searching.

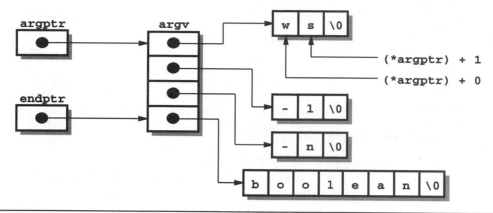

Figure 14.24 Processing the optional arguments. **argptr** points to the argument; **(*argptr)[i]** is the next character in the argument.

14.4   CASE STUDY—SORTING STRINGS

This section is optional!

We conclude this long and detailed chapter with a short but surprisingly useful program that sorts its input. To make the program more useful, we allow several options: -r reverses the sense of the sort, -b*N* begins sorting each string with the *N*th character in the string, and -l*N* limits the sort to a field of *N* characters.

The main program, shown in Figure 14.25, consists almost entirely of function calls. It uses a new function **handleOptions** to process any optional arguments. **handleOptions**, shown in Figure 14.26, is similar to the main function in the searching program we wrote earlier in the chapter. It's passed pointers to the first and last entries in **argv** and uses the first pointer to traverse the argument array. When it encounters a -b or a -l, it uses **sscanf** to turn the subsequent characters into an integer. We could improve **handleOptions** by making it do more error checking, as it currently ignores any unexpected characters. As before, we use a header file, shown in Figure 14.27, that defines various constants and externals shared by these files.

The program uses the function **sortedReadStrings** to read and sort the table of strings. This function, shown in Figure 14.28, extends our earlier **readStrings** function to use an insertion sort algorithm, similar to the one we used in Chapter 8. The program also uses **displayStrings** to display the table in ascending or descending order. This function combines our earlier **printStrings** and **printStringsRev** functions.

SUMMARY

- C allows us to have arrays of pointers, which are often called ragged arrays.

```
/*
 * String-sorting program.
 */
#include "sort.h"

Boolean Reverse;                    /* flag: reverse sense of sort */
int     FieldCol = 0;               /* flag: starting column for sort */
int     FieldLen = MAXLEN;          /* flag: length of field to sort */

int main(int argc, char *argv[])
{
  char *strings[MAXLINES];          /* input lines */
  int   lines;                      /* count of input lines */
  int   status = EXIT_FAILURE;      /* program return status */

  if (argc >= 1 && handleOptions(argv + 1, argv + argc))
    if ((lines = sortedReadStrings(strings, MAXLINES)) < 0)
      printf("Out of memory after %i lines\n\n", -lines);
    else if (lines > MAXLINES)
      printf("%i input lines (max allowed %i).\n\n", lines, MAXLINES);
    else
    {
      displayStrings(strings, lines);
      status = EXIT_SUCCESS;
    }

  return status;
}
```

Figure 14.25   (sort.c)   The main function of our string-sorting program.

- We can initialize ragged arrays at compile time by providing a list of values or at run time by using dynamic allocation.

- Although these ragged arrays are not stored as two-dimensional arrays, we can access their elements using two-dimensional array accessing.

- As with other arrays, we can use either array subscripting or pointer indexing to traverse ragged arrays.

- The arguments we type on the command-line invoking the program are placed into an array of pointers **argv**. The number of arguments is placed into an integer **argc**.

EXERCISES

Explore   **14–1** Compile and run the programs in this chapter.

```c
/*
 * Handle various options.
 */
#include "sort.h"

int handleOptions(char **argptr, char **endptr)
{
  Boolean goodopt = TRUE;                /* flag to indicate bad option */

  for (; argptr < endptr && (*argptr)[0] == '-'; argptr++)
    if ((*argptr)[1] == '\0')
      printf("sort: missing option\n");
    else
      switch ((*argptr)[1])
      {                                  /* process next option */
        case 'b':
          if (sscanf(*argptr + 2, "%i", &FieldCol) != 1)
          {
            printf("sort: invalid starting column\n");
            goodopt = FALSE;
          }
          break;
        case 'l':
          if (sscanf(*argptr + 2, "%i", &FieldLen) != 1)
          {
            printf("sort: invalid field length\n");
            goodopt = FALSE;
          }
          break;
        case 'r':
          Reverse = TRUE;                /* ignore anything after option */
          break;
        default:
          printf("sort: bad option %c\n", *argptr[1]);
          goodopt = FALSE;
      }

  if (argptr < endptr)
  {
    printf("sort: extra arguments\n");
    goodopt = FALSE;
  }

  if (!goodopt)
    printf("Usage: sort [-r] [-bNUM] [-lNUM]\n");
  return goodopt;
}
```

Figure 14.26   (sortopt.c)   The function to handle the various sort options.

```
/*
 * Define useful constants for string searcher.
 */
#include <stdio.h>
#include <stdlib.h>
#include <stddef.h>
#include <string.h>

typedef enum {FALSE, TRUE} Boolean;

#define MAXLINES  1000
#define MAXLEN      80

extern Boolean Reverse;
extern int     FieldCol;
extern int     FieldLen;

extern int  sortedReadStrings(char *table[], int n);
extern void displayStrings(char *table[], int n);
extern int  handleOptions(char **xptr, char **yptr);
extern int  getline(char *line, int n);
```

Figure 14.27 (sort.h) The definitions of constants and externals used by the sorting program.

14–2 Determine how much time it takes for the string-sorting program that makes up this chapter's case study to read, sort, and print 10, 50, 100, and 1000 strings.

Modify

14–3 Rewrite the programs in this chapter to use **const** whenever it's appropriate.

14–4 Rewrite **readStrings** (Figure 14.9) to use a pointer to traverse the array. Do the same for **printStringsRev** (also Figure 14.9).

Extend

14–5 Add a -r option to echo (Figures 14.18 and 14.20) that causes it to print its arguments in reverse order. First use array indexing; then use pointers.

14–6 Add two more options to echo (Figures 14.18 and 14.20): -n causes it to suppress the trailing newline; -s causes it to write each of its arguments on a separate line.

14–7 Add three new options to Chapter 11's uniq program. The first, -c, causes a count of the number of occurrences of any line of output to be printed before the line. The second, -u, causes only those lines that appear uniquely to be output. The last, -d, causes only those lines that are duplicated to appear in the output. What should uniq do when combinations of these options are specified?

14–8 Add an option to the sorting program (Figures 14.25 and 14.26) that allows it to sort numerically.

Code

14–9 Write a function, **tablePrintLen**, that prints the length of each character string in a table of character strings.

14–10 Write a function, **tableReverse**, that reverses each of the strings in a table of strings.

```
/*
 * Functions to read input strings using insertion sort.
 */
#include "sort.h"

static int linecmp(const char *x, const char *y)
{
  int i;

  for (i = 0; i < FieldCol && *x != '\0' && *y != '\0'; i++, x++, y++)
    ;
  return strncmp(x, y, FieldLen);
}

static void insert(char *a[], char *str, int n)
{
  int pos;

  for (pos = n; pos > 0 && linecmp(str, a[pos - 1]) < 0; pos--)
    a[pos] = a[pos - 1];
  a[pos] = str;
}

int sortedReadStrings(char *table[], int max)
{
  char *sptr;                    /* pointer to malloc-allocated space */
  char line[MAXLEN + 1];         /* current input line */
  int  lines = 0;                /* number of lines read */
  int  len;                      /* length of current line */

  for (; (len = getline(line, MAXLEN)) != -1 && lines >= 0; lines++)
    if (lines < max)
      if ((sptr = malloc(len + 1)) != NULL)
        insert(table, strcpy(sptr,line), lines);
      else
        lines = -lines;          /* indicate out-of-memory error */
  return lines;
}

void displayStrings(char *table[], int n)
{
  int i;

  if (!Reverse)
    for (i = 0; i < n; i++)       /* print table in forward order */
      printf("%s\n", table[i]);
  else
    while (--n >= 0)              /* print table in reverse order */
      printf("%s\n",table[n]);
}
```

Figure 14.28   (sortstrs.c)   The heart of our sorting program.

14–11 Write a function, **tableDelete**, that removes and returns a particular string from a table of strings.

14–12 Write a function, **tableCopy**, that is given two tables of strings and copies all the entries in the first into the second. This involves dynamically allocating space for each of the individual strings to be placed in the second table.

14–13 Write array-subscripting and pointer-indexing versions of a pair of functions, **tableInit** and **tableDestroy**. **tableInit** sets each entry in a table of strings to **NULL**. **tableDestroy** runs through a table of strings and deallocates each entry, ignoring **NULL** entries.

14–14 Write a function, **tableBytes**, that returns the total number of bytes used by a table of strings. This size includes the space taken up by pointers and the space used up by the characters in the strings.

14–15 Write a function, **monthName**, that takes a single-integer argument and returns a pointer to the associated month name. The month names should be kept in a **static** table of character strings local to the function.

> **Build**

14–16 Write a program, tail, that prints the last *n* lines of its input (*n* is a program constant). Use the program in Figure 14.8 as a model. Make reasonable assumptions about the maximum line length and the maximum number of lines in the input (using the constants **MAXLEN** and **MAXLINES**, respectively). Be sure to test the return from **malloc** and do something reasonable if it fails.

14–17 Write a program to count the number of words, lines, and characters in its input. Provide options to request any subset of these counts.

14–18 Write a program that reads a sequence of numbers and writes their values out in English. Your program should work for any input value between 0 and 9999. Here's some sample input and output:

```
5
five
16
sixteen
567
five hundred sixty seven
9987
nine thousand nine hundred eighty seven
```

14–19 Write a program that reads a sequence of numeric dates and writes them out in English. The numeric date includes the month, day, and year, as well as the day of the week (with Sunday indicated with a 1 and Saturday with a 7). Here's some sample input and output:

```
4/7/92-3
Tuesday, April 7th, 1992.
12/25/94-6
Friday, December 25th, 1994.
2/19/96-2
Monday, February 19th, 1996.
```

Part IV

ADVANCED PROGRAM STRUCTURE

The next four chapters of this text focus on C's advanced mechanisms for structuring programs.

- Chapter 15 presents the preprocessor in all its glory, focusing on macros and conditional compilation.

- Chapter 16 focuses on more advanced features of functions, such as allowing variable number of arguments, using pointers to functions, and writing recursive functions.

- Chapter 17 discusses generic functions and the generic library routines for searching and sorting.

- Chapter 18 examines the complex declarations that arise when using complex types such as function pointers.

15

THE

PREPROCESSOR

Many useful features of C aren't implemented by the compiler, but instead by a program that processes C source files before the compiler ever sees them. This chapter is a detailed discussion of that program, the C preprocessor. We introduce macros and show how they can make our programs more efficient and more readable. We examine header files in more detail and show how we can use them to effectively extend the language. And we study conditional compilation and show how it aids debugging and portability. This chapter concludes by using the preprocessor to construct a new, more efficient sets package.

15.1   PREPROCESSOR DIRECTIVES

The preprocessor reads a source file, performs various actions on it, and passes the resulting output to the C compiler. To decide what actions to perform, it looks for lines beginning with a *preprocessor directive* in column 1.

Table 15.1 lists the preprocessor directives. Some of them should be familiar; we have already used **#include** and **#define** in many of our programs.

Sometimes we want to examine the preprocessor's output, most often to help us locate problems we've introduced by erroneous preprocessor statements. There's no guarantee, but most C environments provide some way to do so. As you might expect, the details vary from system to system. Usually, we either run the preprocessor as a separate program or provide some special option to the compiler.

15.2   SIMPLE MACRO SUBSTITUTION

We've used **#define** to define various symbolic constants, such as the number of elements in an array. Doing so makes our programs easier to read and easier to change. That's because it can be difficult to decipher what a particular numeric value does, since the same value can mean different things in different places. The value 10 may be the size of an array, or it might be an interest rate or a base for number conversion. When we provide descriptive names for each unique use of a constant, we clarify its purpose and can change its value throughout the program simply by changing the line defining its name.

DIRECTIVE	USE
`#define`	define a macro
`#include`	include text from a file
`#undef`	undefine a macro
`#if`	test if a compile-time condition holds
`#else`	indicate alternatives if a test fails
`#elif`	combine `#else` and `#if`
`#endif`	end a preprocessor conditional (`#if`, `#ifdef`, `#ifndef`)
`#ifdef`	test if a symbol is defined
`#ifndef`	test if a symbol is not defined
`#line`	provide line number (and optional file name) for compiler messages
`#error`	terminate processing early
`#pragma`	implementation-dependent directive

Table 15.1 C preprocessor directives and their uses.

We're not limited to using **#define** to give names to numeric constants. We can use it to give a symbolic name to any arbitrary piece of text. That's because **#define** is more powerful than we have let on—it's actually a general mechanism for text replacement. The preprocessor command-line

#define *NAME TEXT*

instructs the preprocessor to replace all subsequent *unquoted* occurrences of *NAME* with *TEXT*. There are no restrictions on *TEXT*, but *NAME* must be an identifier. We usually write *NAME*s in uppercase to distinguish them from the variable and function names handled by the compiler. A defined name is often called a *macro*, and the process of substituting its replacement text is called *macro substitution*.

One common use for **#define** is to give symbolic names to string constants. After encountering

#define DIGITS "0123456789"

the preprocessor replaces each occurrence of **DIGITS** with the string constant **"0123456789"**. Figure 15.1 contains definitions of some of the more common strings we're likely to use, and Figure 15.2 uses many of those definitions in an extended version of our earlier program to count the number of various characters in its input.

Another common use is to give symbolic names to arbitrary expressions. Figure 15.3 does that in a little program to print the circumference of a circle with a radius it reads from its input. The formula for circumference is $2 * \pi * radius$. To aid readability, we define a constant **TWOPI** and use it in the expression to compute the circumference.

#define TWOPI (3.1415926 * 2.0)

```
/*
 * Generally useful, commonly used string definitions.
 */
#define DIGITS      "0123456789"
#define LOWERS      "abcdefghijklmnopqrstuvwxyz"
#define UPPERS      "ABCDEFGHIJKLMNOPQRSTUVWXYZ"
#define PUNCTS      ",.;:!?"
#define QUOTES      "\'\""
#define BRACKETS    "(){}[]"
```

Figure 15.1   (comstr.h) Definitions of some common strings.

Regardless of how complex a definition we have, the preprocessor simply substitutes the expression for its defined name, *without evaluating it*. So it replaces

```
circumf = TWOPI * radius;
```

with

```
circumf = (3.1415926 * 2.0) * radius;
```

We can define names in terms of other names and in any order, as long as all definitions precede any use. Figure 15.4 is a new version of our circumference program that takes advantage of this ability. Rather than define **TWOPI** directly, it first defines **PI** and uses it to define **TWOPI**.

```
#define   PI       3.1415926
#define   TWOPI    (PI + PI)
```

We can get away with this because the preprocessor simply remembers the replacement text, but does not substitute for any defined names it contains. Later, when we use the name, the preprocessor substitutes the replacement text and then performs macro substitution on any defined names it contains (except for a name appearing in its own replacement text). So when the preprocessor encounters the expression to compute the circumference,

```
circumf = TWOPI * radius;
```

it first substitutes for **TWOPI**

```
circumf = (PI + PI) * radius;
```

and then for both occurrences of **PI**

```
circumf = (3.1415926 + 3.1415926) * radius;
```

Although the preprocessor doesn't evaluate expressions, using names that expand into expressions doesn't slow down our programs. Most C compilers compute the value of expressions involving only constants at compile time.

```c
/*
 * Counts various types of characters.
 */
#include <stdio.h>
#include <stdlib.h>
#include <string.h>
#include <stddef.h>
#include "comstr.h"

const int PrintWidth = 11;                        /* width of counter */
const int LabelWidth = 12;                        /* width of id string */

int main()
{
  void displayCount(const char *label, unsigned long counter);

  int          c;
  unsigned long digits = 0, letters = 0, quotes = 0,
               brackets = 0, delims = 0, others = 0;

  while ((c = getchar()) != EOF)
    if (strchr(DIGITS, c) != NULL)
      digits++;                                    /* digits */
    else if (strchr(LOWERS, c) != NULL || strchr(UPPERS, c) != NULL)
      letters++;                                   /* letters */
    else if (strchr(QUOTES, c) != NULL)
      quotes++;                                    /* single & double quotes */
    else if (strchr(BRACKETS, c) != NULL)
      brackets++;                                  /* punctuation brackets */
    else if (strchr(PUNCTS, c) != NULL)
      delims++;                                    /* usual punctuation */
    else
      others++;                                    /* other characters */

  displayCount("Digits", digits);
  displayCount("Letters", letters);
  displayCount("Quotes", quotes);
  displayCount("Brackets", brackets);
  displayCount("Delimiters", delims);
  displayCount("Other", others);

  return EXIT_SUCCESS;
}

void displayCount(const char *label, unsigned long counter)
{
  printf("%-*s", LabelWidth, label);
  printf("%*lu\n", PrintWidth, counter);
}
```

Figure 15.2   (cntchrs.c)   Count various types of characters.

```
/*
 * Compute the circumference of a circle.
 */
#include <stdio.h>
#include <stdlib.h>

#define TWOPI (3.1415926 * 2.0)

int main()
{
  double radius, circumf;

  printf("Enter radius: ");
  scanf("%lf", &radius);
  circumf = TWOPI * radius;
  printf("Circumference: %g\n", circumf);

  return EXIT_SUCCESS;
}
```

Figure 15.3   (circumf1.c) A program to compute the circumference of a circle.

```
/*
 * Compute the circumference of a circle.
 */
#include <stdio.h>
#include <stdlib.h>

#define PI      3.1415926
#define TWOPI (PI + PI)

int main()
{
  double radius, circumf;

  printf("Enter radius: ");
  scanf("%lf", &radius);
  circumf = TWOPI * radius;
  printf("Circumference: %g\n", circumf);

  return EXIT_SUCCESS;
}
```

Figure 15.4   (circumf2.c) A program to compute the circumference of a circle.

Aside 15.1a: Taking Advantage of Syntactic Replacement

C's syntax is often confusing and error prone. We can use **#define** to hide some of that ugliness. Aside 15.1b does so in yet another version our old **yesOrNo** function. It uses these definitions:

```
#define FOREVER   for(;;)     /* infinite loop */
#define IS        ==          /* equality test */
#define ISNOT     !=          /* inequality test */
```

FOREVER is a more readable way to indicate an infinite loop than **for(;;)**. **IS** prevents the common mistake of using = instead of == in equality tests. And **ISNOT** prevents the Pascal programmer's mistake of using <> instead of !=.

In fact, we can actually hide enough of C's syntax to make it resemble another language, such as Pascal. We can use the definitions in Aside 15.1c to write C programs in a Pascal-like syntax, letting the preprocessor translate them into the form the compiler expects. Aside 15.1d shows a new version of our earlier power-computing functions rewritten to use these definitions.

Our Pascal example is cute, but the major syntactic replacement it takes advantage of has its drawbacks. First, defined names must be identifiers, so we can't redefine operators and other nonalphabetic tokens such as comment delimiters, which limits how much C syntax we can hide. Second, the compiler doesn't know about our extended syntax, so any error messages resulting from using our definitions incorrectly will correspond to C's syntax, making it hard to find these mistakes. And third, most people don't use an extended syntax, so it is hard for them to maintain programs written in one. Despite these limitations, some large programs, including a command interpreter, have been written in an ALGOL-like syntax defined using the preprocessor.

Failing to parenthesize expressions in the replacement text can cause unexpected order-of-evaluation problems. Not parenthesizing **TWOPI**'s definition,

```
#define TWOPI  PI + PI    /* asking for trouble */
```

results in an incorrect expression to compute the circumference:

```
circumf = 3.1415926 + 3.1415926 * radius;
```

> *To avoid problems, always parenthesize the replacement text.*

Syntax errors within a definition are detected when we use the name, not when we define it. The preprocessor does no syntax checking of the results of its substitutions, leaving this task to the compiler. The incorrect definitions

```
#define PI = 3.1415926;   /* Wrong! Don't want "=" or ";" */
#define TWOPI = (2 * PI); /* Wrong! Don't want "=" or ";" */
```

Aside 15.1b (yesorno11.c) Yet another version of our **yesOrNo** function and a small program to use it.

```
/*
 * A version of our yesOrNo function written using syntactic
 * replacement.
 */
#include <stdio.h>
#include <ctype.h>

#define FOREVER    for (;;)                  /* infinite loop */
#define IS         ==                        /* equality test */
#define ISNOT      !=                        /* inequality test */

int yesOrNo(void)
{
  int c;                                     /* input character */

  FOREVER
  {
    if ((c = tolower(getchar())) IS EOF || c IS 'y' || c IS 'n')
      return c IS 'y';
    while (c ISNOT '\n' && c ISNOT EOF)
      c = getchar();                         /* skip rest of line */
    printf("Please answer with a YES or NO: ");
  }
}
```

Aside 15.1c (pascal.h) Definitions used to create a Pascal-like syntax.

```
/*
 * Definitions for Pascal-like keywords
 */
#define INTEGER    int
#define REAL       double
#define IF         if (
#define THEN       )
#define ELSE       else
#define WHILE      while (
#define DO         )
#define BEGIN      {
#define END        }
#define PROCEDURE  void
#define FUNCTION
#define RETURN     return
```

Aside 15.1d (power5.c) Our old **power** function, rewritten using Pascal-like syntax.

```
/*
 * A function to compute powers using Pascal-like keywords.
 */
#include <stdio.h>
#include "pascal.h"                              /* for Pascal keywords */

FUNCTION REAL power(REAL x, INTEGER exp)
BEGIN
  REAL p = 1;

  IF exp > 0 THEN
    WHILE exp-- > 0 DO p *= x;
  ELSE
    WHILE exp++ < 0 DO p /= x;
  RETURN p;
END
```

contain two common syntax errors: following a name with an assignment operator and ending a definition with a semicolon. Following this definition with

        circumf = TWOPI * radius;

will lead to errors for the set of incorrect statements that result from the preprocessor's substitutions.

        circumf = = (2 * = 3.1415926;); * radius;

> *Remember that the preprocessor doesn't know C—it blindly replaces names with replacement text.*

15.3   **MACRO SUBSTITUTION WITH PARAMETERS**

So far we've defined names so that they are always replaced by the same text. There are times, however, when we want the replacement text to act like a template that's filled in differently each time we use the name. We can do this by defining a macro with parameters.

        #define *macro-name* (*name-1*, . . . , *name-n*) *replacement-text*

Subsequent occurrences of the macro name are known as *macro calls*.

        macro-name (*text-1*, . . . , *text-n*)

Macro calls look like function calls but behave differently. When we call a macro, we supply its arguments, and the preprocessor performs *macro expansion*, replacing the call with macro's replacement text and then replacing the macro's parameters with its arguments.

In Chapter 6, we wrote a set of bit-accessing functions and a program that used them to pack employee information into a single word. Figure 15.5 is a header file that contains a set of macro replacements for those bit-accessing functions. **GETBIT**, for example, is a simple macro to return the value of an **int**'s **n**th bit.

```
#define GETBIT(w, n) (((unsigned int) (w) >> (n)) & 01)
```

Once we've defined **GETBIT**, an expression like **GETBIT(value, i)** is a macro call. The preprocessor substitutes **value** for **w** and **i** for **n** in **GETBIT**'s replacement text.

```
(((unsigned int) (value) >> (i)) & 01)
```

Why are there so many parentheses in **GETBIT**'s definition? To prevent order-of-evaluation problems when **GETBIT** is expanded, we not only parenthesize the replacement text but also all occurrences of the macro's parameters.

The macro definitions in Figure 15.5 look like we might expect except for one thing: many of the lines end in a backslash.

```
#define GETBITS(w,n,k) \
        (((unsigned int) (w) & (~(~0 << (k)) << (n))) >> (n))
```

Whenever the preprocessor encounters a backslash immediately followed by a newline character, it joins the two lines together. Here, we're using the backslash so that a complicated macro can extend over multiple lines.

Figure 15.6 is a new version of our earlier bit-packing program that uses these macros. Programs using the macros are more efficient than programs using our earlier functions, since we've eliminated the considerable function call overhead associated with those simple functions. Of course, we didn't have to write macros or functions to get or set bits—we could have used the C bitwise operators directly. But using the macro aids readability without adversely affecting efficiency.

Using Macros in Macro Definitions

Our bit-shifting macros are complex and hard to understand. It would be nice if we could build them up out of smaller, more easily understood pieces. Figure 15.7 shows a new version of our bit-shifting macros that we construct on top of simpler mask-creating macros. With these definitions, when we do a macro call such as

```
SETBIT(word,2,1)
```

the preprocessor initially replaces it with

```
((1 == 0) ? SETBITOFF(word,2) : SETBITON(word,2))
```

Then it expands the macros **SETBITOFF** and **SETBITON**:

```
((1 == 0) ? (UINT(word) | ONBIT(2))
          : (UINT(word) & OFFBIT(2)))
```

```
/*
 * Macro replacements for our earlier bit-accessing functions.
 */
#define GETBIT(w,n)  (((unsigned int) (w) >> (n)) & 01)
#define SETBIT(w,n,v) \
        ((v == 0) ? ((unsigned int) (w) & ~(01 << (n))) \
                  : ((unsigned int) (w) |  (01 << (n))))

#define GETBITS(w,n,k) \
        (((unsigned int) (w) & (~(~0 << (k)) << (n))) >> (n))
#define SETBITS(w,n,k,v) \
        (((unsigned int) (w) & ~(~(~0 << (k)) << (n))) | ((v) << (n)))
```

Figure 15.5　(bits.h)　Macros to get and set bits within a word.

And finally it expands **UINT**, **OFFBIT**, and **ONBIT**, resulting in the expression we want:

```
((1 == 0) ? ((unsigned int) word & ~(01 << (2)))
          : ((unsigned int) word |  (01 << (2))))
```

Some Useful Macros

Macros are much more useful than they might at first appear. That's because they can do things that functions can't. Unlike functions, they can work with many different types of arguments. Consider the macro **INRANGE**, which returns a non-zero value only if its third parameter falls between its other two parameters.

```
#define INRANGE(x,y,v) ((v) >= (x) && (v) <= (y))
```

Following this definition, the macro call **INRANGE(1, 100, i)** expands into

```
((i) >= (1) && (i) <= (100))
```

INRANGE is much more useful as a macro than as a function. Why? Because it can find the minimum of any pair of values with the same data type: **int**s, **double**s, and so on. If we write **INRANGE** as a function, we have to specify a single type for its parameters, which means we end up writing different versions of **INRANGE** for each data type, or suffer through automatic conversions whenever we call it. We also gain efficiency by writing **INRANGE** as a macro, since macro calls are done during preprocessing instead of at run time, eliminating the overhead of a function call (argument passing, variable allocation, calling and returning from the function). Figure 15.8 provides an example of **INRANGE** in an extended version of our earlier program to verify that its input values are legal. This program reads a **double** and an **int** and verifies that they fall within ranges defined by symbolic constants.

Unlike functions, macros can be passed a type as an argument. Figure 15.9 contains a header file containing a set of macros for dynamic allocation that take advantage of this

```c
/*
 * Revised program to pack employee information into a single word.
 * Now uses bit macros rather than bit functions.
 */
#include <stdio.h>
#include <stdlib.h>
#include "bits.h"

enum status {SINGLE, MARRIED, SEPARATED, DIVORCED};
enum genders {MALE, FEMALE};

#define MSBIT     0        /* marital status: bits 0-1 */
#define MSBITS    2
#define AGEBIT    2        /* age: bits 2-8 */
#define AGEBITS   7
#define SEXBIT    9        /* sex: bit 9 */
#define YRSBIT    10       /* year: bits 10-15 */
#define YRSBITS   6

int main()
{
  unsigned int mstat, sex, age, years;
  unsigned int info = 0;          /* holds info on one person */

  printf("male=%i, female=%i? ", MALE, FEMALE);
  scanf("%i", &sex);
  info = SETBIT(info, SEXBIT, sex);

  printf("age? ");
  scanf("%u", &age);
  info = SETBITS(info, AGEBIT, AGEBITS, age);

  printf("single=%i, married=%i, separated=%i, divorced=%i? ",
         SINGLE, MARRIED, SEPARATED, DIVORCED);
  scanf("%i", &mstat);
  info = SETBITS(info, MSBIT, MSBITS, mstat);

  printf("years employed? ");
  scanf("%u", &years);
  info = SETBITS(info, YRSBIT, YRSBITS, years);

  printf("Sex: %u\n", GETBIT(info, SEXBIT));
  printf("Age: %u\n", GETBITS(info, AGEBIT, AGEBITS));
  printf("Marital status: %u\n", GETBITS(info, MSBIT, MSBITS));
  printf("Years employed: %u\n", GETBITS(info, YRSBIT, YRSBITS));

  return EXIT_SUCCESS;
}
```

Figure 15.6 (usebits3.c) Program using our macros to get and set bits within a word.

```
/*
 * New version of our bit macros built up from simpler macros.
 *     UINT(x)            - x cast to unsigned int.
 *     ONBIT(n)           - only bit n on.
 *     OFFBIT(n)          - only bit n off.
 *     ONBITS(n,k)        - only bits n thru n+k on.
 *     OFFBITS(n,k)       - only bits n thru n+k off.
 *     SETBITON(w,n)      - turn bit n on in w.
 *     SETBITOFF(w,n)     - turn bit n off in w.
 *     GETBIT(w,n)        - value of bit n in  w.
 *     GETBITS(w,n,k)     - value of bits n thru n+k in w.
 *     SETBIT(w,n,v)      - give bit n value v in unsigned w.
 *     SETBITS(w,n,k,v)   - give bits n thru n+k value v in w.
 */
#define UINT(x)            ((unsigned int) (x))

#define ONBIT(n)           (01 << (n))
#define OFFBIT(n)          (~ ONBIT(n))
#define ONBITS(n,k)        (~(~0 << (k)) << (n))
#define OFFBITS(n,k)       (~ ONBITS(n,k))
#define SETBITON(w,n)      (UINT(w) | ONBIT(n))
#define SETBITOFF(w,n)     (UINT(w) & OFFBIT(n))
#define GETBIT(w,n)        ((UINT(w) >> (n)) & 01)
#define SETBIT(w,n,v)      (((v) == 0) ? SETBITOFF(w,n) : SETBITON(w,n))
#define GETBITS(w,n,k)     ((UINT(w) & ONBITS(n,k)) >> (n))
#define SETBITS(w,n,k,v)   ((UINT(w) & OFFBITS(n,k)) | ((v) << (n)))
```

Figure 15.7 (bits2.h) New version of our macros to get and set bits within a word.

feature. The first macro, **ALLOC**, allocates an array of **n** items of type **t**, automatically computing the necessary number of bytes.

```
#define ALLOC(n, t) (malloc((n) * sizeof(t)))
```

After this definition, the call **ALLOC(MAX, int)** expands into

```
(malloc(MAX * sizeof(int)))
```

We can't write **ALLOC** as a function, since functions can't take types as arguments. The second macro, **COPY**, is similar. It copies one array into another, given pointers to the new and old arrays, the number of elements, and the type of an element.

```
#define COPY(np,op,n,t) (memcpy(np,op,(n) * sizeof(t))
```

The next macro, **TABLEDUP**, combines calls to these other macros to create a copy of an existing array.

```
#define TABLEDUP(np, op, n, t) \
    (((np = ALLOC(n, t)) != NULL) ? COPY(np, op, n, t) : NULL)
```

It's given a pointer to fill in with a dynamically allocated array, a pointer to an existing

```
/*
 * A version of our range-checking program that uses a macro.
 */
#include <stdio.h>
#include <stdlib.h>

#define INRANGE(x,y,v)   ((v) > (x) && (v) <= (y))

#define MAXINT    1000
#define MININT       0
#define MAXDBL    9999.99
#define MINDBL    -9999.99

int main()
{
  double d;
  int    i;

  printf("Enter values: ");
  scanf("%i %lf", &i, &d);
  printf("%i is %s range!\n",
          i, INRANGE(MININT, MAXINT, i) ? "in" : "out of");
  printf("%f is %s range!\n",
          d, INRANGE(MINDBL, MAXDBL, d) ? "in" : "out of");

  return EXIT_SUCCESS;
}
```

Figure 15.8 (valid.c) A new example of input validation.

```
/*
 * Useful macros for dynamically allocating things.
 */
#include <stdlib.h>
#include <stddef.h>
#include <string.h>

#define ALLOC(n,t)         (malloc((n) * sizeof(t)))
#define COPY(np,op,n,t)    (memcpy(np,op,(n) * sizeof(t)))
#define ZERO(p,n,t)        (memset(p,(n) * sizeof(t),0))

#define TABLEDUP(np,op,n,t) \
        (((np = ALLOC(n,t)) != NULL) ? COPY(np,op,n,t) : NULL)

#define STRALLOC(s)        (malloc(strlen(s) + 1))
#define STRDUP(ns,os)      ((ns = STRALLOC(os)) ? strcpy(ns,os) : NULL)
```

Figure 15.9 (allocs.h) A set of macros useful for dynamically allocating things.

array, the number of elements in the array, and the type of an element. Like the others, it can't be written as a function since it needs to know what kind of elements are in the arrays.

Even when we could use functions, we often use macros to make our program more readable without sacrificing efficiency. **STRALLOC** is a useful variant of **ALLOC** that automatically computes a string's length and allocates sufficient space for the string.

```
#define STRALLOC(s) (malloc(strlen(s) + 1))
```

By using **STRALLOC**, we save ourselves some typing and lessen the chance that we'll forget to allocate space for the string's trailing null character. Of course, we could write **STRALLOC** as a function, but it is much more efficient as a macro.

Figure 15.10 combines all of these macros in a little program to duplicate an array of **int**s and an array of strings. After creating the copies, it zeros out the original arrays and prints the copies.

One other important use of macros is to hide certain confusing language idioms, once again making our programs more readable without losing efficiency. The macros **STREQ**, **STRLT**, and **STRGT** hide the hideousness of **strcmp**'s return value.

```
#define STREQ(x,y) (strcmp((x),(y)) == 0) /* equal? */
#define STRLT(x,y) (strcmp((x),(y)) < 0)  /* x < y? */
#define STRGT(x,y) (strcmp((x),(y)) > 0)  /* x > y? */
```

They test whether one string is lexicographically equal to, less than, or greater than another string. Without these macros, the program's reader must remember the meaning of the various return values of **strcmp** to understand which string comparison is being performed.

Potential Problems

Macros are useful—but they also have several potential pitfalls. One drawback is that a macro's code appears everywhere the macro is called, whereas a function's code appears only once, regardless of how many times the function is called. When minimal program size is important, write large, often-used macros as functions.

Another drawback is that a macro argument, unlike a function argument, may be evaluated more than once. With our definition of **INRANGE**, the call

```
INRANGE(1, 100, i + j)
```

expands into

```
((i + j) >= (1) && (i + j) <= (100))
```

which causes two evaluations of **i + j**. That's not particularly troublesome—but what about when our arguments have side effects? Suppose we pass **i++** instead of **i + j**. Then **INRANGE** expands into

```
((i++) >= (1) && (i++) <= (100))
```

This ends up incrementing **i** twice, rather than just once.

```
/*
 * A program using our memory allocation macros.
 */
#include <stdio.h>
#include <stddef.h>
#include <stdlib.h>
#include "allocs.h"

int main()
{
  int    table[] = {10, 87, 95, 89, 15, 45, 67, 22, 79, 32};
  char   *string = "abcdefghi";
  const int n    =  sizeof(table)/sizeof(table[0]);
  int    *newtable;
  char   *newstr;
  int    i;

  if (TABLEDUP(newtable, table, n, int) == NULL)
    printf("Integer table copy failed...\n");
  else
  {
    ZERO(table, n, int);
    for (i = 0; i < n; i++)                    /* display copied array */
      printf("%i\n", newtable[i]);
  }
  if (STRDUP(newstr, string) == NULL)
    printf("String copy failed...\n");
  else
  {
    int len=strlen(string);

    ZERO(string, len, char);
    printf("%s\n", newstr);
  }

  return EXIT_SUCCESS;
}
```

Figure 15.10 (dup.c) Using macros to create copies of an array of **int**s and an array of strings.

> *Use expressions as macro arguments sparingly, and avoid them entirely when they contain side effects.*

The final drawback is that sloppy parenthesizing can result in incorrect orders of evaluation. Suppose we have a macro to square its arguments, and we don't bother to parenthesize them.

```
#define SQUARE(x) (x * x) /* SLOPPY: underparenthesized */
```

This causes **SQUARE(i + j)** to expand into

```
i + j * i + j
```

which does not return $(i + j)^2$. Carefully parenthesizing eliminates potentially incorrect orders of evaluation.

```
#define SQUARE(x) ((x) * (x))          /* correct */
```

> *Make sure to parenthesize all occurrences of the parameter inside the macro's replacement text.*

Because macro calls can potentially behave differently from function calls, it's a good idea to define macros in all uppercase characters, as we have been doing in this chapter, rather than the mix of lower- and uppercase traditionally used for function names. While uppercase names, such as **GET_BITS**, are not as appealing aesthetically as their mixed-case counterparts, such as **getBits**, they highlight the use of macros in the code and remind the user to avoid certain problematic behaviors in these calls.

Macro Operators

ANSI-C provides two special operators that can appear in macro definitions: **#** and **##**. The first, **#**, precedes a parameter name. It causes double quotes to be placed around the argument substituted for the parameter. We use it in the macro **DUMPINT**, which writes an **int** variable's name and value.

```
#define DUMPINT(x)   printf(#x "=%i\n", x)
```

DUMPINT is especially useful when debugging. The preprocessor expands the call **DUMPINT(i)** into

```
printf("i" "=%i\n", i);
```

The preprocessor places double quotes around the **i** passed as the macro's first argument and takes any quote that appears in it and precedes it with a backslash. The preprocessor (or compiler) then concatenates the resulting strings into a single string.

```
printf("i=%i\n", i);
```

The other operator, **##**, turns two tokens into a single token.[1] We use it to write a more general macro, **DISPLAY**, that takes two arguments: the expression to print and its type. So **DISPLAY(thing, int)** displays **thing**'s value as an **int**, and **DISPLAY(thing, double)** displays its value as a **double**.

How does **DISPLAY** work? It expands into calls to different functions, depending on the type of object it's displaying. **DISPLAY(i, int)**, for example, expands into:

```
printint("i", i)
```

---

[1] A token is a single piece of the program source, such as a keyword, a variable, or an operator.

DISPLAY itself is actually quite simple.

```
#define DISPLAY(x, t)   print ## t (#x, x)
```

It uses **##** to concatenate its second argument onto the word **print** to form the function name. For the macro call **DISPLAY(i, int)**, the preprocessor first substitutes **i** for **x** and **int** for **t**,

```
print ## int("i", i)
```

and then concatenates the two tokens **print** and **int** together, resulting in:

```
printint("i", i)
```

Figure 15.11 is a short example that displays several different variables using these macros. Here's its output:

```
i=69
DEBUG: i (INTEGER) = 69
DEBUG: d (DOUBLE) = 3.141593 (3.141593e+00)
```

Undefining a Name

Once we have defined a name, *all* subsequent occurrences are replaced with its replacement text. Sometimes, however, we want to limit a name definition's scope, either to highlight that the name is used only in a small section of the program or to allow the name to be redefined. We use the directive

```
#undef NAME
```

to undefine a defined name, which stops any further macro substitution for it. We can then use **#define** to redefine the name. Otherwise, the compiler will complain if we try to redefine a name without first undefining it.

#undef lets us select between a macro and a function to accomplish a particular task. Macros give us speed; functions save space. It's usually less harmful to have side effects in a function argument and easier to add debugging code to a function.

15.4   FILE INCLUSION

We have been using file inclusion all along. The directive **#include** instructs the preprocessor to replace the current line with the entire contents of the specified file. If we don't provide a complete file name, the preprocessor searches for the file in various locations determined by the **#include** form used.

We have seen this form:

```
#include  <filename>
```

```
/*
 * Using the preprocessor to obtain readable debugging output.
 */
#include <stdio.h>
#include <stdlib.h>

#define DUMPINT(x)      printf(#x "=%i\n", x)
#define DISPLAY(x, t)  print ## t (#x, x)

int main()
{
  void printint(char *name, int x);
  void printdouble(char *name, double x);

  int     i = 69;
  double d = 3.1415926;

  DUMPINT(i);
  DISPLAY(i, int);  DISPLAY(d, double);

  return EXIT_SUCCESS;
}

void printint(char *name, int x)
  { printf("DEBUG: %s (INTEGER) = %i\n", name, x); }

void printdouble(char *name, double x)
  { printf("DEBUG: %s (DOUBLE) = %f (%e)\n", name, x, x); }
```

Figure 15.11 (debugex.c) Defining and using our **DISPLAY** and **DUMPINT** macros.

The angle brackets tell the preprocessor to look in the usual system locations for the include files. There is an alternative form for include files that we create:

> **#include** *"filename"*

The quotes tell the preprocessor to look in a default directory first and to search the other locations only if the file is not found locally. It's an error if the included file cannot be found. As you might expect, an included file can include other files, but shouldn't include itself or any file that includes it.

File inclusion allows us to create a file of useful definitions that we can include in all our programs. Definitions like those shown in Figure 15.12 require little effort to extend C in a useful way. We've explained most of these definitions and macros already, but we've also defined a pair of macros **MAX** and **MIN** that return the maximum and minimum value of their arguments, respectively, and a macro **PRINT_STRING** that writes a string on a line by itself.

File inclusion allows us to define a set of useful operations entirely within an include file. In fact, we've already done so with the bit-accessing macros we wrote earlier. We

```
/*
 * Our default definitions.
 */
#include <stdio.h>
#include <stddef.h>
#include <stdlib.h>
#include <string.h>
#include <ctype.h>

#define FOREVER for(;;)
#define IS      ==
#define ISNOT   !=

#define MIN(x,y)         ((x) < (y) ? (x) : (y))      /* smaller */
#define MAX(x,y)         ((x) < (y) ? (y) : (x))      /* larger */
#define INRANGE(x,y,v)   ((v) >= (x) && (v) <= (y))

#define STREQ(x,y)       (strcmp(x,y) == 0)           /* hide */
#define STRLT(x,y)       (strcmp(x,y) < 0)            /*  strcmp */
#define STRGT(x,y)       (strcmp(x,y) > 0)            /*  ugliness */
#define PRINT_STRING(s)  (printf("%s\n", s))          /* print string */
```

Figure 15.12 (defs.h) A header file containing generally useful definitions used by many programs.

put them into the header file bits.h and then included this file when we needed these operations. If, after time, we find these macros to be generally useful, we can include bits.h from defs.h. Doing so effectively extends the language to provide additional functions we find useful, while preserving the efficiency of programs that use them.

We can, in fact, define a seemingly new data type completely within a header file. As an example, Figure 15.13 shows the include file boolean.h, which contains definitions that make it appear as though C has a Boolean data type. These definitions help us write more readable code and make it easier to translate programs written in a language that has a Boolean type.

We use **short** to hold **BOOLEAN**s, since we need only store the two values 0 (**FALSE**) and 1 (**TRUE**). For consistency with other languages, we define the constants **NOT**, **AND**, and **OR** as alternatives to C's equivalent logical operators. **BOOLSTR** returns a string representing the **BOOLEAN**'s value, which comes in handy when debugging. The file also makes use of several new preprocessor statements—**#if** and **#endif**—but we'll cover those in the next section.

Any program can pretend that C has **BOOLEAN**s by including boolean.h and using these definitions. We use them in Figure 15.14, a new version of our earlier program to filter duplicate input lines. Before we had these definitions in the source file, but now we just include the header file. We'd already made use of constants for **TRUE** and **FALSE**; this version differs in that the constants are in a header file and do not have to be defined and that **first** is now a **BOOLEAN** rather than **int**. Since we've defined boolean.h ourselves, we surround the **#include** with quotes rather than angle brackets.

```
/*
 * Header file defining BOOLEAN data type.
 */
#if !defined(BOOLEAN)

#define     BOOLEAN         short
#define     TRUE            1
#define     FALSE           0
#define     NOT             !
#define     AND             &&
#define     OR              ||
#define     BOOLSTR(x)      (x) ? "TRUE" : "FALSE"

#endif
```

Figure 15.13 (boolean.h) A header file defining a **BOOLEAN** data type.

```
/*
 * A new version of our program to strip duplicate lines.
 */
#include "defs.h"                /* Our definitions */
#include "boolean.h"            /* Our Boolean type */

#define MAXLEN  80              /* longest line length */

int main()
{
  int getline(char *buf, int size);

  char    curr[MAXLEN + 1],     /* current line */
          prev[MAXLEN + 1];     /* previous line */
  BOOLEAN first = TRUE;         /* first time through? */

  for (; getline(curr, MAXLEN) ISNOT -1; strcpy(prev, curr))
    if (first OR !STREQ(prev, curr))
    {
      PRINT_STRING(curr);
      first = FALSE;
    }

  return EXIT_SUCCESS;
}
```

Figure 15.14 (uniq2.c) Using the **BOOLEAN** definitions in a new version of uniq.

15.5   CONDITIONAL COMPILATION

We can use the preprocessor to select which lines of the source file are actually compiled, a process known as *conditional compilation*. Conditional compilation lets us compile a program's source into different versions, depending on our needs. The directive

```
#if  constant-expression
   first-group-of-lines
#else
   second-group-of-lines
#endif
```

evaluates *constant-expression* and compares its value with zero to determine which group of lines to process. If the expression is non-zero, the preprocessor and compiler process the *first-group-of-lines*; otherwise they process the *second-group-of-lines*. As you might expect, the **#else** and the *second-group-of-lines* is optional.

We can use a simple form of **#if** to "comment out" sections of code that contain comments. This is useful, since comments don't nest.

```
#if 0                    /* begin ignored section */
   lines-to-be-commented-out
#endif                   /* end ignored section */
```

Since the **#if**'s expression is always zero, the *lines-to-be-commented-out* are always ignored.

More typically, we combine **#if** with a new preprocessor operator, **defined**, to test whether a name is known to a preprocessor. **defined** takes a *NAME* (which must be surrounded by parentheses) and returns a non-zero value only if the *NAME* is defined.

Figure 15.15 uses **#if** and **defined** in a new version of our **tableAverage** function. This version conditionally includes statements that provide debugging output. These statements are included only if the name **DEBUG** is defined when the function is compiled. If **DEBUG** is defined when the preprocessor evaluates the final **#if** in **tableAverage**, the compiler receives

```
{
  sum += *ptr;
  printf("*ptr=%i, sum=%li\n", *ptr, sum);
}
```

but doesn't see the statement between the **#else** and the **#endif**. It sees that statement,

```
sum += *ptr;
```

only if **DEBUG** is not defined.

We test whether **DEBUG** is defined to decide whether to include the debugging statements. But how do we make sure **DEBUG** is defined? One way is to simply add the line

```
#define DEBUG
```

```
/*
 * Computing the average of an array, with debugging code.
 */
#if defined(DEBUG)
#include <stdio.h>
#endif

double tableAverage(const int a[], int n)
{
  long      sum = 0L;
  const int *ptr = a;                   /* traversing pointer */
  const int * const endptr = a + n;   /* pointer to just past the end */

#if defined(DEBUG)
  printf("ptr=%p, endptr=%p\n", (void *) ptr, (void *) endptr);
#endif

  for ( ; ptr < endptr; ptr++)
#if defined(DEBUG)
  {
    sum += *ptr;
    printf("*ptr=%i, sum=%li\n", *ptr, sum);
  }
#else
    sum += *ptr;
#endif

  return (n != 0) ? (double) sum / n : 0.0;
}
```

Figure 15.15   (tavg5.c)   Table-averaging routine, complete with debugging statements.

at the top of our source file when we want debugging statements. We then remove it when they are no longer necessary. Most compilers, however, provide an option to define names on the command-line and even to give them a value.

Figure 15.16 is a little program that uses **tableAverage** to compute the average of a small table of values. When we run it with **DEBUG** defined, we can see a trace of the pointer used to run through the array, as well an idea of how many values we're supposed to process:

```
Averaging 5 values.
ptr=68fab31c, endptr=68fab330
*ptr=91, sum=91
*ptr=40, sum=131
*ptr=78, sum=209
*ptr=23, sum=232
*ptr=56, sum=288
57.600000
```

```
/*
 * Using our tableAverage function.
 */
#include <stdio.h>
#include <stdlib.h>

int main()
{
  double tableAverage(const int a[], int n);

  const int table[] = {91, 40, 78, 23, 56};
  const int n        = sizeof(table)/sizeof(table[0]);

#if defined(DEBUG)
  printf("Averaging %i values.\n", n);
#endif

  printf("%f\n", tableAverage(table, n));

  return EXIT_SUCCESS;
}
```

Figure 15.16 (avgmain.c) A program using our new **tableAverage**.

But when we run it without **DEBUG** defined, it simply prints the average:

57.600000

What are the alternatives to having the preprocessor decide whether debugging output should be produced? We could add output statements whenever we want debugging output and remove them once we've debugged the program. But then the debugging statements aren't available when we want to make changes to the program. We could use run-time tests, but then our program is larger, because the debugging statements appear in its object module even when we don't want debugging output, and slower, because the tests are done at run time, not at compile time. The preprocessor approach does have one disadvantage: The many preprocessor tests make the source less readable.

We often combine **defined** with logical negation (**!**) to test whether a name hasn't yet been defined. We use this most often in include files to ensure that even if the file is included more than once, any definitions it contains won't be. We did that in boolean.h, so it defines **BOOLEAN** only if it hasn't already been defined. The file's first line

```
#if !defined(BOOLEAN)
```

causes the various names contained in the file to be defined only if **BOOLEAN** is undefined. If **BOOLEAN** is already defined, we assume that the file has already been included and that we can ignore its definitions.

Remember that **defined** tests only whether the name is defined in the preprocessor. It doesn't test whether the name of an identifier, function, or type has been declared.

One last use of **#if** is to compile things differently depending on the value of some preprocessor constant. We might, for example, want to have several types of debugging output: no output, a sketchy bit of output, and a fuller trace. We can do this by defining **DEBUG** to be 0 for no output, 1 for a dump of each function's parameters or most important variables, and 2 for additional debugging statements and then using **#if** to test for the various values of **DEBUG**. Figure 15.17 does so in a new version of **tableAverage**.

Other Testing Directives

There's one other directive we can use with **#if**: **#elif**. We can use it to write **#if**s of the form

```
#if  test-1
     .  .  .
#else
#if  test-2
     .  .  .
#endif
#endif
```

more compactly:

```
#if  test-1
     .  .  .
#elif  test-2
     .  .  .
#endif
```

We replace any **#else** immediately followed by an **#if** with **#elif** and then remove its **#endif**.

There are also two special directives we can use for testing whether a name is defined. The line

```
#ifdef  NAME
```

is equivalent to

```
#if defined(NAME)
```

and the line

```
#ifndef  NAME
```

is equivalent to

```
#if !defined(NAME).
```

In practice, however, we rarely use either of these directives, since they're really just special cases of **#if**.

```
/*
 * Computing the average of an array, with debugging code.
 */
#if DEBUG > 0
#include <stdio.h>
#endif

double tableAverage(const int a[], int n)
{
  long       sum = 0L;
  const int *ptr = a;                    /* traversing pointer */
  const int * const endptr = a + n;   /* pointer to just past the end */

#if DEBUG > 0
  printf("ptr=%p, endptr=%p\n", (void *) ptr, (void *) endptr);
#endif

  for ( ; ptr < endptr; ptr++)
#if DEBUG > 1
  {
    sum += *ptr;
    printf("*ptr=%i, sum=%li\n", *ptr, sum);
  }
#else
    sum += *ptr;
#endif

  return (n != 0) ? (double) sum / n : 0.0;
}
```

Figure 15.17 (tavg6.c) Compute the average of a table, printing useful debugging information.

Predefined Names

In addition to names we define ourselves, most preprocessors also predefine some names for us. Here are the minimal set of names defined by any ANSI-C conforming compiler.

NAME	VALUE OR TEST
__LINE__	current line number (an integer)
__FILE__	current file name (a string constant)
__DATE__	date source file is translated (string of the form: MMMDDYYYY)
__TIME__	time source file is translated (string of the form: HHMMSS)
__STDC__	defined if ANSI-compatible

Most compilers also define a set of names that describe the particular compiler and the operating system it's running under. A program can test these predefined names to determine what type of environment it's running in and adjust environment dependencies accordingly. There are several ways we can take advantage of these names. We'll present them in detail in Chapter 21, our chapter on portability.

Aside 15.2a: Using the Preprocessor to Aid Debugging

Many bugs are caused because a function makes incorrect assumptions about its parameters. One way to prevent these bugs is to have functions explicitly state what their assumptions are and terminate if the assumptions do not hold.

Aside 15.2b defines a macro, **ASSERT**, that helps us make our assumptions explicit. **ASSERT**'s argument is an expression representing a programmer assumption. If the assumption doesn't hold, it writes a message that includes the line number, and source file where the assertion was made. We can insert a call to **ASSERT** wherever a function makes a critical assumption, documenting the assumption and indicating when it fails. Invariably, a false assumption will cause our program to fail; **ASSERT** helps us find such assumptions.

When **ASSERT** is called, the preprocessor replaces __LINE__ and __FILE__ with the line number and file name of the call. This way the error message indicates where the failed assumption occurred in the source file.

Aside 15.2c contains a new version of **tableAverage** that uses **ASSERT** to make explicit its assumption that it is passed a non-null pointer. If we accidentally pass it a null pointer, we get a useful error message.

```
Assertion (ptr != NULL) failed (tavg7.c,13)
```

This message was generated because the call to **ASSERT**,

```
ASSERT(ptr != NULL);
```

expands into

```
((ptr != NULL) ||
 (printf("Assertion (" "ptr != NULL") failed (%s,%i)\n",
        tavg7.c, 13), exit(1), 0));
```

which causes the error message that's printed when the program runs. Our macro uses **exit** to terminate the program if the assertion fails. (Appendix A describes **exit** in detail.)

The **ASSERT** provides some indication of where the problem lies. An error message from a failed assertion provides a better starting point for locating bugs than missing output or a potentially cryptic system message.

ANSI-C actually provides a system header file assert.h that provides a macro **assert** that behaves similarly to our **ASSERT** macro. One difference is that it writes its error message in a slightly different format. Another is that if the symbol **NDEBUG** is defined, none of the assertions are compiled with the program, effectively turning off checking insertions. There's no need to worry about a conflict between our own include file and the system's, since the double quotation marks in the **#include** guarantee that ours will be used.

Aside 15.2b (assert.h) The definition of our **ASSERT** macro.

```
/*
 * Our version of the ASSERT macro.
 */
#include <stdlib.h>

#define ASSERT(cond) \
  ((cond) || \
    (printf("Assertion (" # cond ") failed (%s,%i)\n", \
            __FILE__, __LINE__), exit(1), 0))
```

Aside 15.2c (tavg7.c) Making an assumption explicit with the **ASSERT** macro.

```
/*
 * Computes the average of an array.  Contains an assertion.
 */
#include <stdio.h>
#include "assert.h"

double tableAverage(const int a[], int n)
{
  long       sum = 0L;
  const int *ptr = a;              /* traversing pointer */
  const int *const endptr = a + n; /* pointer to just past the end */

  ASSERT(ptr != NULL);
  for ( ; ptr < endptr; ptr++)
    sum += *ptr;
  return (n != 0) ? (double) sum / n : 0.0;
}
```

15.6   OTHER PREPROCESSOR DIRECTIVES

There are three other preprocessor directives. The first, **#line**, tells the preprocessor from which input file and line a line in its input was derived.

> **#line** *line-number* **"*filename*"**

#line appears most frequently in C programs that have been generated or modified by other programs before they are seen by the preprocessor or compiler. Because line numbers referred to in a preprocessor or compiler error message may not correspond exactly to the line where the error occurred in the source file used to generate these programs, they use **#line** to make error messages refer to the correct lines in the original source file.

We use **#error** most frequently inside preprocessor conditionals. When the preprocessor encounters a **#error**,

```
#error error-message
```

it writes an error message and terminates preprocessing early. A program could use

```
#if !defined(__STDC__)
#error Requires standard C to compile
#endif
```

to terminate preprocessing unless it's being compiled by an ANSI compiler.

The final directive is **#pragma**, whose behavior differs among compilers. See your compiler manual for details.

15.7   CASE STUDY—IMPLEMENTING SETS WITH MACROS

*This section
is optional!*

Earlier we presented a package implementing some basic set-handling functions. Most of the functions were only one line long and were little more than a **return** statement of a complicated expression. That means they're good candidates for macros.

Figure 15.18 is a header file defining the macros necessary to implement sets. It's divided into several pieces. The first defines the **Set** type and a constant **US_BITS** for the number of bits in an **unsigned short**. The second defines some useful utility macros for determining an element's position within the array representing the set and the number of words needed to store the entire set. These roughly correspond to the **static** functions we had previously. Finally, the last section defines macros for each of the functions in the set package we had before, along with a new macro that switches an item from one set to another. Figure 15.19 is a new version of our program to detect duplicate input values that's written using these macros.

There are some trade-offs in using macros to implement sets. On the positive side, programs using the macro implementation will be more efficient, since they no longer suffer overhead for function calls. They'll also be easier to compile and run, since we no longer need to link in the compiled set functions. On the negative side, however, the header file is hard to read, since the macros cram a lot of code into just a few lines. We've also defined several auxiliary names that make our macros easier to define, but we can't hide these names from the programs using our header file, which may result in various name conflicts.

SUMMARY

- All C programs are first passed through a preprocessor before the compiler ever sees them.

- **#define** is a general mechanism for having the preprocessor substitute text for names.

```
/*
 * Macro package for dynamically allocated sets.
 */
#include <stdlib.h>

typedef void *Set;

#define US_BITS 16                    /* Bits in unsigned short */

/* Utility macros:
 *    WORD:  index of word holding element
 *    BIT:   index of bit holding element
 *    WORDS: number of words needed to hold entire set
 */
#define WORD(e)          ((e) / US_BITS)
#define BIT(e)           ((e) % US_BITS)
#define WORDS(n)         (((n) / US_BITS) + (((n) % US_BITS) != 0))
/*
 * Macros meant for the outside world:
 *    SET_CREATE:  form a new set of n elements.
 *    SET_DESTROY: get rid of existing set.
 *    SET_ADD:     add element to an existing set.
 *    SET_MEMBER:  is item in set?
 *    SET_SWITCH:  move item from one set to another.
 */
#define SET_CREATE(n)    (calloc(WORDS(n),sizeof(unsigned short)))
#define SET_DESTROY(s)   free((s))
#define SET_ADD(s,e) \
        (* ((unsigned short *) (s) + WORD(e)) |= 1 << BIT(e))
#define SET_DELETE(s,e) \
        (* ((unsigned short *) (s) + WORD(e)) &= ~(1 << BIT(e)))
#define SET_MEMBER(s,e) \
        (((unsigned) \
            (* ((unsigned short *) (s) + WORD(e))) >> BIT(e)) & 01)
#define SET_SWITCH(n,o,v)    (SET_DELETE(o,v), SET_ADD(n,v))
```

Figure 15.18 (sets3.h) Defining sets using macros.

- We can define names with parameters, so that the replacement text becomes a template filled in when we use the name.

- We can use **#undef** to stop substituting text for a name.

- **#include** has the preprocessor substitute the contents of the named file, which can be either a system header file or one of our own.

- **#if** (together with **#else** and **#endif**) allows us to pass different code to the compiler depending on whether a particular name is defined at compile time or what value it has.

```
/*
 * Identify duplicates in the input.
 */
#include "defs.h"
#include "sets3.h"                      /* for Sets */

int main()
{
  void        setPrint(const char *name, const Set s, int max);

  const int MAXELEMS = 512;                       /* # of set elements */
  Set         unique = SET_CREATE(MAXELEMS),      /* unique and */
              dup    = SET_CREATE(MAXELEMS);      /*    duplicate sets */
  int         r;                                  /* scanf return */
  int         inp;                                /* input value */

  while ((r = scanf("%i", &inp)) ISNOT EOF)
  {
    if (r ISNOT 1)
    {
      printf("Value in error.\n");
      break;
    }
    if (!INRANGE(0, MAXELEMS - 1, inp))
    {
      printf("Value %i not between %i and %i\n", inp, 0, MAXELEMS - 1);
      continue;
    }
    if (SET_MEMBER(unique, inp))
      SET_SWITCH(dup, unique, inp);
    else if (!SET_MEMBER(dup, inp))
      SET_ADD(unique, inp);
  }
  setPrint("Unique", unique, MAXELEMS);
  setPrint("Duplicate", dup, MAXELEMS);

  return EXIT_SUCCESS;
}

void setPrint(const char *name, const Set set, int max)
{
  int i;                              /* next potential element */

  printf("%s values\n", name);
  for (i = 0; i < max; i++)
    if (SET_MEMBER(set, i))
      printf("%i\n", i);
}
```

Figure 15.19   (usesets3.c)   Using the macro implementation of sets.

EXERCISES

Explore

15–1 Compile and run the programs in this chapter.

15–2 Examine some of the C programs you have written. Are there complicated expressions that could be greatly simplified by using macros? Write these macros.

Modify

15–3 We've been giving our programs the value of π as a constant. It's more accurate to give it the value $4.0 \times \arctan(1.0)$. Write a constant definition for **PI** using this formula. Extend your definition into a macro **N_PI** that computes $n \times \pi$. Modify several of the programs in the text that use the value of π to use your macro rather than a constant.

What's the problem with this approach to defining π? How can we improve it?

Code

15–4 Write the macro **DISPLAY_UL**. It takes a string, an **unsigned long**, and a field width. It prints the string and then prints the value in a field of the specified width. Modify Figure 15.2 to use it.

Provide similar macros for each of C's other basic types.

15–5 Write a macro, **INDEX**, that expands into a **for** loop that indexes a variable from a minimum to a maximum.

```
INDEX(i, 1, 100) printf("This is %i\n", i);
```

expands into

```
for (i = 1; i <= 100; i++) printf("This is %i\n", i);
```

INDEX should work even if the loop bounds are expressions.

15–6 Write the macros **DIV** and **DIVMOD**. **DIV(x,y)** returns the value of x/y for non-zero values of **y**, otherwise it returns zero. **DIVMOD(d,r,x,y)** divides **x** by **y**, storing the result in **d** and the remainder in **r**.

15–7 Write a macro, **MSG(flag,msg)**, that writes the string **msg** only if **flag** is not zero.

15–8 Write a macro, **NULLPTR(type)**, that returns a null pointer correctly cast to the passed type. When is this macro useful?

15–9 Write a macro, **DEREF(ptr, type)**, that dereferences **ptr** only if it is not null. If **ptr** is null, the macro prints an error message and returns zero, cast to the appropriate type.

15–10 Write constant definitions for the maximum and minimum values of the types **short**, **int**, and **long**. These definitions should work for both 16- and 32-bit machines. Write similar constant definitions for their unsigned counterparts.

Build

15–11 Define a header file that provides a group of functions for manipulating sets of small integers (from 0 to 31). Write macros for adding an item to the set, deleting an item from the set, testing whether an item is in the set, and taking the union and intersection of two sets.

15–12 Define a header file that provides a set of macros for traversing arrays. These include

```
INIT(array, elements, ptr, value)
```

which expands into a loop initializing each array element to a particular value,

```
FWALK(array, elements, ptr, func)
```

which expands into a loop executing a function on each array element (going from beginning to end), and

```
RWALK(array, elements, ptr, func)
```

which does the same thing but in the opposite direction.

15–13 Write a program that removes all lines beginning with an at sign (**@**) from C source files. This allows us to have convenient single-line comments. The program should provide **#line**s to ensure that error messages refer to the correct lines in the original source files.

16 FUNCTIONS REVISITED

One of C's strengths is that functions are easy to define and use. However, C functions can be more powerful and complex than we have let on, and this chapter discusses special-purpose features of functions in great detail. In particular, we show how to write functions that can take a variable number of arguments, we introduce pointers to functions and use them to pass functions as parameters, and we present recursive functions, using them to compute factorials and permutations. We also discuss the difference between ANSI-C function prototypes and old-style C function declarations. The chapter concludes with a case study that implements an interesting and useful recursive algorithm, binary search.

16.1   PASSING VARIABLE NUMBERS OF ARGUMENTS

All functions we've written so far take a fixed number of arguments—but we've used functions, such as **scanf** and **printf**, that take a variable number of arguments. To see how these functions are written, we'll write a function, **max**, that returns the largest value in the group of values provided as its arguments. Figure 16.1 contains **max**, along with an example call.

How can **max** figure out how many arguments it was actually passed? **scanf** and **printf** figure out how many arguments they have and what their types are by examining the control string. An alternative is to supply the number of arguments as a parameter, and that's what we've done with **max**. Its first argument is the number of additional arguments. To indicate that these other arguments are arbitrary both in number and type, we use three dots (...) as the last parameter type in both the function header and the prototype.

```
int max(int argcnt, ...)
```

To write functions with variable numbers of arguments, we need to include the system header file stdarg.h. It supplies a new data type, **va_list** (which stands for variable argument list), and a set of functions (macros, actually) that we use to access the undeclared arguments. The idea is that we use a special pointer to traverse the arguments; these functions allow us to obtain and update that pointer.

461

```
/*
 * Illustrate variable-argument "max" function.
 */
#include <stdio.h>
#include <stdlib.h>
#include <stdarg.h>
#include <limits.h>

int main()
{
  int max(int argcnt, ...);

  printf("%i\n", max(5,1,7,3,4,2));
  printf("%i\n", max(10,87,91,18,34,65,89,99,45,99,56));

  return EXIT_SUCCESS;
}

/* Return maximum value of its arguments */

int max(int argcnt, ...)
{
  va_list argptr;                       /* argument pointer */
  int     nextarg;                      /* next variable argument */
  int     i;                            /* argument count */
  int     biggest = INT_MIN;            /* largest value */

  va_start(argptr, argcnt);
  for (i = 0; i < argcnt; i++)
    if ((nextarg = va_arg(argptr, int)) > biggest)
      biggest = nextarg;
  va_end(argptr);
  return biggest;
}
```

Figure 16.1 (max.c) An example function that takes a variable number of arguments.

We begin by declaring this pointer to have type **va_list**. The pointer can have any name, but we like to use **argptr**, which stands for "pointer to an argument list".

```
    va_list argptr;                 /* pointer to argument list */
```

We initialize the pointer with **va_start**, which takes two arguments. The first is the argument pointer (of type **va_list**), and the other is the name of the last parameter in the function definition (the one that appears before the three dots).

```
    va_start(argptr, argcnt);
```

This call makes **argptr** point just past **max**'s first argument, **argcnt**.

> *Be sure to call* **va_start** *before trying to access the variable arguments.*

Figure 16.2 illustrates how we run through **max**'s arguments. We use the macro **va_arg** to do this. It also takes two arguments, the argument pointer, **argptr**, and the *type* of the next argument.[1] It updates **argptr** to point to the next argument and then returns the value of the thing **argptr** used to point to (an item of *type*). This value is the next argument in the variable argument list.

The type can be any of the C's types except **short**, **char**, and **float**. The reason for this restriction is that if C doesn't know what types of parameters a particular function expects, it automatically converts any passed **short** and **char** parameters to **int**s and **float** parameters to **double**s. So if a function taking a variable argument list is passed a **short**, it will actually be passed an **int**.

> *You should not pass a* **short**, **char**, *or* **float** *to* **va_arg**.

Here, *type* is always an **int**.

```
nextarg = va_arg(argptr, int)
```

When we've finished processing arguments, we call **va_end**.

```
va_end(argptr);
```

It turns out this call does nothing in many versions of C. So why do we need it? We don't if our program is compiled with only those versions of C. But on some machines with some compilers, **va_end** may reset some previously changed state information.[2] To be portable, make sure you include the **va_end** when you're done processing the arguments.

> *Be sure to call* **va_end** *after accessing the variable arguments.*

Writing functions that can handle variable numbers of arguments requires extra planning and effort. But these functions are convenient—**max** would be much harder to use if we had to pass it an array of values. The functions in stdargs.h provide a clean interface to these arguments, allowing us to ignore the details of the underlying hardware and leave them to the hardworking compiler writer who has to provide these functions.

Dealing with Differing Argument Types

max only deals with **int** arguments. But functions like **printf** and **scanf** are considerably more complicated because they have to deal with many different types of arguments, and to determine their types from a control string.

---

[1] It must be a macro rather than a function in order to take a type as an argument.
[2] Specifically, it may have to fix up the function call stack to allow a valid return.

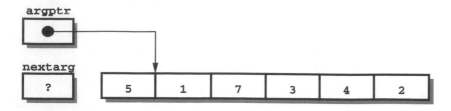

(a) Initially, after **va_start**.

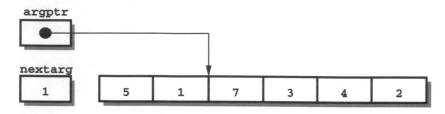

(b) After the first call to **va_arg**.

Figure 16.2   Processing **max**'s arguments.

Figures 16.3 and 16.4 show how to write one of these functions. Figure 16.3 contains the prototype for **getInput**, a function that prompts for and reads input, and Figure 16.4 contains the function itself. Figure 16.5 contains a main program that uses **getInput**.

getInput is similar to **scanf** in that it reads values according to a control string. But it has a pair of important differences: it also takes additional prompt strings as parameters, and it expects each of its input values to be on separate lines. Figure 16.5, for example, uses

```
getInput("sri",  "Name?",  name,
                 "Salary?",  &sal,
                 "Age?",  &age);
```

to prompt for and read a name, a salary, and an age. Unlike **scanf**, **getInput**'s control string is simply an array of one letter type indicators: **s** for strings, **r** for reals, and **i** for integers.

How does **getInput** work? The arguments following the control string are prompt-address pairs. For each pair, it needs to print the prompt and then read a value of the appropriate type into the corresponding address. The function begins by initializing a variable argument pointer to the argument following the control string.

```
va_start(argptr, control);
```

```
/*
 * Prototype and constants for getInput function.
 */
#define MAX_INPUT_LINE    80         /* Longest readable input line */

int getInput(const char *control, ...);
```

Figure 16.3 (getinp.h) The prototype for the **getInput** function.

```
/*
 * Get an input value using a formatting string.
 */
#include <stdio.h>
#include <stdarg.h>
#include <string.h>
#include "getinp.h"

int getInput(const char *control, ...)
{
  int getline(char *, int);

  va_list    argptr;                       /* argument pointer */
  const char *cptr = control;              /* next char in control */
  char       line[MAX_INPUT_LINE + 1];     /* next input line */

  va_start(argptr, control);
  for (; *cptr != '\0'; cptr++)
  {
    printf("%s ", va_arg(argptr, char *));
    if (getline(line, MAX_INPUT_LINE) == -1)
      break;
    switch(*cptr)
    {                                      /* assume successful reads here */
      case 's': strcpy(va_arg(argptr, char *), line);
                break;
      case 'r': sscanf(line, "%lf", va_arg(argptr, double *));
                break;
      case 'i': sscanf(line, "%i", va_arg(argptr, int *));
                break;
    }
  }
  va_end(argptr);
  return cptr - control;                   /* successful reads */
}
```

Figure 16.4 (getinp.c) Using variable numbers of arguments to help us obtain input in a clean way.

```
/*
 * Read an input value according to a provided formatting string.
 */
#include <stdio.h>
#include <stdlib.h>
#include "getinp.h"

int main()
{
  char    name[MAX_INPUT_LINE + 1];
  double  sal;
  int     age;

  getInput("sri", "Name?", name,
                  "Salary?", &sal,
                  "Age?", &age);
  printf("Name: %s\nSalary: %f\nAge: %i\n", name, sal, age);

  return EXIT_SUCCESS;
}
```

Figure 16.5   (useinp.c)   A program that shows how to use **getInput**.

It then processes the control string. For each character, it first obtains and prints the prompt.

```
printf("%s ", va_arg(argptr, char *));
```

Next, it reads the input line into an array **line**. Finally, it obtains the address where the value it read should go and places the value in that address. The address type differs depending on the next character in the control string, so we use a **switch** to decide how to store the value. For a **double**, we obtain the address and store the value with

```
sscanf(line, "%lf", va_arg(argptr, double *));
```

For an **int**, we do the same thing with

```
sscanf(line, "%i", va_arg(argptr, int *));
```

And for a string, we obtain the address and save the string with

```
strcpy(va_arg(argptr, char *), line);
```

Built-in Variable Argument Functions

C provides several library functions that can be passed an argument pointer, a variable of type **va_list**. Two of these are **vprintf** and **vscanf**, which are analogous to **printf** and **scanf**, respectively.

Figure 16.6 shows the function **debug**, a simple debugging aid that uses these functions. Figure 16.7 is a simple main program that shows how to use it. We call it with the name of the function, a formatting string, and a list of variables. It writes the word "DEBUGGING", the function's name, and the variables' values according to the formatting string.

```
DEBUGGING main: x=10, y=20
```

Using **debug** rather than **printf** when debugging helps us obtain consistent debugging output and separates debugging statements from those that produce normal program output.

We want **debug** to take a variable number of arguments, just like **printf** does. That's because we want it to be able to write different numbers of variables in different calls. In fact, **debug** is very similar to **printf**, except that it has an additional first argument, the function name.

```
void debug(const char *funcname, const char *format, ...)
```

debug uses **printf** to write "DEBUGGING" and the function's name. It then wants to write the variable names and values according to its **format** parameter—but it doesn't want to have to process the format parameter itself. That's a lot of work, and we really don't want to duplicate **printf**, deciphering the format string and processing the various arguments. Unfortunately, however, there's no way to pass **printf** a pointer to the remaining arguments.

That's where **vprintf** comes in. **vprintf** takes a formatting string and a pointer to a variable argument list and prints each of the variables in that list appropriately.

```
vprintf(const char *format, va_list argptr);
```

debug works by obtaining the argument pointer with **va_start** and then passing it to **vprintf**.

```
va_start(argptr, format);   /* get argument pointer */
vprintf(format, argptr);    /* print rest */
```

16.2   POINTERS TO FUNCTIONS

It would be nice to be able to pass functions as parameters. To see how we could use this ability, consider a program that maintains a table of structures containing an employee's number, name, phone number, and salary. We might want to search that table for an employee record with a particular employee number or name.

There are several ways to do these searches. One is to write a pair of search functions, **searchEmpNo** and **searchName**, each of which search the table. Figure 16.8 contains a sample declaration for the **Employee** type (as well as **typedefs** for pointers to both **Employee**'s and **const Employee**'s). Figure 16.9 contains the search functions, Figure 16.10 contains a table to search, and Figure 16.11 contains a main program that uses the search functions to search this table. The problem is that these functions duplicate code: they both have to traverse the array. The only difference

```
/*
 * Print function name and the values of various variables.
 */
#include <stdio.h>
#include <stdarg.h>

void debug(const char *funcname, const char *format, ...)
{
  va_list argptr;

  printf("DEBUGGING %s: ", funcname);
  va_start(argptr, format);
  vprintf(format, argptr);    /* print various arguments */
  va_end(argptr);
}
```

Figure 16.6   (debug.c) A debugging aid that makes use of the built-in variable argument functions.

```
/*
 * Illustrates using printf-like debugging function.
 */
#include <stdio.h>
#include <stdlib.h>

int main()
{
  void debug(const char *funcname, const char *format, ...);

  int x = 10, y = 20;

  debug("main", "x=%i, y=%i\n", x, y);

  return EXIT_SUCCESS;
}
```

Figure 16.7   (usedebug.c) An example using showing how to use **debug**.

between them is that one uses the **<** operator to compare an integer with the employee number field, whereas the other uses **strcmp** to compare a string with the name field. Everything else is identical.[3]

An alternate approach is to write a single search function, **searchEmpTable**, that can search the table for any field's value. We can then build **searchEmpNo** and

---

[3]Both functions treat the array they search as a constant to prevent accidentally changing its elements. But the pointer they return isn't a constant; that way their callers can use it to update the array. The problem is that we can't directly assign a pointer to a constant to a pointer to a non-constant, which forces us to use a cast.

```
/*
 * Definition of an employee record.  Differs from our earlier
 * Employee in that we now store a salary rather than an age.
 */
#include <stdio.h>
#include <stddef.h>

typedef struct
{
  long    number;
  char    *name;
  char    *phone;
  double salary;
} Employee, *PtrToEmployee;

typedef const Employee *PtrToConstEmployee;
```

Figure 16.8   (emp.h) Definition of an employee record.

```
/*
 * Employee table-searching functions.
 *    searchEmpNo - find matching employee by number.
 *    searchName - find matching employee by name.
 */
#include <string.h>
#include "emp.h"

PtrToEmployee searchEmpNo(PtrToConstEmployee ptr, int n, long target)
{
  const PtrToConstEmployee endptr = ptr + n;

  for (; ptr < endptr; ptr++)
    if (ptr->number == target)
      return (PtrToEmployee) ptr;
  return NULL;
}

PtrToEmployee searchName(PtrToConstEmployee ptr, int n, char *target)
{
  const PtrToConstEmployee endptr = ptr + n;

  for (; ptr < endptr; ptr++)
    if (strcmp(ptr->name, target) == 0)
      return (PtrToEmployee) ptr;
  return NULL;
}
```

Figure 16.9   (empsrch1.c) Simple-minded search functions.

```
/*
 * A standard array of structures to search through.
 */
#include <string.h>
#include <stdlib.h>
#include "emp.h"

Employee EmpTable[] =
    { {1001, "Daphne Borromeo",    "213-555-2134", 8.78},
      {1011, "Tammy Franklin",     "213-555-1212", 4.50},
      {1140, "Doris Perl",         "213-555-1215", 5.60},
      {2045, "Sally Hong",         "213-555-1219", 7.80},
      {2945, "Diane Goebel",       "213-555-1225", 9.00},
      {3300, "Irene Borromeo",     "213-555-1230", 3.97},
      {4011, "Veronica Ockert",    "213-555-1232", 4.50},
      {4140, "Tony Quilici",       "213-555-1235", 5.60},
      {5045, "Brian Hight",        "213-555-1239", 7.80},
      {5945, "Gisele Pham",        "213-555-1235", 9.00} };

const int EmpTableEntries = sizeof(EmpTable)/sizeof(EmpTable[0]);
```

Figure 16.10 (emptab.c) A sample table to search (ordered by employee number).

searchName on top of it. Doing so eliminates all the unnecessary duplication of code—now only **searchEmpTable** actually traverses the array. But how does this function know when it has found the desired table entry? We pass it a function to perform the comparison, and we replace the direct comparison with a call to this comparison function. So **searchEmpTable** executes this function once for each element in the table, stopping when the function returns an indication that we found a match.

This idea sounds great, but it has a problem: C doesn't let us pass functions as parameters or assign them to variables. But we can pass *pointers* to functions, which can be thought of as the address of the code executed when a function is called or as a pointer to a block of internal information about the function. Dereferencing a pointer to a function calls the function to which it points.

Before we show how to use pointers to functions to implement **searchEmpTable**, we need to know how to declare them, how to obtain them, and how to dereference them to call a function. To declare a pointer to a function, we specify the pointed-to function's return type and its parameters. For example, the declaration

type **(*funcptr)** *(parameter-list)***;**

declares **funcptr** as a pointer to a function that takes parameters of the types specified in *parameter-list* and returns *type*. We need the parentheses around ***funcptr**. Without them we would be declaring it as a function returning *type*, not a pointer to a function.[4]

---

[4]We agree this syntax is gross, but we're stuck with it. We devote a later chapter entirely to dealing with C's declaration syntax, but for now just memorize the form.

```
/*
 * Use standard search on an array of structures.
 */
#include <string.h>
#include <stdlib.h>
#include "emp.h"

int main()
{
  PtrToEmployee searchEmpNo(const Employee tab[], int n, long target);
  PtrToEmployee searchName(const Employee tab[], int n, char *target);

  extern Employee EmpTable[];
  extern const int EmpTableEntries;
  PtrToEmployee matchptr;

  /* Example search for a matching employee number */

  matchptr = searchEmpNo(EmpTable, EmpTableEntries, 1045);
  if (matchptr != NULL)
    printf("1045 is in record %i\n", matchptr - EmpTable);
  else
    printf("1045 wasn't found\n");

  /* Example search for a matching employee name */

  matchptr = searchName(EmpTable, EmpTableEntries, "Tony Quilici");
  if (matchptr != NULL)
    printf("Tony Quilici is in record %i\n", matchptr - EmpTable);
  else
    printf("Tony Quilici wasn't found.\n");

  return EXIT_SUCCESS;
}
```

Figure 16.11   (empmain.c) A main program using our searching functions.

How do we obtain a pointer to a function? You might guess that we simply apply the address operator (**&**) to it—but that's incorrect. Instead, we simply use the function name without following it with a parenthesized parameter list. For example, assuming the declaration

```
double (*funcptr)(double, double);
```

we can use the following assignment to make **funcptr** point to the math library function **pow**.

```
funcptr = pow;
```

Before we do this assignment, however, C must know that **pow** is a function and not a variable. That means we first need to provide a prototype for **pow**. Since **pow** is the math library, we can obtain its prototype simply by including math.h.

To call the function pointed to by **funcptr**, we simply dereference it as we would any other pointer, by following it with a list of parameters. After the previous assignment,

```
(*funcptr)(14.5, 0.5)
```

is equivalent to

```
pow(14.5, 0.5)
```

calling **pow** to compute $14.5^{0.5}$. The parentheses surrounding ***funcptr** are necessary to guarantee the correct order of evaluation.[5]

All we've seen so far is how pointers to functions provide us with a long-winded way of calling functions. But they're useful. Figure 16.12 contains new versions of our earlier search functions (**searchEmpNo** and **searchName**) that take advantage of them.

Our searching function, **searchEmpTable**, takes a collection of parameters. We have to pass it the array of **Employee**s we're searching, an **int** that holds the number of elements in the array, a pointer to the field value we're trying to find (the target), and a pointer to a comparison function (which we use to determine whether we've found the target). Its prototype seems complicated, especially its last two arguments.

```
PtrToEmployee
searchEmpTable(PtrToConstEmployee *ptr,
               int n, const void *tarptr,
               int (*fptr)(const void *,
                           PtrToConstEmployee));
```

Declaring these last two arguments is tricky. What type should the target be? It's hard to decide, since sometimes we search for a **long** and other times we search for a string. The way out of this dilemma is to to pass **searchEmpTable** a pointer to the target. Then we can make this pointer parameter a pointer to **void**, since that indicates a pointer to an unknown type. The final argument must be a pointer to the comparison function—but what are its parameters and what is its return value? When we call it, we need to pass it a pointer to the target and a pointer to the next table entry. That means it takes a pointer to a **void** and a pointer to an **Employee** (actually, a pointer to a **const Employee**). Its return value must indicate whether we found a matching **Employee**, which we can do by returning an **int**, with zero indicating a match.

We can use **searchEmpTable** to search the table for employee number 1045 with

```
i = 1045;
matchptr = searchEmpTable(EmpTable, EmpTableEntries,
                          &i, cmpEmpNo);
```

---

[5]Actually, there's a simpler form. We can call a function through a pointer by using the pointer in place of the function name, as in **funcptr(14.5,0.5)**. What happens in this case is that the compiler is kind enough to automatically stick in the necessary dereference for us. Although this concise form is considerably more convenient, for now we'll use the more wordy form, since it makes the pointer dereference explicit and serves as a reminder that we're dealing with pointers to functions.

```
/*
 * New versions of our search functions.
 *    searchEmpNo - find matching employee by number.
 *    cmpEmpNo - employee-number comparison function.
 *    searchName - find matching employee by name.
 *    cmpName - employee-name comparison function.
 *    searchEmpTable - actual function to search employee table.
 */
#include <string.h>
#include "emp.h"

static PtrToEmployee
searchEmpTable(PtrToConstEmployee ptr, int n, const void *tarptr,
               int (*funcptr)(const void *,
                                PtrToConstEmployee))
{
  PtrToConstEmployee endptr = ptr + n;

  for (; ptr < endptr; ptr++)
    if ((*funcptr)(tarptr, ptr) == 0)
      return (PtrToEmployee) ptr;
  return NULL;
}

static int cmpEmpNo(const void *tarptr, PtrToConstEmployee entryptr)
  { return * (long *) tarptr != entryptr->number; }

static int cmpName(const void *tarptr, PtrToConstEmployee entryptr)
  { return strcmp((char *) tarptr, entryptr->name); }

PtrToEmployee searchEmpNo(PtrToConstEmployee ptr, int n, long num)
  { return searchEmpTable(ptr, n, &num, cmpEmpNo); }

PtrToEmployee searchName(PtrToConstEmployee ptr, int n, char *name)
  { return searchEmpTable(ptr, n, name, cmpName); }
```

Figure 16.12 (empsrch2.c) New versions of our functions to search an array of employee structures.

This call is trickier than it first appears. We can't pass the target employee number directly because **searchEmpTable** expects a pointer. That means we have to place it in a variable and pass its address. And to pass the comparison function, we simply provide its name. We don't follow it with an argument list, since then we would be calling the function and passing its return value. But we do have to provide **cmpEmpNo**'s prototype before calling **searchEmpTable**. That way the compiler knows that it's a function and not an ordinary variable.

It's simpler to search the table for employee name "Tony Quilici".

```
matchptr = searchEmpTable(EmpTable, EmpTableEntries,
                          "Tony Quilici", cmpName);
```

That's because a string is already a pointer, so we don't need to do anything extra to pass it. As before, however, we don't follow the comparison function with any arguments, and we must first provide its prototype.

Actually, in our program we don't call **searchEmpTable** directly. Instead we build our earlier functions on top of it: **searchEmpNo** and **searchName** are simply appropriate calls to **searchEmpTable**.

We've seen how to use **searchEmpTable**, but what does it look like internally? It uses a pointer to traverse the array of **Employee**s and calls our comparison function once for each employee.

```
if ((*funcptr)(tarptr, ptr) == 0)   /* do comparison */
    return (PtrToEmployee) ptr;
```

This calls the function **funcptr** points to, passing it the pointers to the target (which is stored as a pointer to **void**) and to the next **Employee**. The comparison functions must cast the target pointer to an appropriate type before dereferencing it and doing the actual comparison. In **cmpEmpNo**, for example, we cast it to a pointer to a **long** before comparing what it points to against the structure's **number** field.

```
return * (long *) tarptr != entryptr->number;
```

And in **cmpName** we cast the target to a pointer to a **char** and then use **strcmp** to compare it with the **name** field of the structure.

```
return strcmp((char *) tarptr, entryptr->name);
```

This technique of passing pointers to functions hardly seems worth the effort. And for a simple example, like the one we've been discussing, it probably isn't. But imagine that we were using a more complex searching technique or sorting algorithm. Then using pointers to functions helps save us from duplicating a lot of complex code. In the next chapter we'll carry this technique even further to write functions that not only can search and sort based on the values of particular fields, but can actually search and sort any array, regardless of the underlying data type of its elements.

16.3   OLD-STYLE DECLARATIONS AND DEFINITIONS

So far, all our function calls have been preceded by a function prototype that specifies the number and types of its parameters and the type of its return value. These prototypes let the compiler perform extensive type checking and automatic conversions. The compiler can verify that we are calling the function with the correct number of arguments, that these arguments are of the right type, and that we are using the function's return value correctly. They also let the compiler automatically convert the types of the function's arguments to the types of its formal parameters, as well as do any appropriate arithmetic and assignment conversions on the function's return value.

But C hasn't always had function prototypes. They are a new feature of ANSI-C. Earlier versions of C didn't let us specify complete prototypes when declaring functions, only their return values. They also had a slightly different syntax for defining functions. This was problematic, since without complete prototypes the compiler couldn't do type

Aside 16.1a: Recursive Functions

Many algorithms and mathematical definitions are naturally described *recursively*, that is, partially in terms of themselves. One very simple example is the mathematical definition of a factorial. The factorial of n (written $n!$) is the product of all integers between 1 and n (assuming n is non-negative).

$$n! = \begin{cases} 1 & n = 0 \\ n \times (n-1)! & n > 0 \end{cases}$$

Some example factorials are $2! = 2$, $3! = 6$, $4! = 24$, and $5! = 120$.

Notice that to determine the factorial of any $n \geq 0$, we have to determine the factorial of $n - 1$. As with all recursive definitions, we have to know the function's value at one or more points. In this case, we know that $0!$ is 1.

Functions can call themselves recursively—which makes it easy to translate the mathematical definition of a factorial into the function **fact** that can compute a factorial. Aside 16.1b contains **fact**, along with a special version of it that prints additional information allowing us to trace the recursive calls. Aside 16.1c shows its output.

Aside 16.1d is another example of a recursive program. But this one isn't simply an implementation of some recursive formula. Instead, it produces the possible permutations of a string. Given **"alex"**, there are 24 permutations.

```
alex alxe aelx aexl axel axle
laex laxe leax lexa lxea lxae
elax elxa ealx eaxl exal exla
xlea xlae xela xeal xael xale
```

How do we generate these permutations? Our approach is easy to formulate recursively: *For each character in the string, exchange it with the string's first character and generate the permutations of the characters that remain.* We can implement this description in a function **permute** that takes two arguments: a string to permute, and a position within the string to start permuting. Initially, we call **permute** with

```
permute("alex", 0)
```

since we want to permute the whole string. Inside **permute** we exchange the first character with each of the subsequent characters and call permute to generate the permutations of the rest of the string. Our initial call to **permute** results in calls to **permute** with the strings **alex**, **laex**, **elax**, and **xlea**. But these calls to **permute** differ in that they start with a position of 1, rather than 0, and in that the calls they generate start with a position of 2. We print the string only when the position is past the string's end (in this case, 4), since there's nothing left to **permute** at that point.

There's one catch: when we pass a string to **permute**, we don't want **permute** to change it. But within **permute** we are actually exchanging characters in the string. If C passed arrays by value, we wouldn't have a problem. But it doesn't, so we're stuck simulating call by value. We do that by using **malloc** and **strcpy** to create a copy of the string that we then pass to **permute**, and we **free** this copy after the call to **permute**.

Recursion is a powerful technique you will encounter frequently.

Aside 16.1b (fact.c) A pair of functions that recursively compute $n!$.

```c
/*
 * Use factorial function to compute 4!.
 */
#include <stdio.h>
#include <stdlib.h>

int main()
{
  long fact(int n);                    /* compute factorial */
  long factTrace(int n);               /* provides tracing info */

  printf("%li\n", fact(4));            /* test it */
  printf("Here's a trace.\n");
  printf("%li\n", factTrace(4));       /* with trace */

  return EXIT_SUCCESS;
}

long fact(int n)                       /* compute N! for N >= 0 */
  { return (n <= 1) ? 1 : n * fact(n-1); }

long factTrace(int n)                  /* also output tracing info */
{
  long temp;

  printf("Computing %i factorial\n", n);
  temp = (n <= 1) ? 1 : n * factTrace(n-1);
  printf("Computed %i factorial = %li\n", n, temp);
  return temp;
}
```

Aside 16.1c: The program's output when run.

```
24
Here's a trace.
Computing 4 factorial
Computing 3 factorial
Computing 2 factorial
Computing 1 factorial
Computed 1 factorial = 1
Computed 2 factorial = 2
Computed 3 factorial = 6
Computed 4 factorial = 24
24
```

Aside 16.1d (permute.c) Λ program to produce permutations.

```
/*
 * Produce permutations, assuming sufficient memory.
 *    permute - generate all permuations of a string.
 *    swap - exchange two characters.
 */
#include <stdio.h>
#include <string.h>
#include <stdlib.h>

int Len;                                /* length of string to permute */

int main(int argc, char *argv[])
{
  void permute(const char *s, int pos);

  int i;

  for (i = 1; i < argc; i++)
  {
    Len = strlen(argv[i]);
    permute(argv[i], 0);
  }

  return EXIT_SUCCESS;
}

void permute(const char *s, int changepos)
{
  void swap(char *ptr1, char *ptr2);

  char *scopy;
  int  i;

  if (changepos < Len)
    for (i = changepos; i < Len; i++)
    {
      scopy = malloc(Len + 1);     /* assumes malloc succeeds */
      strcpy(scopy, s);
      swap(&scopy[i], &scopy[changepos]);
      permute(scopy, changepos + 1);
      free(scopy);
    }
  else
    printf("%s\n", s);
}

void swap(char *p, char *q)
{
  char temp;

  temp = *p;  *p = *q;  *q = temp;
}
```

checking or automatic conversions. Even so, ANSI-C allows these *old-style* declarations and definitions—after all, there was more than a decade of C development without prototypes. Ideally, all the programs we encounter will use complete prototypes, as in our examples, but they aren't required to do so. That makes it worth taking a look at how to use pre-ANSI functions and what happens when we mix both styles.

In an old-style function definition, we provide only the parameter names, and not their types. On subsequent lines we provide variable declarations for each of the parameters.

```
return-type func-name (name-1, name-2, ..., name-n)
  parm-decl-1;
  parm-decl-2;
    ...
  parm-decl-n;
{
  function-body
}
```

Figure 16.13 contains an old-style definition of **inRange**, a function that returns zero if its last argument doesn't fall between its first two. Here's its header:

```
int inRange(min, max, value)
double min, max, value;
```

ANSI-C's syntax is more compact (we need not list the parameter names and then provide declarations for them) but forces us to declare each parameter's type separately.

In an old-style function prototype, we provide the function's return type, its name, and parentheses, but we don't list the parameter types.

```
return-type func-name ( )
```

We need the parentheses, even if the function has no parameters, since they indicate that we are declaring a function, not just a variable. Figure 16.13 also contains an old-style prototype for **inRange**.

```
int inRange();
```

There's one final difference between the styles. In ANSI-C, when a function takes no parameters, we use **void** as the parameter list in both the function header and prototype. But in pre-ANSI-C, we simply leave the parameter list empty. In ANSI-C, such a declaration is taken to mean that we're providing no information about the function's parameters.[6]

Type-Checking Problems

When we use an old-style function prototype, we aren't supplying information about the types of the function's parameters. This means that there can be no assignment conversions of function arguments—the compiler has no idea what type the function

---

[6]By default, if we fail to provide any prototype at all, C assumes that we provided an old-style prototype declaring the function to return an **int** and providing no information about its parameters.

```
/*
 * A program to check if one value is between two others, using
 * old-style declarations.  But it doesn't work.
 */
#include <stdio.h>
#include <stdlib.h>

int main()
{
  int inRange();                                    /* old-style prototype */

  int v;                                            /* input value */

  printf("Enter a value: ");
  scanf("%i", &v);
  printf("%i is %s range!\n",
         v, inRange(1, 100, v) ? "in" : "out of");

  return EXIT_SUCCESS;
}

int inRange(min, max, value)
double min, max, value;                             /* old-style parameters */
  { return value >= min && value <= max; }
```

Figure 16.13   (inrange.c) An example of C's old-style declarations. This program doesn't work because **inRange**'s arguments aren't automatically converted.

expects. And it means that parameter passing works correctly only when there are no type mismatches—each argument must be the same type as its corresponding parameter. To avoid errors resulting from type mismatches, we must do any needed conversions ourselves.

> *With old-style declarations and definitions, type mismatches usually go undetected at compile time.*

The result is strange run-time behavior, not an informative compiler error message. Consider what happens when we call **inRange** as shown in Figure 16.13. Surprisingly, the "out of range" message is almost always printed, regardless of the value of **v** we pass to **inRange**. Why? Because **inRange** expects its parameters to be **double**s (usually 8 bytes in floating point representation) and instead receives **int**s (usually 2 or 4 bytes in two's complement representation):

```
inRange(1, 100, v)
```

As a result, on many machines, regardless of the values passed, **min** and **max** are always zero—clearly, not what we intended.

What does it take to fix this problem? We simply have to do the conversions ourselves. Here, we can correct things by making sure that all the arguments are **double**s:

```
inRange(1.0, 100.0, (double) v)
```

All floating point constants are **double**s, and the cast converts **v**'s value to a **double** before it is passed as a parameter.

Automatic Conversions

We don't really have to do *all* the conversions ourselves. When we don't supply a function prototype and we use old-style function definitions, C turns any **char** or **short** argument into an **int** and converts any **float** argument into a **double**. That means that we never need to declare **char**, **short**, or **float** parameters—we can declare them as **int** or **double** instead.

Figure 16.14 shows a new call to **inRange** that takes advantage of these conversions. Even though we don't bother to supply a prototype and even though **low**, **high**, and **v** are **float**s, the function call works correctly.

```
inRange(low, high, v)
```

That's because when we pass these values, they are converted automatically to **double**s.

These automatic conversions explain why **printf** has only a single formatting control code for printing real values. Effectively, **printf** is written in the old style, with an old-style function declaration. So when we pass a **float**, it's automatically converted to a **double**. That's also why we can use **%c** and **%i** to print **char**s, **short**s, and **int**s. The compiler is automatically converting these values to **int**s and using the formatting code to decide how to print them.

Do these conversions mean that we can't have **char**, **short**, or **float** parameters? After all, the automatic conversions guarantee that there's no way the value we pass is going to have one of these types. In fact, early C compilers allowed these parameter types, but quietly redeclared them. A **char** parameter, for example, became an **int**, with a cast inserted wherever it was used. If we use old-style declarations, we get the same behavior with ANSI-C compilers.

Prototypes versus Old-Style Declarations

Function prototypes help the compiler catch mismatches between numbers and types of parameters. Prototypes also have several other benefits: they help document a function's arguments, making programs that use them easier to read, and they may make programs run more efficiently, since they prevent automatic conversions of **float** arguments to **double** and of **char** arguments to **int**.

```
/*
 * Another version of our range-checking program that uses
 * old-style declarations.
 */
#include <stdio.h>
#include <stdlib.h>

int main()
{
  int inRange();                             /* old-style prototype */

  float v, low = 0.0, high = 100.0;

  printf("Enter a value: ");
  scanf("%f", &v);
  printf("%f is %s range!\n",
         v, inRange(low, high, v) ? "in" : "out of");

  return EXIT_SUCCESS;
}

int inRange(min, max, value)
double min, max, value;                      /* old-style parameters */
  { return value >= min && value <= max; }
```

Figure 16.14 (inrange2.c) Another call of **inRange** with a parameter type mismatch. This program works correctly because of automatic type promotion.

But there is one big problem with function prototypes: What do we do if we have to port programs written with them to older, pre-ANSI compilers that don't allow them?[7] It is easy to remove all of the prototypes—but it is much more difficult to find all the places where successful parameter passing relies on the automatic conversions that prototypes make possible. When a program has to work with less sophisticated compilers, use explicit casts to ensure that the types of parameters match the function definition.

16.4   CASE STUDY—BINARY SEARCH

This section is optional!

The simplest way to search a table—and the approach we've been taking so far—is *sequential search*: we compare the value we're searching for with each table entry until we've found a match or looked through the entire table. The average successful search examines about half the table's elements—but an unsuccessful search examines them all. Although this method is reasonable for searching small, unordered tables, for large, *sorted* tables we can do much better. Binary search is a much faster (indeed,

---

[7]The general topic of portability—moving programs from machine to machine—is an important one we explore in great depth in Chapter 21. In particular, we'll see how to minimize the problems inherent in moving programs from compilers that support function prototypes to those that don't.

Aside 16.2a: Function Declarations And Portability

Old-style declarations and sloppy programming can lead to all sorts of problems, including programs that work on one machine but fail on another.

Consider the version of **inRange** shown and invoked in Aside 16.2b. This version expects **long** arguments. On 32-bit machines, **int** and **long** are usually the same size (32 bits), and the code works as expected. But we get strange results on machines where **int** is one word and **long** is two. How can we make this program work correctly on all machines? Simply use **long** constants or cast the arguments appropriately:

```
inRange(1L, 100L, (long) v)
```

Another problem happens when we mix declaration styles. There are two different situations to worry about. The first is *failing to provide a prototype*. In Aside 16.2c, we provide an old-style prototype and a ANSI-C definition. There, we're calling **inRange** with three **float** arguments. Since we defined **inRange** to take three **float**s, there shouldn't be a problem, right? Wrong. Because we didn't provide a prototype before the call to **inRange**, C automatically converts the **float**s to **double**s. But because we used an ANSI-C definition, the function expects **float**s, not **double**s, and we get anomalous results. On typical machines, three 64-bit quantities are passed but three 32-bit values are expected within the function. (Strictly speaking, the result is undefined, which means you've done something questionable the C compiler isn't required to catch. Some compilers will catch this error, but not if the function and prototype are placed in separate files.)

The other case is *supplying a prototype with an old-style header*. Aside 16.2d shows another version of **inRange** where we provide a complete prototype but use an old-style function definition. In that case, since we provide a full prototype, when we call **inRange**, C will pass **float**s. But since we declare **inRange** using the old style, the function expects to be passed **double**s, which it will then convert to **float**s—not at all the behavior we want.

In general, avoid mixing styles!

---

optimal) algorithm for searching sorted tables, which happens to be easily expressed by a recursive algorithm.

In binary search, we start by comparing the target value with the table's middle element. The table is sorted, so if the target is larger, we can ignore all values smaller than the middle element and apply binary search recursively to the table's upper half. Similarly, if the target is smaller, we apply binary search recursively to the table's lower half. We stop when we've found the target (it's equal to the middle element) or there are no values left to search.

Figure 16.15 and Figure 16.16 illustrate successful and unsuccessful binary searches on the same seven-element table.

Binary search is significantly faster than sequential search. Every time we compare the target to a table element, we no longer have to consider half of the remaining values.

Aside 16.2b (Inrange3.c) A non-portable version of our range-checking function.

```
/*
 * A non-portable version of our range-checking program.
 */
#include <stdio.h>
#include <stdlib.h>

int main()
{
  int inRange();                            /* old-style prototype */

  int v;

  printf("Enter a value: ");
  scanf("%i", &v);
  printf("%i is %s range!\n",
         v, inRange(1, 100, v) ? "in" : "out of");

  return EXIT_SUCCESS;
}

int inRange(min, max, value)
long min, max, value;                       /* old-style parameters */
  { return value >= min && value <= max; }
```

Aside 16.2c (inrange4.c) Incorrectly mixing styles by failing to use the correct prototype.

```
/*
 * A version of our range-checking program that doesn't work at all.
 */
#include <stdio.h>
#include <stdlib.h>

int main()
{
  float v, low = 1.0, high = 100.0;

  printf("Enter a value: ");
  scanf("%f", &v);
  printf("%f is %s range!\n",
         v, inRange(low, high, v) ? "in" : "out of");

  return EXIT_SUCCESS;
}

int inRange(float min, float max, float value)
  { return value >= min && value <= max; }
```

Aside 16.2d (inrange5.c) Incorrectly mixing styles where the compiler catches the error.

```
/*
 * Another version of our range-checking program that doesn't work.
 * We incorrectly provide a prototype for inRange but define it
 * using an old-style definition.
 */
#include <stdio.h>
#include <stdlib.h>

int main()
{
  int inRange(float min, float max, float value);

  float v, low = 1.0, high = 100.0;

  printf("Enter a value: ");
  scanf("%f", &v);
  printf("%f is %s range!\n",
         v, inRange(low, high, v) ? "in" : "out of");

  return EXIT_SUCCESS;
}

int inRange(min, max, value)
float min, max, value;                          /* old-style parameters */
  { return value >= min && value <= max; }
```

Roughly, its execution time is proportional to $\log_2 n$, where n is the number of values in the table.

We implement binary search in **binarySearch**, shown in Figure 16.17, along with a program that uses it to search a sorted table of **int**s. We pass it the target value and pointers to the table's first and last elements. It returns a pointer to the matching table element or the null pointer if no such element is found.

When we call **binarySearch**, it first calculates the address of the middle element in the unsearched portion of the table (the whole table when it is first called). Because we can't add or divide pointers, we calculate the midpoint with

```
midptr = minptr + (maxptr - minptr) / 2;
```

instead of adding the two pointers together and dividing by two. After we find the midpoint, the first thing we do is check whether the search has succeeded or failed. To do so, we compare the value pointed to by **midptr** with the target. If they're equal, we have found it, so we return **midptr**. Otherwise, we check whether the pointers are pointing to the same element. This happens only when there is one element left to search and that element isn't the target. It means the search has failed, so we return the **NULL** pointer. Otherwise, we know that there are unexamined table elements, so we recursively apply **binarySearch** to the appropriate section of the table.

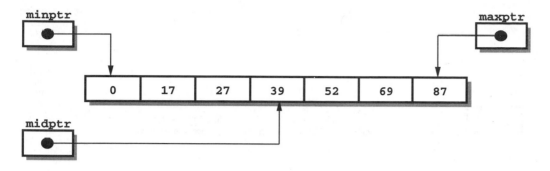

(a) At start, 39 is less than 69, so search top half of table.

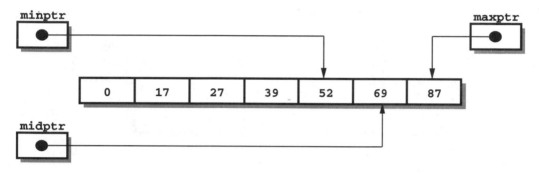

(b) After calling **binarySearch** once, found it.

Figure 16.15 A successful binary search for the value 69.

With every recursive call to **binarySearch**, the pointers **minptr** and **maxptr** move toward each other. The search and recursive calls terminate when the pointers merge or the target value is found.

We can write functions such as **fact** and **binarySearch** more efficiently iteratively than recursively. But using recursion often makes our functions more compact or makes them more closely reflect an algorithm or mathematical definition. Recursion is a powerful technique well worth the trouble of mastering.

SUMMARY

- We can write functions with variable numbers of arguments using the stdargs package. To do so, we include the header file stdarg.h.

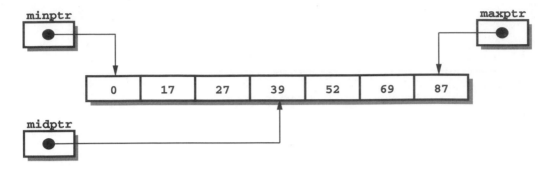

(*a*) At start, 39 is greater than 28, so search lower half of table.

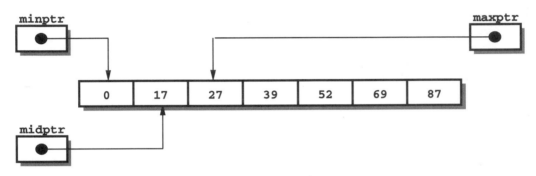

(*b*) After calling **binarySearch** once, 28 greater than 17.

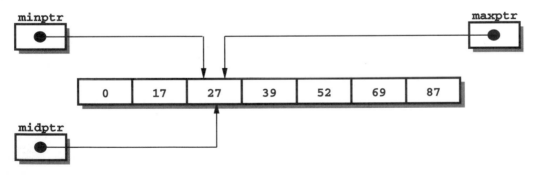

(*c*) Call **binarySearch** again; 28 not equal to 27, so we stop.

Figure 16.16 An unsuccessful binary search for the value 28.

```c
/*
 * Program using binary search for values given to it as arguments.
 */
#include <stdio.h>
#include <stdlib.h>
#include <stddef.h>

#define MAX     100

int main(int argc, char *argv[])
{
  long *binarySearch(const long *min, const long *max, long t);

  long table[MAX];                  /* table to search */
  long t;                           /* target */
  long *fndptr;                     /* pointer to item in array */
  int i;                            /* array index */

  for (i = 0; i < MAX; i++)         /* initialize table with */
    table[i] = i;                   /*    0,1,2,3,... */

  for (i = 1; i < argc; i++)
   if (sscanf(argv[i], "%li", &t) == 1)
   {
     fndptr = binarySearch(&table[0], &table[MAX - 1], t);
     if (fndptr != NULL)
       printf("Found %li as element %i.\n", t, fndptr - table);
     else
       printf("Didn't find %li.\n", t);
   }

  return EXIT_SUCCESS;
}

/* Use binary search to search a table of longs */

long *binarySearch(const long *minptr, const long *maxptr, long target)
{
  const long *midptr = minptr + (maxptr - minptr) / 2;

  if (target == *midptr)            /* middle is target? */
    return (long *) midptr;
  if (maxptr <= minptr)             /* value's not in table? */
    return NULL;

  return (target < *midptr)         /* search correct half */
           ? binarySearch(minptr, midptr - 1, target)
           : binarySearch(midptr + 1, maxptr, target);
}
```

Figure 16.17   (binsrch.c)   A binary search function and a program using it.

- We are allowed to have pointers to functions. We use pointers to functions when we want to pass functions as parameters.

- We can write generic functions by using pointers to functions. These generic functions save us repeating the same code over and over when all that's really different is the type of data we're manipulating.

- We're allowed to have recursive functions—functions that call themselves.

- ANSI-C actually provides two styles for function declarations and definitions. The older style doesn't provide automatic type checking or conversions and is provided for backward compatibility.

EXERCISES

Explore

16–1 Compile and run the programs in this chapter.

16–2 Binary search has considerable overhead in calculating the midpoint. In fact, binary search is often slower than sequential search when searching small tables. Determine the point on your system where both searches take the same amount of time. Then write a single function that always uses the best search method.

Modify

16–3 Rewrite the binary search function (Figure 16.17) nonrecursively. Watch out! It's messier than it seems.

16–4 Rewrite the binary search function (Figure 16.17) using array subscripting rather than pointers. Which version is more compact? Which version is more readable?

Extend

16–5 Modify **getInput** (Figure 16.4) to do error checking on its input values.

16–6 Extend **permute** (Aside 16.1d) into a new function **tracePermute** that traces all of its calls (in the same way we extended **fact** into **traceFact** to trace its calls).

Code

16–7 Write a function, **searchPhone**, that searches for the first employee with a particular phone number. Build it on top of **searchEmpTable**.

16–8 Write **min**, a variable argument function that returns its smallest argument.

16–9 Write **insert**, a function that takes a sorted **int** array, the number of elements in the array, and a variable number of values and then inserts each of these values into their correct place in the array.

16–10 Write **delete**, a function that takes an **int** array, the number of elements in the array, and a variable number of values and deletes all instances of each of these values from the array.

16–11 Write **search**, a variable argument function that searches an array for the first occurrence of any one of a list of arguments. It returns a pointer to the desired element's position in the table or **NULL** if no such element can be found. Its header is

```
int *search(int table[], int argcnt, ...);
```

16–12 Write **count**, which is similar to the **search** function in the previous exercise, except that it returns a count of all instances of the arguments it finds in the provided table.

16–13 The Fibonacci numbers are a famous mathematical sequence that can be defined recursively. For non-negative integers:

$$fib(n) = \begin{cases} 0 & n = 0 \\ 1 & n = 1 \\ fib(n-1) + fib(n-2) & n \geq 2 \end{cases}$$

The first 10 Fibonacci numbers are 0, 1, 1, 2, 3, 5, 8, 13, 21, and 34. Write recursive and iterative functions to compute the nth Fibonacci number and print the 20th number in this sequence. Which version is faster?

Build   **16–14** Write **sumTables**, a variable argument function that returns the sum of a variable number of integer arrays. The function takes two fixed arguments, the number of arrays it should sum and the size of these arrays (we are assuming that all of these arrays are the same size). Its other arguments are then the set of arrays to sum. Assuming that **a**, **b**, and **c** are three **int** arrays containing 10 elements each, we could then use

```
total = sumTables(3, 10, a, b, c);
```

to place the sum of all their elements in **total**.

Extend the **sumTables** function to work with arrays of varying sizes. This requires that the function also be passed the size of each of the arrays.

16–15 Implement Quicksort, a famous recursive sorting algorithm. The idea underlying Quicksort is to sort an array by partitioning the array into two parts, then using the algorithm to recursively sort each of the parts. Quicksort does the partitioning by first picking an array element, **a[m]** (called the *pivot*), which can be any element, such as the first or last element in the array. Then Quicksort uses a pair of indices, one starting on the left and the other on the right, and moves them toward each other by finding the first value less than the pivot (on the left) and the first value greater than the pivot (on the right), exchanging these values, and then continuing on until the indices cross. Finally, Quicksort exchanges the pivot with the value to the right of the crossing point and recursively sorts the partitions less than and greater than the pivot.

16–16 Write a function, **genTable**, to generate a table of x, y points by evaluating another function over a range of x values. **genTable** is passed a pointer to the function to plot, the starting and ending x values, the number of points to plot, and two arrays for the x and y values. For example, we can generate 1000 values of the **sin** function between 0 and 1 radians with

```
genTable(sin, 0, 1, 1000, x, y);
```

Use **getTable** to write a function plotter that generates an array of points, then scales it and actually plots the points.

17   GENERIC
FUNCTIONS

This chapter discusses generic functions: functions that can perform a particular task on any arbitrary C data type. We introduce the built-in generic library functions for searching and sorting arrays and use them to search and sort arrays of integers, arrays of strings, and arrays of structures. We then implement our own generic functions for performing sequential search and insertion sort and show how to build a nice interface on top of them for searching and sorting specific types. The chapter concludes with a case study—an implementation of the standard library's binary search function.

17.1   GENERIC LIBRARY FUNCTIONS

A generic function is one that can perform a particular task on any underlying C data type. Generic functions are a powerful and convenient way to build programs, as they allow us to easily reuse entire algorithms by adding a small amount of type-specific code.

C's standard library provides two of these functions: **bsearch** searches an arbitrary array using the binary search technique we presented in Chapter 16, and **qsort** sorts an arbitrary array using a special sorting technique called *Quicksort*. By arbitrary array, we mean an array with any type of element. We can use these functions to search and sort an array of integers, an array of strings, or even an array of structures. To use these functions, we need to include their prototypes, which are found in the system header file stdlib.h.

The bsearch Library Function

In Chapter 16 we wrote our own binary search routine, **binarySearch**. It took three arguments: pointers to the first and last **long**s in the array, and a **long** to try to find. The problem with **binarySearch** is that we can only use it to search a sorted array of **long**s. It's littered with dependencies on **long**s: it takes pointers to **long**s to delineate the array it's searching, it's passed a **long** to look for, it uses the less than and equality operators to compare **long**s, and it returns a pointer to a **long**. The library's **bsearch** function eliminates this restriction, but at a cost: we now have to provide it additional information about the array we want to search. Specifically, we must also

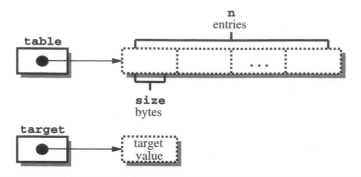

Figure 17.1 The relationship between **bsearch**'s parameters.

pass it the size of an array element and a function to use to determine whether it has found the desired array element. Here's **bsearch**'s prototype:

```
void *bsearch(const void *target,
              const void *table,
              size_t n,
              size_t size,
              int (*cmpfp)(const void *, const void *));
```

bsearch takes five arguments. The first, **target**, is a pointer to the value we're searching for. It's a pointer to **void** because **bsearch** doesn't care at all about the type of object it's trying to find—it could be an **int**, a string, a structure, and so on. As we saw earlier, we use a pointer to **void** to point to an object of unknown type. The target pointer is a **const** because we're not changing its value within the function.

The next three arguments—**table**, **n**, and **size**—describe the array we're searching. **table** is a pointer to the first element in that array. It's a **const** pointer to **void** for the same reasons as **target**: in general, **bsearch** doesn't know what sort of array it's going to be searching. **n** is an **int**, the number of elements in the array. **size** is the size of an array element. We provide this size because **bsearch** uses pointer arithmetic to traverse the array, and it must figure out where each array element begins and ends. Figure 17.1 shows the relationship among all of these parameters.

The final argument, **cmpfp**, is a pointer to a function that **bsearch** uses to determine whether a particular array element matches the target. **bsearch** calls this function each time it examines an array element, passing it a pair of pointers: the first points to the target, the second to the array element it's examining. **bsearch** has no idea what types they actually point to, only how large the objects are, so it passes these as pointers to **void**. That means the comparison function must take a pair of pointers to **void**. **bsearch** expects it to return a negative value if the first pointed-to thing is smaller than the second, zero if they are equal, and a positive value if the first is larger than the second.

bsearch returns a pointer to the matching array element if it finds the value, or **NULL** otherwise. Once again, this pointer is a pointer to **void**.

Figure 17.2 uses **bsearch** to search an array of **long**s, using the call:

```
ptr = bsearch(&t, longTable, MAX,
                    sizeof(longTable[0]), cmpLong);
```

t is a pointer to the target, **longTable** is the table of **long**s we're searching, **MAX** is the number of elements in that table, **sizeof(longTable[0])** is the size of an element, and **cmpLong** is the function we use to compare the target value with an array element. We precede the call to **bsearch** with a prototype for **cmpLong**, so the compiler knows that it's the name of a function and not a variable.

The tricky part is writing the comparison function, **cmpLong**, shown in Figure 17.3. It's passed two pointers to **void**, so it must cast them to pointers to **long** before following them and comparing the values to which they point.

```
target = * (long *) target_ptr;
```

Taking this statement apart, we see that it converts **target_ptr**'s value to a pointer to a **long** and then follows it. It does the same for the other pointer parameter

```
table_entry = * (long *) table_entry_ptr;
```

and finally compares the two **long**s and returns the result.

The nice feature of generic functions like **bsearch** is that we need write only new comparison functions to use it with different data types. Figure 17.4 uses **bsearch** to search an array of strings for a particular string. It's very similar to our previous program, except that now we're using **cmpString**, shown in Figure 17.5, as the comparison function. As with **cmpLong**, it must cast the passed pointers before doing the actual comparison. This time, however, it's comparing strings so it uses the built-in function **strcmp**, instead of the < operator.

```
return strcmp(target, table_entry);
```

This call is straightforward. What's tricky is taking the pointers given to **cmpString** and turning them into the pointers that **strcmp** expects. **cmpString**'s first parameter is actually a pointer to the first character in the target string. Its second parameter is a pointer to an element in the array of strings, and since each element in the array is a pointer to a string, that means it's really a pointer to a pointer to a **char**. Figure 17.6 provides a picture of all of these pointers.

Figures 17.7 and 17.8 provide one final example of **bsearch** in a new implementation of Chapter 16's program to search an array of employees (that assumes the existence of the same employee table that program used). Now, to search by employee number we use **bsearch**, rather than our earlier function **searchEmpNo**.

```
ptr = bsearch(&target, EmpTable, EmpTableEntries,
                  sizeof(EmpTable[0]), cmpEmpNo);
```

This call to **bsearch** is almost identical to the other two. Again, the only real difference lies in the comparison function, **cmpEmpNo**, which casts the pointers appropriately and

```
/*
 * Use generic binary search to search a table of longs.
 */
#include <stdio.h>
#include <stdlib.h>

#define MAX     100

int main(int argc, char *argv[])
{
  int cmpLong(const void *target_ptr, const void *table_entry_ptr);

  long longTable[MAX];                  /* array to search */
  long *ptr;                            /* ptr to found item */
  int  i;                               /* temporary index */
  long t;                               /* target */

  for (i = 0; i < MAX; i++)             /* initialize table with */
    longTable[i] = i;                   /*    0,1,2,3,... */

  for (i = 1; i < argc; i++)            /* are arguments in table? */
    if (sscanf(argv[i], "%li", &t) == 1)
    {
      ptr = bsearch(&t, longTable, MAX,
                        sizeof(longTable[0]), cmpLong);
      if (ptr != NULL)
        printf("Found %li as element %i.\n", t, ptr - longTable);
      else
        printf("Didn't find %li.\n", t);
    }

  return EXIT_SUCCESS;
}
```

Figure 17.2   (lbsearch.c)   A program using **bsearch** to search an array of **long**s.

then compares the target employee number with the **number** field in the structure.

```
return * (long *) target_ptr -
           ((PtrToEmployee) table_entry_ptr)->number;
```

There's one caveat to using **bsearch**: it assumes that the array it's searching is sorted. Our example assumes that the table is ordered, ascending by employee number. That's fine, since we set it up that way. But more realistically we would need to sort the table on whatever field we were looking up. The next section describes a generic sorting function we can use to do just that.

*Use **bsearch** only to search sorted arrays.*

```
/*
 * Compare pointer to target long with pointer to next long in table.
 */
int cmpLong(const void *target_ptr, const void *table_entry_ptr)
{
  long target = * (long *) target_ptr;
  long table_entry = * (long *) table_entry_ptr;

  return (target == table_entry) ? 0
                               : ((target < table_entry) ? -1 : 1);
}
```

Figure 17.3 (cmplong.c) The comparison function provided to **bsearch** to search an array of **long**s.

```
/*
 * Uses generic binary search to search an array of strings.
 */
#include <stdio.h>
#include <stdlib.h>

int main(int argc, char *argv[])
{
  int cmpString(const void *target_ptr, const void *table_entry_ptr);

  const char *stringTable[] =
        {"alex",  "daphne", "doris", "gisele", "irene",
         "sally", "tammy", "tony", "veronica", "vivian"};
  const int n  = sizeof(stringTable)/sizeof(stringTable[0]);

  const char  **ptr;                         /* pointer to found item */
  int    i;

  for (i = 1; i < argc; i++)
  {
    ptr = bsearch(argv[i], stringTable, n,
                        sizeof(stringTable[0]), cmpString);
    if (ptr != NULL)
      printf("Found %s in position %i\n", argv[i], ptr - stringTable);
    else
      printf("Couldn't find %s in table\n", argv[i]);
  }

  return EXIT_SUCCESS;
}
```

Figure 17.4 (sbsearch.c) Using **bsearch** to search an array of strings.

```
/*
 * Compare pointer to target string with pointer to next string
 * in table.
 */
#include <string.h>

int cmpString(const void *target_ptr, const void *table_entry_ptr)
{
  char *target = (char *) target_ptr;
  char *table_entry = * (char **) table_entry_ptr;

  return strcmp(target, table_entry);
}
```

Figure 17.5   (cmpstr.c) The comparison function we pass to **bsearch** to search an array of strings.

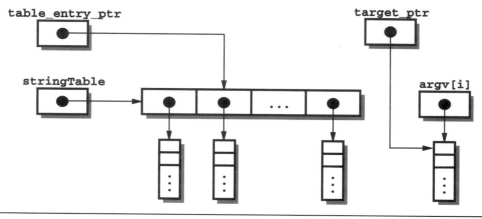

Figure 17.6   The pointers **bsearch** is passing to **cmpString**.

The qsort Library Function

Sorting is ubiquitous in programming. Often we end up writing our own sort routines by rewriting routines written to handle different data types. When the items to be sorted are contained in an array, however, we can use the standard library's generic sorting routine: **qsort**.

```
void qsort(void *table,
           size_t n,
           size_t size,
           int (*cmpfp)(const void *, const void *));
```

```
/*
 * Using bsearch to search an array of structures.
 */
#include <stdio.h>
#include <stdlib.h>
#include "emp.h"

int main(int argc, char *argv[])
{
  int cmpEmpNo(const void *target_ptr, const void *table_entry_ptr);

  extern Employee   EmpTable[];
  extern const int  EmpTableEntries;
  int               i;                /* index into values to search */
  long              target;           /* value we're trying to find */
  PtrToEmployee     ptr;              /* pointer to found item */

  for (i = 1; i < argc; i++)
    if (sscanf(argv[i],"%li",&target) == 1)
    {
      ptr = bsearch(&target, EmpTable, EmpTableEntries,
                  sizeof(EmpTable[0]), cmpEmpNo);
      if (ptr != NULL)
        printf("%li is in record %i\n", target, ptr - EmpTable);
      else
        printf("%li wasn't found\n", target);
    }

  return EXIT_SUCCESS;
}
```

Figure 17.7 (ebsearch.c) Using **bsearch** to search a table of **Employee** structures.

```
/*
 * Comparison function for employee numbers.
 */
#include "emp.h"

int cmpEmpNo(const void *target_ptr, const void *table_entry_ptr)
{
  return * (long *) target_ptr -
         ((PtrToEmployee) table_entry_ptr)->number;
}
```

Figure 17.8 (cmpempno.c) The comparison function we pass to **bsearch** to search an array of **Employee** structures.

```
/*
 * Using Quicksort to sort both an array of longs and an array of
 * character strings.
 */
#include <stdlib.h>
#include "testtabs.h"        /* tables to sort, printing functions */

int main()
{
  int cmpLongs(const void *table_entry_ptr1,
               const void *table_entry_ptr2);
  int cmpStrings(const void *table_entry_ptr1,
                 const void *table_entry_ptr2);

  /* Use qsort to sort a table of longs */

  qsort(LongTable,
        LongTableEntries,
        sizeof(LongTable[0]),
        cmpLongs);

  printLongTable(LongTable, LongTableEntries);

  /* Use qsort to sort a table of strings */

  qsort(StringTable,
        StringTableEntries,
        sizeof(StringTable[0]),
        cmpStrings);

  printStringTable(StringTable, StringTableEntries);

  return EXIT_SUCCESS;
}
```

Figure 17.9   (qsort1.c) Using **qsort** to sort an array of **long**s and an array of character strings.

qsort is similar to **bsearch**. It takes four parameters. The first, **table**, is the address of the first element in the array to sort. **qsort** can sort arrays of any type, so **table** is a pointer to **void**. The second, **n**, is the number of items to sort. The third, **size**, is the size of each item in bytes. The last, **cmpfp**, is a pointer to a comparison function. But this time the comparison function is passed pointers to different array elements, rather than pointers to a target and an array element. It returns the same values as before.

Figure 17.9 shows how to use **qsort** to sort an array of **long**s and an array of character strings. Figure 17.10 contains the necessary comparison functions. Figure 17.11 contains several tables to sort and functions to print these tables. Finally, Figure 17.12 contains external declarations for these tables and functions.

```
/*
 * Comparison function for sorting strings and longs.
 */
#include <string.h>

int cmpLongs(const void *table_entry_ptr1,
             const void *table_entry_ptr2)
{
  long x = * (long *) table_entry_ptr1;
  long y = * (long *) table_entry_ptr2;

  return (x == y) ? 0 : ((x < y) ? -1 : 1);
}

int cmpStrings(const void *table_entry_ptr1,
               const void *table_entry_ptr2)
{
  return strcmp(* (char **) table_entry_ptr1,
                * (char **) table_entry_ptr2);
}
```

Figure 17.10 (qcmps.c) The comparison functions we use with **qsort** to sort arrays of **long**s and arrays of character strings.

To sort **long**s, we could use the same comparison function, **cmpLong**, we used with **bsearch**. That's because we originally wrote it to take a pair of addresses: the address of a table entry and the address of the target **long**. However, our previous parameter-naming scheme (**target** and **table_entry_ptr**) is no longer applicable, since both pointers are now pointers to table entries. So we've rewritten the function with a new name, **cmpLongs**, and more appropriate parameter names.

To sort an array of character strings, however, we use a new comparison function, **cmpStrings**. We can't use our earlier **cmpString** function because it expects to be passed a pointer to a target string and a pointer to an element. **qsort**, however, passes pointers to a pair of array elements.

Figure 17.13 provides one last example of **qsort**, using it to sort our employee records first by phone number and then by employee's first name. Figure 17.14 shows the two new comparison functions, **cmpPhone** and **cmpName**, that it uses. Both cast the two pointers they're passed to pointers to **Employee**s (**PtrToEmployee**) before using **strcmp** to compare their **phone** and **name** fields, respectively.

Coding the comparison functions and getting all of the casts right may seem somewhat difficult—but it is much, much easier than writing Quicksort ourselves.[1]

---

[1] Actually, we haven't been getting the casts exactly right. Within the comparison functions, we should be casting to pointers to constants! To keep things simple, however, all our comparison functions ignore that issue.

```
/*
 * Tables and helper functions to support demonstrating our
 * various generic functions.
 */
#include <stdio.h>
#include <stddef.h>
#include <stdlib.h>
#include "testtabs.h"

long LongTable[] =
    { 17, 10, 89, 26, 30, 99, 78, 11, 91, 16,
      87, 45, 78, 11, 45, 98, 67, 20, 60, 8 };
const int LongTableEntries =
            sizeof(LongTable)/sizeof(LongTable[0]);

char *StringTable[] =
    { "sally", "tammy", "veronica", "daphne", "vivian",
      "tony", "alex", "doris", "irene", "gisele" };
const int StringTableEntries =
            sizeof(StringTable)/sizeof(StringTable[0]);

void printLongTable(long t[], int n)
{
  int i;

  for (i = 0; i < n; i++)
    printf("%li\n", t[i]);
}

void printStringTable(char *t[], int n)
{
  int i;

  for (i = 0; i < n; i++)
    printf("%s\n", t[i]);
}
```

Figure 17.11 (testtabs.c) Some tables with which we can test **qsort** and some functions to print those tables.

17.2   WRITING GENERIC FUNCTIONS

So just how are generic function like **bsearch** and **qsort** written? We'll illustrate by writing our own generic searching and sorting functions. Our functions, however, aren't going to be as elaborate or efficient as their library equivalents. That's because we search the array using sequential search and sort the array using insertion sort. These algorithms aren't as good as the ones used by the library routines; we picked them solely because their implementation is easier to understand.

```
/*
 * Externals for tables and prototypes for helper functions.
 */
extern long LongTable[];
extern const int LongTableEntries;
extern char *StringTable[];
extern const int StringTableEntries;

void printLongTable(long t[], int n);
void printStringTable(char *t[], int n);
```

Figure 17.12 (testtabs.h) External declarations for our testing tables and the functions to print them.

```
/*
 * Using qsort to sort an array of structures.
 */
#include <stdio.h>
#include <stdlib.h>
#include "emp.h"

int main()
{
  int cmpPhone(const void *table_entry_ptr1,
               const void *table_entry_ptr2);
  int cmpName(const void *table_entry_ptr1,
              const void *table_entry_ptr2);

  extern Employee  EmpTable[];
  extern const int EmpTableEntries;
  int i;

  qsort(EmpTable, EmpTableEntries, sizeof(EmpTable[0]), cmpPhone);
  for (i = 0; i < EmpTableEntries; i++)
    printf("%s, %s\n", EmpTable[i].name, EmpTable[i].phone);

  qsort(EmpTable, EmpTableEntries, sizeof(EmpTable[0]), cmpName);
  for (i = 0; i < EmpTableEntries; i++)
    printf("%s, %li\n", EmpTable[i].name, EmpTable[i].number);

  return EXIT_SUCCESS;
}
```

Figure 17.13 (qsort2.c) Using **qsort** to sort an array of **Employee** structures.

```
/*
 * Comparison functions for sorting the employee table.
 */
#include <string.h>
#include "emp.h"

int cmpPhone(const void *table_entry_ptr1,
             const void *table_entry_ptr2)
{
  return strcmp(((PtrToEmployee) table_entry_ptr1)->phone,
                ((PtrToEmployee) table_entry_ptr2)->phone);
}

int cmpName(const void *table_entry_ptr1,
            const void *table_entry_ptr2)
{
  return strcmp(((PtrToEmployee) table_entry_ptr1)->name,
                ((PtrToEmployee) table_entry_ptr2)->name);
}
```

Figure 17.14   (qcmps2.c) The comparison functions for sorting an array of **Employee** structures.

Implementing a Generic Sequential Search

To write our generic sequential search, we'll write a sequential search for **long**s and gradually generalize it. Figure 17.15 contains that function: **longSearch**. It also contains a main program that shows how to use **lon␣Search**. **longSearch** works by running a pointer through the array, comparing the target with what the pointer points to, and stopping when they're equal.

Figure 17.16 contains our generic sequential search function: **search**. It takes the same set of arguments as **bsearch**; the only difference is the algorithm it uses for the search.

The key to turning **longSearch** into **search** is to generalize all the places in **longSearch** that count on its being passed an array of **long**s.

First, we now don't know the type of array we're passed. That means the pointer to the array's starting element must now be a pointer to **void**, and we need an additional parameter that says how big each array element is.

Second, we now have to treat the array as a large sequence of bytes. That means we need to use pointers to **char** to traverse the array rather than pointers to **long**. We make **ptr** point to the first byte in the array, and **endptr** point to the byte just past the array's end. That also means we need to include the size of an element in our pointer computations. We increment **ptr** past one array element by adding the size in bytes of an array element to it.

```
    ptr += size;
```

```
/*
 * Use standard sequential search on an array of integers.
 */
#include <stdio.h>
#include <stdlib.h>
#include "testtabs.h"

int main(int argc, char *argv[])
{
  long *longSearch(const long *ptr, int n, long target);

  const long *ptr;              /* returned pointer to element */
  int        i;                 /* index through arguments */
  long       target;            /* value we're looking for */

  for (i = 1; i < argc; i++)
    if (sscanf(argv[i], "%li", &target) == 1)
    {
      ptr = longSearch(LongTable, LongTableEntries, target);
      if (ptr != NULL)
        printf("%li in tab[%i]\n", *ptr, ptr - LongTable);
      else
        printf("Couldn't find %li\n", target);
    }

  return EXIT_SUCCESS;
}

long *longSearch(const long *ptr, int n, long target)
{
  const long *const endptr = ptr + n;

  for (; ptr < endptr; ptr++)
    if (target == *ptr)
      return (long *) ptr;                /* found it */
  return NULL;                            /* failure, return null */
}
```

Figure 17.15 (lsearch.c) Sequential search of an array of **long** integers.

And we initialize **endptr** by adding the number of bytes in the array to **ptr**.

```
endptr = ptr + size * n;
```

Finally, we can no longer use **==** to determine whether the target is in the array. Instead, we need to pass a comparison function two pointers to the target and the next array element. Figure 17.17 shows how to use **search** to search an array of strings. Because **search** works just like **bsearch**, we can pass it the same comparison function, **cmpString**, that we used earlier to search a table of strings with **bsearch**.

```
/*
 * Generic sequential search function.
 */
#include <stddef.h>

void *search(const void *tarptr, const void *tabptr,
             int n, size_t size,
             int (*funcptr)(const void *, const void *))
{
  const char *ptr          = tabptr;
  const char *const endptr = ptr + size * n;

  for (; ptr < endptr; ptr += size)
    if (funcptr(tarptr, ptr) == 0)
      return (void *) ptr;       /* found it, return pointer */
  return NULL;                   /* failure, return null */
}
```

Figure 17.16 (search.c) Our generic sequential search function.

Implementing a Generic Insertion Sort

When writing any generic function, it helps to base it on some earlier function written for a particular type. So we would like to base our generic insertion sort on the insertion sort programs we've written in earlier chapters. In Chapter 8, for example, we wrote a program that used insertion sort to sort an array of **int**s, and in Chapter 14, we rewrote it to sort an array of strings. The problem with these earlier programs is that they combined the sorting with reading the input values. Now we want an insertion sort that can sort an array in place. Figure 17.18 contains a new insertion sort function that does just that, but only for arrays of **long**s, and Figure 17.19 contains a main program that uses it.

Writing a generic sort is considerably more complicated than writing a generic search. To see why, let's think about what sorting is all about. It's really just a matter of *comparing* and *copying* (exchanging out-of-order values). To write a generic sorter, we need the array to sort, a method for *comparing* values, and a method for *copying* or *exchanging* two values. We'll do the comparing with a comparison function, as we've been doing all along with the built-in searching and sorting routines and our own generic searching routine. But now we also need a function for *copying* values. Fortunately, we don't have to provide this function to the sorting routine as a parameter. That's because if we want to copy any value from one location to another, regardless of type, all we really need to know is the locations and how many bytes to copy. Given that information, we can use **memcpy** (the standard library routine we first saw in Chapter 10) to actually do the copy.

```
/*
 * Use generic sequential search to search a table of strings.
 */
#include <stdio.h>
#include <stdlib.h>
#include <stddef.h>
#include "testtabs.h"

int main(int argc, char *argv[])
{
  int cmpString(const void *elptr, const void *tarptr);
  void *search(const void *tarptr, const void *tabptr, int n,
               size_t size, int (*cmpfp)(const void *, const void *));

  char  **ptr;                    /* array, ptr to an item */
  int   i;                        /* temporary index */

  for (i = 1; i < argc; i++)
  {
    ptr = search(argv[i], StringTable, StringTableEntries,
                 sizeof(StringTable[0]), cmpString);
    if (ptr != NULL)
      printf("Found %s as element %i.\n", argv[i], ptr - StringTable);
    else
      printf("Didn't find %s.\n", argv[i]);
  }

  return EXIT_SUCCESS;
}
```

Figure 17.17   (ssearch.c) A program that uses generic sequential search on a table of strings.

Figure 17.20 contains our generic insertion sort routine and Figure 17.21 contains a main program using it. It takes the same set of arguments as **qsort**. We created it by making several changes to our earlier code.

One change is that we now use pointers to traverse the array, just as we did with **search**. Since we now treat the array as an array of bytes, all of these pointers are pointers to **char**. **startptr** points to the first byte, and **endptr** to the first byte just past the array's end. We initialize these in the same way we initialized their counterparts in **search**. We also use two other pointers: **pi** to traverse the table, and **pj** to help us move out-of-place elements. These replace our earlier index variables **i** and **j**.

Just like before, when we do arithmetic with these pointers, we have to account for the size of an array element ourselves. So when we increment a pointer, we have to increment it by the number of bytes in an array element. That's important both when we initialize **pi** to point to the table's second element,

```
        pi = startptr + size;
```

```
/*
 * Insertion sort an existing array of longs in place.
 */
void isortLongTable(long vals[], int n)
{
  int i;

  for (i = 1; i < n; i++)
  {
    long temp = vals[i];
    int j;

    for (j = i; j > 0 && temp < vals[j-1]; j--)
      vals[j] = vals[j-1];
    vals[j] = temp;
  }
}
```

Figure 17.18   (isort1.c)   Insertion sorting routine that sorts an array of **long**s in place.

```
/*
 * Using insertion sort to sort an existing array of longs.
 */
#include <stdlib.h>
#include "testtabs.h"

int main()
{
  void isortLongTable(long vals[], int n);

  isortLongTable(LongTable, LongTableEntries);
  printLongTable(LongTable, LongTableEntries);

  return EXIT_SUCCESS;
}
```

Figure 17.19   (useis1.c)   A main program that uses our **long**-specific insertion sort.

and when we move it along the array:

```
        pi += size;
```

pj is similar to **pi**, but it moves backward from the current value of **pi** to the front of the array:

```
        pj -= size;
```

```
/*
 * Sort long integers using generic insertion sorting routine.
 */
#include <stddef.h>                          /* for size_t */
#include <stdlib.h>                          /* for malloc */
#include <string.h>                          /* for memcpy */

void isort(void *table,
           int n,
           size_t size,
           int (*cmpfp)(const void *, const void *))
{
  char *startptr      = table;                 /* ptrs to array start */
  char *const endptr = startptr + (n * size); /*   and end */
  char *pi, *pj;                               /* loop pointers */

  void *const temp    = malloc(size);          /* space for 1 element */

  for (pi = startptr + size; pi < endptr; pi += size)
  {
    memcpy(temp, pi, size);                         /* store into temp space */
    for (pj = pi; pj > startptr; pj -= size)
    {
      if (cmpfp(temp, pj - size) >= 0)
        break;
      memcpy(pj, pj - size, size);
    }
    memcpy(pj, temp, size);
  }

  free(temp);                                   /* free up the space */
}
```

Figure 17.20 (isort2.c) Generic version of our insertion sorting routine.

Another change is that we now replace the comparison between array elements using < with a call to the comparison function, just as we've had to do in all our other generic routines.

There's one more catch. Our previous version exchanged variables using an assignment and a temporary variable, **temp** (which we declared as an **int**), to hold the current array element. Here, we don't know how large to make **temp** at compile time. Our only choice is to declare it as a pointer to **void**, to use **malloc** to allocate enough space for an array element, and to use **memcpy** to store an array element in it.[2] We then also have to remember to free up this space before exiting our sorting function. This dynamic allocation is a pain, but that's the price we pay to play with generic functions.

---

[2]To make the sorting program fit on a single page, we're a little sloppy here and don't bother to check to see whether **malloc** actually succeeded.

```
/*
 * Sort long integers using generic insertion sorting routine.
 */
#include <stdlib.h>
#include <stddef.h>
#include "testtabs.h"

int main()
{
  void isort(void *tab,
             int n,
             size_t size,
             int (*cmpfp)(const void *, const void *));
  int  cmpLongs(const void *table_entry_ptr1,
                const void *table_entry_ptr2);

  isort(LongTable, LongTableEntries, sizeof(long), cmpLongs);
  printLongTable(LongTable, LongTableEntries);

  return EXIT_SUCCESS;
}
```

Figure 17.21   (useis2.c) A main program using our generic insertion sort.

17.3   MAKING GENERIC FUNCTIONS EASIER TO USE

Generic functions such as **bsearch** and **qsort** are powerful and make our job of coding complex programs much easier. But they aren't the easiest functions in the world to use. To use **bsearch**, for example, we not only provide a target value, an array, and the number of elements in the array but also extra information describing the size of each element and the function to use to compare elements. We would prefer, however, to hide all of this extra detail and to be able to perform searches with a simple call, such as[3]

```
ptr = SEARCH_STRINGS(argv[i],
                     StringTable,
                     StringTableEntries);
```

We would also like a similar interface for using **qsort**.

We can do this by taking advantage of header files and macros. For each type we're going to search and sort, we create a header file that provides a pair of interface macros (one for searching, the other for sorting), as well as prototypes for any comparison functions we need. And we put the comparison functions in a separate source file, which we can compile separately. Once we have done that, all we have to do to search and sort is include the header file, use the macros, and link in the comparison functions.

---

[3]This call assumes that we are searching for a command-line argument in a table of strings.

Aside 17.1: Generic Functions—How Fast?

Generic functions are great—they allow us to use one routine that works with any data type. Unfortunately that power comes at a price: generic routines don't run—they crawl. We compiled and ran the two versions of insertion sort on files of **int**s and timed the programs for files of 100 and 1000 values (on an 8600 VAX using the GNU C compiler under Berkeley 4.3 UNIX). For 100 values, the times were similar: 0.05 seconds versus 0.07 seconds. But for 1000 values, things were much different: 0.75 seconds for the "conventional" insertion sort versus almost 5 seconds for the generic version.

The table below shows where the generic version is spending its time: almost 30% in **memcpy** and almost a quarter million calls!

PERCENT TIME	TOTAL TIME (SECONDS)	NUMBER OF CALLS	TIME PER CALL (MICROSECONDS)	ROUTINE
29.6	1.47	242762	0.01	`memcpy`
27.2	2.82	1	1350.32	`isort`
21.4	3.88			`mcount` †
14.1	4.58	241749	0.00	`cmpInt`
2.8	4.72			`monstartup` †
2.2	4.83	1001	0.11	`doscan` †
1.6	4.91	1000	0.08	`doprnt` †

We have shown only those routines accounting for more than 1% of the total time. The routines marked with a † are C run-time routines compiled automatically with the program. The table also includes calls to two routines, **mcount** and **monstartup**, accounting for almost 25% of the program's total time. These two routines are included when execution profiling is turned on.

Despite their performance problems, we use generic routines wherever we can. Why? Simply because they're an easy way to reduce the time we spend programming. Only if a generic function turns out to be a primary performance bottleneck in our program do we replace it with something that's less general but more efficient.

We illustrate this technique with examples of searching and sorting tables of **long**s and tables of strings.

Figure 17.22 contains a header file for searching and sorting tables of **long**s. Figure 17.23 contains **cmpLong** and **cmpLongs**, our **long** comparison functions. Figure 17.24 is a short program that uses the macros to sort a table of **long**s and then perform several searches of it. Similarly, Figure 17.25 contains a header file for searching and sorting tables of strings. Figure 17.26 contains **cmpString** and **cmpStrings**, our string comparison functions. And Figure 17.27 is a short program that uses the macros to sort a table of strings and then perform several searches of it.

These changes make searching and sorting tables of **long**s and strings a breeze.

```
/*
 * Interface for searching and sorting tables of longs.
 */
#include <stdlib.h>

#define SEARCH_LONGS(tar,t,n) \
        bsearch(&(tar),t,n,sizeof(char *),cmpLong)

#define SORT_LONGS(t,n) \
        qsort(t,n,sizeof(char *),cmpLongs)

int cmpLong(const void *table_entry_ptr1,
          const void *table_entry_ptr2);
int cmpLongs(const void *table_entry_ptr1,
            const void *table_entry_ptr2);
```

Figure 17.22   (longgens.h)   Searching and sorting macros for arrays of **long**s.

```
/*
 * Comparison functions for longs.
 *    cmpLong - compare target long with long in table (search)
 *    cmpLongs - compare two longs in table (sort)
 */
int cmpLong(const void *target_ptr, const void *table_entry_ptr)
{
  long target = * (long *) target_ptr;
  long table_entry = * (long *) table_entry_ptr;

  return (target == table_entry) ? 0
                                 : ((target < table_entry) ? -1 : 1);
}

int cmpLongs(const void *table_entry_ptr1, const void *table_entry_ptr2)
{
  long x = * (long *) table_entry_ptr1;
  long y = * (long *) table_entry_ptr2;

  return (x == y) ? 0 : ((x < y) ? -1 : 1);
}
```

Figure 17.23   (longgens.c)   Comparison functions for **long**s.

```
/*
 * Table searching and sorting a table of longs using nice interface.
 */
#include <stdio.h>
#include <stddef.h>
#include "testtabs.h"
#include "longgens.h"

int main(int argc, char *argv[])
{
  long *ptr;                  /* pointer to target's position in table */
  int  i;
  long target;

  SORT_LONGS(LongTable, LongTableEntries);

#if defined(DEBUG)
  printLongTable(LongTable, LongTableEntries);
#endif

  for (i = 1; i < argc; i++)
  {
    target = atol(argv[i]);
    ptr = SEARCH_LONGS(target, LongTable, LongTableEntries);
    if (ptr == NULL)
      printf("Search failed.\n");
    else
      printf("Found %li at position %i\n", target, ptr - LongTable);
  }

  return EXIT_SUCCESS;
}
```

Figure 17.24 (lsrchsrt.c) Using our new interface to the generic search and sorting functions to sort a table of **long**s.

17.4 CASE STUDY—IMPLEMENTING A GENERIC BINARY SEARCH

This section is optional!

Figure 17.28 concludes the chapter with an implementation of **bsearch**. We've based it on **binarySearch**, the recursive binary search function we wrote in Chapter 16. In fact, all **bsearch** does is set up a call to a generic version of **binarySearch**.

As before, **binarySearch** takes three parameters: a pointer to the table's first byte, a pointer to just past the table's last byte, and a pointer to the target value. But we now make the first two arguments pointers to **char**. That's because within **binarySearch** we're treating the array as an array of bytes. The last argument is a pointer to **void**, because **binarySearch** doesn't care about the target's actual type. We pass the starting pointer and a target pointer to **bsearch**, so it can pass them

```
/*
 * Interface for searching and sorting tables of strings.
 */
#include <stdlib.h>

#define SEARCH_STRINGS(tar,t,n) \
          bsearch(tar,t,n,sizeof(char *),cmpString)
#define SORT_STRINGS(t,n) \
          qsort(t,n,sizeof(char *),cmpStrings)

int cmpString(const void *table_entry_ptr1,
              const void *table_entry_ptr2);
int cmpStrings(const void *table_entry_ptr1,
              const void *table_entry_ptr2);
```

Figure 17.25   (strgens.h) Searching and sorting macros for arrays of strings.

```
/*
 * Comparison functions for strings.
 *    cmpString - compare target string with string in table (search)
 *    cmpStrings - compare two strings in table (sort)
 */
#include <string.h>

int cmpString(const void *target_ptr,
              const void *table_entry_ptr)
{
  return strcmp((char *) target_ptr,
                * (char **) table_entry_ptr);
}

int cmpStrings(const void *table_entry_ptr1,
               const void *table_entry_ptr2)
{
  return strcmp(* (char **) table_entry_ptr1,
                * (char **) table_entry_ptr2);
}
```

Figure 17.26   (strgens.c) Comparison functions for strings.

```
/*
 * Table searching and sorting using nice interface.
 */
#include <stdio.h>
#include <stddef.h>
#include "testtabs.h"
#include "strgens.h"

int main(int argc, char *argv[])
{
  char **ptr;                  /* pointer to target's position in table */
  int   i;

  SORT_STRINGS(StringTable, StringTableEntries);

#if defined(DEBUG)
  printStringTable(StringTable, StringTableEntries);
#endif

  for (i = 1; i < argc; i++)
  {
    ptr = SEARCH_STRINGS(argv[i],
                         StringTable,
                         StringTableEntries);
    if (ptr == NULL)
      printf("Search failed.\n");
    else
      printf("Found %s at position %i\n", argv[i], ptr - StringTable);
  }

  return EXIT_SUCCESS;
}
```

Figure 17.27   (ssrchsrt.c) Using our new interface to the generic search and sorting functions to sort a table of strings.

unchanged to **binarySearch**. But we don't pass an ending pointer, so **bsearch** must compute it from the starting pointer and the size of the array.

Like our sequential search function, **binarySearch** needs a comparison function to determine whether it has found the target, and it needs to know the size of an array element to do pointer arithmetic. But we aren't passing it either, so how does **binarySearch** know which comparison function to use and what the size of an element is? **bsearch** places the comparison function and the array size in **static** global variables, so **binarySearch** simply uses these variables. Why not pass them as parameters? Because **binarySearch** is recursive, and all the recursive calls to **binarySearch** use the same size and comparison function. Putting that information in global variables eliminates the unnecessary overhead of passing them as parameters.

```
/*
 * An implementation of the standard library's binary search function.
 */
#include <stddef.h>

static int (*CmpFp)(const void *xptr, const void *yptr);
static int Size;            /* int rather than possibly unsigned size_t */

static void *
binarySearch(const char *minptr, const char *maxptr, const void *tptr)
{
  const char *midptr = minptr + ((maxptr - minptr)/(Size * 2)) * Size;
  int cmpres = CmpFp(tptr, midptr);

  if (cmpres == 0)                    /* got it! */
    return (void *) midptr;
  if (maxptr <= minptr)              /* value's not in table? */
    return NULL;
  return (cmpres < 0) ? binarySearch(minptr, midptr - Size, tptr)
                      : binarySearch(midptr + Size, maxptr, tptr);
}

void *bsearch(const void *tptr, const void *ptr, size_t n, size_t s,
              int (*fp)(const void *xptr, const void *yptr))
{
  CmpFp = fp;                        /* store in globals to simplify calls */
  Size = (int) s;
  return binarySearch(ptr, (char *) ptr + (n - 1) * s, tptr);
}
```

Figure 17.28   (bsearch.c) Our implementation of the library's generic binary search routine.

Within **binarySearch**, we have to make only a few changes from our earlier version. We use a comparison function rather than a direct comparison. And now we can no longer simply subtract or add one to **midptr** before we recursively call **binarySearch** to search subsections of the table. Instead, we have to add or subtract the size of an element instead. There is one place we don't have to change: our computation of the **midptr** is exactly the same as before.

SUMMARY

■ Generic functions are functions that can perform a particular task with any data type.

■ C's standard library comes complete with a generic binary search function, **bsearch**, and a generic Quicksort function, **qsort**.

- We use the generic functions by providing them with pointers to comparison functions. These functions take pointers to the target or table entries and convert them to pointers to the underlying data type.

- We can write our generic functions that process arrays by treating arrays as collections of bytes and carefully doing all of the pointer arithmetic ourselves.

- By using macros, we can write a nice interface on top of generic functions that allows us to forget the painful details of comparison functions and size computations.

EXERCISES

Explore

17–1 Compile and run the programs in this chapter.

17–2 There is no guarantee that **qsort** is really a "quick" sorting routine at all, only that it will order the elements in the array according to the supplied comparison function. Run **qsort** on input data sets of size 100, 200, 400, 800, and 1600 elements and plot the sorting time. A well-written **qsort** will have computing time proportional to $n \times \log_2 n$. A poor sorting routine, such as our very own insertion sort, has computing time on the order of n^2.

17–3 **bsearch** is said to be an order of $\log_2 n$ algorithm, where n is the number of elements in the table. Linear search (start the search from the beginning of the table and continue until either a match is found or the end of the table is reached) is order of n. Compare the search times when using **search** and **bsearch** to search tables that vary in size from 5 to 5000 elements on your own computer. Is **bsearch** always faster? If not, what is the break point in the number of elements below which linear search should be used?

Modify

17–4 Write a nonrecursive, generic version of **bsearch** (Figure 17.28).

Code

17–5 Write a program that uses binary search to search our employee table for matching names.

17–6 Write a program that uses **qsort** to sort our employee database by salary and then by employee name.

17–7 Write a function to determine whether a generic array is already sorted.

17–8 Write a function to reverse any type of array. How can we combine this with Quicksort to sort in descending order rather than ascending order?

17–9 Write a function, **traverseArray**, that will execute a pointer to a function on each element in an array of any type. Use it to print each element in a table of integers and to print each of the records in our employee database.

17–10 Provide a nice interface for searching and sorting arrays of strings and arrays of **double**s.

Build

17–11 Provide a set of functions for manipulating arrays. This set should include **walkArray**, which applies a function to every array element, and **mapArray**, which is just like

walkArray, but quits if the function it applies returns zero. Provide a nice interface for using them with arrays of **int**s and arrays of **double**s.

17–12 Write a generic table package that provides functions for adding and deleting table elements, as well as for running through the table. Then rewrite Chapter 12's employee database program to use these functions.

17–13 Write a program that reads input lines in the form of *lastname*, *firstname*, one name per line. Sort the input based on *two* sorting keys: last name, then first name, then print the results to the terminal. The two-key sort should yield all names in order by last name; two or more last names that are the same should then also be sorted by first name.

18 COMPLEX DECLARATIONS

This chapter discusses how to understand and construct complex type declarations. We present some types even more complex than those we've so far declared and show where we might want to use them. We provide algorithms for understanding and formulating C's type declarations—no matter how complex. And we show tricks that can help us avoid most of the material in this chapter most of the time. The chapter concludes with a case study: a program takes an abbreviated English type description and produces an appropriate C declaration for it.

18.1 SOME NEW COMPLEX TYPES

So far we've presented a bewildering collection of types: arrays of arrays, pointers to arrays, arrays of pointers, pointers to pointers, pointers to functions, functions returning pointers, and so on. And each new type declaration seems to be more complex than the last. But we're not limited to only those types we've been discussing. Despite all our efforts, we have merely skimmed the surface of the types C allows us to declare and use. We can, in fact, declare arbitrarily complex data types; we're limited only by our imagination and our ability to read and understand the resulting declarations. To give you an idea of the true power of C, we now present two new complex data types: arrays of pointers to functions, and functions returning pointers to functions.

Arrays of Pointers to Functions

Why would we ever want an array of pointers to functions? We'll use them to write a small program that repeatedly prints a menu,

```
Your choices are:
        1) Add record
        2) Delete record
        3) Print record
Or type a 0 to quit:
```

obtains the user's choice, and then executes a function corresponding to the user's choice.

The program stores a menu as an array of strings:

```
const char *const MenuEntries[] =
  { "Add record", "Delete record", "Print record" };
```

It also stores the functions implementing the user's choices in an array of pointers to functions.

```
void (*MenuFptrs[])(void) =
  { addRecord, delRecord, printRecord };
```

This declares **MenuFptrs** as an array of pointers to functions, each of which takes no parameters and returns no value. It also initializes the array to hold pointers to three of these functions: **addRecord**, **delRecord**, and **printRecord**. This initialization must be preceded with the functions' prototypes so that the compiler knows they are function names and not variable names. In general, these functions would do things such as add records to a data base, but for now they simply print a message announcing that they've been called successfully. Figure 18.1 shows this array. Figure 18.2 contains the prototypes for these functions, and Figure 18.3 contains the functions themselves.

Figure 18.4 contains the **main** program and the tables of strings and function pointers that make up the menu. **main** doesn't do much—it simply sets up the tables and calls a function, **menuProcess**, to do all the real work.

Figure 18.5 contains **menuProcess**. It repeatedly calls another function, **menuChoice**, to print the menu and obtain a valid user choice. It quits when the user's choice is 0. Otherwise, the user's choice is between 1 and the number of menu entries, and **menuProcess** uses it as an index into the table of function pointers.

```
fptrs[choice - 1]();   /* execute the function */
```

fptrs[choice - 1] is a pointer to a function, so supplying an argument list executes the function to which it points. The compiler automatically dereferences the pointer for us, saving us a ***** and a set of parentheses. We subtract 1 from **choice** because C arrays start at zero and the user's choice starts at 1.

Functions That Return Pointers to Functions

Our functions so far either have returned a simple type, such as **int** or **double**, or a pointer to one of these types. There are times, however, when we want to have a function return a pointer to another function. We do so in a more sophisticated implementation of our menu program. This time the menu is an array of structures, with each structure containing a string to print and a pointer to a function to execute. And now the user selects a menu entry by typing its first few characters, not by entering a number.

Figure 18.6 contains the definition of a menu structure, Figure 18.7 contains a new main program that initializes the menu structures, and Figure 18.8 contains the new version of **menuProcess**.

Before, we directly indexed the menu with the user's choice: **menuProcess** called **menuChoice** to print the menu and return the user's choice and then used it to index a table of function pointers. Now, however, we have **menuChoice** search the menu for a matching entry and then return its corresponding function pointer. **menuProcess** then

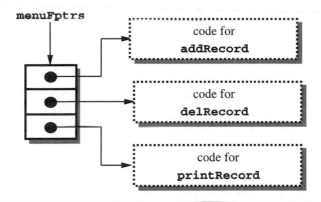

Figure 18.1 What the table of pointers to functions looks like.

```
/*
 * Prototypes for dummy functions used to test the menu.
 */
extern void addRecord(void);
extern void delRecord(void);
extern void printRecord(void);
```

Figure 18.2 (record.h) Prototypes for dummy functions used to test **menuProcess**.

```
/*
 * Dummy functions to test our menu program.
 */
#include <stdio.h>
#include "record.h"

#define ANNOUNCE(x) printf("In %s\n", x)

void addRecord(void)   { ANNOUNCE("addRecord"); }
void delRecord(void)   { ANNOUNCE("delRecord"); }
void printRecord(void) { ANNOUNCE("printRecord"); }
```

Figure 18.3 (record.c) Dummy functions used to test **menuProcess**.

```
/*
 * Print menu and then obtain and execute the user's choice.
 */
#include <stdio.h>
#include <stdlib.h>
#include "record.h"

const char *const MenuEntries[] =
  { "Add record", "Delete record", "Print record" };

void (*MenuFptrs[])(void) =
  { addRecord, delRecord, printRecord };

int main()
{
  void menuProcess(int, const char *const[], void (*[])(void));

  const int choices = sizeof(MenuFptrs)/sizeof(MenuFptrs[0]);

  menuProcess(choices, MenuEntries, MenuFptrs);
  return EXIT_SUCCESS;
}
```

Figure 18.4   (usemenu.c)   Storing a menu as an array of strings plus an array of pointers to functions.

simply calls the function through this pointer. The problem is that we now must declare **menuChoice** as a function returning one of these pointers. Here is its prototype:

```
void (*menuChoice(int n, const MenuItem menu[]))(void);
```

This declares **menuChoice** as a function that takes two arguments—an **int** and an array of **MenuItem**s—and returns a pointer to a function that takes no arguments and returns no value. That's a mouthful, but it's easily understandable. Just replace **menuChoice** and its parameter list with a variable, say **choiceptr**.

```
void (*choiceptr)(void);
```

That results in the familiar declaration for a pointer to a function with no parameters and no return value. And that's what **menuChoice** returns.

    menuProcess calls **menuChoice** just like any other function and assigns its return value to **choiceptr**.

```
choiceptr = menuChoice(n, menu)
```

And we execute the returned function simply by calling it through **choiceptr**.

```
choiceptr();
```

Once again, we take advantage of C's automatically dereferencing function pointers when we follow them with an argument list.

```c
/*
 * Display menu and obtain and execute user choices.
 *    menuProcess - obtain and execute user's choice.
 *    menuChoice - request and get the user's choice.
 *    menuDisplay - print menu of user choices.
 */
#include <stdio.h>
#include <stdlib.h>

#define MAXLEN 80

static void menuDisplay(int n, const char *const items[])
{
  int i;

  printf("Your choices are:\n");
  for (i = 1; i <= n; i++)
    printf("\t%i) %s\n", i, items[i - 1]);
  printf("Or type a 0 to quit: ");
}

static int menuChoice(int n, const char *const items[])
{
  int  getline(char *buf, int buflen);
  void menuDisplay(int n, const char *const items[]);

  int  num;                          /* index, selection */
  char line[MAXLEN + 1];

  menuDisplay(n, items);             /* display menu */

  while (getline(line, MAXLEN) != -1)
    if (sscanf(line, "%i", &num) == 1 && 0 <= num && num <= n)
      return num;
    else
      printf("Enter a value between 0 and %i: ", n);

  return EXIT_SUCCESS;
}

void menuProcess(int n,
                 const char *const items[],
                 void (*fptrs[])(void))
{
  int choice;                        /* holds user's choice */

  while ((choice = menuChoice(n, items)) != 0)
    fptrs[choice - 1]();             /* execute the function */
}
```

Figure 18.5 (prmenu.c) Functions to prompt the user for a menu selection and then use the user's choice to select and execute the appropriate function.

```
/*
 * Definition of a menu structure.
 */
typedef struct menu_item
{
  char *entry;                          /* string to write */
  void (*fptr)(void);                   /* function to execute */
} MenuItem;

void menuProcess(int n, const MenuItem tab[]);
```

Figure 18.6 (menu.h) Definition of a menu structure.

```
/*
 * Menu processor, rewritten to represent menus with structures.
 */
#include <stdlib.h>
#include "menu.h"
#include "record.h"

MenuItem Menu[] =
{
  {"Add record",    addRecord},
  {"Delete record", delRecord},
  {"Print record",  printRecord}
};

int main()
{
  const int choices = sizeof(Menu)/sizeof(Menu[0]);

  menuProcess(choices, Menu);

  return EXIT_SUCCESS;
}
```

Figure 18.7 (usemenu2.c) Program to use a menu defined as a structure.

18.2   CONSTRUCTING TYPE DECLARATIONS

We've now seen some fairly complex type declarations—but how do we construct them?

A type declaration consists of a basic type followed by a *declarator* and specifies the type of the identifier contained within the declarator. In the declaration

```
double (*funcptr)(void);
```

```
/*
 * Display menu and obtain/execute user choices.
 *    menuProcess - get and execute user's choice.
 *    menuChoice - read and verify choice from user.
 *    menuSearch - search menu to find user's choice.
 */
#include <stdio.h>
#include <stddef.h>
#include <string.h>
#include "menu.h"

#define MAXLEN 80

static const MenuItem *menuSearch(const MenuItem *ptr,
                                  const MenuItem *endptr,
                                  const char *target)
{
  for (; ptr < endptr; ptr++)
    if (strncmp(target, ptr->entry, strlen(target)) == 0)
      return ptr;
  return NULL;
}

static void (*menuChoice(int n, const MenuItem menu[]))(void)
{
  int    getline(char *buf, int buflen);

  char   line[MAXLEN + 1];
  const MenuItem *ptr;
  const MenuItem *const endptr = menu + n;

  printf("Your choices are:\n");
  for (ptr = menu; ptr < endptr; ptr++)
    printf("\t%s\n", ptr->entry);
  printf("Or type QUIT to quit: ");
  while (getline(line, MAXLEN) != -1 && strcmp(line, "QUIT") != 0)
  {
    if ((ptr = menuSearch(menu, endptr, line)) != NULL)
      return ptr->fptr;
    printf("Select an appropriate menu entry: ");
  }
  return NULL;
}

void menuProcess(int n, const MenuItem menu[])
{
  void (*choiceptr)(void);                /* user-selected function */

  while ((choiceptr = menuChoice(n, menu)) != NULL)
    choiceptr();                          /* execute user's choice */
}
```

Figure 18.8   (prmenu2.c)   Prompting for a menu selection and executing the corresponding function.

double is the basic type, **(*funcptr)(void)** is the declarator, and **funcptr** is the identifier contained in the declarator. As we saw earlier, this declares **funcptr** as a pointer to a function that takes no arguments and returns a **double**.

The problem is to come up with the correct declarator. It's easy if we're declaring a variable with one of the basic types: it's simply a single identifier.

```
int     i;              /* an int */
double d;               /* a double */
```

We can declare several more complicated types by combining the identifier with a single *****, **()**, and **[]**. Prefacing the identifier with ***** declares a pointer to the base type.

```
int  *iptr;             /* pointer to an int */
char *cptr;             /* pointer to a char */
```

Following the identifier with **[]** declares an array of the base type.

```
double dtab[10];        /* array of 10 doubles */
char    ctab[10];       /* array of 10 characters */
```

We need to include a subscript only if we're defining storage and we're not following the declaration with an initialization expression. Following the identifier with a **()**, possibly with an enclosed list of types, declares a function.

```
int     ifunc(void);    /* function returning an int */
double dfunc(void);     /* function returning a double */
```

Here, we're assuming we want to declare functions that take no parameters. Otherwise, of course, we would replace the **void** with a list of type declarations for these parameters.

We declare even more complex types, such as pointers to functions and arrays of pointers, by combining the pieces used to form the previous declarators. Now, however, we have to worry about operator precedence.

The simplest combinations are an array of pointers:

```
int *iptrtab[10];       /* array of 10 pointers to int */
char *cptrtab[10];      /* array of 10 pointers to char */
```

and a function returning a pointer:

```
char *cptrfunc(void);   /* function returning ptr to char */
int  *iptrfunc(void);   /* function returning ptr to int */
```

Why are these arrays of pointers and functions returning pointers rather than pointers to arrays or pointers to functions? Because when we combine declarators, ***** has lower precedence than either **()** or **[]**. If we want the latter types, we need to use parentheses to override the normal precedence. We declare a pointer to an array with

```
char (*crowptr)[10];    /* ptr to array of 10 characters */
int  (*irowptr)[10];    /* ptr to array of 10 integers */
```

and we declare a pointer to a function with

```
int    (*iptr)(void);  /* ptr to function returning int */
double (*dptr)(void);  /* ptr to function returning double */
```

How do we declare even more complex types? It helps to think of the English description of an identifier's type as being composed of several pieces. Each piece, except for the base type, is "an array of," "a pointer to," or "a function returning." Suppose, for example, that we want to declare an array of pointers to functions that take no arguments and return **void**. That's the type we used in the first version of our menu-processing program. We break its description into

> *an array of*
> *pointers to*
> *functions taking no arguments and returning*
> **void**

The last part of this description, **void**, is the base type of the identifier, and we can ignore it while we're trying to construct the declarator.

We compose the declarator in three steps. First, we examine each of the remaining lines in the description and decide on a C declarator for a variable with that type.

```
table[]
*ptr
func(void)
```

Second, we work our way through these declarators, substituting the topmost declarator for the identifier in the declarator beneath it. So we initially substitute **table[]** for **ptr** in ***ptr**, which leaves

```
*table[]
func(void)
```

We keep repeating the process until only a single declarator remains. In this case, we have only one more substitution to do, replacing **func** with ***table[]**:

```
(*table[])(void)
```

We've done something sneaky here—we surrounded ***table[]** with parentheses. But where did they come from? As we just saw, the precedence of ***** is less than that of either **()** or **[]**, so we have to parenthesize pointer declarators whenever we substitute them into an array or function declarator.

The final step is to precede the declarator by the base type, **void** in this case.

```
void (*table[])(void)
```

And, lo and behold, this is the type declaration we used for the array of pointers in our original menu-processing program.

Let's do one more example. How can we construct the declaration for a function that takes an **int** and an array of **MenuItem**s and returns a pointer to a function that takes no arguments and returns no value? That's exactly the type we used in the structure-based version of our menu-processing program.

As with any other declaration, no matter how complex, we start out with an English description.

> *a function taking two parameters and returning*
> *a pointer to*
> *a function taking no parameters and returning*
> **void**

And then we formulate the declarations for objects with each of these types.

> **func1**(*two-parameters*)
> ***ptr**
> **func2(void)**

To keep things simple, we're ignoring the parameters of the functions for now and we'll throw them in once we've figured out the rest of the declarator.

Now we go through the same process as before, substituting the topmost declarator for the variable in the declarator following it. Here, that's substituting **func1**(*two-parameters*) for **ptr**.

> ***func1**(*two-parameters*)
> **func2(void)**

We repeat the process for the remaining declarators, this time substituting the topmost declarator for **func2**.

> **(*func1**(*two-parameters*)**)(void)**

Again, because we're substituting a pointer, we have to parenthesize it. Once we have only a single declarator left, we precede it with the base type. At this point, we can also fill in any missing parameter declarations.

> **void (*func1(int n, MenuItem menu[]))(void)**

Fortunately, this declaration matches the one we used in the previous section.

18.3 UNDERSTANDING COMPLEX TYPE DECLARATIONS

How do we understand complex type declarations? This task turns out to be considerably trickier than constructing the declaration.

We start by taking the type declaration and finding its innermost declarator. We write down its type, substitute an identifier for this innermost declarator, and repeat the process until only a single identifier remains. At that point, we have determined the identifier's type.

That sounds straightforward enough, but the hard part is locating the innermost declarator. The rule is that it's the identifier and an immediately following **[]** or **()** or, if neither of these is present, an immediately preceding *****. Once we have determined the type of the innermost declarator, we can ignore any parentheses surrounding it.

To see how this works, suppose we're suddenly confronted with this confusing type declaration.

```
void (*table[])(void)
```

First, we need to locate the innermost declarator. Here, it's **table[]** (since **[]** has higher precedence than *****), so we note that we have an array of some kind. But what kind? To find out, we substitute a variable for **table[]** and repeat the process.

```
void (*x)(void);
```

Now the innermost declarator is ***x**, so we know we have an array of pointers to something. But what's the something? We repeat the process one last time, substituting a variable for ***x** and the parentheses that surround it.

```
void y(void);
```

This leaves us with a familiar declaration: **y** is a function taking no arguments and returning **void**. So combining that with what we'd figured out before, we can see that we have an array of pointers to functions taking no arguments and returning **void**.

Here's a summary of the process. The innermost declarator is in italics.

void (**table[]*)(**void**)	*an array of*
void (*x)(**void**)	*pointers to*
void *y(void)*	*functions returning*
void *z*	**void**

We'll try the process on one more declaration. What does the declaration below declare?

```
void (*function(int x, MenuItem m[]))(void)
```

To find out, we repeat the above process. The innermost declarator is

```
function(int x, MenuItem m[])
```

This is a function that takes two arguments, an **int** and an array of **MenuItem**s, and returns some unknown value. We replace it with a variable, resulting in a simpler declaration.

```
void (*x)(void)
```

The innermost declarator is now ***x**, which is a pointer. We replace it with a variable, which leaves a declaration we recognize:

```
void y(void);
```

This declares a function that takes no arguments and returns no value. So putting all this together, we have a function taking an **int** and an array of **MenuItem**s and returning a pointer to a function taking no arguments and returning no value. We've summarized the process on the top of the next page.

void (*_function(two-params)_)(**void**)	*a function returning*
void (*_x_)(**void**)	*a pointer to*
void _y(void)_	*a function returning*
void _z_	**void**

18.4   TYPE SPECIFICATIONS

When a declarator does not contain an identifier, we have a type specification rather than a variable declaration. These type specifications show up in three places: **sizeof**, function prototypes, and casts. The trick to writing a type specification is to first declare a variable of that type and then to omit the variable from the declaration.

Suppose we want to know how many bytes are required by a pointer to function taking an **int** and returning a **double**. One way to find this out is to pass an appropriate type specifier to **sizeof**. But how do we form that type specifier?

We start by declaring a variable with that type.

```
double (*fp)(int);
```

We then remove the variable to form the type specifier.

```
double (*)(int)
```

And all that remains is to add the **sizeof** operator.

```
sizeof(double (*)(int))
```

Similarly, suppose we want to write a function prototype for Chapter 13's **testAvg** function. It takes three arguments—a pointer to an array containing three elements, and a pair of **int**s—and returns a **double**. We come up with its type specifier by first writing the declaration for a pointer to a row containing three elements as

```
int (*rowp)[3];
```

And we obtain the type specifier by removing the variable.

```
double testAvg(int (*)[3], int, int);
```

As one final example, suppose we want to pass a **NULL** pointer to a function that is expecting a table of pointers to functions taking no arguments and returning **void**. We might do so to indicate that **menuProcess** is supposed to obtain choices but not execute them. (Of course, we would have to rewrite the function to test for a **NULL** pointer, but we've left that as an exercise.) We can declare such an array as

```
void (*functab[])(void)
```

We obtain the type specifier by eliminating the variable.

```
void (*[])(void)
```

And we obtain the cast by wrapping parentheses around the resulting type specifier.

```
(void (*[])(void))
```

18.5   CASE STUDY—ENGLISH TO C

This section is optional!

This chapter concludes with a simple program to turn an abbreviated description of a type into an appropriate C type declaration. Here's some sample input and output from the program.

```
pf void
void (*thing)()
apf void
void (*thing[])()
fpfp void
void *(*thing())()
pfpa int
int (*(*thing)())[]
papfpa double
double (*(*(*thing)[])())[]
```

To keep things simple, we use single letter abbreviations for English type descriptions: *p* stands for "pointer to," *f* stands for "function returning," and *a* stands for "array of." So *pf* **void** is a shorthand way to write pointer to functions returning **void**, and *apf* **void** is a shortcut for array of pointers to functions returning **void**. We make several other simplifications. First, we expect the input to be in the form of our sample input, but we don't bother to do any error checking. Second, we don't bother to report whether a particular type makes sense: the program will come up with a type declaration for *af* even though we aren't allowed to have an array of functions. And finally, we don't provide any mechanism for specifying what arguments a function takes. These have to be added by hand later.

Figure 18.9 contains our English-to-C translator. It simply reads a line of input containing a type description and a base type and works its way through the type description, gradually building up the declarator. To do so, it uses our earlier algorithm: working left to right, declaring each item, and then wrapping it in the declaration for the item to its right. When it's all done, it prints the base type followed by the newly created declarator. Figure 18.10 contains the function that wraps the type information around the current item.

SUMMARY

- C allows us to declare arbitrarily complex data types, including types such as arrays of pointers to functions, and functions that return pointers to functions.

- These type declarations appear in numerous places, including variable declarations, function headers, and type casts.

- There are algorithms we can use both to turn an English description of a type into its declaration and to turn a declaration into its English description.

```c
/*
 * Pseudo-English-to-C converter.
 */
#include <stdio.h>
#include <string.h>
#include <stdlib.h>
#include <stddef.h>

#define MAXLEN    80

char Declarator[MAXLEN * 5];              /* more than enough room */

int main()
{
  int  getline(char *buf, int len);
  void wrap(char *towrap, const char *frontptr, const char *backptr);

  char line[MAXLEN + 1];               /* input line */
  char desc[MAXLEN + 1];               /* description of type */
  char type[MAXLEN + 1];               /* base type */
  char *descptr;                       /* ptr to next piece */

  while (getline(line, MAXLEN) != -1)
    if (sscanf(line, "%s %s\n", desc, type) != 2)
      printf("Need description and type, ie \"pfp int\"\n");
    else
    {
      strcpy(Declarator, "thing");
      for (descptr = desc; *descptr != '\0'; descptr++)
        switch (*descptr)
        {
          case 'p':  wrap(Declarator, "*", NULL);
                     break;
          case 'f':  if (Declarator[0] != '*')
                        wrap(Declarator, NULL, "()");
                     else
                        wrap(Declarator, "(", ")()");
                     break;
          case 'a':  if (Declarator[0] != '*')
                        wrap(Declarator, NULL, "[]");
                     else
                        wrap(Declarator, "(", ")[]");
                     break;
        }
      printf("%s %s\n", type, Declarator);
    }

  return EXIT_SUCCESS;
}
```

Figure 18.9   (etoc.c) A program to turn English descriptions of C data types into an appropriate C declaration.

```
/*
 * Function to wrap one string inside two other strings.
 */
#include <stddef.h>
#include <string.h>

void wrap(char *string, const char *fstr, const char *bstr)
{
  char *endptr = string + strlen(string);   /* initial end */
  char *ptr = endptr;                        /* traversing ptr */
  int   flen;

  if (fstr != NULL)
  {
    flen = strlen(fstr);
    while (ptr-- > string)          /* move over to make room */
      *(ptr + flen) = *(ptr);
    while (*fstr != '\0')           /* do insert */
      *string++ = *fstr++;
    *(endptr += flen) = '\0';
  }
  if (bstr != NULL)                 /* append trailing string */
    while ((*endptr++ = *bstr++) != '\0')
      ;
}
```

Figure 18.10 (wrap.c) A utility function to wrap type information around a declarator.

- Having to use an algorithm to figure out how to declare something or to decipher a declaration means the code is too complex. We should use **typedef** to make these types considerably easier to read and declare.

EXERCISES

Explore

18–1 Compile and run the programs in this chapter.

18–2 How can we declare an array of **N** elements, each a pointer to a function that returns a pointer to an **int** and takes two arguments: a **double** and a pointer to a function taking a **double** and returning a **double**?

18–3 How can we declare a pointer to a function that takes a pointer to an array of 10 **int**s and an **int** and returns a pointer to an array of 10 **int**s?

18–4 How would we declare a two-dimensional array of 10 rows of 20 elements, each of which is a pointer to a function that takes a pointer to **void** and returns no value?

Aside 18.1a: Using Type Definitions to Aid Readability

The compiler can easily process arbitrarily complex type declarations and type specifiers—but most people can't. To keep declarations readable, use **typedef** when declaring types more complex than arrays of pointers and pointers to arrays.

Aside 18.1b contains several type definitions that we can use to make our menu-processing program more readable. The first is the easiest to understand:

```
typedef char *String;
```

As we saw earlier, to use **typedef**, we pretend we're declaring a variable with the type's name and throw **typedef** in front of it to turn that variable declaration into a type definition. So this **typedef** declares a new type **String** that's a synonym for a pointer to **char**. **String** is useful when declaring things such as a table of menu entries:

```
const String MenuEntries[] =
   { "Add record", "Delete record", "Print record" };
```

The second is a bit more complex.

```
typedef void (*PfrVoid)(void);
```

This **typedef** declares a type **PfrVoid** that's a synonym for a pointer to a function that takes no arguments and returns **void**. To see why, just eliminate the **typedef**—we are then declaring a variable **PfrVoid** with that type.

The final **typedef** simply makes **MenuFuncPtr** a synonym for **PfrVoid**.

```
typedef PfrVoid MenuFuncPtr;
```

Since these types are now identical, why do we bother to declare them both? **MenuFuncPtr** describes the type's use in the program: it's the type of the functions we execute when the user chooses a menu entry. In contrast, **PfrVoid** describes the underlying type, which makes the **typedef** easier to understand. Having both types leads to a more readable program. In any case, it's a lot easier to understand

```
const MenuFuncPtr MenuFptrs[] =
   { addRecord, delRecord, printRecord };
```

than the equivalent raw declaration

```
void (*MenuFptrs[])(void) =
   { addRecord, delRecord, printRecord };
```

Asides 18.1c and 18.1d use these **typedef**s in a more readable rewrite of our original array-based menu-processing program. This version is much easier to understand than the original.

typedef's are never absolutely necessary, but a little care in using them goes a long way toward writing readable code.

Aside 18.1b (typedefs.h) Useful type definitions for our menu program.

```
/*
 * Useful typedefs for menu program.
 */
typedef char *String;
typedef void (*PfrVoid)(void);
typedef PfrVoid MenuFuncPtr;
```

Aside 18.1c (usemenu3.c) Our original menu program rewritten more readably using type definitions.

```
/*
 * Print menu and then obtain and execute the user's choice.
 */
#include <stdio.h>
#include <stdlib.h>
#include "record.h"
#include "typedefs.h"

const String MenuEntries[] =
  { "Add record", "Delete record", "Print record" };

const MenuFuncPtr MenuFptrs[] =
  { addRecord, delRecord, printRecord };

int main()
{
  void menuProcess(int, const String [], const MenuFuncPtr []);

  const int choices = sizeof(MenuFptrs)/sizeof(MenuFptrs[0]);

  menuProcess(choices, MenuEntries, MenuFptrs);

  return EXIT_SUCCESS;
}
```

18–5 How would we declare a pointer to a function that returns a pointer to a function that takes a pointer to **void** and an **int** and returns a pointer to **void**? The function takes a table of pointers to these functions and an **int**. What might we use this type for?

18–6 Using **typedef**s, write a declaration for an array of **M LINE**s, each of which is an array of **N** chars. Write a declaration for a pointer to one of the arrays of **N** chars.

Modify **18–7** Modify Chapter 12's database program to use this chapter's array-based menu-processing package.

18–8 Modify Chapter 12's database program to use this chapter's structure-based menu-processing package.

Aside 18.1d (prmenu3.c) Menu-processing functions rewritten using type definitions.

```c
/*
 * Display menu and obtain and execute user choices.
 *    menuProcess - obtain and execute user's choice.
 *    menuDisplay - display the menu choices.
 *    menuChoice - request and get the user's choice.
 */
#include <stdio.h>
#include <stdlib.h>
#include "typedefs.h"

#define MAXLEN 80

static void menuDisplay(int n, const String items[])
{
  int i;

  printf("Your choices are:\n");
  for (i = 1; i <= n; i++)
    printf("\t%i) %s\n", i, items[i - 1]);
  printf("Or type a 0 to quit: ");
}

static int menuChoice(int n, const String items[])
{
  int   getline(String buf, int buflen);
  void menuDisplay(int n, const String items[]);

  int  num;                              /* index, selection */
  char line[MAXLEN + 1];

  menuDisplay(n, items);
  while (getline(line, MAXLEN) != -1)
    if (sscanf(line, "%i", &num) == 1 && 0 <= num && num <= n)
      return num;
    else
      printf("Enter a value between 0 and %i: ", n);

  return EXIT_SUCCESS;
}

void menuProcess(int n,
                 const String items[],
                 const MenuFuncPtr fptrs[])
{
  int choice;                            /* holds user's choice */

  while ((choice = menuChoice(n, items)) != 0)
    fptrs[choice - 1]();
}
```

Extend   **18–9**   Improve our program to turn an English description of a type into its type declaration (Figure 18.9). Allow the user to specify types of the arguments of any functions by enclosing them in parentheses and appending them to the *f* indicating the function. Your program should also verify that the user's input is legal and print an appropriate error message if it isn't. You have to worry about two types of errors: an invalid letter (other than 'a', 'p', or 'f') or an invalid type (there's no such type as an array of functions).

Code   **18–10**   Write a function **execute** that runs through a generic array, executing a series of functions for each element. **execute** is passed a generic array, the number of elements in the array, and the size of each element, along with an array of pointers to functions and the number of functions in that array. **execute** should pass each function the current array element and its size. Write this program with and without **typedef**s.

18–11   Rewrite the previous exercise to use a pointer to traverse the table of functions.

Build   **18–12**   Write a program to take a C type declaration and return an English description of the type it declares.

Extend this program to print English descriptions of all type declarations in a C source or header file. Make whatever simplifying assumptions you need.

Part V

C AND THE REAL WORLD

The next three chapters of this text focus on C's advanced mechanisms for structuring programs.

- Chapter 19 examines the standard library functions for accessing files.

- Chapter 20 shows how to implement common data structures such as lists, trees, queues, and stacks.

- Chapter 21 discusses how to write portable programs.

19 EXTERNAL FILES

Our earlier programs have accessed files solely through their standard input and output. But that's a severe limitation—those programs can access only one input and one output file. Fortunately, C provides a well-stocked library of functions for manipulating external files. This chapter presents most of these functions and uses them to write useful file-handling utilities. We also write a small package that allows us to use "virtual arrays," data structures that behave like arrays but are actually stored in files rather than memory. The chapter concludes with an electronic address book that stores the addresses and phone numbers in an indexed external file.

19.1   ACCESSING EXTERNAL FILES

Up to now, whenever we've wanted a program to read or write an external file, we've redirected its standard input or output. But to access more than one file at one time, we also need a way to access external files directly. In C, we do so using library functions.

Before we can access a file, we must *open* it. Opening a file gives us a handle that we can use to conveniently identify the file when calling I/O library functions.[1] We open a file with the standard I/O function **fopen**, which takes two string parameters—a file name and a mode—and returns a pointer to a **FILE**. Unlike **int** and **float**, **FILE** is not one of C's basic data types. Instead, it is usually a structure (defined in stdio.h) that contains information useful to the library routines that process files. **fopen** returns **NULL** if there is an error and the file can't be opened.

The mode specifies how we plan to use the file. The basic modes are **"r"** (open for reading), **"w"** (open for writing), and **"a"** (open for appending). So after declaring **fp** as a pointer to a file,

```
FILE *fp;
```

we can use

```
fp = fopen("phonenos", "r");   /* open phone number file */
```

to open the file phonenos for reading.

---

[1]It also causes the system to set up any internal data structures, such as buffers, that are necessary for processing the file.

Aside 19.1: Text Files versus Binary Files

C distinguishes between text files and binary files. What's the difference?

A *text* file is assumed to contain a sequence of characters, and the I/O operations we apply to text files convert back and forth between a data type's internal representation and its printable representation as a sequence of characters. The standard input and output files are text files, and we have already seen how **scanf** takes sequence of characters, such as the six-character sequence 123.45, and converts it to an internal representation, such as an 8-byte **double**.

A *binary* file, on the other hand, is assumed to simply be a stream of bytes. The I/O operations we apply to a binary file do not do any conversions. In essence, we use binary files when we want to move data directly from memory to disk, exactly as is. We use text files when we want to convert data in memory to sequences of characters.

There are also some specific differences between how text files and binary files are processed. In some operating systems (such as MS-DOS), text files use a special combination of characters (a carriage return followed by a newline) to indicate the end of a line. When reading from a *text* file on those systems, C automatically ignores any carriage return (**\r**) that immediately precedes a newline (**\n**). And similarly, when writing to a *text* file, C inserts a carriage return before every newline. But for a *binary* file or on operating systems (such as UNIX) that use a newline to indicate the end of a line, C doesn't do this conversion.

In general, it's more efficient to work with binary files, since we aren't wasting time converting back and forth between different representations. However, binary files have several drawbacks. One is that they're not portable, as each machine and, in fact, each compiler can provide different internal representations. Another is that binary files are not easily viewable; in fact, to examine them, we usually need to use special tools.

In general, we use text mode when we think of the file as being divided into lines, as in a program that prints every line containing a particular pattern. We use binary files when we don't care how the file is organized, as in a file-copying program or when we treat the file as being divided into records.

We can open a file for reading only if it already exists. But there is no such restriction when we open a file for writing or appending. If the file doesn't exist, it is automatically created for us. If it does exist, opening it for writing wipes out its previous contents and opening it for appending causes new writes to take place at the file's end.

> *Don't open a file for writing unless you're sure you no longer need the data it contains.*

We can open files as either *text* or *binary*, with *text* as the default. To open a file as a specific type, we append a **t** or a **b** to the basic mode, as in **"rt"**, **"wt"**, or **"at"** for text files and **"rb"**, **"wb"**, or **"ab"** for binary files.

After we open a file, we can use any one of a large set of library functions to access its contents. When we're finished with a file, we use **fclose** to *close* it. This forces out any buffered output and frees up the file's **FILE** structure. **fclose** takes a single file-pointer argument and returns **EOF** if there is an error in closing the file. Because most systems have a maximum number of files that can be open simultaneously,[2] we habitually close a file as soon as we no longer need it. All files, however, are automatically closed when our program terminates.

Character File I/O

There are several ways to access an open file. The simplest is a character at a time, using the *macros* **getc** and **putc**, which are analogous to **getchar** and **putchar**. (There are also a couple of equivalent functions, **fgetc** and **fputc**, which we can use when the macros are undesirable.) **getc** takes a file pointer and returns the integer representation of the next character in the file, or **EOF** if it encounters an end of file. **putc** takes the integer representation of a character and a file pointer and writes the character to the file. All of these return **EOF** if an error occurs.

With **getc** and **putc**, we now have the pieces to write a useful utility program to copy files. Figure 19.1 contains this program, called filecopy. It takes two file names as arguments, copying the file named by its first argument into the file named by its second. For example,

    filecopy paper paper.bak

copies the contents of the file paper into the file paper.bak.

filecopy begins by verifying that it was passed three arguments (the program name and the two file names) and prints an error message if it wasn't. Otherwise, it prints the names of the files involved in the copy. It uses a function, **fileCopy**, to perform the copy, passing it the two file names. **fileCopy**, shown in Figure 19.2, opens the files, copies one into the other with **getc** and **putc**, and then closes the files. It returns the number of characters it copied or -1 if it couldn't open both files successfully.

We don't care whether the files are divided into lines, so we open both of them in binary mode. Since opening a file for writing destroys the file's contents, we are careful to do the open for writing only after the open for reading has succeeded. In this way, we destroy the previous contents of the destination file only if there is something to copy. Finally, we also take care to perform the copy only if both opens are successful.

fileCopy checks for only one error, a failed open, and ignores the possibility of other errors, such as a failed read or write. Although this is standard practice, it can cause problems in the unlikely event that an I/O error does occur, and we can make our programs more robust by checking for that possibility.[3] The standard I/O output functions return **EOF** if they detect a write error, so **fileCopy** should print an error

---

[2] On UNIX, for example, we can have at least 20 per program. On MS-DOS, we can specify the maximum number of open files by setting the *files* variable in config.sys.

[3] Usually such failures are caused by hardware errors, but write errors can also occur when a device becomes full and there is no room for the newly written characters.

```
/*
 * File-copying utility.  Usage is: filecopy source dest.
 */
#include <stdio.h>
#include <stdlib.h>

int main(int argc, char *argv[])
{
  long fileCopy(const char *dest, const char *source);

  long copycnt;                     /* number of characters copied */
  int  status = EXIT_FAILURE;       /* program return value */

  if (argc != 3)
    printf("Usage: %s source dest\n", argv[0]);
  else
  {
    printf("Copying %s into %s\n", argv[1], argv[2]);
    if ((copycnt = fileCopy(argv[2], argv[1])) == -1L)
      printf("Copy failed\n");
    else
    {
      printf("Copied %li characters\n", copycnt);
      status = EXIT_SUCCESS;
    }
  }
  return status;
}
```

Figure 19.1   (filecopy.c)   A program to copy one file into another.

message if **putc**'s return value is **EOF**. It should also check **fclose**'s return value, since output is usually buffered and it is possible that the final few characters aren't really written to the file until the file is closed.

Detecting read errors is more difficult, since **EOF** can indicate either an error or end of file. There are two library functions, **feof** and **ferror**, that help us distinguish between these two meanings. **feof** takes a file pointer and returns a non-zero value only when the end of the file has been reached. **ferror** is similar, taking a file pointer and returning non-zero only if an error has occurred in processing that file.

To keep our examples simple, we avoid the added complication of file I/O error handling—but at a cost. When an error does occur, our programs may behave abnormally without indicating any error. Typically, an unchecked input error as **EOF** prematurely terminates input processing, and an unchecked output error results in lost output. In fact, filecopy now simply prints the number of characters in the source file and relies on the user's verifying that the destination file actually has this length. Production-quality programs check the values returned by the standard input and output library functions and provide appropriate error indications.

```
/*
 * Actually copy one file into another.
 */
#include <stdio.h>
#include <stddef.h>

long fileCopy(const char *dest, const char *source)
{
  FILE *sfp;                           /* source file pointer */
  FILE *dfp;                           /* destination file pointer */
  int  c;                              /* next input character */
  long cnt = -1L;                      /* count of characters copied */

  if ((sfp = fopen(source,"rb")) == NULL)
    printf("Can't open %s for reading\n", source);
  else
  {
    if ((dfp = fopen(dest,"wb")) == NULL)
      printf("Can't open %s for writing\n", dest);
    else
    {
      for (cnt = 0L; (c = getc(sfp)) != EOF; cnt++)
        putc(c,dfp);
      fclose(dfp);
    }
    fclose(sfp);
  }
  return cnt;
}
```

Figure 19.2 (filecpy1.c) A function, **fileCopy**, to copy one file into another.

Formatted File I/O

As you might have guessed, both **printf** and **scanf** have counterparts that do formatted I/O on files. **fprintf** is like **printf**, with an additional file-pointer argument that specifies the file to which we write.

> **fprintf** (*file-pointer*, *control-string*, ...)

And **fscanf** is like **scanf**, with an additional file-pointer argument that specifies the file from which we read.

> **fscanf** (*file-pointer*, *control-string*, ...)

Because of their similarity to **printf** and **scanf**, it is easy to forget to pass the file pointer to **fprintf** or **fscanf**. But if we've remembered to include stdio.h, which supplies prototypes for the various library functions, the compiler catches this error for us.

```
/*
 * Read up to "max" values into "a" from file "name".
 */
#include <stdio.h>
#include <stdlib.h>
#include "getints.h"

#define TESTFILE   "table"
#define MAX        20

int main()
{
  int table[MAX];
  int i;
  int status = EXIT_FAILURE;

  for (i = 0; i < MAX; i++)            /* some sample values to write */
    table[i] = i;
  if (filePutInts(TESTFILE, table, MAX) != MAX)
    printf("Couldn't write array to file\n");
  else if (fileGetInts(TESTFILE, table, MAX) != MAX)
    printf("Couldn't read array from file\n");
  else
  {
    printf("Wrote and read %i ints using %s\n", MAX, TESTFILE);
    status = EXIT_SUCCESS;
  }

  return status;
}
```

Figure 19.3   (fints.c) A program to read and write arrays of integers into a file.

Figure 19.3 provides an example use of **fprintf** and **fscanf** in a small program to write an array to a file and then read the file back into the array. It uses two functions, **fileGetInts** and **filePutInts**. **fileGetInts** uses **fscanf** to read an array of integers from a file; **filePutInts** uses **fprintf** to write an array of integers to a file. Figure 19.4 contains their prototypes, and Figure 19.5 contains the functions.

Line-Oriented File I/O

Many programs, such as Chapter 11's uniq, most naturally process their input a line at a time. The standard I/O library provides four functions that do line-at-a-time I/O. The most general of these functions are **fgets** and **fputs**.

fgets takes three parameters: a character array, its size, and a file pointer. It reads characters into the array, stopping when it encounters a newline or finds that the array is full. Unlike our function **getline**, **fgets** includes the newline in the array. **fgets** terminates the array with a null, so it reads at most 1 less than the number of characters

```
/*
 * Prototypes for table-reading and -writing functions.
 */
int filePutInts(const char *name, int *ptr, int max);
int fileGetInts(const char *name, int *ptr, int max);
```

Figure 19.4   (getints.h)   The prototypes for table-reading functions.

```
/*
 * Reading and writing arrays using formatted I/O.
 *   fileGetInts - read values from file into an array.
 *   filePutInts - write values from array into a file.
 */
#include <stdio.h>
#include "getints.h"

int fileGetInts(const char *name, int a[], int max)
{
  int  cnt = 0;
  FILE *fp = fopen(name, "r");

  if (fp != NULL)
  {
    for (; cnt < max && fscanf(fp, "%i", &a[cnt]) == 1; cnt++)
      ;            /* read values while there's room */
    fclose(fp);
  }
  return cnt;     /* number of values actually read */
}

int filePutInts(const char *name, int a[], int num)
{
  int  cnt = 0;
  FILE *fp = fopen(name, "w");

  if (fp != NULL)
  {
    for (; cnt < num; cnt++)
      fprintf(fp, "%i\n", a[cnt]);
    fclose(fp);
  }
  return cnt;          /* assumes write successful */
}
```

Figure 19.5   (getints1.c)   A pair of functions for reading and writing arrays.

in the array. So the call

```
fgets(buffer, MAXLEN + 1, fp)
```

reads up to **MAXLEN** characters, placing them into **buffer**. **fgets** returns **NULL** when the end of file is reached; otherwise, it returns its first argument, a pointer to a character.

If the line (including the trailing newline) is too long, we can keep calling **fgets** to read the rest of the line. Unfortunately, with **fgets** there is no way to determine if the entire input line was read without examining the returned string. This makes **fgets** much less useful than it would be if it returned the line length as **getline** does.

fputs takes a string and a file pointer and writes the string to the file.

```
fputs("Hi Mom! Hi Dad! Send money!\n", fp);
```

writes a single line to the file specified by **fp**. It does not automatically terminate its output with a newline. **fputs** provides a convenient and more efficient way to print a string than **fprintf**, since it eliminates the overhead of parsing the control string. Its one drawback is that the file pointer is its last argument instead of its first argument, as with **fprintf**.

Figure 19.6 uses **fgets** and **fputs** in a new version of **fileCopy**. This line-copying version produces the same result as the character-copying version, albeit somewhat slower. It's not as fast because **fgets** and **fputs** are usually built on top of **getc** and **putc** and because we have to determine the length of each line in the file.

The other two line-oriented functions, **gets** and **puts**, are closely related to **fgets** and **fputs**. Unfortunately, they are also just different enough to cause confusion. **gets** takes a character array, reads a line from the standard input, places it into the array, and terminates the array with a null. It returns a pointer to the array's first character, or **NULL** if it encounters an end of file. Unlike **fgets**, **gets** does not place the terminating newline into the array. **puts** is simpler and more useful, taking a string and writing it and a trailing newline to the standard output.

It would seem that we would use **puts** and **gets** most frequently to prompt the user for input and to read the response, as shown below.

```
puts("What's your name? ");
if (gets(name) != NULL)
  printf("Hi %s!  Do you like C?\n", name);
```

But we don't. One problem is that there is no way to limit the number of characters **gets** reads. That means the program "bombs" if the user enters more characters than the array can accommodate. And **puts** has a problem too: it automatically writes a newline after it writes the string. This means we can't use it to write prompts if we want the cursor to remain on the prompt line.

19.2   THE STANDARD FILES

When our programs start, three text files are automatically opened for us: the standard input, the standard output, and the standard error output. The corresponding file pointers

```
/*
 * Copy one file into another, a line at a time.
 */
#include <stdio.h>
#include <stddef.h>
#include <string.h>

#define MAXLEN  80

long fileCopy(const char *dest, const char *source)
{
  FILE *sfp, *dfp;                /* source and destination files */
  char line[MAXLEN + 1];         /* next input line */
  long cnt = -1L;                /* count of characters written */

  if ((sfp = fopen(source,"rb")) == NULL)
    printf("Can't open %s for reading\n", source);
  else
  {
    if ((dfp = fopen(dest,"wb")) == NULL)
      printf("Can't open %s for writing\n", dest);
    else
    {
      for (cnt = 0L;
           fgets(line, sizeof(line), sfp) != NULL;
           cnt += strlen(line))
        fputs(line,dfp);
      fclose(dfp);
    }
    fclose(sfp);
  }
  return cnt;
}
```

Figure 19.6 (filecpy2.c) A function to copy files line by line. Surprisingly, this is slower than character by character.

are **stdin**, **stdout**, and **stderr** and are defined in stdio.h. These file pointers are constants, so we can't assign to them.

We've already been using **stdin** and **stdout**, even though we didn't know it. That is because **getchar** and **putchar** are defined as macros that expand into calls to **getc** and **putc**.

```
#define getchar()      getc(stdin)
#define putchar(c)     putc(c, stdout)
```

Similarly, we can read from the standard input with either **scanf(...)** or with **fscanf(stdin, ...)**, and we can write to the standard output with either **printf(...)** or with **fprintf(stdout, ...)**.

One other common explicit use of **stdout** is to write prompts with **fputs**, since it doesn't automatically write a newline and **puts** does.

We haven't used **stderr** yet. **stderr** is the place where we write error messages, since they will then show up on the display, even if the standard output has been redirected. That is, **stderr** is an output file like **stdout**, but it isn't redirected when we redirect **stdout**.

We use **stderr** in the functions **fileOpen** and **fileClose**. Figure 19.7 supplies their prototypes, and Figure 19.8 contains the functions themselves. **fileOpen** is an extension to **fopen** that not only opens the file for us but also writes an error message to **stderr** if it fails. **fileClose** takes a file name and a file pointer, closing the file if it wasn't passed a **NULL** pointer and writing an error message if necessary. These two functions simplify our file-handling functions, since they take care of the messy error handling. Later in this chapter, we'll see just how convenient they are.

19.3   RANDOM FILE ACCESS

All our file processing has been sequential. That is, we started reading at the beginning of the file and read characters one after the other until we hit its end. But we are sometimes interested in only part of a file, and we want to avoid reading all the preceding data. In effect, we want to treat a file like an array, indexing any byte in the file as we would an array element. Three standard I/O functions support this random file access: **fseek**, **rewind**, and **ftell**.

fseek moves the internal file pointer, which points to the next character in the file, to a specified location within the file. It takes three arguments—a file pointer, a **long** offset, and an **int** specifier—and computes the new location by adding the offset to the part of the file specified by the specifier.

For text files, the offset must come from the function **ftell**, discussed below. For binary files, the offset is simply some number of bytes. In either case, however, the offset is a **long**.

The specifier must have one of three values: **SEEK_SET** (0) means the beginning of the file, **SEEK_CUR** (1) means the current position, and **SEEK_END** (2) means the end of the file. Here are some example **fseek**s:

```
fseek(fp, 0L, SEEK_SET); /* go to the start of the file */
fseek(fp, 0L, SEEK_CUR); /* don't move (not too useful!) */
fseek(fp, 0L, SEEK_END); /* go to the end of the file */
fseek(fp, n,  SEEK_SET); /* go to the nth byte in the file */
fseek(fp, n,  SEEK_CUR); /* skip ahead n bytes */
fseek(fp, -n, SEEK_CUR); /* go backward n bytes */
fseek(fp, -n, SEEK_END); /* go to n bytes before the end */
```

fseek returns −1 if there is an error and zero otherwise. In most systems, errors include attempting to seek past the file's boundaries, as well as trying to seek on a closed file. But on some systems, such as MS-DOS, it will return a failure only if the file isn't open. We have ignored **fseek**'s return value in these examples, but by checking it we can verify that the file position was changed.

```
/*
 * Prototypes for fileOpen/fileClose functions.
 */
#include <stdio.h>
#include <stddef.h>

extern FILE *fileOpen(const char *name, const char *mode);
extern void fileClose(const char *name, FILE *fp);
```

Figure 19.7 (fileopen.h) Prototypes for our file-opening and -closing functions.

```
/*
 * Open/close files, with error message on failure.
 *    fileOpen - open a file (built on top of fopen).
 *    fileClose - close a file (built on top of fclose).
 */
#include "fileopen.h"

FILE *fileOpen(const char *name, const char *mode)
{
  FILE *fp = fopen(name, mode);              /* open the file */

  if (fp == NULL)                            /* did open fail? */
  {
    fprintf(stderr, "Can't open %s for ", name);
    switch(mode[0])
    {
      case 'r': fprintf(stderr, "reading\n");
                break;
      case 'w': fprintf(stderr, "writing\n");
                break;
      case 'a': fprintf(stderr, "appending\n");
                break;
      default:  fprintf(stderr, "some strange mode\n");
                break;
    }
  }
  return fp;
}

void fileClose(const char *name, FILE *fp)
{
  if (fp != NULL && fclose(fp) == EOF)
    fprintf(stderr, "Error closing %s\n", name);
}
```

Figure 19.8 (fileopen.c) The functions **fileOpen** and **fileClose** that open and close files, printing any necessary error message to the standard error output.

rewind is a special case **fseek** that moves the internal file pointer to the beginning of the file. That is,

```
rewind(fp)
```

is the equivalent of

```
fseek(fp, 0L, SEEK_SET)
```

except that **rewind** returns no value and clears the internal **EOF** and error indicators. A **rewind** happens implicitly during any **fopen** for reading or writing (but not, of course, during an **fopen** for appending). Any input function immediately following a **rewind** begins its reading with the file's first character. **rewind** lets a program read through a file more than once without having to repeatedly open and close the file.

The final function, **ftell**, takes a file pointer and returns a **long** containing the current offset in the file, the position of the next byte to be read or written. So an **ftell** at the beginning of the file returns the position of the file's first byte, and an **ftell** at the end of the file returns the number of bytes in the file. Typically, programs use **ftell** to save their current position in a file so that they can easily return to it later, without having to read all the intervening data.

We use **ftell** and **fseek** in two programs. Figure 19.9 prints the number of bytes in the files provided as its arguments. It uses a function **fileLength** to compute each file's length. **fileLength**, in turn, uses **ftell** to save the current position in the file, **fseek** to go to the end of the file, **ftell** to record that position (which is the file's length), and another **fseek** to return to the previous position within the file. We are careful to test **fseek**'s return value, because the file pointer's position doesn't change if we specify an invalid location to which to move.

Figure 19.10 contains a program to print the last 10 lines of each of the files specified as its arguments. It is especially useful for examining files, such as log files, in which new information is always appended to the end.

There is an especially easy way to write this program. We can use **fseek** to get to the file's end and then read the file backward until the desired number of newlines have been seen. We can read backward by first saving the current offset with **ftell**, reading a character with **getc**, and then using **fseek** to move to the character before the saved offset. Once we find the beginning of the appropriate line, we simply read and display the rest of the characters in the file. The problem with this simple-minded solution is that it is slow—we execute several library calls each time we read a character.

We improve this scheme by reading a *block* of characters each time and then counting the newlines within each block. Figure 19.11 contains the functions that actually handle reading a block and counting the newlines. The program's surprising length arises from its substantial error checking.

19.4   BLOCK INPUT AND OUTPUT

The standard I/O library functions we've seen so far are used to read and write characters. C also provides two functions to read and write blocks of bytes: **fread** reads an array of

```
/*
 * Find each file's length in bytes. Usage: filelen file1 ...
 */
#include <stdlib.h>
#include "fileopen.h"

int main(int argc, char *argv[])
{
  long fileLength(FILE *fp);

  int  i;                            /* argument length */
  long len;                          /* next file's length */
  FILE *fp;                          /* file pointer */

  for (i = 1; i < argc; i++)
  {
    if ((fp = fileOpen(argv[i], "rb")) != NULL)
      if ((len = fileLength(fp)) == -1)
        fprintf(stderr,"Can't compute length of %s\n", argv[i]);
      else
        printf("%s: %li\n", argv[i], len);
    fileClose(argv[i], fp);
  }

  return EXIT_SUCCESS;
}

long fileLength(FILE *fp)
{
  long oldpos = ftell(fp);              /* save old position */
  long length;

  if (fseek(fp, 0L, SEEK_END) == -1)    /* go to end of file */
    return -1;

  length = ftell(fp);                    /* compute length */
  return (fseek(fp, oldpos, SEEK_SET) == -1) ? -1 : length;
}
```

Figure 19.9   (filelen.c) A program to rapidly determine the size in bytes of a file.

bytes from a file, and **fwrite** writes an array to a file. Both require four parameters: a pointer to the array's first element (a pointer to **void**), the size (in bytes) of an element, the number of elements in the array, and a file pointer. Both return the number of elements successfully read or written; zero indicates the end of file or an error.

Figure 19.12 uses **fread** and **fwrite** in new versions of **fileGetInts** and **filePutInts**. Now **fileGetInts** reads the array with a single **fread**, and **filePutInts** writes the array with a single **fwrite**.

```
/*
 * Print last 10 lines of each file.
 */
#include <stdlib.h>
#include "fileopen.h"

#define LAST       10              /* last 10 lines of the file */

int main(int argc, char *argv[])
{
  long findPosition(FILE *fp, int lastline);
  void displayUntilEOF(FILE *fp);

  int  i;                          /* index */
  long pos;                        /* position of newline within block */
  FILE *fp;                        /* file we're reading through */

  for (i = 1; i < argc; i++)
    if ((fp = fileOpen(argv[i],"rb")) != NULL)
    {
      if ((pos = findPosition(fp, LAST)) == -1L ||
          fseek(fp, pos, SEEK_SET) == -1)
        fprintf(stderr,"Couldn't tail %s\n", argv[i]);
      else
        displayUntilEOF(fp);
      fileClose(argv[1], fp);
    }

  return EXIT_SUCCESS;             /* no special return value for error */
}

void displayUntilEOF(FILE *fp)
{
  int c;                           /* next character to display */

  while ((c = getc(fp)) != EOF)            /* display lines */
    putc(c, stdout);
}
```

Figure 19.10   (tail.c) A program to print the last 10 lines of each of the files specified as its arguments.

The new versions aren't exactly equivalent, however. To see why, note that our call to **fwrite** simply writes **sizeof(int)** $\times$ **num** bytes to the file, the first byte coming from **&x[0]**. And similarly, our call to **fread** reads the next **sizeof(int)** $\times$ **max** bytes from the file into the array **a**. No translation to and from ASCII characters takes place. This means the file is a binary file rather than a text file, and we are careful to specify the **rb** and **wb** modes when we open it.

fread and **fwrite** provide a convenient and efficient way to save internal tables between program runs. We often use **fwrite** to save an internal table when a program

```c
/*
 * Utility functions for tail program.
 *    findPosition - locate first character in file to print.
 *    nextBlock - read next block of characters in file.
 */
#include <stdio.h>

#define MAXBUF 512              /* characters in block */

long findPosition(FILE *fp, int lines)
{
  int  nextBlock(FILE *fp, int max, int *cnt, int target);

  int  count = 0;              /* newlines seen */
  long pos;                    /* position of desired newline in file */
  long blkend;                 /* position of last char in block */
  int  blksize;                /* # of characters within block */

  if (fseek(fp, 0L, SEEK_END) == -1)
     return -1;                /* get to end of file */

  for (blkend = ftell(fp); blkend >= 0; blkend -= MAXBUF)
  {
    blksize = (MAXBUF > blkend) ? (int) blkend : MAXBUF;
    if (fseek(fp, blkend - blksize, SEEK_SET) == -1)
       return -1;              /* couldn't go back a block - error */
    if ((pos = nextBlock(fp, blksize, &count, lines)) != -1)
       return blkend - blksize + pos;
  }

  return 0L;                   /* start at beginning */
}

int nextBlock(FILE *fp, int max, int *cnt, int target)
{
  char buffer[MAXBUF];               /* to hold block */
  char *ptr    = buffer;             /* pointer into buffer */
  char *endptr = buffer + max;       /* pointer to end of buffer */
  int  c;

  for (; ptr < endptr && (c = getc(fp)) != EOF; *ptr++ = c)
    ;                                /* read next block */
  *ptr = '\0';
  for (; ptr >= buffer; ptr--)
    if (*ptr == '\n' && (*cnt)++ == target)
      return ptr - buffer + 1;       /* where to start reading */
  return -1;                         /* have to read another block */
}
```

Figure 19.11   (tailutls.c)   Functions to determine where in the file we need to begin printing.

```
/*
 * New versions of our earlier functions to read and write arrays.
 * Now they use fread/fwrite to read/write the arrays all at once.
 *
 * The resulting files are not readable in text-based editors and
 * viewers.
 */
#include "fileopen.h"
#include "getints.h"

int fileGetInts(const char *name, int a[], int max)
{
  FILE *fp = fileOpen(name, "rb");
  int   cnt = -1;

  if (fp != NULL)
    cnt = fread((void *) a, sizeof(int), max, fp);
  fileClose(name, fp);
  return cnt;                       /* # of elements written or -1 */
}

int filePutInts(const char *name, int a[], int num)
{
  FILE *fp = fileOpen(name, "wb");
  int   cnt = -1;

  if (fp != NULL)
    cnt = fwrite((void *) a, sizeof(int), num, fp);
  fileClose(name, fp);
  return cnt;                       /* # of elements written or -1 */
}
```

Figure 19.12   (getints2.c) New version of our functions to read and write arrays of integers.

finishes and **fread** to read it the next time the program starts. This method is much more efficient than using **fprintf** and **fscanf** but has the disadvantage that the saved table is not text and cannot be easily examined.

> **fread** *and* **fwrite** *are portable, but the files they read and write aren't.*

To see why, consider a file containing 100 **int**s written using **fwrite**. If **int**s are 2 bytes, this file takes 200 bytes. Now suppose we move the file to a machine with 4-byte **int**s, and we try to read it using **fread** and telling **fread** to read 100 **int**s. **fread** will try to read 400 bytes, which it won't be able to do. The moral: Don't use **fwrite** to create files to be transferred between machines.

19.5   FILE UPDATING

There are three file modes we haven't yet mentioned: **r+**, **w+**, and **a+**. The trailing **+** means "open for update". When we open a file for update we are allowed to both read and write to it—with one important restriction. We can't immediately follow a read with a write or a write with a read; there must be an intervening **fseek**. Except for the ability to update, the modes have the same effects as their earlier counterparts. That is, when we open a file for **"r+"**, the file must already exist. When we open a file for **"w+"**, the file is either created or truncated. And when we open a file for **"a+"**, the file is created if it doesn't exist, and the internal file pointer moved to the end of the file.

The update modes allows us to change a file's contents without completely rewriting it. We'll show how useful this is by writing a little package that allows us to create and access an array of any type, with its elements stored in a file rather than in memory. We call such an array a *virtual* array. Virtual arrays are a convenient—but slow—way to store a large table when we have a limited amount of available memory. The package also makes it easy for us to use files as arrays without forcing us to sprinkle lots and lots of **fseek**s, **fread**s, and **fwrite**s throughout our code.

Our package lets us access these virtual arrays in the same way we access files. We first open them, which gives us a handle that we then pass to the functions that access or change an element's value. And when we are done, we close them.

How do we open a virtual array? We provide two possibilities: **vaCreate** and **vaOpen**. We use **vaCreate** to create a new virtual array. It takes two arguments: the name of the file in which the array is to be stored and the size in bytes of one of its elements. The function opens the file using mode **w+b**, which wipes out any previous contents and allows us to subsequently read or write the file. **vaCreate** returns a pointer to a **Varray**. A **Varray** is a structure, like **FILE**, that contains information needed by the other functions in our package. Specifically, it contains a file pointer, the file's name, and the size of an element.

We use the other function, **vaOpen**, to access an existing virtual array. Like **vaCreate**, it takes a pair of arguments: the name of the file and the size in bytes of an element. Unlike **vaCreate**, however, **vaOpen** opens the file with mode **r+b**, which succeeds only if the file already exists. Like **vaCreate**, **vaOpen** returns a pointer to a **Varray**.

Once we've opened a virtual array, we use **vaGet** and **vaPut** to access or change the values of its elements. Both take similar parameters: a pointer to a **Varray**, the index of the desired element, and a pointer to a buffer the size of an array element. **vaGet** determines the element's location within the file, uses **fseek** to move to that location, and then uses **fread** to read its value into the provided buffer. **vaPut** does the opposite: it writes the buffer's contents to the appropriate position in the file. Both functions (actually macros) return zero if they can't access the specified array element.

There's one restriction on using **vaPut**: we can use it only to assign a new value to an existing array element or to append a single new element onto the end of the array. This restriction arises because we can't use **fseek** to move the internal file pointer past the end of the file. This isn't a terrible limitation, however, since we can create and initialize the elements of a virtual array by repeatedly using **vaPut**.

```
/*
 * Define virtual array type, prototypes, and macros.
 */
#include <stdio.h>
#include <stddef.h>
#include <stdlib.h>

typedef struct varray
{
  FILE *fp;        /* pointer to external file */
  int  size;       /* size of an element */
} Varray;

Varray *vaCreate(const char *name, int size);
Varray *vaOpen(const char *name, int size);

#define vaClose(vaptr) ((void) fclose(vaptr->fp), free(vaptr))

#define vaEntries(vaptr) \
  (fseek((vaptr)->fp, 0L, SEEK_END) == -1L \
      ? -1 : (int) (ftell((vaptr)->fp) / (vaptr)->size))

#define vaGet(vaptr, i, ptr)  \
  (fseek((vaptr)->fp, (long) (i) * (vaptr)->size, SEEK_SET) != -1 && \
        fread((ptr), (vaptr)->size, 1, (vaptr)->fp) == 1)

#define vaPut(vaptr, i, ptr)  \
  (fseek((vaptr)->fp, (long) (i) * (vaptr)->size, SEEK_SET) != -1 && \
        fwrite((ptr), (vaptr)->size, 1, (vaptr)->fp) == 1)
```

Figure 19.13 (varray.h) Header file for virtual array package.

The package's final function, **vaClose**, closes a virtual array. It takes a pointer to a **Varray**, closes its file, and deallocates its **Varray** structure.

We divide our virtual array package into two parts. Figure 19.13 is a header file that defines the **Varray** type and provides prototypes and macros for the various virtual array operations. Figure 19.14 contains the operations themselves. We use these virtual arrays in this chapter's case study.

19.6   CASE STUDY—AN ELECTRONIC ADDRESS BOOK

This section is optional!

We bring together many of the concepts covered in this text by implementing a small indexed file containing names, addresses, and phone numbers—a computerized little black book. Our address book consists of two files, bb and bb.idx. bb is a text file that holds records that contain names, addresses, and phone numbers. The only requirements are that the each record's first line contain the person's name and its last line contain

```
/*
 * Operations for creating or opening a virtual array.
 */
#include "allocs.h"                    /* Our memory macros (Chapter 15) */
#include "varray.h"

static Varray *makeVarray(const char *name, const char *mode, int size)
{
  FILE    *fp  = fopen(name, mode);
  Varray *new = (fp != NULL) ? ALLOC(1, Varray) : NULL;

  if (new != NULL)
  {
    new->fp = fp;
    new->size = size;
  }
  else if (fp != NULL)
    (void) fclose(fp);
  return new;
}

Varray *vaCreate(const char *name, int size)   /* create a new Varray */
  { return makeVarray(name, "w+b", size); }

Varray *vaOpen(const char *name, int size)     /* open existing Varray */
  { return makeVarray(name, "r+b", size); }
```

Figure 19.14   (varray.c) Several functions for creating and opening virtual arrays.

a '.' on a line by itself. bb.idx is a binary file that contains a person's name and the starting position of its corresponding record in bb. We keep this index file sorted by name. Figure 19.15 shows a sample address book.

The idea is that we create and maintain bb using any ordinary text editor, but look up addresses and phone numbers using a special program. This program, lookup, doesn't simply do a slow sequential search of bb. Instead, it does a fast binary search through bb.idx to determine exactly where in bb the desired record is located and then goes directly to this location to retrieve it. Unlike bb, however, we don't access bb.idx directly. We construct it by running another special program. This program, index, travels through bb, building a table of names and record locations. It then sorts the table and writes it to bb.idx. To ensure that the index file is up to date, we must run index whenever we modify the file containing the names and addresses.

Both of these programs need the definition of an index structure, so we've placed it in a header file, index.h. Figure 19.16 shows this file, which also contains constants for the address book file names, the input line length, and the end-of-record delimiter. Both programs treat the index file as a virtual array, so index.h includes varray.h.

Figures 19.17, 19.18, and 19.19 contain index, which is surprisingly straightforward, despite its long length. It opens the file provided as its argument, and calls

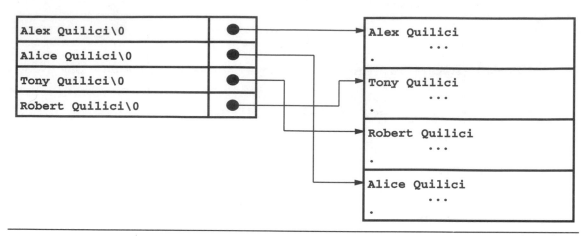

Figure 19.15 Our address book: one file contains the data and the other a sorted index.

```
/*
 * Definitions to use indexes.
 */
#include <string.h>
#include "varray.h"                       /* for external array */

#define MAXLEN      80                     /* maximum line length */
#define MAXKEY      40                     /* maximum key size */
#define INDEXFILE   "idx"                  /* the index file */
#define ENDREC(x)   ((*x) == '.')          /* end of a record */
#define MAXIDX      100                    /* max number of records */

struct index_rec                           /* index record: */
{
  char key[MAXKEY];                        /*    name */
  long pos;                                /*    position */
};

typedef struct index_rec Index, *IndexPtr;
```

Figure 19.16 (index.h) The address book header file.

```
/*
 * Create the index table for a file.
 */
#include "index.h"                        /* definition of INDEX */
#include "fileopen.h"                     /* fileOpen, fileClose */

int main(int argc, char *argv[])
{
  int processTable(FILE *fp, char *filename);

  FILE   *fp;                             /* text file name */
  int    status = EXIT_FAILURE;           /* exit status */

  if (argc != 2)
    fprintf(stderr, "Usage: %s file\n", argv[0]);
  else
  {
    if ((fp = fileOpen(argv[1], "rb")) == NULL)
      fprintf(stderr, "Can't open index file\n");
    else if (processTable(fp,argv[1]))
      status = EXIT_SUCCESS;
    fileClose(argv[1], fp);
  }

  return status;
}
```

Figure 19.17   (index.c)   The program that creates the indexed address book.

processTable to build the name-location table with **makeTable**, sort it with **qsort**, and then write it to an external file with **saveTable**. **saveTable** uses our **Varray** functions to create and save this table as an external array.

Figures 19.20, 19.21, and 19.22 contain lookup, which is also surprisingly straightforward. It repeatedly prompts for names and prints the corresponding addresses and phone numbers. lookup also treats the index file as a virtual array, but uses a new function, **vaSearch**, to look up locations. **vaSearch** is simply a binary search routine that uses **vaGet** to access the desired record in the file.

SUMMARY

- C allows us to access external files through library functions.

- We use **fopen** to open files and **fclose** to close them. To open a file, we need to specify the file name and how we're going to use it. The three files **stdin**, **stdout**, and **stderr** are automatically opened for us.

```
/*
 * Build index, sort it, and save it to a file.
 */
#include "index.h"

int processTable(FILE *fp, char *filename)
{
  int   makeTable(FILE *fp, Index table[]);
  int   saveTable(char *name, Index table[], int n);
  int   cmpKey(const void *, const void *);

  Index itable[MAXIDX];                /* holds index table */
  int   items;                         /* items in table */
  char  iname[MAXLEN + 1];             /* index file name */
  int   status = 0;                    /* assume failure */

  if ((items = makeTable(fp, itable)) == -1)
    fprintf(stderr, "Too many index entries\n");
  else
  {
    qsort(itable, items, sizeof(itable[0]), cmpKey);
    sprintf(iname,"%s.%s", filename, INDEXFILE);
    if (saveTable(iname, itable, items) != items)
      fprintf(stderr, "Couldn't build index file\n");
    else
      status = 1;                      /* worked */
  }
  return status;
}

int cmpKey(const void *xptr, const void *yptr)
  { return strcmp(((IndexPtr) xptr)->key, ((IndexPtr) yptr)->key); }
```

Figure 19.18   (indexp.c)   A table that constructs an index table.

- We can use **getc** and **putc** to do character-at-a-time I/O to files. **getchar** and **putchar** are macros defined on top of these routines.

- We can use **fgets** and **fputs** to do line-at-a-time I/O to files. These usually are slower than **getc** and **putc**, and they weren't designed with ease of use in mind, so we tend not to use them very much.

- We can use **fseek** to move to any byte in a file, **rewind** to move to the beginning of a file, and **ftell** to find out where in the file we actually are.

- We use **fread** and **fwrite** to read and write blocks of bytes to a file.

- There are special update modes, indicated with a '+' sign, that allow us to both read from and write to the same file.

```
/*
 * Functions to construct and save the index table.
 *    saveTable - write index table into file.
 *    makeTable - build index table from reading file.
 */
#include "index.h"

int saveTable(char *name, Index table[], int n)
{
  int i = -1;                   /* indicates create-failed error */
  Varray *vaptr;                /* the virtual array we create */

  if ((vaptr = vaCreate(name, sizeof(table[0]))) != NULL)
  {
    for (i = 0; i < n; i++)
      if (vaPut(vaptr, i, &table[i]) == -1)
        break;
    vaClose(vaptr);
  }
  return i;
}

int makeTable(FILE *fp, Index table[])
{
  char line[MAXLEN + 1];        /* next line */
  long pos;                     /* record's pos in file */
  int  linecnt = 0;             /* # of lines in record */
  int  cnt = 0;                 /* count of records */
  int  last;                    /* index to last character in line */

  while (pos = ftell(fp), fgets(line, sizeof(line), fp) != NULL)
  {
    if (linecnt++ == 0)         /* add a table entry */
    {
      if (cnt == MAXIDX)
        return -1;
      last = strlen(line) - 1;            /* strip non-key chars */
      if (line[last - 1] == '\r')         /* \r\n ends line */
        line[last - 1] = '\0';
      else                                /* \n ends line */
        line[last] = '\0';
      strncpy(table[cnt].key, line, MAXKEY);
      table[cnt++].pos = pos;             /* store position */
    }
    if (ENDREC(line))
      linecnt = 0;
  }
  return cnt;
}
```

Figure 19.19   (indextab.c)   The functions to build and save an index table.

```
/*
 * Look up addresses/phone numbers given name.
 */
#include "index.h"
#include "fileopen.h"

int main(int argc, char *argv[])
{
  int   findNames(FILE *fp, char *name);

  FILE *fp;                               /* address book */
  char iname[MAXLEN + 1];                 /* index name */
  int  status = EXIT_FAILURE;             /* return value */

  if (argc != 2)
    fprintf(stderr, "usage: %s file\n", argv[0]);
  else if ((fp = fileOpen(argv[1], "rb")) != NULL)
  {
    sprintf(iname, "%s.%s", argv[1], INDEXFILE);
    if (findNames(fp, iname))
      status = EXIT_SUCCESS;
      fileClose(argv[1],fp);
  }

  return status;
}
```

Figure 19.20   (lookup.c) Program to look up records in the address book.

EXERCISES

Explore

19–1 Compile and run the programs in this chapter.

19–2 Determine how to view the binary files produced by this chapter's programs.

Modify

19–3 Rewrite **fileCopy** to use **fread** and **fwrite**.

19–4 To find an address with lookup (Figure 19.20), we have to specify an entire name. Modify it to allow partial matches and to print all records matching the given name.

19–5 Modify lookup (Figure 19.20) so that it obtains the names it searches for from its command-line arguments.

19–6 Modify index (Figure 19.17) and lookup (Figure 19.20) to allow fast access to records by phone number. You'll have to impose some additional structure on the file: the line containing the phone number must be easily identifiable.

19–7 Rewrite Chapter 12's program to store employee information to store its data in a file rather than an array. The program should keep an internal index table so that it can

```
/*
 * Interact with the lookup program's user
 */
#include "index.h"

int findNames(FILE *fp, char *name)
{
  long    vaSearch(Varray *ep, int first, int last, char *target);
  long    displayRecord(FILE *fp, long pos);
  int     getline(char *, int);

  int     entries;                          /* # of entries in file */
  Varray *vaptr;                            /* virtual array */
  char    line[MAXLEN + 1];                 /* user input line */
  long    pos;                              /* position of record */

  if ((vaptr = vaOpen(name, sizeof(Index))) == NULL)
  {
    fprintf(stderr,"Can't access index file %s\n", name);
    return 0;    /* oops... */
  }
  entries = vaEntries(vaptr);
  while (fputs("Name? ", stdout), getline(line, MAXLEN) != -1)
    if ((pos = vaSearch(vaptr, 0, entries - 1, line)) == -1)
      fprintf(stderr, "Couldn't find: %s\n", line);
    else if (displayRecord(fp, pos) == -1)
      fprintf(stderr, "Couldn't display record at %li\n", pos);
  vaClose(vaptr);
  return 1;      /* success */
}
```

Figure 19.21   (lookupn.c) A function that interacts with the user.

access records quickly. When the program terminates, it writes this index table to a file. When the program starts, it begins with the existing index table.

19–8 We can speed up our array-accessing functions by keeping a cache of the most recently accessed array elements. The cache is a small in-memory array, and whenever we access an array element, we first check the cache. If the value is there, we've saved a file access. If it isn't, we access the file element as before, except that we also add it to the cache, removing whatever item has been in the cache the longest (writing it to the file if its value has changed).

Extend

19–9 Rewrite `fileCopy` (Figure 19.2) to use `fileOpen` and `fileClose` and to check for both read and write errors.

19–10 Make uniq (Figure 11.17) work with external files provided as command arguments. When no arguments are provided, it should use the standard input, as before.

```
/*
 * Get name from user, look it up, and display record.
 */
#include <string.h>
#include "index.h"

long displayRecord(FILE *fp, long pos)
{
  int   rval;                          /* fseek's return value */
  char line[MAXLEN + 1];               /* holds user input */

  if ((rval = fseek(fp, pos, SEEK_SET)) != -1)
    while (fgets(line, sizeof(line), fp) && !ENDREC(line))
      fputs(line,stdout);
  return rval;
}

long vaSearch(Varray *vaptr, int first, int last, char *target)
{
  int    mid = (first + last) / 2;     /* mid item */
  Index next;                          /* to hold record */
  int    cmp;                          /* holds comparison result */

  if (last < first || !vaGet(vaptr, mid, (void *) &next))
    return -1L;                        /* not there */
  if ((cmp = strncmp(target, next.key, MAXKEY)) == 0)
    return next.pos;                   /* found it */
  return (cmp < 0)  ? vaSearch(vaptr, first, mid - 1, target)
                    : vaSearch(vaptr, mid + 1, last, target);
}
```

Figure 19.22   (find.c) Functions that actually search file for name and display record.

19–11 Modify tail (Figure 19.10) to provide a command-line option that allows the user to select the number of lines to display.

Code **19–12** Write a function, **fileAppend**, that appends one file to the end of another. Can **fileCopy** and **fileAppend** be combined into a single function? Is this a good idea?

19–13 Implement **fgets**, **fputs**, **puts**, **gets**, **fread**, and **fwrite** using only **getc** and **putc**.

19–14 Write a function, **filegetline**, that is just like **getline** except that it reads its input from a file rather than the standard input.

19–15 Write a program to print the line number of the first byte where two files differ.

19–16 Write a program that counts the number of words, lines, and characters in each of the files supplied as its arguments.

19–17 Write a little program that prints the indexing information for the address book. It should print each entry in the index file in a readable format. It should verify that the indexed entry is indeed there and print its length in bytes. And finally, it should print some summary information, including the total number of entries in the address book and the average size of an entry.

19–18 Write a program that takes three arguments—a file name, a byte offset, and a byte count—and prints the specified bytes within the specified file.

19–19 Write a program, rev, that reverses the files provided as its arguments, one character at a time. This program is a useful April Fools' Day substitute for the DOS type and UNIX cat commands.

19–20 Write a program keep that prints only certain lines in the files provided as its arguments. The lines to print are specified as options. The command

keep -1-10 -50,52,54 *filename*

prints the first 10 lines of filename followed by lines 50, 52, and 54. keep should work with the standard input if no files are specified.

19–21 Write an insertion sort that works with virtual arrays. Use any of the earlier insertion sort programs as a starting point.

Build **19–22** Write a program, cut, that prints only certain characters in the lines of the files provided as its arguments. As with keep, the relevant characters are provided as options. The command

cut -1-10 -50,52 *file*

prints each line without printing its first 10 characters and without characters 50 and 52.

19–23 Write a program that allows a user to examine any specified line in a file. It should construct an index table, an array whose items hold the starting position of the corresponding line in the file. To get to the user-specified line, it uses it as an index into the table and then uses **fseek** to move to that position in the file.

19–24 Write a program to manage student grades. The program should keep these grades in a single file, with one record per student. The record should include a name, an ID number, room for 10 numeric grades, and room for a final letter grade. You should provide operations to add and delete students, to change information about a student, and to add, delete, and change grades. Index the file by student ID number. You also need to provide operations to assign grades, to print the information on various students, and to print a grading summary for the entire file.

20 LISTS AND TREES

This chapter examines two linked data structures: linked lists and binary search trees. We introduce linked lists and present a set of functions for managing ordered lists, stacks, and queues, regardless of the data stored in a list element. And we introduce binary search trees and present a set of functions for managing them. We end the chapter with a case study that uses both lists and trees—a cross-referencer that produces a listing of all the words in its input, along with the line numbers on which they appear.

20.1   LINKED LISTS

Up to now we've been using arrays to store tables of values. But arrays have a pair of problems.

First, there's no easy way to maintain an array in sorted order. Instead, we're stuck with shifting array elements to make room for a new element or to close up the space used by an deleted element. That's troublesome if we're constantly updating an array's elements, since when we're unlucky and have to insert or delete one of the first few elements of the array, we're going to end up moving almost all of its elements.

Second, there's no convenient and efficient way to change an array's size at run time. To do so, we're stuck with allocating a larger table and then copying our original table into it. That's an expensive operation, so we're really forced to guess accurately how many elements an array is going to need. But if we guess wrong, we're in trouble. Underestimating our storage requirements leads to our running out of space when an array fills up. And overestimating them leads to wasting space or to writing programs that may not compile on some machines because there isn't sufficient storage.

Linked lists are dynamic data structures that help us get around these problems. A linked list consists of a collection of objects called *nodes*. Each node contains two fields: a *data* field, which corresponds to an array element, and a *pointer* field, which contains a pointer to the next node in the linked list. A **NULL** pointer field marks the end of the list.

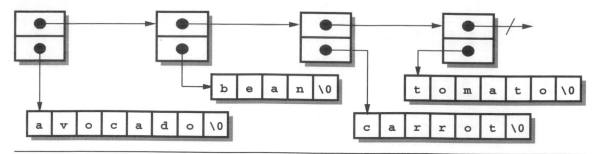

Figure 20.1 Linked list of nodes with pointers to a character string.

Figure 20.1 shows a typical linked list of strings. Here the data field is a pointer to a character, rather than a character array itself. That's because strings can vary in length, and storing them this way eliminates wasted space and allows the space for the node itself to be a small fixed amount: room for the string pointer, plus room for the pointer to the next node. The trade-off is that we must now not only create nodes, but also allocate space for the string.

Linked lists have a pair of advantages over arrays. We can insert an element into the list without shifting all of the elements that follow: we simply adjust the pointers appropriately. And we can have an unlimited number of values in the list—unlike arrays, where we had to predeclare a maximum number of values. The disadvantage is that we must sequentially search the list to find the elements we want, a potentially time-consuming operation, rather than directly indexing it.

Representing Linked Lists

We can represent linked list nodes in a structure containing two fields.

```
typedef struct listnode
{
  void *dataptr;             /* ptr to node's data */
  struct listnode *nextptr;  /* ptr to next list node */
} ListNode;
```

The **dataptr** field holds a pointer to the data corresponding to the node. It's a pointer to **void** so it can hold a pointer to any type of data. **nextptr** holds the pointer to the next node in the list. To clarify and simplify the use of this structure, we use **typedef** to define **ListNode** as a synonym for a **listnode** structure.

Unlike array elements, we have to allocate space for each individual list node. And when we no longer need a node, it's our responsibility to free it up if we plan on reusing the storage.

Figure 20.2 is a header file defining the **ListNode** type, and Figure 20.3 defines a pair of functions for creating and destroying list nodes: **listNodeCreate** and **listNodeDestroy**.

```
/*
 * Linked list node type and prototypes.
 */
#include <stddef.h>                   /* for NULL */
#include <stdlib.h>                   /* for malloc/free */

typedef struct listnode
{
  void *dataptr;                      /* ptr to node's data */
  struct listnode *nextptr;           /* ptr to next list node */
} ListNode;

ListNode *listNodeCreate(void *dataptr, ListNode *nodeptr);
void listNodeDestroy(ListNode *nodeptr);
```

Figure 20.2 (lnodes.h) Definition of linked list nodes.

```
/*
 * Manage linked list nodes.
 *    listNodeCreate - create new list node.
 *    listNodeDestroy - free space used by existing list node.
 */
#include "lnodes.h"                          /* node type, prototypes */

ListNode *listNodeCreate(void *dataptr, ListNode *nodeptr)
{
  ListNode *nptr = malloc(sizeof(ListNode));

  if (nptr != NULL)
  {
    nptr->dataptr = dataptr;               /* points to data */
    nptr->nextptr = nodeptr;               /* points to next node */
  }
  return nptr;
}

void listNodeDestroy(ListNode *nptr)
  { free(nptr); }                          /* destroy node, not data */
```

Figure 20.3 (lnodes.c) Functions to create and destroy linked list nodes.

listNodeCreate allocates space for a node and fills in the node's fields. It takes two arguments: a pointer to the data to be contained in this node, and a pointer to the node that will follow it. It uses **malloc** to allocate space for a single **ListNode** and then assigns its arguments to the node's fields. **listNodeCreate** assumes that space has already been allocated for the data pointed to by the node and that we've already decided where in the list the node should go. It then returns the pointer to the new node.

listNodeDestroy frees up the space used by a node. It takes one argument, a pointer to a node, which it passes to **free**. This frees the node itself, but not the data it points to. **listNodeDestroy** assumes that this data has already been freed.

Common Linked-List Operations

We'll use linked lists to write a program that sorts strings. This requires four list-manipulating functions: **listCreate** creates an empty list, **listTraverse** does an action on each data value in the list, **listInsert** inserts a new node into its correct place in the list, and **listDestroy** removes all the nodes in the list.

Although for now we're only going to manipulate lists of strings, we really want our list operations to be general enough to support lists of any data type. That way we have to write the messy pointer manipulations only once. But to do that, we'll need to pass the various list operations pointers to functions for doing things such as comparing and printing values, just as we did with our generic functions for searching and sorting arrays. To keep our programs readable, we've defined and used several type definitions for these pointers. Figure 20.4 contains these **typedef**s, Figure 20.5 provides the prototypes for our list operations, and Figure 20.6 defines the operations themselves. We now discuss each of these functions, starting with the simplest and finishing with the most complex.

Creating an Empty List

Before we can do anything to a list, we need to create it. **listCreate** takes no arguments and returns a new, empty list. We represent an empty list with a **NULL** pointer, so that's what **listCreate** actually returns. We then assign this pointer to a **List** variable, where **List** is a type we've defined as a synonym for a pointer to a **ListNode**.

Since **listCreate** is so simple, why do we bother making it a function at all? Why don't we directly assign **NULL** to the **List** variable and skip the overhead of a function call? Because using **listCreate** contributes to making our program more readable and more maintainable. There are many reasons why we might assign **NULL** to a variable, so without the function it's not clear that we're initializing a list. Besides, it's possible that in the future we'll want a different representation for our list, such as adding a special *header* node containing a count of elements or pointers to the first and last elements. Using **listCreate** makes it easier to make changes to programs using lists.

```
/*
 * Useful typedefs for pointers to functions that create, update,
 * compare, and access nodes in linked lists.
 */
#if !defined(POINTER_TYPEDEFS)
#define POINTER_TYPEDEFS

enum status {UPDATE, CREATE};        /* controls whether update function
                                        creates or updates list node */

/* Pointer to comparison function */
typedef int  (*PtrToCompFunc)(const void *, const void *);

/* Pointer to action function */
typedef void (*PtrToActionFunc)(void *);

/* Pointer to update function */
typedef void *(*PtrToUpdateFunc)(void *, enum status);

#endif
```

Figure 20.4 (ptrfuncs.h) Type definitions for some useful pointers to functions.

```
/*
 * Definitions of list type and prototypes for list operations.
 */
#include "lnodes.h"                    /* list node and prototypes */
#include "ptrfuncs.h"                  /* pointer to function typedefs */

typedef ListNode *List;                /* list is ptr to first list node */

List listCreate(void);
void listTraverse(List l, PtrToActionFunc action);
List listInsert(List l, void *dataptr, PtrToCompFunc cmp);
void listDestroy(List l);
List listUpdate(List l, void *dataptr,
                PtrToCompFunc cmp, PtrToUpdateFunc upd);
```

Figure 20.5 (lists.h) Definitions of list data type.

```
/*
 * Basic functions implementing List data type.
 *   listCreate - create a new, empty list.
 *   listTraverse - do action on each list node's data.
 *   listInsert - insert new node in correct place in list.
 *   listDestroy - remove all list nodes.
 */
#include "lists.h"

List listCreate(void)
{
  return NULL;
}

void listTraverse(List list, PtrToActionFunc actfptr)
{
  ListNode *curr;                            /* ptr to current node */

  for (curr = list; curr != NULL; curr = curr->nextptr)
    actfptr(curr->dataptr);                  /* do action to node's data */
}

List listInsert(List list, void *target, PtrToCompFunc cmpfptr)
{
  ListNode *nptr;                            /* ptr to new node */
  ListNode *curr = list;                     /* ptr to current node */
  ListNode *prev = NULL;                     /* ptr to previous node */

  for (; curr != NULL; prev = curr, curr = curr->nextptr)
    if (cmpfptr(curr->dataptr, target) > 0)
      break;                                 /* found place for node */
  nptr = listNodeCreate(target, curr);
  if (prev == NULL)
    list = nptr;                             /* insert at front */
  else
    prev->nextptr = nptr;                    /* insert in middle or at end */
  return list;                               /* return updated list */
}

void listDestroy(List list)
{
  ListNode *curr = list;                     /* ptr to current node */
  ListNode *temp;                            /* ptr to next node */

  for ( ; curr != NULL; curr = temp)
  {
    temp = curr->nextptr;
    listNodeDestroy(curr);
  }
}
```

Figure 20.6   (lists1.c) Our functions to create, destroy, and traverse linked lists.

Traversing an Existing List

The next operation is to run through an existing list, the task handled by **listTraverse**. When we traverse a list, we "process" each node in the list, from the first to the last. Processing a node could involve printing its data, returning the data items to the free storage pool, and so on. That means we need to tell **listTraverse** which list we're working on and what action we want to do for each list element. We do that by passing **listTraverse** a pair of arguments: a **List** to traverse and a pointer to a function. **listTraverse** executes the function once for each node, passing it the current node's **dataptr**.

How do we actually traverse the list? Simply by moving a pointer along the list. In particular, **listTraverse** uses a pointer called **curr** to traverse the list and uses **curr->dataptr** to access each node's data field. When we're done with the current node, we move **curr** along the list with the assignment

```
curr = curr->nextptr
```

We stop the traversing when **curr** finally becomes **NULL**.

> *Don't forget to make sure that all lists are properly **NULL** terminated.*

Forgetting to terminate a list with a **NULL** is likely to lead to disaster, just as if we forget to terminate a string with a null character.

Inserting in a Sorted Linked List

Another important operation is inserting a new element in the correct place in the list, the task handled by **listInsert**. It takes three arguments: a **List**, a pointer to the data item we want to insert, and a pointer to a comparison function it uses to determine where to insert this item. It returns the list with the new data item inserted in the appropriate place. **listInsert**'s caller is responsible for allocating storage for the data to be inserted in the list, and for placing a copy of that data into this storage. That means that to insert a string into the list, we have to **malloc** sufficient storage for it, copy it into this storage, and then pass **listInsert** a pointer to it. So what does **listInsert** do for us? It determines where this string belongs, creates a node whose **dataptr** field points to the storage we allocated, and hooks the node into the list. Figure 20.7 shows how it locates the correct place for a new value and how we actually insert the node.

To search the list, we use two pointers, **curr** and **prev**. We initialize **curr** to point to the list's first node and **prev** to **NULL** and move both down the list, one trailing the other. Why do we need two pointers? Because we know we've found the correct place to insert only when we've gone one node past it. That is, as we move **curr** through the list, we compare the value it points to with the value to insert. When the value we're inserting is larger, we know we should insert it in front of the current node. But since our list contains only pointers to the next node, we need to keep this *trailing link pointer*, **prev**, one node behind **curr**.

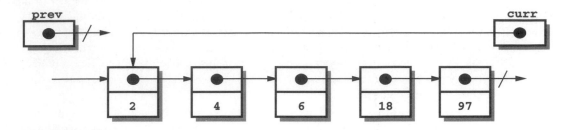

(*a*) Before searching the list.

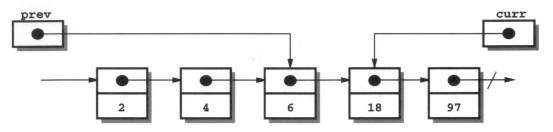

(*b*) When we find the desired node.

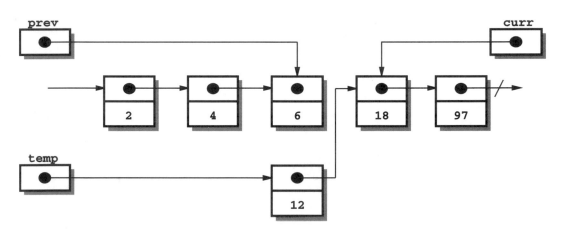

(*c*) Halfway through inserting 12.

Figure 20.7   Inserting the value 12 into a sorted linked list of numbers.

To do a comparison, **listInsert** calls the comparison function, passing it a pointer to the data item we're inserting and a pointer to the current node's **dataptr**. That function is responsible for dereferencing the passed pointers and comparing the pointed-to values. It should return zero if the values are the same, something positive if the item we're inserting is the larger value, and something negative if it's smaller.

To create a new node, we use **listNodeCreate**, passing it a pair of pointers. The first is a pointer to its new data value—the value we used to determine where in the list we wanted to insert the new node. The other is **curr**, which points to the node that should follow the new node. We then make the previous node's **nextptr** field point to this new node and return a pointer to the beginning of the list. There is only one exception to this simple scenario: when we insert an item into the beginning of the list, there is no previous item, so we simply return a pointer to the new node, which becomes the first item in the list.

Destroying a Linked List

Printing a list is not the only operation that requires its traversal. Another example is deallocating all of the nodes in a list. Because we dynamically allocate linked list nodes with **malloc**, we must deallocate them with **free** once we no longer need them, so that the space they use is available for other purposes. You might think we could deallocate a list simply by **free**ing the node's first element. But we requested space a node at a time for our linked list, so we must free it a node at a time, which means that we're forced to traverse an entire list to deallocate all of its nodes.

listDestroy is a slight variant on **listTraverse** in which "process the node" becomes a call to **listNodeDestroy** (which calls **free**). Since they're so similar, why didn't we just use **listTraverse**, passing it **free** as the function to execute? Because that would deallocate the space used by the data in each node, not the space used by the nodes themselves.

freeing nodes in a linked list is actually a little tricky. We have to be careful to save a copy of the node's **nextptr** field before we **free** the node. Why? Because once we **free** something, we aren't allowed to access it again.

Sorting Strings Using Linked Lists

Figure 20.8 puts all of these functions together in a program that uses a single linked list to sort its input lines. Figure 20.9 contains two additional functions to compare and print strings that this sorting program needs.

The program itself is surprisingly simple. It uses **listCreate** to create an empty list, storing it in the **List** variable, **sl** (for string list).

```
sl = listCreate();
```

It then repeatedly uses **getline** to read the next input line, **malloc** and **strcpy** to dynamically allocate a copy of it, and **listInsert** to store the copy in the correct place in the list.

```
sl = listInsert(sl, ptr, cmpString);
```

```
/*
 * Sort strings using generic linked lists.
 */
#include <stdio.h>
#include <string.h>
#include "lists.h"                              /* for list data type */

#define MAXLEN 80

int main()
{
  int  getline(char *line, int max);
  int  cmpString(const void *ptr1, const void *ptr2);
  void printString(void *ptr);

  char line[MAXLEN + 1];                        /* input line */
  char *ptr;                                    /* ptr to input line copy */
  int  len;                                     /* length of input line */
  List sl = listCreate();                       /* list of strings */

  while ((len = getline(line, MAXLEN)) != -1)
    if ((ptr = malloc(len + 1)) != NULL)
      sl = listInsert(sl, strcpy(ptr,line), cmpString);
    else
    {
      printf("Out of memory reading line %s\n", line);
      break;
    }
  listTraverse(sl, printString);                /* print elements */
  listTraverse(sl, free);                       /* free data */
  listDestroy(sl);                              /* free nodes */

  return EXIT_SUCCESS;                          /* always return success */
}
```

Figure 20.8   (strlists.c)   Insertion sort of input strings using linked lists.

We pass **listInsert** the current list, a pointer to the string we want to insert, and a pointer to the comparison function **cmpString**. **cmpString** simply casts the passed pointers as pointers to characters and then uses **strcmp** to compare those strings. **listInsert** returns a pointer to the modified list, which we store back in **sl**.

To print the list, we use **listTraverse**, passing it **sl** and a pointer to the function **printString**. **listTraverse** calls **printstr** once for each node, passing it a pointer to the node's data.

```
        listTraverse(sl, printString);
```

printString simply casts the pointer as a pointer to a character and uses **printf** to write that string.

```
/*
 * Comparison and printing functions.
 *    cmpString - given generic pointers, compare strings.
 *    printString - given generic pointer, print string.
 */
#include <stdio.h>
#include <string.h>

int cmpString(const void *xptr, const void *yptr)
  { return strcmp((const char *) xptr, (const char *) yptr); }

void printString(void *ptr)
  { printf("%s\n", (const char *) ptr); }
```

Figure 20.9   (strfuncs.c) Comparison and printing functions for our string utilities.

To free the list, we make two passes through it. The first uses **listTraverse** to free the node's data field—the strings we allocated before we inserted them into the list. We simply pass it **sl** and a pointer to **free**.

```
    listTraverse(sl, free);
```

The second uses **listDestroy** to remove the nodes in the list. We simply pass **listDestroy** the list.

```
    listDestroy(sl);
```

There are several places we can improve this program. First, we really don't need to destroy the list, since we don't need to reuse its space before we finish. So we can simply remove the calls dealing with deallocating nodes and their data. Second, we're not using the world's most efficient sorting algorithm. Although linked-list insertion sort avoids the time-consuming process of shifting data to make room for a new item, it isn't substantially faster than the array-based insertion sort. Whenever we insert a value, we still must search the list for the correct place to insert, an operation that takes time proportional to m, if there are m values in the list or array. For all n input values, this takes a total amount of time proportional to n^2. If n doubles, for example, sorting time goes up by a factor of 4.

Updating a Linked List

Our string sort always inserts an item in its correct place in the list. But how do we update an existing list item?

Suppose we want to print the number of occurrences of each word in the input. One approach is to maintain a list in which each item contains a word and a count of the number of times it appears. Whenever we see an existing word, we update its count. And whenever we see a new word, we insert it in the list with a count of zero. To do this, we need one other operation, **listUpdate**, shown in Figure 20.10. It takes the

```
/*
 * Update a list item or create it if it's not already there.
 */
#include "lists.h"

List listUpdate(List list, void *target, PtrToCompFunc cfptr,
                PtrToUpdateFunc ufptr)
{
  ListNode *nptr;                        /* pointer to new node */
  ListNode *curr;                        /* pointer to current node */
  ListNode *prev = NULL;                 /* pointer to previous node */
  int cmp = -1;                          /* result of list comparison */

  for (curr = list; curr != NULL; prev = curr, curr = curr->nextptr)
    if ((cmp = cfptr(target, curr->dataptr)) <= 0)
      break;
  if (cmp == 0)                          /* found it in list; do update */
    curr->dataptr = ufptr(curr->dataptr, UPDATE);
  else
  {                                      /* not in list, so create */
    nptr = listNodeCreate(ufptr(target, CREATE), curr);
    if (prev == NULL)
      list = nptr;                       /* insert at front */
    else
      prev->nextptr = nptr;              /* insert at middle or end */
  }
  return list;                           /* return updated list */
}
```

Figure 20.10   (lists2.c)   The function **listUpdate** for updating a linked list element.

same arguments as **listInsert**, plus one additional argument: a pointer to a function capable of updating an existing data field or creating a new one.

Like **listInsert**, **listUpdate** searches the list for a place to insert the new item. But unlike **listInsert**, it also worries about whether the item is already there. If it finds the item, **listUpdate** calls the update function, passing it the matching node's **dataptr** and a flag telling it to update the data. The function does the update and returns a pointer to the changed data, which **listUpdate** stores back into **dataptr**. We use a function to perform the update, since different types of data will be updated in different ways.

If **listUpdate** can't find the item, it needs to insert a new node in the list, just as **listInsert** did. When we used **listInsert**, we created the new data item before we called it. But we can't do that with **listUpdate**, since we're usually not creating a new node. Instead, **listUpdate** calls the update function to create the new data item, passing it the value we were trying to find and a flag telling it that we didn't find it.

Figure 20.11 contains a program to print the number of times each input line appears. We can use it to count different words in our input by combining it with our Chapter 5

```
/*
 * Prints number of times each word appears in input, sorted by word
 * (assumes one word per input line).
 */
#include <stdio.h>
#include <string.h>
#include "items.h"

int main()
{
  int getline(char *line, int max);        /* for reading input line */

  char line[MAXLEN + 1];                    /* input line */
  List sl = listCreate();                   /* list of strings */

  while (getline(line, MAXLEN) != -1)
    if (line[0] != '\0')
      sl = listUpdate(sl, line, cmpItem, updItem);
  listTraverse(sl, printItem);

  return EXIT_SUCCESS;
}
```

Figure 20.11   (cntwords.c)   Count different words in input using a linked list to hold them.

program that takes its input and prints it to the output, one word at a time. It differs from our earlier string sort in two ways. The data items are **Item** structures containing a word and a count, rather than strings. And it uses **listUpdate** to add and update list items, rather than **listInsert**.

Figure 20.12 contains the definition of an **Item**, and Figure 20.13 provides the functions to update, compare, and print items. We use **updItem** as our node-updating function. It has two jobs: creating a new data item and updating an existing item. To create a new item, it **malloc**s a structure, fills in the word field with the value we were trying to find, and sets the count of appearances to one. To update an existing item, it simply increments its count field.

Since we're dealing with **Item**s rather than strings, we've had to write new comparison and printing functions: **cmpItem** determines whether an **Item** contains our target word, and **printItem** prints an **Item**'s word and count fields.

20.2   STACKS AND QUEUES—SPECIAL-PURPOSE LISTS

We've shown how to manage ordered linked lists. But there are other useful organizations for linked lists. The most common ones are *stacks* and *queues*. Both are lists, but with restrictions. With a stack, we can only access its first element. That is, we can only put new values at the start of the list, and we can only examine and remove the value at

```
/*
 * Item definition and prototypes.
 */
#include "lists.h"

#define  MAXLEN    80                       /* longest input line */

typedef struct item
{
    char wordtext[MAXLEN + 1];              /* text of word */
    int cnt;                                /* count of appearances */
} Item, *ItemPtr;

int  cmpItem(const void *ptr1, const void *ptr2);
void *updItem(void *ptr, enum status updtype);
void printItem(void *ptr);
```

Figure 20.12   (items.h) Definition of the **Item** type and prototypes for the functions that access it.

the start of the list. And with a queue, we can only insert items at the front and remove them from the rear, as we saw when we implemented queues using an array.

We'll now show how to implement stacks and queues of any data type. They are much easier to implement than ordered lists: we don't need to do any comparisons or traversals, so we don't have to pass around any pointers to functions.

Stacks

We need to provide several stack operations: **stackCreate** creates an empty stack, **stackPush** places a new item on the top of the stack, **stackPop** removes the top item, **stackTop** returns the top item's value (without removing it), and **stackEmpty** returns a non-zero value if the stack is empty. We need not implement an operation to destroy a stack, since we can do that by repeated calls to **stackPop**.

Figure 20.14 contains the prototypes for these operations, and Figure 20.15 contains the operations themselves. To aid readability, we define a type **Stack** that's a synonym for a pointer to a **ListNode**.

Actually, some of our stack functions are so simple that for efficiency we've made them macros. **stackCreate** takes no arguments and returns an empty **Stack**. Since an empty stack corresponds to an empty list, it simply returns a **NULL** pointer. **stackEmpty** takes a **Stack** and determines whether it is empty by testing whether it is **NULL**. **stackTop** returns the **dataptr** of the first element in the **Stack**.

stackPush and **stackPop** are slightly more complex. **stackPush** takes a **Stack** and a pointer to new data, inserts a new node at the front of the list, and returns a pointer to it. That's easy to do: it simply calls **listNodeCreate** to create a new node, passing it a pointer to the new data item and a pointer to the front of the list. **stackPop** takes a **Stack**, frees the first node in the list, and then returns a pointer

```
/*
 * Functions managing Item type.
 */
#include <stdio.h>
#include <stdlib.h>
#include <string.h>
#include "items.h"

void *updItem(void *target, enum status todo)   /* update/create item */
{
  ItemPtr itemptr = target;

  if (todo == CREATE)                            /* not already there, create */
    if ((itemptr = malloc(sizeof(Item))) == NULL)
      printf("Couldn't allocate space for item\n");
    else
    {
      strncpy(itemptr->wordtext, target, MAXLEN + 1);
      itemptr->cnt = 1;
    }
  else                                           /* already there, update */
    itemptr->cnt++;
  return itemptr;
}

int cmpItem(const void *xptr, const void *yptr)  /* compare items */
  { return strcmp((const char *) xptr, ((ItemPtr) yptr)->wordtext); }

void printItem(void *ptr)                         /* print item */
{
  printf("%s %i\n", ((ItemPtr) ptr)->wordtext, ((ItemPtr) ptr)->cnt);
}
```

Figure 20.13   (items.c) The functions for updating, comparing, and printing items.

to the next node as the new **Stack**. We have to be careful to save the first node's **nextptr** before we free the node.

Figure 20.16 reverses its input using a stack. It repeatedly reads input lines, pushing each input line onto the top of the stack. Once it hits the end of the input, it keeps printing the top stack element and popping the stack until it's empty.

Queues

There is a small set of basic queue operations: **queueCreate** creates a new queue, **enqueue** adds a new element to the end of a queue, **dequeue** removes the first element from the queue, and **queueEmpty** tells us whether the queue is empty.

We could represent a queue in the same way we represent a stack: as a pointer to the first node in a linked list. **dequeue** is then just like **stackPop**, returning the first

```
/*
 * Definitions of stack data type and prototypes.
 */
#include "lists.h"

typedef ListNode *Stack;

#define stackCreate()   NULL             /* create an empty stack */
#define stackEmpty(s)   ((s) == NULL)    /* is stack empty? */
#define stackTop(s)     ((s)->dataptr)   /* first item on stack */

Stack stackPush(Stack s, void *dataptr);
Stack stackPop(Stack s);
```

Figure 20.14 (stacks.h) Definitions of stack and stack prototypes.

```
/*
 * Stack operations.
 */
#include "stacks.h"                       /* Stack type and prototypes */

Stack stackPush(Stack s, void *dptr)      /* add new item to stack */
  { return listNodeCreate(dptr, s); }

Stack stackPop(Stack s)                   /* delete top item from stack */
{
  ListNode *topptr    = s;
  ListNode *secondptr = topptr->nextptr;

  listNodeDestroy(topptr);
  return secondptr;
}
```

Figure 20.15 (stacks.c) Definitions of stack functions.

node in the list. But then **enqueue** is prohibitively expensive, because we have to run through the entire list every time we add an item to it. A better way to represent a queue is with a pair of pointers: one to the front of a linked list and the other to the rear. Both **enqueue** and **dequeue** can do their jobs simply by changing a few pointers. Figure 20.17 shows how these functions work, Figure 20.18 contains their prototypes, and Figure 20.19 contains the functions themselves. As with stacks, we define a special type **Queue**, but this time it's not merely a synonym for a pointer to a **ListNode**. Instead, it's a pointer to a structure containing two pointers to **ListNode**s: **frontptr**, which points to the first node in the queue, and **rearptr**, which points to the last.

```
/*
 * Reverse input strings using a stack.
 */
#include <stdio.h>
#include <stdlib.h>
#include <string.h>
#include "stacks.h"                    /* Stack type and prototypes */

#define MAXLEN 80

int main()
{
  int    getline(char *buf, int len);

  char   line[MAXLEN + 1];             /* input line */
  char *ptr;                           /* copy of input line */
  Stack s = stackCreate();             /* our stack */
  int len;

  while ((len = getline(line, MAXLEN)) != -1)
    if ((ptr = malloc(len + 1)) != NULL)
      s = stackPush(s, strcpy(ptr,line));
    else
    {
      printf("Out of memory processing line %s\n", line);
      break;
    }
  for (; !stackEmpty(s); s = stackPop(s))
  {
    printf("%s\n", ptr = stackTop(s));
    free(ptr);
  }
  return EXIT_SUCCESS;
}
```

Figure 20.16   (strrev.c) Reverse input using a stack.

queueCreate differs from our functions to create lists and stacks in that it doesn't simply return a NULL pointer. Instead, it allocates a queue structure and returns a pointer to it. enqueue takes this pointer and a pointer to the new data item. It allocates a new node with listNodeCreate and then updates the queue's rearptr to point to this node. If the queue is empty, it also updates the queue's frontptr. dequeue takes a pointer to the queue structure and returns the first node's dataptr. It destroys the first node and updates frontptr to point to the next node. If the queue is now empty, it also updates the queue's rearptr. We'll use these functions in our end-of-chapter case study.

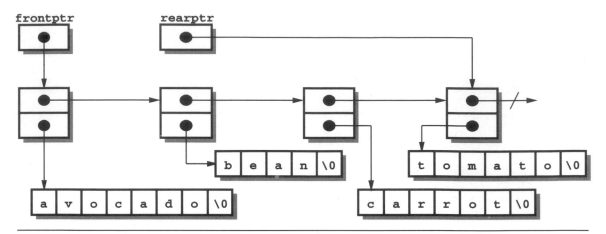

Figure 20.17   Representing a queue with pointers to first and last elements. **enqueue** adds an element at the end; **dequeue** deletes an element from the beginning.

```
/*
 * Queue type and prototypes.
 */
#include "lists.h"                       /* list type and prototypes */

typedef struct queue
{
  ListNode *frontptr;                    /* pointer to first list node */
  ListNode *rearptr;                     /* pointer to last list node */
} *Queue;

Queue queueCreate(void);
void  enqueue(Queue q, void *dataptr);
void  *dequeue(Queue q);

#define queueEmpty(qptr) \
        ((qptr)->frontptr == NULL)    /* is queue empty? */
```

Figure 20.18   (qs.h) Definitions of the **Queue** structure and prototypes.

```
/*
 * Queue-manipulating functions.
 */
#include "qs.h"                         /* Queue type and prototypes */

Queue queueCreate(void)                 /* create new, empty queue */
{
  Queue qptr = malloc(sizeof(struct queue));

  if (qptr != NULL)
    qptr->frontptr = qptr->rearptr = NULL;
  return qptr;
}

void enqueue(Queue qptr, void *ptr)     /* add item to rear of queue */
{
  ListNode *nptr = listNodeCreate(ptr, NULL);

  if (qptr->frontptr == NULL)           /* empty queue */
    qptr->frontptr = nptr;
  else                                  /* non-empty queue */
    qptr->rearptr->nextptr = nptr;
  qptr->rearptr = nptr;
}

void *dequeue(Queue qptr)               /* remove first item in queue */
{
  ListNode *nptr   = qptr->frontptr;    /* first node */
  void     *dataptr = nptr->dataptr;    /* data in first node */

  if ((qptr->frontptr = nptr->nextptr) == NULL)
    qptr->rearptr = NULL;               /* now queue empty */
  free(nptr);                           /* destroy node */
  return dataptr;
}
```

Figure 20.19 (qs.c) Definitions of queue functions.

20.3 BINARY SEARCH TREES

In a linked list, each node contains a pointer to the next node in the list. A binary tree is an extension to lists in which each node has two pointers, where each pointer is either **NULL** or a pointer to a binary tree. The top node in the tree is called the *root*.

Figure 20.20 shows a particularly useful type of binary tree, a *binary search tree* (BST). In a BST, the data value at each node partitions its subtrees into two subsets. In the left subtree, every data item is smaller than the current node; in the right subtree, every data item is larger than (or equal to) the current node. We'll now use BSTs to construct another, more efficient, sorting program, called *tree sort*.

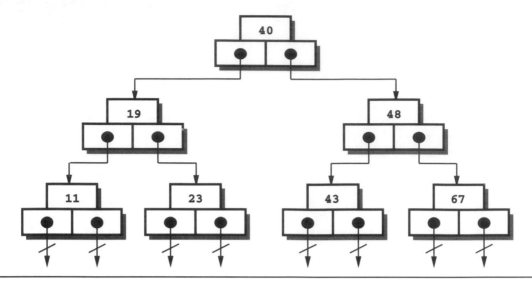

Figure 20.20   An example binary search tree. For every node, all of the items in its left subtree are less than the node, and all of the items in its right subtree are greater than the node.

As you might expect, we can define a node in a binary tree as a structure. As with lists, we store a pointer to the data. But unlike lists we store two pointers in each node, not just one. Figure 20.21 shows the definition of a tree node, and Figure 20.22 provides the functions, **treeNodeCreate** and **treeNodeDestroy**, for creating and destroying them.

Binary Search Tree Operations

We implement the same operations for trees that we did for lists: **treeCreate** creates an empty tree, **treeInsert** inserts a new item in its correct place in the tree, **treeUpdate** updates an existing item or adds it if it's not there, **treeTraverse** runs through a tree in sorted order, and **treeDestroy** frees up the nodes used by the tree. Figure 20.23 provides the prototypes for these functions, and Figures 20.24 and 20.25 provide the functions themselves.

Building a Binary Search Tree

Creating an empty tree is easy. An empty tree is really nothing more than a **NULL** pointer, so **treeCreate** is just **listCreate**: it returns a **NULL** pointer.

Inserting a node into a tree is more difficult. **treeInsert** uses a technique similar to **listInsert** to insert a node into the tree. Again, we use two pointers, **curr** and **prev**. Assuming the tree is not empty, we first set **curr** to its root, and **prev** to **NULL**. We then compare the value with the current node. If the value is less, we set **curr** to

```
/*
 * Definitions and prototypes for a tree node.
 */
typedef struct treenode
{
  void             *dataptr;
  struct treenode *left;
  struct treenode *right;
} TreeNode;

TreeNode *treeNodeCreate(void *dataptr);
void treeNodeDestroy(TreeNode *dataptr);
```

Figure 20.21   (tnodes.h) Tree node declarations.

```
/*
 * Manage a tree node.
 *    treeNodeCreate - create a new tree node.
 *    treeNodeDestroy - remove an existing tree node.
 */
#include <stdlib.h>
#include <stddef.h>
#include "tnodes.h"

TreeNode *treeNodeCreate(void *ptr)
{
  TreeNode *nptr = malloc(sizeof(TreeNode));

  if (nptr != NULL)
  {
    nptr->dataptr = ptr;
    nptr->left = nptr->right = NULL;
  }
  return nptr;
}

void treeNodeDestroy(TreeNode *ptr)
  { free(ptr); }
```

Figure 20.22   (tnodes.c) Tree node creation.

```
/*
 * Definition of a tree and protoypes for its operations.
 */
#include <stdio.h>
#include <stdlib.h>
#include <string.h>
#include <stddef.h>
#include "tnodes.h"                        /* tree node and prototypes */
#include "ptrfuncs.h"                      /* pointer to function defs */

typedef TreeNode *Tree;

#define treeCreate()  NULL                 /* create an empty tree */

Tree treeInsert(Tree t, void *dataptr, PtrToCompFunc cmp);
void treeTraverse(Tree t, PtrToActionFunc action);
void treeDestroy(Tree t);
Tree treeUpdate(Tree t, void *dataptr,
             PtrToCompFunc cmp, PtrToUpdateFunc upd);
```

Figure 20.23   (trees.h) Tree declarations.

point to its left subtree. If the value is greater (or equal), we set **curr** to point to its right subtree. In either case, before changing **curr**, we save its value in **prev**. We keep repeating this process until **curr** becomes **NULL**, at which point we allocate a new node and make the appropriate pointer field of **prev** point to it. If the tree's empty, it's even easier. The new node becomes the root of the tree.

Suppose we want to insert 27 into our tree. We first compare it with the value at the root; since 27 is less than 40, we move to the left. We then compare 27 with 19; it is greater, so now we move to the right. Finally, we compare 27 with 23 and again find that it is greater. We can't move right, since the right subtree of 23 is **NULL**, so we get a new node and attach 27 as the new right subtree of 23.

treeUpdate works just as **treeInsert**, except that it updates the node if it's there and inserts it only if it isn't.

Traversing a Binary Search Tree

treeTraverse tackles the hard job of running through the tree in sorted order. Once we've created a binary search tree, it isn't obvious how we can retrieve the values in a useful way. But we can do so by traversing the tree in a systematic way that corresponds to the way we constructed the tree. The idea is that, since all of the nodes in the left subtree of any node are less than its value, and all of the nodes in its right subtree are greater than its value, we can process the tree in sorted order by processing a node's left subtree, then processing the node, and then processing its right subtree. So **treeTraverse** calls itself recursively on the left subtree, executes its action on the current node's data, and then calls itself recursively on its right subtree (processing

```
/*
 * Manage a binary search tree.
 *    treeInsert - insert a new node in a tree.
 *    treeDestroy - remove all nodes in tree.
 *    treeTraverse - traverse tree in order, doing action.
 */
#include "trees.h"

Tree treeInsert(Tree root, void *target, PtrToCompFunc cmpfptr)
{
  TreeNode *curr = root;                   /* current node in tree */
  TreeNode *prev = NULL;                   /* parent node in tree */
  TreeNode *temp = treeNodeCreate(target); /* new node */
  int cmp;                                 /* result of comparison */

  for (; curr != NULL; curr = cmp < 0 ? curr->left : curr->right)
  {
    cmp = cmpfptr(target, curr->dataptr);
    prev = curr;
  }
  if (prev == NULL)                        /* node is parent of tree */
    root = temp;
  else if (cmp < 0)
    prev->left = temp;                     /* left child */
  else
    prev->right = temp;                    /* right child */
  return root;
}

void treeDestroy(Tree root)
{
  if (root != NULL)
  {
    treeDestroy(root->left);
    treeDestroy(root->right);
    treeNodeDestroy(root);
  }
}

void treeTraverse(Tree root, PtrToActionFunc fptr)
{
  if (root != NULL)
  {
    treeTraverse(root->left, fptr);
    fptr(root->dataptr);
    treeTraverse(root->right, fptr);
  }
}
```

Figure 20.24 (trees1.c) Constructing, destroying, and traversing a tree.

```
/*
 * A function to update a node or insert a new node.
 */
#include "trees.h"

Tree treeUpdate(Tree root, void *target,
                PtrToCompFunc cfptr, PtrToUpdateFunc ufptr)
{
  TreeNode *curr = root;                  /* current tree node */
  TreeNode *prev = NULL;                  /* parent tree node */
  TreeNode *temp;                         /* new tree node */
  int cmp;                                /* result of comparison */

  for (; curr != NULL; curr = cmp < 0 ? curr->left : curr->right)
  {
    if ((cmp = cfptr(target, curr->dataptr)) == 0)
    {                                     /* found match, so update */
      curr->dataptr = ufptr(curr->dataptr, UPDATE);
      return root;
    }
    prev = curr;
  }
  temp = treeNodeCreate(ufptr(target, CREATE));
  if (prev == NULL)                       /* insert new node, like before */
    root = temp;
  else if (cmp < 0)
    prev->left = temp;
  else
    prev->right = temp;
  return root;
}
```

Figure 20.25   (trees2.c) Updating a tree.

those values). The traversal is called "in order" because accessing the value at a node comes in between the traversals of the subtrees. There are also preorder (the node is processed first) and postorder (the node is processed last) traversals.

treeDestroy traverses the tree, but does it in a slightly different order than **treeTraverse**. That's because it can't destroy a node until it has destroyed both its subtrees. So it first calls itself to destroy the node's right subtree, then the node's left subtree, and then finally the node itself.

A Tree Sort Program

Figure 20.26 uses tree sort to sort its input. As it reads each value, it calls **treeInsert** to place the value in its correct place in the tree. When it has read and inserted all values, it calls **treeTraverse** to display the tree. We use the same comparison and printing functions we used for linked lists of strings.

```
/*
 * Insertion sort strings using trees.
 */
#include "trees.h"                            /* tree type and prototypes */

#define MAXLEN 80

int main()
{
  int  getline(char *line, int len);
  void printString(void *ptr);
  int  cmpString(const void *ptr1, const void *ptr2);

  char line[MAXLEN + 1];                      /* input line */
  char *ptr;                                  /* ptr to input line copy */
  Tree st = treeCreate();                     /* tree of strings */
  int  len;

  while ((len = getline(line, MAXLEN)) != -1)
    if ((ptr = malloc(len + 1)) != NULL)
      st = treeInsert(st, strcpy(ptr,line), cmpString);
    else
    {
      printf("Out of memory processing line %s\n", line);
      break;
    }
  treeTraverse(st, printString);
  treeTraverse(st, free);                     /* not really needed */
  treeDestroy(st);
  return EXIT_SUCCESS;
}
```

Figure 20.26 (tsort.c) Sort input strings using tree sort.

20.4   CASE STUDY—A CROSS-REFERENCE PROGRAM

This section is optional!

When debugging, it often helps to have a listing of the program's identifiers and the line numbers on which they appear. Such a listing is called a *cross-reference*, and a program to produce it is called a *cross-referencer*. To give you an idea of what such a program should produce, Figure 20.27 is the output of a cross-referencer run on Chapter 1's initial price-computing program.

Basically, all a cross-referencer needs to do is maintain a table of words and the line numbers on which they appear. Whenever the program reads a word, it updates the table. After the program has read all of the words in its input, it prints the table in sorted order. The key question is: How do we organize this table of words?

We've chosen to use a tree, where each node contains a word and a queue of line numbers on which the word appeared (just like our previous trees, except that now we

Aside 20.1: Data Structures, Algorithms, and Efficiency

What does it mean for an algorithm or data structure to be more efficient than another?

We usually measure algorithmic efficiency by an order of magnitude characterization of the number of operations performed. Sorting algorithms, for example, are usually characterized by the number of comparisons they must perform. By this measure, tree sort is, in general, faster than insertion sort. Why? Because assuming that we're lucky and the binary tree is complete—that is, each node has exactly two nonempty subtrees, except for nodes at the bottom level—each comparison of an input value to a tree node reduces the search space by half. As a result, we only have do a few ($\log_2 N$) comparisons to decide where to put the new node, much less than the $N/2$ comparisons required by insertion sort. For a binary search tree, sorting time for N values averages $N \log_2 N$; for insertion sort, it's N^2. As N gets large, so does the difference in speed between the two sorting methods.

We usually use something called big O notation (which stands for "Order") to describe the running time of an algorithm. So, in the average case, tree sort is $O(N \log_2 N)$, whereas insertion sort is $O(N^2)$.

It turns out that the average case is not the only one of interest. We also have to be concerned with the worst case. With tree sort, for example, we're not always going to get lucky and have a complete tree. If we're really unlucky, with already sorted input the tree degenerates into a list; each node will have, at most, one non-empty subtree. In this worst case, tree sort is no better than insertion sort, and is also an $O(N^2)$ algorithm. There are ways, however, to modify tree sort to prevent this degenerate case from happening—any data structures book has the details.

have a queue in the node rather than a string). Why this data structure? We use a tree because we want to be able to store an arbitrary number of words, to quickly locate a particular word, and to easily print the words in order. And we store the line numbers in a queue because we need to print the line numbers in the order they appear.

Figures 20.28, 20.29, and 20.30 contain our cross-referencer. We've built it on top of our generic routines for trees and queues. All we've had to do is to provide an appropriate definition for the data stored in the trees and queues, and functions for comparing, updating, and printing this data.

SUMMARY

- By using structures, pointers, and dynamic allocation, we can implement data structures other than arrays.

- Linked lists consist of a list of nodes. Each node contains a pointer to a data item and a pointer to the next node in the list. The last node in the list contains a **NULL** pointer.

```
Compute            2
EXIT               37
List               29 30
Price              31
SUCCESS            37
Sales              33
Total              35
We                 2
a                  3
actual             2
after              31
all                14 15
amount             16
an                 2
and                3
assume             2
at                 2 33
bought             10
buying             2
cost               2 17 17 27 35 35
discount           3 12 12 15 15 21 25 25 26 27 31 32 32
double             11 12 13 14 15 16 17
f                  29 30 31 31 33 33 35
final              17 27 35
h                  5 6
i                  30
include            5 6
including          17
int                8 10
item               11 29
items              2 10 10 14 15 19 24 30 30
list               11 11 20 24 29
main               8
n                  29 30 31 33 35
of                 2 10 11 14 15 16 30
per                29
percentage         12 13
price              11 11 14 14 15 15 20 24 24 25 25 25 26 27 29 29 30 30 32
printf             29 30 31 33 35
rate               3 12 13 21 22 25 26 32 34
return             37
sales              3 13 13 16 16 17 22 26 26 27 34 34
stdio              5
stdlib             6
tax                3 13 13 16 16 17 22 26 26 27 33 34 34
the                2
total              14 14 24 25 25 30
```

Figure 20.27   The output of running the cross-referencer on Chapter 1's initial price-computing program.

```
/*
 * Define cross-referencer tree items and prototypes.
 */
#include "trees.h"
#include "qs.h"

#define MAXWORD 20

typedef struct item                     /* WORD NODE */
{
  char wordtext[MAXWORD + 1];           /* value of the word */
  Queue lines;                          /* list of line numbers */
} Item, *ItemPtr;

void *updItem(void *dataptr, enum status updtype);
int  cmpItem(const void *ptr1, const void *ptr2);
void printItem(void *dataptr);

extern char CurrentWord[];
extern int CurrentLineNo;
```

Figure 20.28   (xref.h)   Defines cross-referencer tree items.

- A stack is a last-in, first-out data structure, easily implemented as a list in which all items are added and deleted to the front of the list.

- A queue is a first-in, first-out data structure, easily implemented as a list in which all items are added to the end and deleted from the front.

- Binary trees consist of a set of nodes, each node containing a pointer to a data item and two other pointers: one to a node containing a larger item, the other to a node containing a smaller item.

EXERCISES

Explore

20–1 Compile and run the programs in this chapter.

20–2 Compare the execution times of linked-list insertion sort (Figure 20.8) and tree sort (Figure 20.26). Make sure you try sorting 10, 50, 100, 500, and 1000 strings. You may want to consider writing a program to generate the input (since typing 1000 strings can take a *long* time).

Modify

20–3 Rewrite Chapter 9's bus-stop simulating program to use the queues we implemented in this chapter (Figures 20.18 and 20.19).

20–4 Rewrite Chapter 12's database program to maintain the database as a sorted list. Then rewrite it to use a tree.

```
/*
 * The cross-referencing program.
 */
#include <stdio.h>
#include <stdlib.h>
#include <ctype.h>
#include "xref.h"

char CurrentWord[MAXWORD + 1];
int  CurrentLineNo = 0;

int main()
{
  int wordGet(void);
  Tree words = treeCreate();

  while (wordGet() != 0)
    words = treeUpdate(words, CurrentWord, cmpItem, updItem);
  treeTraverse(words, printItem);
  return EXIT_SUCCESS;
}

/* Read next character, updating line count */

int getNextChar(void)
{
  static int lastc = '\n';
  int c = getchar();

  if (lastc == '\n')
    CurrentLineNo++;
  return lastc = c;
}

/* Read next word, storing into CurrentWord */

int wordGet(void)
{
  int next;                                 /* next character */
  char *ptr    = CurrentWord;               /* start of word */
  char *endptr = CurrentWord + MAXWORD;     /* end of word */

  while ((next = getNextChar()) != EOF && !isalpha(next))
    ;                                       /* skip non-letters */
  for (; next != EOF && isalpha(next); next = getNextChar())
    if (ptr < endptr)                       /* save up to max chars */
      *ptr++ = next;
  *ptr = '\0';
  return ptr - CurrentWord;                 /* return chars in word */
}
```

Figure 20.29   (xref.c)   The cross-referencer program itself.

```
/*
 * The cross-referencer's comparison and update functions.
 */
#include "xref.h"

int cmpItem(const void *xptr, const void *yptr)    /* compare items */
{
  return strcmp((const char *) xptr, ((ItemPtr) yptr)->wordtext);
}

void *updItem(void *ptr, enum status todo)         /* update item */
{
  ItemPtr iptr = ptr;
  int *lptr = malloc(sizeof(int));                 /* holds line # */

  if (todo == CREATE)
  {                                                /* new word */
    iptr = malloc(sizeof(Item));
    strcpy(iptr->wordtext, CurrentWord);
    iptr->lines = queueCreate();
  }
  *lptr = CurrentLineNo;                           /* add line # */
  enqueue(iptr->lines, lptr);
  return iptr;
}

void printItem(void *ptr)
{                               /* write word and count to standard output */
  ItemPtr iptr = ptr;                       /* item in current node */

  printf("%-*s", MAXWORD, iptr->wordtext);
  while (!queueEmpty(iptr->lines))
    printf(" %i", * (int *) dequeue(iptr->lines));
  putchar('\n');
}
```

Figure 20.30 (utils.c) Some utility functions used by the cross-referencer.

20–5 Rewrite **treeTraverse** (Figure 20.24) without using recursion. Use a stack to hold pointers to the nodes as you move down the tree.

20–6 A doubly linked list is one in which each node has not only a pointer to the following node, but also one to the preceding node. Rewrite our list-manipulating functions to work with doubly linked lists.

20–7 Rewrite our Chapter 9's sets package to represent sets using a tree.

Extend **20–8** We can modify our string sort program (Figure 20.8) to sort in descending order simply by changing the comparison function. Add an option, **-r**, to our string sort program to indicate that the values should be printed in reverse order.

20–9 Add the operations **stackCount** and **stackTraverse** to our stack data type (Figures 20.14 and 20.15). **stackCount** returns the number of items in the stack, and **stackTraverse** runs through the stack and executes a function once for each node.

20–10 Add the **listLength** and **listDelete** operations to our list data type. **listLength** returns the number of elements in the list. **listDelete** removes all matching nodes in the list. It takes a list, a pointer to a comparison function, and a pointer to a function to be called before the node is actually deleted and to be passed the current node's **dataptr**. Typically this function deallocates the node's data item.

20–11 xref (Figure 20.29) has a very simple idea of what a word is (now just a sequence of letters). Modify it to treat any legal C identifier as a word. Of course, this change still won't let it handle file names such as stdio.h correctly. Extend your solution to deal with filenames in **#includes** and quoted strings.

20–12 Modify xref (Figure 20.29) to also include the position of a word on the line.

20–13 Make xref (Figure 20.29) specific to C. That is, have it ignore C reserved words and words inside C comments and strings. Keep the reserved words in a separate table that is searched for each identifier. What is the most appropriate form for this table?

20–14 Rewrite xref (Figure 20.29) to use a different organization for the word table. Have it use an array of linked lists with one array element for each possible first letter of a word.

Code

20–15 Write a function, **listReverse**, that takes a pointer to a linked list and reverses the order of the nodes. If the list contains nodes with 1, 2, 5, and 7, the list will point to the node with 7, which points to 5, and so on. No data movement should occur, only appropriate alteration of pointers.

20–16 Write a function, **listSplice**, that takes two linked lists and appends the second list to the first.

20–17 Write **treeDelete**. It takes a pointer to a binary search tree and a value. It removes the first node in the tree containing the value, maintaining the BST property. There are three cases: the node has no children, the node has one child, and the node has two children.

20–18 Write **treeCombine**. It takes a pair of pointers to binary search trees and inserts all of the values in the second binary search tree into the first.

20–19 Write a program that maintains a list of events (event name and date) in sorted order by date. Rewrite it to use a tree.

20–20 Write a routine that visits the nodes in a binary tree in *level order*. That is, first the value at the root is visited, then all direct children of the root, then all their children, etc. *Hint*: Use a queue to hold the pointers to the nodes as you move along a given level.

Build

20–21 One classic use of stacks is in postfix or "reverse Polish" (RPN) calculators. In postfix, the values come first, and then the operator. For example, to add 15 and 21, we enter **15 21 +**, and to evaluate $(17 + 19) \times 55$, we enter **17 19 + 55 ***. This last one means "enter 17; enter 19; add these values and put back the result; enter 55; multiply the top two values and put back the result." To build an RPN calculator, we get each item; if it's an operand, we push it on the stack, and if it's an operator, we pop the items from stack and perform the operation, pushing the result back on the stack. At the end we display the top value. Implement a simple calculator that can do addition, subtraction, multiplication, and division.

21 PORTABILITY

By now you're familiar with C and should feel fairly comfortable programming in it. But what about when you want to take one of your programs and compile it with a different compiler or run it on a different machine or use it with some other operating system? This chapter discusses the problems you're likely to run into and how you can best avoid them. We present a series of problems that arise when porting programs, along with a set of reasonable solutions. The chapter concludes with a case study that develops some portable input and output routines.

21.1   PRINCIPLES OF PORTABILITY

What do we mean by portability? Ideally, a portable program need not be changed to run under a different compiler or operating system, to run on a different computer, or to run with different input or output devices. Unfortunately, however, the ideal is almost always impossible to attain. Compilers differ in how much of the language they implement and which additional features they provide. Linkers differ in the length of variable names they allow. Operating systems differ in the system calls that are available. Computers differ in word sizes, character sets, amount of available memory, available external storage, and in the I/O devices they provide. Input can be typed on the keyboard, entered with a mouse, or selected with cursor input keys. And displays can be black and white or color, and they can be character- or bit-mapped. There are so many differences that we must carefully design and code our programs to achieve any degree of portability between different systems.

Since writing portable programs requires extra effort, why do we care about portability at all? If we *always* develop and run our programs using the same compiler on the same machine, we don't. But few of us will write programs that spend their entire lifetime on a single machine. We've found that many programs we've written on the PC are just as useful running on a Macintosh, a workstation, or even a minicomputer or a mainframe. And because we work so hard to write large programs, we want to be able to move them effortlessly from one environment to another.

So, assuming that we care about portability, how can we attain it? By doing two things: avoiding, wherever possible, constructs that are known to be nonportable and, when that's impossible, packaging any nonportable constructs within a portable interface. We can't achieve portability painlessly, but with careful design and an awareness of portable and nonportable constructs, we can at least minimize the changes we have to do when we move our code from one platform to another. So now we'll look at some common portability problems and how we get around them.

21.2   PORTING ACROSS ANSI-C COMPILERS

Ideally, any program that compiles successfully under one ANSI-C compiler should compile successfully under any other ANSI-C compiler. But not all ANSI-C compilers are created equal. Although there are certain minimum limits they all must meet, many exceed these limits. These minimums are shown below; any conforming ANSI-C compiler may exceed them.

TYPE	LIMIT
Nesting levels of compound statements	15
Nesting levels in conditional compilation	6
Nested declarations for a basic type	6
Expressions nested by parentheses	127
Significant characters in a macro or *internal* name	31
Significant characters in any *external* name	6
External identifiers in a source file	511
Identifiers with block scope in one block	127
Macro identifiers simultaneously defined	1024
Parameters in a function definition or call	31
Parameters in a macro definition or call	31
Characters in a logical source line	509
Characters in a string literal	509
Bytes in an object	32K
Levels of nested `#include` files	8
Case labels in `switch`	255

To be truly portable, our programs can't exceed any of these limits. There may in truth be few "strictly conforming" programs. The limit most likely to be exceeded is the one relating to the number of significant characters in an external name: six. This small size was chosen because C programs, after being compiled, must be linked via a linking loader. Many (older) linkers place this restriction—from the FORTRAN days—on the number of characters in an identifier.

These limits are large enough that it's unlikely we'll run up against them—except for the amount of an external name that's significant. The standard states that the first 31 characters in an internal name but only the first 6 characters in an external name are significant (the distinction arises because many linkers weren't written with C in mind and can't be easily changed). This is problematic, because our functions often share common prefixes longer than six characters, as with **stackPush** and **stackPop**. It's possible that a linker will treat these names as identical.

To ensure portability, we must write our program so that all our external names differ somewhere within the first six characters. When two names are identical in the first five characters, we can rename them slightly so they vary. Renaming **stackPush** as **pushStack** and **stackPop** as **popStack** makes them differ in their second character, rather than their eighth.

The problem is that this approach forces us to use short, often unreadable names, and it flies in the face of our convention of building names that start with the data type and end with the operation. Another solution uses **#define**. We simply redefine the troublesome longer names into short names and place the definitions in a header file included by the program containing the long names. We then go ahead and freely use the long names.

Figure 21.1 is a header file that does that for our stack-managing functions. It defines the macros only if the linker doesn't provide long names. How do we test for this situation? We check whether a symbol **SHORTNAMES** is defined. **SHORTNAMES** isn't a built-in name. Instead, we're assuming that we define this symbol ourselves before including this header file, but only if we're compiling in an environment with a linker that can handle only short external names.[1]

There are several potential problems with this practice. The first is that only the preprocessor ever sees the longer names, so that error messages will refer to the shorter names. And the other is that we might accidentally **#define** two long names to the same short name, a mistake that may be hard to detect.

21.3   PORTABILITY ACROSS OPERATING SYSTEMS

Most of the programs we've written are useful running under many different operating systems: UNIX, MS-DOS, VMS, and OS/2, among others. So far, our programs have managed to avoid operating-system-specific calls. But in the real world that's not so easy, since we have often to go through the operating system to access specialized devices, to communicate over a network, to have one executing program talk to another, and so on.

Obviously, it's not a good idea to simply thread these calls throughout our code, as it makes porting programs much more difficult. We would have to thoroughly examine our code, flushing out these calls and replacing them with the appropriate calls for the new operating system. It's a much better idea to place all system calls in higher-level functions whose names indicate the actual tasks they perform. The idea is that the higher-level function takes account of any operating system dependencies, limiting any nonportable code to a small part of our program.

Figures 21.2 and 21.3 contain a portable function to print the size of a file and its prototypes, and Figure 21.4 contains a main program that uses it. We wrote one version of this function earlier. It computed the length of a file by opening it, seeking to the end, and returning that position. That's a completely portable way of doing it, since it uses only the standard C library functions. But MS-DOS and UNIX provide special system calls that find a file's length in a more efficient way. On these systems we want to use these calls. To keep our program portable, as well as efficient, when we need the length of a file, we don't include direct references to these system calls. Instead we call the function **fileSize**. We provide several different versions of **fileSize**—one for MS-DOS, another for UNIX, and a default version—and we use **#if** to select the most appropriate version.

---

[1] We can usually accomplish this with command-line compilers by using the -D option. The idea is that we follow -D with the name of the symbol we want to define, as with -DSHORTNAMES.

```
/*
 * Definitions of stack data type and prototypes.
 */
#include "lists.h"

typedef ListNode *Stack;

#define stackCreate()   NULL
#define stackEmpty(s)   ((s) == NULL)
#define stackTop(s)     ((s)->dataptr)

#if defined(SHORTNAMES)
#define stackPush(s,i)  stpsh(s,i)
#define stackPop(s)     stpop(s)
#endif

Stack stackPush(Stack s, void *dataptr);
Stack stackPop(Stack s);
```

Figure 21.1 (stacks.h) The header file for our stack-managing routines.

```
/*
 * Prototype and necessary definition for fileSize function.
 */
#include <stdio.h>

#define FILESIZE_UNKNOWN  -1L

long fileSize(const char *file);
```

Figure 21.2 (filesize.h) Header file for the function **fileSize**.

This approach relies on the compiler having predefined a name for the operating system it's running under, such as **_MSDOS_** or **unix**. If our compiler doesn't do this, we're stuck with defining the appropriate name ourselves.[2]

Placing all of the operating-system-specific code within the file in which we define **fileSize** makes that code harder to read. But the main program itself is actually more readable, since the purpose of the strangely named system calls is now clearer.

There's one other place besides system calls where we frequently run into operating system dependencies: specifying path names. On UNIX, we use a forward slash to separate the different components of a file name. But on MS-DOS, we use a backslash.

---

[2]Some compilers and environments are particularly nasty and go out of their way to undefine symbols that programmers tend to count on. The standard HP/UX include files, for example, undefine **unix**, even if we've defined it ourselves! In order to get around this behavior, on these systems we're forced to define **_HPUX_SOURCE**. Yuck! Be on the lookout for similar behavior on your system.

```c
/*
 * Determine the size of the given file.  Returns the special
 * value FILESIZE_UNKNOWN if it can't do so.
 */
#include <stdio.h>
#include "filesize.h"

#if defined(__MSDOS__)
#include <io.h>                          /* MS-DOS-specific include file */

long fileSize(const char *file)
{
  FILE *fp = fopen(file, "rb");
  long len = FILESIZE_UNKNOWN;

  if (fp != NULL)
  {
    len = fileLength(fileno(fp));
    fclose(fp);
  }
  return len;
}
#elif defined(unix)
#include <sys/types.h>                   /* UNIX-specific include files */
#include <sys/stat.h>

long fileSize(const char *file)
{
  struct stat s;

  return (stat(file, &s) != -1) ? s.st_size : FILESIZE_UNKNOWN;
}
#else    /* default version */
long fileSize(const char *file)
{
  FILE *fp = fopen(file, "rb");
  long len = FILESIZE_UNKNOWN;

  if (fp != NULL)
  {
    if (fseek(fp, 0L, 2) != -1)
      len = ftell(fp);
    fclose(fp);
  }
  return len;
}
#endif
```

Figure 21.3   (filesize.c)   A function to determine the number of bytes in a file.

```
/*
 * Print size in bytes for each of its arguments.
 */
#include <stdio.h>
#include <stdlib.h>
#include "filesize.h"

int main(int argc, char *argv[])
{
  long fs;                                  /* next file's size */
  int i;                                    /* index through args */

  for (i = 1; i < argc; i++)
    if ((fs = fileSize(argv[i])) == FILESIZE_UNKNOWN)
      fprintf(stderr,"Can't get size of %s\n", argv[i]);
    else
      printf("Size of %s: %li\n", argv[i], fs);

  return EXIT_SUCCESS;
}
```

Figure 21.4   (testfs.c) A main program using **fileSize** to determine the length of a file.

That doesn't affect us when we read file names from the input, since we can assume the user will provide names in an appropriate form. But it does affect us if we're using absolute file names built into our program. Once again, the trick is to use the preprocessor. Whenever we have a name, we define a constant for it and let the preprocessor select the appropriate value.

21.4   MACHINE DEPENDENCIES

C differs from most high-level languages in that it was designed to help us implement programs efficiently and to let us directly access the underlying machine. Although these are two of its most attractive features, they are also a source of several machine dependencies that lead to portability problems.

Data Type Sizes

Most machines work most efficiently on integers when they are stored in a single word. But the size of a word can differ from machine to machine. This means that **int**s vary in size from 16 bits (as on the PC) to 32 bits (as on VAXs, Suns, and 386-based UNIX systems), to 60 bits (on the Cray). The result is that we must never assume that an **int** can hold a value outside the range of −32768 to 32767.

chars also vary in size from machine to machine. They range from 6 bits on older CDC machines, to 7 bits on the PDP-7, to 8 bits on most minicomputers, to 9 bits on many older UNISYS, Honeywell, and DEC machines, to 10 bits on the Cray. How can this cause portability problems? Suppose we're using an **unsigned char** to hold small integers in the range of 0 to 255. That's safe if our characters are 8 bits, but what if we go to a machine with 6- or 7-bit characters? Once again, we're in trouble.

The easiest way to minimize portability problems is to use **long**s for all our integers. But the drawbacks to this approach should be obvious—our programs will run more slowly and take up more space. A better way is to carefully define types that reflect their uses and to define these types differently on different machines.

Suppose, for example, that we want a type for dealing with small counters, that is, counters that range in size from 0 to 255. And further suppose that we have an array of 1000 of these. That means on most machines we can save at least 1000 bytes by declaring these types as **unsigned char**s instead of **short**s or **int**s. But then we would have a problem if we tried to port our program to a machine such as the PDP-7 that has 7-bit characters. So we instead define a new type, **SmallCounter**, and use it to declare all our counters. On some machines we can define this type as an **unsigned char**; on others we should define it as a **short**. We decide by examining the maximum value of an **unsigned char**, and if it's not big enough to hold the values we want, we use **unsigned short** instead. This extra work lets us use space efficiently without hurting portability.

Figure 21.5 defines this type, and Figure 21.6 provides an example use of it.

Character Set Differences

Different machines can have different underlying representations for characters. The two most common are ASCII and EBCDIC. This causes problems when we make direct use of the underlying representation. Clearly, it isn't portable to compare a variable directly with 48 to determine whether it holds the character '0'. Although 48 is the ASCII representation for the character '0', it represents a different character in EBCDIC. The solution is to always use the character rather than its integer representation. When we need a nonprinting character, we can use its octal code, but to aid portability, we should define a symbolic name for it.

Not only shouldn't we assume that the integer representation of a character is the same across different character sets, but we shouldn't even assume that a particular group of characters is always contiguous. That assumption shows up in relational expressions such as

```
c >= 'a' && c <= 'z'
```

In ASCII, this assumption holds for lowercase letters, for uppercase letters, and for digits. In EBCDIC, however, the assumption only holds for digits.

The functions in the character-testing library discussed in Chapter 5, such as **islower**, provide a more portable way of making these comparisons. In fact, their use leads to more readable code as well. The only possible sacrifice we may be making is in efficiency. But since these functions are actually macros and they usually expand into an index to a table of information about various characters, they may be at least as efficient as the nonportable comparison.

```
/*
 * Defining a "SmallCounter" type.
 */
#include <limits.h>

#if UCHAR_MAX >= 255
  typedef unsigned char SmallCounter;          /* 8-bit chars */
#else
  typedef unsigned short SmallCounter;         /* 7-bit chars */
#endif
```

Figure 21.5   (ourtypes.h) Header file defining names for our types.

```
/*
 * Using the "SmallCounter" type.
 */
#include <stdio.h>
#include <stdlib.h>
#include "ourtypes.h"                          /* type definitions */

#define MAXCNT 10

int main()
{
  SmallCounter table[MAXCNT];                  /* array of that type */
  SmallCounter i;

  for (i = 0; i < MAXCNT; i++)                 /* some initial values */
    table[i] = i;
  for (i = 0; i < MAXCNT; i++)                 /* print them */
    printf("%u\n", (unsigned int) table[i]);

  return EXIT_SUCCESS;
}
```

Figure 21.6   (ourtypes.c) Using the defined types to isolate the underlying types.

Unfortunately, there are no library functions for two common tasks: converting a character digit (such as '0') to the digit's underlying value (0) and converting the underlying value to the corresponding character. In Chapter 5's case study, we wrote nonportable functions to perform these tasks: **toDecimal** converted a character representing a digit to an integer; **toChar** went the other way. These functions relied on both the letters' and digits' being contiguous, which is a property of the ASCII character set, but not of other character sets. Figure 21.7 shows portable versions of these functions that instead do the conversions through table lookup.

```
/*
 * Functions to convert digits to and from characters.
 *   toDecimal - convert char to equivalent decimal number.
 *   toChar - convert decimal number to equivalent character.
 */
#include <ctype.h>
#include <string.h>

#define OFFSET(c,s) ((const char *const) strchr(s,c) - (s))

static const char *const Digits = "0123456789";
static const char *const LowerCase = "abcdefghijklmnopqrstuvwxyz";
static const char *const UpperCase = "ABCDEFGHIJKLMNOPQRSTUVWXYZ";

int toDecimal(int c, int toobig)
{
  int value = -1;                        /* simplify later decimal handling */

  if (isdigit(c))
    value = OFFSET(c, Digits);
  else if (islower(c))
    value = OFFSET(c, LowerCase) + 10;
  else if (isupper(c))
    value = OFFSET(c, UpperCase) + 10;
  if (value >= toobig)                   /* make sure result is legal */
    value = -1;
  return value;
}

int toChar(int value)
  { return (value < 10) ? Digits[value] : UpperCase[value - 10]; }
```

Figure 21.7 (convchar2.c) More portable version of our earlier conversion functions.

Sign-Related Problems

Another source of portability problems arises when we compare **signed** and **unsigned** values. These problems show up most often when we compare **char**s with integers—but only if we've stored a value in the **char** that's outside the range of values for a legal character in the machine's character set.

Figure 21.8 is a nonportable version of Chapter 5's display program. What's wrong with it? It uses a **char** to hold **getchar**'s return value. The problem is that **char**s are sometimes **signed** by default and other times **unsigned**.

This program works when we have **signed char**s and we're dealing with 7-bit ASCII characters. There, the high bit of the character represents its sign, and when we compare a character with an integer, C converts it using sign extension (filling its new high bytes with 1 bits if the value is negative). We need this behavior because we're storing **EOF** (-1) into a **char** and later comparing it with **EOF**.

```
/*
 * A nonportable version of our display program.
 */
#include <stdio.h>
#include <stdlib.h>

int main()
{
  char c;

  while ((c = getchar()) != EOF)
    putchar(c);

  return EXIT_SUCCESS;
}
```

Figure 21.8   (baddisp.c) A nonportable version of our program to display its input.

Unfortunately, our program fails miserably if **char**s are **unsigned**. When we compare an **unsigned char** with an integer, its high bit is part of its value and isn't sign extended. Instead, C fills the new high bytes with zero bits, which means the test for equality with **EOF** always fails. The solution is simple: store the character into an **int** rather than a **char**.

We can also get into trouble comparing **signed** and **unsigned** values with their integral types. That's because when we compare an **unsigned int** with a **long**, the conversions that take place are machine dependent. If **int**s are smaller than **long**s, the **unsigned int** is converted to a **long**. But if they're the same size both are converted to **unsigned long**s.

Figure 21.9 illustrates the problem. On a machine where **int**s are smaller than **long**s, **-1L** is less than **1U**, just as we would expect. But on a machine where **int**s and **long**s are the same size, we're in trouble: **-1L** is greater than **1U**. That's because both are converted to **unsigned long**s and **-1L** is all bits on, a very large value. The fix is to cast both operands to a particular type ourselves before doing the comparison.

There's one other related time we can get into trouble: when we do right shifts on negative numbers. That's because some machines fill with zeros and other machines propagate the sign bit. The solution is to do right shifts only on **unsigned** quantities. Luckily we don't have a problem with left shifts, since they always shift in zeros.

Sometimes we want to ensure the machine shifts in zeros. In the days before limits.h, we calculated special values such as the largest **int** ourselves. One trick was to fill a word with all one bits (with ~**0**) and then shift it over one bit to the right. On two's complement machines, the leftmost bit is the sign bit and the remaining bits are the value, so as long as a zero is shifted in as the new high-order bit, the result is the largest possible positive value. Some machines, however, shift in a one, which results in a word of all ones, or −1. To fix this, we cast the value to **unsigned** before shifting. Figure 21.10 shows correct and incorrect calculations for the largest positive value.

```
/*
 * Comparing signed and unsigned values.
 */
#include <stdio.h>
#include <stdlib.h>

int main()
{
  unsigned int i = 1U;
  long l = -1L;

  printf((i > 1) ? "Expected: 1U > -1L\n"
                 : "Unexpected: 1U < -1L\n");

  printf(((long) i > 1) ? "Expected: 1L > -1L\n"
                        : "Impossible: 1L < -1L\n");

  return EXIT_SUCCESS;
}
```

Figure 21.9 (unport.c) An illustration of the problems that arise when we compare **signed** and **unsigned** values.

```
/*
 * Computing the largest integer, correctly and incorrectly.
 */
#include <stdio.h>
#include <stdlib.h>

#define BAD_MAXINT   ~0 >> 1                /* not portable */
#define MAXINT       (unsigned) ~0 >> 1     /* portable */

int main()
{
  printf("~0 >> 1 = %i\n", BAD_MAXINT);
  printf("(unsigned) ~0 >> 1 = %i\n", MAXINT);

  return EXIT_SUCCESS;
}
```

Figure 21.10 (shifts.c) Correct and incorrect calculations of the largest positive **int**.

Byte Ordering

Unfortunately, the order of bytes in a word also differs among machines. On some the high byte is most significant; on others the low byte is most significant. Figure 21.11 illustrates the difference.

Figure 21.12 shows how this difference results in a portability problem if we access the individual bytes within a word. This program declares a variable that's a **union** of a **short** and a 2-byte character array. It assigns the **short** the value 0x08F0 and then prints the values of the two entries in the byte array. On some machines the output will be 0x08 followed by 0xf0; on others the values will be reversed. The solution is to avoid directly accessing bytes within integers.

Byte Alignment Problems

Different machines have different alignment constraints. As we saw in Chapter 12, this can lead to empty space being placed in structures in order to line up fields. That means it's not portable to compute the offset of a field in the structure simply by summing the sizes of the preceding fields in the structure definition. Instead, the system header file stddef.h provides a special macro, **offsetof**, that returns the field's offset in bytes from the start of a structure. It takes two arguments, the structure type and the field name (which shouldn't be the name of a bitfield):

```
size_t offsetof(type,member)
```

Figure 21.13 shows a simple program that uses it to print out the byte offsets for each of the fields in a **struct employee**. Here's its output when we run it.

```
Offset to number:      0 bytes
Offset to name:        4 bytes
Offset to phone:       44 bytes
Offset to age:         60 bytes
```

Pointer Problems

Pointers are another area where portability problems frequently arise. The problems stem from a pair of common, but false, assumptions. The first is that all pointers are the same size. But on some word-oriented machines, pointers to characters are larger than pointers to other types. That means that, in general, we can't count on assigning a pointer to one type to a pointer to another type without losing information. The only exception is a pointer to **void**: the language guarantees that it's large enough to hold a pointer to any object.

The other assumption is that pointers and integers are the same size. But there are plenty of machines where **int**s are 16 bits and pointers are 32 bits. We get into trouble on these machines if we assign an integer to a function expecting a pointer. Most often, that's because we passed **NULL** to a function expecting a pointer without supplying a prototype. The solution is to either provide a prototype or to cast **NULL** into an appropriate pointer type.

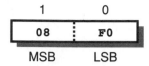

(*a*) On some machines the most significant byte (MSB) is the high byte.

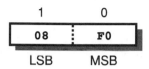

(*b*) On other machines, it's the low byte.

Figure 21.11 Differences in most significant versus least significant bytes.

```
/*
 * Nonportable program with byte-order assumptions built in.
 */
#include <stdio.h>
#include <stdlib.h>

union word
{
  short x;                           /* use as word */
  unsigned char bytes[2];            /* use as bytes */
};

int main()
{
  union word w;

  w.x = 0x08F0;                      /* 08 F0 */
  printf("LSB=%x, MSB=%x.\n", w.bytes[0], w.bytes[1]);

  return EXIT_SUCCESS;
}
```

Figure 21.12 (bytetest.c) A program with a nonportable assumption about byte ordering.

```c
/*
 * A program that prints each field's starting byte within
 * a structure.
 */
#include <stdio.h>
#include <stdlib.h>
#include <stddef.h>

#define MAXNAME 40

typedef struct employee
{
  long number;                          /* employee number */
  char name[MAXNAME];                   /* first and last name */
  char phone[13];                       /* xxx-xxx-xxxx\0 */
  int age;                              /* age */
} Employee;

#define displayOffset(field, bytes) \
  printf("Offset to " #field ":  \t%li bytes\n", (long) bytes)

int main()
{
  size_t number_off = offsetof(Employee, number);
  size_t name_off   = offsetof(Employee, name);
  size_t phone_off  = offsetof(Employee, phone);
  size_t age_off    = offsetof(Employee, age);

  displayOffset(number, number_off);
  displayOffset(name,   name_off);
  displayOffset(phone,  phone_off);
  displayOffset(age,    age_off);

  return EXIT_SUCCESS;
}
```

Figure 21.13   (offset.c)   A simple program showing how to use the **offsetof** macro.

We also get into trouble on these machines if we assume that the difference between two pointers is an **int**. It's entirely possible that it will instead be a **long**. However, the system header file stddef.h defines a type **ptrdiff_t** that's defined as the appropriate type to hold a pointer difference. Using **ptrdiff_t** to store the results of pointer subtractions helps make programs using pointers more portable.

Evaluation Order

Another portability problem results from assuming a particular order of evaluation. This problem is especially noticeable in function calls. Many programs assume that function arguments are evaluated left to right. If that's the case, with **i** equal to 0,

```
printf("%i, %i, %i\n", ++i, ++i, ++i);
```

prints

```
1, 2, 3
```

But C makes no such guarantee. It could just as well evaluate the arguments right to left or, in fact, inside out.

The solution is to perform all side effects before the function call. The correct way to do this would be to assign the various values of **i** to temporary variables and then pass these variables to **printf**. Figure 21.14 shows some example incorrect function calls and how to correct them.

Libraries and Machines

One very subtle machine-dependent portability problem can arise from assuming that library calls never fail. It arises most frequently when dealing with dynamic allocation and when opening files.

When we assume that **malloc** (or one of its derivatives) always succeeds, we're assuming that there will always be some available memory. This may be reasonable in a small program running on a machine with many megabytes of memory. But it is much less reasonable if the program is running on a machine with 64K. Why is not checking **malloc**'s return value a portability problem? Because our program will usually bomb if it runs out of memory, which will happen on some machines but not on others.

Similarly, we shouldn't assume that a file open or write can never fail. It is possible for a file open to fail if the file doesn't exist and for a file write to fail if there isn't sufficient room on the disk. And while one machine may have a 100-megabyte hard disk that never fills up, another may be running with a 320K floppy disk that is nearly always full. Not checking these return values could make our program work fine on one machine but fail miserably on another. We would hate to use a text editor that promptly died if it couldn't open our file or allocate enough space to hold it in memory or that failed to at least warn us if a disk was full and it couldn't write the file. To write portable programs, we must always check the return values of system calls and library functions.

21.5   PORTING TO NON-ANSI COMPILERS

The C language covered in this text is the "official" C language, as blessed by the American National Standards Institute.[3] One of the biggest portability problems at this time is actually one that will soon go away: not every compiler implements the entire ANSI-standard, but instead implements only the C language as originally defined by Brian Kernighan and Dennis Ritchie in their book *The C Programming Language*. That

---

[3] *American National Standard for Information Systems—Programming Language—C*, ANSI X3.159-1989, published by the American National Standards Institute, 1430 Broadway, New York, NY 10018, copyright 1990.

```
/*
 * Portable and nonportable function calls.
 */
#include <stdio.h>
#include <stdlib.h>

int main()
{
  int func1(void), func2(void);

  int i, tmp1, tmp2, tmp3;

  i = 0;
  printf("%i, %i, %i\n", ++i, ++i, ++i);           /* nonportable */

  i = 0;
  tmp1 = ++i;  tmp2 = ++i;  tmp3 = ++i;
  printf("%i, %i, %i\n", tmp1, tmp2, tmp3);        /* portable */

  printf("%i, %i\n", func1(), func2());            /* nonportable */

  tmp1 = func1();  tmp2 = func2();
  printf("%i, %i\n", tmp1, tmp2);                  /* portable */

  return EXIT_SUCCESS;
}

int func1(void)
{
  printf("Called func1.\n");
  return 1;
}

int func2(void)
{
  printf("Called func2.\n");
  return 2;
}
```

Figure 21.14   (funccall.c) Some example function calls and their portable replacements.

leads to problems because programs written using the full range of ANSI features won't compile under "traditional" (K&R) C compilers.

In a few years, these old compilers will gracefully fade away, and we'll be able to safely ignore this problem. For now, however, we can't simply bury our head in the sand and assume the programs we write will only be compiled with ANSI compilers. One way to ensure that our programs are portable to these old-style compilers is to avoid completely any special ANSI features. But features like function prototypes and the type checking and automatic conversions they support are extremely useful, and we hate to give them up when they're available on our compiler. What we really want is a way to write our programs so they take advantage of these features when they're present and struggle along without them when they're not.

Dealing with Function Prototypes

How can we use complete function prototypes on an ANSI compiler and avoid them on an old-style compiler? Essentially, we let the preprocessor decide which to use. We illustrate the technique with a new version of **getline** that compiles successfully under both types of compilers. Figure 21.15 contains the header file defining **getline**'s prototype; Figure 21.16 contains **getline** itself.

We start by modifying the header file so that it defines complete prototypes when we're running under the standard C compiler and partial prototypes when we're running on a nonstandard C compiler. To determine which kind of compiler we're running under, we check whether **__STDC__** is defined. As we saw in Chapter 15, ANSI compilers define **__STDC__**; other compilers don't.

Next, we define a macro **getline** that expands into a call to the actual function **getline2** with its arguments cast to their proper type. **getline2** is the original **getline** function renamed to prevent an infinite macro expansion. Why do we do that? Because when we provide prototypes, C automatically converts the function's arguments to the types the function expects. The macro allows **getline**'s callers to assume that this is still happening, even if they aren't compiled with an ANSI compiler.

Finally, when we define the functions, we use the preprocessor to select between the old and new styles of parameter declarations.

```
#ifdef __STDC__
int getline(char *ptr, int max)
#else
int getline2(ptr, max)
   char *ptr; int max;
#endif
```

When we're not compiling under an ANSI compiler, we're actually defining a function named **getline2**. But that's OK because its users actually call the **getline** macro, which expands into the appropriate call to **getline2**.

Why are we using **#ifdef** rather than **#if** and **defined**? Because we're now assuming that our program may be compiled on an old-style compiler and **defined** is an ANSI addition.

Generic Pointers

The availability of complete function prototypes is a big difference between ANSI and old-style compilers. But that's not the only difference we need to worry about. Generic pointers are another feature unavailable in many old-style compilers. On these compilers we're stuck with using the type pointer to **char** as a rough approximation to a pointer to **void**. This works reasonably well, as it's usually safe to store any pointer type in a pointer to **char**.

```
/*
 * Defining getline's prototype.
 */
#ifdef __STDC__
int getline(char *, int);
#else
int getline2();
#define getline(1,m)  getline2((char *) (1), (int) (m))
#endif
```

Figure 21.15   (getline.h) Header file defining **getline**'s prototype.

```
/*
 * Defines a function to read an input line into an array.
 */
#include <stdio.h>
#include "getline.h"

#ifdef __STDC__
int getline(char *ptr, int max)
#else
int getline2(ptr, max)
  char *ptr; int max;
#endif
{
  int  c;                       /* current character */
  char *startptr = ptr;         /* pointer to start of line */
  char *endptr = ptr + max;     /* pointer to end of line */

  while ((c = getchar ()) != '\n' && c != EOF)
    if (ptr < endptr)
      *ptr++ = c;
  *ptr = '\0';                  /* terminate with null */
  return (c == EOF) ? -1 : ptr - startptr;
}
```

Figure 21.16   (getline.c) A version of **getline** portable to both ANSI and non-ANSI compilers.

To aid portability, we usually define a type **GenericPtr** and use it whenever we need a generic pointer. Figure 21.17 shows its definition. On old-style compilers, we define it as a pointer to **unsigned char** and on ANSI compilers we define it as a pointer to **void**.

Unfortunately, that's not all we have to do to write portable code. The one big problem is that there are no automatic conversions to and from pointers to **unsigned char**, as there are with pointers to **void**. That means that on old-style compilers we have to

```
/*
 * Definition of generic pointer type.
 */
#ifdef __STDC__
typedef void *GenericPtr;              /* ANSI generic pointer */
#else
typedef unsigned char *GenericPtr;     /* no generic pointer */
#endif
```

Figure 21.17 (gens.h) Definition of a generic pointer type.

do these casts ourselves. For portability, however, we cast *all* our assignments to and from **GenericPtr**s.

We also increase portability by hiding inside macros any calls to functions that access generic pointers. On old-style compilers, we define the macros to take care of any necessary type casting. But on ANSI compilers the macros map directly into the low-level call. Figure 21.18 provides an example in a revision of Chapter 15's allocs.h header file. It defines a set of macros, including **ALLOC**, **ALLOC_ZERO**, and **DEALLOC**, which provide a friendly interface to **malloc**, **calloc**, and **free**, respectively.

Figures 21.19 and 21.20 put all of this advice together in a new version of our basic set-managing functions that compiles and runs successfully under both types of compilers. We've changed the header file to supply complete prototypes under ANSI compilers and to supply partial prototypes and macros to handle the argument casting for old-style compilers. We've also made **Set** a **GenericPtr**, rather than a pointer to **void**. Finally, since many old-style compilers do not allow **const**, we have **#define**d it to nothing, so it is ignored by these compilers. Within the set operations, we're now using our **ALLOC_ZERO** and **DEALLOC** macros rather than **calloc** and **free**. And anywhere we assign a **Set** to another type of pointer, we're careful to use a cast. Figures 21.21 and 21.22 show the similar changes we have to make to the utility function for printing sets, and Figure 21.23 contains a main program using the **Set** type.

When we have straightforward, extremely short functions, it's often easier to write them as macros than to try to write them as functions that we can compile and use correctly under both types of compilers. We could, for example, rewrite our set functions as macros, as we did in Chapter 15's case study. That approach, however, has several drawbacks. One is that macros are usually less readable than the functions, since they are dense and lack type information. Macros are also less modular, and the details of how a set is implemented would no longer be kept hidden from its users.

Missing Header Files

ANSI compilers provide a set of header files with prototypes for all library functions. Old-style C compilers, however, provided only partial prototypes for a small subset of these functions. With one of these compilers, we're often stuck with declaring a library function's return value explicitly and supplying any casts necessary to guarantee

```
/*
 * Useful macros for dynamically allocating things.
 */
#include "gens.h"                    /* for generic pointer */

#ifdef __STDC__         /* ANSI C */

#include <stdlib.h>                  /* for malloc/calloc/free */
#include <stddef.h>                  /* for NULL */
#include <string.h>                  /* for memcpy, memset, strcpy */

#define ALLOC(n,t)       (malloc((n) * sizeof(t)))
#define ALLOC_ZERO(n,t)  (calloc(n, sizeof(t)))

#else                   /* Old-style C */

#include <stdio.h>                   /* for NULL */

extern GenericPtr malloc();
extern GenericPtr calloc();
extern int free();

#define ALLOC(n,t)       ((t *) (malloc((n) * sizeof(t))))
#define ALLOC_ZERO(n,t)  ((t *) (calloc(n, sizeof(t))))

#endif

#define DEALLOC(x)       (free((GenericPtr) x))
#define COPY(np,op,n,t)  (memcpy(np,op,(n) * sizeof(t)))
#define ZERO(p,n,t)      (memset(p,(n) * sizeof(t),0))

#define STRALLOC(s)      (malloc(strlen(s) + 1))
#define STRDUP(ns,os)    ((ns = STRALLOC(os)) ? strcpy(ns,os) : NULL)

#define TABLEDUP(np,op,n,t) \
        (((np = ALLOC(n,t)) != NULL) ? COPY(np,op,n,t) : NULL)
```

Figure 21.18 (allocs.h) A more portable memory allocation package.

that we're passing it the expected arguments. This problem is solvable using the preprocessor: when compiling under ANSI-C, we include the usual header file, but when compiling under old-style compilers, we declare the return values ourselves.

Figure 21.24 shows a new version of our earlier program to compute powers that can run under both ANSI and old-style compilers. When we're compiling with a standard compiler, we include math.h and define a macro **POW** that simply expands into a call to the math library's **pow** function. Otherwise we define **pow**'s return value ourselves and define another version of the **POW** macro that appropriately casts its arguments. In either case we use **POW** to compute powers and rely on the preprocessor to map it to the appropriate library call.

```
/*
 * A definition of "sets" of integers that is portable to
 * non-ANSI-C compilers.
 */
#include "allocs.h"

typedef GenericPtr Set;

#ifdef __STDC__                     /* ANSI-C */

extern Set    setCreate(unsigned int n);
extern void   setAdd(Set s, int e);
extern void   setDelete(Set s, int e);
extern int    setMember(const Set s, int e);

#else                               /* OLD-STYLE C */

extern Set    setCreate2();
extern void   setAdd2();
extern void   setDelete2();
extern int    setMember2();

#define setCreate(n)        setCreate2((unsigned int) n)
#define setAdd(s, e)        setAdd2((Set) s, (int) e)
#define setDelete(s, e)     setDelete2((Set) s, (int) e)
#define setMember(s, e)     setMember2((Set) s, (int) e)

#define const                       /* No const in old-style C */

#endif

#define setDestroy(s)       (DEALLOC(s))
#define setSwitch(s, t, e)  (setDelete(t, e), setAdd(s, e))
```

Figure 21.19 (sets.h) More portable set function prototypes.

21.6   CASE STUDY—PORTABLE I/O DEVICE HANDLING

*This section
is optional!*

The one major portability concern we've so far ignored deals with I/O. There are a multitude of I/O devices out there, each of which is handled in different ways on different systems. Our problem is that we don't want a program wedded to a particular input or output device. But if we directly call the low-level functions needed to manipulate the keyboard or display, we're going to be in trouble once we change to a different device or to a system with different calls. To avoid this problem, we have to treat keyboards and displays as *virtual* devices. Rather than directly calling whatever low-level functions are required to access the display, we make use of a package of high-level functions that do things such as reading a keystroke or moving the cursor. This gives us the flexibility to reimplement these functions for many different devices on different systems.

```
/*
 * Functions to handle dynamically allocated sets.
 */
#include "sets.h"

#define US_BITS 16

#define WORD(elem)    ((elem) / US_BITS)
#define BIT(elem)    ((elem) % US_BITS)

#ifdef __STDC__
Set setCreate(unsigned int n)            /* create an empty set */
#else
Set setCreate2(n)
  unsigned int n;
#endif
{
  return (Set) ALLOC_ZERO(n / US_BITS + (n % US_BITS != 0),
                          unsigned short);
}

#ifdef __STDC__
void setAdd(Set s, int elem)             /* add element to set */
#else
void setAdd2(s, elem)
  Set s; int elem;
#endif
  { * ((unsigned short *) s + WORD(elem)) |= 1 << BIT(elem); }

#ifdef __STDC__
void setDelete(Set s, int elem)          /* delete element from set */
#else
void setDelete2(s, elem)
    Set s; int elem;
#endif
  { * ((unsigned short *) s + WORD(elem)) &= ~(1 << BIT(elem)); }

#ifdef __STDC__
int setMember(const Set s, int elem)    /* is item in set? */
#else
int setMember2(s, elem)
  Set s; int elem;
#endif
{
  const unsigned int temp = * ((const unsigned short *) s + WORD(elem));

  return (temp >> BIT(elem)) & 01;
}
```

Figure 21.20   (sets.c)   A more portable version of our set operations.

```
/*
 * Prototypes for set utilities.
 */
#include "sets.h"

#ifdef __STDC__
void setPrint(char *msg, const Set s, int max);
#else
void setPrint2(msg, s, max)
  char *msg; const Set s; int max;
#endif
```

Figure 21.21   (setutils.h) More portable set utility prototypes.

```
/*
 * Set utility functions.
 */
#include <stdio.h>
#include "sets.h"

#ifdef __STDC__
void setPrint(char *msg, const Set set, int max)
#else
void setPrint2(msg, set, max)
  char *msg; const Set set; int max;
#endif
{
  int i;                                 /* next potential element */

  printf(msg);
  for (i = 0; i < max; i++)
    if (setMember(set, i))
      printf("%i\n", i);
}
```

Figure 21.22   (setutils.c) A more portable version of our set utilities.

This chapter concludes by looking at how we can portably implement several display and keyboard I/O functions that C doesn't naturally provide for us. These include functions for reading a character as soon as it's typed, clearing the screen, and moving the cursor to a particular screen location. We implement these functions for programs compiled with Turbo C++ and for programs running on the most common versions of UNIX.

```
/*
 * Identify duplicates in the input (more portable version).
 */
#include <stdio.h>
#include <stdlib.h>
#include "setutils.h"
#include "getline.h"

#define MAXLEN       80
#define ELEMENTS     512

int main()
{
  Set  unique = setCreate(ELEMENTS);
  Set  dup = setCreate(ELEMENTS);
  int  value;                              /* current input value */
  char line[MAXLEN + 1];                   /* current input line */

  while (getline(line, MAXLEN) != -1)
    if (sscanf(line, "%i", &value) != 1)
      fprintf(stderr,"Skipping bad input item\n");
    else if (value < 0 || value >= ELEMENTS)
      fprintf(stderr,"Out of range item %i\n", value);
    else if (setMember(unique, value))
      setSwitch(dup, unique, value);       /* move to dup */
    else if (!setMember(dup, value))
      setAdd(unique, value);
  setPrint("Unique values\n", unique, ELEMENTS);
  setPrint("Duplicate values\n", dup, ELEMENTS);

  return EXIT_SUCCESS;
}
```

Figure 21.23   (usesets3.c)   A new version of our program to detect duplicate input values.

Immediate Input

getchar doesn't read characters as soon as they're typed. Instead, it waits until the user has typed in an entire input line. That allows the system to handle backspace characters so our programs don't have to worry about them. But there are times when we want to read characters *immediately*—just as soon as our user types them. Our **yesOrNo** function, for example, shouldn't wait until the user has typed a whole line, since it really needs only to process a single input character. Unfortunately, C doesn't provide any such mechanism. Instead, we have to rely on special, operating-system-dependent system calls. The problem, of course, is that our code becomes very operating system dependent.

We take a more portable approach and provide a set of functions that together let us read characters as soon as they arrive on the standard input: **icharInit**, **icharGet**,

```
/*
 * Using the math library function to compute exponents.
 */
#include <stdio.h>
#include <stdlib.h>

#ifdef __STDC__

#include <math.h>                    /* grab prototypes */
#define POW(x,y)     pow(x,y)

#else

double pow();                        /* supply prototypes ourselves */
#define POW(x,y)     pow((double) (x), (double) (y))

#endif

int main()
{
  printf("10^6 = %g\n",    POW(10, 6));
  printf("3.3^-2 = %g\n",  POW(3.3, -2));

  return EXIT_SUCCESS;
}
```

Figure 21.24   (power.c) A program that uses **pow** to compute exponents and that works appropriately under both old-style and ANSI compilers.

and **icharDone**. **icharInit** puts us in a mode where we can read characters as soon as they appear. **icharGet** reads the next char. And **icharDone** puts us back in our original mode of reading characters only after the user has entered a complete line. In between calls to **icharInit** and **icharDone**, we're not allowed to use any of the other standard I/O functions on the standard input. Figure 21.25 provides their prototypes, and Figure 21.26 provides the functions themselves.

With Turbo C++, our job is surprisingly easy, because there is already a library function, **getche**, we can call to read the next character immediately. So **icharGet** is simply a macro that calls **getche**, and **icharInit** and **icharDone** are macros that return 1, since they're not needed here. With UNIX, however, our job is more complicated, and we have to use a set of system calls to set things up so we can read one character at a time with **getchar**. These calls involve turning off standard I/O buffering for **stdin**, as well as turning off any internal buffering the operating system does for terminal I/O. And when we no longer want to read characters one at a time, we have to restore the default behavior. Our job is particularly difficult because there are two different flavors of UNIX, and slightly different system calls are needed for both.

Figure 21.27 shows a final version of **yesOrNo** that uses these functions. Each time we call it, it uses **icharInit** to obtain the special input processing, **icharGet**

```
/*
 * Prototypes for read-immediately functions.
 */
#if defined(__TURBOC__)

#include <conio.h>

#define icharGet()      getche()        /* built-in insta-char */
#define icharInit()     1               /* fake function return */
#define icharDone()     1               /* fake function return */

#elif defined(unix)

#define icharGet()      getchar()

int icharInit(void);
int icharDone(void);

#else
#error Can only handle Turbo C (under MS-DOS) and UNIX
#endif
```

Figure 21.25   (ichars.h)   Prototypes for our read-character-immediately functions.

to read the user's responses, and **icharDone** to return to normal character-at-a-time input.

Cursor Control

Real-world programs can't get by with the simple or almost nonexistent user interfaces we've so far provided to our programs. They need the ability to manage the screen directly. At the very least, they must be able to clear the screen and to move the cursor around it. The underlying code to handle this stuff is messy and system dependent, so we'll provide a small set of functions to do the work for us: **displayInit**, **displayClear**, and **displayGoTo**. **displayInit** handles any necessary initialization, **displayClear** clears the screen, and **displayGoTo** moves the cursor to a particular x, y coordinate. Figure 21.28 contains the prototypes for our functions, Figure 21.29 contains the functions that work under MS-DOS, and Figure 21.30 contains the same functions written to work under UNIX.

These functions are simply a nice interface on top of system-specific display functions. On MS-DOS, we access the display through a low-level hardware interrupt function, **int86**. Essentially, we pass it a structure that describes the operation we want, and it takes care of the rest for us. On UNIX, it's actually more complicated because we have to handle many different kinds of terminals. There, we access the terminal through a package of library calls.

```
/*
 * Package for reading characters immediately.
 *    icharInit - set things up for character-at-a-time I/O.
 *    icharDone - restore things to the normal start-up state.
 */
#include <stdio.h>
#include "ichars.h"

#if defined(unix)

#if defined(sys5)                       /* ATT UNIX */
#include <sys/termio.h>
#define GETTERMINFO TCGETA
#define SETTERMINFO TCSETAF

struct termio oldt, t;                  /* old and new terminal status */
#else                                   /* otherwise assume Berkeley UNIX */
#include <sgtty.h>
#define GETTERMINFO TIOCGETP
#define SETTERMINFO TIOCSETN

struct sgttyb oldt, t;                  /* old and new terminal status */
#endif

int icharInit(void)
{
  setvbuf(stdin, NULL, _IONBF, NULL);
  if (ioctl(0, GETTERMINFO, &t) == -1)
    return -1;
  oldt = t;                             /* save terminal settings */

#if defined(sys5)
  t.c_lflag &= ~ICANON;                 /* set up for one char read */
  t.c_cc[4] = 1;
  t.c_cc[5] = 0;
#else
  t.sg_flags |= CBREAK;                 /* set up for one char read */
#endif

  return ioctl(0, SETTERMINFO, &t) != -1 ? 0 : -1;
}

int icharDone(void)
{
  setvbuf(stdin, NULL, _IOFBF, BUFSIZ);
  return ioctl(0, SETTERMINFO, &oldt) != -1 ? 0 : -1;
}
#endif
```

Figure 21.26   (ichars.c) Immediate character input.

```
/*
 * Program using immediate input to get a yes or no answer.
 */
#include <stdio.h>
#include <ctype.h>
#include "ichars.h"

int yesOrNo(const char *prompt)
{
  int answer;                          /* user-entered character */

  (void) icharInit();                  /* assume worked */
  for (;;)
  {
    printf(prompt);
    answer = tolower(icharGet());
    putchar('\n');
    if (answer != 'y' && answer != 'n')
      printf("Please enter Y, y, N, or n.\n");
    else
      break;
  }
  (void) icharDone();                  /* assume worked */
  return answer == 'y';
}
```

Figure 21.27 (yesorno12.c) A version of **yesOrNo** that reads characters as soon as they are typed in.

```
/*
 * Prototypes for direct screen access.
 */
#if defined(__MSDOS__)
#define displayInit()    displayClear()
#else
void displayInit(void);
#endif

void displayClear(void);
void displayGoTo(int, int);
```

Figure 21.28 (screen.h) Prototypes for functions implementing screen operations.

```
/*
 * Screen output operations (for MS-DOS).
 *    displayClear - clear the screen.
 *    displayGoTo - move to a particular x,y location.
 */
#include <stdio.h>
#include "screen.h"

#if !defined(__MSDOS__)
#error This file should only be compiled under MS-DOS
#else
#include <dos.h>
void displayClear(void)
{
  union REGS regs;

  regs.h.ah = 0;                        /* OP: set text mode */
  regs.h.al = 2;                        /* clear as side effect */
  int86(0x10, &regs, &regs);
}

void displayGoTo(int row, int col)
{
  union REGS regs;

  regs.h.ah = 2;                        /* OP: set cursor position */
  regs.h.bh = 0;                        /* page to move to (always 0) */
  regs.h.dl = col;                      /* row to move to */
  regs.h.dh = row;                      /* column to move to */
  int86(0x10, &regs, &regs);
}
#endif
```

Figure 21.29   (dosscr.c) Functions implementing screen operations under MS-DOS.

What we've tried to do here is localize the nonportable code in a few specialized routines. That way, only these routines have to be changed and recompiled to use a different display, not the remainder of our program. Figure 21.31 illustrates their use in a new version of our earlier Life program's output routine.

SUMMARY

- An important goal is to maximize the portability of the programs we write. This involves ensuring that our programs can be compiled under a variety of compilers and run on a variety of different machines, under the control of different operating systems, and with different I/O devices.

```
/*
 * Screen output operations (for UNIX).
 *    displayInit - initialize display.
 *    displayClear - clear display.
 *    displayGoTo - tmove to a particular x,y coordinate.
 */
#include <stdio.h>
#include "screen.h"

#if !defined(unix)
#error This file can only be compiled under UNIX
#else
#include <stdlib.h>                      /* for getenv */

extern int tgetent(const char *, const char *);
extern char *tgetstr(const char *, char **);
extern int tputs(const char *, int, int(*)(int));
extern char *tgoto(const char *, int, int);

static char *tn = NULL;                  /* terminal name */
static char tc[1024];                    /* terminal controls */
static char *ptr = tc;                   /* ptr to terminal controls */

static char *clearscreen;                /* clear-screen chars */
static char *movecursor;                 /* move-cursor chars */
static char td[1024];                    /* termcap description */

void displayClear(void)
  { printf(clearscreen); }

void displayInit(void)
{
  if ((tn = getenv("TERM")) != NULL && tgetent(td, tn) == 1)
  {
    clearscreen = tgetstr("cl", &ptr);
    movecursor = tgetstr("cm", &ptr);
  }
  displayClear();
}

static int putcontrol(int c)
  { return putchar(c); }                 /* need function, not macro */

void displayGoTo(int r, int c)
  { (void) tputs(tgoto(movecursor, c, r), 1, putcontrol); }
#endif
```

Figure 21.30 (unixscr.c) Functions implementing screen operations under UNIX.

```
/*
 * Print generation using direct cursor addressing.
 */
#include <stdio.h>
#include "life.h"
#include "screen.h"

#define HEADER_ROW          0    /* row containing header */
#define BORDER_ROW          1    /* row containing top border */
#define BORDER_COL          0    /* col containing left border */
#define TOP_CELL_ROW        2    /* first row with cells */
#define LEFT_CELL_COL       1    /* first column with cells */

static void displayChar(int row, int col, int n, char ch)
{
  for (displayGoTo(row,col); n-- > 0; putchar(ch))
    ;
}

void putWorld(PtrToConstWorld world)
{
  int c, r;
  static int printed = FALSE;       /* first printing? */
  extern int Rows, Cols, Gen, EndGen;

  if (!printed)
  {
    displayInit();
    displayChar(BORDER_ROW, BORDER_COL, Cols + 2, BORDER);
    displayChar(BORDER_ROW + Rows + 1, BORDER_COL,
                Cols + 2, BORDER);
    for (r = TOP_CELL_ROW; r <=  TOP_CELL_ROW + Rows; r++)
    {                                  /* other borders */
      displayChar(r, BORDER_COL, 1, BORDER);
      displayChar(r, LEFT_CELL_COL + Cols, 1, BORDER);
    }
    printed = TRUE;
  }
  displayGoTo(HEADER_ROW, BORDER_COL);
  printf("Generation %i out of %i", Gen, EndGen);
  for (r = TOP_CELL_ROW; r < TOP_CELL_ROW + Rows; r++)
  {
    displayGoTo(r, LEFT_CELL_COL);
    for (c = 1; c <= Cols; c++)
      putchar(world[r][c] ? MARKER : ' ');
  }
  displayGoTo(BORDER_ROW + Rows + 3, BORDER_COL);
}
```

Figure 21.31 (outworld.c) A new version of Life output routines using our portable display functions.

- When our programs must also compile on non-ANSI compilers, our biggest worries are function prototypes, generic pointers, and missing header files.

- The biggest difference between ANSI compilers is in the lengths of external names that are allowed. We use the preprocessor to define short names for any long, potentially conflicting function names.

- Operating systems differ in the low-level system calls they provide. We need to define higher-level functions that internally use the appropriate low-level calls.

- There are a variety of different machine dependencies that can creep into C programs. To write portable code we must avoid using these troublesome constructs.

EXERCISES

Explore

21–1 Compile and run the programs in this chapter with at least two different compilers and on two different machines.

21–2 How portable are the programs in the book? Pick two or three of the case studies and run them on another machine. Make whatever changes are necessary to guarantee that these programs work on both ANSI and old-style compilers.

Tune

21–3 Make the changes necessary to port our display package to a system that supports only five significant characters in an identifier name.

21–4 Find out what the machine-dependent operations (such as right shifts of negative integers) actually do on your machine. Do any of your programs take advantage of them? If any do, can you rewrite your programs to avoid these operations?

21–5 If you have access to more than one machine, take a sizable program that you have written and used on one machine and port it to another. Where were your portability problems? Does the program have identical run-time behavior on both machines?

Code

21–6 Write **exists**, a function that takes a single file name argument and returns 1 if a file with that name exists and a 0 otherwise. Write it so that it works with MS-DOS and UNIX. The UNIX version should use **stat**, which returns −1 if the file doesn't exist. The MS-DOS version can simply try to open the file for reading.

21–7 Write a program that prints the contents of a **long**, one byte at a time, using a **union** as we did in Figure 21.12.

21–8 Write a function that can print the contents of any type, including structures, one byte at a time. What might such a function be useful for?

Build

21–9 Suppose you have to write a program that requires a 100,000-element array of integers and that, in addition, must be able to run both on a machine with 16 megabytes of memory and on a machine with only 128K of memory where arrays are limited to 64,000 bytes. Assume that the only operations on the table are to access an element and to store a value in an array element. Write functions for these operations that use an in-memory array if there is enough room or store the array in an external file if there is not. Should the callers of these functions be aware of how the array is actually accessed?

Part VI

MOVING FROM C TO C++

The final three chapters of this text focus on how C++ extends C into a powerful object-oriented programming language.

- Chapter 22 discusses a collection of non-object-oriented C++ features we can use to improve our C programs.

- Chapter 23 discusses the basic C++ features that support objects.

- Chapter 24 discusses the basic C++ features that support inheritance, polymorphism, and dynamic binding.

22 C++

BASICS

C++ is an extension of C designed to support object-oriented programming. For now, however, we defer discussion of its object-oriented features and instead focus on introducing special C++ features that allow us to use it as a better way to write C programs. We first focus on likely problems with taking C programs and compiling them under C++, and then introduce a set of useful C++ features, such as references, inline functions, default function parameters, and function and operator overloading. To illustrate the use of these features, we rewrite some of our earlier C functions and programs to take advantage of them.

22.1 COMPILING C PROGRAMS WITH C++ COMPILERS

The real-world appears to be moving from C to C++. It's likely that in the future, our C programs will be maintained and extended using C++ compilers. That means it is important to write our C programs so that they can compile under C++. In fact, a good quick test of the quality of our C code is to try to compile it using a C++ compiler. That's because C++ is essentially a superset of C, but with a compiler that's much more picky about type checking.

Function Prototypes

One difference is that C++ *requires* a complete function prototype before the function call, unlike C, where a prototype is optional and the compiler quietly assumes that the function returns an **int** if you fail to provide a prototype. In addition, if you leave out parameter type specifications, as you can do in C, C++ interprets the declaration as specifying *no* parameters (the equivalent of providing a parameter list of **void** in C). That is,

```
int inRange();
```

is interpreted in C++ as if we wrote

```
int inRange(void);
```

The result is that the first thing we need to do to get a C program to compile under C++ is to provide complete prototypes for all functions. The ideal way to do this in C, as we saw earlier, is to place prototypes in header files that are included both where the function is used and where it is defined. There is often a tendency to cheat, however, and to simply supply the prototype where the function is called. In C, this can lead to a nasty little run-time problem when a function's prototype does not match its definition. In C++, however, this mistake merely leads to a link-time error.

Figure 22.1 is a new version of our earlier main program using our **power** function that provides an *incorrect* prototype. In particular, it's declaring **power** as a function taking a pair of **int** parameters, when **power** actually takes a **double** base and an **int** exponent. In C, this program compiles and links, but produces incorrect results when run. In C++, however, we get a linker error. This is called *type-safe* linkage and by itself is reason enough to migrate from C to C++![1]

Pointer Usage

Another difference related to type checking is in how C++ handles assignments involving pointers to **void**.

In C, we can quietly assign a pointer to **void** to a pointer to **char** or any other type without using a cast. One place where this often causes trouble is in C programs that use **malloc**. An example is the **makeDupStr** function from Figure 14.9, a function in which we assign the result of using **malloc** (a pointer to **void**) to a pointer to a character.

```
char *newstr = malloc(strlen(str) + 1);
```

In C++, this assignment is an error, and we must instead cast the pointer when we do the assignment.

```
char *newstr = (char *) malloc(strlen(str) + 1);
```

We also need to use a cast when we pass a **void** * pointer to a function expecting a different pointer type, and when we return a **void** * pointer from a function returning a different pointer type.

It is not necessary to cast going the other way. That is, we can safely assign any pointer type a **void** *. The idea is that a **void** * is always large enough to hold any type of pointer, so we don't need to use a cast to specify what type we are storing. But when we access the stored pointer, we're making an assumption that an appropriate pointer type was stored there in the first place, the type of which is specified in the cast, highlighting that assumption.

Naming Problems

There is one more likely trouble spot when compiling C programs with C++ due to C++'s more sizable set of keywords (which were listed at the beginning of Chapter 4). A C identifier that just so happens to have the name of a C++ keyword, such as **delete**

---

[1]There are a variety of ways for C++ to accomplish this. A common one is by name mangling, wherein the compiler generates new names for all our functions that encode information about the types of their parameters. In our example, the underlying name for **power** when it is called differs from the underlying name generated for **power** when it was defined, so the linker can't resolve the call.

```
/*
 * Using our function to compute exponents (with incorrect prototype).
 */
#include <stdio.h>
#include <stdlib.h>

int main()
{
  double power(int base, int exp);          /* ERROR: Incorrect Prototype */

  double x;                                 /* user-supplied base */
  int    y;                                 /* user-supplied exponent */

  while (scanf("%lf %i", &x, &y) == 2)
    printf("%g^%i = %g\n", x, y, power(x, y));

  return EXIT_SUCCESS;
}
```

Figure 22.1   (usepower.C) An incorrect version of our main program using our earlier **power** function.

or **new**, is going to produce streams of error messages! The solution here is simply to rename those variables or functions (unfortunately, doing so often turns out to be not all that simple).

22.2   SIMPLE BUT USEFUL C++ EXTENSIONS TO C

This section introduces a collection of minor but useful extensions to C. These include a new way of writing comments, an improved **const**, and the ability to declare variables just when we need them, a shortcut for declaring variables that have a constructed type, and a boolean data type.

C++ Comments

Figure 22.2 is a new version of the main program in our earlier input-reversal program (Figure 8.4). This version uses the C++ commenting style. A pair of slashes (**//**) tells the compiler to ignore the remainder of the line.

```
    int   table[MaxValues];          // array to hold input values
```

This has the advantages of not requiring us to remember to terminate comments, as well as allowing us to easily comment out lines that already contain comments.

C++ still allows us to use C comments, but it's considered better style to use C++ comments instead, as this helps the user recognize at a glance that the program must be compiled with a C++ and not a C compiler.

```
//
// Read values and print them in reverse order using functions.
//
#include <stdio.h>
#include <stdlib.h>

const int MaxValues = 100;    // max number of values we can reverse

int main()
{
  int  tableFill(int a[], int max);
  void tablePrintRev(int a[], int max);

  int  table[MaxValues];                    // array to hold input values
  int  n = tableFill(table, MaxValues);     // number of values in "table"

  tablePrintRev(table, n);

  return EXIT_SUCCESS;
}
```

Figure 22.2   (revint2.C)   A C++ version of a program to reverse an array.

An Improved const

C++ eliminates one of C's restrictions on using **const**. In C, for example, we cannot use a **const** variable to specify a value that appears as the subscript in an array declaration (or, more generally, in any place the language requires a constant expression). In C++, however, we can. In Figure 22.2, we declare **MaxValues** as a **const int** and then use it in the declaration of the array **table**:

```
    int table[MaxValues];            // array to hold input values
```

This would be illegal in C.

const variables are statically scoped, so we can include them in header files to share their value among different source files.

The result is that in C++ we can usually use **const** instead of **#define**, which eliminates hard-to-find syntax errors that can result from incorrectly using **#define**.

> *Use* **const** *instead of* **#define** *to define constants.*

Variable Declarations

C++ allows us to declare variables whenever we need them, rather than only at the beginning of a block. That is, a variable declaration is legal any place a statement is legal. The variable is visible from the point of its declaration to the end of the nearest enclosing block.

Figure 22.3 takes advantage of this in a new version of our earlier input-averaging program (Figure 6.26). We declare the variable **avg** after the loop that reads the input and computes its sum, but not within a separate block, as we would have had to do in C. We have also declared **avg** as a **const**, since we use the variable solely to clarify the meaning of the complex expression that computes the average and because we do not plan on modifying it later. We would not have been able to declare it as a **const** if we declared it at the program's start, since we would not know what value to initialize it with and we're not allowed to assign to **const**s.

C++ also allows us to declare variables within a **for**'s initialization expression.[2] Figure 22.4 takes advantage of this feature in a new version of **tablePrintRev**, our function to print an array in reverse order. The printing loop now takes care of declaring the index variable **i**.

```
for (int i = n - 1; i >= 0; i--)
    printf("%i\n", table[i]);
```

This declares **i** right where it is used, making the code more readable.

C++ limits the scope of a variable declared within a **for** to its body, so the variable becomes undefined after the loop.[3] Above, this means that **i**'s scope extends to the end of the loop only, so we can't access **i** after the loop. That scoping restriction is why we don't declare the **cnt** used to index the loop in **tableFill**, as we need **cnt**'s value after the loop in order to return it. If we had, we would be stuck saving its value in another variable declared outside of the loop so we could use it later.

Structure Tags as Type Names

Another convenient C++ feature is that the tag in a compound type is a type name in its own right, without the need for the preceding **struct**, **union**, or **enum**. That is, if we declare a type **struct Employee**, we can declare variable of type **Employee**, as in

```
Employee emp;
```

This eliminates the need for the common C trick of using a **typedef** to declare a special type, **EMPLOYEE**, and then declaring variables with this type. We'll take advantage of this feature throughout the rest of this chapter's examples.

A Boolean Type

In C, we often use boolean-like data types, usually a **short** or **int**, and ones and zeros to store information about *true* and *false* conditions. Also, though the relational

---

[2]The language standard now actually allows us to declare variables in expressions that appear in other statement types as well.

[3]Earlier versions of C++ made the variable visible throughout the block in which it was declared. However, since this behavior has only recently been standardized, current compilers vary in their treatment of variables declared within loops.

```
//
// Compute average of input values (no error checking).
//
#include <stdio.h>
#include <stdlib.h>

int main()
{
  int          next;                   // next input value
  unsigned int n = 0;                  // number of input values

  long sum = 0;
  for (n = 0; scanf("%i", &next) == 1; n++)
    sum += next;

  const double avg = (n == 0) ? 0.0 : (double) sum / n;
  printf("Average of %u values is %f.\n", n, avg);

  return EXIT_SUCCESS;
}
```

Figure 22.3   (avg.C)   A program to compute an average.

operators (**<**, **<=**, and the others) are indicating a true or false result, in C they actually return an **int**: zero for false, one for true. Similarly, the loop control variable, though often thought of as a boolean (true or false), can be any integral type, where zero is treated as false, non-zero as true.

C++ addresses this not entirely clear use of integers for truth values with a new type, **bool**. **bool** is a type with just two values, **true** and **false**. In C++, relational operators and the equality operators (**==**, **!=**) give back a **bool**, and loop control expressions (**while**, **do-while**, **for**) evaluate to a **bool**. C++ supports automatic conversions, so code using integers instead, such as that using an integer as a loop control variable, still works.

bool is a relatively recent addition to C++, and if your compiler doesn't support it, you can still get much of its behavior simply by defining an enumerated type:

```
enum bool {false, true};
```

22.3   IMPROVEMENTS TO FUNCTIONS

C++ has a variety of features that make functions easier to write and use. These include parameter passing using references, default parameters, inline functions, and function and operator overloading.

```
//
// Functions to fill a table and print it in reverse order.
//    tableFill - read values into a table
//    tablePrintRev - print a table in reverse order
//
#include <stdio.h>

int tableFill(int a[], int max)
{
  int next;                  // next input value
  int r;                     // return from trying to read values
  int cnt;                   // count of values read

  for (cnt = 0; (r = scanf("%i", &next)) != EOF; cnt++)
  {
    if (r != 1)              // bad return from scanf
    {
      printf("Error in the input after reading %i values.\n", cnt);
      break;
    }
    if (cnt == max)          // no room to store this value
    {
      printf("No more room in array after reading %i values.\n", cnt);
      break;
    }
    a[cnt] = next;           // save element in array
  }
  return cnt;
}

void tablePrintRev(int a[], int n)
{
  for (int i = n - 1; i >= 0; i--)
    printf("%i\n", a[i]);
}
```

Figure 22.4 (tabfill.C) C++ functions to read and reverse an array.

Reference Parameters

As we saw earlier, C's argument passing method is always "call by value." C copies the actual arguments, and the copies are accessed within a function. Actually changing a value in the caller requires passing its address and dereferencing that pointer within the function body. That's simple enough, except that it's easy to forget an **&** or *****.

C++, however, allows us to have reference variables, which we can use to extend the calling method to include "call by reference." We obtain a reference parameter by following the variable's type with an **&** when we declare the variable. A reference parameter indicates that a reference to an item is passed, not the item itself. That is, the parameter is just another name for the variable being passed to it from the calling function. Within the function, we don't have to do anything special to access the item, but any changes affect the referenced object.

Figure 22.5 shows how to rewrite our earlier **swap** function to take advantage of this feature. In its header we declare the parameters **x** and **y** as references.

```
void swap(int& x, int& y)
```

Within **swap**, we just exchange **x** and **y** using a temporary variable but no pointers. Finally, when we call **swap**, we just pass it **s** and **t**.

```
swap(s, t);
```

The result is that when **swap** is called, **x** becomes a reference to **s** and **y** a reference to **t**, so exchanging **x** and **y** is really exchanging **s** and **t**.

Despite some superficial similarities, however, references are *not* pointers, and we cannot use them interchangeably. The correct way to understand the above program is simply to view the **x** in **swap** as another name for **s** in **main** (and **y** as another name for **t**).

> *Use references rather than pointers in functions that modify values in their callers.*

The reference-based version of **swap** is simpler both to write and to use than our earlier pointer-based version. The caller doesn't have to do any extra work whatsoever (no addresses to pass). And the only tricky part in writing the function is turning its parameters into references. The one drawback is that we can no longer guarantee that functions we use will not modify the variables we pass to them. Instead, we now have to carefully examine the prototypes of each function we call to determine which parameters are references and therefore might be modified by the function.

Another use for references is to pass large structures. In C, to avoid copying a large structure, we often pass an address. We have to write the call carefully so that we don't neglect the address-of operator, and to make sure we dereference the structure pointer in the function body. Passing a reference saves this hassle, although we should still be careful to make it a **const** reference so that the compiler will catch inadvertent changes to the referenced structure. Figure 22.6 provides an example in a new version of our earlier program to print an employee's number, name, phone, and age (Figure 12.1).

Inline Functions

In C, we often rewrote short functions as preprocessor macros. Unfortunately, there is no type checking of macro arguments, and macro names are not available at run time, making it difficult to track down error messages or to use a symbolic debugger. In C++, we can preface short function definitions with **inline**. This asks the compiler to insert the function's body into the code each time the function is called. However, the compiler preserves all of the normal function behavior (performing type checking and conversions on arguments, and so on). The result is that we eliminate the function call overhead while preserving the readability and structural advantages of using functions.

```
//
// Using a swap function to exchange two int values.
//
#include <stdio.h>
#include <stdlib.h>

int main()
{
  void swap(int& x, int& y);

  int s = 10, t = 20;

  printf("Before swap, s=%i, t=%i\n", s, t);
  swap(s, t);
  printf("After swap, s=%i, t=%i\n", s, t);

  return EXIT_SUCCESS;
}

void swap(int &x, int &y)
{
  int temp;

  temp = x;
  x = y;
  y = temp;
}
```

Figure 22.5 (swap.C) A C++ function to exchange two values using references.

Figure 22.7 is a new, inline version of **swap** and Figure 22.8 is the main program that uses it. We've now prefaced **swap**'s definition with **inline** and placed its definition in a header file (and we therefore provide only the definition and do not bother providing a prototype). We do this because the compiler needs to have the definition of an inline function available whenever it sees a call to the function. Fortunately, inline functions are treated as static functions, and so their names aren't exported to the linker. As a result, we need not worry about the linker getting confused if we include **swap**'s definition in more than one source file.

We use inline functions in the same places we would use macros: for functions that are really little more than named expressions. Inline functions tend to lead to more efficient programs but have the disadvantage that they also can often lead to slightly larger programs (since the body of the function is essentially repeated everywhere we call it). In addition, **inline** is only a hint, like **register**. The compiler is free to ignore your request if it considers the routine too big or too complex to inline.[4] In that case, the compiler treats the **inline** function as if it were declared as **static**, generating and calling a local copy of the function in each object module.

---

[4]Most compilers, for example, refuse to inline functions containing loops.

```
//
// Display Employee information.
//
#include <stdio.h>
#include <stdlib.h>

struct Employee
{
  long number;                          // Employee number
  char *name, *phone;                   // Employee name and phone
  int age;                              // Employee age
};

int main()
{
  void printEmp(const Employee& emp);

  Employee emp = {1001, "borromeo, daphne", "310-555-2042", 26};

  printEmp(emp);                        // write our Employee

  return EXIT_SUCCESS;
}

void printEmp(const Employee& e)        // reference to Employee
{
  printf("Employee: %li\n", e.number);
  printf("Name:     %s\n",  e.name);
  printf("Age:      %i\n",  e.age);
  printf("Phone:    %s\n",  e.phone);
}
```

Figure 22.6   (prstruct.C)   A C++ function to print a structure using references to pass the structure.

```
//
// An inline version of our swap function to exchange two values.
//
inline void swap(int& x, int& y)
  { int temp = x; x = y; y = temp; }
```

Figure 22.7   (swap.h)   An inline C++ function to exchange two values using references.

```
//
// Using an inline swap function to exchange two int values.
//
#include <stdio.h>
#include <stdlib.h>
#include "swap.h"

int main()
{
  int s = 10, t = 20;

  printf("Before swap, s=%i, t=%i\n", s, t);
  swap(s, t);
  printf("After swap, s=%i, t=%i\n", s, t);

  return EXIT_SUCCESS;
}
```

Figure 22.8   (useswap.C) Using our inline **swap** function.

Regardless, inline functions significantly reduce the need for function-like macros; because their arguments are counted and type checked, there is also an important reduction in run-time type errors, along with easier debugging.

> *Use inline functions rather than macros.*

Default Function Parameters

Many times we write a function with one or more parameters that will almost always be the same value. We still require these parameters, though, for those times when the function's caller may want to provide a different value. In C++ we can write such a function by specifying default parameters as part of the function's prototype. When we call the function with those parameters missing, it uses their default values. Otherwise, it simply uses the values we provide in the function call.

Figure 22.9 uses default arguments in a function to print an array, with a specified number of elements on each output line. The first (required) argument is the array to print; the second (also required) is the number of elements in that array. The third and final argument is the number of items to print on each line, for which we provide a default value of 1.

```
void display(const int a[], int n, int count = 1);
```

We usually place the prototype in a header file, which ensures that all callers who include it will have access to the default value. The default parameters must follow the required parameters.

```
//
// Print an array, several elements per line.
//
#include <stdio.h>
#include <stdlib.h>

main()
{
  void display(const int a[], int n, int count = 1);

  int a[10] = {81, 78, 45, 78, 91, 45, 76, 87, 54, 99};

  printf("Here's the array, one per line.\n");
  display(a, 10);          // one per line
  printf("Here's the array, three per line.\n");
  display(a, 10, 3);       // three per line

  return EXIT_SUCCESS;
}

void display(const int a[], int n, int count)
{
  for (int i = 1; i <= n; i++)
  {
    printf("%i", a[i - 1]);
    if (i % count == 0 || i == n)
      putchar('\n');
    else if (i != 0)
      putchar(' ');;
  }
}
```

Figure 22.9   (array.C)   A C++ program using default function arguments.

Function Overloading

C++ lets us write multiple versions of a function, each taking different numbers or types of arguments, a technique known as function *overloading*. We can, for example, write a single function, **display**, that writes any sort of object on the standard output. To do so, we write one version to handle an **Employee**, another a string, another an **int**, and so on.

Figure 22.10 rewrites our employee printing program to provide three different versions of **display**: one takes an employee, another a string, and the last an integer. When we call **display**, the compiler decides which version to call by examining the types of the parameters we're passing. With **display(emp)**, for example, we're passing an **Employee**, so we execute the version of **display** that expects an **Employee**. But with **display(e.age)**, we're passing an **int**, so we execute the version of **display** that expects to be passed an **int**.

```
//
// Use overloaded functions to display Employee info.
//
#include <stdio.h>
#include <stdlib.h>

struct Employee
{
  long number;                        // Employee number
  char *name, *phone;                 // Employee name and phone
  int age;                            // Employee age
};

int main()
{
  void display(const Employee& e);         // display Employee

  Employee emp = {1001, "borromeo, daphne", "310-555-2042", 26};

  display(emp);                            // write our Employee

  return EXIT_SUCCESS;
}

void display(const Employee& e)            // display an Employee
{
  void display(char *s), display(int i), display(long l);

  display("Employee: "); display(e.number); display("\n");
  display("Name:     "); display(e.name);   display("\n");
  display("Age:      "); display(e.age);    display("\n");
  display("Phone:    "); display(e.phone);  display("\n");
}

void display(char *s) { printf("%s", s); }   // display a string
void display(int i) { printf("%i", i); }     // display an integer
void display(long l) { printf("%li", l); }   // display a long
```

Figure 22.10 (prstrct2.C) A version of our employee printing program using function overloading.

Function overloading based on type is a powerful addition to the language. However, there's a "gotcha" to watch out for. When the types of a function's parameters match one of the prototypes exactly, the compiler can easily determine the correct function to call. On the other hand, when the types do not match, the compiler must apply rules to make this determination—and that's where the problem creeps in. Occasionally, these rules produce different results than we intend or result in the compiler being unable to tell which function to call. Of course, we can always get around these problems by casting the parameters in the call to the type we want, forcing an exact match.

Operator Overloading

C++ also allows us to overload operators so that they will apply to new user-defined types. In fact, the C++ library overloads the **<<** (left-shift) operator to perform output and so eliminates much of the need for **display**. Similarly, the **>>** (right-shift) operator is overloaded to perform input.

Before we discuss these operators in more detail, however, we'll take a look at a simpler example of operator overloading. In particular, let's look at how we can provide comparison operators for Chapter 12's functions for comparing dates. Figure 22.11 is a header file defining a set of overloaded operators as inline functions. In particular, it defines the comparison operators (such as equals, not equals, and so on) so that we can compare dates the same way we compare integers or any other basic type. Given that **x** and **y** are **Date**s, we can check whether **x** comes before **y** simply by using the expression:

```
x < y
```

Figure 22.12 is a new version of our earlier C program to test the various date comparisons, this time rewritten in C++ to use these operators.

To overload an operator, we need to define a function with the name

operator *op-name*

where *op-name* is replaced by the operator we are trying to overload. If it's a binary operator, the function will take two arguments: the first argument is the operand to the left of the operator, the second argument is the operand to the right. (If it's a unary operator, there will be only one argument.) Here's the definition of the operator **==** for comparing dates:

```
inline bool operator==(const Date& x, const Date& y)
  {
    return x.year == y.year &&
           x.month == y.month &&
           x.day == y.day;
  }
```

In this case, the function name is **operator==**, and it takes two **Date**s as parameters (actually references to **Date**s, for efficiency). It returns a **bool**, since that's what **==** is expected to return. The body of the function simply does the usual comparison to see if the year, month, and day are the same.

That's it! It's actually no different than defining our original **areDatesEqual** function in C, except that because of its special name, the compiler will map any use of **==** that involves a pair of **Date**s into a call to this function.

There are some restrictions on overloading operators. The most important is that we can't overload operators unless one of their parameters is *not* a basic type (so, for example, we can't change the meaning of **+** for integers). But even when you can overload an operator, it doesn't always make sense to do so. Make sure any operator you overload is an obvious shortcut, and avoid being overly clever in the operators you choose to overload.

```
//
// A Date type and prototypes for functions to compare Dates.
//
struct Date { int month, day, year; };

inline bool operator==(const Date& x, const Date& y)
   {
     return x.year == y.year &&
            x.month == y.month &&
            x.day == y.day;
   }

inline bool operator!=(const Date& x, const Date& y)
   { return x != y; }

inline bool operator<(const Date& x, const Date& y)
   {
     if (x.year < y.year)
       return true;
     if (x.year > y.year)
       return false;
     return (x.month < y.month || (x.month == y.month && x.day < y.day));
   }

inline bool operator<=(const Date& x, const Date& y)
   { return x < y || x == y; }

inline bool operator>(const Date& x, const Date& y)
   { return ! (x <= y); }

inline bool operator>=(const Date& x, const Date& y)
   { return ! (x < y); }
```

Figure 22.11 (date.h) A version of our date comparison functions using operator overloading.

22.4 INPUT AND OUTPUT OPERATORS

The standard I/O library is available in C++, but the C++ I/O stream library is generally simpler, more flexible, and more powerful. The basic C++ mechanism for performing most I/O operations is to use an *operator*. We can do all input and output using the *extraction* and *insertion* operators: >> and <<, respectively. We use >> for input and << for output. Since these are just the left- and right-shift operators (overloaded to perform I/O), we can also overload these operators to work on user-defined data types.

For output, the left operand is a file (called a *stream* in C++ terms) and the right is a value or expression. C++ writes the value to the stream, based on its type, using a default format, so we no longer need formatting codes. For input, the left operand is an input stream, and the right operand is a variable. The input is read and converted into

```
//
// A program to test the Date comparison routines.   Uses:
//    cmpDates - compare two Dates and print message describing results.
//    dateStr - convert Date to string format for output.
//
#include <stdio.h>
#include <stdlib.h>
#include "date.h"

const int MonthChars = 2, DayChars = 2, YearChars = 4;

int main()
{
  void cmpDates(const Date& x, const Date& y);

  Date day1 = {10,4,1965}, day2 = {10, 18, 1963};
  Date day3 = {6,24,1963}, day4 = day1;

  cmpDates(day1, day2);   cmpDates(day1, day3);
  cmpDates(day2, day1);   cmpDates(day2, day3);
  cmpDates(day3, day2);   cmpDates(day2, day3);
  cmpDates(day4, day1);

  return EXIT_SUCCESS;
}

void cmpDates(const Date& x, const Date& y)
{
  const char *dateStr(const Date& x);

  printf("Comparing %s ", dateStr(x));
  printf("with %s: ", dateStr(y));
  if (x < y)
    printf("it's earlier.\n");
  if (x > y)
    printf("it's later.\n");
  if (x == y)
    printf("they're the same.\n");
}

const char *dateStr(const Date& x)
{
  static char d[MonthChars + DayChars + YearChars + 3];

  sprintf(d, "%0*i/%0*i/%*i",
          MonthChars, x.month, DayChars, x.day, YearChars, x.year);
  return d;
}
```

Figure 22.12   (datetest.C) A program to test these comparison functions.

Aside 22.1: Portability and C++ Header Files

In C, the standard header files all end with **.h**. That particular way of naming header files has permeated the C language from the beginning. In the C++ community, however, there have been a variety of different naming schemes: ending names with .hh, .hpp, and others.

C++ also provides a brand new way to specify standard header files: we include them with no suffix at all. As a result, the library header files now use names such as **<iostream>**, **<stddef>**, **<stdlib>** and the like. Most compilers today don't yet support this way of naming header files, but when they do, most will also support the more traditional C names also, so you could include **<iostream>** or **<iostream.h>**. For maximum portability, use the standard names. You may still name your own headers with whatever dot names you like.

Another difference is that in C header files are text files, and text file inclusion is used whenever **#include** is processed by the compiler. It's exactly as if the contents of the file had been typed right then and there. But no such requirement exists with C++ headers, and this allows compiler environments to "precompile" headers into some (presumably faster-to-process) intermediate form.

the proper form for the variable; again we don't need any formatting codes. **>>** returns the stream it read from.

Our programs start with one input stream and two output streams already open. The input stream is **cin**, which corresponds to **stdin**. The output streams are **cout** and **cerr** (corresponding to **stdout** and **stderr**; **cerr** is unbuffered).

We can read into a single variable with a single extractor (**operator >>**):

```
cin >> x
```

This reads a value into **x**, interpreting it with whatever type **x** happens to be. That is, if **x** is a **double**, then it reads a single floating pointer number from the input and stores it into **x**.

If we have a series of values to read into various program variables, we can chain extractors:

```
cin >> x >> y
```

Here, we have chained two extractors together, but we can chain however many we want. This works left to right, reading the first value into **x** and the next into **y**. It works as we would hope because **>>** associates left to right and it returns the stream from which it read (**cin**, in this case), which means the stream it returns becomes the left argument of the next **>>**.

Using **>>** is considerably simpler than the comparable **scanf**, which would involve specifying the types of the values and passing pointers:

```
scanf("%lf %lf", &x, &y)
```

It's also easier to maintain code using **>>**, as the input-reading statement does not depend at all on the types of particular values being read. This allows us to change the types of the input variables without having to modify the input-reading statement.

We can check for errors or **EOF** by testing the return value of the extractor. We write our code as if it returns **true** if it successfully read the value and **false** otherwise.[5]

Output works similarly. For example,

```
cout << x << '^' << y
```

writes two values separate by a caret, where the values are written in an appropriate format for their type; we don't need any percent-sign formatting codes.

For output, we can also write a special item, **endl**, which writes a newline and flushes any output buffer. This often appears at the end of a series of insertion operators, although it doesn't have to.

Figure 22.13 puts all this together in a rewrite of our earlier exponent-computing program (Figure 4.6) that uses these operators to request x, y pairs from the user and then display x^y.

We include the header file iostream.h to define these overloaded I/O operators. We don't include stdio.h because we no longer use any standard I/O functions.

Overloading I/O Operators

C++ overloads **<<** and **>>** to handle its basic data types. Extraction (**>>**) has been overloaded to take an input stream on the left and any of the built-in types on the right. Similarly, insertion (**<<**) has been overloaded to take an output stream on the left. Consequently, there are unique two-argument operator functions for **int**s, **long**s, and **short**s, both signed and unsigned, **float**s and **double**s, **bool**s, the various character types, **char ***s (used for strings), and **void ***s (used for all other pointer types).[6]

We're forced, however, to overload them ourselves to handle other types, such as structures we define. Figure 22.14 does so in a final version of our program to print employee information.

We do this overloading in a stylized way that's just like how we've overloaded other operators. One key difference is that now the return value and the first parameter are references to an appropriate stream (**ostream** for **<<** and **istream** for **>>**). A second difference is that the other argument is a **const** reference to whatever type we want to display. So the prototype for our output operator for **Employee**s looks like this:

```
ostream& operator<<(ostream& s, const Employee& e);
```

Providing a definition for an input or output operator is straightforward, since it looks like any normal function definition. Writing one of our **Employee**s involves simply writing each of the fields in a reasonable way.

---

[5]What actually happens is that the **cin** it returns is automatically converted to **true** or **false** when it is used in tests (or more generally, used in contexts where a **bool** is expected).

[6]For **bool**s, the insertion operator prints true for **true**, false for **false**, and the extraction operator interprets any mixed case of TRUE for **true** and FALSE for **false**.

```
//
// Using the math library to compute exponents.
//
#include <iostream.h>
#include <stdlib.h>
#include <math.h>

int main()
{
  double x, y;                        // user-supplied base and exponent

  while (cin >> x >> y)
    cout << x << '^' << y << " = " << pow(x,y) << endl;

  return EXIT_SUCCESS;
}
```

Figure 22.13 (usepower2.C) An exponent-computing program written in C++.

There is one difference, however. The input and output operators should always return the stream they are passed. Doing so is what allows us to string multiple input or output operations together.

22.5 STORAGE ALLOCATION AND DEALLOCATION

Storage allocation is handled through two *operators* (they're operators even though they have names): **new** and **delete**. They function much like C's **malloc** and **free** (which are also available, but generally avoided in C++ programs).

We can use **new** in two ways. One is to allocate a single item, using one of these two forms. The first simply allocates an item of the provided type:

> **new** *type*

The other also initializes it to a provided value:

> **new** *type* (*value*)

Assuming **new** succeeds, it returns a pointer to the allocated storage. So

> `int *ptr = new int;`

allocates a single **int** without initializing it, and

> `int *countptr = new int(0);`

allocates a single **int** and initializes it to 0.

```
//
// Using an overloaded output operator to display Employee info.
//
#include <iostream.h>
#include <stdlib.h>

struct Employee
{
  long number;                        // Employee number
  char *name, *phone;                 // Employee name and phone
  int  age;                           // Employee age
};

ostream& operator<<(ostream& output, const Employee &e);

int main()
{
  Employee emp = {1001, "borromeo, daphne", "310-555-2042", 26};

  cout << emp;                        // write our Employee

  return EXIT_SUCCESS;
}

ostream& operator <<(ostream& output, const Employee &e)
{
  output << "Employee: " << e.number << endl;
  output << "Name:     " << e.name   << endl;
  output << "Age:      " << e.age    << endl;
  output << "Phone:    " << e.phone  << endl;
  return output;
}
```

Figure 22.14   (prstrct3.C)   A program that overloads the output operator.

The other form allocates an array:

>   **new** *type* [*number of items*]

For example,

>   `int *table = new int[tableEntries];`

will assign **table** a pointer to the first element in a dynamically allocated array of **tableEntries** integers.

There are also two forms of **delete**. The simplest is

>   **delete** *ptr-to-space*

where *ptr-to-space* is a pointer to a single object that had previously been allocated with

new. The other form of **delete** is

> **delete []** *ptr-to-space*

We use this form only if the pointed-to space is an array (which was allocated with the second form of **new**).

Figure 22.15 is a main program that illustrates the various forms of the calls to **new** and **delete**. All it does is dynamically allocate several different types of values and then deallocate them.

new is nice because we simply provide it a type and it does all the underlying calculations to determine how much space we actually require. **delete** is nice because it automatically checks whether we're passing it a null pointer before attempting to delete the pointed-to storage.

new's behavior if it can't allocate the requested space is a little complicated to explain. Originally, like **malloc**, **new** returned zero if it couldn't allocate the requested space. On newer compilers, it generates something called an exception.[7] Most compilers, however, provide an option to request the original behavior. On top of that, the language has since been changed, so there's now a way to specify the desired behavior for a given **new**. Our examples take the easy way out and assume that **new** always succeeds!

22.6   CASE STUDY—A FIRST IMPLEMENTATION OF SETS IN C++

This section is optional!

We conclude the chapter with a C++ implementation of sets. As with our earlier C version, we will use an array of bits to represent set values. One difference, however, is that now we define a **BitVector** type for arrays of bits, and build a **Set** type on top of it, rather than constructing sets directly on top of unsigned values and complicated expressions for accessing and modifying bits.

Implementing Arrays of Bits

Figure 22.16 is a header file bitvec.h that provides the declaration of a **BitVector**. In particular, a **BitVector** consists of a pointer to a dynamically allocated array of bits (actually, an array of **unsigned int**s), the number of array elements, and the total number of bits the bit vector represents.

This header file also provides inline implementations for almost all of the functions users will use to manipulate **BitVector**s. **Init** initializes a **BitVector** by using **new** to allocate an array of **unsigned int**s and set them all to zero. **CleanUp** destroys a bit vector by using **delete** to deallocate that array. Both functions are passed a reference to the **BitVector** they are accessing (rather than a pointer, considerably simplifying their internals). **IsOn** and **IsOff** return a **bool** indicating whether a particular bit is on or off, respectively. Since they don't modify the **BitVector** they're passed, they are passed **const** references to that **BitVector**. **TurnOn** and **TurnOff** turn on or off a particular sequence of bits in the **BitVector**. Both have

---

[7]Exceptions are an advanced topic that we do not cover in this text.

```
//
// Some examples of array allocation with new.
//
#include <iostream.h>
#include <stdlib.h>

const int tableEntries = 100;

int main()
{
  int *iptr      = new int;                 // make an uninitialized int
  int *countptr = new int(0);               // make an initialized int (0)
  int *table     = new int[tableEntries]; // make an array of 100 ints

  *iptr = 20;
  cout << "1st int (allocated and assigned): " << *iptr << endl;
  cout << "2nd int (initialized when allocated): " << *countptr << endl;

  for (int i = 0; i < tableEntries; i++) // put some values in table
    table[i] = i;

  cout << "20th entry (in allocated table): " << table[20] << endl;

  delete [] table;                          // free an entire table
  delete countptr;                          // free an int
  delete iptr;                              // free another int

  return EXIT_SUCCESS;
}
```

Figure 22.15   (newex.C) An example using **new** and **delete**.

a parameter for the length of the sequence that defaults to 1 if it is not provided (so the same functions can deal with a single bit or a sequence of bits). The one function that can't be inlined is the overloaded **operator<<** that displays a **BitVector** as a sequence of 1s and 0s (since it requires a loop).

All of these functions take advantage of C++'s function overloading. Rather than preface their names with an explicit indication of the **BitVector** type they work with, as in **BvInit** or **BvCleanUp**, we give the functions simple names reflecting the action they perform and rely on C++ to call the right function based on the parameter types we pass.

Most of these functions require access to the underlying bits in the array of **unsigned int**s representing a **BitVector**. They obtain this access through the collection of **inline** functions, shown in Figure 22.17, which reside in a header file included by the bitvec.h header file declaring the **BitVector** type. **WordIndex** returns an index to the particular word containing a desired bit; **BitIndexInWord** returns the index of the bit within that word; **GetBit** and **SetBit** get and set a

```
//
// BitVector type and related functions.
//
#include <iostream.h>
#include <limits.h>

struct BitVector
{
  unsigned int *bits;            // dynamically allocated bits
  int num_words, num_bits;       // # of words, bits for BitVector
};

#include "bitutils.h"

inline void Init(BitVector& b, int n)
  {
    b.num_words = RequiredWords(b.num_bits = n);
    b.bits = new unsigned int[b.num_words];
    SetBits(b.bits, 0, n, 0);
  }

inline void CleanUp(BitVector& b)
  { delete [] b.bits; }

inline bool IsOn(const BitVector& b, int target)
  { return GetBit(b.bits, target) != 0; }

inline bool IsOff(const BitVector& b, int target)
  { return GetBit(b.bits, target) == 1; }

inline void TurnOn(BitVector& b, int target, int n = 1)
  { SetBits(b.bits, target, n, 1); }

inline void TurnOff(BitVector& b, int target, int n = 1)
  { SetBits(b.bits, target, n, 0); }

ostream& operator<<(ostream& output, const BitVector& b);
```

Figure 22.16   (bitvec.h)   The declaration of **BitVector** and the functions that manipulate it.

particular bit's value, respectively; **SetWord** sets an entire word to all 0s or all 1s; and **RequiredWords** determines how many words are necessary to store a particular number of bits

In fact, only two functions in the entire **BitVector** package can't reasonably be made inline: the utility function **SetBits**, which needs a loop to set all of the bits to either 0 or 1, and the output operator, which needs a loop to run through and print the entire array of bits. Figure 22.18 contains the definitions of these functions.

Finally, Figure 22.19 provides a main program that uses these functions.

```
//
// Inline utility functions for BitVectors:
//
#include <limits.h>

const WordBits = CHAR_BIT * sizeof(unsigned int);

void SetBits(unsigned int bitarray[], int start, int n, int value);

inline int WordIndex(int desired_bit)
  { return desired_bit / WordBits; }

inline int BitIndexInWord(int desired_bit)
  { return desired_bit % WordBits; }

inline int GetBit(const unsigned int bitarray[],  int desired_bit)
  {
    return (bitarray[WordIndex(desired_bit)]
               >> BitIndexInWord(desired_bit)) & 01;
  }

inline void SetBit(unsigned int bitarray[], int desired_bit, int value)
  {
    if (value)
      bitarray[WordIndex(desired_bit)] |=
         (01 << BitIndexInWord(desired_bit));
    else
      bitarray[WordIndex(desired_bit)] &=
         (~ (01 << BitIndexInWord(desired_bit)) );
  }

inline void SetWord(unsigned int bitarray[], int desired_bit, int value)
  { bitarray[WordIndex(desired_bit)] = (value == 0) ? 0 : ~0; }

inline int RequiredWords(int desired_bits)
  { return desired_bits / WordBits + 1; }
```

Figure 22.17   (bitutils.h)   The definition of the useful inline utility functions for **BitVector**s.

Using Arrays of Bits to Implement Sets

Given our **BitVector** type, we can easily implement sets. The idea is that if a user wants to create a set that can represent the possible values 25 through 50, we create a bit vector large enough to hold 26 values ($50 - 25 + 1$), with bit 0 representing the element 25 and bit 25 representing the element 50. Each time we want to add or delete an element, we access the appropriate bit.

Figure 22.20 contains the definition of the **Set** type and inline definitions for most of its functions. A **Set** contains a **BitVector**, along with the values of the first and

```
//
// Non-inlinable functions for processing BitVectors.
//
#include "bitvec.h"

void SetBits(unsigned int bitarray[], int start, int n, int value)
{
  int finish = start + n;
  int next = start;

  while (next < finish)
    if (GetBit(bitarray, next) == 0 && n >= WordBits)
    {          // Do whole word at once
      SetWord(bitarray, next, value);
      next += WordBits;
    }
    else       // Just do next bit
      SetBit(bitarray, next++, value);
}

ostream& operator<<(ostream& output, const BitVector& b)
{
  for (int i = 0; i < b.num_bits; i++)
    output << GetBit(b.bits, i);
  return output;
}
```

Figure 22.18   (bitvec.C)   The definition of the non-inline functions for manipulating **BitVector**s.

last possible values in the set. As with **BitVector**s, we provide the functions **Init** and **CleanUp**, where **Init** initializes the **Set** by initializing its internal **BitVector** and **CleanUp** destroys a **Set** by cleaning up that internal **BitVector**. We also provide functions to add an element to the set, to delete an element from the set, and to check whether a set element is actually in the set. These functions use a new function, **BitForElement**, to map the element value to the bit representing it.

Figure 22.21 contains the overloaded output operator for **Set**s, the only non-inline function in the **Set** package. And finally, Figure 22.22 is a new version of our program to detect duplicate input values using sets.

SUMMARY

- C++ is much stricter on type checking than C. As a result, compiling our C programs with C++ can help us find errors due to mismatched types.

- C++ provides references, which we can use to simulate call-by-reference parameter passing and to efficiently pass large structures.

```
//
// Simple main program using BitVectors.
//
#include <stdlib.h>
#include "bitvec.h"

const int DesiredBits = 48;

int main()
{
  BitVector b;

  Init(b, DesiredBits);              // Allocate space and initialize
  cout << "Created bitvector: " << b << endl;

  TurnOn(b, 32, 16);                 // Turn on several sets of bits
  TurnOn(b, 0, 8);
  cout << "Turned on some bits: " << b << endl;

  TurnOff(b, 40, 4);                 // Turn off part of those sets
  TurnOff(b, 4, 4);
  cout << "Turned off some bits: " << b << endl;

  // Check whether bits on/off

  cout << "Bit 7 is " << (IsOn(b, 7) ? "on" : "off") << endl;
  cout << "Bit 46 is " << (IsOff(b, 46) ? "off" : "on") << endl;

  CleanUp(b);                        // Clean up allocated space

  return EXIT_SUCCESS;
}
```

Figure 22.19   (bitmain.C) A main program that uses **BitVector**s.

- C++ provides a variety of minor features that are nice extensions to C. These include end-of-line comments, statically scoped **const**s, constructed type tags as type names, and variable declarations anywhere a statement is legal.

- C++ provides default parameters, which we can use to write very general functions whose parameters are by default filled in to the most common way we call the function.

- C++ provides function and operator overloading, which allows us to have the same functions and operators work with a variety of different types.

- C++ provides **inline** functions, which allow us to trade size for speed with small functions.

- C++ input and C++ output are done with operators. We are allowed to overload these operators for types we define.

```
//
// Improved definitions to use "sets" of integers.
//
#include <iostream.h>
#include <stdlib.h>
#include "bitvec.h"

struct Set                         // Build sets on top of BitVectors
{
  BitVector bv;                    // Internal BitVector
  int first, last;                 // First and last elements in Set
};

inline int BitForElement(const Set& s, int element)
  { return element - s.first; }

inline void Init(Set& s, int start, int finish)  // Create empty set.
  { Init(s.bv, (s.last = finish) - (s.first = start) + 1); }

inline void CleanUp(Set& s)                       // Remove existing set.
  { CleanUp(s.bv); }

inline void Add(Set& s, int elem)                 // Add element to set.
  { TurnOn(s.bv, BitForElement(s, elem)); }

inline void Delete(Set& s, int elem)              // Delete set element.
  { TurnOff(s.bv, BitForElement(s, elem)); }

inline int Member(const Set& s, int elem)         // Is item in set?
  { return IsOn(s.bv, BitForElement(s,elem)); }

ostream& operator <<(ostream& output, const Set& s);
```

Figure 22.20 (sets.h) The declaration of a **Set** type.

```
//
// Utility functions for manipulating sets.
//
#include "sets.h"

ostream& operator <<(ostream& output, const Set &s)
{
  for (int i = s.first; i < s.last; i++)
    if (Member(s, i))
      output << i << endl;
  return output;
}
```

Figure 22.21 (sets.C) The non-inline functions for **Set**s.

```
//
// Identify duplicates in the input.
//
#include <stdio.h>
#include <stdlib.h>
#include "sets.h"

const int FirstElement = 0;
const int LastElement = 511;

inline bool inRange(int value, int min, int max)
  { return (value >= min && value <= max); }

inline void Switch(Set& newer, Set& older, int value)
  {
    Delete(older, value);
    Add(newer, value);
  }

int main()
{
  Set unique, dup;                        // unique and duplicate sets

  Init(unique, FirstElement, LastElement);
  Init(dup, FirstElement, LastElement);

  int inp;

  while (cin >> inp)
  {
    if (!inRange(inp, FirstElement, LastElement))
    {
      cout << "Value out of range." << endl;
      continue;
    }
    if (Member(unique, inp))
      Switch(dup, unique, inp);
    else if (!Member(dup, inp))
      Add(unique, inp);
  }
  cout << "Unique values " << endl;
  cout << unique;
  cout << "Duplicate values " << endl;
  cout << dup;

  CleanUp(unique);
  CleanUp(dup);

  return EXIT_SUCCESS;
}
```

Figure 22.22   (usesets.C) A program to detect duplicate input values using **Set**s.

■ C++ provides **new** and **delete** for storage allocation and deallocation. These operators are superior to **malloc** and **free** because we use them in terms of types and not bytes.

EXERCISES

Explore

22–1   Compile and run the programs in this chapter.

22–2   Pick three C programs from earlier in the text and compile them using a C++ compiler. Do they still compile and run correctly?

22–3   Take two C programs you have written and compile them using a C++ compiler. Do they still compile and run correctly?

Modify

22–4   Rewrite Figure 22.2 to take full advantage of the C++ features we have so far discussed. Do not worry about distinguishing between errors and end of file for ending the input.

22–5   Rewrite Figure 22.3 to take full advantage of the C++ features we have so far discussed.

22–6   Rewrite **minmax** (Figure 10.6) to use references rather than pointer parameters.

22–7   Rewrite the array-allocating and -deallocating part of the group reversal program (Figure 10.24) to use **new** and **delete**.

Code

22–8   Provide suitable definitions for an overloaded function named **fetch** that takes as arguments a prompt and a reference to a value to read. Here's the prototype for a version of **fetch** to read an **int**:

```
int fetch(int& x, const char *prompt);
```

22–9   Write a C++ function for computing and returning the smallest, largest, and average values in an array.

Define versions of **fetch** for reading an **int**, a string (which should be an entire input line), and an **Employee**. Allow the **prompt** to default to the string "**Enter Value:**".

22–10   Overload the equality operator **==** to determine whether two **Employee**s are the same. Also overload the **!=** operator.

22–11   Define overloaded input and output operators for **Date**s.

22–12   Define overloaded equality and inequality operators for **BitVector**s.

22–13   Provide a function for determining how many **bits** with a particular value are present in a given **BitVector**. That is, we should be able to use your function to determine how many 0s there are in a **BitVector** or how many 1s.

22–14   Define overloaded equality and inequality operators for **Set**s.

23 ENCAPSULATION

WITH

CLASSES

C++ extends C to support object-oriented programming. There are many definitions for what we mean by "object-oriented," but generally it encompasses encapsulation, inheritance, polymorphism, and dynamic binding. This chapter discusses encapsulation, explaining what it is, why it's important, and how to write C++ programs that take advantage of it. As part of this discussion, we introduce the C++ notions of classes, member functions, constructors, copy constructors, destructors, and assignment operators. We also introduce the concept of layering and the member initialization lists that support it. The chapter concludes with a case study in which we rewrite the previous chapter's BitVector and Set types in an object-oriented way.

23.1   INTRODUCTION TO ENCAPSULATION

C++ expands on the C language by providing direct programming language support for *encapsulation*: the ability to hide the internals of a data type's representation and limit access to it through a well-defined set of operations.

The concept of encapsulation is not completely novel to us. We've used the notion of *abstract data type* (ADT) in several places throughout this book. In Chapters 9 and 10 we developed functions for manipulating sets (for adding and deleting elements, for checking set membership). Similarly, in Chapter 20 we developed a collection of functions for managing stacks and queues, including functions to push and pop stack elements and to enqueue and dequeue queue elements. In all of these cases, the idea is that a program creates and initializes the data structure, then accesses and updates it solely through calling the appropriate functions.

Our sets, stacks, and queues are *abstract* data types because we can describe their behavior and a programmer can use them without needing to know how they are represented. We can implement sets with bit vectors, regular arrays, or linked lists, and we can also have a variety of choices for implementing stacks and queues. This property—the hidden nature of the underlying representation, along with the appropriate access functions—is what we mean by an abstract data type.

C gives us many—but not really enough—of the tools to do this right. The big problem is that C data structures are pure representation—the structure itself does not hint at what we can and cannot do with it. That is, when we define a structure that describes a **Queue**, we don't state that **Queue**s exist so that we can enqueue and dequeue elements, but instead describe the internals of a **Queue** (the needed pointers and counters and so on). This is troublesome since we would like to think the only access to the queue's internals is through enqueue and dequeue functions. However, there is nothing but good coding practice preventing the programmer from accessing the internals directly. Since programmers have to include queues.h to declare a **Queue** variable, they might very well take advantage of particular fields within a **Queue** structure that depend on exactly how a stack or queue is built. Later, should we decide to change the representation, the programmer using **Queue**s will have to change his or her code: a maintenance nightmare and a potential source of latent program bugs.

C++ (and other object-oriented programming languages—OOPLs for short) provide mechanisms for enhancing data type abstraction and reducing the likelihood of inadvertent messing around with a variable's privates. Two closely related features support improved encapsulation or data hiding. First, as part of defining a data type, we are able to specify the *operations* or functions that work on it. And second, we have the ability to specifically tag its internal data fields so that only those operations have access to them.

In this chapter, we show how we encapsulate behavior (what something can do) and representation (how it goes about doing it) in a *class*.

23.2 THE BASICS OF CLASSES

A *class* is a C-like structure with a really big difference: not only do we declare data members, but we can also declare member functions and state that these member functions are the *only* way to access the data members.

Declaring a Class

When we declare a class, we typically provide two pieces of information. One is that we describe the *operations* on the object and their interfaces (the number and types of their arguments, and what they return, just like normal functions). The other is we describe the data fields (*instance data*) that will be used by their implementation. The class declaration is called the "interface specification," since it defines how other functions or objects can interface with (or use) this class. We usually place this declaration in a header file so that it can be used by other programs.

As an example, let's consider a **Queue**. Given a **Queue**, there are five key actions we can do on it: create an empty queue, place a value on the end of the queue, take the front value off the queue, check whether the queue is empty, and determine how many items are in the queue. There are a variety of ways of implementing these operations, one of which is an array with indices to the start and end of the queue and with a counter that keeps track of how many elements are in the queue.

Figure 23.1 is the header file queues.h, and it shows how we can declare this **Queue** type in C++. It's declared as a **class**, whose general form is:

```
class Name
{
  public:
      prototypes for generally usable operations

  private:
      data fields for implementation

      prototypes of internal operations
};
```

Name is the class's name, which, like a structure's name, automatically becomes a type we can use to create variables. Those variables are called *objects*. So after the **Queue** class declaration, we will be able to declare variables of type **Queue**.

The **public** section provides prototypes for the operations that can be invoked on objects of the class. Operations are often called *member functions*, *methods*, and *messages*. These member functions can *only* be applied to objects of the class. In this case, we are defining **Enqueue**, **Dequeue**, and so on as the only member functions that can be applied to **Queue** objects.

The **private** section declares the data fields each instance of the class will have (just as we declared fields within a structure). Here, that includes an array of integers that will hold elements of the queue, integer indices to the front and rear of the queue, and an integer count of queue elements. The key idea here is that only **Queue** member functions (**Enqueue**, **Dequeue**, and so on) can access this implementation information, not ordinary C functions and not member functions of other objects.

The **private** section can also declare operations that are local to the member functions of the class (that is, that cannot be invoked outside of the class). This is often useful for defining helper functions used in the implementation of class operations. In our case, that code is an operation to update an index appropriately, taking into account the circular nature of the queue.

Using a Class

Before we get into the details of implementing the **Queue** class, let's look at how we use it. Figure 23.2 is a simple program that creates a queue, enqueues a set of elements into it, then dequeues and prints all of these elements.

There are two important things we can do with classes: one is to create an object that is an instance of the class, the other is to invoke an operation. Creating an instance is easy. All we do is declare a variable with that type:

```
Queue q;
```

This declares **q** as an instance of **Queue**.

```
//
// Initial Queue class declaration.
//
const int MaxQueueSize = 100;

class Queue
{
  public:
    Queue();                        // Construct empty queue

    void Enqueue(int value);        // Add element to end of queue
    int  Dequeue();                 // Delete queue's first element
    bool IsEmpty();                 // Return true if queue is empty
    int  Length();                  // # of elements in queue

  private:
    int  elements[MaxQueueSize];    // Items in queue
    int  f, r;                      // Indices to first and last element
    int  elementCount;              // Count of number of queue elements

    int  NextIndex(int current);    // Update internal queue index
};
```

Figure 23.1   (queues.h)   Declaring a **Queue** class.

Invoking an operation is a bit trickier. We do this by using the dot selection operator, preceding it with the object and following it with the name of the operation and any parameters the operation requires. For example,

```
q.Enqueue(next);
```

invokes the **Enqueue** operation on the **q** object, passing it **next** as its parameter. Similarly,

```
cout << "Dequeuing: " << q.Dequeue() << endl;
```

invokes the **Dequeue** operation on the **q** object, displaying its return value.

Defining Class Operations

All in all, declaring and using classes is pretty easy. Defining their operations, however, takes a little getting used to.

Figure 23.3 shows the definition of the operations in the **Queue** class. The simplest is the **Length** operation: all it has to do is return the number of elements stored in the **Queue**'s **elementCount** field.

```
int Queue::Length()
  { return elementCount; }
```

```
//
// A simple program showing how to use queues.
//
#include <iostream.h>
#include <stdlib.h>
#include "queues.h"

const int DesiredElements = 20;

main()
{
  Queue q;

  for (int next = 0; next < DesiredElements; next++)
  {
    cout << "Enqueuing: " << next << endl;
    q.Enqueue(next);
  }
  cout << "There are " << q.Length() << " elements." << endl;
  while (!q.IsEmpty())
    cout << "Dequeueing: " << q.Dequeue() << endl;

  return EXIT_SUCCESS;
}
```

Figure 23.2 (useqs.C) A simple program showing how to use **Queue**s.

This is a normal function definition, except for two strange things. The first is the **Queue::** preceding the name **Length**. This means we are defining the **Length** operation for the **Queue** type. Whenever we define an operation, we precede it with the class name and the C++ scope resolution operator, **::**. We have to do this because other objects may have defined identically named member functions, so we have to specify that we are defining **Length** for **Queue**s, as opposed to **Length** for **List**s or **BitVector**s or some other type (or, in fact, just a C-style **Length** function).

In fact, it's standard practice in the C++ world to use this fully qualified name in documentation that describes a class's behavior. We'll often do that from now on to make it clear to which function we are referring.

The other strange thing is that we reference **elementCount** without declaring it (or preceding it with a dot selection operator). The thing to remember here is that member functions are always invoked on an object. As a result, C++ lets member functions access members in that object without qualifying them, so, within **Queue::Length**, **elementCount** is assumed to mean the **elementCount** in the particular **Queue** that **Length** is being applied to. That is, when we call **Queue::Length** with

```
cout << "There are " << q.Length() << " elements." << endl;
```

during that call to **Length**, **elementCount** is referring to **q.elementCount**.

```
//
// Definitions of Queue operations.
//
#include "queues.h"

Queue::Queue()                          // Initialize Queue
  { f = r = elementCount = 0; }

inline int Queue::NextIndex(int i)      // Bump index to next spot
  { return (i + 1 < MaxQueueSize) ? i + 1 : 0; }

void Queue::Enqueue(int value)          // Add element to queue
{                                       //   Assumes enough room
  elements[r] = value;
  elementCount++;
  r = NextIndex(r);
}

int Queue::Dequeue(void)                // Remove queue element
{                                       //   Assumes queue not empty
  int value = elements[f];

  f = NextIndex(f);
  elementCount--;
  return value;
}

int Queue::Length()                     // Return queue length
  { return elementCount; }

bool Queue::IsEmpty()                   // True if queue empty
  { return Length() == 0; }
```

Figure 23.3 (queues.C) The definitions of the operations in the **Queue** class.

We can take advantage of this behavior with function names as well, and the **IsEmpty** operation does so.

```
bool Queue::IsEmpty()
  { return Length() == 0; }
```

When it calls **Length**, it is calling **Queue::Length** and applying that function to the same object on which we invoked **Queue::IsEmpty**. Having several operations call another operation is a common technique for minimizing redundant code. Both **Enqueue** and **Dequeue** call **Queue::NextIndex** to bump up the indices to the front and rear of the queue, taking into account the circular nature of the queue.

Our **Enqueue** and **Dequeue** both have an important flaw: **Enqueue** assumes there is sufficient room to insert elements into the queue and **Dequeue** assumes that the queue is not empty. Relaxing these assumptions is left as an exercise.

Constructors

We are almost done with the **Queue** class definition. The final thing we have to worry about is this strange little function:

```
Queue::Queue()
  { f = r = elementCount = 0; }
```

A function with the same name as the class is called a *constructor* and plays a special role. Whenever we create instances of the class (either by declaring a variable or, as we'll see shortly, by allocating an object with **new**), C++ tries to find a constructor it can use to initialize the object's fields. In particular, if we declare a variable,

```
Queue q;
```

C++ automatically looks for a **Queue::Queue** function that takes no parameters to initialize the fields of this variable. In this case, it's simply a matter of setting all of the fields to zero. If we fail to provide this function, by default the compiler will simply not initialize any of the fields.

Constructors are optional, but we generally supply them in most objects, since most objects have fields that must be initialized. Automatic constructor invocation ensures that this initialization takes place, and it saves the programmer the bother of explicitly calling a specific initialization function, which programmers are likely to forget to call.

Constructors have one very peculiar property: they do not have a return value. It's not that they have a return type of **void**, but instead that they are not allowed to have any kind of return type at all. That's because C++ sets things up to call them whenever a variable of the constructed type is declared—we never call constructors directly and so they therefore have no place where they can return a value.

Some More Detail on Private and Public

What exactly do **public** and **private** mean? From a high-level point of view, **public** is something that is intended to be accessible by the object's users, while **private** is something that is intended to be used only in the object's implementation.

From a language-specific point of view, **public** operations (or data) can be accessed by any function. That's why the main program in our earlier example could do

```
q.Enqueue(next);
```

Since **Enqueue** is public, anyone can access it. In contrast, **private** operations or data can only be accessed by member functions. So because **elementCount** and the other data fields are private, we can't try to sneakily empty the queue by doing:

```
q.elementCount = q.f = q.r = 0;
```

That's illegal and leads to a compiler warning message. Because **f** and **r** and **elementCount** are private data fields within a **Queue** we can't access them, except within the member functions of **Queue**. Similarly, because **NextIndex** is a private operation of **Queue**, we can only call it from the other operations within **Queue**.

At first, private data and operations may seem problematic. We can imagine times, for effiency perhaps, where we would like to take advantage of a **Queues**'s internal structure. For example, we may want to enqueue the same item a specific number of times (not just once). A clever trick would be to use a pointer loop to directly stick copies of the value into the internal **elements** array, and then update **r** just once after doing the copy. But this trick is forbidden because we've made the data fields private. Moreover, even if we could sneakily do this trick somewhere, any code using it would become dependent on the internals of the **Queue**. If we change the internal layout of **Queue**s (to use explicit pointers rather than indices, or to modify the internals to use a linked list, and so on), we must find all of these dependencies and update the code. That's tremendously time-consuming.

One of the benefits of making data fields private is that we keep the details of the implementation hidden from a class's users. As a result, even though it's possible to have public data, we never want to do so. Allowing direct access to an object's internals violates a basic tenet of object-oriented programming: an object is something that is only accessed through its operations, and the details of a class's implementation should be kept hidden. By following this principle, we can freely change an object's internal representation without breaking code that uses it, since we are guaranteed that its user has no dependencies on its internals. The ability to have public member functions (accessible outside the structure) and private fields (accessible only within the structure) allows the compiler to enforce the separation of an object's implementation and its use.

> *Make all data fields private.*

Another place where the desire for public data creeps in is when we have a field in the object that might be useful just to examine. For example, with a **Queue**, users may want to know how many elements it currently contains or whether the queue has any elements at all. This information could conceivably be directly accessed by examining the **elementCount** field. However, we have instead provided the functions **Length** and **IsEmpty**. The reason for providing these functions is that we can change the internals of the **Queue** (perhaps deleting the **elementCount** field to save space), without affecting the user's code. In addition, **Length** and **IsEmpty** are more readable, since they make clear the overall reason why **elementCount** is being accessed.

> *All access to data members should be through member functions.*

There are a few other details about **private** and **public**. In C++, all members within a **class** default to **private** unless we make them **public**. It turns out that **struct** is just like **class**, except that all the members are **public** by default. That means we can define our objects using **struct** as well as **class**, although **class** is generally the preferred method. We aren't restricted to having the **public** come first, followed by the **private**; they can come in any order, appear multiple times, and be mixed. For readability, our preference is to put the public members first, then the private fields.

23.3   SOME MORE FEATURES OF CLASSES

Our initial implementation of the **Queue** class had a single constructor that took no arguments. However, we are allowed to have multiple constructors for a given object, and these constructors are allowed to take parameters. In addition, we can have a special cleanup function called a destructor, and we are allowed to define what it means to assign one instance of a class to another. Finally, as part of providing a class, we can define friend functions, which are functions that need access to the class's internals but for one reason or another cannot be members of the class.

Constructors That Take Parameters

Our original **Queue** class provided a single constructor that initializes an empty **Queue** with a fixed maximum size. Suppose, however, we instead wanted dynamically allocated queues where we could specify the initial size when we create the queue. In that case, we would need a **Queue** constructor that could be supplied a parameter: the number of elements to allocate. Figure 23.4 is a new version of **Queue**s that declares such a constructor, Figure 23.5 shows how that constructor is defined, and Figure 23.6 contains definitions of the basic queue operations.

We declare the new constructor in a straightforward fashion:

```
Queue(int size = MaxQueueSize);
```

Because this member function has the same name as the class in which it is declared, it's a constructor. It takes a single parameter, the requested size for the queue, which defaults to the constant **MaxQueueSize** if left unspecified.

We can create a **Queue** and initialize it with this constructor with this declaration:

```
Queue q(DesiredElements);
```

This declaration invokes this particular **Queue** constructor to initialize **q**, passing it the constant **DesiredElements** as the number of elements to initialize. In general, to invoke a particular constructor, we follow the variable with the arguments for that constructor.

As usual, we have to provide a definition for this constructor. It's similar to the original, except that it uses **new** to allocate space for the array. However, to do that, we've changed the **elements** field within the **Queue** object to be a pointer, rather than an array. We've also added a new field in each **Queue** that contains the maximum elements it can contain, along with a function **IsFull** that determines whether the **Queue** is out of room for new elements.

In this case, because we supply a default parameter, our **Queue** constructor can be called with no arguments, just like before.

```
Queue q;
```

In fact, because we have only changed the internals to the **Queue** and not the interface, we can use this new implementation in our earlier example programs using **Queue**s and it will still work correctly.

```
//
// Queue class declaration for extended queue.
//
#include <iostream.h>

const int MaxQueueSize = 100;

class Queue
{
  public:
    Queue(int initsize = MaxQueueSize);       // Construct empty queue
    Queue(const Queue& other_q);              // Construct from queue
    ~Queue();                                 // Destruct queue

    Queue& operator=(const Queue& other_q);   // Assign queues

    void Enqueue(int value);                  // Add element at end
    int  Dequeue();                           // Delete first element
    bool IsEmpty();                           // True if no elements
    bool IsFull();                            // True if full
    int  Length();                            // # of elements

  friend ostream& operator<<(ostream& output, const Queue& q);

  private:
    int  *elements;                           // Actual queue elements
    int  f, r;                                // Indices to start/finish
    int  elementCount;                        // Number of elements
    int  maxElements;                         // Max number of elements

    int  NextIndex(int current);              // Update queue index

    void Init(const Queue& other_q);          // Initialize by copying
    void CleanUp();                           // Deallocate fields
};
```

Figure 23.4 (queues2.h) An improved **Queue** definition.

Copy Constructors

If you look carefully at our new **Queue** class, you'll see that we have added one other constructor declaration.

```
Queue(const Queue& other_q);
```

What is this?

Whenever you create a new object that's a copy of an existing one, C++ automatically calls a "copy constructor" that initializes it by copying the contents of the existing object, one field at a time. There are three places where this happens: when you pass an object

```
//
// Definitions of Queue constructors, destructors, and assignment
// operator.
//
#include "queues2.h"

inline void Queue::Init(const Queue& other_q)
{
  elements = new int [maxElements = other_q.maxElements];
  f = other_q.f;    r = other_q.r;
  elementCount = other_q.elementCount;
  memcpy(elements, other_q.elements, maxElements * sizeof(int));
}

inline void Queue::CleanUp()
  { delete [] elements; }

Queue::Queue(int initsize)              // Initialize queue to specified
{                                       //    number of entries
  elements = new int[maxElements = initsize];
  f = r = elementCount = 0;
}

Queue::Queue(const Queue &other_q)      // Initialize queue to copy
  { Init(other_q); }                    //    existing queue

Queue::~Queue()                         // Clean up queue before removal
  { CleanUp(); }

Queue& Queue::operator=(const Queue& other_q)
{
  if (this != &other_q)
  {
    CleanUp();
    Init(other_q);
  }
  return *this;
}
```

Figure 23.5 (qs2a.C) Definitions of **Queue** constructors, destructors, and assignment operators.

by value (rather than by reference), when you return an object by value, and when you initialize one object from another object in the same class. For example, we might do the following:

```
Queue q(DesiredElements);
   ...
Queue q2 = q;
```

```
//
// Definitions of other Queue operations.
//
#include "queues2.h"

inline int Queue::NextIndex(int i)
  { return (i + 1 < maxElements) ? i + 1 : 0; }

void Queue::Enqueue(int value)
{
  elements[r] = value;
  elementCount++;
  r = NextIndex(r);
}

int Queue::Dequeue(void)
{
  int value = elements[f];

  f = NextIndex(f);
  elementCount--;
  return value;
}

int Queue::Length()
  { return elementCount; }

bool Queue::IsEmpty()
  { return Length() == 0; }

bool Queue::IsFull()
  { return Length() == maxElements; }

ostream& operator<<(ostream& output, const Queue& q)
{
  if (q.f < q.r)
  {
    for (int i = q.f; i < q.r; i++)
      cout << q.elements[i] << endl;
  }
  else
  {
    for (int i = q.f; i < q.maxElements; i++)
      cout << q.elements[i] << endl;
    for (int j = 0; j < q.r; j++)
      cout << q.elements[j] << endl;
  }
  return output;
}
```

Figure 23.6   (qs2b.C)   Definitions of the basic **Queue** operations.

This says to create a **Queue** named **q2** and initialize it to be a copy of **q**. **Queue**'s default copy constructor is used to do this initialization. For many objects, such as our original **Queue** class, this default behavior of field-at-a-time copying is fine. However, when objects contain handles to resources, such as a pointer to dynamically allocated storage, this default copying can cause trouble. With **Queue**s, the default behavior would lead to **q2.elements** pointing to the same thing as **q.elements**. That's bad, since when we enqueue something to **q2**, we would be modifying **q**'s internal array as well! That's not what we want at all.

So how do we deal with this problem? It turns out that C++ lets us override the default by defining our own copy constructor. The copy constructor is always declared as:

```
T(const T& other_t);
```

Here, **T** is replaced with the class name. For **Queue**s, that's the

```
Queue(const Queue& other_q);
```

declaration we saw earlier.

What does our **Queue** copy constructor actually do? It dynamically allocates an array with the same number of items as there are in the **Queue** it is to copy, copies the items in that **Queue**, and then initializes the other fields to copies of the values they had in that **Queue**.

There are a couple of things to note about copy constructors. Another way to invoke the copy constructor is using the same syntax for invoking other constructors:

```
Queue q3(q);
```

In fact, this is exactly the same as using the **=** when declaring the object.

The other is that if you don't feel like providing a copy constructor for a class that needs one, you can simply provide a prototype for it in the private section and then fail to provide an implementation. If the user doesn't do any copies, everything works just fine. If the user does do a copy, there will be a compile-time error about an illegal attempt to use the copy constructor.

Destructors

For each class, we can specify a *destructor*—a member function with the same name as the class, with a ~ in front. The destructor for our **Queue** class is declared as:

```
~Queue();
```

The destructor is called whenever an object goes out of scope (or is deallocated). This happens at the end of the block containing the object's declaration, so if we declared **q**, **q2**, and **q3** at the top of a function, their destructors would be called at the end of that function.

Since destructors get called when objects go away, their job is to clean up any mess attached to that object. In our new **Queue** class, for example, each of its constructors dynamically allocates storage for its elements. That storage needs to be deallocated, which is exactly what the destructor does (calling **delete** on the **elements** array).

Like constructors, destructors are automatically called by the system and so do not have a return value.

What's really nice about destructors is that we don't leave the task of freeing up storage (or other cleanup details) to the user. Instead, they happen automatically, preventing the common user mistake of not cleaning things up (which eventually leads to problems such as running out of memory).

Assignment Operators

C++ provides a default assignment operator for every class. It individually assigns each of the fields of the class (this is the normal assignment operator for structures in C). The problem is that this default behavior often leads to the same problems as that of the copy constructor. For example, consider assigning one queue to another:

```
q = q2;
```

If we don't do anything special, we'll have **q.elements** and **q2.elements** pointing to the same underlying array of queue elements. We don't want this situation, since it gives results in all the same problems that led us to defining our own copy constructor.

Fortunately, C++ lets us redefine the assignment operator. That is, we can declare an assignment operator as a member of the class and then provide an implementation for it. Its declaration in the **Queue** class looks like:

```
Queue& operator=(const Queue& other_q);
```

When we provide this prototype and its implementation, C++ will use it rather than the default assignment operator.

It should seem weird that **operator=** is a binary operator, but its corresponding member function only takes one argument. This works because when we write

```
q = q2
```

the compiler translates the call into:

```
q.operator=(q2);
```

The result is that we're applying a normal member function with a funny name (in this case, **operator=**) to an object, just as we did with functions with more normal names, such as **Enqueue**. In this case, the object is the one we're assigning to, and the parameter is the one we're assigning from.

operator= usually behaves very similarly to the copy constructor, except that it must first clean up the object that it is assigning to. That is, in the assignment above, we want to clean up **q**, then make it a copy of **q2**. In this case, that means freeing up the storage allocated for **q**'s elements, allocating sufficient storage for **q2**'s elements, and copying them over.

You may be tempted to implement **operator=** simply by calling the destructor (to clean up the object we're assigning to) and then calling the copy constructor (to reinitialize it to a copy of the object we're assigning from). The problem is that we're not allowed to call constructors and we're not supposed to call destructors. However, there's a useful trick. We first define private member functions **CleanUp** and **Init** to do the cleanup and the copy, respectively. We then have the destructor call **CleanUp** and the copy constructor call **Init**. Then we implement assignment by first calling **CleanUp**, then calling **Init**.

The complete implementation of **operator=** is actually a bit more complex. One reason is that we have to worry about the case where it's used to assign an object to itself. It's not so much that we expect programmers to intentionally write:

```
q = q;
```

It's instead that they may have references or pointers to objects and not be aware they are assigning an object to itself.

To see why we have to worry about this case, consider how we implemented **Queue::operator=**. We destroy the array of elements in the queue on the left, allocate it to the size of the queue on the right, and then copy the elements. If both queues are the same, then we're destroying the same internal array that we are trying to copy, a sure-fire recipe for disaster. So we need to make sure we don't do the delete and copy if we're assigning a queue to itself.

But how do we tell that the object on the left is the same as the object on the right? To do so, we use a new keyword, **this**. Within a member function, **this** is defined to point to the object on which that member function was invoked. We can therefore compare **this** to the address of the parameter—if they're the same, then we're assigning an object to itself.

Keeping this in mind, here's the complete implementation of **operator=**:

```
Queue& Queue::operator=(const Queue& other_q)
{
  if (this != &other_q)
  {
    CleanUp();
    Init(other_q);
  }
  return *this;
}
```

This still has some strangeness to it. Why does the **operator=** return a reference to ***this**? The short answer is that doing so allows us to write expressions like:

```
q = q1 = q2;
```

That is, we want assignment to return the object assigned so that we can cascade assignments and pass that object on to the next assignment. We return a reference for efficiency; returning an entire object would require a call to the copy constructor to return it by value. The trick is that we need to refer to the object we assigned to. But that's the object pointed to by **this**, so ***this** refers to the object itself.

Whenever we redefine the copy constructor, we usually find ourselves redefining the assignment operator as well. It can seem amazingly complex at first, but almost all assignment operators can simply follow the template above.

Figure 23.7 puts all of this together in a short program that shows how the copy constructor and assignment operator are used.

> *When defining a class that does resource acquistion, such as dynamic allocation, provide a copy constructor and assignment operator.*

Friend Functions

There's one last detail we have ignored in our **Queue** class. We have provided an output operator for that class. To do so, it runs through the **elements** array, displaying the values, starting with the front of the queue and ending with the rear. There's a catch though: we can't reasonably define this operator as a member function! The reason is that the output operator is always used like this:

> *output-stream* **<<** *item-to-output*

If we defined **<<** as a member function, the object would have to appear on the left and the output stream on the right—exactly the opposite of how we would like to use it.

As a result, we have to define it as a normal, global function (the same way we overloaded the various operators for **Date**s in the previous chapter). The catch is that the output operator needs access to the internals of a **Queue**. However, those internals are private and therefore inaccessible.

Fortunately, C++ provides us with a way out of this dilemma. When we provide a class declaration, we can declare certain functions as *friends* of the class. These functions have access to the class internals, just as if they were member functions.

To make a function a friend of a class, we include the function's prototype in the class declaration, preceded by the keyword **friend**, as in:

```
friend ostream& operator<<(ostream& output, const Queue& q);
```

Where we place this in the class declaration doesn't matter, as **private** and **public** do not apply to friends.

That's it. Now this particular function can access the internals of the queue, with **q.f**, **q.r**, and so on (assuming that **q** is the name of the particular queue we want to access). If it wasn't a friend, those accesses would generate compiler error messages.

It's often said that in life one can't have too many friends. That may well be true of people, but it's not true of classes. Every function that's a friend of a particular class may have dependencies on its internal implementation. That means that if we make changes to that implementation, we have to check all of those functions to see if they are affected. In some sense, friend functions violate the basic principle of encapsulation that classes are designed to support. While they are useful in situations like this one, where the syntax of the language forces us to define a particular function outside of the class, you should think carefully before adding friend functions to a class.

> *Avoid friend functions when member functions are sufficient.*

```
//
// Examples of using the copy constructor and assignment operator.
//
#include <iostream.h>
#include <stdlib.h>
#include "queues2.h"

const int DesiredElements = 10;

int main()
{
  Queue q(DesiredElements);

  // Initialize queue with 0...DesiredElements - 1 and print it

  for (int next = 0; next < DesiredElements; next++)
    q.Enqueue(next);
  cout << "The initial queue: " << endl << q;

  // Make copies and print them

  Queue q2 = q;
  Queue q3(q2);
  cout << "The first copy: " << endl << q2;
  cout << "The second copy: " << endl << q3;

  // Dequeue and enqueue some elements and print queues

  q2.Dequeue();
  q2.Dequeue();
  q2.Dequeue();
  q2.Enqueue(DesiredElements + 1);
  q2.Enqueue(DesiredElements + 2);
  cout << "The first copy minus 3 elements plus 2 new elements: "
       << endl << q2;

  // Print the original and second copy to make sure they aren't
  // changed

  cout << "The original: " << endl << q;
  cout << "The second copy: " << endl << q3;

  // Assign to original queue and then print it

  q = q2;
  cout << "The original after assigning the 1st copy: " << endl << q;

  return EXIT_SUCCESS;
}
```

Figure 23.7   (useqs2.C)   An example program using the copy constructor and assignment operator.

23.4   LAYERING

Objects are not used in isolation. We often have objects that contain other objects, a powerful technique called *layering*.

We will illustrate layering with a new version of Chapter 9's bus-stop simulator. The original program used a single queue (represented as a static array) to hold the arrival times of the people waiting for a bus, adding elements to the queue when people arrived at the bus stop and deleting elements from the queue whenever a bus arrived. In addition, we updated counters for the number of riders and the time they waited.

There are a variety of problems with that original implementation. The main one is that the program is not easily extensible. Since its queue and counters are either static or global, it's not easy to modify to simulate multiple bus stops. The program also has readability problems, in that it's not immediately obvious which variables are used solely for input and which are used to keep track of the simulation.

One way to address these problems is to rewrite the program using a **BusStop** object. Figure 23.8 contains its class declaration. A **BusStop** provides operations to record arrivals of people and buses, as well as to determine how many riders there have been, how long they have been waiting, and how many people remain at the bus stop. It also provides operations to turn on and off tracing of arrivals. To implement these operations, the object contains several pieces of data: a **Queue**, counters for riders and waiting time, and a flag to indicate whether tracing is taking place.

As soon as we layer, we have to worry about the process of constructing a layered object. To construct a **BusStop**, we need to initialize the fields it contains. The catch is that any field that is itself an object needs to be initialized by one of its constructors. As a result, when we initialize a **BusStop**, we need to invoke the **Queue** constructor to initialize the **Queue** it contains.

By default, C++ automatically initializes all contained objects using their *default* constructor (the constructor that can be invoked with no arguments). So, without our having to do anything special, when we declare a **BusStop**, C++ calls the default **Queue** constructor on the **Queue** it contains (which initializes it to a default size), then executes the code in the appropriate **BusStop** constructor (which presumably initializes the non-object fields in a **BusStop** object).

That's certainly reasonable behavior. However, it's not always sufficient. Suppose we want to be able to specify the number of slots a **BusStop** should have, as in:

```
BusStop b(BusStopSize);
```

That is, we want to specify that **b** is a **BusStop** that can have up to **BusStopSize** people waiting at any given time. The problem is that the **BusStop** constructor needs a way to specify that size to the **Queue** constructor.

Member Initialization Lists

In C++, initialization of contained objects is done by member initialization lists. The **BusStop** constructor's implementation is shown on the top of the next page.

```
//
// BusStop object.
//
#include "queues2.h"

const int DefaultCapacity = 100;

class BusStop
{
  public:
    BusStop(int desiredCapacity = DefaultCapacity);

    bool ArrivePeople(int time, int newPeople = 1);
    void ArriveBus(int time, int capacity);

    int PeopleRemaining();           // # of people still at bus stop
    unsigned long PeopleBoarded();      // people who have boarded so far
    unsigned long PeopleWaitingTime(); // time they waited.

    void TraceArrivals();      // set things up to trace arrivals
    void NotraceArrivals();    //    or to not trace arrivals

  private:
    Queue q;
    unsigned long total_boarders, total_waiting_time;
    bool tracing;
};

#include "busin1.h"
```

Figure 23.8 (busstop.h) Header file for **BusStop** class.

```
inline BusStop::BusStop(int desiredCapacity)
  : q(desiredCapacity),
    total_boarders(0), total_waiting_time(0),
    tracing(false)
{}
```

The member initialization list goes between the constructor header and its body. It consists of a colon, followed by the names of each field and the arguments to supply to its constructor. C++ uses the types of the arguments in parentheses to select the appropriate constructor. For example, the line

```
q(desiredCapacity);
```

says to initialize the **q** field of a **BusStop** by calling the **Queue::Queue(int)** constructor and passing it **desiredCapacity**.

How all this works is this. Before executing the body of an object's constructor, C++ runs through all fields in the object in the order they were declared. It checks whether each field appears in the member initialization list and, if it does, C++ invokes the appropriate constructor to initialize it, passing that constructor the arguments following the variable's name. If the field's name doesn't appear in the member initializion list, C++ calls the object's default constructor to initialize it (and generates an error if there is no default constructor).

For a basic type, C++ initializes it to the value in the the parentheses following its name (or leaves it uninitialized if the name doesn't appear there).

Member initialization lists often eliminate the need for the constructor's body to take any action. That's the case with the **BusStop** constructor, as all of the fields have been initialized in its member initialization list.

The rest of the implementation is similar to code we have already seen. Figure 23.9 defines the inline access operations and Figure 23.10 defines the remaining **BusStop** operations. Finally, Figure 23.11 is simulation program using the **BusStop** class.

Destructors, Copy Constructors, and Assignment

If you look closely at the declaration and implementation of the **BusStop** class, you should notice something a little suspicious. There's no destructor, copy constructor, or assignment operator for the class—but this is not an oversight on our part.

Let's consider each of these operations in order. When we go to destruct an object, C++ automatically executes the code inside its destructor, then recursively calls the destructors of each of the objects it contains. With **BusStop** objects, the only cleanup that's needed is to free up the dynamically allocated array for its internal **Queue**, but that's a task handled by the destructor for **Queue**s, which is called automatically. As a result, there's no need to provide a destructor for **BusStop**s.

What about when we initialize an object in a way that requires a copy constructor? The default copy constructor for any object copies each of its fields, calling each of their copy constructors. So if we initialize one **BusStop** as a copy of another, we automatically copy each of its fields, using the **Queue** copy constructor to copy the **Queue** field. As a result, we need not provide a copy constructor for **BusStop**s.

By now you can probably guess how assignment works. The default assignment operator automatically assigns each of the fields within an object by calling each of their assignment operators. So assigning one **BusStop** to another causes the assignment operator for **Queue**s to be used to assign the **Queue** fields they contain. That's just what we want, so there's no need to provide an assignment operator for **BusStop**s either.

In fact, it turns out that one reason layering is so powerful is that only the low-level classes, such as **Queue**, that actually do things such as dynamic allocation have to provide destructors, copy constructors, and assignment operators. The higher-level classes, such as **BusStop**, are in large part insulated from these issues.

23.5   ## USING BUILT-IN CLASSES—ADDITIONAL I/O OPERATORS

We have seen how to do input and output through the overloaded **<<** and **>>** operators. But **cin** and **cout** are objects (of type **istream** and **ostream**, respectively) and

```
//
// BusStop inline operations.
//
inline BusStop::BusStop(int desiredCapacity)
  : q(desiredCapacity),
    total_boarders(0), total_waiting_time(0),
    tracing(false)
  {}

inline int BusStop::PeopleRemaining()
  { return q.Length(); }

inline unsigned long BusStop::PeopleBoarded()
  { return total_boarders; }

inline unsigned long BusStop::PeopleWaitingTime()
  { return total_waiting_time; }

inline void BusStop::TraceArrivals()
  { tracing = true; }

inline void BusStop::NotraceArrivals()
  { tracing = false; }
```

Figure 23.9   (businl.h)   The header file defining the inline **Queue** operations.

have a variety of operations that we can apply to them. This section describes a few of the most important ones.

Character-at-a-Time I/O

Figure 23.12 is a C++ reworking of our Chapter 5 display program that copies its input to its output. It relies on two new operations. Each **istream** object provides a **get** operation that's essentially identical to C's **getchar** function. It takes no parameters and returns the internal code of the next input character (or **EOF** if there's no more input). Each **ostream** object provides a **put** operation that's identical to C's **putchar** function. It takes an internal code and displays the corresponding character. This means we can copy the input to the output with this C-like loop:

```
while ((c = cin.get()) != EOF)
  cout.put(c);
```

C++ also provides a second **get** operation for **istream** objects. This one takes a character as an argument and fills it in with next character in the input. It returns a non-zero value if the operation succeeded and a zero if it failed.[1] That means we can

---

[1]Actually, most I/O operations return the object they were invoked on and rely on special conversion operations to convert the object to an appropriate integer.

```
//
// Definitions of non-inlinable BusStop operations.
//
#include "busstop.h"

bool BusStop::ArrivePeople(int time, int newPeople)
{
  if (tracing)
    cout << newPeople << " people arrived at time " << time << endl;

  for (; newPeople > 0; newPeople--)  // put people in queue
  {
    if (q.IsFull())
      return false;
    q.Enqueue(time);
    total_boarders++;
  }
  return true;
}

void BusStop::ArriveBus(int time, int capacity)
{
  if (tracing)
    cout << "Bus arrived at time " << time
         << " (" << capacity << " seats)" << endl;

  while (! q.IsEmpty() && capacity-- > 0)
    total_waiting_time += time - q.Dequeue();
}
```

Figure 23.10 (busstop.C) The source file defining the non-inline **Queue** operations.

also copy the input to the output with this simpler loop, as we have done in Figure 23.13.

```
while (cin.get(ch))
  cout.put(ch);
```

Figure 23.14 is a final version of the display program. It uses the input and output operators to read and write each input character. Unfortunately, this program doesn't work as expected, because reading into a single character variable with **>>** *skips white space*, while using **get** reads the next character even if it is a space.

Line-at-a-Time Input and Output

C++ also provides a **getline** operation for input streams. It takes three parameters: a pointer to a place to put the characters it reads, the number of characters it can safely read into that array, and a delimiter that tells it when to stop reading (which defaults to a newline character). It stops after reading the delimiter or filling the array. It then

```
//
// Simulation using BusStop object.
//
#include <iostream.h>
#include <stdlib.h>
#include "busstop.h"

const int BusStopSize = 100;

int main()
{
  BusStop b(BusStopSize);
  int code;                        // transaction code
  int time;                        // event time
  int count;                       // # of people or capacity

  b.TraceArrivals();
  while (cin >> code >> time >> count)
    switch(code)
    {
      case 0:  if (! b.ArrivePeople(time, count))
                  cout << "Couldn't record all " << count
                       << " arrivals." << endl;
               break;
      case 1:  b.ArriveBus(time, count);
               break;
      default: cout << "Invalid code of " << code << endl;
               break;
    }
  if (b.PeopleBoarded() == 0)
    cout << "No people ever boarded a bus " << endl;
  else
    cout << b.PeopleBoarded() << " riders waited "
         << b.PeopleWaitingTime() << ", average wait "
         << (double) b.PeopleWaitingTime() / b.PeopleBoarded() << endl;
  if ( b.PeopleRemaining() )
    cout << b.PeopleRemaining() << " people still at bus stop" << endl;
  return EXIT_SUCCESS;
}
```

Figure 23.11   (usebs.C) The simulation program written using the **BusStop** object.

terminates the array with a trailing null, so its second argument should be no more than one less than the size of the array. It returns a non-zero value if the input was read successfully, or a zero if it encounters end of file or an input error.

Figure 23.15 is our line numbering program, rewritten using **getline**.[2] This program introduces one new I/O library feature: the **setw** manipulator. The library

[2]This program only works correctly if all input lines are smaller than the size array we've allocated. If we enter a longer line, **getline** treats it as an error and returns a zero, terminating our loop.

```
//
// Copy input to output a character at a time, initial C++ version
//
#include <iostream.h>
#include <stdlib.h>

int main()
{
  int c;

  while ((c = cin.get()) != EOF)
    cout.put(c);

  return EXIT_SUCCESS;
}
```

Figure 23.12   (display.C)   A C++ program that copies its input to its output.

```
//
// Copy input to output a character at a time, second C++ version
//
#include <iostream.h>
#include <stdlib.h>

int main()
{
  char ch;

  while (cin.get(ch))
    cout.put(ch);

  return EXIT_SUCCESS;
}
```

Figure 23.13   (display2.C)   A second C++ program to copy its input to its output.

provides a variety of manipulators we can use to specify the formatting of our input and output. **setw** sets the width of the *next* item read or written to its argument. So:

```
cout << setw(MaxWidth) << lines
```

writes **lines** in a field of width **MaxWidth** (which is 8 in the line-numbering program). To use manipulators we need to include **<iomanip.h>**.

```
//
// Copy input to output a character at a time, skipping white space.
//
#include <iostream.h>
#include <stdlib.h>

int main()
{
  char  c;

  while (cin >> c)
    cout << c;

  return EXIT_SUCCESS;
}
```

Figure 23.14 (display3.C) A C++ program that doesn't quite copy its input to its output.

```
//
// Line-number its input, one line at a time.
//
#include <iostream.h>
#include <iomanip.h>
#include <stdlib.h>

const int MaxLineLen = 80;                   // longest expected input line
const int MaxWidth = 8;                      // line-number field width

int main()
{
  char line[MaxLineLen + 1];                 // input line (plus \0)

  for (unsigned long lines = 0L;
       cin.getline(line, MaxLineLen);
       lines++)
    cout << setw(MaxWidth) << lines << " " << line << endl;

  return EXIT_SUCCESS;
}
```

Figure 23.15 (lineno.C) A program to line-number its input.

23.6   CONSTANT OBJECTS

In C++, we are allowed to have constant objects. These are objects that are initialized to a value when they are created and then remain unchanged until they are destroyed.

Figure 23.16 is an example. It's a program showing how to use a new object type, **Word**. A **Word** is an object containing a single machine word of data with operations to access it to get and set the value of bits. It's a nice abstraction over the equivalent C code, which does those operations with combinations of low-level operators.

We construct a word by providing an initial value for the word. The declaration

```
const Word zero(0);
```

constructs a **Word** object, initializing it to 0. The **const** in front indicates that it's a constant **Word**, so we can't change the variable after we declare it. It's obvious that **const** means we can't assign to it, but with objects **const** also means something else. We can't apply any member function to the object that could potentially change the object's internals. Unfortunately, by default, any member function is allowed to change the object's internals, so unless we do something special we can't apply any member functions to the object.

Figure 23.17 shows the declaration of the **Word** class and how it gets around this problem. The declarations of member functions that do not modify the object on which they are invoked are terminated with a **const**.

```
int GetBit(int desired_bit) const;
```

This **const** is a promise that the member function will not try to assign or otherwise change the fields within the object. Here, that means **GetBit** won't change the **data** field in the **Word** we are applying it to.

Figure 23.18 shows the definitions of the various inline **Word** operations, and Figure 23.19 shows the definition of the non-inline operations. The trailing **const** is also applied to the operation's definition, as with **GetBit**'s definition:

```
inline int Word::GetBit(int desired_bit) const
  { return (data >> desired_bit) & 01; }
```

It's easy to be misled into thinking that all of **Word**'s operations should be made **const**, but that's not true. In particular, those that modify a **Word**, such as **SetBit**, cannot.

When we define a class, we have to very carefully examine each operation and determine whether it changes the internals of an object. If it doesn't, we should make it **const**, as we did with **GetBit** and **GetValue** within **Word**. It's important to make these functions **const**, not only for explictly declared constant objects, but also for parameters that are passed as references to constants, as we can't apply non-**const** member functions to these objects either. One place this matters is the output operator for **Word**s. Its second parameter is a reference to a **const** word (the **Word** to display). If **GetBit** were not **const**, we couldn't apply it to this parameter.

```
//
// An example using the Word class.
//
#include <stdlib.h>
#include "word.h"

main()
{
  const Word zero(0);          // Create a constant byte of all 0s.
  cout << "Zero is: " << zero << endl;

  int x;                       // Read, modify, and print input words.
  while (cin >> x)
  {
    Word test(x);
    cout << "The original word: " << test << endl;

    test.SetBit(4, 1);         // turn bit 4 on
    test.SetBit(5, 0);         // turn bit 5 off
    cout << "With bit 4 on and bit 5 off: " << test << endl;

    test = ~ test.GetValue(); // flip bits
    cout << "With bits then flipped: " << test << endl;
  }

  return EXIT_SUCCESS;
}
```

Figure 23.16 (useword.C) A C++ program using a new **Word** type.

> *Examine each member function carefully to see if should be made* **const**.

23.7   CASE STUDY—A LAYERED IMPLEMENTATION OF SETS

This section is optional!

We conclude this chapter with a case study that provides a layered implementation of the previous chapter's **Set**s. In particular, we implement **Set**s on top of **BitVector**s, and we use our **Word** object to help us implement **BitVector**s.

Figure 23.20 is our declaration of the **BitVector** class. It provides the same general functionality as the previous chapter's **BitVector** type. We have, however, improved it significantly by declaring it as a class. The internal implementation of a **BitVector** is now hidden from its users. In fact, not only have we hidden the particular data we've used to implement **BitVector**s, but also the many helper functions we've used to perform tasks like locating the word containing a particular bit. These functions are now private operations and can no longer be accessed by class users. They are now also much simpler. Because they are now **BitVector** operations, they can access the

```
//
// Class declaration for Words.
//
#include <iostream.h>
#include <limits.h>

const int WordBits = CHAR_BIT * sizeof(int);  // Bits in word

class Word
{
  public:
    Word(unsigned int value = 0);

    int GetBit(int desired_bit) const;          // Return bit's value
    unsigned int GetValue() const;              // Word's integer value

    void SetBit(int desired_bit, int value);    // Set bit on/off.
    void SetBits(int value);                     // Set all bits.
    Word& operator=(unsigned int value);         // Assign integer to Word.

  private:
    unsigned int data;                           // Word is unsigned int.
};

ostream& operator<<(ostream& output, const Word& w);

#include "wordinl.h"
```

Figure 23.17 (word.h) The declaration of the **Word** class.

internal data they need without our having to pass that data explicitly. This is also true for the functions the users use to manipulate **BitVectors**. Since they too are now operations, they no longer have to declare and access the **BitVector** they work on as an explicit parameter.

Our particular implementation for **BitVector**s is as a dynamically allocated array of **Word**s. The **BitVector** itself contains a pointer to a **Word**, and its constructors fill in this pointer by using **new** to allocate an array of **Word**s.

```
words = new Word[num_words = RequiredWords(num_bits)];
```

When we allocate arrays of objects with **new**, it automatically calls the no-argument constructor to initialize each object. For **Word**, that constructor initializes the **Word** to all zero bits, which is just what we want. However, because we are using dynamic allocation, one drawback is that we are forced to provide a copy constructor, assignment operator, and destructor for our **BitVector** class. Figure 23.21 contains the definitions of the private inline functions, Figure 23.22 contains the definitions of the inline **BitVector** operations, and Figure 23.23 contains the definitions for the non-inline **Bitvector** operations.

```
//
// Inline operations on Words.
//
inline Word::Word(unsigned int value) : data(value)
  {}

inline int Word::GetBit(int desired_bit) const
  { return (data >> desired_bit) & 01; }

inline unsigned int Word::GetValue() const
  { return data; }

inline void Word::SetBit(int desired_bit, int value)
  {
    if (value)
        data |= (01 << desired_bit);
    else
        data &= ~(01 << desired_bit);
  }

inline void Word::SetBits(int value)
  { data = (value == 0) ? 0 : ~0; }

inline Word& Word::operator=(unsigned int value)
  {
    data = value;
    return *this;
  }
```

Figure 23.18 (wordinl.h) The definition of the inline **Word** operations.

```
//
// Non-inline Word functions.
//
#include "word.h"

ostream& operator<<(ostream& output, const Word& w)
{
  for (int i = WordBits - 1; i >= 0; i--)
    output << w.GetBit(i);
  return output;
}
```

Figure 23.19 (word.C) The declaration of the **Word** class.

```
//
// BitVector type and related functions.
//
#include <iostream.h>
#include "word.h"

class BitVector
{
  public:
    BitVector(int n = WordBits);
    BitVector(const BitVector& other_b);
    ~BitVector();

    BitVector& operator=(const BitVector& other_b);

    // Access-only operations.

    bool IsOn(int target) const;
    bool IsOff(int target) const;

    // Object-modifying operations.

    void TurnOn(int target, int n = 1);
    void TurnOff(int target, int n = 1);
    int Length() const;

  private:
    Word *words;                   // Dynamically allocated bits
    int num_words;                 // # of words actually used
    int num_bits;                  // # of bits needed in BitVector

    void Init(int n);
    void Init(const BitVector& other_b);
    void CleanUp();

    int  WordIndex(int desired_bit) const;
    int  BitIndexInWord(int desired_bit) const;
    int  RequiredWords(int desired_bits) const;

    int  GetBit(int desired_bit) const;

    void SetBit(int desired_bit, int value);
    void SetBits(int start, int n, int value);
};

ostream& operator<<(ostream& output, const BitVector& b);

#include "bitin1.h"
```

Figure 23.20 (bitvec.h) Declaration of the **BitVector** class.

```
//
// Useful BitVector utility functions.
//
#include <limits.h>

inline int BitVector::WordIndex(int desired_bit) const
  { return desired_bit / WordBits; }

inline int BitVector::BitIndexInWord(int desired_bit) const
  { return desired_bit % WordBits; }

inline int BitVector::GetBit(int desired_bit) const
  {
    Word &w = words[WordIndex(desired_bit)];
    return w.GetBit(BitIndexInWord(desired_bit));
  }

inline void BitVector::SetBit(int desired_bit, int value)
  {
    Word &w = words[WordIndex(desired_bit)];
    w.SetBit(BitIndexInWord(desired_bit), value);
  }

inline int BitVector::RequiredWords(int desired_bits) const
  { return desired_bits / WordBits + 1; }

inline void BitVector::Init(int n)
  {
    num_bits = n;
    words = new Word[num_words = RequiredWords(num_bits)];
  }

inline void BitVector::CleanUp()
  { delete [] words; }
```

Figure 23.21 (bitutils.h) Definition of inline utility **BitVector** operations.

The implementation of most of the **BitVector** operations is straightforward. We have taken advantage of only one new variant of a previously presented C++ feature. That's the ability to declare reference variables (not just reference parameters). One place we use this feature is in **BitVector::GetBit**:

```
Word &w = words[WordIndex(desired_bit)];
return w.GetBit(BitIndexInWord(desired_bit));
```

This code declares **w** as a reference to a **Word** and initializes it as a reference to the word containing the bit we're trying to access. We then apply **Word::GetBit** to **w** to actually access that bit. We do this simply to make our code more readable than a direct

```
//
// Inline BitVector operations.
//
#include "bitutils.h"

inline BitVector::BitVector(int n)
  { Init(n); }

inline BitVector::BitVector(const BitVector& other_b)
  { Init(other_b); }

inline BitVector::~BitVector()
  { CleanUp(); }

inline BitVector& BitVector::operator=(const BitVector& other_b)
  {
    if (this != &other_b)
    {
      CleanUp();
      Init(other_b);
    }
    return *this;
  }

inline bool BitVector::IsOn(int target) const
  { return GetBit(target) != 0; }

inline bool BitVector::IsOff(int target) const
  { return GetBit(target) == 1; }

inline void BitVector::TurnOn(int target, int n)
  { SetBits(target, n, 1); }

inline void BitVector::TurnOff(int target, int n)
  { SetBits(target, n, 0); }

inline int BitVector::Length() const
  { return num_bits; }
```

Figure 23.22   (bitinl.h)   Definition of inline **BitVector** operations.

application of the **Word::GetBit**:

```
return words[WordIndex(desired_bit)] .
           GetBit(BitIndexInWord(desired_bit));
```

Figure 23.24 contains the declaration of our **Set** class. This class contains a **BitVector** and two integers that represent the lowest and highest values that can be stored in the **Set**. We provide a constructor to initialize the **Set** and rely on a member initialization list to specify the needed size to the constructor for the internal

```
//
// Non-inlinable functions for processing BitVectors
//
#include "bitvec.h"

void BitVector::SetBits(int next_bit, int n, int value)
{
  const int past_end_bit = next_bit + n;

  while (next_bit < past_end_bit)
  {
    Word& target_word = words[WordIndex(next_bit)];

    if (BitIndexInWord(next_bit) == 0 && n >= WordBits)
    {          // Do whole word at once
      target_word.SetBits(value);
      next_bit += WordBits;
    }
    else       // Just do next bit
      target_word.SetBit(next_bit++, value);
  }
}

void BitVector::Init(const BitVector& other_b)
{
  num_bits = other_b.num_bits;
  words = new Word[num_words = other_b.num_words];
  for (int i = 0; i < num_words; i++)
    words[i] = other_b.words[i];
}

ostream& operator<<(ostream& output, const BitVector& b)
{
  for (int i = 0; i < b.Length(); i++)
    output << (b.IsOn(i) ? 1 : 0);
  return output;
}
```

Figure 23.23 (bitvec.C) Definitions of non-inline **BitVector** operations.

BitVector. We include prototypes for the standard **Add**, **Delete**, and **Member** operations. We also provide two operations to access the minimum and maximum possible **Set** values. However, we take advantage of C++ support for layering and rely on the default copy constructor, assignment operator, and destructor.

Figure 23.25 contains the definitions of the **Set** operations, all of which are defined as inline. Figure 23.26 contains the definitions of the overloaded output operator for **Set**s, which cannot be defined as inline. We have carefully written it to use only the

```
//
// Improved definitions to use "sets" of integers.
//
#include <iostream.h>
#include <stdlib.h>
#include "bitvec.h"

class Set                          // Build sets on top of BitVectors
{
  public:
    Set(int start, int finish);

    void Add(int elem);
    void Delete(int elem);
    int Member(int elem) const;

    int MinPossElement() const;
    int MaxPossElement() const;

  private:
    BitVector bv;                  // Internal BitVector
    int first, last;               // First and last elements in Set

    int BitForElement(int element) const;
};

#include "setsin1.h"
```

Figure 23.24   (sets.h) Declaration of the **Set** class and the inline **Set** operations.

public interface to **Set**s, however, so there is no need for it to be a **friend** of the **Set** class. Finally, Figure 23.27 is a new version of our program that uses the **Set** class to determine which input values are unique. This object-oriented version is considerably simpler than the original version in the previous chapter.

SUMMARY

- Classes are the C++ mechanism that supports encapsulation. Within a class declaration, we supply prototypes for the operations on objects of the class and declare the variables that each object contains.

- We control access to the internals of a class through the **private** and **public** tags.

- Every object can have constructors to initialize it and a destructor to clean up any resources it uses.

```
//
// Inline Set functions.
//
inline Set::Set(int start, int finish) :
  bv(finish - start + 1), first(start), last(finish)
  {}

inline int Set::BitForElement(int element) const
  { return element - first; }

inline void Set::Add(int elem)         // Add element to set
  { bv.TurnOn(BitForElement(elem)); }

inline void Set::Delete(int elem)          // Delete element from set
  { bv.TurnOff(BitForElement(elem)); }

inline int Set::Member(int elem) const    // Is item in set?
  { return bv.IsOn(BitForElement(elem)); }

inline int Set::MinPossElement() const
  { return first; }

inline int Set::MaxPossElement() const
  { return last; }

ostream& operator<<(ostream&, const Set &s);

inline void Switch(Set& newer, Set& older, int value)
  {
    older.Delete(value);
    newer.Add(value);
  }
```

Figure 23.25   (setsinl.h) Definition of the inline **Set** operations.

```
//
// Utility functions for manipulating sets.
//
#include "sets.h"

ostream& operator <<(ostream& output, const Set &s)
{
  for (int i = s.MinPossElement(); i < s.MaxPossElement(); i++)
    if (s.Member(i))
      output << i << endl;
  return output;
}
```

Figure 23.26   (sets.C) Definition of the output operator for **Set**s.

```
//
// Identify duplicates in the input.
//
#include <stdio.h>
#include <stdlib.h>
#include "sets.h"

const int FirstElement = 0, LastElement = 511;

inline int inRange(int value, int min, int max)
  { return (value >= min && value <= max); }

int main()
{
  Set unique(FirstElement, LastElement);    // unique and
  Set dup(FirstElement, LastElement);       //   duplicate sets
  int inp;

  while (cin >> inp)
  {
    if (!inRange(inp, FirstElement, LastElement))
    {
      cout << "Value out of range." << endl;
      continue;
    }
    if (unique.Member(inp))
      Switch(dup, unique, inp);
    else if (!dup.Member(inp))
      unique.Add(inp);
  }
  cout << "Unique values " << endl;
  cout << unique;
  cout << "Duplicate values " << endl;
  cout << dup;

  return EXIT_SUCCESS;
}
```

Figure 23.27 (usesets.C) A program using the **Set** class to determine which input values are unique.

- Objects have a default copy constructor and assignment operator. Objects that contain handles to resources need to override these default operations, since their default behavior is inappropriate.

- The C++ standard I/O library is implemented in terms of objects. This design makes it much simpler to use than the C library.

- Objects can contain other objects. This is called layering and is a powerful technique for quickly constructing software.

- We can have constant objects. To write a class that allows them, we need to use **const** to specify which member functions can work on constants.

EXERCISES

Explore

23–1 Compile and run the programs in this chapter.

23–2 What happens if you create a **Queue** and try to directly access its internals from the main program? Why does this behavior lead to more maintainable programs?

Modify

23–3 Rewrite Chapter 12's database program in an object-oriented style.

23–4 Rewrite Chapter 13's Game of Life in an object-oriented style.

Extend

23–5 In our **Queue** class implementations, **Enqueue** assumes there is sufficient room to insert elements, and **Dequeue** assumes that the queue is not empty. Fix their implementations to relax these assumptions.

23–6 Add **RotateRight** and **RotateLeft** operations for the **Word** class. Both operations should take as a parameter the number of bits to rotate. Then add **RotateRight** and **RotateLeft** operations to the **BitVector** class.

23–7 Implement **FirstBit** and **LastBit** operations for the **BitVector** class. These functions each take a value as an argument, either 0 or 1, and return the bit number of the first bit (or last bit) with that value, or -1 if no bit has that value. Modify the **Set** class to use these functions to provide **MinElement** and **MaxElement** functions that return the value of the **Set**'s actual smallest and largest elements, respectively. Use these functions to optimize the **Set** output operator.

23–8 Implement **Word::CountBits**. This operation takes as an argument a 1 or 0, the value of the bit to count, and it returns the number of 1s or 0s in a given **Word**. Use this function to implement **BitVector::CountBits**, and then use that to implement a **Cardinality** function for **Set**s. This function returns the number of elements in a set.

23–9 Provide another constructor for the **Word** class that takes two arguments: an array of booleans and the number of entries in that array. This constructor initializes the word by initializing each bit to the value of the corresponding array entry. Any leftover bits are initialized to zero by default.

Build

23–10 Define a class **StringTable** that maintains a sorted array of strings, where each string is simply a C string, declared as a **char ***. Provide a constructor that allows the user to specify the size of this array, provide a reasonable default, and allocate the desired-size array dynamically. Provide operations to add and delete items and to search for a particular item. Overload **<<** to print the table. Finally, provide a destructor that frees the space allocated for the array table.

Use the **StringTable** class you have defined to write a program that sorts its input lines.

Then redefine **StringTable** to use a linked list rather than an array.

23–11 Implement a **String** class. Provide operations for constructing and comparing strings. Also provide operations for determining the length of a string, accessing a particular character within a string, and displaying a string. The **String** should be implemented internally with a single field: a dynamically allocated array of characters.

23–12 Implement a **Date** class that provides operations for constructing and comparing **Date**s. Each **Date** should contain fields for the month, day, and year.

23–13 Implement a **Time** class that provides operations for constructing, comparing, and displaying **Time**s. Each **Time** should contain fields for the hour, minute, and second. You should also provide an operation for calculating the difference in seconds between two **Time**s, and converting a time into seconds.

23–14 Implement a **Money** class that contains fields for dollars and cents and does exact arithmetic using them, even for large amounts. It should provide operations for constructing **Money** objects, for comparing them, for performing basic arithmetic on them, and for displaying them.

24   INHERITANCE

C++ and other object-oriented languages provide not just the ability to package behavior into encapsulated classes, but also the facility, called inheritance, for defining new classes as extensions or variants of existing ones. This chapter explores the details of inheritance, including the notions of virtual functions, abstract classes, polymorphism, and dynamic binding. We concentrate on two traditional examples of inheritance: we illustrate inheritance to support code reuse by defining a hierarchy of window classes and we illustrate inheritance to support design reuse by implementing a graphics drawing package.

24.1   A SIMPLE EXAMPLE OF INHERITANCE

Often an application requires several data types that are very closely related.

Consider the problem of producing text-based windows for creating a drawing area on the display. We can easily think of three different types of windows we would like to have: plain windows (without any kind of border), bordered windows (which are plain windows, except that they add a frame around the window when they display its contents), and titled windows (which are bordered windows, except that they add a title as well as the border). All of these windows share some basic capabilities, such as displaying themselves, adding an element at a given location, erasing the window, and so on. They really differ only in how they display themselves and in exactly what data we require to implement their functionality. The vanilla window, for example, needs to internally contain a two-dimensional array of characters and the height and width of the window, while the bordered window also needs to store the character used to write the border, and the titled window also needs to store the string to be written as the title.

One way to approach this problem is to implement each of these window types as the separate classes **Window**, **BorderedWindow**, and **TitledWindow**. The end result, however, is likely to be considerable duplication in the code and no guarantee that we can successfully substitute one window for another (such as replacing a **Window** with a **BorderedWindow**). What we really want is a way to take advantage of the commonalities between these different types of windows.

The mechanism that allows us to take advantage of these commonalities is inheritance. The idea is that we define classes as *derived classes* of other classes. These derived classes, or *subclasses*, are said to *inherit* all of the members—data members and function members—of another class. We're allowed to add new members and methods (functions), and we can even *overload* members from the *parent* or *base* class.

Figure 24.1 shows how our windowing classes would be defined in an inheritance hierarchy. The **Window** class serves as the root or base class of this hierarchy; the **BorderedWindow** class is *derived* from it, and **TitledWindow** class is in turn derived from **BorderedWindow**. We often diagram these hierarchies using boxes and arrows, with the base or root class at the top, and the derived classes beneath.

In Figure 24.1, the large boxes are the classes (**Window**, **BorderedWindow**, and **TitledWindow**). The smaller boxes within each class are the class's local variables. For **Window** these are **actual_rows** and **actual_columns** (to store the size of the window) and **cells** (to store the characters contained in the window). The named arrows (such as **PutRow** and **Display**) indicate operations that can be applied to class. The light font indicates inherited data and operations and the boldface font indicates data and operations defined in that class. In **BorderedWindow**, for example, we inherit the various **PutRow** and **PutColumn** operations, as well as **Erase**, but we have to define our own **Display** because the **Display** we would inherit doesn't write a border. And within a **BorderedWindow**, we add an additional field, **border_char**, to hold the character used to display the border.

Finally, Figure 24.1 illustrates one other feature of C++. It's possible in C++ to distinguish between operations that can be used by any function (public), operations that can only be used by member functions of the class (private), and operations that can be used only by member functions of a class or any class derived from it (protected). In our diagram, the operations on the left are the public interface of the class and the operations listed on the right are protected. For example, the **Window** class provides **Rows** and **Columns** to return the number of rows and number of columns actually used by the window, and it provides **ValidRow** and **ValidColumn** to verify that a particular row or column is within the **Window**'s boundaries. These are accessible only by the **Window**, **BorderedWindow**, and **TitledWindow** classes.

24.2   DEFINING INHERITED CLASSES

Figure 24.1 can be thought of as describing an inheritance-based design for our windowing classes. But what does the program that corresponds to this design look like?

Defining a Base Class

Figure 24.2 shows the **Window** class declaration, Figure 24.3 contains the definitions of the inline operations, and Figure 24.4 contains the definitions of the non-inline operations. The **Window** class illustrates something that may be surprising. It takes extra effort to produce a class from which other classes can be derived. This effort shows up in three places.

The first effort is that we have to decide which functions can be overloaded (that is, redefined) in derived classes. For **Window**s, we are assuming that most of the functions will not be redefined in derived classes—the **Erase**, **PutRow**, and **PutColumn** operations seem sufficient for any type of window we might come up with. However, the **Display** operation is going to be customized for each of the derived classes. When we have a function like this, we need to precede its prototype with the keyword

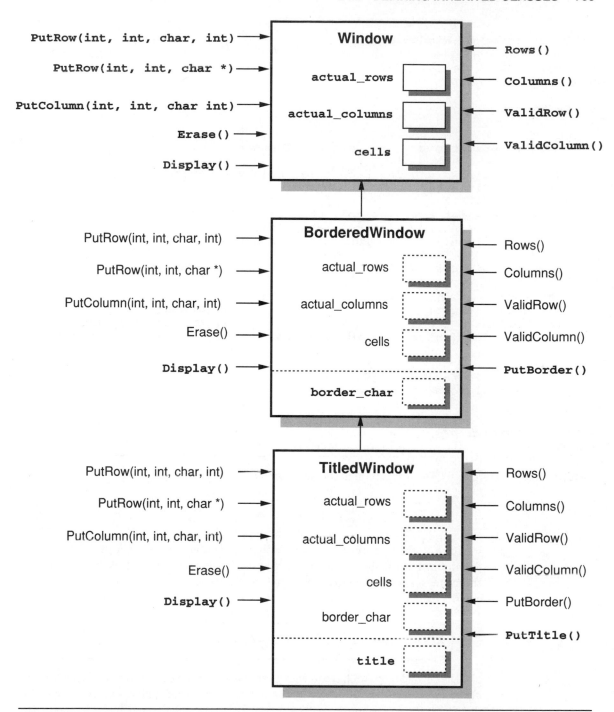

Figure 24.1 A hierarchy of windowing classes.

```
//
// Declaration of Window class.
//
#if !defined (CLASS_WINDOW)
#define CLASS_WINDOW

class Window
{
  public:
    enum { DefaultRows = 24, DefaultColumns = 80 };

    Window(int rows = DefaultRows, int cols = DefaultColumns);
    virtual ~Window();

    void PutRow(int row, int col, char c = ' ', int n = 1);
    void PutRow(int row, int col, char *s);
    void PutColumn(int row, int col, char c = ' ', int n = 1);
    void Erase();
    virtual void Display();                     // Overridable

  protected:
    int Rows() const;                           // Number of rows
    int Columns() const;                        // Number of columns
    bool ValidRow(int r), ValidColumn(int c);   // Is row/column valid?

  private:
    char cells[DefaultRows][DefaultColumns];
    int  actual_rows, actual_columns;
};

#include "winin1.h"
#endif
```

Figure 24.2   (window.h) The declaration of the **Window** class.

virtual. The **virtual** appears only in the prototype and not in the function's definition. Later in the chapter, we'll see exactly what **virtual** does, but for now it's sufficient to simply remember that it means that we can safely redefine the function in a derived class.[1]

> *Redefine only inherited* **virtual** *functions.*

The second thing we have to worry about is whether we need to provide the derived classes with access to the object's data fields. In this case, public operations provide the necessary access to the **cells** array. However, the derived functions may also

---

[1] It's possible to redefine non-**virtual** functions as well, but whether or not that works depends on exactly how you are using the function.

```
//
// Definition of inline Window operations.
//
inline Window::Window(int rows, int cols)
  : actual_rows(rows),
    actual_columns(cols)
  { Erase(); }

inline Window::~Window() {}

inline int Window::Rows() const
  { return actual_rows; }
inline int Window::Columns() const
  { return actual_columns; }

inline bool Window::ValidRow(int r)
  { return r >= 0 && r <= Rows(); }
inline bool Window::ValidColumn(int c)
  { return c >= 0 && c <= Columns(); }
```

Figure 24.3 (wininl.h) The inline **Window** operations.

need to know the size of the window. The most reasonable way to provide this access is by providing **protected** functions that return the values of the **actual_rows** and **actual_columns** data fields. In this case, we are assuming that these functions shouldn't be public (to keep the public interface as simple as possible), but rather available only to this class and its derived classes.

The final thing we have to do is provide a virtual destructor for the class. We have to do this even if the destructor doesn't have anything to do, in which case we supply an implementation with an empty body. We'll explain exactly why later in the chapter.

Deriving a New Class

We now turn to creating the derived class **BorderedWindow**. We create a derived class from an existing class using this simple syntax:

> **class** *Derived-Class* **:** **public** *Base-Class*
> **{**
>   *Additional data/operations for Derived-Class*
> **};**

The new, derived class has all the methods and data attributes of the existing class, plus whatever else we add in.

Figure 24.5 shows the declaration of the **BorderedWindow** class, and Figure 24.6 shows the definition of its operations. We define the **BorderedWindow** class as a class derived from **Window**. From **BorderedWindow**'s class declaration, we can see it provides one new piece of data and three operations. That piece of data is the

```
//
// Definition of Window operations.
//
#include <iostream.h>
#include "window.h"

void Window::PutRow(int row, int col, char c, int n)
{
  if (ValidRow(row))
    for (int i = 0; i < n; i++)
      if (ValidColumn(col + i))
        cells[row][col + i] = c;
}

void Window::PutRow(int row, int col, char *s)
{
  if (ValidRow(row))
    for (int i = 0; s[i] != '\0'; i++)
      if (ValidColumn(col + i))
        cells[row][col + i] = s[i];
}

void Window::PutColumn(int row, int col, char c, int n)
{
  if (ValidColumn(col))
    for (int i = 0; i < n; i++)
      if (ValidRow(row + i))
        cells[row + i][col] = c;
}

void Window::Display()
{
  for (int r = 0; r < Rows(); r++)
  {
    for (int c = 0; c < Columns(); c++)
      cout << cells[r][c];
    cout << '\n';
  }
}

void Window::Erase()
{
  for (int r = 0; r < Rows(); r++)
    PutRow(r, 0, ' ', Columns());
}
```

Figure 24.4   (window.C)   The non-inline **Window** operations.

```
//
//   Declaration of BorderedWindow class.
//
#include "window.h"

class BorderedWindow : public Window
{
  public:
    enum { DefaultBorder = '+' };

    BorderedWindow(int rows = DefaultRows, int cols = DefaultColumns,
                   char border_char = DefaultBorder);

    virtual void Display();

  protected:
    void PlaceBorder();

  private:
    char border_char;           // character for drawing border
};

#include "bwininl.h"
```

Figure 24.5   (bwindow.h) The declaration of the **BorderedWindow** class.

border_char field, which holds the character to write as the border. The operations
are a constructor, an overloaded **Display** operation, and a protected member function,
PlaceBorder, to place the border in the internal array (which we provide in case a
class derived from this one might find it useful).

Defining Derived Class Constructors

Derived class objects contain storage for all of the fields in their base classes, as well as
any new fields they declare.[2] The derived class constructor is responsible for ensuring
that the entire object (both derived part and base part) is properly constructed.

As a result, any **BorderedWindow** constructor must ensure that the **Window** part
is properly constructed, as well as initializing any new fields. You might think we could
simply initialize the **Window** fields directly from the **BorderedWindow** constructor.
We can't, however, and even if we could, we wouldn't want to. We can't because the
data fields in **Window** are **private** and therefore accessible only to member functions
of the **Window** class. We wouldn't want to because doing so violates the principle of
encapsulation—ideally, only **Window** constructors worry about constructing **Window**
objects, not every constructor for every object derived from **Window**.

---
[2]This storage is typically laid out with their base class part first, then the derived part.

```
//
//  Declaration of BorderedWindow class.
//
inline
BorderedWindow::BorderedWindow(int rows, int cols,
                               char border)
  : Window(rows, cols), border_char(border)
  {}

inline void BorderedWindow::Display()
{
  PlaceBorder();
  Window::Display();
}

inline void BorderedWindow::PlaceBorder()
{
  PutColumn(0, 0, border_char, Rows());
  PutColumn(0, Columns() - 1, border_char, Rows());
  PutRow(0, 1, border_char, Columns() - 2);
  PutRow(Rows() - 1, 1, border_char, Columns() - 2);
}
```

Figure 24.6 (bwininl.h) The definition of the **BorderedWindow** operations.

What all this means is that **BorderedWindow** must somehow invoke an appropriate **Window** constructor. But how?

If we do nothing special when we construct a **BorderedWindow** object, C++ will automatically call the default, no-argument **Window** constructor, **Window::Window**, to initialize the **Window** part. In our program, however, there is no such constructor! What we really want to do is call the **Window** constructor. Fortunately, C++ makes this easy for us. Any derived class constructor can invoke a base class constructor in the member initialization list by referring to it by name and passing the appropriate parameters. So we can define our **BorderedWindow** constructor this way:

```
inline
BorderedWindow::BorderedWindow(int rows, int cols,
                               char border)
  : Window(rows, cols), border_char(border)
  {}
```

Here, we invoke the **Window** constructor, passing it the number of rows and columns in the window.

So what happens when we go to construct a **BorderedWindow**, by declaring one like the following?

```
BorderedWindow bw(5, 10, '*');
```

In general, when we create a derived class object, C++ first calls the base class constructor (either the one selected on the member initialization list, or, if none is provided, the default, no-argument constructor for the base class). Then it calls the appropriate constructor for each object the derived class contains (again, either the one selected on the member initialization list or the default one if no constructor is explicitly requested). Finally, it calls the body of the derived class constructor.

In this case, the declaration invokes the **BorderedWindow** constructor, which first calls the **Window** constructor to initialize the **Window** part of the object, passing it 5 and 10 (the number of rows and columns), and then initializes the **border_char** field to a '*'.

The **BorderedWindow** constructor is similar to most derived class constructors in that it takes the same set of parameters as its base class constructor, plus additional parameters to use to initialize its own private data (in this case, just one parameter, the value of the border chararacter).

Defining Derived Class Operations

The **BorderedWindow** operations are simple enough to be defined as **inline**s. One reason for this simplicity is that they rely on **Window** operations to do the real work.

BorderedWindow::PlaceBorder is an example. It's the operation that places the border inside a window. It works by using **Window::PutColumn** to write the border characters down the first and last columns, and it uses **Window::PutRow** to display the first and last rows.

```
inline void BorderedWindow::PlaceBorder()
{
  PutColumn(0, 0, border_char, Rows());
  PutColumn(0, Columns() - 1, border_char, Rows());
  PutRow(0, 1, border_char, Columns() - 2);
  PutRow(Rows() - 1, 1, border_char, Columns() - 2);
}
```

Because **PutColumn** and **PutRow** are inherited, we can call them as if they were member functions of the **BorderedWindow** class.

In general, whenever C++ sees a name within a member function, it attempts to locate the definition of the name by searching up through the hierarchy. So when it sees **PutColumn**, it first looks for **BorderedWindow::PutColumn** and then **Window::PutColumn**, which it finds. This is essentially how inheritance works: whenever we use a function (or field) name that's not defined in the derived class, C++ tries to find the function (or field) in a base class.

There's one common case where the usual behavior for resolving names can get us into trouble. This incorrect **BorderedWindow::Display** illustrates the problem.

```
inline void BorderedWindow::Display()
{
  PlaceBorder();
  Display();                 // Incorrect recursive call!
}
```

The idea is that we can display a **BorderedWindow** by writing the border into the window with **PlaceBorder** and then using the **Display** operation for **Window**s to display the contents on the standard output. The problem comes in if we simply call **Display**. C++ finds a **Display** associated with **BorderedWindow** and assumes that's the display we want. Unfortunately, that's the *wrong* **Display** and causes a recursive call to our function. To fix the problem, we have to provide the class as part of the operation name.

```
inline void BorderedWindow::Display()
{
  PlaceBorder();
  Window::Display();      // Correct call!
}
```

More Details on Deriving Classes

To complete the hierarchy, we need to provide the definition of a **TitledWindow**. Figure 24.7 contains the declaration of a **TitledWindow** and Figure 24.8 contains the definition of its operations.

There are several tricky aspects to this class. One is that we have chosen to store the title as a dynamically allocated string. This means we need to provide a destructor, copy constructor, and assignment operator for the class.

Whenever C++ goes to destruct a derived object, it calls destructors in the reverse order of constructors. More specfically, C++ first executes the body of the derived object's destructor. Then it calls the destructors on any objects that are fields in the derived object. And then it precedes to recursively call the destructor for its base class, and so on. In our case, only **TitledWindow** has a destructor—there aren't any layered objects, and the **BorderedWindow** and **Window** base class objects do not provide destructors—so only **TitledWindow**'s destructor needs to be executed when a **TitledWindow** goes out of scope.

C++ does something similar with copy constructors. By default, when we construct a derived object as a copy of another derived object, C++ copies the base class part of the object using its copy constructor, then copies the derived class part, one field at a time, using their copy constructors. So, for example, when we need to copy-construct a **BorderedWindow**, for example, C++ calls the **Window** copy constructor (which defaults to copying all of its fields), then the **BorderedWindow** copy constructor (which defaults to copying all of its fields).

However, things are more complex when we provide our own copy constructor for a derived class. It is responsible for explicitly invoking the copy constructor for its base class as part of its member initialization list.

```
inline TitledWindow::TitledWindow(const TitledWindow& other)
  : BorderedWindow(other)
  { Init(other.actual_title); }
```

This first calls the **BorderedWindow** constructor that is specified to take a **const TitledWindow&** as a parameter, and then calls the **Init** function to take care of

```
//
// Declaration of the TitledWindow class.
//
#include "bwindow.h"

class TitledWindow : public BorderedWindow
{
  public:
    TitledWindow(char *title,
                    int rows = DefaultRows, int cols = DefaultColumns,
                    int border_char = DefaultBorder);
    TitledWindow(const TitledWindow& other);
    ~TitledWindow();
    TitledWindow& operator=(const TitledWindow& other);

    void Display();

  protected:
    void PlaceTitle();

  private:
    char *actual_title;

    void Init(char *string);
    void CleanUp();
};

#include "twinin1.h"
```

Figure 24.7   (twindow.h)   Declaration of the **TitledWindow** class.

initializing the **TitledWindow** part of the object. But there is no **BorderedWindow** constructor that takes a reference to a **TitledWindow** as a parameter—or is there?

It turns out that pointers or references to a derived class objects can automatically be converted to pointers or references to the base class (but not the other way around). So we can pass a reference to **TitledWindow** anyplace code is written to expect a reference to a **Window** or **BorderedWindow**. That's what's going on here. The default copy constructor for **BorderedWindow** is written to take a reference to a **BorderedWindow**, but we are passing it a reference to a **TitledWindow**. This works because a **BorderedWindow** can be thought of as part of a **TitledWindow**— the copy constructor is therefore aware only of the **BorderedWindow** part of the object, which is all it needs to know about to be able to make the copy.

There is a similar issue for the assignment operator. By default, everything works correctly. C++ assigns the base class part of the object, then assigns each of the fields in the derived class part. When we provide our own assignment operator for a derived class, as we have done for **TitledWindow**, it must explicitly call the base class (**BorderedWindow**) assignment operator before assigning the fields in the derived

```
//
// Declaration of TitledWindow operations (all inline).
//
#include <string.h>

inline void TitledWindow::Init(char *string)
  {
    actual_title = new char[strlen(string) + 1];
    strcpy(actual_title, string);
  }

inline void TitledWindow::CleanUp()
  { delete [] actual_title; }

inline TitledWindow::TitledWindow(char *title,
                                  int rows, int cols,
                                  int border_char)
  : BorderedWindow(rows, cols, border_char)
  { Init(title); }

inline TitledWindow::TitledWindow(const TitledWindow& other)
  : BorderedWindow(other)
  { Init(other.actual_title); }

inline TitledWindow::~TitledWindow()
  { delete [] actual_title; }

inline TitledWindow&
TitledWindow::operator=(const TitledWindow& other)
  {
    if (this != &other)
    {
      BorderedWindow::operator=(other);
      CleanUp();
      Init(other.actual_title);
    }
    return *this;
  }

inline void TitledWindow::PlaceTitle()
  { PutRow(0, (Columns() - strlen(actual_title)) / 2, actual_title); }

inline void TitledWindow::Display()
  {
    PlaceBorder();
    PlaceTitle();
    Window::Display();
  }
```

Figure 24.8   (twininl.h)   Definition of the **TitledWindow** operations.

class (**TitledWindow**) part, as shown below.

```
inline TitledWindow&
TitledWindow::operator=(const TitledWindow& other)
  {
    if (this != &other)
    {
      BorderedWindow::operator=(other);
      CleanUp();
      Init(other.actual_title);
    }
    return *this;
  }
```

There is one final tricky part to implementing **TitledWindow**. Its **Display** operation winds up using operations from all three windowing classes to do its job. It places the border using **PlaceBorder** for **BorderWindow**s, it places the title in the border using **PlaceTitle**, and it uses **Display** for **Window**s to do the actual display. Why all this complexity? Because it can't first place the title and then use **Display** for **BorderWindow**s because that places the border before displaying, which would overwrite the title.

Using Our Class Hierarchy

Figure 24.9 is an example program showing how to use the window classes. It creates one window of each type, places text in the windows, and then displays them. Figure 24.10 shows the program's output.

24.3   POLYMORPHISM AND DYNAMIC BINDING

The final place object-oriented programming gets its power is from the combination of polymorphism and dynamic binding.

The word "polymorphism" is derived from Greek and means "many shapes." The idea, in C language terms, is simply this: *any pointer or reference to a base class can hold a pointer or reference to one of its derived classes.* For example, suppose we declare a variable as a pointer to a **Window**:

```
Window *wptr;
```

We're allowed to set this pointer to point to a **Window**, a **BorderedWindow**, or a **TitledWindow**. This allows us, for example, to construct an array of pointers to **Window**s, where each array element is a pointer to a different type of window.

```
Window w(3, 5);
BorderedWindow bw(4, 10, '*');
TitledWindow tbw("A Cute Title", 6, 20, '*');
Window *window_table[] = { &w, &bw, &tbw};
```

```
//
// A program using the various window classes.
//
#include <iostream.h>
#include <stdlib.h>
#include "twindow.h"

int main()
{
  Window w(3, 5);
  for (int i = 0; i < 3; i++)
    w.PutRow(i, 0, '$', 5);
  w.Display();              // 3 x 5, filled with $s
  cout << endl;

  BorderedWindow bw(4, 10, '*');
  bw.PutRow(1, 1, "Hello.");
  bw.PutRow(2, 1, "Goodbye.");
  bw.Display();            // 4 x 10, with border and "Hello/Goodbye"
  cout << endl;

  TitledWindow tbw("A Cute Title", 6, 20, '*');
  tbw.PutRow(3, 6, "Hello.");
  tbw.PutRow(4, 11, "Goodbye.");
  tbw.Display();           // 6 x 20, with title and "Hello/Goodbye"

  return EXIT_SUCCESS;
}
```

Figure 24.9   (usewin.C) An example program using the **Window** class hierarchy.

```
$$$$$
$$$$$
$$$$$

**********
*Hello.  *
*Goodbye.*
**********

****A Cute Title****
*                  *
*                  *
*      Hello.      *
*           Goodbye.*
********************
```

Figure 24.10   The output of our example program using the **Window** class hierarchy.

This allows us to represent a collection of different windows in a single data structure. One real-world use of this capability would be to keep track of all the different windows found on a single display.

Dynamic binding is closely related to polymorphism. It refers to the compiler's binding the name of an inherited function to a particular instance of the function. Consider what we want to have to happen when we invoke an operation through a pointer. That is, suppose we invoke the **Display** operation this way:

```
wptr->Display();
```

What **Display** operation do we want to call?

The answer is, it depends. If, when this call is executed, **wptr** actually points to a **Window**, then we want to call **Window::Display**. But if it instead points to a **BorderedWindow**, then we want to call **BorderedWindow::Display**. And if it points to a **TitledWindow**, we want to call **TitledWindow::Display**. Which function we want the **Display** to refer to is now *dynamic*: it depends entirely on the type of the object to which the pointer points at the time we make the call.

This seems a bit strange, since we're used to compile-time, or *static* binding. In that case, the compiler determines exactly which function to call at compile time. For example, it's not what we want in this case, but with static binding the call

```
wptr->Display();
```

would always call **Window::Display**. That's because *static* binding always works with the declared type, called the *static* type, and ignores what the type actually refers to, called the *dynamic* type. That is, static binding only cares about **wptr**'s static type, **Window**, and not its *dynamic* type, which might be **Window**, **BorderedWindow**, or **TitledWindow**.

You might get the idea that we always want dynamic binding. That's reasonable, except for one thing. There's an additional run-time cost to dynamic binding. To execute a function call like the one above, the system has to somehow determine what type the pointer is pointing to. No matter how clever the compiler writer is, this requires some cost at run time. As a result, for efficiency C++ uses static binding by default and forces us to request dynamic binding when we require it.

So when do we need dynamic binding? The one place is when we overload a function in a derived class, as with **Display**, and we invoke it through a base class reference or pointer. What we need then is a mechanism for informing the compiler that a function can be overloaded and that it therefore needs to use dynamic binding when calling that function. And that's exactly what the **virtual** we saw earlier does.

```
class Window
{
    ...
    virtual void Display();
    ...
};
```

Specifically, **virtual** tells the compiler to use dynamic binding to call the function if we are invoking the function through a pointer or reference. Once we label a member function as virtual, any function with the same prototype in a derived class is automatically virtual as well. That means we only have to put the **virtual** keyword in the base class declaration, but we are free to also put it in the derived class declaration, which we tend to do to make the program more readable.

An Example of Dynamic Binding

It's easy to wonder what all of this stuff is good for. One compelling use of polymorphism and dynamic binding arises when we want to maintain and process collections of objects that share the same base class. Figure 24.11 is a simple example. It's a new version of an earlier program to display windows. This time, however, we treat the windows as a collection. That is, we create each window and place its address in an array of pointers. Then, when we wish to display all the windows, we simply run through the array:

```
for (i = 0; i < num_windows; i++)
{
  Window *wptr = window_table[i];
  wptr->Display();
  cout << endl;
}
```

This program produces output identical to that of our previous example. But it has the big advantage that the code to display windows doesn't care about which type of window we are displaying. That gives us freedom to place whatever windows we want into the collection, even adding new types of windows. The end result is that this code is easy to extend and easy to maintain.

Figure 24.12 shows the output that results when we change **Window::Display**'s declaration so that it is not virtual. It's quite different—and not at all what we want. Removing the **virtual** turns off the dynamic binding when **Display** is called, which results in always invoking **Window::Display** and displaying whatever type of window we are pointing to as a **Window**.

Why We Need Virtual Destructors

Figure 24.13 is a main program that shows why we need virtual destructors. It is a new version of Figure 24.11 that dynamically allocates the various windows. To do that, we take advantage of a feature of **new** we have so far ignored: if we request that **new** allocate an object, it not only allocates the space we require, but also invokes a constructor to initialize it. For example, the expression

```
new Window(3, 5)
```

allocates a **Window**, initializes it with the **Window** constructor that takes two integer parameters, and returns a pointer to it.

The program in Figure 24.13 stores the allocated windows in the array **window_table**, which is declared as an array of pointers to **Window**s. As in Figure 24.11, this array winds up containing pointers to various different types of windows.

```
//
// A program using dynamic binding to display a set of windows.
//
#include <iostream.h>
#include <stdlib.h>
#include "twindow.h"

int main()
{
  Window w(3, 5);
  BorderedWindow bw(4, 10, '*');
  TitledWindow tbw("A Cute Title", 6, 20, '*');

  Window *window_table[] = {&w, &bw, &tbw};
  const int num_windows = sizeof(window_table)/sizeof(Window *);

  for (int i = 0; i < 3; i++)
    w.PutRow(i, 0, '$', 5);
  bw.PutRow(1, 1, "Hello.");
  bw.PutRow(2, 1, "Goodbye.");
  tbw.PutRow(3, 6, "Hello.");
  tbw.PutRow(4, 11, "Goodbye.");

  for (i = 0; i < num_windows; i++)
  {
    Window *wptr = window_table[i];
    wptr->Display();
    cout << endl;
  }

  return EXIT_SUCCESS;
}
```

Figure 24.11 (usewin2.C) Our window display program, rewritten to use dynamic binding.

However, since we have dynamically allocated each of these windows, we have to return their storage (and call their destructors, if any) by using **delete**.

```
delete wptr;
```

By default **delete** uses static binding. Here, that means unless we do something special, it's going to assume that it's been given a pointer to a **Window** (since that's **wptr**'s type) and it will call the **Window** destructor. That's bad, since if it really points to a **TitledWindow**, the **TitledWindow** destructor will not be called. What we really want is for **delete** to determine what type of object we are really deleting. To do that, we make the destructor for the base class virtual.

Make all base class destructors `virtual`.

```
$$$$$
$$$$$
$$$$$


Hello.
Goodbye.




     Hello.
          Goodbye.
```

Figure 24.12   The output of our example program using the **Window** class hierarchy when **Display** is not declared as **virtual**.

24.4   **ABSTRACT BASE CLASSES**

Another example where polymorpism and dynamic binding come in quite handy is in implementing computer drawing systems (for pictures, CAD diagrams, and the like). These systems place on the screen graphic images that can be manipulated by the user— moved, rotated, scaled, displayed, filled, and many more. Even the simplest graphics drawing system has many special graphic objects it can deal with: points, lines, squares, rectangles, circles, and polygons. Regardless of which objects they provide, however, all of them need to provide the same basic image/graphics operations.

One common approach to implementing such a system is to create a class for each type of graphic object and to have each class provide the customized functions for those objects. Figure 24.14 shows how a few of the more common of these classes could quite naturally be represented as a hierarchy. In this simple shape hierarchy, we have a base class, **Shape**, and three specific shapes we derive from it: **Square**, **Triangle**, and **Line**.

We assume that when we create any of these objects, we specify a particular coordinate where the object resides, plus additional information particular to each object (such as the length of a square's side, the triangle's height, and the line's length). Since every shape will have a location, we capture this generalization in **Shape**, which declares the variables **row** and **column** to hold the location, and operations **Row** and **Column** to return their value. We also assume that every one of the more specific shapes (and any additional shapes we might add later) will provide a **Draw** operation, which simply displays the object on the standard output. That means **Shape** needs to provide a prototype for a **Draw** operation and declare it as a **virtual** function. If it didn't, we couldn't have collections of different **Shape**s as we had collections of different **Windows**.

```
//
// A program using dynamic binding to display a set of
// dynamic allocated windows.
//
#include <iostream.h>
#include <stdlib.h>
#include "twindow.h"

int main()
{
  const int num_windows = 3;
  Window *window_table[num_windows];

  window_table[0] = new Window(3, 5);
  window_table[1] = new BorderedWindow(4, 10, '*');
  window_table[2] = new TitledWindow("A Cute Title", 6, 20, '*');

  for (int i = 0; i < 3; i++)
    window_table[0]->PutRow(i, 0, '$', 5);
  window_table[1]->PutRow(1, 1, "Hello.");
  window_table[1]->PutRow(2, 1, "Goodbye.");
  window_table[2]->PutRow(3, 6, "Hello.");
  window_table[2]->PutRow(4, 11, "Goodbye.");

  for (i = 0; i < num_windows; i++)
  {
    Window *wptr = window_table[i];
    wptr->Display();
    cout << endl;
    delete wptr;
  }

  return EXIT_SUCCESS;
}
```

Figure 24.13 (usewin3.C) Our window display program, rewritten to dynamically allocate the windows it displays.

Actually, in some ways, **Shape** is strange. After all, in a real drawing system, there really isn't anything as amorphous as a "shape." There are only concrete kinds of shapes: our graphic images are made up of squares or triangles or lines. Yet the **Shape** class serves two important purposes in our design. We need it as a placeholder for data, such as its row/column location, that all of our more specific shapes require. And we need to declare as **virtual** those operations that we expect derived classes to supply without necessarily being able to provide a sensible default implementation.

As a result, we would like **Shape** to have two additional properties. One is that we don't want users to ever be able to create an instance of a **Shape**; it serves a valuable role

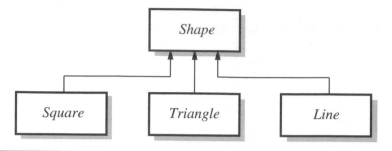

Figure 24.14 A hierarchy of shape classes.

but only in terms of its ability to aid our definitions of more specific classes. Technically speaking, this means we want **Shape** to be an *abstract* class: it serves solely to capture an abstraction of what shapes are all about, but it's not ever intended to be instantiated. The other property is to have **Shape** be able to specify that classes derived from it must provide certain operations. That is, we want to treat **Shape** as a specification, so that every class that inherits from **Shape** must provide a **Draw** operation.

We can get both properties in one fell swoop: any class that contains at least one pure virtual function is an abstract class. A pure virtual function is a virtual function with an **= 0** used to terminate its declaration (it appears after the prototype and before the trailing semicolon). Any derived class must provide an implementation for all of the pure virtual functions it inherits, or it is automatically an abstract class itself.

Figure 24.15 declares the **Shape** class. Within the **Shape** class declaration, **Draw** is declared pure virtual:

```
virtual void Draw() = 0;
```

One consequence of this is that it now becomes illegal to try to create an instance of **Shape**, even though **Shape** provides a constructor.

```
Shape s(10, 20);
```

That constructor, however, is there solely to be invoked by derived class constructors to initialize the **Shape** base class part of their object. However, it is perfectly legal to declare a pointer to an abstract class and then set it up to point to instances of derived classes. Another consequence is that any class that is derived from **Shape**, such as **Square**, **Triangle**, or **Line**, must define a **Draw** function (or users won't be able to create instances of those classes).

Figure 24.16 contains the definition for the **Square** class, Figure 24.17 contains the definition for the **Triangle** class, and Figure 24.18 contains the definition of the **Line** class. In all of these the **Draw** function simply writes the type of object, any internal variables, and its row/column location.[3]

---

[3] In the chapter's case study, we will extend these objects to actually draw themselves within the **Window**s we saw previously.

```
//
// Complete definition of the Shape abstract class.
//
#if !defined(CLASS_SHAPE)
#define CLASS_SHAPE

class Shape
{
  public:
    Shape(int init_x, int init_y);

    virtual void Draw() = 0;        // Every shape must supply a draw!
    int Row() const;                // Row shape is in.
    int Column() const;             // Column shape is in.

  private:
    int row, column;                // Location of shape.
};

inline Shape::Shape(int init_r, int init_c)
  : row(init_r), column(init_c)
  {}

inline int Shape::Row() const
  { return row; }
inline int Shape::Column() const
  { return column; }
#endif
```

Figure 24.15 (shape.h) The definition of the **Shape** class.

Figure 24.19 shows how we can have an array of **Shape**s to represent a composite image. We use exactly the same technique we used in the **Windows** example. We have an array of pointers to **Shape**, initialize it to point to individual, concrete types of shapes, and then run through it invoking the draw function on whatever shapes are contained there. Our program has one of each type of shape and produces this output:

```
Square[r=3,c=5,length=10]
Triangle[r=4,c=6,height=5]
Line[r=7,c=3,length=2,direction=2]
```

24.5   THE INPUT/OUTPUT HIERARCHY

The C++ I/O library really takes advantage of the power of object-oriented programming, including inheritance.

```
//
// Complete definition of Square class.
//
#include "shape.h"

class Square : public Shape
{
  public:
    Square(int init_r, int init_c, int init_len);
    virtual void Draw();

  private:
    int side_length;
};

inline Square::Square(int init_r, int init_c, int init_len)
  : Shape(init_r, init_c), side_length(init_len) {}

inline void Square::Draw()
  { cout << "Square[r=" << Row() << ",c=" << Column()
         << ",length=" << side_length << "]"; }
```

Figure 24.16 (square.h) The definition of the **Square** class.

```
//
// Complete definition of the Triangle class.
//
#include "shape.h"

class Triangle : public Shape
{
  public:
    Triangle(int init_r, int init_c, int init_height);
    virtual void Draw();

  private:
    int height;
};

inline Triangle::Triangle(int init_r, int init_c, int init_height)
  : Shape(init_r, init_c), height(init_height) {}

inline void Triangle::Draw()
  { cout << "Triangle[r=" << Row() << ",c=" << Column()
         << ",height=" << height << "]"; }
```

Figure 24.17 (triangle.h) The definition of the **Triangle** class.

```
//
// Complete definition of the Line class.
//
#include "shape.h"

class Line : public Shape
{
  public:
    enum Direction {up, down, left, right};

    Line(int init_r, int init_c, int init_length, Direction init_dir);
    virtual void Draw();

  private:
    int        length;
    Direction direction;
};

inline Line::Line(int init_r, int init_c,
                  int init_length, Direction init_dir)
  : Shape(init_r, init_c), length(init_length), direction(init_dir) {}

inline void Line::Draw()
  { cout << "Line[r=" << Row() << ",c="<< Column()
         << ",length=" << length
         << ",direction=" << (unsigned int) direction << "]"; }
```

Figure 24.18   (line.h) The definition of the **Line** class.

We have already seen that we use operations on the classes **istream** and **ostream** to perform input and output, respectively. It turns out that we manipulate files using the special classes **ifstream** for input files and **ofstream** for output files. These classes inherit from the **istream** and **ostream** classes, which in turn inherit from a common "I/O stream" class **ios**. Figure 24.20 shows what this hierarchy looks like.

As a result, our programs are using *objects* for input files and for output files. One thing that's especially nice is that their constructors and destructors take care of opening and closing the files for us. In addition, since file objects inherit from the general stream objects, any code we write to work with streams automatically works for files as well.

Figure 24.21 shows how we can use file classes to write a simple program to copy one file to another. The program takes the names of the files from the command line, so

filecopy *file1 file2*

copies from *file1* into *file2*. The program is superficially similar to the C version. First we open *file1* for reading and then *file2* for writing. If both opens succeed, we continue and copy *file1* into *file2*, one character at a time. But that's where the similarity with C ends and the object-oriented features of C++ shine.

```
//
// Main program using the various shapes.
//
#include <iostream.h>
#include <stdlib.h>

#include "square.h"
#include "triangle.h"
#include "line.h"

int main()
{
  Square s(3, 5, 10);            // square s of length 10, at 3,5
  Triangle t(4, 6, 5);           // triangle t of height 5 at 4,6
  Line l(7, 3, 2, Line::left);   // line l of length 2, left, at 7,3

  Shape *shape_table[] = {&s, &t, &l};
  const int numShapes = sizeof(shape_table)/sizeof(Shape *);

  for (int i = 0; i < numShapes; i++)
  {
    shape_table[i]->Draw();
    cout << endl;
  }

  return EXIT_SUCCESS;
}
```

Figure 24.19   (usedraw.C)   A program that uses the **Shape** hierarchy.

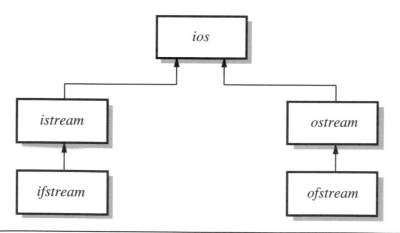

Figure 24.20   Part of the IOStreams library class hierarchy.

```
//
// Copy one file to another.  The first argument is name of the
// source file, the second argument is the name of the destination.
//
#include <iostream.h>           // For basic I/O
#include <fstream.h>            // For file I/O
#include <stdlib.h>

inline int usageError(const char *prog, const char *args)
  { cerr << "Usage: " << prog << " " << args << endl;
    return EXIT_FAILURE; }

inline int openError(const char *fname, const char *access)
  { cerr << "Can't open " << fname << " for " << access << endl;
    return EXIT_FAILURE; }

int main(int argc, char *argv[])
{
  int copyFile(istream& in, ostream& out);

  int   status;

  if (argc > 3)
    status = usageError(argv[0], "source-file destination-file");
  else if (argc == 1)                      // one arg--copy stdin to stdout
    status = copyFile(cin, cout);
  else if (argc > 1)
  {
    ifstream src(argv[1]);

    if (!src)
      status = openError(argv[1], "reading");
    else if (argc == 2)
      status = copyFile(src, cout);    // two arg--copy file to stdout
    else
    {
      ofstream dst(argv[2]);        // open output file

      status = !dst ? openError(argv[2], "writing") : copyFile(src, dst);
    }
  }
  return status;
}

int copyFile(istream& in, ostream& out)
{
  for (char ch; in.get(ch); out.put(ch))
    ;
  return EXIT_SUCCESS;
}
```

Figure 24.21   (filecopy.C) Copy from one file to another.

We open a file for reading by giving its name along with the variable that we declare to be of type **ifstream**:

```
ifstream src(argv[1]);
```

This declares **src** to be an **ifstream** and also attempts to open the file named in **argv[1]** for reading. It does that by invoking the constructor for an **ifstream**, which takes as its argument the name of the file to open. We determine whether the open succeeded by testing **src**:

```
if (!src)
  openError(argv[1], "reading");
```

And we do a similar declaration and test for **dst**:

```
ofstream dst(argv[2]);

if (!dst)
  openError(argv[2], "writing");
```

src and **dst** are objects of the **ifstream** or **ofstream** classes, yet the **if** statement tests **src** and **dst** with logical not. This shouldn't work: logical not is defined only for built-in types. For this to work the **!** operator must be overloaded for the stream classes. Check your own versions of iostream to see how this operator is defined.

We're careful to attempt to open the second file for writing only if we can open the first for reading. That way we don't wipe out an existing file if the source file can't be opened.

The program uses a function, **copyFile**, to handle the file copying. It takes references to an **istream** and an **ostream** as its parameters. This allows us to pass instances of that class or any of its derived classes. We take advantage of that by passing **cin** and **cout** when the program is given no files to copy:

```
status = copyFile(cin, cout);
```

And we pass in **src** and **dst** (which are objects of type **ifstream** and **ofstream**, respectively) when the user has supplied us with file names:

```
status = copyFile(src, dst);
```

The function reads a character at a time from **src** and writes it to **dst**, using the **get** and **put** operations. Because of inheritance, we can apply **get** and **put** to any stream or file object.

24.6   CASE STUDY—A SIMPLE TEXT-BASED DRAWING LIBRARY

This section is optional!

We conclude this chapter by extending our shape classes to actually draw objects in windows. Figure 24.22 is an example window containing a line, a triangle, and a square.

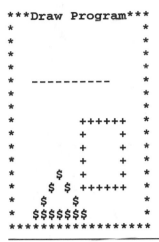

```
***Draw Program***
*                 *
*                 *
*                 *
*                 *
*   ----------    *
*                 *
*                 *
*       ++++++    *
*       +    +    *
*       +    +    *
*       +    +    *
*    $  +    +    *
*    $ $ ++++++   *
*    $   $        *
*   $$$$$$$       *
*****************
```

Figure 24.22   An example window filled in by using the drawing library.

Figure 24.23 shows the **Shape** class that supports this extension. It now has two additional fields: the **Window** into which shapes will be drawn and the character that should be used to draw them. When we create a shape, we tie it to a window and put it in a specific place in that window. Since a particular shape in our simple design will always be tied to a particular window, we store in the object a reference to the window rather than a pointer. As before, we don't want **protected** data, so we provide accessor functions for the window, the location, and the drawing character.

We have also extended **Shape** to provide a bit more functionality. Besides **Draw**, we now also have **Erase** and **Move** functions. **Erase** is pure virtual, so we are requiring each particular type of **Shape** to provide its own **Erase**. **Move**, however, is implemented as part of **Shape**: it erases the object, changes its location internally, and redraws it. Since **Erase** and **Move** are **virtual**, when we invoke them on an object from the inherited **Move**, we call the appropriate **Erase** and **Move** for our particular type of object. Our **Move** can be thought of as a framework: erase, update, and move, with the details of erasing and moving filled in by the derived class.

Figure 24.24 contains our **Square** class, which can still be completely defined with inline operations. It must provide **Draw** and **Erase** operations specific to a **Square**. These operations are actually very similar: they both involve drawing a square; it's just that we erase a **Square** by drawing a **Square** out of blanks. As a result, we provide a private **PlaceSquare** operation that is given a **Window** and a drawing character and draws a square in that window using that character. It uses **PutRow** and **PutColumn** to actually draw into the **Window**. We can then trivially implement **Draw** and **Erase** on top of **PlaceSquare**.

Our other derived classes all share the same architecture, with a private function to do the actual drawing and public **Draw** and **Erase** functions implemented on top

```
//
// Complete definition of the Shape abstract class.
//
#if !defined(CLASS_SHAPE)
#define CLASS_SHAPE
#include "window.h"

class Shape
{
  public:
    Shape(Window& init_w, char init_marker, int init_x, int init_y);

    virtual void Draw() = 0;        // Every shape must supply a draw!
    virtual void Erase() = 0;       // Every shape must supply an erase!

    void Move(int xoff, int yoff);  // Move supplied by default.

  protected:
    int Row() const;                // Row location.
    int Column() const;             // Column location
    char Marker() const;            // Marker
    Window& DrawWindow() const;     // Drawing Window

  private:
    int row, column;                // Location in Window
    Window &w;                      // Window object is in
    char marker;                    // Character used to write object
};

inline Shape::Shape(Window &init_w, char init_m, int init_r, int init_c)
  : marker(init_m), w(init_w), row(init_r), column(init_c)
  {}

inline int Shape::Row() const
  { return row; }
inline int Shape::Column() const
  { return column; }
inline char Shape::Marker() const
  { return marker; }
inline Window& Shape::DrawWindow() const
  { return w; }

inline void Shape::Move(int rowoff, int coloff)
  {
    this->Erase();
    row += rowoff;
    column += coloff;
    this->Draw();
  }
#endif
```

Figure 24.23   (Draw/shape.h) An expanded version of our **Shape** class.

```
//
// Complete definition of Square class.
//
#include "shape.h"

class Square : public Shape
{
  public:
    Square(Window& init_w, char init_m,
           int init_r, int init_c, int init_len);
    virtual void Draw();
    virtual void Erase();

  private:
    void PlaceSquare(Window& w, char m);

    int side_length;
};

inline Square::Square(Window& init_w, char init_m,
                      int init_r, int init_c, int init_len)
  : Shape(init_w, init_m, init_r, init_c), side_length(init_len)
  {}

inline void Square::PlaceSquare(Window& w, char drawchar)
  {
    w.PutRow(Row(), Column(), drawchar, side_length);
    w.PutRow(Row() + side_length - 1, Column(),
             drawchar, side_length);
    w.PutColumn(Row(), Column(), drawchar, side_length);
    w.PutColumn(Row(), Column() + side_length - 1,
                drawchar, side_length);
  }

inline void Square::Draw()
  { PlaceSquare(DrawWindow(), Marker()); }

inline void Square::Erase()
  { PlaceSquare(DrawWindow(), ' '); }
```

Figure 24.24 (Draw/square.h) An expanded version of our **Square** class.

of them. Figure 24.25 is the declaration of the **Triangle** class, along with its inline operations; Figure 24.26 is its private drawing function, which contains a loop and therefore generally can't be inlined. Figure 24.27 contains our new implementation of the **Line** class.

Finally, Figure 24.28 is an example program that creates a collection of **Shapes**, places them into the **Window**, and then moves them to a new location.

```
//
// Triangle class declaration and definitions of inline operations.
//
#include "shape.h"

class Triangle : public Shape
{
  public:
    Triangle(Window& init_w, char init_m,
             int init_r, int init_c, int init_height);
    virtual void Draw();
    virtual void Erase();

  private:
    void PlaceTriangle(Window &w, char drawchar);

    int height;
};

inline Triangle::Triangle(Window& init_w, char init_m,
                          int init_r, int init_c, int init_height)
  : Shape(init_w, init_m, init_r, init_c), height(init_height)
  {}

inline void Triangle::Draw()
  { PlaceTriangle(DrawWindow(), Marker()); }

inline void Triangle::Erase()
  { PlaceTriangle(DrawWindow(), ' '); }
```

Figure 24.25   (Draw/triangle.h)   An expanded version of our **Triangle** class.

SUMMARY

- C++ lets us define classes that are derived from other classes. These derived classes automatically inherit instance data and member functions from their base classes.

- We are allowed to have **protected** data and operations, which are accessible only by the current class and those classes derived from it. However, we generally avoid using **protected** data.

- We are allowed to redefine inherited functions in the derived class. However, we should do so only if they have been declared **virtual**.

- **virtual** functions are dynamically bound when called through a pointer or reference. All other calls are statically bound.

```
//
// Non-inlinable functions in Triangle class.
//
#include "triangle.h"

void Triangle::PlaceTriangle(Window &w, char drawchar)
{
  w.PutRow(Row(), Column(), drawchar);
  for (int i = 1; i < height; i++)
  {
    w.PutRow(Row() + i, Column() - i, drawchar);
    w.PutRow(Row() + i, Column() + i, drawchar);
  }
  w.PutRow(Row() + height - 1, Column() - height + 1,
        drawchar, height * 2 - 1);
}
```

Figure 24.26 (Draw/triangle.C) The non-inlinable **Triangle** operations.

■ An abstract class is a class that serves to hold default data and operations and to specify required operations in derived class, but is itself never meant to be instantiated. We obtain an abstract class by declaring one or more of its operations as pure virtual.

EXERCISES

24–1 Compile and run the programs in this chapter.

24–2 What happens when we execute Figure 24.11 if we eliminate the **virtual** from our **Display** function's declaration?

24–3 Extend our **Window** class to provide operations to **Fill** the window and to **Fill** a box within the window with a particular character.

24–4 Extend the **Window** class to provide a general **Put** operation. The **Put** operation is like **PutRow**, but also takes two additional arguments: a row increment and a column increment. After **Put** writes each character, it updates its idea of the current row and column by the row and column increments. **Put** is now powerful enough it can be used for diagonal, horizontal, or vertical lines. Provide **Put** for a single character written N times, and **Put** for a **String**.

24–5 Use the **Put** operation defined in the previous exercise to reimplement our earlier **PutRow** and **PutColumn** operations. Modify the **Triangle** drawing routine to use the **Put** written in the earlier exercise. Also, modify **Line** so that it uses **Put** to provide lines drawn as diagonals.

24–6 Imagine we want to have filled and unfilled objects. For example, a square or triangle could have the outside lines drawn with one character and its inner contents drawn with

```
//
// Complete definition of the Line class.
//
#include "shape.h"

class Line : public Shape
{
  public:
    enum Direction {up, down, left, right};

    Line(Window& init_w, char init_m,
         int init_r, int init_c, int init_length, Direction init_dir);
    virtual void Draw();
    virtual void Erase();

  private:
    void PlaceLine(Window& w, char drawchar);

    int length;
    Direction direction;
};

inline Line::Line(Window &init_w, char init_m, int init_r, int init_c,
                  int init_length, Direction init_dir)
  : Shape(init_w, init_m, init_r, init_c),
    length(init_length), direction(init_dir)
  {}

inline void Line::PlaceLine(Window &w, char drawchar)
{
  switch (direction)
  {
    case up:
      w.PutColumn(Row() - length + 1, Column(), drawchar, length);
      break;
    case down:
      w.PutColumn(Row(), Column(), drawchar, length);
      break;
    case left:
      w.PutRow(Row(), Column() - length + 1, drawchar, length);
      break;
    case right:
      w.PutRow(Row(), Column(), drawchar, length);
      break;
  }
}

inline void Line::Draw()
  { PlaceLine(DrawWindow(), Marker()); }
inline void Line::Erase()
  { PlaceLine(DrawWindow(), ' '); }
```

Figure 24.27   (Draw/line.h) An expanded version of our **Line** class.

```
//
// Main program using the various shapes.
//
#include <iostream.h>
#include <stdlib.h>

#include "twindow.h"
#include "square.h"
#include "line.h"
#include "triangle.h"

int main()
{
  TitledWindow tbw("Draw Program", 17, 18, '*');

  // Square in window tbw, drawn with '+', at 8, 9, sides of length 6
  Square s(tbw, '+', 8, 9, 6);
  // Line in window tbw, drawn with '-' at 5, 3, length 10, to the right
  Line l(tbw, '-', 5, 3, 10, Line::right);
  // Triangle in window tbw, drawn with '$' at 12, 6, height 4
  Triangle t(tbw, '$', 12, 6, 4);

  Shape *shape_table[] = {&s, &l, &t};
  const int numShapes = sizeof(shape_table)/sizeof(Shape *);

  for (int i = 0; i < numShapes; i++)
    shape_table[i]->Draw();        // put shapes in window
  tbw.Display();                   // actually display window

  for (int j = 0; j < numShapes; j++)
    shape_table[j]->Move(-2,-2);   // move shapes 2 places up and left
  tbw.Display();                   // display window again

  return EXIT_SUCCESS;
}
```

Figure 24.28   (Draw/usedraw.C) A program that draws several shapes into a **Window**.

another character. Add a **FilledObject** class to the **Shape** hierarchy that takes care of the details of filling (such as storing the character used to **Fill** an object).

24–7   Update our **Shape** hierarchy to include **Rectangle**s, **Point**s, and **Diamond**s.

Allow filled or unfilled versions of these objects.

| Code | 24–8   Define a **List** class that maintains an unsorted linked list of integers. It should provide **Insert**, **Delete**, **Find**, **Sort**, **Length**, and **Nth** operations.

Now define a **SortedList** class that's derived from **List** but maintains the list in sorted order. Which operations need to be redefined?

Build

24–9 Write a class hierarchy for a simple banking system. There should be an abstract base class **BankAccount** with methods such as **Deposit** and **Withdraw**. Then create new concrete classes **CheckingAccount** and **SavingsAccount** derived from **BankAccount**.

A LIBRARY DETAILS

There are a variety of different library functions and header files that come with any ANSI-C compiler. Throughout the text we've discussed the most important of these. This appendix provides pointers to these earlier discussions and discusses the details of the header files and library functions we ignored.

A.1 THE STANDARD HEADER FILES

Table A.1 lists the header files in the standard library, their purpose, and where, if anywhere, we discuss them in the text. Each header file provides prototypes for a different set of library functions, as well as definitions of other useful macros and types. Most systems have all of these header files in a standard location, and there's usually nothing to prevent you from examining them. You'll find doing so quite helpful when you need to know exactly what types a particular library function takes or returns or when you are curious about how a particular constant or type is defined.

A.2 ERROR HANDLING

The header file errno.h contains the symbolic names and values for a global integer **errno** that's set when various library functions fail. These library functions indicate errors in two ways: they set **errno** to a value that indicates what type of error occurred, and they return a failure indication, such as -1. That means that when a function fails, we can test **errno**'s value and write an appropriate error message.

There are a couple of cautions. Library functions don't automatically set **errno** to zero (no error), so we need to to do that ourselves before calling them. Furthermore, not all library functions set **errno**: only the functions in the math library and a few others.

Figure A.1 provides an example that uses **errno** to determine whether the natural logarithm function (**log**) succeeded or failed. The next section describes more about the particular error codes that the math library functions, such as **log**, can return.

There are two functions from the standard libraries that are often useful in error handling. The string library provides **strerror**.

```
char *strerror(int errnum);
```

HEADER FILE	ITS USE	WHERE DESCRIBED
assert.h	debugging aid	Chapter 15
ctype.h	character-testing macros	Chapter 5
errno.h	error handling	Appendix A
float.h	floating point ranges	Chapter 4
limits.h	integral ranges	Chapters 4 and 5
locale.h	locales	Appendix A
math.h	mathematical functions	Chapter 4, Appendix A
setjmp.h	nonlocal gotos	Appendix A
signal.h	interrupt handling	Appendix A
stdlib.h	generally useful functions	Chapters 1 and 10, Appendix A
stdarg.h	variable arguments	Chapter 16
string.h	string manipulation	Chapters 10 and 11
stddef.h	useful types and constants	Chapter 10, Appendix A
stdio.h	performing I/O	Chapter 1 through Chapter 5, Chapter 19, Appendix A
time.h	dealing with time	Appendix A

Table A.1   The standard header files.

```
/*
 * A program to check for errors that uses the math routines.
 */
#include <stdio.h>
#include <stdlib.h>
#include <math.h>
#include <errno.h>

int main(void)
{
  double  d, x;

  while (printf("Value: "), scanf("%lf", &x) == 1)
  {
    errno = 0;
    d = log(x);
    if (errno == EDOM)
      fprintf(stderr, "Domain error (bad argument) with log(%g)\n", x);
    else
      printf("log(%g) = %g\n", x, d);
  }

  return EXIT_SUCCESS;
}
```

Figure A.1   (uselog.c) An example using **errno**.

strerror returns a pointer to a string containing an *implementation-defined* error message corresponding to its integer parameter, normally **errno**. The standard I/O library provides **perror**.

```
void perror(const char *string)
```

It writes its string parameter to the standard error output (**stderr**), along with a message describing the most recent system error (corresponding to the global variable **errno**). The output format is:

> *string*: *system error message*

It terminates its output with a newline.

A.3   THE MATH LIBRARY

Chapter 4 discussed most of the functions in the math library. To use them, we saw that we had to include math.h and request that the math library be linked with our program. What we haven't discussed is the errors these functions can return. We also skipped a pair of math library functions that require an additional pointer argument.

Many of the math routines require that their argument be in a certain range. If an argument is out of the specified range, the math routine sets the global variable **errno** to **EDOM** (defined in errno.h) and returns an *implementation-defined* value. The call **log(-1)** is a domain error, since the natural log of a negative number isn't defined.

If the value computed by a math library function is outside the range that can be represented as a **double**, the function sets **errno** to **ERANGE**. In addition, on underflow it returns a 0.0, and on overflow it returns **HUGE_VAL** (a constant defined in math.h) with its sign set correctly. The call **exp(x)** with a large enough **x** will result in a range error.

The two math library functions we skipped are **frexp** and **modf**. **frexp** breaks the floating point value **val** into a *normalized* fraction and an integer power of 2.

```
double frexp(double val, int *exp);
```

It stores the power of 2 in the location pointed to by **exp**. If **val** is zero, it sets both the fraction and the power of 2 to zero. A *normalized* fraction means that the leading bit is 1. That is, the fraction is in the range $[\frac{1}{2}, 1)$ and is exactly zero if **val** is zero. Figure A.2 is an example program using **frexp**. For the input

```
-123 123 0.5 2 4.0 78.0
```

it produces the output:

```
-123.000000 = -0.960938 x 2^7
 123.000000 =  0.960938 x 2^7
   0.500000 =  0.500000 x 2^0
   2.000000 =  0.500000 x 2^2
   4.000000 =  0.500000 x 2^3
  78.000000 =  0.609375 x 2^7
```

```
/*
 * Using the frexp math library function.
 */
#include <stdio.h>
#include <stdlib.h>
#include <math.h>

int main()
{
  int     exp;
  double  val, x;

  while (printf("Value: "), scanf("%lf", &val) == 1)
  {
    x = frexp(val, &exp);
    printf("%f = %f x 2^%i\n", val, x, exp);
  }

  return EXIT_SUCCESS;
}
```

Figure A.2   (usefrexp.c)   An example program using **frexp**.

The other math library function, **modf**, returns the integer and fractional parts of its first parameter.

```
double modf(double val, double *iptr);
```

It stores the integer part as a **double** in the location pointed to by **iptr**. And it returns the fractional part as the value of the function. Both ***iptr** and the value returned from the function will have the same sign—the sign of **val**.

A.4   THE STRING LIBRARY

Chapter 10 describes all of the string library functions for manipulating byte arrays, and Chapter 11 describes almost all of the library functions for manipulating null-terminated character strings. As we saw earlier, we need to include string.h to use any of these functions.

There are only a few functions we haven't discussed. **strcoll** compares the two strings **s1** and **s2** and returns an **int** with the same interpretation as for **strcmp**.

```
int strcoll(const char *s1, const char *s2);
```

strcoll differs from **strcmp** in that it bases the comparison on the collating sequence in the current locale (discussed later in this appendix). Since many compilers support only the **"C"** locale, these two functions are often identical.

strxfrm transforms up to **n** characters from string **s2** into the space pointed to by **s1**.

```
size_t strxfrm(char *s1, const char *s2, size_t n);
```

The transformation depends on the current locale. Since many compilers support only the **"C"** locale, **strxfrm** is often identical to **strncpy**. It returns the same value as does **strncpy**.

strtok is a complex function used to break up a string into *tokens*.

```
char *strtok(char *s1, const char *s2);
```

Tokens are groups of characters in **s1** terminated by any of the characters in **s2**. When **strtok** is first called, it returns a pointer to the first token in **s1** and places a null character at the end of the token (actually modifying **s1**). On subsequent calls, token scanning begins at the place it left off. Second and further calls to **strtok** should pass the null pointer as the first argument. The second argument need not be the same between calls. **strtok** returns a null pointer when there are no more tokens in **s1**.

strtok has many uses. One is to simplify what would otherwise be a rather difficult job: breaking an input line into individual numbers. Suppose that we have a series of input lines, each consisting of a name and zero or more scores, and that we want to break out the name, sum up the scores, and print a total for the name. This task is surprisingly messy for **scanf**, since we don't know how many values appear on each line. Figure A.3 is a program that does this task using **strtok**. With this input:

```
Miller, Larry 89 123
Grant, Rita 105 88 60 70
Quilici, Alex 12 55 23 123 87
Borromeo, Daphne 84 20 6
Cohen, Danny 61 8 9
```

it generates this output:

Name	N	Sum
Miller, Larry	2	212
Grant, Rita	4	323
Quilici, Alex	5	300
Borromeo, Daphne	3	110
Cohen, Danny	3	78

A.5   THE STANDARD C LIBRARY

The standard C library contains a set of macros and function declarations for a hodge-podge collection of generally useful functions that don't seem to fit well in other libraries. We've already examined some of these functions. Chapter 10 presented its memory management functions, and Chapter 17 discussed its generic searching and sorting functions. However, there are also string conversion functions, random number generators, functions for interfacing with the environment, and functions for manipulating multibyte

```
/*
 * Break a line into individual integral values.   The input file
 * format is (0 or more values on each line):
 *     Last-Name    First-Name    n1   n2   n3 ...
 */
#include <stdio.h>
#include <stdlib.h>
#include <string.h>
#include <ctype.h>

#define  MAX     256                  /* max input line length */
#define  SEP     " \t"                 /* blank or tab--for strtok */

int main(void)
{
  int       getline(char *buf, int max);
  int       count;                    /* number of values on this line */
  long      lno = 0;                  /* current line number */
  long      sum;                      /* total for this line */
  char      line[MAX];                /* current line */
  char      *p;                       /* token pointer from strtok */

  puts("Name                    N             Sum");
  while (getline(line, MAX) != -1)
  {
    lno++;
    if ((p = strtok(line, SEP)) != NULL)
    {
      printf("%s ", p);               /* print last name if there */
      if ((p = strtok(NULL, SEP)) != NULL)
      {
        printf("%s\t", p);            /* print first name if there */
        sum = count = 0;              /* sum and values for this line */
        while ((p = strtok(NULL, SEP)) != NULL)
          if (isdigit(*p) || *p == '-'|| *p == '+')
          {
            count++;
            sum += atol(p);           /* atol is a library function */
          }
          else
            fprintf(stderr, "Line %li: %s not a number\n", lno, p);
        printf("%4i\t%10li\n", count, sum);
      }
      else
        fprintf(stderr, "Line %li: no name found\n", lno);
    }
  }

  return EXIT_SUCCESS;
}
```

Figure A.3   (strtok.c)   Using **strtok** to parse simple input lines.

and wide characters. As we saw earlier, we need to include the header file stdlib.h to use any of these functions. That file also defines the macros and types listed in Table A.2.

String Conversion

The standard library provides two sets of string conversion functions. The first set takes a string **s** and converts it to a number.

```
double atof(const char *s);
int    atoi(const char *s);
long   atol(const char *s);
```

atof (ASCII to floating point number) returns the value of the string **s** converted to a **double**. The results are undefined if the conversion can't occur. **atoi** and **atol** are similar, but they convert **s** to an **int** or **long**, respectively. All assume that **s** contains a set of characters representing an appropriate base 10 value.

The other set allows us to determine whether errors took place and to handle values in other bases.

```
double strtod(const char *s, char **endp);
long   strtol(const char *s, char **endp, int base);
unsigned long strtoul(const char *s, char **endp, int base);
```

strtod converts the string **s** to a **double**, just like **scanf** using the **%g** format. That is, it skips leading space characters (any character for which **isspace** is true) then reads an optional sign (+ or −), digits, an optional decimal point followed by more digits, and an optional exponent (letter 'e' or 'E') followed by a signed integer. It stops converting on the first character that's not part of a floating point number. If **endp** is not **NULL**, it points to this character.

strtod returns the converted number; if it encounters an unrecognized character before the first digit, it returns a zero. If conversion causes overflow, it returns **HUGE_VAL** with the correct sign. If the conversion causes underflow, it returns zero. On either overflow or underflow, it sets **errno** to **ERANGE**.

strtol and **strtoul** convert the string **s** to a **long** or **unsigned long**, respectively. Both skip leading space characters (any character for which **isspace** is true) and then expect an optional sign (+ or −) followed by digits. Both stop converting on the first character that cannot be part of a signed **long**. If **endp** is not **NULL**, it points to this character.

Both of these functions use **base** as a base of conversion. Valid values are 0, or 2 through 36. For a **base** of 0, a base 10 integer is assumed, base 8 if there is a leading **0**, or base 16 if there is a leading **0x** or **0X**. For **base** greater than 10, the letters 'a' through 'z' (or 'A' through 'Z') represent the values 10 through 35, respectively. Any character that is greater than or equal to **base** terminates conversion. If **base** is 16, a leading "0x" or "0X" is allowed.

Both functions return the converted value or zero if the first nonspace character cannot be part of a number. If conversion causes overflow, they both set **errno** to **ERANGE**, and **strtol** returns **LONG_MAX** or **LONG_MIN** and **strolul** returns **ULONG_MAX** or zero, as appropriate.

Macro or Type	Function
size_t	type returned by **sizeof**
wchar_t	type to hold a wide or multibyte character
div_t	type of structure returned by **div**
ldiv_t	type of structure returned by **ldiv**
RAND_MAX	maximum value returned from **rand**
NULL	the null pointer
EXIT_FAILURE	argument for **exit** indicating failed return
EXIT_SUCCESS	argument for **exit** indicating successful return
MB_CUR_MAX	number of bytes in a multibyte character

Table A.2   The macros and types defined in stdlib.h.

Random Number Generation

There are two functions that deal with random numbers, **rand** and **srand**.

```
int rand(void);
void srand(unsigned seed);
```

rand returns a random number in the range 0 to **RAND_MAX**. We often use **rand() % n** to obtain a random number between 0 and $n-1$. **srand** "seeds" the random number generator. Calling a sequence of **rand**s after **srand** with the same seed produces the same sequence of random numbers. We can use the **time** function (discussed later in this appendix) to produce a unique seed.

Environment Communication

There are several functions we can use to communicate with a program's environment. The first two, **exit** and **abort**, terminate our program, although they do it in very different ways.

```
void exit(int status);
void abort(void);
```

exit returns **status** to the calling environment and does not return to its caller. An exit status of **EXIT_SUCCESS** (or 0) implies successful termination; **EXIT_FAILURE** implies unsuccessful termination. Other return values are *implementation defined*.

Before terminating the program, **exit** does several tasks. First, it calls the functions registered using **atexit** (discussed below) as if they were called from the host environment. Second, it flushes all output buffers and closes all open files. And third, it removes all files created via a call to **tmpfile**.

abort generates the signal **SIGABRT**.[1] If this signal is not being caught or is ignored, the program's execution terminates with an unsuccessful exit status. The handling of open files, removing temporary files, and flushing output buffers is *implementation defined*.

The closely related function **atexit** "registers" the function pointed to by **f** to be called when the program terminates (either through a specific **return** from **main** or a call to **exit**).

```
int atexit(void (*f)(void));
```

atexit returns zero on success and non-zero otherwise. If we register a function more than once, it will be called more than once.[2] Upon termination, the functions are called in reverse order of registration. An implementation must be able to register at least 32 functions. Figure A.4 provides an example. Here's its output:

```
About to rejoin the real world.
Adios and goodbye.
```

The next function, **system**, allows us to execute operating system commands from within our C program.

```
int system(const char *s);
```

It passes the command **s** to the operating system to be executed. The return value is *implementation defined* but generally corresponds to the exit status of the called command **s**. Figure A.5 shows a simple program using **system** to execute the ls command on UNIX or the dir command on MS-DOS, both of which by default list the contents of the current directory.

Finally, **getenv** obtains the value of the environment variable corresponding to **name**.

```
char *getenv(const char *name);
```

Environment variables are stored in lists provided to the program by the host environment and are generally of the form **name=value**. The **name** argument must match a name in the environment list exactly. If it does, **getenv** returns a pointer to the corresponding value; otherwise, it returns **NULL**. The particular variables supported by an environment are *implementation defined*.

Integer Arithmetic

The standard library contains a small set of functions that perform integer arithmetic (the math library functions all perform floating point arithmetic). The first two compute absolute values:

```
int  abs(int i);
long labs(long i);
```

---

[1] This is similar to the call **raise(SIGABRT)**. We discuss these signals and how to handle them later in this appendix.

[2] This implies **exit** can be called more than once. If that happens, the result is *undefined*.

```c
#include <stdio.h>
#include <stdlib.h>
#include <stddef.h>

int main(void)
{
  void adios(void);
  void goodbye(void);

  if ((atexit(adios) != 0) || (atexit(goodbye) != 0))
    fprintf(stderr, "Can't register both functions!\n");

  return EXIT_SUCCESS;
}

void adios(void)
  { fprintf(stderr, "Adios and goodbye.\n"); }

void goodbye(void)
  { fprintf(stderr, "About to rejoin the real world.\n"); }
```

Figure A.4   (useatex.c)   An example use of **atexit**.

```c
/*
 * Using system to list a directory's contents.
 */
#include <stdio.h>
#include <stdlib.h>

#if defined(unix)
#define DIRECTORY_LISTER "/bin/ls"
#elif defined(__msdos__)
#define DIRECTORY_LISTER "dir"
#else
#error "Don't know how to list directories on this system."
#endif

int main()
{
  printf("Contents of current directory:\n");

  return system(DIRECTORY_LISTER);
}
```

Figure A.5   (usesys.c)   Using **system** to print the contents of the current directory.

abs returns the absolute value of **i**. The result is *undefined* in the rare case that the result is too large for an **int** (for example, on a 16-bit PC, the largest negative value **INT_MIN** is −32,768, while the largest positive value **INT MAX** is 32,767). **labs** is similar, except that its argument and return values are **long**s.

There are two other functions that perform integer division:

```
div_t div(int n, int d);
ldiv_t ldiv(long n, long d);
```

div computes both the quotient and remainder of **n** divided by **d**. It stores the result in a **div_t**, a structure defined to have these fields (in either order):

```
typedef struct
{
  int quot, rem;
} div_t;
```

ldiv is the same as **div**, except the arguments are **long**s and the return type is type **ldiv_t**, a structure with the same named fields as a **div_t**, but with **long** types. Their result is *undefined* if we try to divide by zero, so we need to check **d** before calling **div** or **ldiv**.

The library provides these functions for two reasons. One is that division in C produces *implementation-defined* results if one of the operands is negative (that is, **−9/5** could evaluate to −1 or −2). The result of **div(-9, 5)** always has a quotient of −1 and a remainder of −4. The other is that they provide a convenient way to obtain the quotient and remainder simultaneously, rather than with two separate arithmetic expressions.

Multibyte Characters

The C library provides a set of functions for converting back and forth between multibyte and wide characters.

```
int    mblen(const char *s, size_t n);
int    mbtowc(wchar_t *p, const char *s, size_t n);
int    wctomb(char *s, wchar_t w);
size_t mbstowcs(wchar_t *p, const char *s, size_t n);
size_t wcstombs(char *s, const wchar_t *p, size_t n);
```

Multibyte characters are of necessity *implementation defined* and depend on the current locale. Since many compilers only support the **"C"** locale, multibyte characters may not be supported on your compiler.

mblen returns the number of bytes required for the multibyte character pointed to by **s** (but only up to **n** bytes). If **s** is **NULL**, **mblen** returns non-zero or zero indicating that multibyte characters do or do not have state dependencies, respectively. If **s** points to an invalid multibyte character, **mblen** returns −1.

mbtowc ("multibyte to wide character") is similar to **mblen**, except that it stores the encoding for the multibyte character pointed to by **s** into the space pointed to by **p**.

wctomb ("wide character to multibyte") is the inverse of **mctowc**. It takes a wide character **w** and stores the corresponding multibyte character into the space pointed to by **s** (up to a maximum of **MB_CUR_MAX** characters). It returns the number of bytes required for the wide character **w**, or −1 if **w** isn't a valid multibyte character.

mbstowcs converts up to **n** multibyte characters from **s** into wide characters and stores them in **p**. Conversion stops after **n** characters or an all-zero byte. It returns the number of characters converted, not counting the null character, or −1 if **s** contains an illegal multibyte character.

wcstombs is the opposite of **mbstowcs**: it converts up to **n** wide characters into multibye characters. It returns the same value as **mbstowcs**.

A.6   THE STANDARD I/O LIBRARY

Chapters 1, 2, 3, 4, 5, and 19 have described functions in the standard input/output library. To use any of these functions, we need to include the file stdio.h, which defines the macros and types listed in Table A.3.

Removing and Renaming Files

There are a pair of functions for removing and renaming files.

```
int remove(const char *name)
int rename(const char *old_name, const char *new_name)
```

remove removes the named file, so it can no longer be accessed by the name. A call to **remove** on an open file produces *implementation-defined* behavior. **remove** returns zero on success and non-zero on error.

rename changes the name of an existing file **old_name** to the new name **new_name**. If a file with **new_name** already exists, the behavior is *implementation defined*. **rename** returns zero on success and non-zero on error. If **rename** fails, the original file with its original name is still accessible.

Temporary Files

There are pair of library functions that deal with temporary files.

```
FILE   *tmpfile(void)
char   *tmpnam(char *name)
```

tmpfile creates a *temporary* file preopened for reading and writing (opened for **"wb+"**). It's just like **fopen** in that it returns a **FILE *** or **NULL** if it can't create and open the temporary file. The file is temporary in the sense that it will be automatically removed when it's closed (either by a call to **fclose** or normal program termination). On abnormal program termination, however, the file may or may not be removed: the action is *implementation defined* (abnormal termination includes a call to the function **abort**, an uncaught signal, and so on).

CONSTANT/TYPE	DESCRIPTION
NULL	*null* pointer
BUFSIZ	size of **setbuf**'s buffer
_IOFBF	argument to **setvbuf** requesting full buffering
_IOLBF	argument to **setvbuf** requesting line buffering
_IONBF	argument to **setvbuf** requesting no buffering
FILE	type used for file access
EOF	return value indicating end of file
FOPEN_MAX	minimum number of files that can be open simultaneously (at least eight)
FILENAME_MAX	longest file name
TMP_MAX	minimum number of file names that **tmpnam** can generate (at least 25)
L_tmpnam	length of a file name generated by **tmpnam**
SEEK_CUR	tells **fseek** to seek relative to the current position in a file
SEEK_END	tells **fseek** to seek relative to the end of a file
SEEK_SET	tells **fseek** to seek relative to the start of a file
fpos_t	type used to indicate a position within a file

Table A.3   Macros defined in the header file stdio.h.

tmpnam generates a new, unique name that can be used as the name of a temporary file. Each call, up to **TMP_MAX** times, generates a new name; after that, the result is *implementation defined*. The name is unique in the sense that each call produces a new name that is guaranteed not to be the name of any existing file. We can call **tmpnam** in two ways. If we pass it a null pointer, **tmpnam** returns a pointer to the new name. If we pass it a nonnull argument, it places the name in that character array (which must be at least **L_tmpnam** characters long) and also returns a pointer to that space.

Since **tmpnam** generates only a string, it is necessary to open and close the file in the usual way. Despite the implication in the function's name that it gives the name of a *temporary* file, any files opened with names generated by **tmpnam** must still be removed via calls to **remove**, or they will continue to exist after the program terminates.

Error Detection

There are three functions we can use to detect and clear errors.

```
int   feof(FILE *stream)
int   ferror(FILE *stream)
void  clearerr(FILE *stream)
```

feof tests an input stream for end-of-file indication. Subsequent reads will continue to return end of file until a call to **rewind**, **clearerr**, or the file is closed. **feof** returns non-zero if end of file was detected on the last read on the stream.

ferror tests the stream for a read or write error. Once an error occurs, **ferror** remains true until a call to **clearerr** or **rewind** or until the file is closed. **ferror** returns non-zero if any error was detected on the last read or write on the stream. Errors can occur if the file becomes full, if a read operation cannot be performed because some other operation has changed the permission on the file, and so on.

clearerr resets the end of file and error indicators to zero.

Input/Output Redirection

Usually, we redirect I/O before starting the program, but we can also redirect the input or output from within the program with **freopen**.

```
FILE *freopen(const char *name,
              const char *mode,
              FILE *stream)
```

freopen creates a new file pointer for an already opened file. It returns a file pointer or **NULL**, as with **fopen**. The old file is closed, even if **freopen** fails. We use **freopen** most often for associating **stdin**, **stdout**, or **stderr** with another named file. The following call causes all reads involving **stdin** to come from a file named **data.txt**.

```
FILE  *stdin_ptr = freopen("data.txt", "r", stdin);
```

We need **freopen** because even though we think of the names **stdin**, **stdout**, and **stderr** as being type **FILE** *, we can't assign to them.[3] The following is illegal:

```
stdin = fopen("data.txt", "r");
```

Moving the File Pointer

The functions **fgetpos** and **fsetpos** are used to get and set the internal file position when we're manipulating files that are longer than can be represented in a **long**.[4]

```
int fgetpos(FILE *stream, fpos_t *where)
int fsetpos(FILE *stream, const fpos_t *where)
```

fgetpos gets the current position of the file, in a form suitable for a subsequent call to **fsetpos**. The location is returned in the space pointed to by **where**, a pointer to an **fpos_t**. This type could be a simple type on systems incapable of supporting very large files, or it could be a structured type. **fgetpos** returns zero on success and non-zero on error.

fsetpos positions the file pointer to the location in the file, as specified by the value pointed to by **where**. This value must have been set by a previous call to **fgetpos**. As with **fseek**, a call to **fsetpos** erases the end-of-file indication on the file and any

---

[3]On many systems, these are defined using **#define** as addresses of operating system buffers associated with the appropriate files.

[4]Both **ftell** and **fseek** return and use **long**s for reporting the size of a file. With very large files this is inadequate.

memory of pushed-back characters. **fsetpos** returns zero on success, non-zero on error. On error, both **fgetpos** and **fsetpos** set **errno** to indicate the error.

Putting Characters Back

The function **ungetc** pushes its character parameter back to the stream (after first converting it to type **unsigned char**).

```
int ungetc(int c, FILE *stream)
```

If **c** is **EOF**, **ungetc** fails, and no character is pushed back. The size of the push-back buffer is at least one character. Subsequent reads on the file will return the pushed-back characters in reverse order of being pushed. **fseek** and **fsetpos** erase the pushed-back characters. It's an error if the stream isn't open for reading. **ungetc** returns **c**, the pushed-back character; on failure, it returns **EOF**.

Controlling Buffering

There are several library functions we can use to control the size of input/output buffers and when they're actually written out to the file.

```
int   fflush(FILE *stream)
void  setbuf(FILE *stream, char *buf)
int   setvbuf(FILE *stream, char *buf,
              int type, size_t size)
```

fflush causes a file's buffer to be written out. It returns zero on success.

setbuf and **setvbuf** cause a named buffer to be used for input or output buffering on an open file, instead of a system-allocated buffer. In **setbuf**, if **buff** is **NULL**, I/O will be unbuffered. If it's not, the named buffer is used, which must be at least **BUFSIZ** bytes (given in stdio.h). For **setvbuf**, a buffer will be automatically allocated using **malloc**, requesting **size** bytes.

In **setvbuf**, **type** controls the type of buffering we have. There are three choices. **_IOFBF** causes the file to be *fully* buffered. The next input operation on an *empty* buffer will attempt to fill the entire buffer. On output, the buffer must be completely filled before the file is actually written. **_IOLBF** causes the file to be *line* buffered. If the buffer is empty, the next input will attempt to fill the entire buffer. On output, the buffer is written to the file when a newline character is written. **_IONBF** causes the file to be *unbuffered* and both **size** and **buffer** to be ignored. **setvbuf** returns zero if successful and non-zero otherwise.

Formatted Output

We've seen an entire collection of functions that perform formatted output, but we've left out lots of gory details. These functions are listed on the top of the next page.

```
int printf(const char *format, ...)
int fprintf(FILE *stream, const char *format, ...)
int sprintf(char *string, const char *format, ...)
int vprintf(const char *format, va_list param)
int vfprintf(FILE *stream, const char *format, va_list param)
int vsprintf(char *string, const char *format, va_list param)
```

Each of these functions requires a format specification given in the **format** parameter and a list of expressions to print. All **printf** family routines return the number of characters printed or, if an error occurs, a negative value. The functions differ as to where output goes (standard output, a file, or another string) and whether or not they're provided expressions to display directly or through variable argument lists.

The format string in the **printf** family indicates how a value or expression is to be formatted. It's usually a constant string (provided in double quotes). Characters in the format string are written as is, except for those beginning with the percent character (**%**). The format string thus consists of two types of objects: *plain characters* and *format specifiers*.

format specifiers begin with the percent character (**%**); for each format specifier there must be one value or expression in the comma-separated expression list or variable argument list. One expression is "consumed" for each format specifier. The syntax of a format specifier is

% [flags] [width] [.precision] [size] type

flags is an optional list of flag characters indicating justification, plus or minus sign, decimal point, trailing zeros, or octal or hex prefix.

width is an optional value that indicates the *minimum* number of characters to print (more characters are printed if a value is too large for the given width). Padding is done with blanks or zeros depending on an appropriate flag character. If no width is specified, a default width is used.

precision is the *maximum* number of characters to print. Again, padding is done with blanks or zeros depending on an appropriate flag character.

size (**h**, **l**, or **L**) overrides the default size of an argument. The size characters are **h** for a **short int**, **l** for a **long int**, and **L** for a **long double**. To print a short hex integer, use **%hx**; a long octal, use **%lo**; and so on.

type indicates the type of the expression or value. Table A.4 lists the various legal types (although many compilers have extensions to this table—see your compiler write-up for details). Most of the various formatting types have defaults associated with them; these are described in Table A.5.

A *flag* is one of the characters **-**, **+**, blank, or **#**. Any combination and order of flag characters is allowed (but **+** will take precedence over a blank if both are given). A minus-sign flag left-justifies the value, padded to the right with blanks; otherwise the value is right justified and padded on the left with zeros or blanks (zeros for numerical values or blanks for strings). A plus-sign flag uses a plus sign for positive values (default is a blank) and a minus sign for negative values (signed expressions). A blank flag uses a space instead of a plus sign for positive values; negative values still have a minus sign. Finally, the **#** flag uses an alternate output format, as described in Table A.6.

TYPE	EXPRESSION	OUTPUT FORMAT OR ACTION
d	integer	signed decimal integer
i	integer	signed decimal integer
u	integer	unsigned decimal integer
o	integer	unsigned octal integer
x	integer	unsigned hex integer (uses **a–f** for the values 10 through 15)
X	integer	unsigned hex integer (uses **A–F** for the values 10 through 15)
f	floating point	signed value in form **[-]dddd.ddd**
e	floating point	signed value in form **[-]d.dddd e [+ | -]ddd** (scientific notation)
E	floating point	same as **e** but prints **E** instead.
g	floating point	signed value using either **e** or **f** form, based on value and precision, with trailing zeros and decimal point only if necessary
G	floating point	same as **g** but prints **E** instead
c	character	single character (the integer argument is converted to **unsigned char**, then printed)
s	pointer to **char**	characters in string up until a null character or until precision number of characters have been printed
%	none	single percent character
n	pointer to **int**	stores count of characters written so far in the location pointed to by the next argument (which must be the address of an **int**)
p	pointer	address is an *implementation-defined* format

Table A.4 **printf** format types and their meaning.

TYPE	DEFAULT FORMAT
e or **E**	Prints a minus sign for negative numbers and a plus or minus sign for the exponent. Prints one digit before the decimal point. The number of digits after the decimal point is given by the precision (default six). The exponent contains at least two digits.
f	Prints a minus sign for negative numbers and a blank for positive. The number of digits after the decimal point is given by the precision (default six).
g or **G**	Uses the default style of **e**, **E**, or **f**. The precision indicates the number of significant digits (default six). Removes trailing zeros and includes the decimal point only if needed.
x or **X**	Uses the letters **a–f** for the **x** format, and **A–F** for **X**.

Table A.5 Default formats for the **printf** format types.

TYPE	EFFECT OF **#**
c, s, d, i, u	no effect
o	**0** is prepended to a non-zero value
x, X	**0x** or **0X** is prepended to a non-zero value
e, E, f	output always contains a decimal point
g, G	same as **e** and **E**, except trailing zeros are not removed

Table A.6 Alternate **printf** format using the **#** alternate format specifier.

The width specifier sets a minimum width for the output field. If the expression requires more than the minimum, it overflows the output field (that is, truncation does not occur nor is the output marked with special "field too small" characters as in FORTRAN). The width is given as a number of characters, such as **%10i** or **%010i**, indicating that if the value requires less than 10 characters, it is padded on the left with blanks in the first case and zeros in the second. The width can also be specified as the special character *****: **%*i**. For the ***** width, the expression list provides the width. It is taken from the next argument in the list, which must be an integer preceding the argument being formatted. This call:

```
printf("Val: %*i", width, val);
```

prints the value of **val** (an integer) using the width given as the value of **width** (also an integer).

A *precision* specifier is used to indicate the amount of space for the decimal part of a floating point value or for zero-padding for integers. If no precision or a precision of **.0** is given, the default is used (one for **d**, **i**, **o**, **u**, **x**, and **X**; six for **e**, **E**, and **f**; all significant digits for **g** and **G**; and all characters up to the null for **s**). If the precision is **.n** (where **n** is a constant), *n* characters or decimal places are printed as specified in Table A.7. Finally, if the precision is *****, the next value in the expression list specifies the precision (this must be an integer expression). If an ***** is used for both the width and the precision, the width expression precedes the precision expression and the value to be printed:

```
printf("Val: %*.*f\n", width, precision, val);
```

There is one oddity for values whose precision is stated as **.0**: if the format specifies one of the integer formats (**d**, **i**, **o**, **u**, **x**, or **X**) *and* the value is zero, then no numeric characters are printed: the field will contain blanks.

Table A.8 shows some examples of the various formatting strings, assuming the following declarations and values:

```
int     val = -14;
int     val2 = 87;
float   fval =  43.718;
char    *s = "I love rock and roll";
```

TYPE	EFFECT OF PRECISION SPECIFIER
d, i, o, u, x, X	Prints at least n digits. If the value has less than n digits, it pads the output on left with zeros. If the value has more than n digits, it doesn't truncate.
e, E, f	Prints n digits after the decimal point; rounds the least significant digit.
g, G	Prints at most n digits.
c	No effect.
s	Prints no more than n characters. (This is how we print long strings in a short field.)

Table A.7 Effect of *precision specifier* on **printf** formats.

FORMAT STRING	EXPRESSION	OUTPUT
"[%15i]"	val	[-14]
"[%-15i]"	val	[-14]
"[%15i]"	val2	[87]
"[%+15i]"	val2	[+87]
"[%-15i]"	val2	[87]
"[%-+15i]"	val2	[+87]
"[%f]"	fval	[43.717999]
"[%15.0f]"	fval	[44]
"[%-15.0f]"	fval	[44]
"[%+15.0f]"	fval	[+44]
"[%10.5f]"	fval	[43.71800]
"[%.5f]"	fval	[43.71800]
"[%30s]"	s	[I love rock and roll]
"[%-30s]"	s	[I love rock and roll]
"[%-10.6s]"	s	[I love]
"[%10.6s]"	s	[I love]
"[%15x]"	val	[fff2]
"[%#15x]"	val	[0xfff2]

Table A.8 **printf** format strings, expressions, and output.

Formatted Input

We've also seen a variety of functions for performing formatted input.

```
int scanf(const char *format, ...)
int fscanf(FILE *stream, const char *format, ...)
int sscanf(char *string, const char *format, ...)
int vscanf(const char *format, va_list param)
int vfscanf(FILE *stream, const char *format, va_list param)
int vsscanf(char *string, const char *format, va_list param)
```

Each of these functions takes two sets of parameters. The first is a formatting string, describing the types and number of input values to be read (in a manner similar to the **printf** family). The second set is a list of *addresses* where values are to be stored. As with **printf**, input formats are indicated using a **%** format code. For each **%** format of the appropriate type, one address from the address list is used to store an input value.

The options available for **scanf**'s formatting codes are lengthy and rather complex. Table A.9 summarizes their use.

The conversions in Table A.9 also have certain conventions associated with them. The **%c** code reads the next input character, including white space (blank, tab, or newline). An optional count can be used with the **%c** format; in this case, the indicated number of characters is read, and the variable to which characters go should be an array of **char**, rather than pointer to **char**. For example, **%c** reads a single character, **%10c** reads 10 characters.

String input using **%s** requires that the array have enough space for the input. Reading continues until a space (blank or tab) or a newline. This often leads to confusion; if you really don't want to stop reading on a space, but only on a newline, use **gets** or **fgets** instead (or the **getline** function we wrote in Chapter 11).

The **scanf** input formats allow for integer and long types. **short**s can be read using the **h** modifier (**%hi**, **%ho**, or **%hx**). Similarly, **long**s can be read by using the **l** modifier (**%li**, **%lo**, or **%lx**). Here are some examples.

```
scanf("%i", &a);          /* read an int */
scanf("%li", &a);         /* read a long */
scanf("%hi", &a);         /* read a short */
scanf("%ho", &a);         /* read a short octal integer */
scanf("%lx", &a);         /* read a long hex integer */
```

The **scanf** functions return the number of input values successfully scanned and stored or **EOF** if end of file is read. Scanning will terminate if the input does not match the type of the **%** format specifier. This typically occurs when a numeric input format is specified, but the input contains invalid alphabetics.

The general form of the format control string is

% [*] [width] [size] type

The * is an *assignment suppression* character, which we use most often when we know that input meets a rigid format and we don't need to keep all values. As an example, if the input consists of blank-separated fields containing last name, first name,

TYPE	INPUT TYPE	ADDRESS TYPE
d	integer	`int *`
o	octal integer	`int *`
i	decimal, octal, or hex integer	`int *`
u	unsigned integer	`unsigned int *`
x	hexadecimal integer	`int *`
X	hexadecimal integer	`int *`
e	floating point	`float *`
E	floating point	`float *`
f	floating point	`float *`
g	floating point	`float *`
G	floating point	`float *`
s	string	`char []` (array of `char`)
c	character	`char *`
%	character	no input (`%` symbol stored)
n	no input is read	`int *` (number of values successfully stored)
p	hex number in address form	implementation-defined pointer

Table A.9 `scanf` variations and what they do.

and three values and we only want the last name and the third value, we can read and throw away the unwanted ones like this:

```
scanf("%s %*s %*i %*i %i", lname, &v3);
```

Here we read two string values and three decimal integer values, but we only store two values: the first string into **lname** and the third decimal integer into **v3**. We expect **scanf** to return 2.

The *width* is used to indicate the maximum number of characters to read. **scanf** will read fewer values if it reaches a character for which **isspace** is true, end of file, or a character it can't convert. With the input abcdefghijklmnopq, the call

```
scanf("%6s%6s", s1, s2);
```

will read and assign the string **abcdef** to **s1** and **ghijkl** to **s2**. Similarly, the input 123456789123456 and the program

```
scanf("%6li%6li", &v1, &v2);
```

will assign the value 123456 to **v1** and 789123 to **v2** (assuming **v1** and **v2** are **long**s).

The **%n** format does not consume input; instead it assigns to the next address in the address list the number of items successfully converted and stored up to, but not including, this **%n**. So

```
scanf("%d %d %n %d\n", &v1, &v2, &how_many, &v3);
```

should store 2 into **how_many**. Since **scanf** returns as its value the number of items correctly read from the input, converted, and stored, it does not count any of the **%n** conversions. **scanf** should return 3 in the above example.

A format specification given in brackets will match any character between the brackets: **%[**_list_**]**. _list_ can be a list of individual characters, a range of characters separated by a dash (the first character must be smaller than the second in the local character set collating sequence), or a list beginning with a caret (^). If the list _begins_ with a caret, then the meaning is reversed: we match only the characters _not_ in the list. If the caret appears other than at the start of the list, then it is part of the _matching set_. Matched characters are assigned to an array of characters, which should be large enough to hold the largest possible match. So

```
scanf("%[a-z]", s);
```

will store "now" into **s** if the input is "now is the time." Table A.10 provides some additional examples.

If the format string contains a character other than a **%** format code or a blank, the character must match the input exactly. To read two integer values separated by a colon, use

```
scanf("%i:%i", &v1, &v2)
```

Here the first value must be immediately followed by a colon (no intervening spaces). Compare this with:

```
scanf("%i :%i", &v1, &v2)
```

Now the first value must be followed by a colon, but there may be zero or more spaces before the colon.

A.7   LOCALES

The header file locale.h helps a program tailor itself to the individual system or _locale_. A _locale_ means a set of capabilities in reading and printing numbers and money that is specific to a country or region. In the United States, we use a comma to separate thousands, and a period for the fractional part of floating point numbers. We use a negative sign or parentheses for negative dollar amounts, and a dollar sign for money. But some other countries use a comma for fractional amounts and place the minus sign after the monetary amount for negative values.

There are two functions dealing with locales. The first is **setlocale**:

```
char *setlocale(int category, const char *locale);
```

It sets the program's locale in one of the areas specified by the **category** to the value specified by **locale**. That value is either **"C"**, **""**, or an _implementation-defined_ specification. A null string for **locale** indicates an _implementation-defined_ local environment.

FORMAT	MATCHES
%[abc]	any string made up of the characters *a*, *b*, or *c*
%[a-z]	any string made up of the lowercase alphabetic characters
%[A-Z]	any string made up of the uppercase alphabetic characters
%[a-zA-Z]	any string made up of alphabetic characters
%[0-9]	any string made up of numeric characters
%[0-9a-fA-F]	any string made up of numeric characters, *a* through *f*, *A* through *F*
%[^0-9]	any string made up of nonnumeric characters
%[^a-zA-Z]	any string made up of the nonalphabetic characters
%[0-9^]	any string made up of the numeric characters or carets

Table A.10 **scanf** string matches.

"**C**" is the default and indicates that the source and execution locales are the same. The equivalent of

```
setlocale(LC_ALL, "C");
```

happens automatically before the program starts.

Table A.11 lists the possible values for the **category** and their meaning. These values are defined in locale.h.

On success, **setlocale** returns a pointer to a string associated with locale information for the given **category**; otherwise the null pointer is returned.

We can also use **setlocale** to determine what the current **locale** is. We do this by providing **NULL** as its second argument. **setlocale** then returns a pointer to a string associated with locale information for the given **category**. The information in this string is *implementation defined*, but must be in a form appropriate for a subsequent call to **setlocale** with the string as the second argument and the same first argument.

The information on **setlocale** is of necessity hazy, since the meaning of a **locale** argument other than "**C**" is *implementation defined*. You're stuck scanning your compiler documentation for the specifics for your implementation.

The other locale-related function is **localeconv**.

```
struct lconv  *localeconv(void);
```

It returns a pointer to a structure describing how numbers are formatted for reading and printing, the separator between thousands, the decimal point, the monetary symbol, how negative monetary values are formatted, how time is formatted, and on and on. These values are all set in terms of the current locale. The name stands for *locale convention*.

Table A.12 lists the fields in a **struct lconv** and what they're used for. By default, **decimal_point** is "**.**", the other strings are null strings, and the **char** fields are **CHAR_MAX**. If any field is the null string or has the **char** value **CHAR_MAX**, its value is not available in the current locale. The **char** values are interpreted as small nonnegative numbers.

CATEGORY	AREAS FOR WHICH LOCALE IS SET
LC_ALL	all areas
LC_COLLATE	**strcoll** and **strxfrm**
LC_CTYPE	*ctype* character-testing routines
LC_MONETARY	monetary conversions (from **localeconv**)
LC_NUMERIC	type/placement of decimal point in formatted input and output
LC_TIME	only for **strftime** type

Table A.11   The possible categories and their effect on locales.

A few fields need additional description. The **grouping** and **mon_grouping** fields describe the size of "thousands" groups in a tricky way. If an element of the string is **CHAR_MAX**, no more grouping occurs; if **0**, then the previous value is repeated for all remaining groups; otherwise, the character is interpreted as an integer and is the number of characters to be grouped. For example, the value **"\0\3"** indicates that grouping is by threes. **"\0\2\3"** indicates that grouping is by twos, except the rightmost, which groups by threes:

    12,45,89,999.903232

This is certainly odd, but the locale mechanism supports this if such a method is supported in the local environment (through an appropriate call to **setlocale**).

    p_sign_posn and **n_sign_posn** are also somewhat tricky. Depending on their value, different methods are used to display the positive or negative sign with monetary amounts. A 0 causes parentheses to surround the value and the currency symbol. A 1 causes the sign to precede the value and the currency symbol. A 2 causes it to follow them. A 3 causes the sign to precede the currency symbol. And a 4 causes the sign to follow it.

A.8   **SIGNAL HANDLING**

The standard C library provides a function, **signal**, to allow us to handle interrupts and other asynchronous events. Our programs are informed of these events, such as a user hitting the interrupt key, by being sent a signal. These signals may be generated by system, hardware, or software methods or by calling the **raise** function.

    C allows us to do one of three things when a signal occurs. The first is to simply ignore it. Our processing continues as if the signal never occurred. The second is to let the system handle the signal in its default way. Each signal has some default action associated with it that is established at the beginning of program execution.[5] The last is to

---

[5]The specific default action for any given signal is *implementation defined*. Operating systems and compilers vary substantially on this, and the documentation for **signal** in the local environment should be examined carefully. Under both UNIX and MS-DOS, most—but not all—signals cause our program to terminate.

FIELD AND TYPE	MEANING
`char *decimal_point;`	Decimal point for *nonmonetary* quantities in formatted I/O.
`char *thousands_sep;`	Separator between groups of digits for *nonmonetary* quantities in formatted I/O. Only used before the decimal point. The number of digits in a group is given by **grouping**.
`char *grouping;`	String indicating the number of characters in each "thousands" grouping for nonmonetary quantities.
`char *int_curr_symbol;`	*International* currency symbol for the current locale. It consists of three symbols for the currency symbol specified in *ISO 4217 Codes for the Representation of Currency and Funds*. Its fourth character separates the currency symbol from the monetary amount (usually a blank or period). For the US, this string is `"USD "`; for Italy, `"ITL."`
`char *currency_symbol;`	*Local* currency symbol. For the US, this is `"$"`; for Italy, `"L."`.
`char *mon_decimal_point;`	Decimal point for monetary quantities. For the US, this is `"."`; for Italy, `""`.
`char *mon_thousands_sep;`	"Thousands" separator for monetary quantities (before the decimal point). **mon_grouping** determines the number of digits grouped as "thousands."
`char *mon_grouping;`	Same as **grouping**, but applied only to monetary quantities.
`char *positive_sign;`	Sign used for nonnegative monetary quantities in formatted I/O (usually the null string). The **p_sign_posn** field describes where the **positive_sign** goes.
`char *negative_sign;`	Sign used for negative monetary quantities in formatted I/O. Usually `"-"`; for Switzerland it is `"C"`. The **n_sign_posn** field describes where the **negative_sign** goes.
`char int_frac_digits;`	Number of digits to the right of the decimal point in a monetary quantity displayed in *international* format. For the US, this is two; for Italy, zero.
`char frac_digits;`	Number of digits to the right of the decimal point in a monetary quantity display in *local* format. For the US, this is two; for Italy, zero.
`char p_cs_precedes;`	One or zero, depending on whether the currency symbol *precedes* or *follows* a nonnegative monetary quantity. For the US and most other countries, this is one.
`char n_cs_precedes;`	Same as **p_cs_precedes**, but for negative quantities.
`char p_sep_by_space;`	One or zero, depending on whether the currency symbol is, or is not, separated by a space from a nonnegative monetary quantity. For the US, this is one; for Italy, zero.
`char n_sep_by_space;`	Same as **p_sep_by_space**, but for negative quantities.
`char p_sign_posn;`	Describes formatting of positive sign for nonnegative monetary values. Values given on previous page.
`char n_sign_posn;`	Same as **p_sign_posn**, but for negative monetary values.

Table A.12   The fields in a `localeconv` and their meaning.

SIGNAL	SIGNAL DESCRIPTION
SIGABRT	abnormal termination has occurred
SIGFPE	arithmetic error (floating point exception) has occurred
SIGILL	illegal instruction has occurred
SIGINT	interactive interrupt (attention) has occurred
SIGSEGV	invalid access to data has occurred (called a *segmentation violation*)
SIGTERM	termination request has been sent to the program

Table A.13 Constants for signals that every implementation must provide.

provide a piece of code (called a *handler*) to be executed when the signal occurs. When the signal happens, our program is interrupted and control is automatically transferred to this handler. When the handler returns, control automatically goes back to the place where our program was interrupted.

In general, to process signals we need to include signal.h. We specify the behavior we want for a particular signal by calling **signal**.

```
void (*signal(int sig, void (*f)(int)))(int)
```

It takes an integer identifying a particular signal and a pointer to a handling function. The integers are constants defined in signal.h and are listed in Table A.13. The language requires that at least these six be available, but most environments provide additional *implementation-defined* ones. The handling function must take an **int** argument and return **void**.

To ignore subsequent occurrences of a signal, we pass the special constant **SIG_IGN** as the handler. To restore the default action for subsequent occurrences of a signal, we pass **SIG_DFL** as the handler. The only other choice is to pass the name of a function to be used as a handler. This requests that this handler be invoked for the *next* occurrence of the given signal. The handler takes an **int** and returns **void**. It's automatically passed the number of the signal that caused it to be invoked (so we can have the same function handle more than one signal). As soon as the handler is invoked, the action for the signal is automatically reset to **SIG_DFL** (except for a **SIGILL**, for which the reset to **SIG_DFL** is *implementation defined*). If it exits via a call to **return**, execution continues at the exact point at which the signal occurred (except for a **SIGFPE**, where a **return** will cause *undefined* behavior).

signal returns the value of the function from the previous call or, if it fails, the special pointer **SIG_ERR**.

Figure A.6 provides a simple program that shows how to ignore signals and to supply handlers. It ignores **SIGTERM** and catches **SIGINT**. The result is an infinite loop that we can stop only by hitting an interrupt three times.

If you look at our handler for **SIGINT** closely, you'll see that the first thing it does is ignore the signal that caused it to be invoked. User-supplied handlers generally don't want the signal handler to be reset to **SIG_DFL**, since receipt of the same signal while in the handler will invoke the default action—usually terminating the program. Usually

```
/*
 * Only way to kill this program is to send it three interrupts!
 */
#include <stdio.h>
#include <signal.h>
#include <stdlib.h>

#define REALLY_QUIT    3              /* 3 interrupts kill it */

int main(void)
{
  void       int_handler(int);
  unsigned sleep(unsigned);          /* nonstandard but portable */

  signal(SIGTERM, SIG_IGN);          /* ignore termination signals */
  signal(SIGINT, int_handler);       /* provide interrupt handler */
  for (;;)                           /* infinite loop */
  {
    printf("Stop me before I print again!\n");
    (void) sleep(1);
  }
}

void int_handler(int sig)
{
  static int count = 0;

  signal(SIGINT, SIG_IGN);                /* turn off interrupts */
  fprintf(stderr,"That's %i interrupts (signal %i).\n", ++count, sig);
  if (count >= REALLY_QUIT)
    exit(EXIT_FAILURE);

  fprintf(stderr,"I'm not quitting until you hit three interrupts\n");
  signal(SIGINT, int_handler);       /* reset interrupt handling */
}
```

Figure A.6 (catchsig.c) A signal-handling example.

we reset the action for the given signal to **SIG_IGN** at the start of the handler (leaving only a tiny bit of vulnerability) and then set it back to call our own handler just before exiting.

Since a signal can occur anywhere, including system or library routines, resuming in the middle of what we were doing when the signal occurred may cause unexpected results. In this program, for example, it's possible for the **printf** in **main** to be interrupted in the middle before writing all its output. On some implementations, it may start writing its output again; on others, it may ignore the unwritten output. The most appropriate, safe, portable behavior for a user-supplied interrupt handler is to ignore subsequent occurrences of the signal, do its task, and then call **exit** or perform a **longjmp** (discussed in the next section), bringing the program to a known state.

We can use **raise** to generate a signal from our program:

```
int raise(int sig);
```

raise sends the signal **sig** to the program, returning zero on success, non-zero otherwise. So **raise(SIGINT)** is suicide, unless we have a handler set up for **SIGINT**. We often use **raise** to test our program's behavior when it's sent different signals.

The header file also defines a special type, **sig_atomic_t**, which is a synonym for an object of integral type that can be accessed *atomically*. This means that any object of this type will be completely accessed even during a signal.

Programs written using interrupts are necessarily system specific and will require some recoding when they're moved to a different system. But we can minimize the damage by localizing signal handling in a few specific modules. Ideally, only those modules will need to be converted to match the requirements of a new environment.

A.9   NONLOCAL GOTOS

The library provides a pair of functions, **setjmp** and **longjmp**, that let us portably jump out of one function and into another.

```
int setjmp(jmp_buf state);
void longjmp(jmp_buf state, int val);
```

We use these functions most frequently to have an interrupt handler jump back to the main program, rather than return to the function that was interrupted by the signal. To use them, we need to include setjmp.h, which also defines the **jmp_buf** type.

The idea behind **setjmp** and **longjmp** is simple. Most C implementations use a *stack* to store information about a called function and its caller. As functions are called from within other functions, the stack grows deeper and deeper. In order to jump to an earlier function, we need to restore the stack to the way it was when we were in that function. **setjmp** provides a way of saving the information necessary to restore the stack to a particular state. **longjmp** provides a way to exit a function and request the change to the stack to a previously saved state. A **jmp_buf** is usually an array of **int**s used to contain the registers or other structures necessary for restoring the stack.

setjmp saves the current state so that a later call to **longjmp** restores it. Its return value depends on how **setjmp** was called. It turns out that **setjmp** can be called in two ways: directly or through a **longjmp**. If called directly, **setjmp** returns zero. If called through **longjmp**, it returns the value of the **longjmp**'s second argument.

We should call **setjmp** only in the context of a direct comparison with an integral expression (such as in a **switch** statement or relational test). Whether **setjmp** is allowed in any other context is *implementation defined.*[6]

---

[6]This is because using **setjmp** in a more complex expression may involve optimizations that can affect the success of what a **setjmp** is trying to do.

longjmp restores the state given in the argument **state**, which must have been previously stored by a call to **setjmp**. We're usually in big trouble if **state** has not been set with a call to **setjmp** or if the routine that called **setjmp** has returned before the call to **longjmp**. We also may get strange results if we call **longjmp** in a nested signal-handling function. A nested signal handler is one that is called on receipt of a signal while in a routine that was called via another signal.

After the return from **longjmp**, all variables have values as of the time of the call to **longjmp**. But automatic variables that are not **volatile** and that have been changed between the call to **setjmp** and **longjmp** have *indeterminate* values.

longjmp does not return a value, but the result of a **longjmp** is the same as if the corresponding **setjmp** had just returned with the value of the second argument to **longjmp**. However, if **val** is 0, **setjmp** will return as if it were 1. **longjmp** can be thought of as a goto to the corresponding **setjmp**. The effect is as if **setjmp** returns with value **val**.

Figures A.7 and A.8 are an example. The main program is a simple loop that requests file names from the user and displays those files. If an interrupt happens at any time during that loop, the program uses **longjmp** to exit a signal-handling routine.[7] We're careful to make **fp**, the file pointer, a global variable, since we need to know its value after the **longjmp** in order to close the file.

A.10 TIME FUNCTIONS

The standard library provides a rich and somewhat strange collection of time-related functions. They're a bit bizarre because they are mainly adopted from UNIX and don't necessarily follow the conventions of other operating systems. To use these functions, we include the header file time.h. It defines the "broken-down" time structure **struct tm**, the **time_t** and **clock_t** times, and a constant, **CLOCKS_PER_SEC** (the number of "clock ticks" equal to one second).

There are a pair of functions that return a time, **clock** and **time**.

```
clock_t  clock(void);
time_t   time(time_t *t);
double   difftime(time_t t2, time_t t1);
```

clock returns the time (in units of **CLOCKS_PER_SEC**) since some initial time. We use it when we need a relative time but not an absolute one. If the processor time can't be determined, **clock** returns −1.

Figure A.9 uses **clock** to compute a program's total execution time. It calls **clock** at the start and at the end, subtracts the two times, and divides the result by **CLOCKS_PER_SEC**.[8]

time gets the absolute time. Due to the historical association with UNIX, **time** often returns the time in seconds since some distant past. In UNIX, this is midnight, January 1, 1970 (GMT). But there's no guarantee that a **time_t** will be a time in

---

[7]Control-C is the usual keyboard character for sending interrupts on many interactive systems.

[8]This program calls **sleep**, available in many systems but not part of ANSI-C, to suspend execution (but keep the clock ticking) for the specified number of seconds.

```c
/*
 * Print files, going to next file at interrupt.
 */
#include <stdio.h>
#include <stdlib.h>
#include <stddef.h>
#include <signal.h>
#include <setjmp.h>

jmp_buf state;                         /* for setjmp and longjmp */
FILE    *fp = NULL;                    /* currently open file */

int main(void)
{
  int  getline(char *buf, int len);
  void display_file(FILE *fp);
  void intr_handler(int sig);

  char name[BUFSIZ + 1];

  setjmp(state);                                /* return here on longjmps */
  signal(SIGINT, intr_handler);         /* catch interrupts */
  while (printf("File: "), getline(name,BUFSIZ) != EOF && name[0] != '\0')
  {
    if (fp != NULL)              /* close file that may still be open */
    {
      fclose(fp);
      fp = NULL;
    }
    if ((fp = fopen(name, "r")) != NULL)
      display_file(fp);
    else
      fprintf(stderr,"Can't open %s\n", name);
  }

  return EXIT_SUCCESS;
}
```

Figure A.7   (jump.c)   An example of **setjmp/longjmp**.

seconds. As a result, if we want portable code we need to use the library functions discussed below to manipulate **time**'s return value. If the time is not available, **time** returns **(time_t)(-1)**.

What about **time**'s argument, the **time_t ***? That's another historical artifact. If the argument is nonnull, just for the heck of it, **time** also stores the result in the pointed-to location. Just call **time** with a null pointer and forget this oddity.[9]

---

[9]It stems from times back when C had no **long**s and the time had to be represented as an array of two **int**s.

```
/*
 * Functions to handle interrupts and display file contents.
 */
#include <stdio.h>
#include <stdlib.h>
#include <stddef.h>
#include <signal.h>
#include <setjmp.h>

extern jmp_buf state;                     /* for setjmp and longjmp */
extern FILE    *fp;                        /* currently open file */

void intr_handler(int sig)
{
  signal(SIGINT, SIG_IGN);                /* ignore interrupts */
  fprintf(stderr, "Interrupted (by signal %i)!\n", sig);
  signal(SIGINT, intr_handler);           /* ignore interrupts */
  longjmp(state, 1);                       /* now back to a known state */
}

void display_file(FILE *fp)
{
  int c;

  while ((c = getc(fp)) != EOF)
    putchar(c);
}
```

Figure A.8 (jumputls.c) Functions to handle an interrupt and to display a file.

difftime returns the difference (in seconds) of **t2** and **t1**. **time_t** is usually a **long**, so we could do this ourselves. But it's conceivable that it could be implemented as a structure, in which case we couldn't do direct subtraction.

Another UNIX carryover, **ctime** (for "character time"), takes a **time_t** returned from **time** and returns a pointer to a string with the time formatted nicely and neatly.

```
char *ctime(const time_t *when);
```

This string is the current date and *local* time, accounting for time zone and daylight savings time. The string returned from **ctime** is always exactly 26 characters, like this:

```
DDD MMM dd hh:mm:ss yyyy\n\0
```

Notice that it sneakily stuffs a newline at the end of the string.

Figure A.10 uses these functions to nicely print today's date. Here is its output:

```
Today's date: Mon Aug 31 14:01:55 1992
```

```c
/*
 * Print amount of time program takes to run.
 */
#include <stdio.h>
#include <stdlib.h>
#include <time.h>

#define   DEFL_SLEEP_MAX       10u
#define   SLEEP_MAX            100

int main(void)
{
  unsigned sleep(unsigned);                          /* nonstandard */

  unsigned how_long;
  clock_t  t1;
  int      status = EXIT_SUCCESS;

  if ((t1 = clock()) == (clock_t) -1)
  {
    fprintf(stderr, "Can't get processor clock.  Exiting...\n");
    status = EXIT_FAILURE;
  }
  else
  {
    printf("Sleep time: ");
    if (scanf("%u", &how_long) != 1 || how_long > SLEEP_MAX)
      fprintf(stderr, "Time in error.  Defaulting to %u secs.\n",
            how_long = DEFL_SLEEP_MAX);
    (void) sleep(how_long);                          /* nonstandard */
    printf("Program took %.2f seconds to run.\n",
          (double)(clock()-t1)/CLOCKS_PER_SEC);
  }
  return status;
}
```

Figure A.9   (timeprog.c) Program that prints its execution time.

There are also a pair of library functions for converting a **time_t** into a structure. **gmtime** takes a **time_t** and returns the current Greenwich Mean Time (now called Coordinated Universal Time).

```c
struct tm *gmtime(const time_t *tp);
```

It returns a pointer to a **struct tm**. **localtime** is similar, but it converts the time to the local time, accounting for time zone and daylight savings time.

```c
struct tm *localtime(const time_t *tp);
```

```
/*
 * A program to print today's date.
 */
#include <stdio.h>
#include <stdlib.h>
#include <time.h>

int main(void)
{
  time_t now;

  now = time(NULL);
  printf("Today's date: %s", ctime(&now));

  return EXIT_SUCCESS;
}
```

Figure A.10 (dumpdate.c) Print today's date.

The structure they return looks like this:

```
struct tm
{
    int  tm_sec;   /* 0 ... 61 (leap seconds too) */
    int  tm_min;   /* 0 ... 59 */
    int  tm_hour;  /* hours since midnight: 0 ... 23 */
    int  tm_mday;  /* day of month: 1 ... 31 */
    int  tm_mon;   /* month: Jan = 0, etc. */
    int  tm_year;  /* year since 1900 */
    int  tm_wday;  /* Sunday = 0, Monday = 1, etc. */
    int  tm_yday;  /* day of year (Jan 1 = 0, through 365) */
    int  tm_isdst; /* daylight savings time */
};
```

tm_sec ranges from 0 to 61 to account for leap seconds added from time to time; **tm_isdst** is zero if daylight savings time is not in effect, positive for daylight savings time, and negative if the time in effect can't be determined.

The last thing we may want to do is take one of the structures and turn it into a string. To do that, we use **asctime**, which is similar to **ctime**.

```
char *asctime(const struct tm *tp);
```

It takes a pointer to a **struct tm** and returns a pointer to a string. In fact, **asctime(localtime(&now))** gives the same string as **ctime(&now)**.

Figure A.11 is a little program to print the current time in both GMT and local versions, adding the suffix DST or GMT. Rather than decoding the parts of the **struct tm**, we'll use the string from **asctime**, remove the trailing newline, and then append DST or GMT as appropriate.

```
/*
 * Print current local time and Greenwich Mean Time.
 */
#include <stdio.h>
#include <stdlib.h>
#include <string.h>
#include <time.h>

int main(void)
{
  struct tm  *tp;
  char       *p;
  time_t     now = time(NULL);

  *(strchr(p = asctime(tp = localtime(&now)), '\n')) = '\0';
  printf("%s", p);
  if (tp->tm_isdst > 0)
    printf(" DST");
  putchar('\n');

  *(strchr(p = asctime(gmtime(&now)), '\n')) = '\0';
  printf("%s GMT\n", p);

  return EXIT_SUCCESS;
}
```

Figure A.11   (currtime.c)   Program that prints the time and adds DST for daylight savings time and GMT for Greenwich Mean Time.

Most of the program is straightforward except for the statement

```
*(strchr(p = asctime(tp = localtime(&now)), '\n')) = '\0';
```

This grungy mess assigns the result of **localtime** to **tp**, passes this value to **asctime**, and saves the result in **p**. Finally, since **asctime**'s string ends with a newline, we use **strchr** to replace it with the null character. The output, run during daylight savings time, was

```
Mon Aug 31 15:44:16 1992 DST
Mon Aug 31 22:44:16 1992 GMT
```

There are only two functions left. **mktime** converts the time components in the structure pointed to by **tp** into a **time_t**.

```
time_t mktime(struct tm *tp);
```

It sets the values of **tp->tm_wday** and **tp->tm_yday** to correspond to the converted time. It returns the converted time or −1 if conversion cannot be accomplished. Figure A.12 is an example.

```
/*
 * Determine day of the week for December 7, 1941.
 */
#include <stdio.h>
#include <stdlib.h>
#include <time.h>

char *days[] = {"Sun", "Mon", "Tues", "Wednes", "Thurs", "Fri", "Sat"};

int main(void)
{
  struct tm any_day =                          /* 7th of December 1941 */
    {
      0, 0, 0,          /* seconds, minutes, hours */
      7, 11,            /* day of month, month (0 ... 11) */
      1941 - 1900,      /* year since 1900 */
      -1                /* day of year */
    };

  if(mktime(&any_day) == -1)
  {
    fprintf(stderr, "Can't convert given date.\n");
    return EXIT_FAILURE;
  }
  printf("Dec. 7, 1941, occurred on a %sday\n", days[any_day.tm_wday]);

  return EXIT_SUCCESS;
}
```

Figure A.12 (usemktim.c) Example program making use of **mktime**.

The last function is **strftime** (for "string format time"), which converts the time in the structure pointed to by **tp** into a locale-specific representation according to the format string **format**.

```
size_t strftime(char *s, size_t n, const char *format,
                const struct tm *tp);
```

It writes the characters into the string **s** as with **sprintf**. Characters in the format string are copied as is into **s**, except for % format characters. For format characters in Table A.14, it uses the appropriate field in the **struct tm** pointed to by **tp**.

The function returns the number of characters stored into **s**. The second argument, **n**, specifies that no more than **n** characters can be stored. However, if the conversion requires more than **n** characters, zero is returned and the contents of **s** are not specified.

Figure A.13 uses it to print when a famous event took place at Pearl Harbor. Here's its output:

```
Pearl harbor day: Sunday, December 7, 1941 (12/07/41)
```

FORMAT	COPIES
%a, %A	abbreviation of the weekday name, full weekday name
%b, %B	abbreviated month name, full month name
%c	date and time
%d	day of the month (01–31)
%H, %I	hour in 24-hour notation (00–23), hour in 12-hour notation (01–12)
%j, %m	day of the year (001–366), month of the year (01–12)
%M	minute (00–59)
%p	AM or PM designator for a 12-hour clock
%s	seconds (00–61)
%U	week of the year (00–53), based on week 0 starting on a Sunday
%w	weekday as a number (Sunday = 0, Monday = 1, and so on)
%W	week of the year (00–53), based on week 1 starting on a Monday
%x, %X	date, time
%y, %Y	year with only two digits (00–99), year with all four digits
%z	time zone name if the time zone can be determined
%%	% sign

Table A.14 Format codes and their meaning for the format string in the **strftime** routine.

```
/*
 * Display in a nice format when Pearl Harbor was bombed (12/7/1941).
 */
#include <stdio.h>
#include <stdlib.h>
#include <time.h>

int main()
{
  char      s[BUFSIZ];
  struct tm day = { 0, 0, 0, 7, 11, 1941-1900, 0, 0, -1 };

  if (strftime(s, BUFSIZ, "Pearl harbor day: %A, %B 7, %Y (%x)", &day))
    puts(s);

  return EXIT_SUCCESS;
}
```

Figure A.13 (pearl.c) Using **strftime** to print when a famous event took place at Pearl Harbor.

B CHARACTER SETS

Each implementation uses some underlying representation for characters, called a character set. The two most common character sets are ASCII and EBCDIC. This appendix provides a pair of tables that you can use to determine a character's integer representation in either of these sets. Given a character, first locate it in the appropriate table, then add its row number to the number at the top of its column. For example, the ASCII representation for the character 'A' is 64 plus 1, or 65.

THE ASCII CHARACTER SET

	0	16	32	48	64	80	96	112
0	^@	^P	[SP]	0	@	P	'	p
1	^A	^Q	!	1	A	Q	a	q
2	^B	^R	"	2	B	R	b	r
3	^C	^S	#	3	C	S	c	s
4	^D	^T	$	4	D	T	d	t
5	^E	^U	%	5	E	U	e	U
6	^F	^V	&	6	F	V	f	v
7	^G	^W	'	7	G	W	g	w
8	^H	^X	(	8	H	X	h	x
9	^I	^Y	)	9	I	Y	i	y
10	^J	^Z	*	:	J	Z	j	z
11	^K	ESC	+	;	K	[	k	{
12	^L		,	<	L	\	l		
13	^M		–	=	M	]	m	}
14	^N		.	>	N	^	n	~
15	^O		/	?	O	_	o	[DEL]

B.2   THE EBCDIC CHARACTER SET

	0	32	64	96	128	160	192	224
0	NUL	DS	SP					
1	SOH	SOS		/	a		A	
2	STX	FS			b	s	B	S
3	ETX				c	t	C	T
4	PF	BYP			d	u	D	U
5	HT	LF			e	v	E	V
6	LC	ETB			f	w	F	W
7	DEL	ESC			g	x	G	X
8					h	y	H	Y
9					i	z	I	Z
10	SMM	SM	¢					
11	VT	CU2	.	'				
12	FF		<	%				
13	CR	ENQ	(	~				
14	SO	ACK	+	>				
15	SI	BEL			?				
16	DLE		&					0
17	DC1				j		J	1
18	DC2	SYN			k		K	2
19	TM				l		L	3
20	RES	PN			m		M	4
21	NL	RS			n		N	5
22	BS	UC			o		O	6
23	IL	EOT			p		P	7
24	CAN				q		Q	8
25	EM				r		R	9
26	CC		!	:				
27	CU1	CU3	$	#				
28	IFS	DC4	*	@				
29	IGS	NAK	)	'				
30	IRS		;	=				
31	IUS	SUB	corner					

INDEX

Our index contains all the usual key terms and topics, as well as every type, macro, function, and header file that appears in the standard libraries or that we implemented in the text. Those that we implemented are followed by a †. In addition, C++-related terms are followed by a ◇. Finally, italic page numbers indicate interesting examples of language concepts that occur away from where the concept is discussed in detail.